Integrated Mathematics 3

Volume 1

TIMOTHY D. KANOLD
EDWARD B. BURGER
JULI K. DIXON
MATTHEW R. LARSON
STEVEN J. LEINWAND

Printed in the U.S.A.

ISBN 978-0-544-38988-5

14 15 16 17 18 19 20 0928 24 23 22 21 20 19 18

4500747196 E F G H I

Authors

Timothy D. Kanold, Ph.D., is an award-winning international educator, author, and consultant. He is a former superintendent and director of mathematics and science at Adlai E. Stevenson High School District 125 in Lincolnshire, Illinois. He is a past president of the National Council of Supervisors of Mathematics (NCSM) and the Council for the Presidential Awardees of Mathematics (CPAM). He has served on several writing and leadership commissions for NCTM during the past decade. He presents motivational professional development seminars with a focus on developing professional learning communities (PLC's) to improve the teaching, assessing, and learning of students. He has recently authored nationally recognized articles, books, and textbooks for mathematics education and school leadership, including *What Every Principal Needs to Know about the Teaching and Learning of Mathematics*.

Edward B. Burger, Ph.D., is the President of Southwestern University, a former Francis Christopher Oakley Third Century Professor of Mathematics at Williams College, and a former vice provost at Baylor University. He has authored or coauthored more than sixty-five articles, books, and video series; delivered over five hundred addresses and workshops throughout the world; and made more than fifty radio and television appearances. He is a Fellow of the American Mathematical Society as well as having earned many national honors, including the Robert Foster Cherry Award for Great Teaching in 2010. In 2012, Microsoft Education named him a "Global Hero in Education."

Juli K. Dixon, Ph.D., is a Professor of Mathematics Education at the University of Central Florida. She has taught mathematics in urban schools at the elementary, middle, secondary, and post-secondary levels. She is an active researcher and speaker with numerous publications and conference presentations. Key areas of focus are deepening teachers' content knowledge and communicating and justifying mathematical ideas. She is a past chair of the NCTM Student Explorations in Mathematics Editorial Panel and member of the Board of Directors for the Association of Mathematics Teacher Educators.

Matthew R. Larson, Ph.D., is the K-12 mathematics curriculum specialist for the Lincoln Public Schools and served on the Board of Directors for the National Council of Teachers of Mathematics from 2010 to 2013. He is a past chair of NCTM's Research Committee and was a member of NCTM's Task Force on Linking Research and Practice. He is the author of several books on implementing the Common Core Standards for Mathematics. He has taught mathematics at the secondary and college levels and held an appointment as an honorary visiting associate professor at Teachers College, Columbia University.

Steven J. Leinwand is a Principal Research Analyst at the American Institutes for Research (AIR) in Washington, D.C., and has over 30 years in leadership positions in mathematics education. He is past president of the National Council of Supervisors of Mathematics and served on the NCTM Board of Directors. He is the author of numerous articles, books, and textbooks and has made countless presentations with topics including student achievement, reasoning, effective assessment, and successful implementation of standards.

Performance Task Consultant

Robert Kaplinsky
Teacher Specialist, Mathematics
Downey Unified School District
Downey, California

STEM Consultants

Science, Technology, Engineering, and Mathematics

Michael A. DiSpezio
Global Educator
North Falmouth, Massachusetts

Michael R. Heithaus
Executive Director, School of Environment, Arts, and Society
Professor, Department of Biological Sciences
Florida International University
North Miami, Florida

Reviewers

Mindy Eden
Richwoods High School
Peoria School District
Peoria, IL

Dustin Johnson
Badger High School Math Teacher
Department Chair
Lake Geneva-Genoa City Union High School District
Lake Geneva, WI

Ashley D. McSwain
Murray High School
Murray City School District
Salt Lake City, UT

Rebecca Quinn
Doherty Memorial High School
Worcester Public Schools District
Worcester, MA

Ted Ryan
Madison LaFollette High School
Madison Metropolitan School District
Madison, WI

Tony Scoles
Fort Zumwalt School District
O'Fallon, MO

Cynthia L. Smith
Higley Unified School District
Gilbert, AZ

Phillip E. Spellane
Doherty Memorial High School
Worcester Public Schools District
Worcester, MA

Mona Toncheff
Math Content Specialist
Phoenix Union High School District
Phoenix, AZ

Methods for Reasoning with Geometry

UNIT 1

Volume 1

MODULE 1

Constructions

MODULE 2

Coordinate Proof Using Slope and Distance

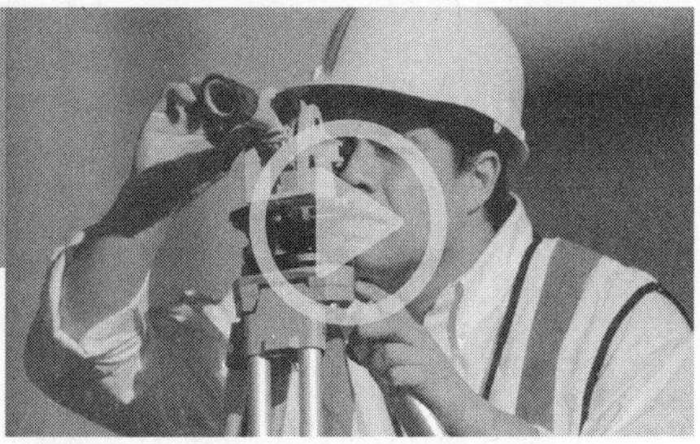

UNIT 2

Volume 1

Measurement and Modeling in Two and Three Dimensions

MODULE 3

Visualizing Solids

MODULE 4

Modeling and Problem Solving

Polynomial Functions, Expressions, and Equations

UNIT 3

Volume 1

MODULE 5

Polynomial Functions

MODULE 6

Polynomials

MODULE 7

Polynomial Equations

Exponential and Logarithmic Functions and Equations

UNIT 6

Volume 2

MODULE 12 Sequences and Series

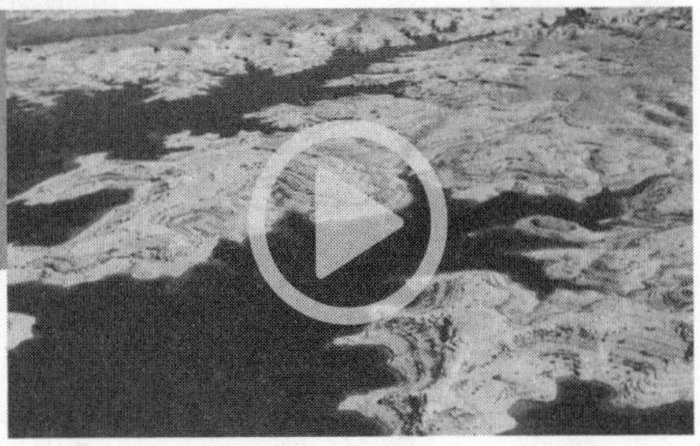

MODULE 13

Exponential Functions

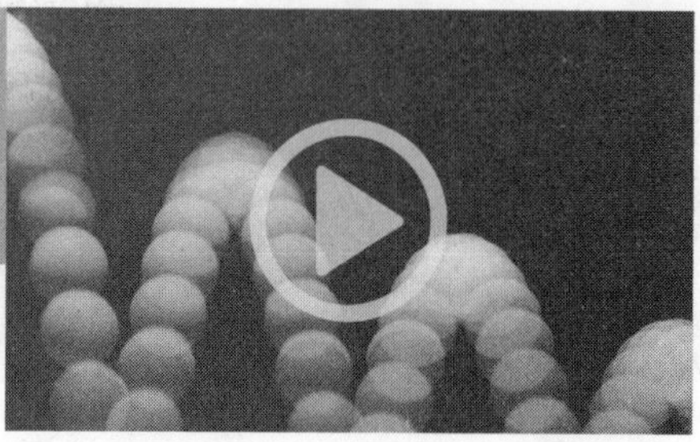

MODULE 14 Modeling with Exponential and Other Functions

MODULE 15 Logarithmic Functions

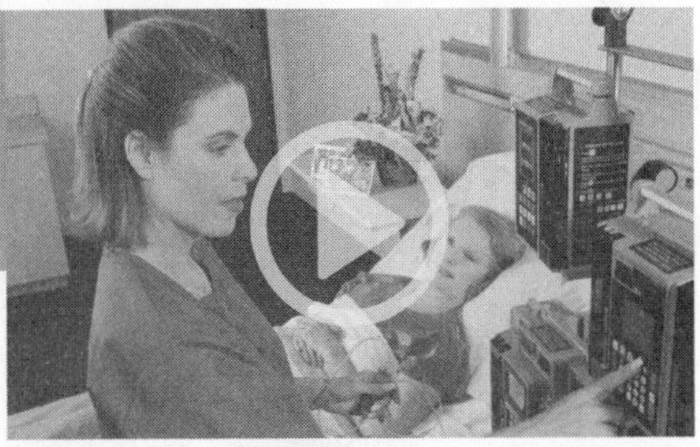

MODULE 16

Logarithmic Properties and Exponential Equations

Trigonometric Functions

UNIT 7

Volume 2

MODULE 17 Trigonometry with All Triangles

MODULE 18 Unit-Circle Definition of Trigonometric Functions

MODULE 19

Graphing Trigonometric Functions

Statistics and Decision Making

UNIT 8

Volume 2

MODULE 20 Gathering and Displaying Data

MODULE 21 Data Distributions

MODULE 22

Making Inferences from Data

MODULE 23

Probability and Decision Making

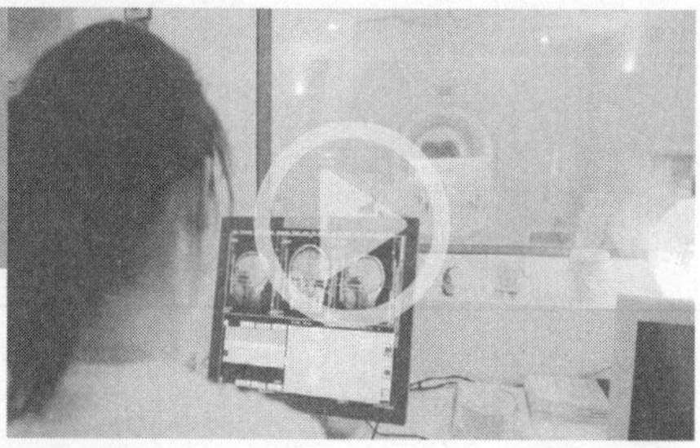

Properties of Circles

UNIT 9

Volume 2

MODULE 24 Angles and Segments in Circles

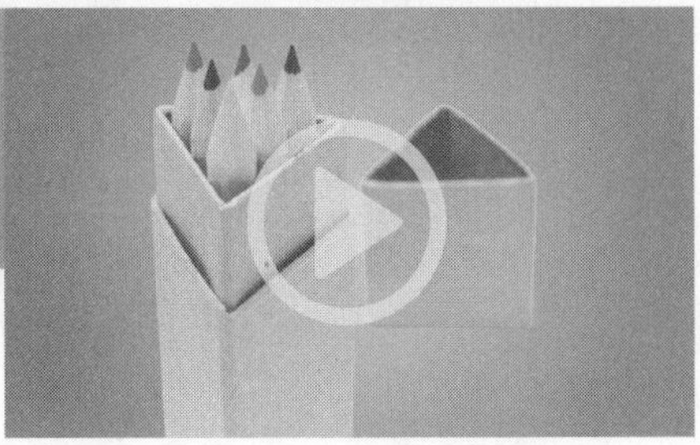

MODULE 25 Arc Length and Sector Area

MODULE 26

Equations of Circles and Parabolas

HMH Integrated Math 3

Online State Resources

Scan the QR code or visit:
my.hrw.com/nsmedia/osp/2015/ma/hs/tempint
for correlations and other state-specific resources.

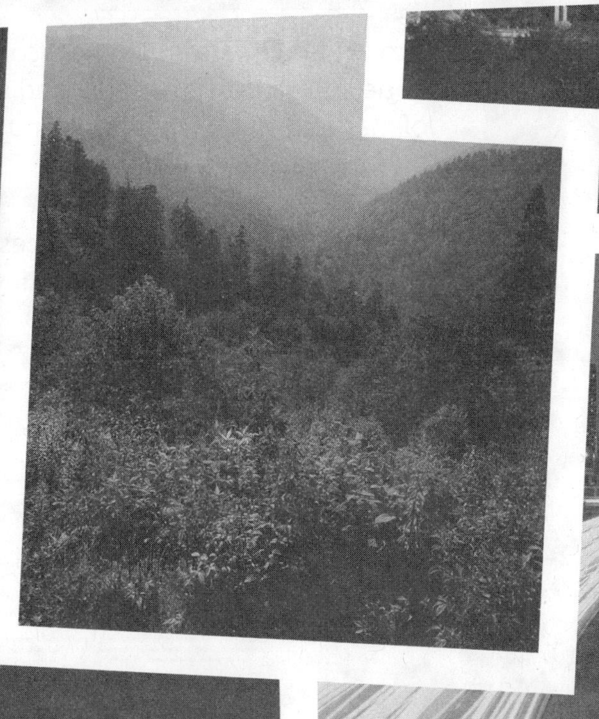

Succeeding with HMH Integrated Math 3

HMH Integrated Math 3 is built on the 5E instructional model–Engage, Explore, Explain, Elaborate, Evaluate–to develop strong conceptual understanding and mastery of key mathematics standards.

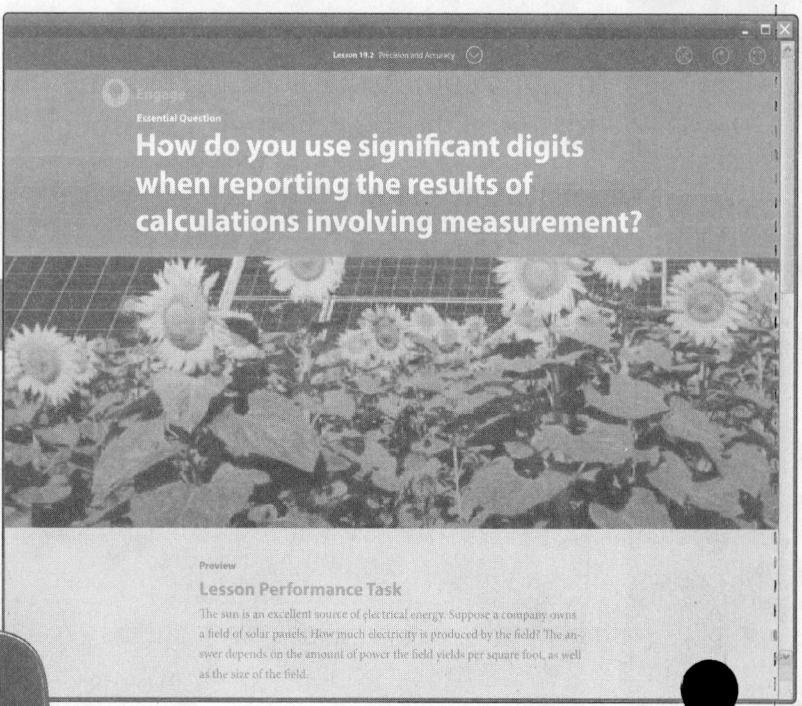
Lesson 19.2 Precision and Accuracy
Engage
Essential Question
How do you use significant digits when reporting the results of calculations involving measurement?
Preview
Lesson Performance Task
The sun is an excellent source of electrical energy. Suppose a company owns a field of solar panels. How much electricity is produced by the field? The answer depends on the amount of power the field yields per square foot, as well as the size of the field.

ENGAGE

Preview the Lesson Performance Task in the Interactive Student Edition.

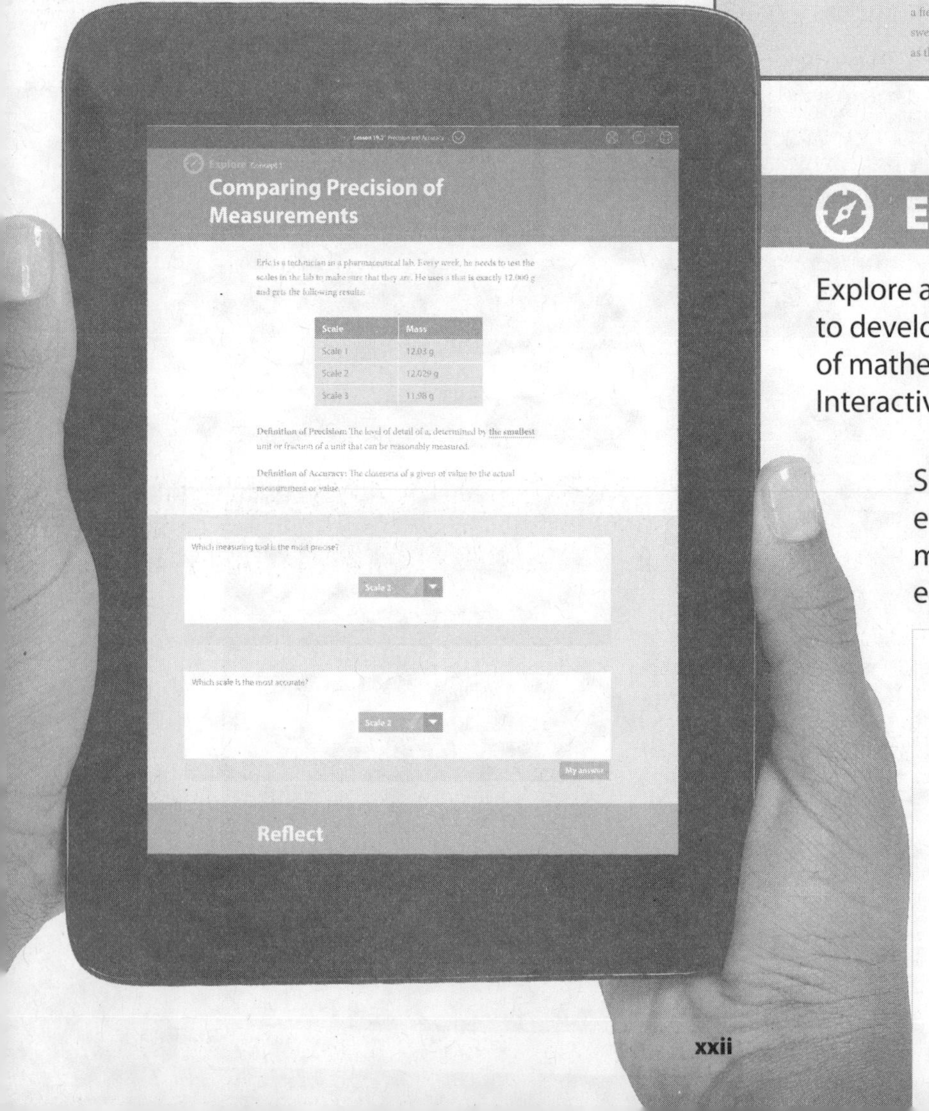
Comparing Precision of Measurements
Scale
Mass
Scale 1
12.03 g
Scale 2
12.029 g
Scale 3
11.98 g
Reflect

EXPLORE

Explore and interact with new concepts to develop a deeper understanding of mathematics in your book and the Interactive Student Edition.

Scan the QR code to access engaging videos, activities, and more in the Resource Locker for each lesson.

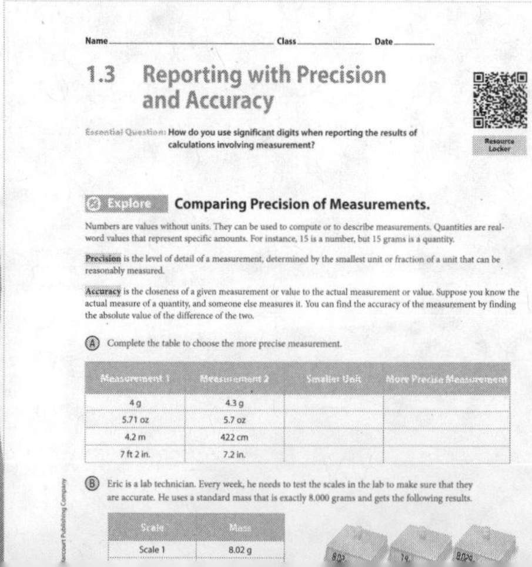

Name________ Class________ Date________

1.3 Reporting with Precision and Accuracy

Resource Locker

Essential Question: How do you use significant digits when reporting the results of calculations involving measurement?

Explore Comparing Precision of Measurements.

Numbers are values without units. They can be used to compute or to describe measurements. Quantities are real-word values that represent specific amounts. For instance, 15 is a number, but 15 grams is a quantity.

Precision is the level of detail of a measurement, determined by the smallest unit or fraction of a unit that can be reasonably measured.

Accuracy is the closeness of a given measurement or value to the actual measurement or value. Suppose you know the actual measure of a quantity, and someone else measures it. You can find the accuracy of the measurement by finding the absolute value of the difference of the two.

(A) Complete the table to choose the more precise measurement.

Measurement 1	Measurement 2	Smaller Unit	More Precise Measurement
4 g	4.3 g		
5.71 oz	5.7 oz		
4.2 m	422 cm		
7 ft 2 in.	7.2 in.		

(B) Eric is a lab technician. Every week, he needs to test the scales in the lab to make sure that they are accurate. He uses a standard mass that is exactly 8.000 grams and gets the following results.

Scale	Mass
Scale 1	8.02 g

EXPLAIN

Learn concepts with step-by-step interactive examples. Every example is also supported by a Math On the Spot video tutorial.

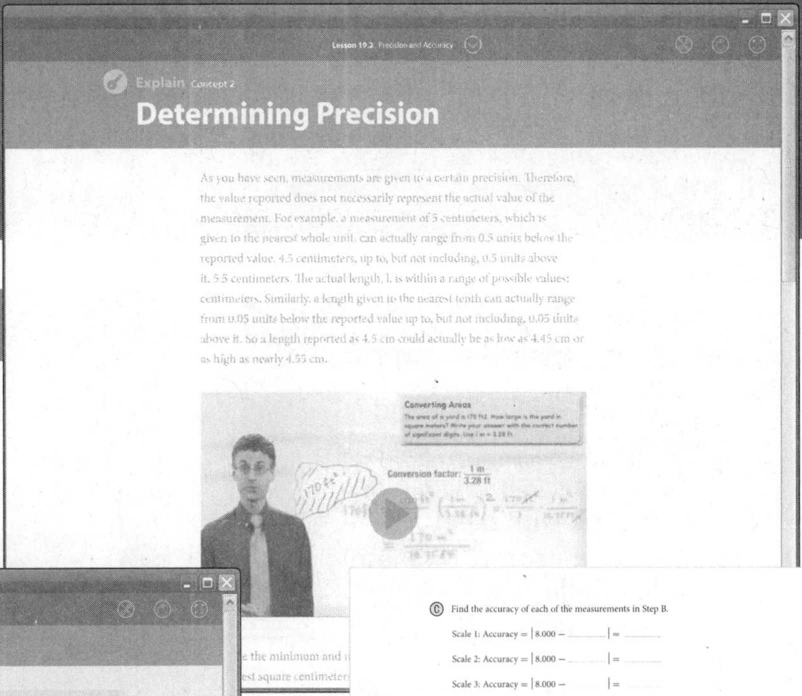

Lesson 19.2 Precision and Accuracy
Explain Concept 2
Determining Precision
As you have seen, measurements are given to a certain precision. Therefore, the value reported does not necessarily represent the actual value of the measurement. For example, a measurement of 5 centimeters, which is given to the nearest whole unit, can actually range from 0.5 units below the reported value, 4.5 centimeters, up to, but not including, 0.5 units above it, 5.5 centimeters. The actual length, l, is within a range of possible values: centimeters. Similarly, a length given to the nearest tenth can actually range from 0.05 units below the reported value up to, but not including, 0.05 units above it. So a length reported as 4.5 cm could actually be as low as 4.45 cm or as high as nearly 4.55 cm.
Converting Areas
Conversion factor: 1 m / 3.28 ft

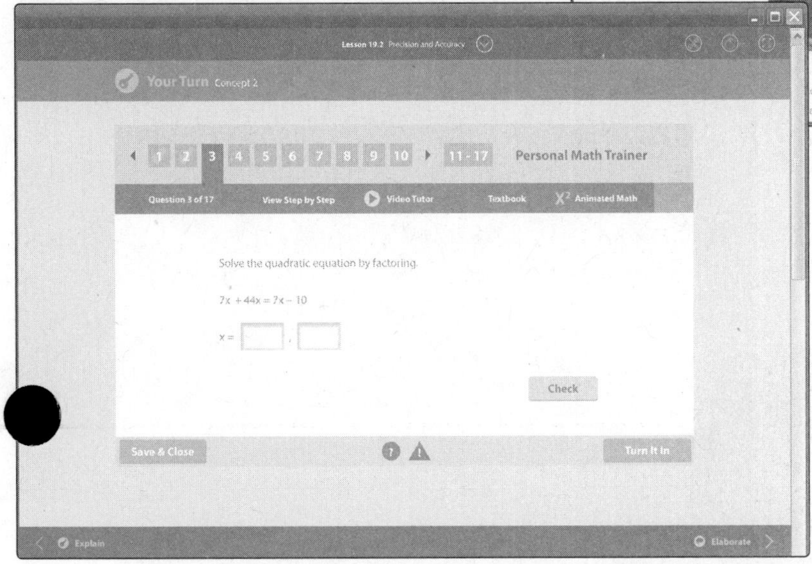

Lesson 19.2 Precision and Accuracy
Your Turn Concept 2
1 2 3 4 5 6 7 8 9 10 11-17
Personal Math Trainer
Question 3 of 17
View Step by Step
Video Tutor
Textbook
Animated Math
Solve the quadratic equation by factoring.
7x + 44x = 7x − 10
x =
Check
Save & Close
Turn It In
Explain
Elaborate

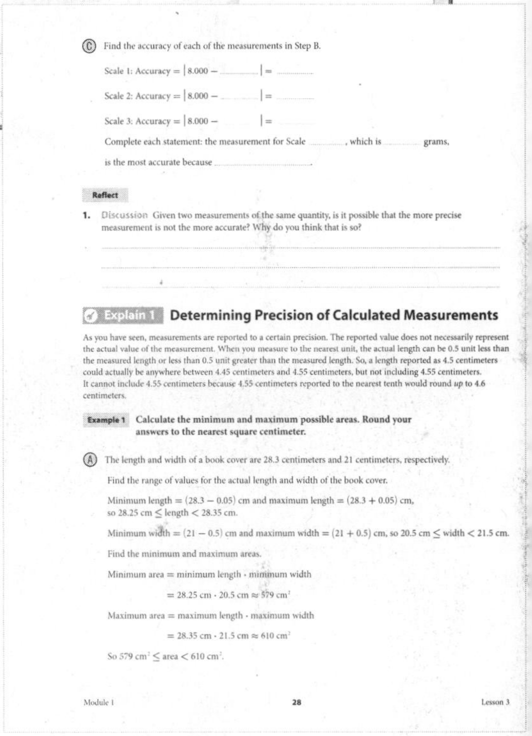

(C) Find the accuracy of each of the measurements in Step B.

Scale 1: Accuracy = |8.000 − ______| = ______

Scale 2: Accuracy = |8.000 − ______| = ______

Scale 3: Accuracy = |8.000 − ______| = ______

Complete each statement: the measurement for Scale ______, which is ______ grams, is the most accurate because ______.

Reflect

1. Discussion Given two measurements of the same quantity, is it possible that the more precise measurement is not the more accurate? Why do you think that is so?

Explain 1 Determining Precision of Calculated Measurements

As you have seen, measurements are reported to a certain precision. The reported value does not necessarily represent the actual value of the measurement. When you measure to the nearest unit, the actual length can be 0.5 unit less than the measured length or less than 0.5 unit greater than the measured length. So, a length reported as 4.5 centimeters could actually be anywhere between 4.45 centimeters and 4.55 centimeters, but not including 4.55 centimeters. It cannot include 4.55 centimeters because 4.55 centimeters reported to the nearest tenth would round *up* to 4.6 centimeters.

Example 1 **Calculate the minimum and maximum possible areas. Round your answers to the nearest square centimeter.**

(A) The length and width of a book cover are 28.3 centimeters and 21 centimeters, respectively.

Find the range of values for the actual length and width of the book cover.

Minimum length = $(28.3 - 0.05)$ cm and maximum length = $(28.3 + 0.05)$ cm, so 28.25 cm $\leq$ length $<$ 28.35 cm.

Minimum width = $(21 - 0.5)$ cm and maximum width = $(21 + 0.5)$ cm, so 20.5 cm $\leq$ width $<$ 21.5 cm.

Find the minimum and maximum areas.

Minimum area = minimum length · minimum width

$= 28.25 \text{ cm} \cdot 20.5 \text{ cm} \approx 579 \text{ cm}^2$

Maximum area = maximum length · maximum width

$= 28.35 \text{ cm} \cdot 21.5 \text{ cm} \approx 610 \text{ cm}^2$

So $579 \text{ cm}^2 \leq \text{area} < 610 \text{ cm}^2$.

Module 1 28 Lesson 3

Check your understanding of new concepts and skills with Your Turn exercises in your book or online with Personal Math Trainer.

Personal Math Trainer

ELABORATE

Show your understanding and reasoning with Reflect and Elaborate questions.

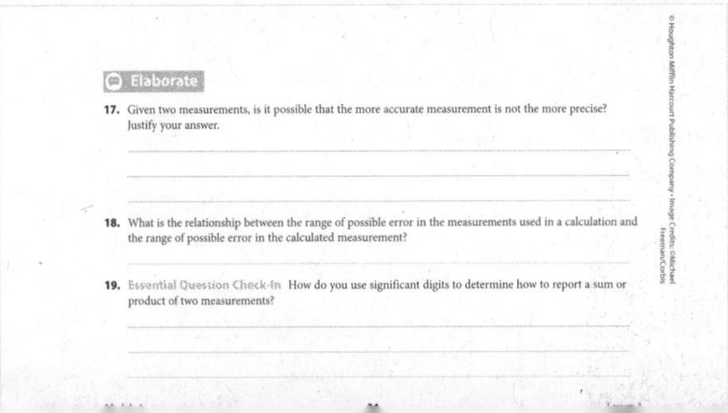

Elaborate

17. Given two measurements, is it possible that the more accurate measurement is not the more precise? Justify your answer.

18. What is the relationship between the range of possible error in the measurements used in a calculation and the range of possible error in the calculated measurement?

19. Essential Question Check-In How do you use significant digits to determine how to report a sum or product of two measurements?

© Houghton Mifflin Harcourt Publishing Company • Image Credits: ©Michael Freeman/Corbis

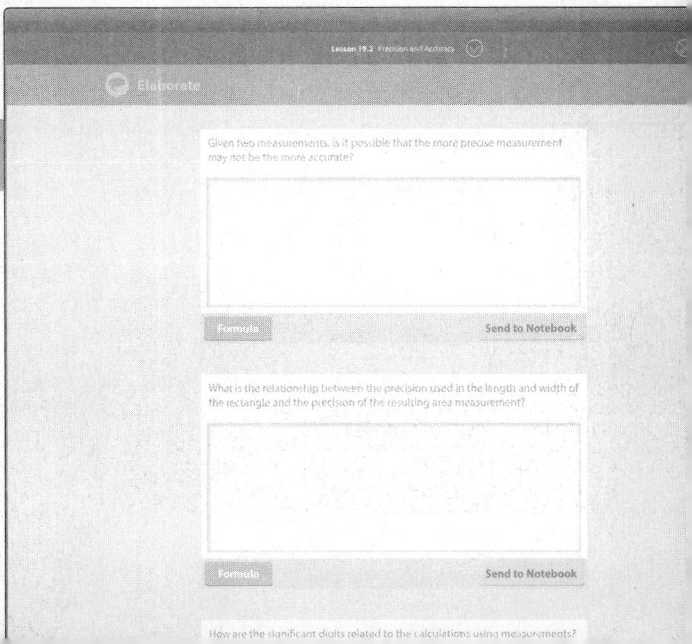

Lesson 19.2 Precision and Accuracy
Elaborate
Given two measurements, is it possible that the more precise measurement may not be the more accurate?
Formula
Send to Notebook
What is the relationship between the precision used in the length and width of the rectangle and the precision of the resulting area measurement?
Formula
Send to Notebook
How are the significant digits related to the calculations using measurements?

EVALUATE

Practice and apply skills and concepts with Evaluate exercises and a Lesson Performance Task in your book with plenty of workspace, or complete these exercises online with Personal Math Trainer.

Personal
Math
Trainer

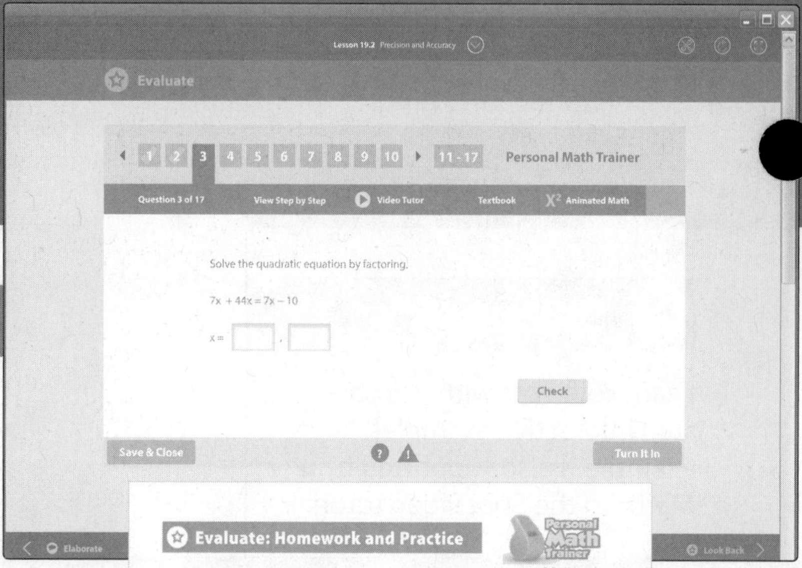

Lesson 19.2 Precision and Accuracy
Evaluate
1 2 3 4 5 6 7 8 9 10 11 - 17
Personal Math Trainer
Question 3 of 17
View Step by Step
Video Tutor
Textbook
Animated Math
Solve the quadratic equation by factoring.
7x + 44x = 7x − 10
x =
Check
Save & Close
Turn It In
Elaborate
Look Back

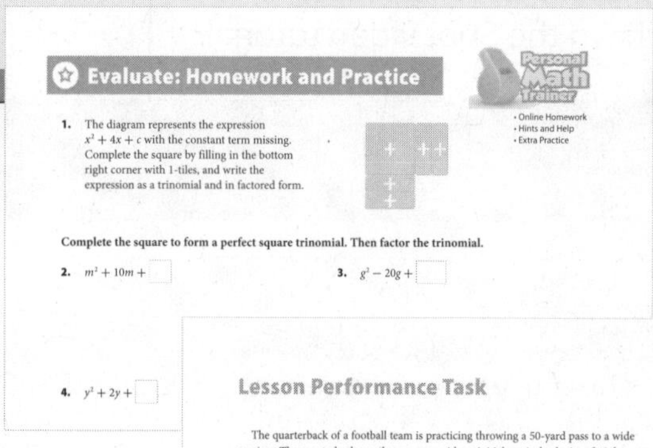

Evaluate: Homework and Practice
Personal Math Trainer
• Online Homework
• Hints and Help
• Extra Practice
1. The diagram represents the expression x² + 4x + c with the constant term missing. Complete the square by filling in the bottom right corner with 1-tiles, and write the expression as a trinomial and in factored form.
Complete the square to form a perfect square trinomial. Then factor the trinomial.
2. m² + 10m +
3. g² − 20g +
4. y² + 2y +

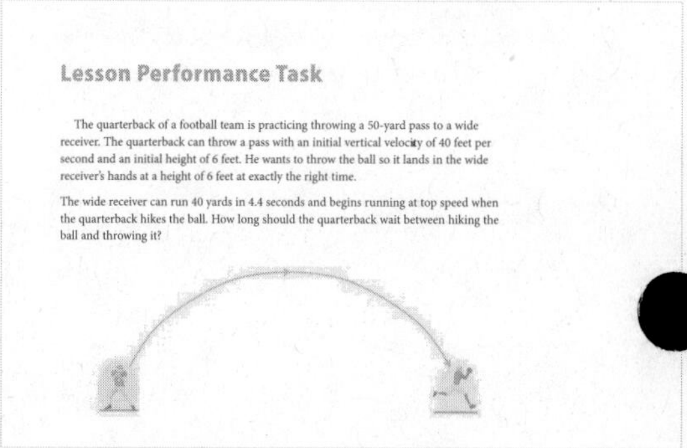

Lesson Performance Task
The quarterback of a football team is practicing throwing a 50-yard pass to a wide receiver. The quarterback can throw a pass with an initial vertical velocity of 40 feet per second and an initial height of 6 feet. He wants to throw the ball so it lands in the wide receiver's hands at a height of 6 feet at exactly the right time.
The wide receiver can run 40 yards in 4.4 seconds and begins running at top speed when the quarterback hikes the ball. How long should the quarterback wait between hiking the ball and throwing it?

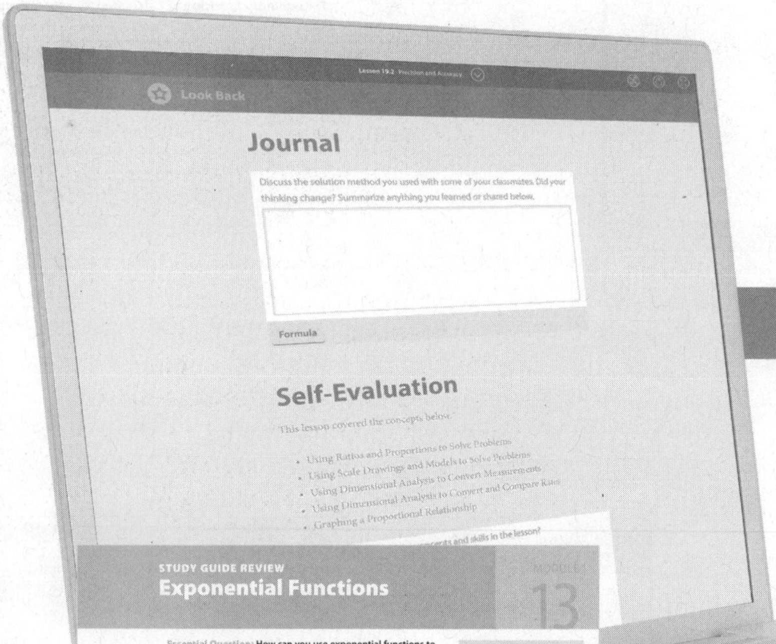

Look Back
Journal
Discuss the solution method you used with some of your classmates. Did your thinking change? Summarize anything you learned or shared below.
Formula
Self-Evaluation

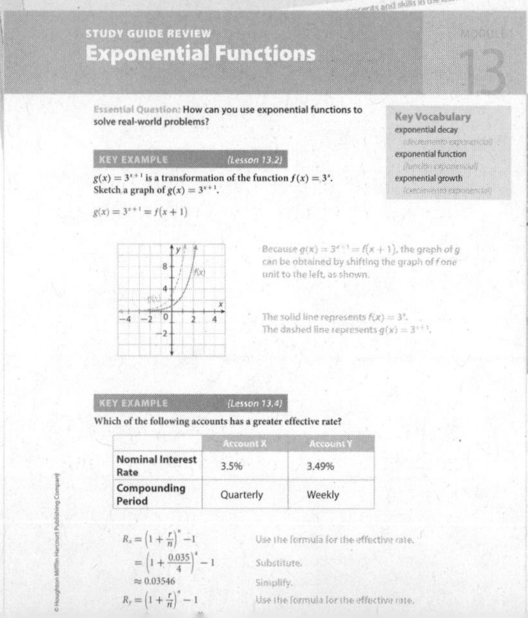

STUDY GUIDE REVIEW
Exponential Functions
MODULE 13
Essential Question: How can you use exponential functions to solve real-world problems?
Key Vocabulary
exponential decay
exponential function
exponential growth
KEY EXAMPLE (Lesson 13.2)
KEY EXAMPLE (Lesson 13.4)
Which of the following accounts has a greater effective rate?
Account X
Account Y
Nominal Interest Rate
3.5%
3.49%
Compounding Period
Quarterly
Weekly

LOOK BACK

Review what you have learned and prepare for high-stakes tests with a variety of resources, including Study Guide Reviews, Performance Tasks, and Assessment Readiness test preparation.

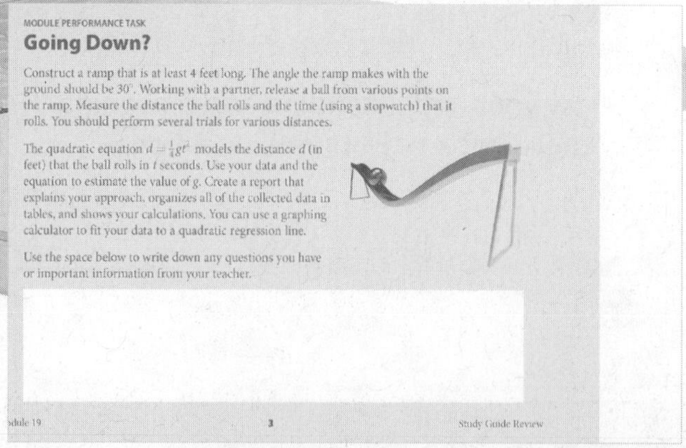

MODULE PERFORMANCE TASK
Going Down?
Construct a ramp that is at least 4 feet long. The angle the ramp makes with the ground should be 30°. Working with a partner, release a ball from various points on the ramp. Measure the distance the ball rolls and the time (using a stopwatch) that it rolls. You should perform several trials for various distances.
Use the space below to write down any questions you have or important information from your teacher.
Study Guide Review

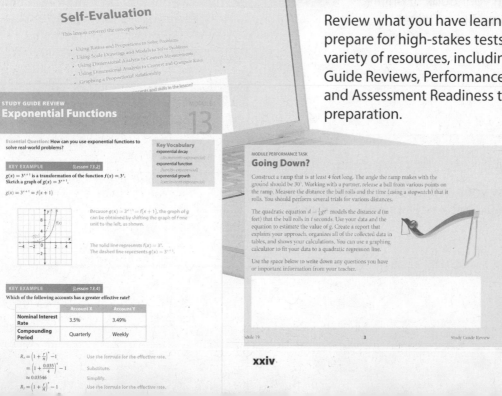

UNIT 1

Methods for Reasoning with Geometry

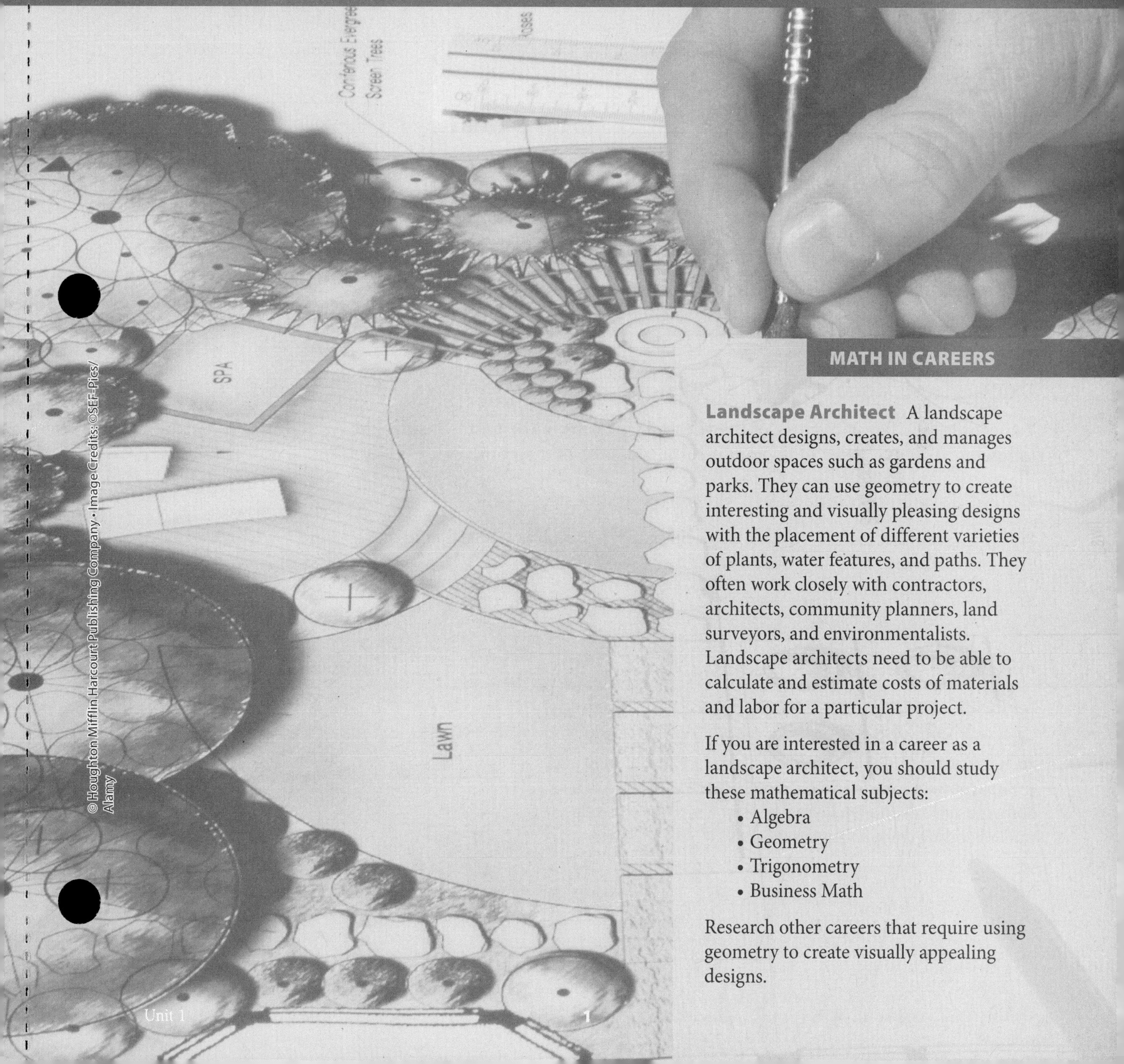

MATH IN CAREERS

Landscape Architect A landscape architect designs, creates, and manages outdoor spaces such as gardens and parks. They can use geometry to create interesting and visually pleasing designs with the placement of different varieties of plants, water features, and paths. They often work closely with contractors, architects, community planners, land surveyors, and environmentalists. Landscape architects need to be able to calculate and estimate costs of materials and labor for a particular project.

If you are interested in a career as a landscape architect, you should study these mathematical subjects:

- Algebra
- Geometry
- Trigonometry
- Business Math

Research other careers that require using geometry to create visually appealing designs.

Reading Start-Up

Visualize Vocabulary

Use the review words to complete the chart.

	A formula that finds the distance between two points, written as $(x_2 - x_1)^2 + (y_2 - y_1)^2 = d^2$.
	Two lines that lie in the same plane and never intersect.
	A formula that finds the midpoint of a line segment, written as $M = \left(\frac{x_1 + x_2}{2}, \frac{y_1 + y_2}{2}\right)$.
	A ratio that is used to determine how steep a line is.
	When two lines intersect, four angles result. This refers to either pair of angles that are not adjacent to each other.

Vocabulary

Review Words

✔ distance formula *(fórmula de la distancia)*
✔ midpoint formula *(fórmula de punto medio)*
✔ opposite angles *(ángulos opuestos)*
✔ parallel *(paralelo)*
✔ slope *(pendiente)*

Preview Words

composite figure *(figura compuesta)*
coordinate proof *(demostración coordenado)*
parallelogram *(paralelogramo)*
quadrilateral *(cuadrilátero)*
rhombus *(rombo)*
transversal *(transversal)*

Understand Vocabulary

To become familiar with some of the vocabulary terms in the unit, consider the following. You may refer to the module, the glossary, or a dictionary.

1. A __________ is a quadrilateral with four congruent sides.

2. A ______________ is made up of simple shapes, such as triangles and quadrilaterals.

3. A ______________ is any quadrilateral whose opposite sides are parallel.

Active Reading

Before beginning the unit, create a booklet to help you organize what you learn. Write a main topic from each module on each page of the booklet. Write details of each main topic on the appropriate page to create an outline of the module. The ability to reword and retell the details of a module will help in understanding complex materials.

Constructions

MODULE 1

Essential Question: How can you use constructions to solve real-world problems?

REAL WORLD VIDEO
Check out how properties of parallel and perpendicular lines and angles can be used to create real-world illusions in a mystery spot building.

MODULE PERFORMANCE TASK PREVIEW

Mystery Spot Building

In this module, you will use properties of parallel lines and angles to analyze the strange happenings in a mystery spot building. With a little bit of geometry, you'll be able to figure out whether mystery spot buildings are "on the up-and-up!"

Are YOU Ready?

Complete these exercises to review skills you will need for this module.

Personal Math Trainer
- Online Homework
- Hints and Help
- Extra Practice

Angle Relationships

Example 1

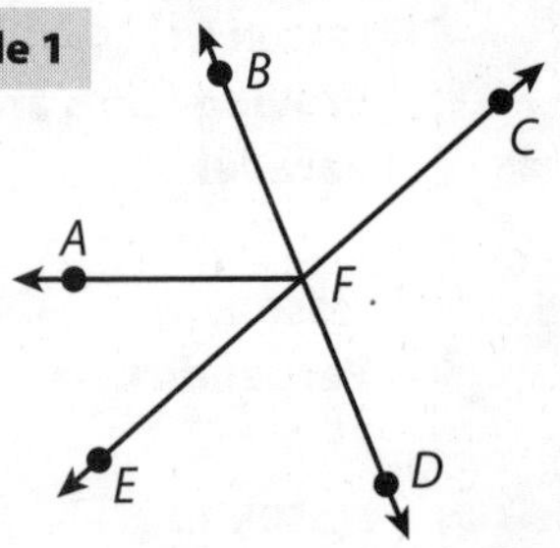

The measure of $\angle AFB$ is 70° and the measure of $\angle AFE$ is 40°. Find the measure of angle $\angle BFE$.

$m\angle BFE = m\angle AFB + m\angle AFE$ Angle Addition Postulate

$m\angle BFE = 70° + 40°$ Substitute.

$m\angle BFE = 110°$ Solve for $m\angle BFE$.

Find the measure of the angle in the image from the example.

1. The measure of $\angle BFE$ is 110°. Find $m\angle CFD$.

$m\angle CFD =$ ______

2. The measure of $\angle BFE$ is 110°. Find $m\angle EFD$ and $m\angle BFC$.

$m\angle EFD = m\angle BFC =$ ______

Parallel Lines Cut by a Transversal

Example 2 The measure of $\angle 7$ is 110°. Find $m\angle 3$. Assume $p \parallel q$.

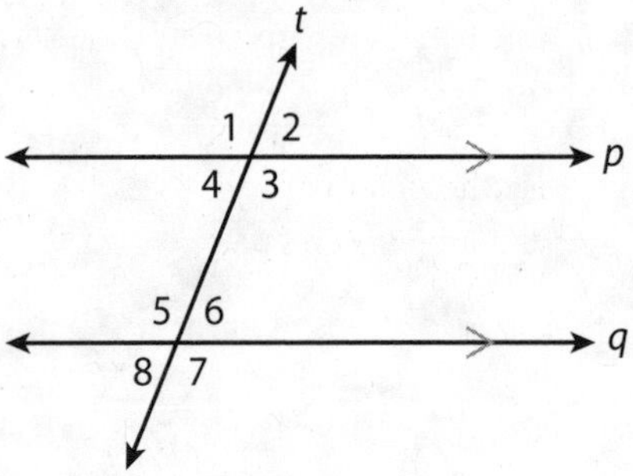

$m\angle 3 = m\angle 7$ Corresponding Angles Theorem

$m\angle 3 = 110°$ Substitute.

Find the measure of the angle in the image from the example. Assume $p \parallel q$.

3. The measure of $\angle 3$ is 110°. Find $m\angle 1$. $m\angle 1 =$ ______

4. The measure of $\angle 3$ is 110°. Find $m\angle 6$. $m\angle 6 =$ ______

Writing Equations of Parallel, Perpendicular, Vertical, and Horizontal Lines

Example 3 Find the line parallel to $y = 2x + 7$ that passes through the point (3, 6).

$(y - y_1) = m(x - x_1)$ Use point-slope form.

$(y - 6) = 2(x - 3)$ Substitute for m, x_1, y_1. Parallel lines have the same slope, so $m = 2$.

$y - 6 = 2x - 6$ Simplify.

$y = 2x$ Solve for y.

Find the equation of the line described.

5. Perpendicular to $y = 3x + 5$; passing through the point $(-6, -4)$ ______

6. Parallel to the x-axis; passing through the point $(4, 1)$ ______

Name ________________________ Class ______________ Date ________

1.1 Proving Lines are Parallel

Essential Question: How can you prove that two lines are parallel?

Resource Locker

Explore Writing Converses of Parallel Line Theorems

You form the **converse** of and if-then statement "if *p*, then *q*" by swapping *p* and *q*. The converses of the postulate and theorems you have learned about lines cut by a transversal are true statements. In the Explore, you will write specific cases of each of these converses.

The diagram shows two lines cut by a transversal *t*. Use the diagram and the given statements in Steps A–D. You will complete the statements based on your work in Steps A–D.

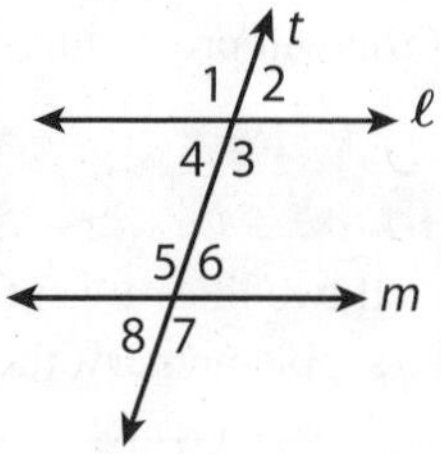

Statements	
lines ℓ and m are parallel	$\angle 4 \cong \angle$ ☐
$\angle 6$ and $\angle$ ☐ are supplementary	$\angle$ ☐ $\cong \angle 7$

Ⓐ Use two of the given statements together to complete a statement about the diagram using the Same-Side Interior Angles Postulate.

By the postulate: If ______________________________, then $\angle 6$ and $\angle$ ☐ are supplementary.

Ⓑ Now write the converse of the Same-Side Interior Angles Postulate using the diagram and your statement in Step A.

By its converse: If ______________________________,

then ______________________________.

Ⓒ Repeat to illustrate the Alternate Interior Angles Theorem and its converse using the diagram and the given statements.

By the theorem: If ______________________________, then $\angle 4 \cong \angle$ ☐.

By its converse: If ______________________________,

then ______________________________.

Ⓓ Use the diagram and the given statements to illustrate the Corresponding Angles Theorem and its converse.

By the theorem: If ______________________________, then $\angle$ ☐ $\cong \angle 7$.

By its converse: ______________________________.

Reflect

1. How do you form the converse of a statement?

2. What kind of angles are ∠4 and ∠6 in Step C? What does the converse you wrote in Step C mean?

Explain 1 Proving that Two Lines are Parallel

The converses from the Explore can be stated formally as a postulate and two theorems. (You will prove the converses of the theorems in the exercises.)

Converse of the Same-Side Interior Angles Postulate

If two lines are cut by a transversal so that a pair of same-side interior angles are supplementary, then the lines are parallel.

Converse of the Alternate Interior Angles Theorem

If two lines are cut by a transversal so that any pair of alternate interior angles are congruent, then the lines are parallel.

Converse of the Corresponding Angles Theorem

If two lines are cut by a transversal so that any pair of corresponding angles are congruent, then the lines are parallel.

You can use these converses to decide whether two lines are parallel.

Example 1 **A mosaic designer is using quadrilateral-shaped colored tiles to make an ornamental design. Each tile is congruent to the one shown here.**

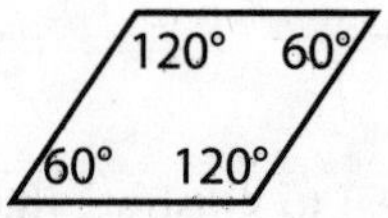

The designer uses the colored tiles to create the pattern shown here.

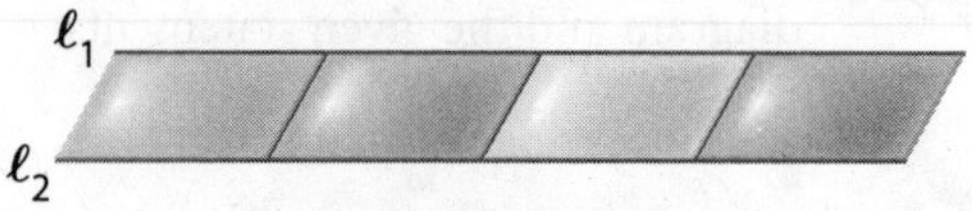

Ⓐ Use the values of the marked angles to show that the two lines ℓ_1 and ℓ_2 are parallel.

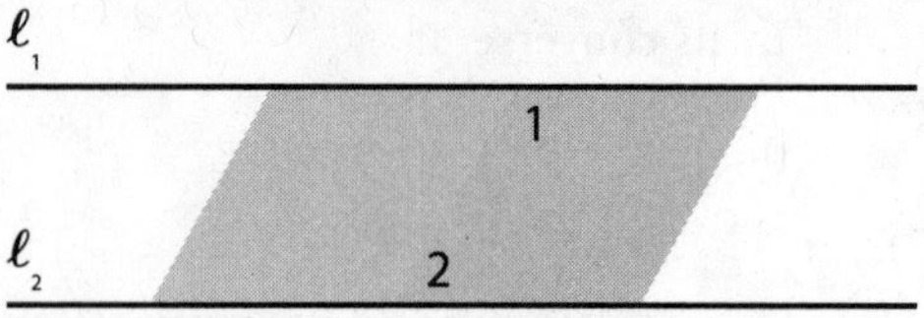

Measure of ∠1: 120° Measure of ∠2: 60°

Relationship between the two angles: They are supplementary.

Conclusion: $\ell_1 \parallel \ell_2$ by the Converse of the Same-Side Interior Angles Postulate.

(B) Now look at this situation. Use the values of the marked angles to show that the two lines are parallel.

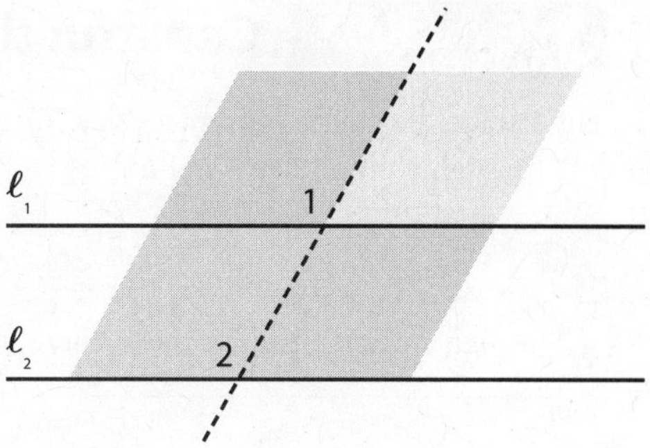

Measure of ∠1: ____________ Measure of ∠2: ____________

Relationship between the two angles: ____________

Conclusion:

____

Reflect

3. **What If?** Suppose the designer had been working with this basic shape instead. Do you think the conclusions in Parts A and B would have been different? Why or why not?

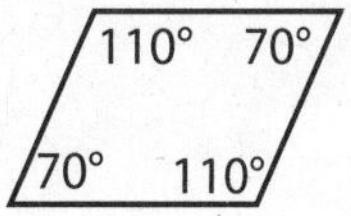

____

____

Your Turn

Explain why the lines are parallel given the angles shown. Assume that all tile patterns use this basic shape.

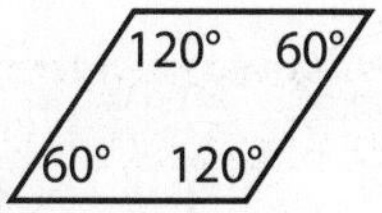

4.

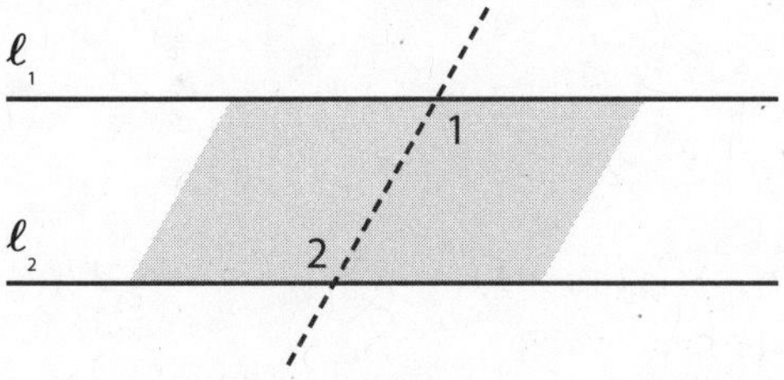

5.

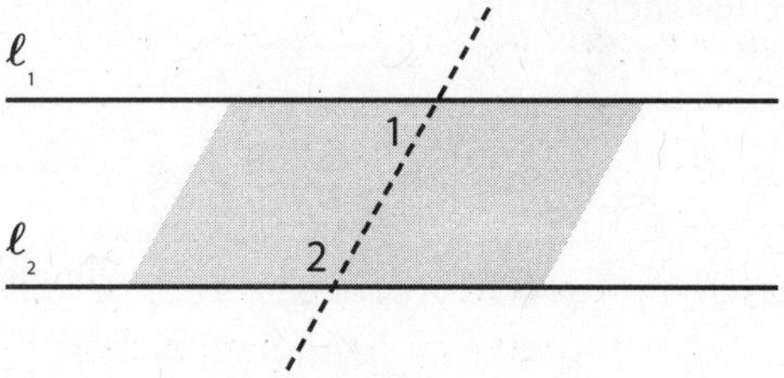

Explain 2 Constructing Parallel Lines

The Parallel Postulate guarantees that for any line ℓ, you can always construct a parallel line through a point that is not on ℓ.

The Parallel Postulate
Through a point P not on line ℓ, there is exactly one line parallel to ℓ.

Example 2 **Use a compass and straightedge to construct parallel lines.**

(A) Construct a line m through a point P not on a line ℓ so that m is parallel to ℓ.

Step 1 Draw a line ℓ and a point P not on ℓ.

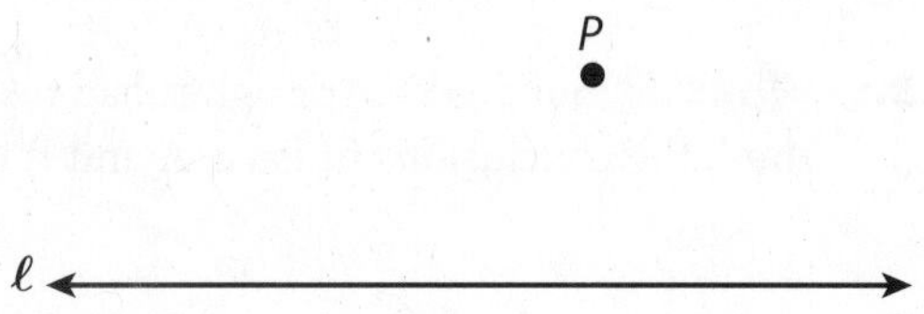

Step 2 Choose two points on ℓ and label them Q and R. Use a straightedge to draw $\overleftrightarrow{PQ}$.

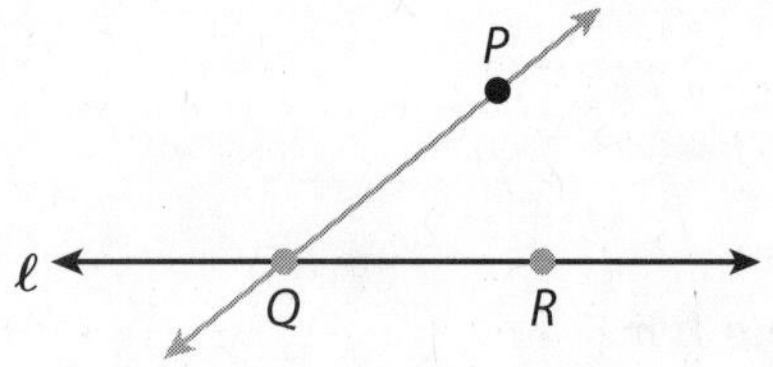

Step 3 Use a compass to copy $\angle PQR$ at point P, as shown, to construct line m.

line $m \parallel$ line ℓ

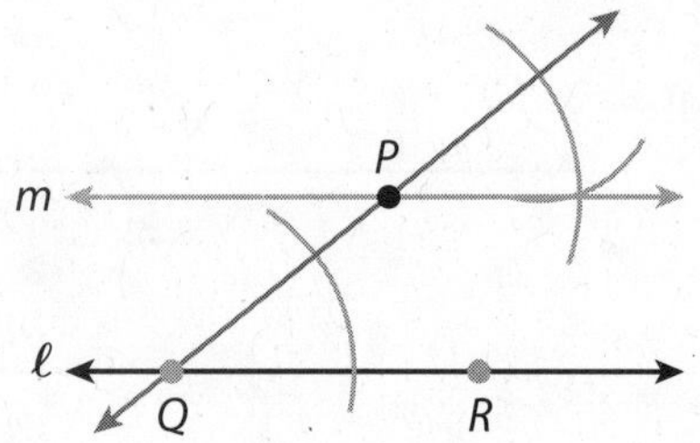

(B) In the space provided, follow the steps to construct a line r through a point G not on a line s so that r is parallel to s.

Step 1 Draw a line s and a point G not on s.

Step 2 Choose two points on s and label them E and F. Use a straightedge to draw $\overleftrightarrow{GE}$.

Step 3 Use a compass to copy $\angle GEF$ at point G. Label the side of the angle as line r.
line $r \parallel$ line s

Reflect

6. **Discussion** Explain how you know that the construction in Part A or Part B produces a line passing through the given point that is parallel to the given line.

____

____

____

Your Turn

7. Construct a line m through P parallel to line ℓ.

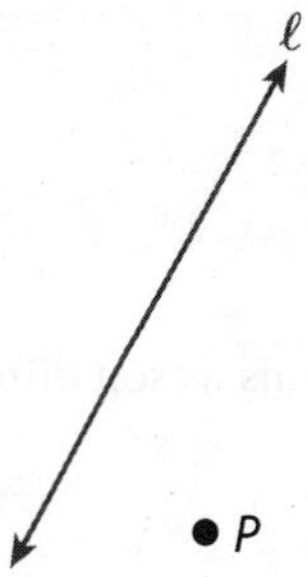

Explain 3 Using Angle Pair Relationships to Verify Lines are Parallel

When two lines are cut by a transversal, you can use relationships of pairs of angles to decide if the lines are parallel.

Example 3 **Use the given angle relationships to decide whether the lines are parallel. Explain your reasoning.**

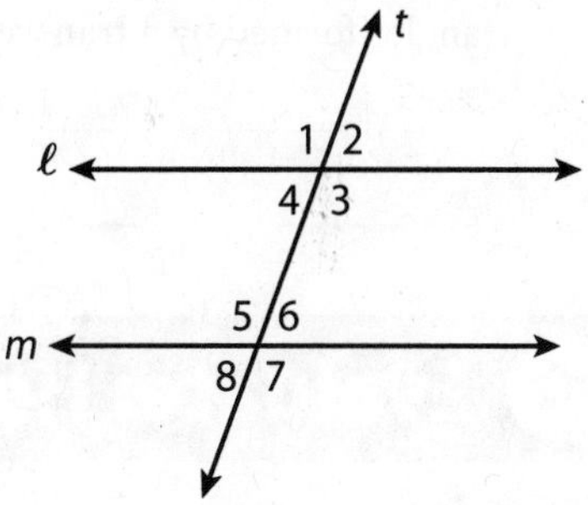

Ⓐ $\angle 3 \cong \angle 5$

Step 1 Identify the relationship between the two angles.
$\angle 3$ and $\angle 5$ are congruent alternate interior angles.

Step 2 Are the lines parallel? Explain.
Yes, the lines are parallel by the Converse of the Alternate Interior Angles Theorem.

Ⓑ $m\angle 4 = (x + 20)°$, $m\angle 8 = (2x + 5)°$, and $x = 15$.

Step 1 Identify the relationship between the two angles.

$m\angle 4 = (x + 20)°$ $\quad$ $m\angle 8 = (2x + 5)°$

$= (\square + 20)° = \square$ $\quad$ $= (2 \cdot \square + 5)° = \square$

So, ______ and ______ are ______________________ angles.

Step 2 Are the lines parallel? Explain.

____

Your Turn

Identify the type of angle pair described in the given condition. How do you know that lines ℓ and m are parallel?

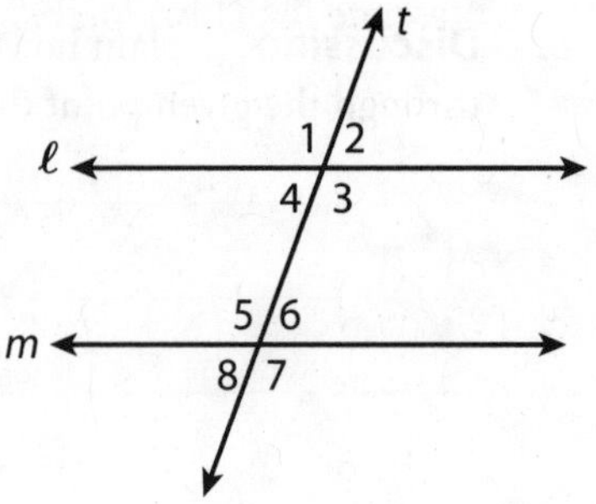

8. $m\angle 3 + m\angle 6 = 180°$

9. $\angle 2 \cong \angle 6$

Elaborate

10. How are the converses in this lesson different from the postulate/theorems in the previous lesson?

11. **What If?** Suppose two lines are cut by a transversal such that alternate interior angles are both congruent and supplementary. Describe the lines.

12. **Essential Question Check-In** Name two ways to test if a pair of lines is parallel, using the interior angles formed by a transversal crossing the two lines.

Evaluate: Homework and Practice

- Online Homework
- Hints and Help
- Extra Practice

The diagram shows two lines cut by a transversal t. Use the diagram and the given statements in Exercises 1–3 on the facing page.

Statements
lines ℓ and m are parallel
$m\angle$ ☐ $+ m\angle 3 = 180°$
$\angle 1 \cong \angle$ ☐
$\angle$ ☐ $\cong \angle 6$

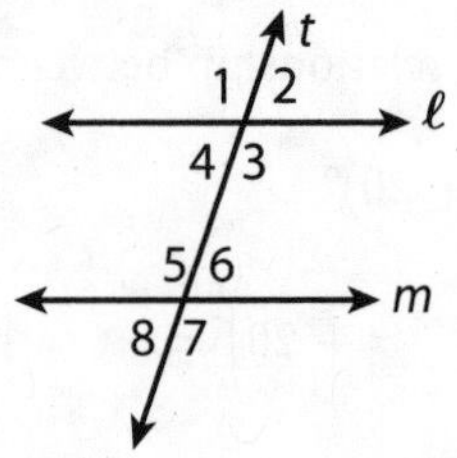

1. Use two of the given statements together to complete statements about the diagram to illustrate the Corresponding Angles Theorem. Then write its converse.

By the theorem: If ______________________________, then $\angle 1 \cong \angle$ ☐.

By its converse: ______________________________

2. Use two of the given statements together to complete statements about the diagram to illustrate the Same-Side Interior Angles Postulate. Then write its converse.

By the postulate: If ______________________, then $m\angle$ ☐ $+ m\angle 3 = 180°$.

By its converse: ______________________________

3. Use two of the given statements together to complete statements about the diagram to illustrate the Alternate Interior Angles Theorem. Then write its converse.

By the theorem: If ______________________________, then $\angle$ ☐ $\cong \angle 6$.

By its converse: ______________________________

4. **Matching** Match the angle pair relationship on the left with the name of a postulate or theorem that you could use to prove that lines ℓ and m in the diagram are parallel.

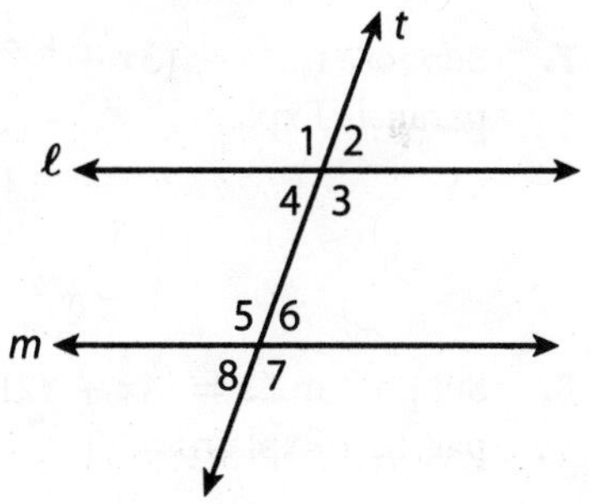

A. $\angle 2 \cong \angle 6$

B. $\angle 3 \cong \angle 5$

C. $\angle 4$ and $\angle 5$ are supplementary.

D. $\angle 4 \cong \angle 8$

E. $m\angle 3 + m\angle 6 = 180°$

F. $\angle 4 \cong \angle 6$

________ Converse of the Corresponding Angles Theorem

________ Converse of the Same-Side Interior Angles Postulate

________ Converse of the Alternate Interior Angles Theorem

Use the diagram for Exercises 5–8.

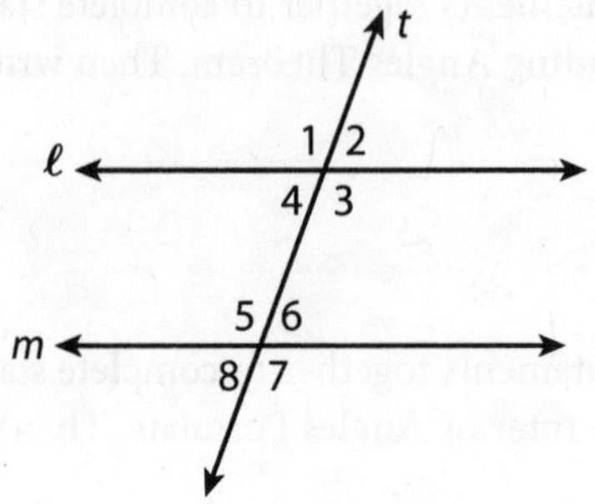

5. What must be true about $\angle 7$ and $\angle 3$ for the lines to be parallel? Name the postulate or theorem.

6. What must be true about $\angle 6$ and $\angle 3$ for the lines to be parallel? Name the postulate or theorem.

7. Suppose $m\angle 4 = (3x + 5)°$ and $m\angle 5 = (x + 95)°$, where $x = 20$. Are the lines parallel? Explain.

8. Suppose $m\angle 3 = (4x + 12)°$ and $m\angle 7 = (80 - x)°$, where $x = 15$. Are the lines parallel? Explain.

Use a converse to answer each question.

9. What value of x makes the horizontal parts of the letter Z parallel?

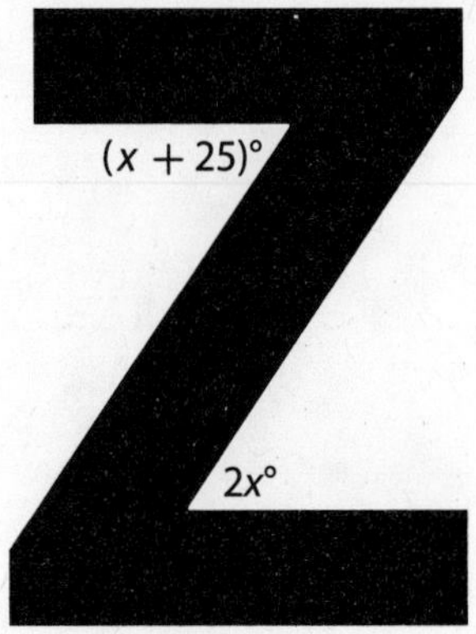

10. What value of x makes the vertical parts of the letter N parallel?

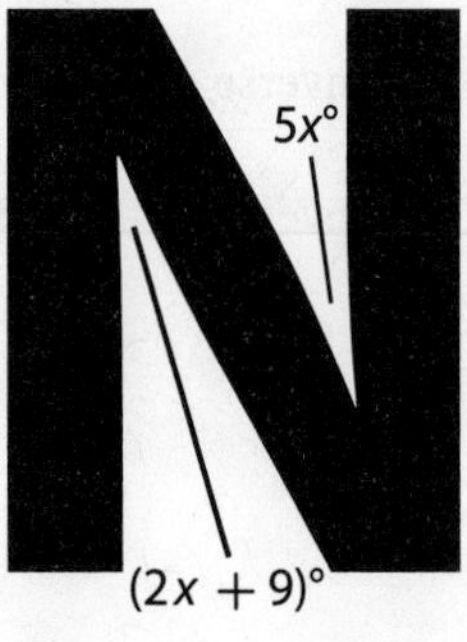

11. Engineering An overpass intersects two lanes of a highway. What must the value of x be to ensure the two lanes are parallel?

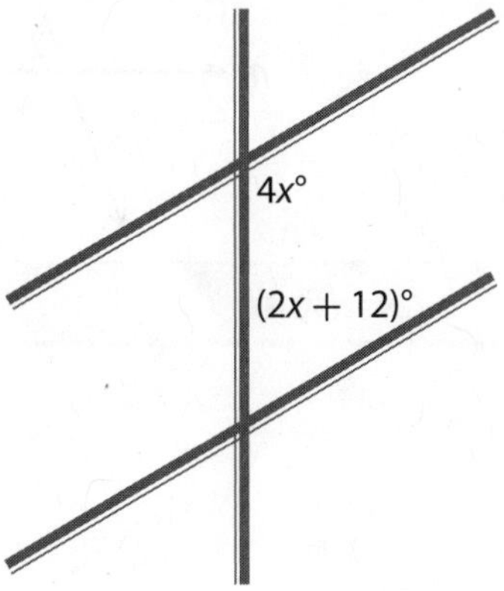

12. A trellis consists of overlapping wooden slats. What must the value of x be in order for the two slats to be parallel?

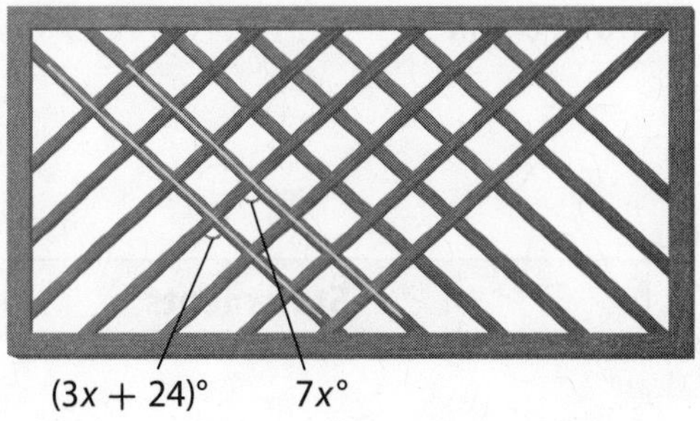

13. Construct a line parallel to ℓ that passes through P.

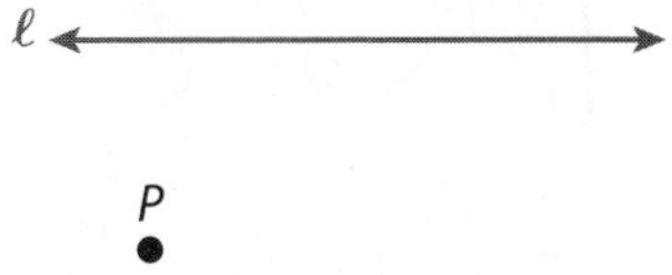

14. Communicate Mathematical Ideas In Exercise 13, how many parallel lines can you draw through P that are parallel to ℓ? Explain.

H.O.T. Focus on Higher Order Thinking

15. Justify Reasoning Write a two-column proof of the Converse of the Alternate Interior Angles Theorem.

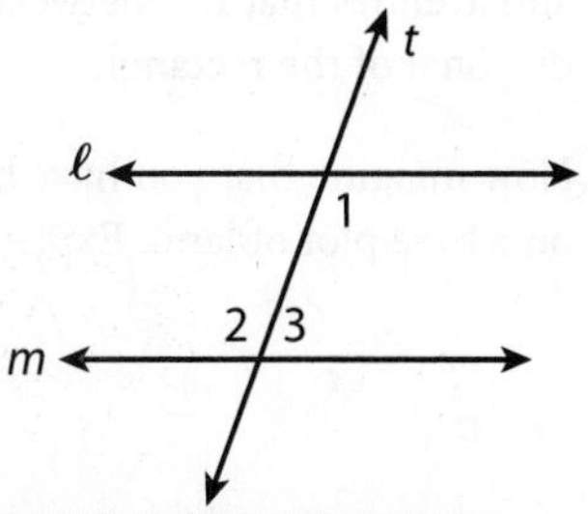

Given: lines ℓ and m are cut by a transversal t; $\angle 1 \cong \angle 2$

Prove: $\ell \parallel m$

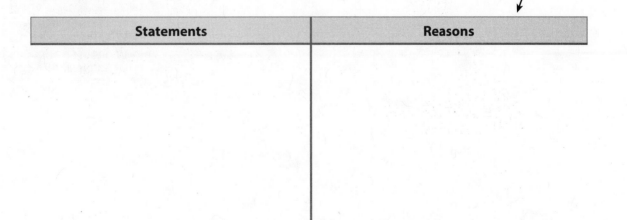

Statements	Reasons

16. Justify Reasoning Write a two-column proof of the Converse of the Corresponding Angles Theorem.

Given: lines ℓ and m are cut by a transversal t; $\angle 1 \cong \angle 2$

Prove: $\ell \parallel m$

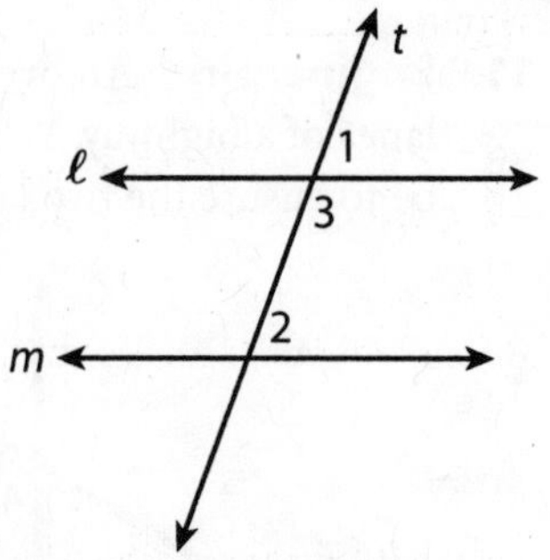

Statements	Reasons

Lesson Performance Task

A simplified street map of a section of Harlem in New York City is shown at right. Draw a sketch of the rectangle bounded by West 110th Street and West 121st Street in one direction and Eighth Avenue and Lenox Avenue in the other. Include all the streets and avenues that run between sides of the rectangle. Show St. Nicholas Avenue as a diagonal of the rectangle.

Now imagine that you have been given the job of laying out these streets and avenues on a bare plot of land. Explain in detail how you would do it.

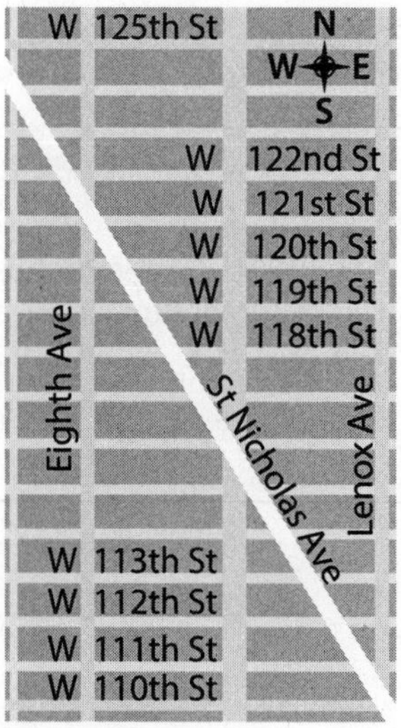

Name ______________________ Class ______________ Date __________

1.2 Perpendicular Lines

Essential Question: What are the key ideas about perpendicular bisectors of a segment?

Resource Locker

Explore Constructing Perpendicular Bisectors and Perpendicular Lines

You can construct geometric figures without using measurement tools like a ruler or a protractor. By using geometric relationships and a compass and a straightedge, you can construct geometric figures with greater precision than figures drawn with standard measurement tools.

In Steps A–C, construct the perpendicular bisector of $\overline{AB}$.

(A) Place the point of the compass at point A. Using a compass setting that is greater than half the length of $\overline{AB}$, draw an arc.

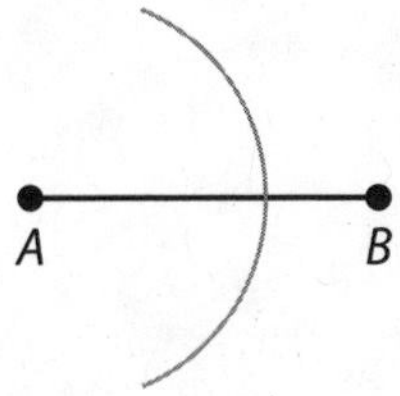

(B) Without adjusting the compass, place the point of the compass at point B and draw an arc intersecting the first arc in two places. Label the points of intersection C and D.

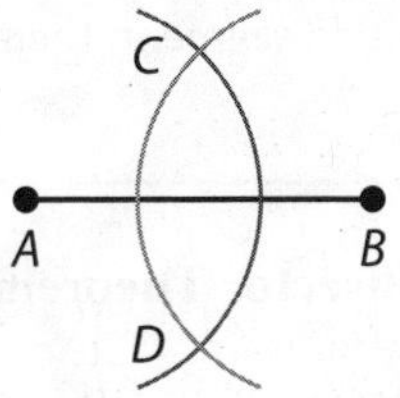

(C) Use a straightedge to draw $\overline{CD}$, which is the perpendicular bisector of $\overline{AB}$.

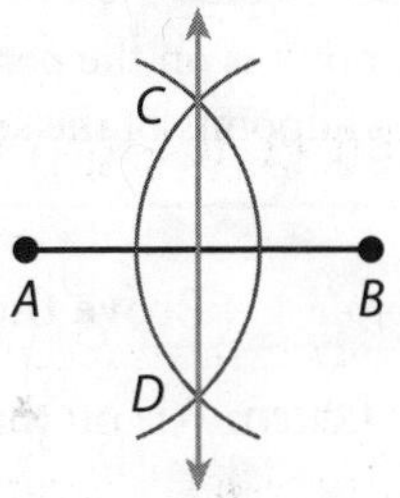

In Steps D–E, construct a line perpendicular to a line ℓ that passes through some point P that is not on ℓ.

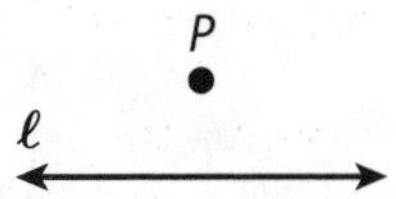

(D) Place the point of the compass at P. Draw an arc that intersects line ℓ at two points, A and B.

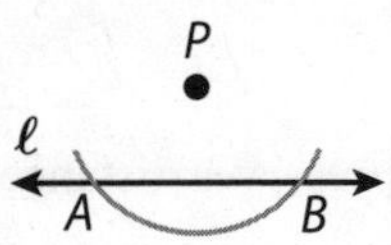

(E) Use the methods in Steps A–C to construct the perpendicular bisector of $\overline{AB}$.

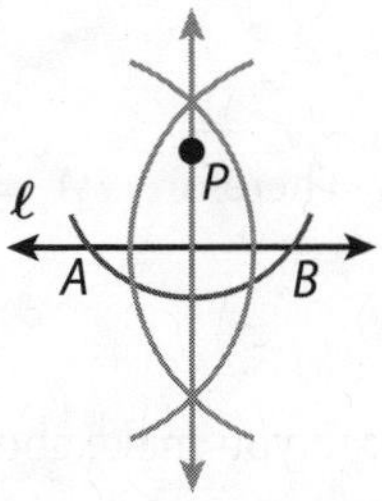

Because it is the perpendicular bisector of $\overline{AB}$, then the constructed line through P is perpendicular to line ℓ.

Reflect

1. In Step A of the first construction, why do you open the compass to a setting that is greater than half the length of $\overline{AB}$?

____

2. **What If?** Suppose Q is a point *on* line ℓ. Is the construction of a line perpendicular to ℓ through Q any different than constructing a perpendicular line through a point P *not* on the line, as in Steps D and E?

____

____

____

____

Explain 1 Proving the Perpendicular Bisector Theorem Using Reflections

You can use reflections and their properties to prove a theorem about perpendicular bisectors. These theorems will be useful in proofs later on.

Perpendicular Bisector Theorem

If a point is on the perpendicular bisector of a segment, then it is equidistant from the endpoints of the segment.

Example 1 **Prove the Perpendicular Bisector Theorem.**

Given: P is on the perpendicular bisector m of $\overline{AB}$.

Prove: $PA = PB$

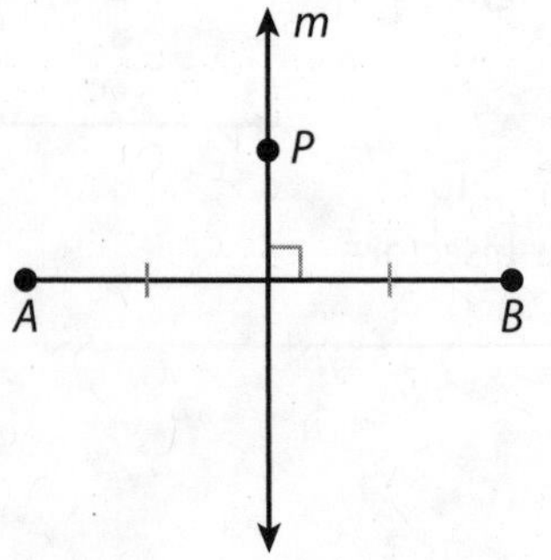

Consider the reflection across __________. Then the reflection of point P across line m is also __________ because point P lies on __________, which is the line of reflection.

Also, the reflection of __________ across line m is B by the definition of __________.

Therefore, $PA = PB$ because __________ preserves distance.

Reflect

3. **Discussion** What conclusion can you make about $\triangle KLJ$ in the diagram using the Perpendicular Bisector Theorem?

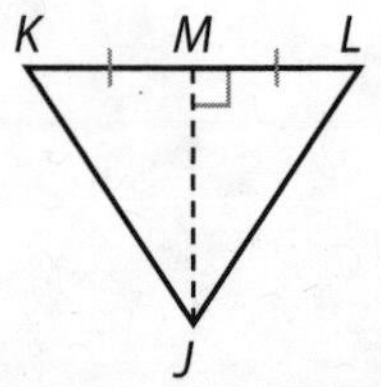

____

____

Your Turn

Use the diagram shown. $\overline{BD}$ is the perpendicular bisector of $\overline{AC}$.

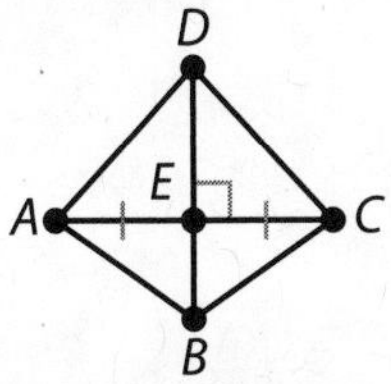

4. Suppose $ED = 16$ cm and $DA = 20$ cm. Find DC.

5. Suppose $EC = 15$ cm and $BA = 25$ cm. Find BC.

Explain 2 Proving the Converse of the Perpendicular Bisector Theorem

The converse of the Perpendicular Bisector Theorem is also true. In order to prove the converse, you will use an *indirect proof* and the *Pythagorean Theorem*.

In an **indirect proof**, you assume that the statement you are trying to prove is false. Then you use logic to lead to a contradiction of given information, a definition, a postulate, or a previously proven theorem. You can then conclude that the assumption was false and the original statement is true.

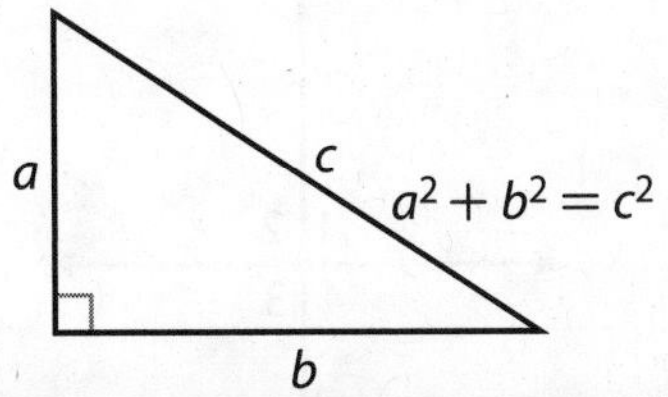

Recall that the Pythagorean Theorem states that for a right triangle with legs of length a and b and a hypotenuse of length c, $a^2 + b^2 = c^2$.

Converse of the Perpendicular Bisector Theorem

If a point is equidistant from the endpoints of a segment, then it lies on the perpendicular bisector of the segment.

Example 2 **Prove the Converse of the Perpendicular Bisector Theorem**

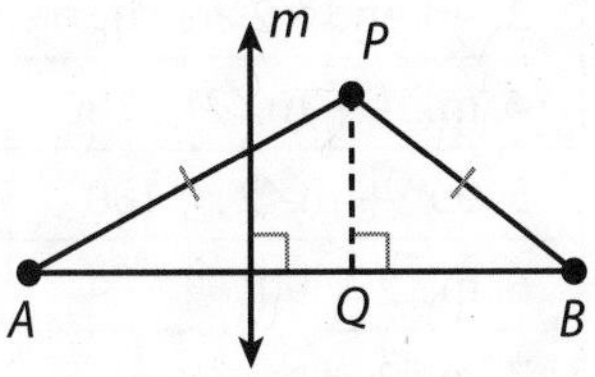

Given: $PA = PB$

Prove: P is on the perpendicular bisector m of $\overline{AB}$.

Step A: Assume what you are trying to prove is false.

Assume that P is *not* on the perpendicular bisector m of ______________.
Then, when you draw a perpendicular line from P to the line containing A and B, it intersects $\overline{AB}$ at point Q, which is not the ______________ of $\overline{AB}$.

Step B: Complete the following to show that this assumption leads to a contradiction.

$\overline{PQ}$ forms two right triangles, $\triangle AQP$ and ______________.

So, $AQ^2 + QP^2 = PA^2$ and $BQ^2 + QP^2 =$ ☐ by the ______________ Theorem.

Subtract these equations:

$AQ^2 + QP^2 = PA^2$

$BQ^2 + QP^2 = PB^2$

$AQ^2 - BQ^2 = PA^2 - PB^2$

However, $PA^2 - PB^2 = 0$ because ______________.

Therefore, $AQ^2 - BQ^2 = 0$. This means that $AQ^2 = BQ^2$ and $AQ = BQ$. This contradicts the fact that Q is not the midpoint of $\overline{AB}$. Thus, the initial assumption must be incorrect, and P must lie on the ______________ of $\overline{AB}$.

Reflect

6. In the proof, once you know $AQ^2 = BQ^2$, why can you conclude that $AQ = BQ$?

____

Your Turn

7. $\overline{AD}$ is 10 inches long. $\overline{BD}$ is 6 inches long. Find the length of $\overline{AC}$.

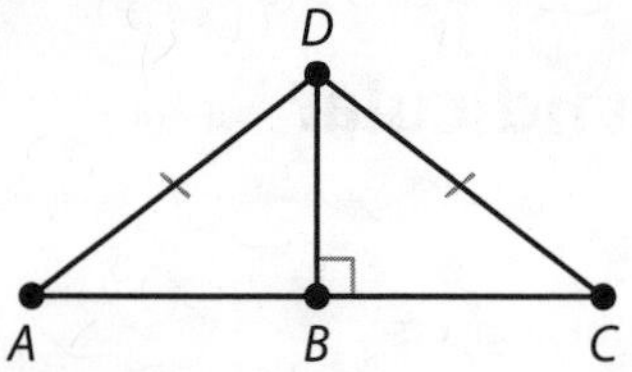

Explain 3 Proving Theorems about Right Angles

The symbol ⊥ means that two figures are perpendicular. For example, $\ell \perp m$ or $\overleftrightarrow{XY} \perp \overline{AB}$.

Example 3 **Prove each theorem about right angles.**

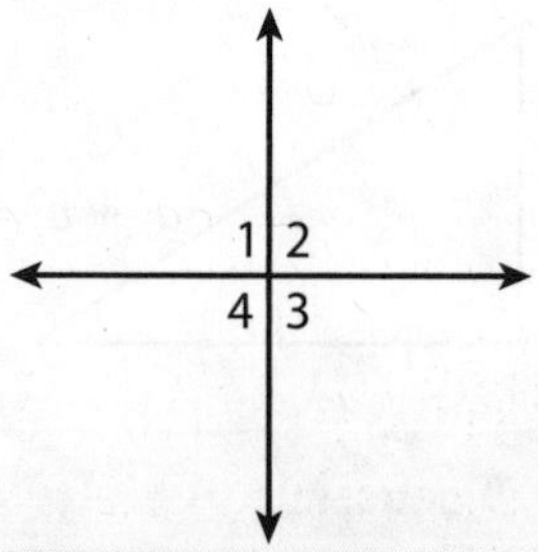

(A) If two lines intersect to form one right angle, then they are perpendicular and they intersect to form four right angles.

Given: m∠1 = 90° **Prove:** m∠2 = 90°, m∠3 = 90°, m∠4 = 90°

Statement	Reason
1. m∠1 = 90°	1. Given
2. ∠1 and ∠2 are a linear pair.	2. Given
3. ∠1 and ∠2 are supplementary.	3. Linear Pair Theorem
4. m∠1 + m∠2 = 180°	4. Definition of supplementary angles
5. 90° + m∠2 = 180°	5. Substitution Property of Equality
6. m∠2 = 90°	6. Subtraction Property of Equality
7. m∠2 = m∠4	7. Vertical Angles Theorem
8. m∠4 = 90°	8. Substitution Property of Equality
9. m∠1 = m∠3	9. Vertical Angles Theorem
10. m∠3 = 90°	10. Substitution Property of Equality

(B) If two intersecting lines form a linear pair of angles with equal measures, then the lines are perpendicular.

Given: m∠1 = m∠2 **Prove:** $\ell \perp m$

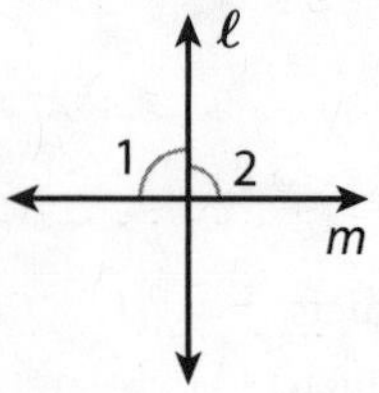

By the diagram, ∠1 and ∠2 form a linear pair so ∠1 and ∠2 are supplementary by the ______________. By the definition of supplementary angles, m∠1 + m∠2 = ______. It is also given that ______________, so m∠1 + m∠1 = 180° by the ______________. Adding gives 2 · m∠1 = 180° and m∠1 = 90° by the Division Property of Equality. Therefore, ∠1 is a right angle and $\ell \perp$ m by the ______________.

Reflect

8. State the converse of the theorem in Part B. Is the converse true?

Your Turn

9. Given: $b \parallel d$, $c \parallel e$, $m\angle 1 = 50°$, and $m\angle 5 = 90°$. Use the diagram to find $m\angle 4$.

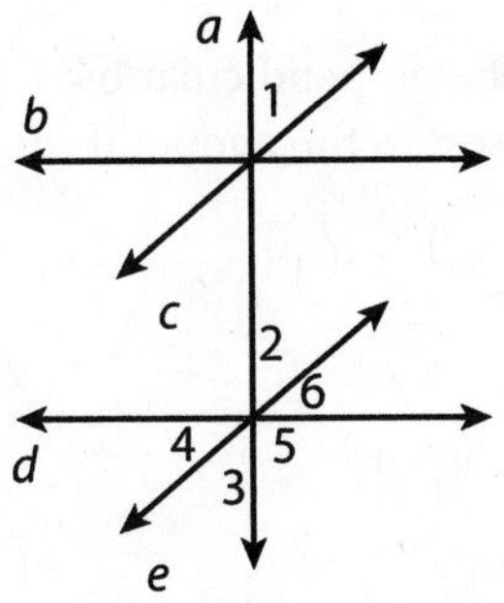

Elaborate

10. Discussion Explain how the converse of the Perpendicular Bisector Theorem justifies the compass-and-straightedge construction of the perpendicular bisector of a segment.

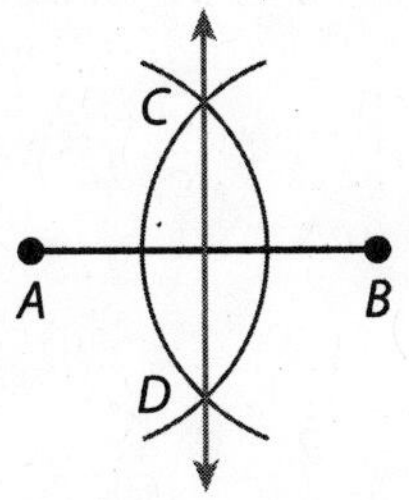

11. Essential Question Check-In How can you construct perpendicular lines and prove theorems about perpendicular bisectors?

Evaluate: Homework and Practice

Personal Math Trainer
- Online Homework
- Hints and Help
- Extra Practice

1. How can you construct a line perpendicular to line ℓ that passes through point P using paper folding?

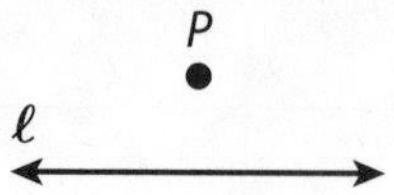

2. **Check for Reasonableness** How can you use a ruler and a protractor to check the construction in Elaborate Exercise 11?

3. Describe the point on the perpendicular bisector of a segment that is closest to the endpoints of the segment.

4. **Represent Real-World Problems** A field of soybeans is watered by a rotating irrigation system. The watering arm, $\overline{CD}$, rotates around its center point. To show the area of the crop of soybeans that will be watered, construct a circle with diameter CD.

Use the diagram to find the lengths. $\overline{BP}$ is the perpendicular bisector of $\overline{AC}$. $\overline{CQ}$ is the perpendicular bisector of $\overline{BD}$. $AB = BC = CD$.

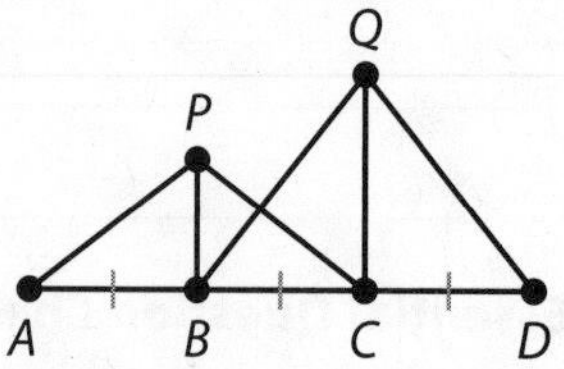

5. Suppose $AP = 5$ cm. What is the length of $\overline{PC}$?

6. Suppose $AP = 5$ cm and $BQ = 8$ cm. What is the length of $\overline{QD}$?

7. Suppose $AC = 12$ cm and $QD = 10$ cm. What is the length of $\overline{QC}$?

8. Suppose $PB = 3$ cm and $AD = 12$ cm. What is the length of $\overline{PC}$?

Given: $PA = PC$ and $BA = BC$. Use the diagram to find the lengths or angle measures described.

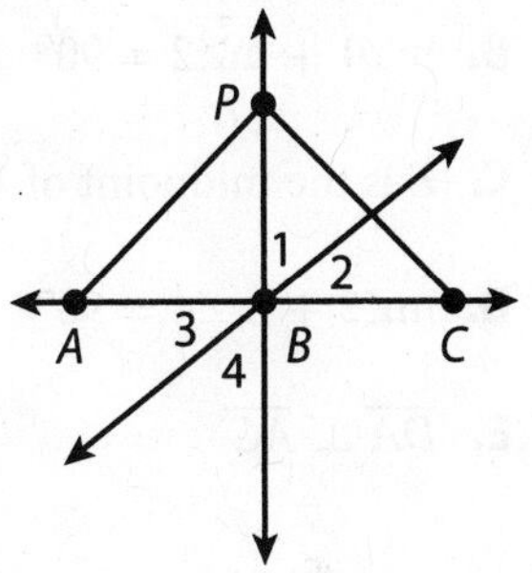

9. Suppose $m\angle 2 = 38°$. Find $m\angle 1$.

10. Suppose $PA = 10$ cm and $PB = 6$ cm. What is the length of $\overline{AC}$?

11. Find $m\angle 3 + m\angle 4$.

Given: $m \parallel n$, $x \parallel y$, and $y \perp m$. Use the diagram to find the angle measures.

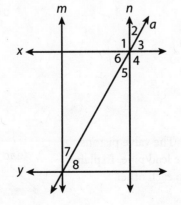

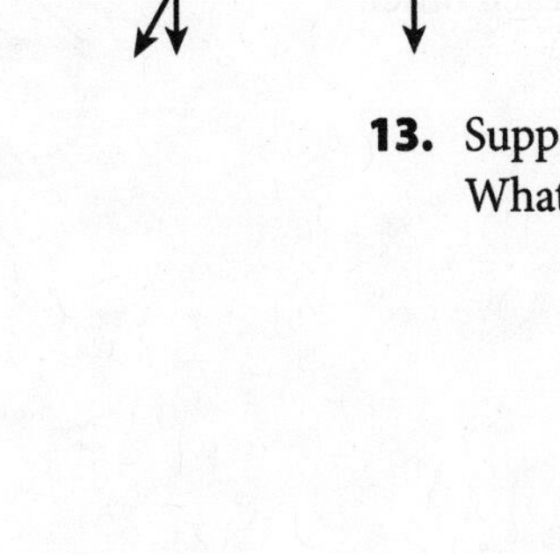

12. Suppose $m\angle 7 = 30°$. Find $m\angle 3$.

13. Suppose $m\angle 1 = 90°$. What is $m\angle 2 + m\angle 3 + m\angle 5 + m\angle 6$?

Use this diagram of trusses for a railroad bridge in Exercise 14.

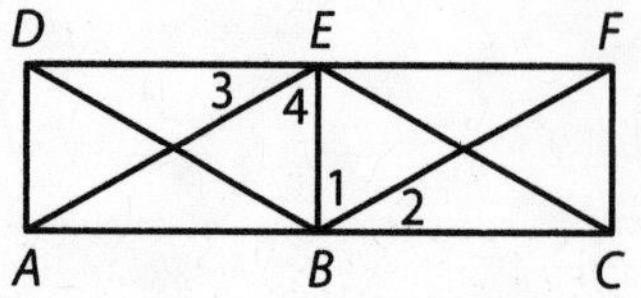

14. Suppose $\overline{BE}$ is the perpendicular bisector of $\overline{DF}$. Which of the following statements do you know are true? Select all that apply. Explain your reasoning.

A. $BD = BF$

B. $m\angle 1 + m\angle 2 = 90°$

C. E is the midpoint of $\overline{DF}$.

D. $m\angle 3 + m\angle 4 = 90°$

E. $\overline{DA} \perp \overline{AC}$

15. Algebra Two lines intersect to form a linear pair with equal measures. One angle has the measure $2x°$ and the other angle has the measure $(20y - 10)°$. Find the values of x and y. Explain your reasoning.

16. Algebra Two lines intersect to form a linear pair of congruent angles. The measure of one angle is $(8x + 10)°$ and the measure of the other angle is $\left(\frac{15y}{2}\right)°$. Find the values of x and y. Explain your reasoning.

H.O.T. Focus on Higher Order Thinking

17. Communicate Mathematical Ideas The valve pistons on a trumpet are all perpendicular to the lead pipe. Explain why the valve pistons must be parallel to each other.

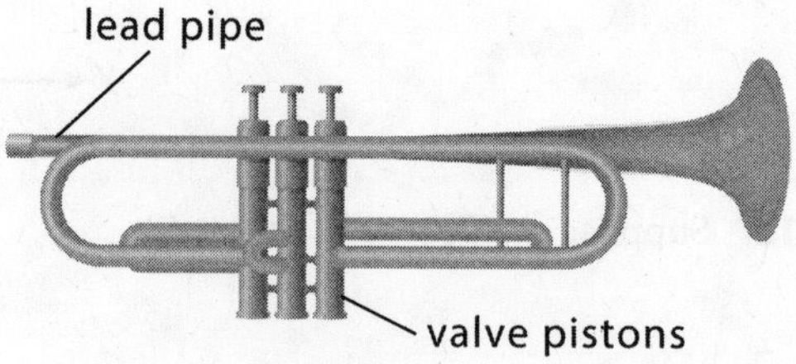

18. Justify Reasoning Prove the theorem: In a plane, if a transversal is perpendicular to one of two parallel lines, then it is perpendicular to the other.

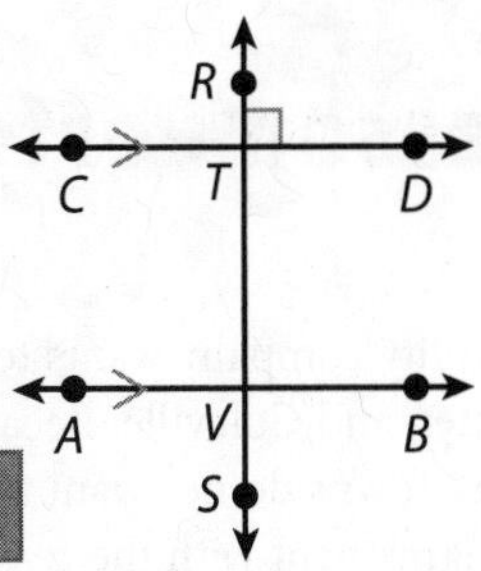

Given: $\overline{RS} \perp \overline{CD}$ and $\overline{AB} \parallel \overline{CD}$ Prove: $\overline{RS} \perp \overline{AB}$

Statements	Reasons

19. Analyze Mathematical Relationships Complete the indirect proof to show that two supplementary angles cannot both be obtuse angles.

Given: $\angle 1$ and $\angle 2$ are supplementary.

Prove: $\angle 1$ and $\angle 2$ cannot both be obtuse.

Assume that two supplementary angles *can* both be obtuse angles. So, assume that $\angle 1$ and $\angle 2$ ________________. Then $m\angle 1 > 90°$ and $m\angle 2 >$ ☐ by ____________________. Adding the two inequalities, $m\angle 1 + m\angle 2 >$ ☐. However, by the definition of supplementary angles, ________________. So $m\angle 1 + m\angle 2 > 180°$ contradicts the given information.

This means the assumption is ______, and therefore ____________________.

Lesson Performance Task

A utility company wants to build a wind farm to provide electricity to the towns of Acton, Baxter, and Coleville. Because of concerns about noise from the turbines, the residents of all three towns do not want the wind farm built close to where they live. The company comes to an agreement with the residents to build the wind farm at a location that is equally distant from all three towns.

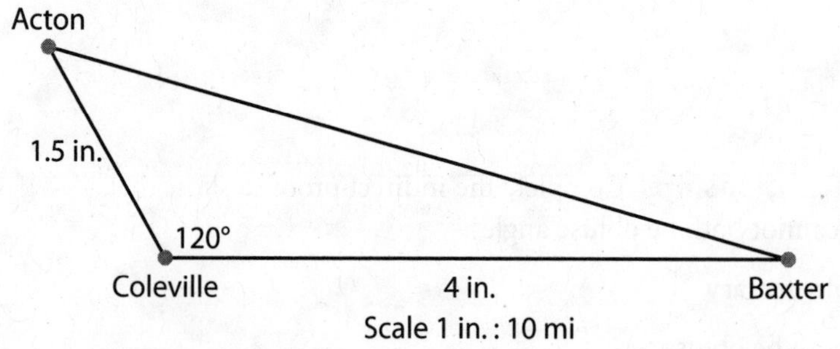

a. Use the drawing to draw a diagram of the locations of the towns using a scale of 1 in. : 10 mi. Draw the 4-inch and 1.5-inch lines with a 120° angle between them. Write the actual distances between the towns on your diagram.

b. Estimate where you think the wind farm will be located.

c. Use what you have learned in this lesson to find the exact location of the wind farm. What is the approximate distance from the wind farm to each of the three towns?

Name ______________________ Class ____________ Date ________

1.3 Justifying Constructions

Essential Question: How can you be sure that the result of a construction is valid?

Resource Locker

Explore 1 Using a Reflective Device to Construct a Perpendicular Line

You have constructed a line perpendicular to a given line through a point not on the line using a compass and straightedge. You can also use a reflective device to construct perpendicular lines.

(A) **Step 1** Place the reflective device along line ℓ. Look through the device to locate the image of point P on the opposite side of line ℓ. Draw the image of point P and label it P'.

Step 2 Use a straightedge to draw $\overleftrightarrow{PP'}$.

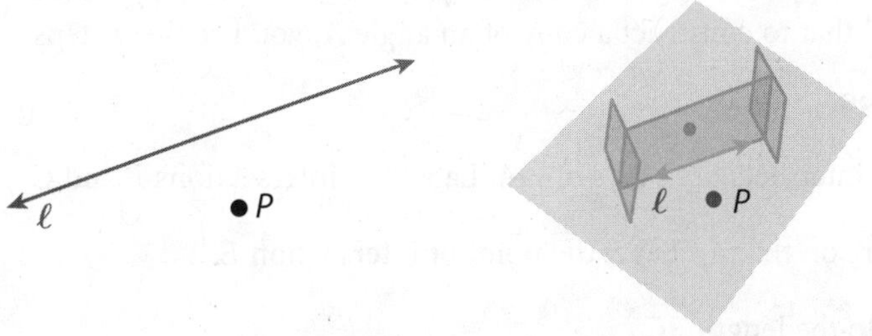

Explain why $\overleftrightarrow{PP'}$ is perpendicular to line ℓ.

____

(B) Place the reflective device so that it passes through point Q and is approximately perpendicular to line m. Adjust the angle of the device until the image of line m coincides with line m. Draw a line along the reflective device and label it line n. Explain why line n is perpendicular to line m.

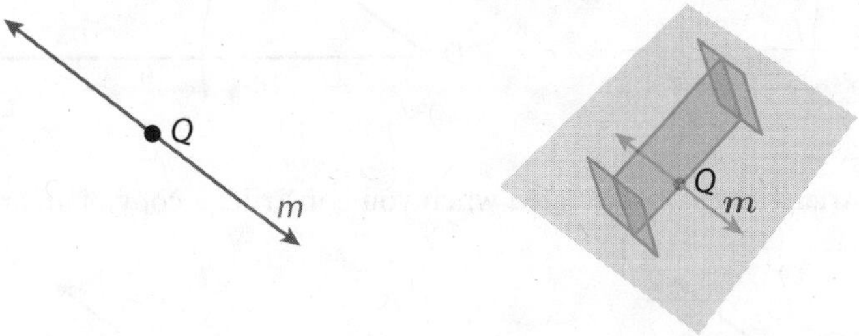

____

____

____

Reflect

1. How can you check that the lines you drew are perpendicular to lines ℓ and m?

2. Use the reflective device to draw two points on line ℓ that are reflections of each other. Label the points X and X'. What is true about PX and PX'? Why? Use a ruler to check your prediction.

3. Describe how to construct a perpendicular bisector of a line segment using paper folding. Use a rigid motion to explain why the result is a perpendicular bisector.

Explore 2 Justifying the Copy of an Angle Construction

You have seen how to construct a copy of an angle, but how do you know that the copy must be congruent to the original? Recall that to construct a copy of an angle A, you use these steps.

Step 1 Draw a ray with endpoint D.

Step 2 Draw an arc that intersects both rays of $\angle A$. Label the intersections B and C.

Step 3 Draw the same arc on the ray. Label the point of intersection E.

Step 4 Set the compass to the length BC.

Step 5 Place the compass at E and draw a new arc. Label the intersection of the new arc F. Draw $\overrightarrow{DF}$. $\angle D$ is congruent to $\angle A$.

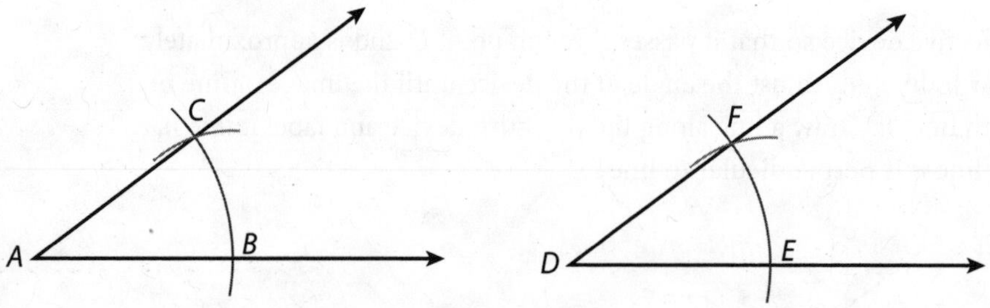

(A) Sketch and name the two triangles that are created when you construct a copy of an angle.

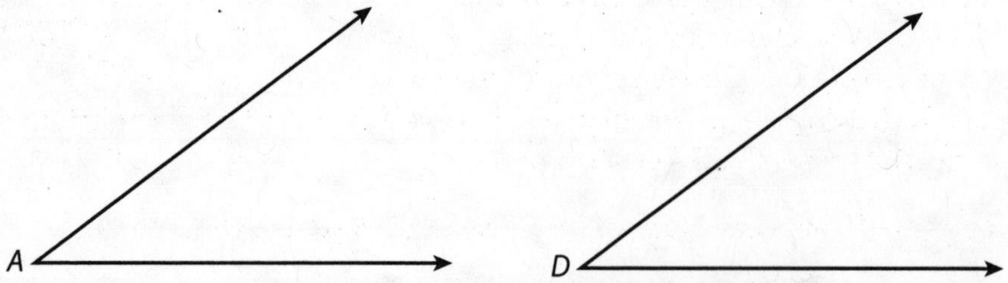

(B) What segments do you know are congruent? Explain how you know.

(C) Are the triangles congruent? How do you know?

Reflect

4. **Discussion** Suppose you used a larger compass setting to create $\overline{AB}$ than another student when copying the same angle. Will your copied angles be congruent?

5. Does the justification above for constructing a copy of an angle work for obtuse angles?

Explain 1 Proving the Angle Bisector and Perpendicular Bisector Constructions

You have constructed angle bisectors and perpendicular bisectors. You now have the tools you need to prove that these compass and straightedge constructions result in the intended figures.

Example 1 **Prove two bisector constructions.**

(A) You have used the following steps to construct an angle bisector.

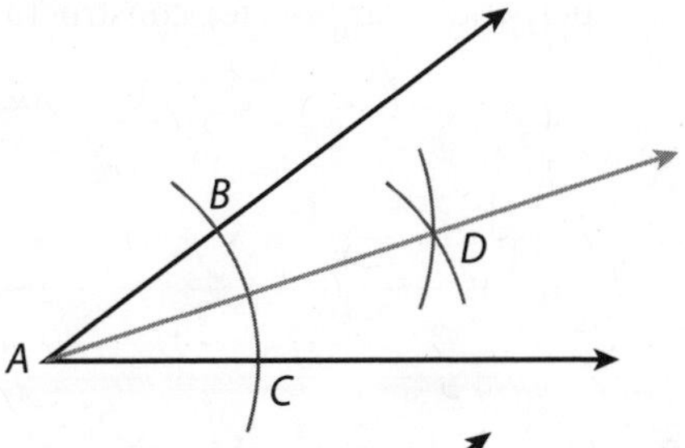

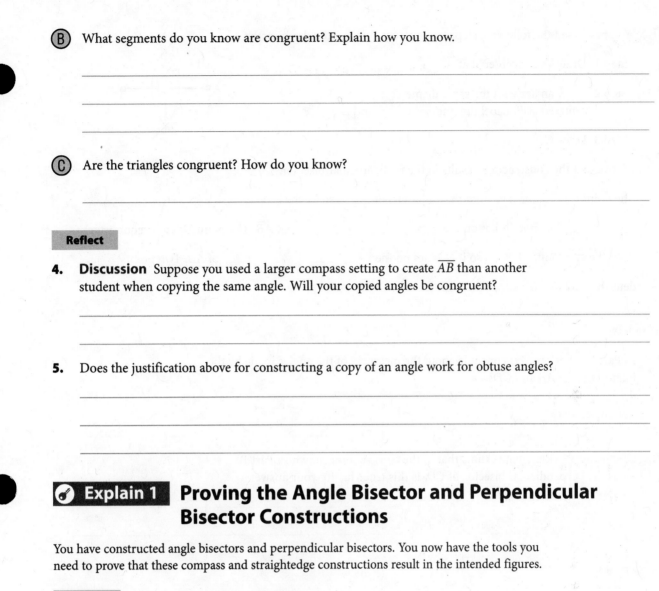

Step 1 Draw an arc intersecting the sides of the angle. Label the intersections *B* and *C*.

Step 2 Draw intersecting arcs from *B* and *C*. Label the intersection of the arcs as *D*.

Step 3 Use a straightedge to draw $\overline{AD}$.

Prove that the construction results in the angle bisector.

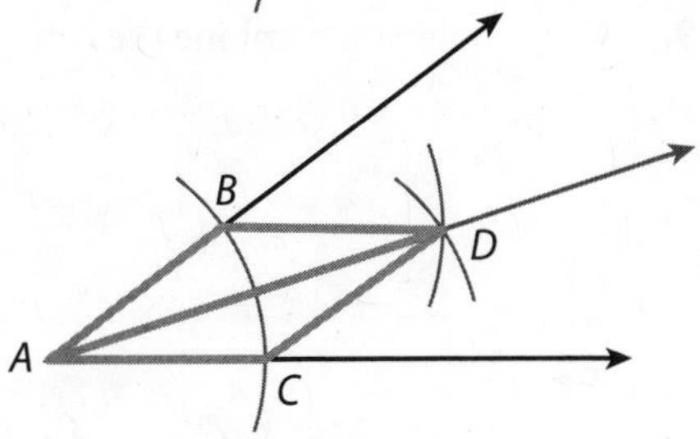

The construction results in the triangles *ABD* and *ACD*. Because the same compass setting was used to create them, $\overline{AB} \cong \overline{AC}$ and $\overline{BD} \cong \overline{CD}$. The segment $\overline{AD}$ is congruent to itself by the Reflexive Property of Congruence. So, by the SSS Triangle Congruence Theorem, $\triangle ABD \cong \triangle ACD$.

Corresponding parts of congruent figures are congruent, so $\angle BAD \cong \angle DAC$.

By the definition of angle bisector, $\overrightarrow{AD}$ is the angle bisector of $\angle A$.

(B) You have used the following steps to construct a perpendicular bisector.

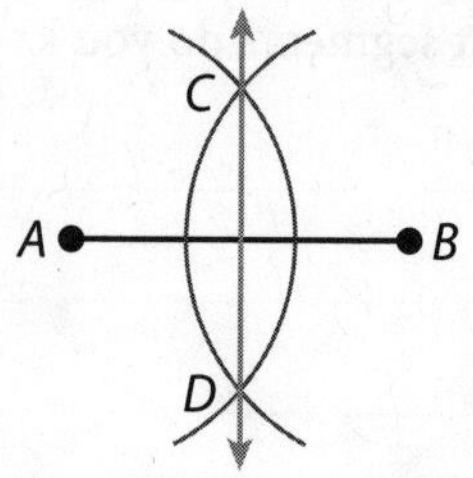

Step 1 Draw an arc centered at A.

Step 2 Draw an arc with the same diameter centered at B. Label the intersections C and D.

Step 3 Draw $\overline{CD}$.

Prove that the construction results in the perpendicular bisector.

The point C is equidistant from the endpoints of ______, so by the ____________________ ____________ Theorem, it lies on the ____________________ of $\overline{AB}$. The point D is also equidistant from the endpoints of ______, so it also lies on the ____________________ of $\overline{AB}$. Two points determine a line, so ____________________

Reflect

6. In Part B, what can you conclude about the measures of the angles made by the intersection of $\overline{AB}$ and $\overline{CD}$?

7. Discussion A classmate claims that in the construction shown in Part B, $\overline{AB}$ is the perpendicular bisector of $\overline{CD}$. Is this true? Justify your answer.

Your Turn

8. The construction in Part B is also used to construct the midpoint R of $\overline{MN}$. How is the proof of this construction different from the proof of the perpendicular bisector construction in Part B?

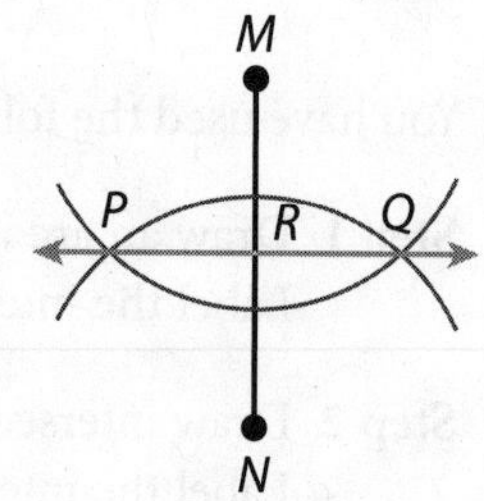

9. How could you combine the constructions in Example 1 to construct a 45° angle?

Elaborate

10. Describe how you can construct a line that is parallel to a given line using the construction of a perpendicular to a line.

11. Use a straightedge and a piece of string to construct an equilateral triangle that has AB as one of its sides. Then explain how you know your construction works. (*Hint*: Consider an arc centered at A with radius AB and an arc centered at B with radius AB.)

12. **Essential Question Check-In** Is a construction something that must be proven? Explain.

Evaluate: Homework and Practice

Personal Math Trainer

- Online Homework
- Hints and Help
- Extra Practice

1. Julia is given a line ℓ and a point P not on line ℓ. She is asked to use a reflective device to construct a line through P that is perpendicular to line ℓ. She places the device as shown in the figure. What should she do next to draw the required line?

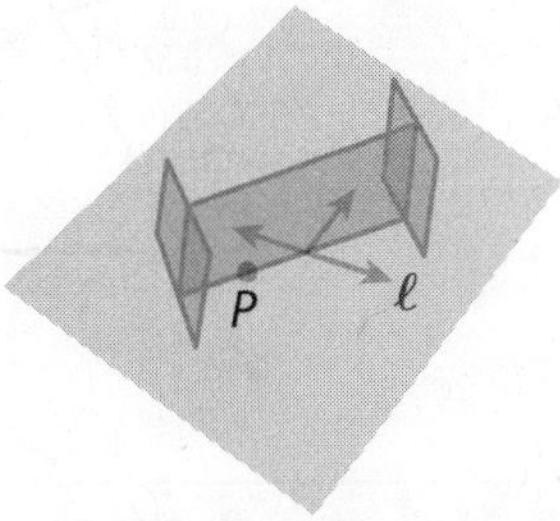

2. Describe how to construct a copy of a segment. Explain how you know that the segments are congruent.

Complete the proof of the construction of a segment bisector.

3. **Given:** the construction of the segment bisector of $\overline{AB}$

Prove: $\overline{CD}$ bisects $\overline{AB}$

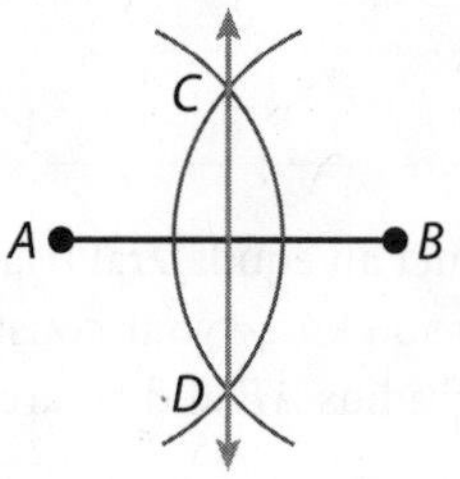

Statements	Reasons
1. $AC =$ ____ and $AD =$ ____ .	1. Same compass setting used
2. C is on the perpendicular bisector of $\overline{AB}$.	2. ____________
3. D is on the perpendicular bisector of $\overline{AB}$.	3. ____________
4. ____ is the perpendicular bisector of $\overline{AB}$.	4. Through any two points, there is exactly one line.
5. ____________	5. Definition of ____________

4. Complete the proof of the construction of a congruent angle.

Given: the construction of $\angle CAB$ given $\angle HFG$

Prove: $\angle CAB \cong \angle HFG$

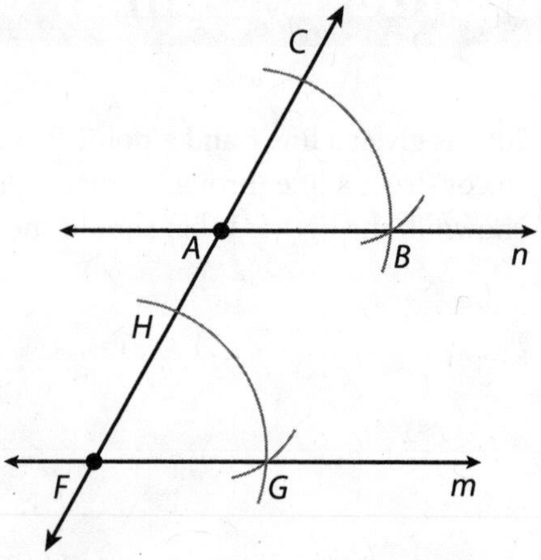

Statements	Reasons
1. $FG = FH =$ ____ $= AC$	1. same compass setting
2. $GH = CB$	2. ____________
3. $\triangle FGH \cong \triangle ABC$	3. ____________
4. $\angle CAB \cong \angle HFG$	4. ____________

To construct a line through the given point *P*, parallel to line ℓ, you use the following steps.

Step 1 Choose a point *Q* on line ℓ and draw $\overline{QP}$.

Step 2 Construct an angle congruent to ∠1 at *P*.

Step 3 Construct the line through the given point, parallel to the line shown.

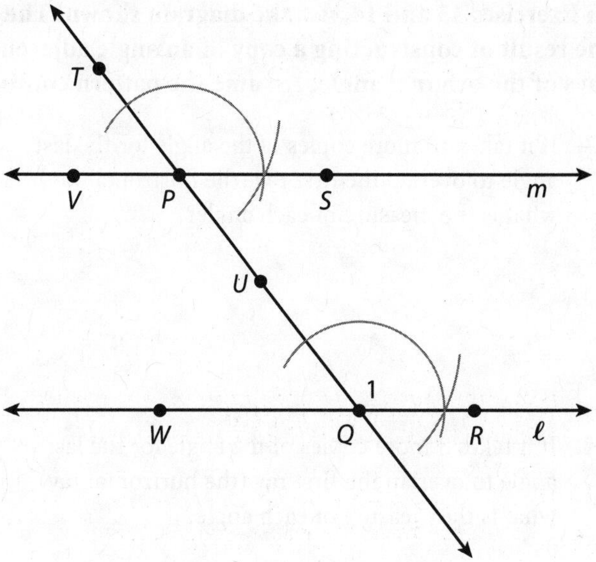

Describe the relationship between the given angles or segments. Justify your answer.

5. ∠*TPS* and ∠*UQR*

6. ∠*SPU* and ∠*RQU*

7. ∠*VPU* and ∠*UQR*

8. ∠*TPS* and ∠*WQU*

9. $\overline{QU}$ and $\overline{PS}$

10. $\overline{QU}$ and $\overline{PT}$

11. To construct a line through the given point *P*, parallel to line ℓ, you use the
following steps.

Step 1 Draw line *m* through *P* and intersecting line ℓ.

Step 2 Construct an angle congruent to ∠1 at *P*.

Step 3 Construct the line through the given point, parallel to the line shown.

How do you know that lines ℓ and *n* are parallel? Explain.

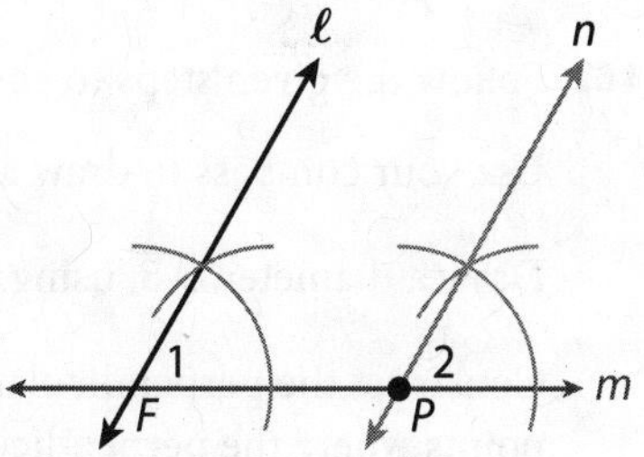

12. Construct an angle whose measure is $\frac{1}{4}$ the measure of ∠*Z*. Justify the construction.

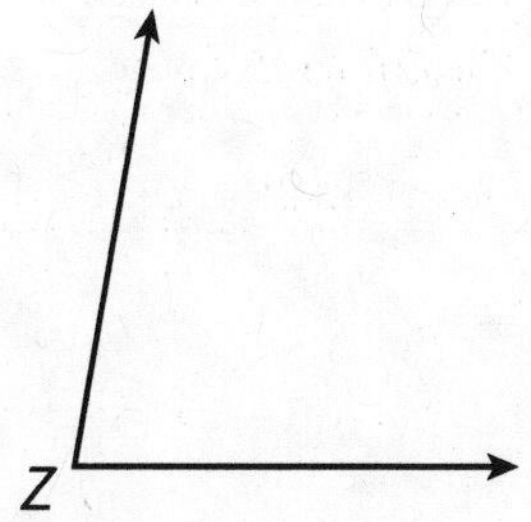

In Exercises 13 and 14, use the diagram shown. The diagram shows the result of constructing a copy of an angle adjacent to one of the rays of the original angle. Assume the pattern continues.

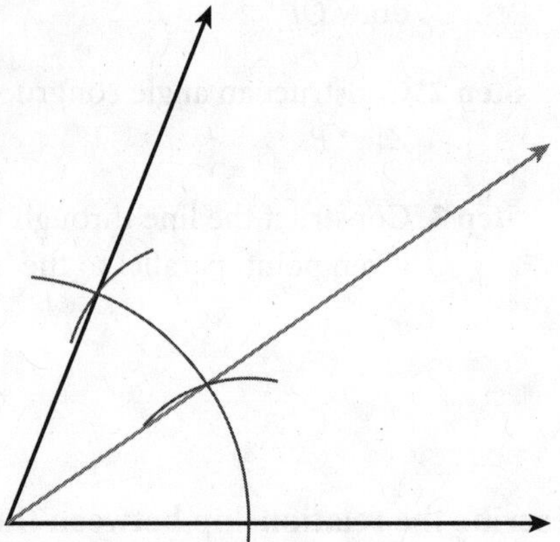

13. If it takes 10 more copies of the angle for the last angle to overlap the first ray (the horizontal ray), what is the measure of each angle?

14. If it takes 8 more copies of the angle for the last angle to overlap the first ray (the horizontal ray), what is the measure of each angle?

15. Sonia draws a segment on a piece of paper. She wants to find three points that are equidistant from the endpoints of the segment. Explain how she can use paper folding to help her locate the three points.

In Exercises 16–18, a polygon is inscribed in a circle if all of the polygon's vertices lie on the circle.

16. Follow the given steps to construct a square inscribed in a circle.

Use your compass to draw a circle. Mark the center.

Draw a diameter, $\overline{AB}$, using a straightedge.

Construct the perpendicular bisector of $\overline{AB}$. Label the points where the perpendicular bisector intersects the circle as C and D.

Use the straightedge to draw $\overline{AC}$, $\overline{CB}$, $\overline{BD}$, and $\overline{DA}$.

17. Suppose you are given a piece of tracing paper with a circle on it and you do not have a compass. How can you use paper folding to inscribe a square in the circle?

18. Follow the given steps to construct a regular hexagon inscribed in a circle.

Tie a pencil to one end of the string.

Mark a point O on your paper. Place the string on point O and hold it down with your finger. Pull the string taut and draw a circle. Mark and label a point A.

Hold the point on the string that you placed on point O, and move it to point A. Pull the string taut and draw an arc that intersects the circle. Label the point as B.

Hold the point on the string that you placed on point A, and move it to point B. Draw an arc to locate point C on the circle. Repeat to locate points D, E, and F. Use your straightedge to draw $ABCDEF$.

H.O.T. Focus on Higher Order Thinking

19. Your teacher constructed the figure shown. It shows the construction of line PT through point P and parallel to line AB.

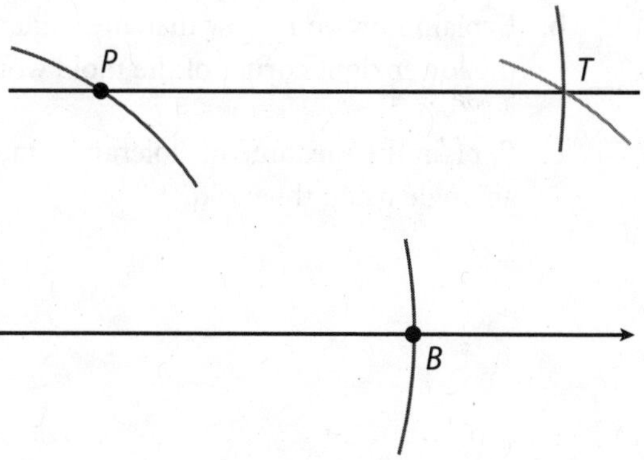

a. Compass settings of length AB and AP were used in the construction. Complete the statements:

With the compass set to length AP, an arc was drawn with the compass point at point ____.

With the compass set to length ____, an arc was drawn with the compass point at point ____.

The two arcs intersect at point ____.

b. Write two congruence statements involving segments in the construction.

c. Write a proof that the construction is true. That is, given the construction, prove $\overline{PT} \parallel \overline{AB}$. (*Hint*: Draw segments to create two congruent triangles.)

20. Use the segments shown. Construct and label a segment, $\overline{XY}$, whose length is the average of the lengths of $\overline{AB}$ and $\overline{CD}$. Justify the method you used.

Lesson Performance Task

A plastic "mold" for copying a 30° angle is shown here.

a. If you drew a 30°—60°—90° triangle using the mold, how would you know that your triangle and the mold were congruent?

b. Explain how you know that any angle you would draw using the lower right corner of the mold would measure 30°.

c. Explain the meaning of "tolerance" in the context of drawing an angle using the mold.

Name_______________________ Class_____________ Date________

1.4 Properties of Parallelograms

Resource Locker

Essential Question: What can you conclude about the sides, angles, and diagonals of a parallelogram?

Explore Investigating Parallelograms

A **quadrilateral** is a polygon with four sides. A **parallelogram** is a quadrilateral that has two pairs of parallel sides. You can use geometry software to investigate properties of parallelograms.

(A) Draw a straight line. Then plot a point that is not on the line. Construct a line through the point that is parallel to the line. This gives you a pair of parallel lines.

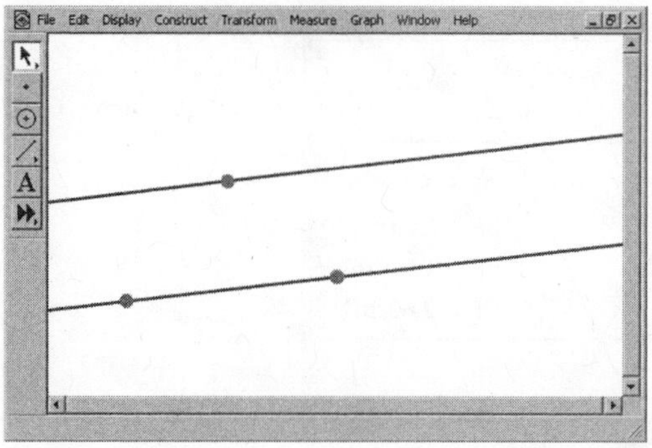

(B) Repeat Step A to construct a second pair of parallel lines that intersect those from Step A.

(C) The intersections of the parallel lines create a parallelogram. Plot points at these intersections. Label the points *A*, *B*, *C*, and *D*.

Identify the *opposite sides* and *opposite angles* of the parallelogram.

Opposite sides: ______________________

Opposite angles: ______________________

Ⓓ Measure each angle of the parallelogram.

Measure the length of each side of the parallelogram. You can do this by measuring the distance between consecutive vertices.

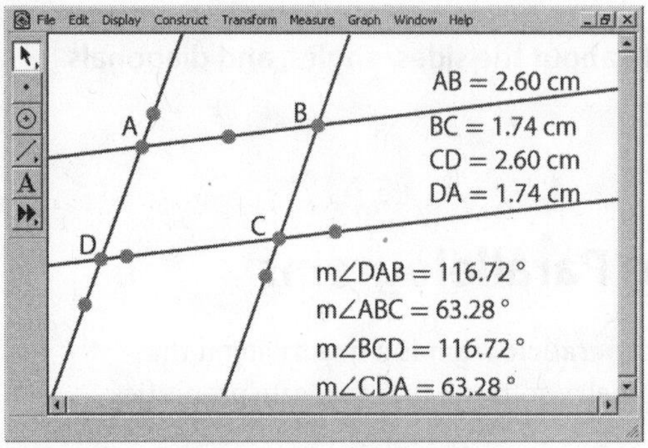

Ⓔ Then drag the points and lines in your construction to change the shape of the parallelogram. As you do so, look for relationships in the measurements. Make a conjecture about the sides and angles of a parallelogram.

Conjecture: ____

____

Ⓕ A segment that connects two nonconsecutive vertices of a polygon is a **diagonal**. Construct diagonals $\overline{AC}$ and $\overline{BD}$. Plot a point at the intersection of the diagonals and label it *E*.

Ⓖ Measure the length of $\overline{AE}$, $\overline{BE}$, $\overline{CE}$, and $\overline{DE}$.

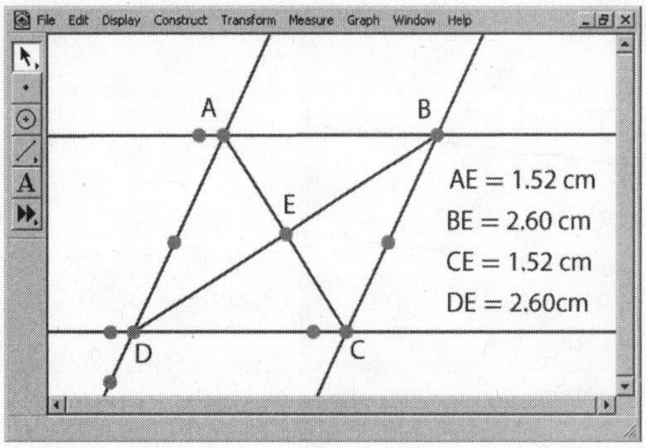

Ⓗ Drag the points and lines in your construction to change the shape of the parallelogram. As you do so, look for relationships in the measurements in Step G. Make a conjecture about the diagonals of a parallelogram.

Conjecture: ____

Reflect

1. *Consecutive angles* are the angles at consecutive vertices, such as ∠*A* and ∠*B*, or ∠*A* and ∠*D*. Use your construction to make a conjecture about consecutive angles of a parallelogram.

Conjecture: ____

2. **Critique Reasoning** A student claims that the perimeter of $\triangle AEB$ in the construction is always equal to the perimeter of $\triangle CED$. Without doing any further measurements in your construction, explain whether or not you agree with the student's statement.

Explain 1 Proving Opposite Sides Are Congruent

The conjecture you made in the Explore about opposite sides of a parallelogram can be stated as a theorem. The proof involves drawing an *auxiliary line* in the figure.

Theorem

If a quadrilateral is a parallelogram, then its opposite sides are congruent.

Example 1 **Prove that the opposite sides of a parallelogram are congruent.**

Given: *ABCD* is a parallelogram.

Prove: $\overline{AB} \cong \overline{CD}$ and $\overline{AD} \cong \overline{CB}$

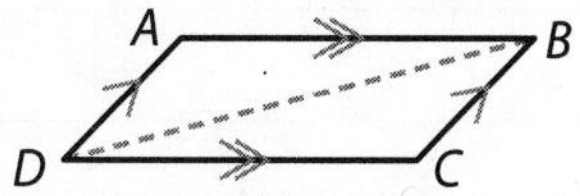

Statements	Reasons
1. *ABCD* is a parallelogram.	1.
2. Draw $\overline{DB}$.	2. Through any two points, there is exactly one line.
3. $\overline{AB} \parallel \overline{DC}$, $\overline{AD} \parallel \overline{BC}$	3.
4. $\angle ADB \cong \angle CBD$ $\angle ABD \cong \angle CDB$	4.
5. $\overline{DB} \cong \overline{DB}$	5.
6.	6. ASA Triangle Congruence Theorem
7. $\overline{AB} \cong \overline{CD}$ and $\overline{AD} \cong \overline{CB}$	7.

Reflect

3. Explain how you can use the rotational symmetry of a parallelogram to give an argument that supports the above theorem.

Explain 2 Proving Opposite Angles Are Congruent

The conjecture from the Explore about opposite angles of a parallelogram can also be proven and stated as a theorem.

Theorem

If a quadrilateral is a parallelogram, then its opposite angles are congruent.

Example 2 **Prove that the opposite angles of a parallelogram are congruent.**

Given: *ABCD* is a parallelogram.

Prove: $\angle A \cong \angle C$ (A similar proof shows that $\angle B \cong \angle D$.)

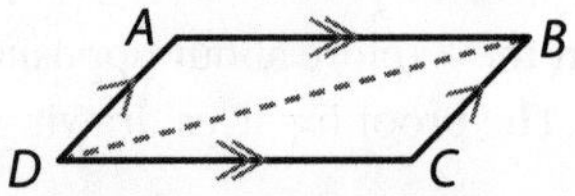

Statements	Reasons
1. *ABCD* is a parallelogram.	1.
2. Draw $\overline{DB}$.	2.
3. $\overline{AB} \parallel \overline{DC}$, $\overline{AD} \parallel \overline{BC}$	3.
4.	4. Alternate Interior Angles Theorem
5.	5. Reflexive Property of Congruence
6.	6. ASA Triangle Congruence Theorem
7.	7.

Reflect

4. Explain how the proof would change in order to prove $\angle B \cong \angle D$.

5. In Reflect 1, you noticed that the consecutive angles of a parallelogram are supplementary. This can be stated as the theorem, *If a quadrilateral is a parallelogram, then its consecutive angles are supplementary.*

Explain why this theorem is true.

Explain 3 Proving Diagonals Bisect Each Other

The conjecture from the Explore about diagonals of a parallelogram can also be proven and stated as a theorem. One proof is shown on the facing page.

Theorem

If a quadrilateral is a parallelogram, then its diagonals bisect each other.

Example 3 **Complete the flow proof that the diagonals of a parallelogram bisect each other.**

Given: $ABCD$ is a parallelogram.

Prove: $\overline{AE} \cong \overline{CE}$ and $\overline{BE} \cong \overline{DE}$

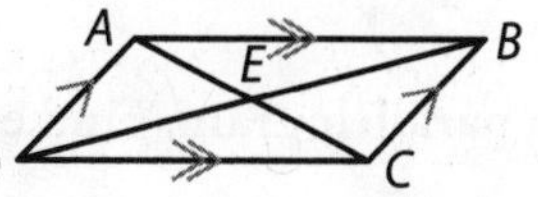

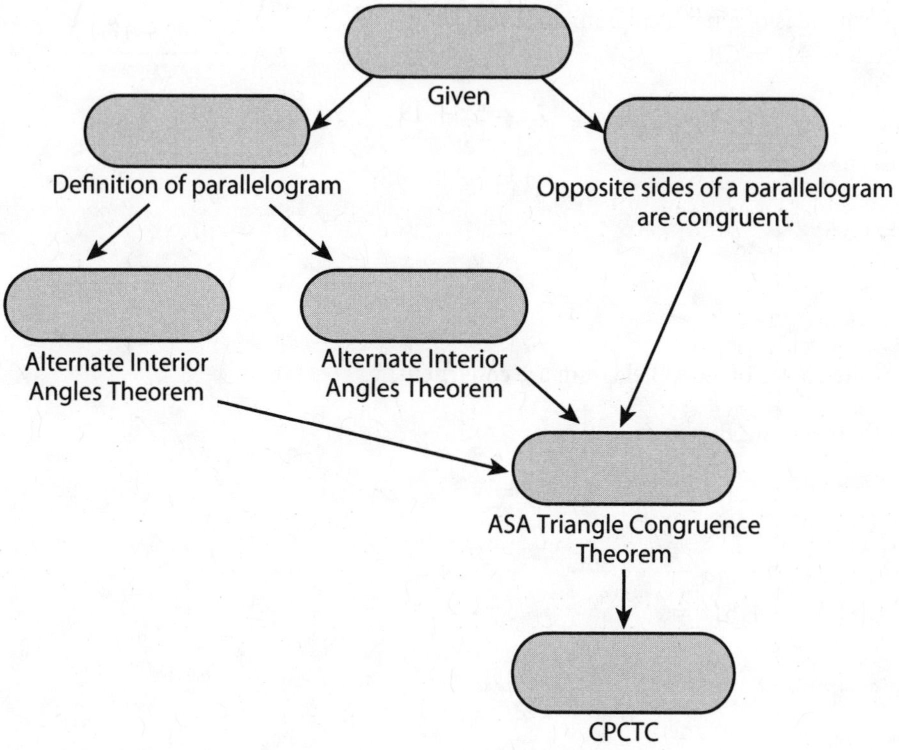

Reflect

6. **Discussion** Is it possible to prove the theorem using a different triangle congruence theorem? Explain.

Explain 4 Using Properties of Parallelograms

You can use the properties of parallelograms to find unknown lengths or angle measures in a figure.

Example 4 ***ABCD* is a parallelogram. Find each measure.**

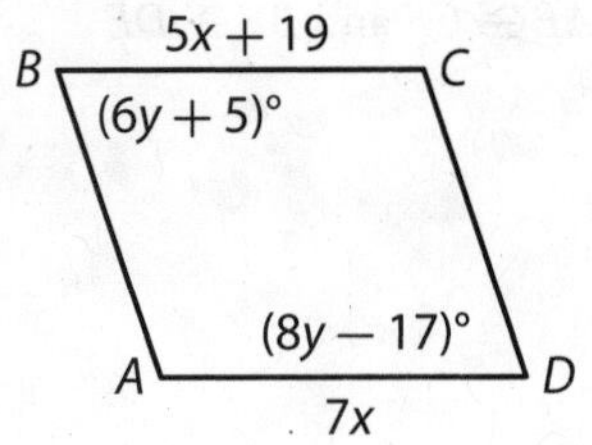

Ⓐ *AD*

Use the fact that opposite sides of a parallelogram are congruent, so $\overline{AD} \cong \overline{CB}$ and therefore $AD = CB$.

Write an equation. $7x = 5x + 19$

Solve for x. $x = 9.5$

$AD = 7x = 7(9.5) = 66.5$

Ⓑ $m\angle B$

Use the fact that opposite angles of a parallelogram are congruent,

so $\angle B \cong \angle$ ☐ and therefore $m\angle B = m\angle$ ☐.

Write an equation. $6y + 5 =$ ______

Solve for y. ______ $= y$

$m\angle B = (6y + 5)° = \left(6\left(\square\right) + 5\right)° = \square°$

Reflect

7. Suppose you wanted to find the measures of the other angles of parallelogram *ABCD*. Explain your steps.

______

______

______

______

______

Your Turn

***PQRS* is a parallelogram. Find each measure.**

8. *QR*

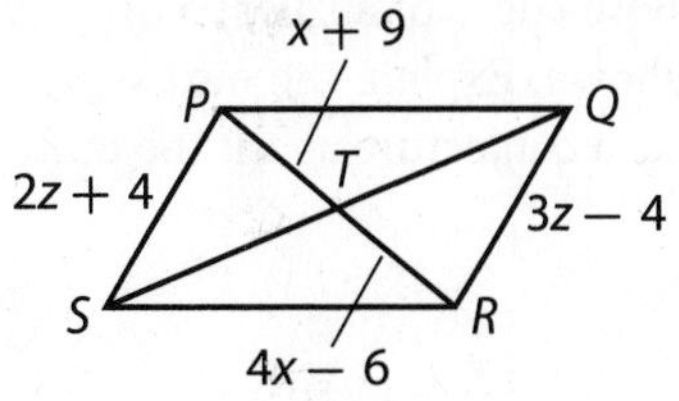

9. *PR*

Elaborate

10. What do you need to know first in order to apply any of the theorems of this lesson?

11. In parallelogram *ABCD*, point *P* lies on $\overline{DC}$, as shown in the figure. Explain why it must be the case that $DC = 2AD$. Use what you know about base angles of an isosceles triangle.

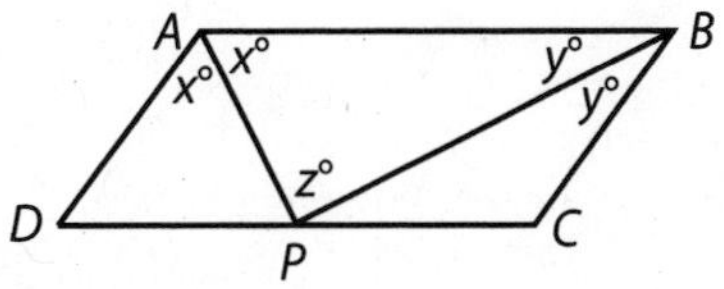

12. **Essential Question Check-In** *JKLM* is a parallelogram. Name all of the congruent segments and angles in the figure.

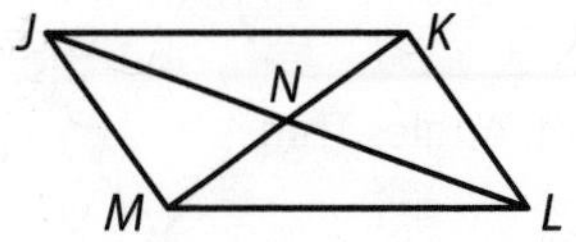

Evaluate: Homework and Practice

Personal Math Trainer

- Online Homework
- Hints and Help
- Extra Practice

1. Pablo traced along both edges of a ruler to draw two pairs of parallel lines, as shown. Explain the next steps he could take in order to make a conjecture about the diagonals of a parallelogram.

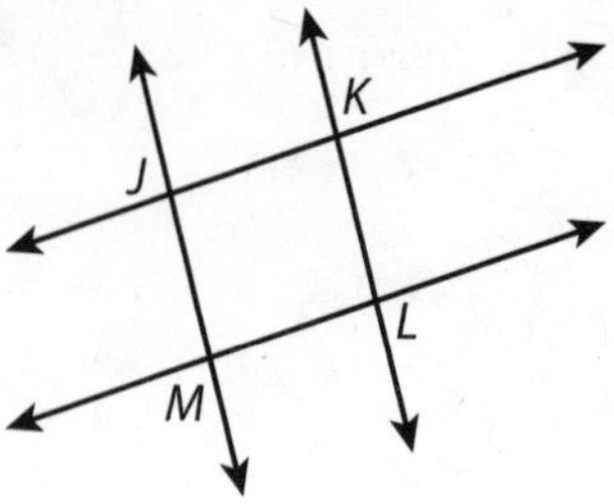

2. Sabina has tiles in the shape of a parallelogram. She labels the angles of each tile as $\angle A$, $\angle B$, $\angle C$, and $\angle D$. Then she arranges the tiles to make the pattern shown here and uses the pattern to make a conjecture about opposite angles of a parallelogram. What conjecture does she make? How does the pattern help her make the conjecture?

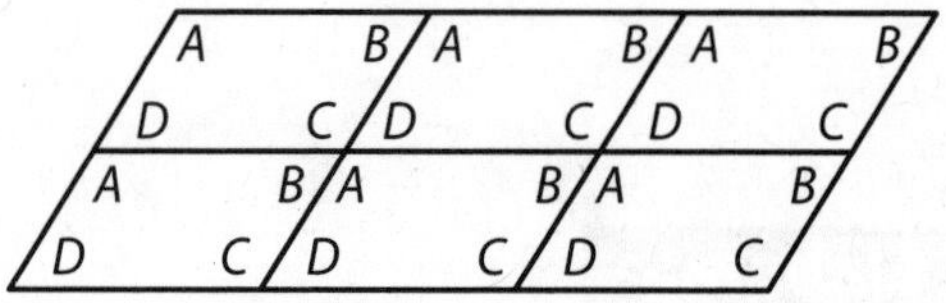

3. Complete the flow proof that the opposite sides of a parallelogram are congruent. Given: *ABCD* is a parallelogram. Prove: $\overline{AB} \cong \overline{CD}$ and $\overline{AD} \cong \overline{CB}$

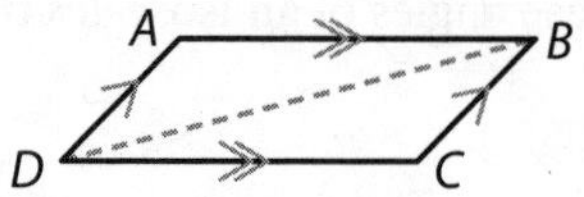

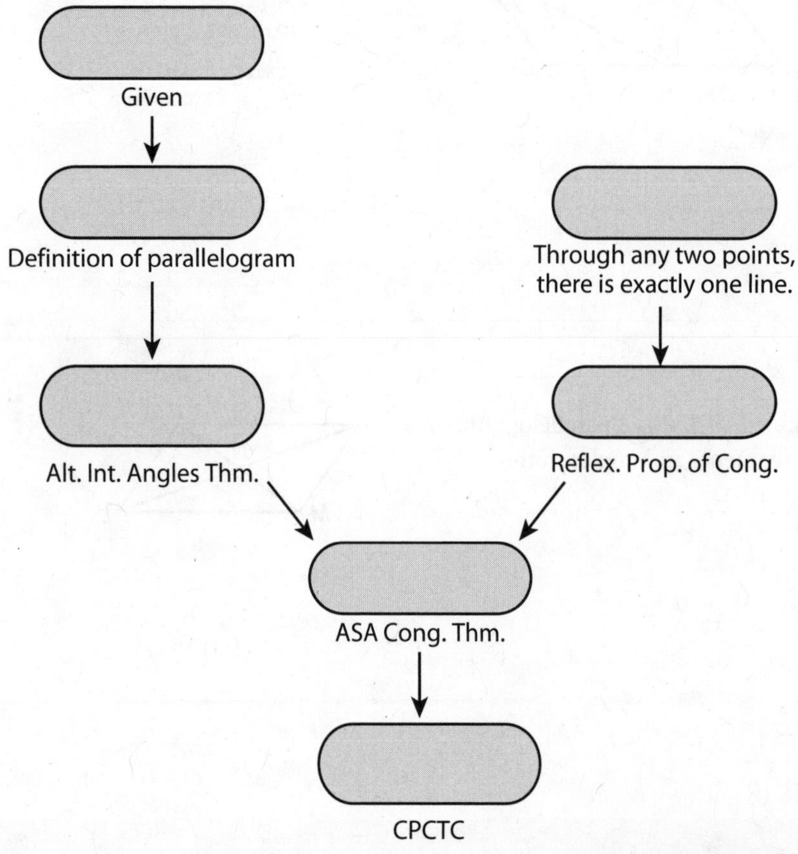

4. Write the proof that the opposite angles of a parallelogram are congruent as a paragraph proof.

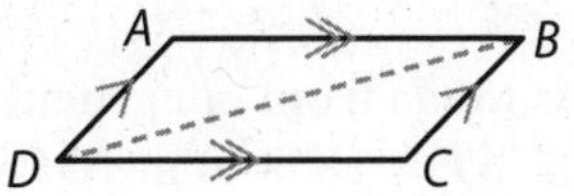

Given: *ABCD* is a parallelogram.

Prove: $\angle A \cong \angle C$ (A similar proof shows that $\angle B \cong \angle D$.)

5. Write the proof that the diagonals of a parallelogram bisect each other as a two-column proof.

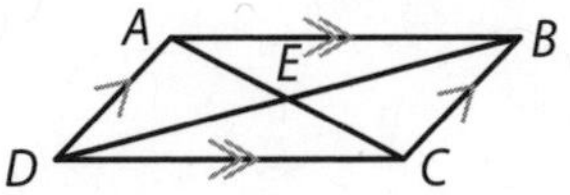

Given: *ABCD* is a parallelogram.

Prove: $\overline{AE} \cong \overline{CE}$ and $\overline{BE} \cong \overline{DE}$

Statements	Reasons
1.	1.

***EFGH* is a parallelogram. Find each measure.**

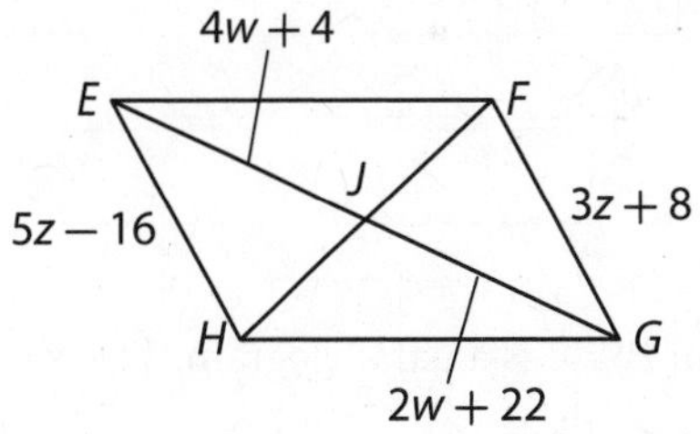

6. *FG*

7. *EG*

***ABCD* is a parallelogram. Find each measure.**

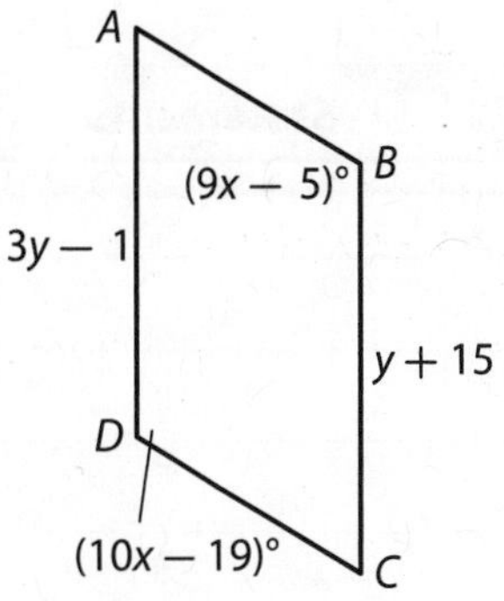

8. $m\angle B$

9. *AD*

A staircase handrail is made from congruent parallelograms. In ▱$PQRS$, $PQ = 17.5$, $ST = 18$, and $m\angle QRS = 110°$. Find each measure. Explain.

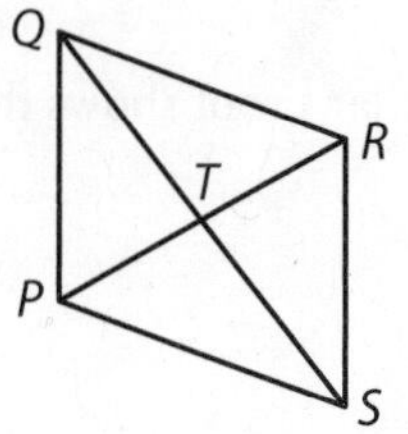

10. RS

11. QT

12. $m\angle PQR$

13. $m\angle SPQ$

Write each proof as a two-column proof.

14. Given: $GHJN$ and $JKLM$ are parallelograms.
Prove: $\angle G \cong \angle L$

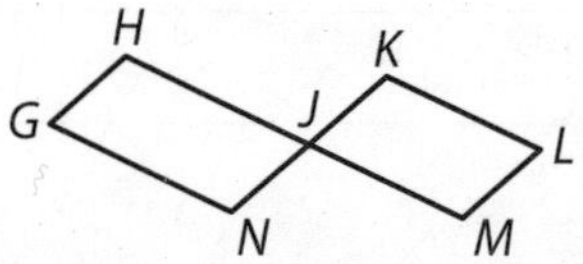

Statements	Reasons
1.	1.

15. Given: $PSTV$ is a parallelogram. $\overline{PQ} \cong \overline{RQ}$
Prove: $\angle STV \cong \angle R$

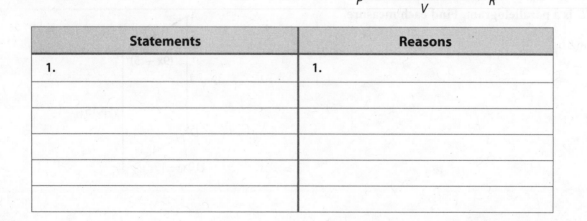

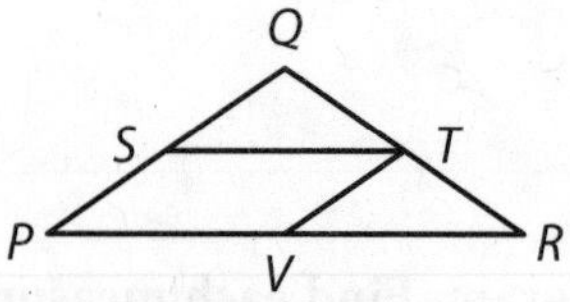

Statements	Reasons
1.	1.

16. Given: *ABCD* and *AFGH* are parallelograms.
Prove: $\angle C \cong \angle G$

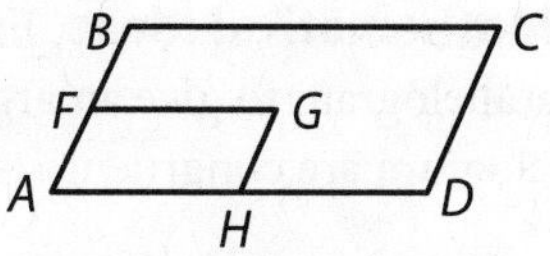

Statements	Reasons
1.	1.

Justify Reasoning **Determine whether each statement is always, sometimes, or never true. Explain your reasoning.**

17. If quadrilateral *RSTU* is a parallelogram, then $\overline{RS} \cong \overline{ST}$.

18. If a parallelogram has a 30° angle, then it also has a 150° angle.

19. If quadrilateral *GHJK* is a parallelogram, then $\overline{GH}$ is congruent to $\overline{JK}$.

20. In parallelogram *ABCD*, $\angle A$ is acute and $\angle C$ is obtuse.

21. In parallelogram *MNPQ*, the diagonals $\overline{MP}$ and $\overline{NQ}$ meet at *R* with $MR = 7$ cm and $RP = 5$ cm.

22. Communicate Mathematical Ideas Explain how you can use the rotational symmetry of a parallelogram to give an argument that supports the fact that opposite angles of a parallelogram are congruent.

23. To repair a large truck or bus, a mechanic might use a parallelogram lift. The figure shows a side view of the lift. *FGKL*, *GHJK*, and *FHJL* are parallelograms.

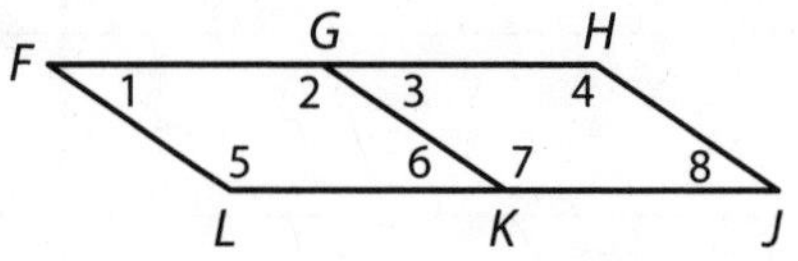

a. Which angles are congruent to $\angle 1$? Explain.

b. What is the relationship between $\angle 1$ and each of the remaining labeled angles? Explain.

24. Justify Reasoning *ABCD* is a parallelogram. Determine whether each statement must be true. Select the correct answer for each lettered part. Explain your reasoning.

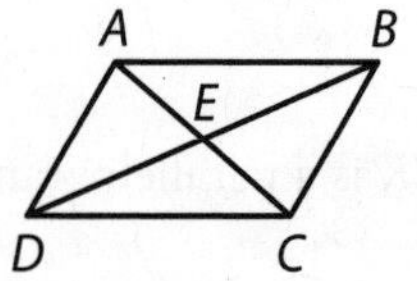

A. The perimeter of *ABCD* is $2AB + 2BC$. ○ Yes ○ No

B. $DE = \frac{1}{2}DB$ ○ Yes ○ No

C. $\overline{BC} \cong \overline{DC}$ ○ Yes ○ No

D. $\angle DAC \cong \angle BCA$ ○ Yes ○ No

E. $\triangle AED \cong \triangle CEB$ ○ Yes ○ No

F. $\angle DAC \cong \angle BAC$ ○ Yes ○ No

H.O.T. Focus on Higher Order Thinking

25. Represent Real-World Problems A store sells tiles in the shape of a parallelogram. The perimeter of each tile is 29 inches. One side of each tile is 2.5 inches longer than another side. What are the side lengths of the tile? Explain your steps.

26. Critique Reasoning A student claims that there is an SSSS congruence criterion for parallelograms. That is, if all four sides of one parallelogram are congruent to the four sides of another parallelogram, then the parallelograms are congruent. Do you agree? If so, explain why. If not, give a counterexample. Hint: Draw a picture.

27. Analyze Relationships The figure shows two congruent parallelograms. How are x and y related? Write an equation that expresses the relationship. Explain your reasoning.

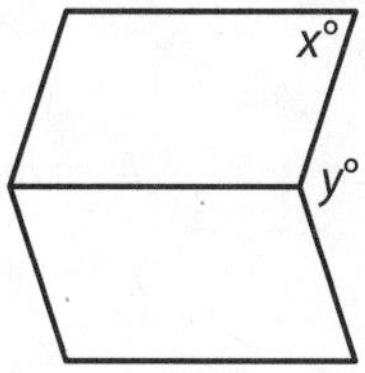

Lesson Performance Task

The principle that allows a scissor lift to raise the platform on top of it to a considerable height can be illustrated with four popsicle sticks attached at the corners.

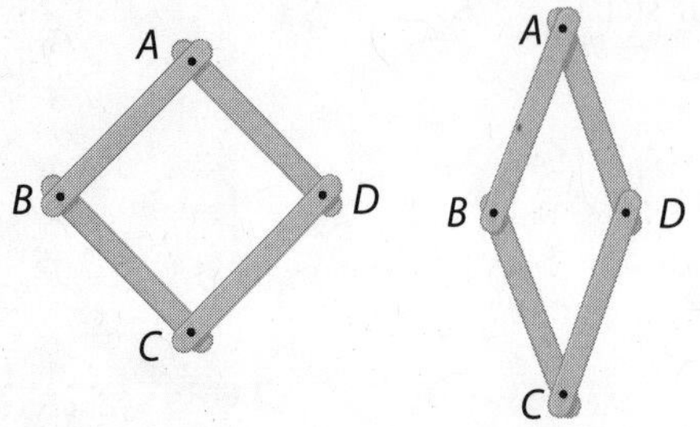

Answer these questions about what happens to parallelogram *ABCD* when you change its shape as in the illustration.

a. Is it still a parallelogram? Explain.

b. Is its area the same? Explain.

c. Compare the lengths of the diagonals in the two figures as you change them.

d. Describe a process that might be used to raise the platform on a scissor lift.

Constructions

Essential Question: How can you use constructions to solve real-world problems?

Key Vocabulary
diagonal (*diagonal*)
indirect proof (*prueba indirecta*)
isosceles trapezoid (*trapecio isósceles*)
kite (*el deltoide*)
parallelogram (*paralelogramo*)
quadrilateral (*cuadrilátero*)
rectangle (*rectángulo*)
rhombus (*rombo*)
square (*cuadrado*)
transversal (*transversal*)
trapezoid (*trapecio*)

KEY EXAMPLE (Lesson 1.1)

Determine whether the lines $\overleftrightarrow{DE}$ and $\overleftrightarrow{FG}$ are parallel given that $\overleftrightarrow{AB}$ intersects them at the points P and Q, respectively, $m\angle APE = 60°$, and $m\angle BQF = 60°$.

Lines $\overleftrightarrow{AB}$ and $\overleftrightarrow{DE}$ intersect, so they create two pairs of vertical angles. The angle which is the opposite of $\angle APE$ is $\angle DPB$, so they are called vertical angles.

$\angle APE \cong \angle DPB$	Vertical Angles Theorem
$m\angle APE = m\angle DPB$	Definition of congruence
$m\angle DPB = 60°$	Solve.
$m\angle BQF = m\angle DPB = 60°$	
$\angle BQF \cong \angle DPB$	Definition of congruence

Thus, the lines $\overleftrightarrow{DE}$ and $\overleftrightarrow{FG}$ are parallel by the converse of the Corresponding Angles Theorem because their corresponding angles are congruent.

KEY EXAMPLE (Lesson 1.3)

Construct the bisector of the angle shown.

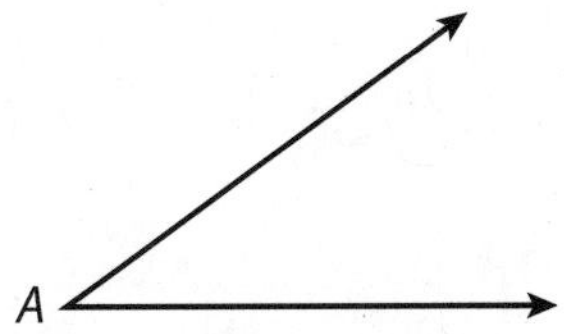

Place the point of the compass at A and draw an arc intersecting the sides of the angle. Label its points of intersection as B and C.

Use the same compass setting to draw intersecting arcs from B and C. Label the intersection of the arcs as point D.

Use a straight edge to draw $\overrightarrow{AD}$.

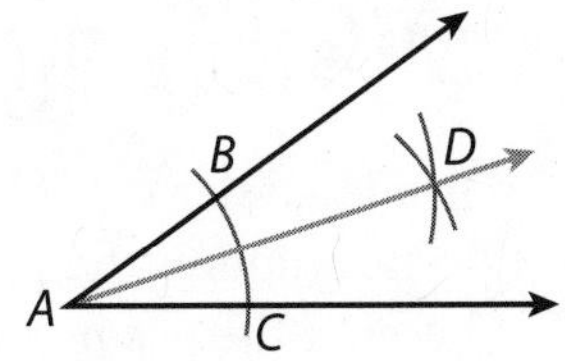

KEY EXAMPLE (Lesson 1.4)

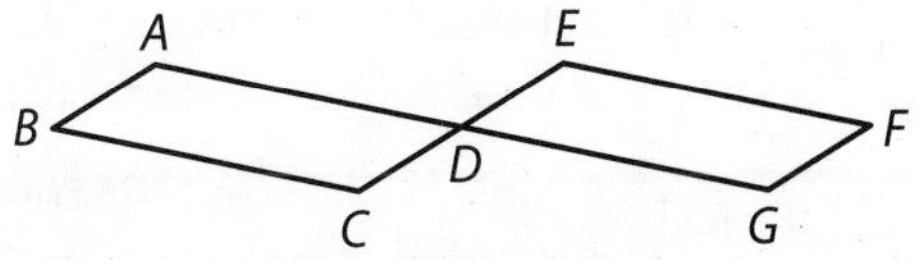

Given: $ABCD$ and $EDGF$ are parallelograms.

Prove: $\angle A \cong \angle G$

Proof	Reason
$ABCD$ and $EDGF$ are parallelograms.	Given
$\angle A \cong \angle C$	Opposite angles of a parallelogram are congruent.
$\overline{AB} \parallel \overline{CE}$	Definition of a parallelogram
$\overline{CE} \parallel \overline{FG}$	Definition of a parallelogram
$\angle C \cong \angle CDG$	Alternate interior angles theorem
$\angle CDG \cong \angle G$	Alternate interior angles theorem
$\angle A \cong \angle G$	Transitive property of congruence

EXERCISES

Determine whether the lines are parallel. (Lesson 1.1)

1. $\overleftrightarrow{DE}$ and $\overleftrightarrow{FG}$, given that $\overleftrightarrow{AB}$ intersects them at the points P and Q, respectively, $m\angle APD = 60°$, and $m\angle BQG = 120°$.

Find the distance and angle formed from the perpendicular bisector. (Lesson 1.2)

2. Find the distance of point D from B given that D is the point at the perpendicular bisector of the line segment $\overline{AB}$, $\overleftrightarrow{DE}$ intersects $\overline{AB}$, and $AD = 3$. Find $m\angle ADE$.

Refer to the diagram, which shows isosceles triangle *ABC*, to find the measure of the angle. $\overline{AD}$ and $\overline{CD}$ are angle bisectors. (Lesson 1.3)

3. $m\angle BAC$ ________

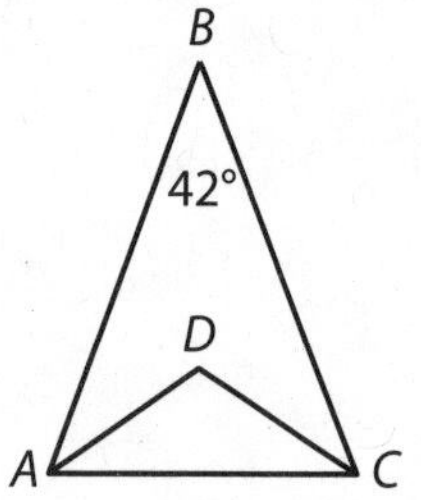

4. $m\angle ADC$ ________

***EFGH* is a parallelogram. Find the given side length.** (Lesson 1.4)

5. EF

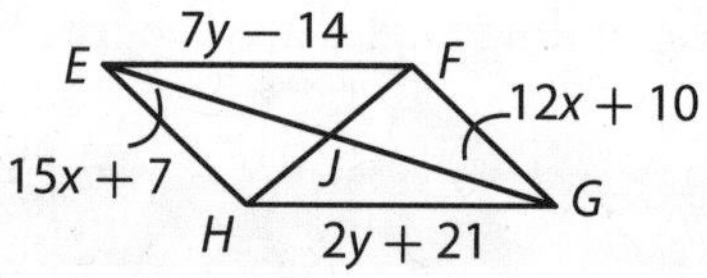

6. EG

MODULE PERFORMANCE TASK

Mystery Spot Geometry

Inside mystery spot buildings, some odd things can appear to occur. Water can appear to flow uphill, and people can look as if they are standing at impossible angles. That is because there is no view of the outside, so the room appears to be normal.

The illustration shows a mystery spot building constructed so that the floor is at a 25° angle with the ground.

- A table is placed in the room with its legs perpendicular to the floor and the tabletop perpendicular to the legs. Sketch or describe the relationship of the tabletop to the floor, walls, and ceiling of the room. What would happen if a ball were placed on the table?
- A chandelier hangs from the ceiling of the room. How does it appear to someone inside? How does it appear to someone standing outside of the room?

View from outside

View from inside

Use your own paper to complete the task. Use sketches, words, or geometry to explain how you reached your conclusions.

Ready to Go On?

1.1–1.4 Constructions

Personal Math Trainer

- Online Homework
- Hints and Help
- Extra Practice

Use the diagram to find lengths. $\overline{PB}$ is the perpendicular bisector of $\overline{AC}$. $\overline{QC}$ is the perpendicular bisector of $\overline{BD}$. $AB = BC = CD$. *(Lesson 1.2)*

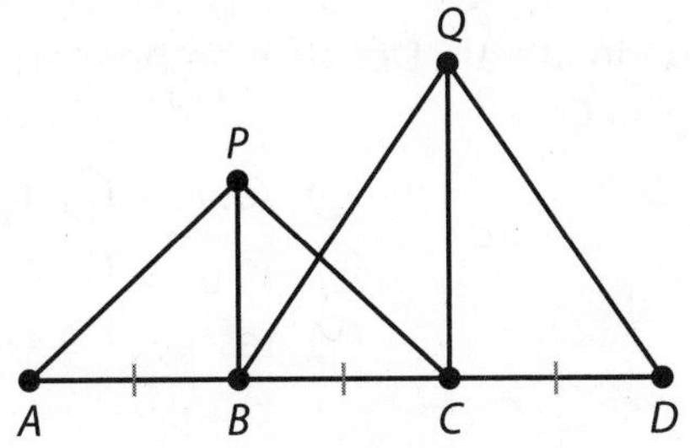

1. Given $BD = 24$ and $PC = 13$, find PB.

2. Given $QB = 23$ and $PC = 12$, find QD.

Solve the problem using the given information. *(Lesson 1.3)*

3. Given: $\overline{BC}$ bisects $\angle ACD$ and $m\angle ACB$ is 36°. Find $m\angle BCD$.

RSTU* is a parallelogram. Find each indicated measurement. *(Lesson 1.4)

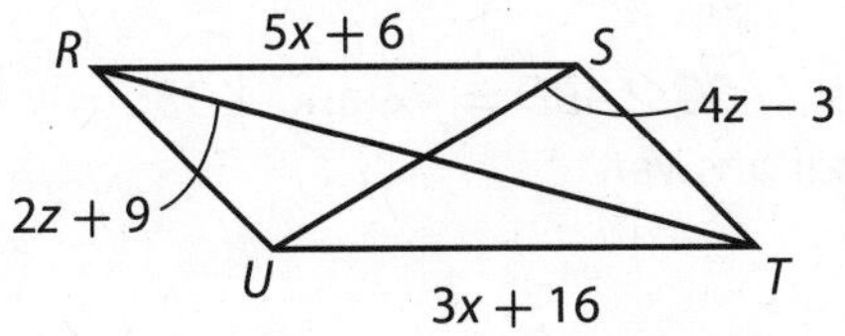

4. x

5. z

6. RS

7. RT

ESSENTIAL QUESTION

8. Say you want to create a ladder. Why would it be important to know if lines are parallel or perpendicular to each other?

MODULE 1
MIXED REVIEW

Assessment Readiness

1. Consider each equation. Is it the equation of a line that is parallel or perpendicular to $y = 3x + 2$?
Select Yes or No for A–C.

A. $y = -\frac{1}{3}x - 8$ ○ Yes ○ No
B. $y = 3x - 10$ ○ Yes ○ No
C. $y = 2x + 4$ ○ Yes ○ No

2. Consider each of the following quadrilaterals. Decide whether each is also a parallelogram. Select Yes or No for A–C.

A. Trapezoid ○ Yes ○ No
B. Rhombus ○ Yes ○ No
C. Square ○ Yes ○ No

3. Which conclusions are valid given that *ABCD* is a parallelogram? Choose True or False for each statement.

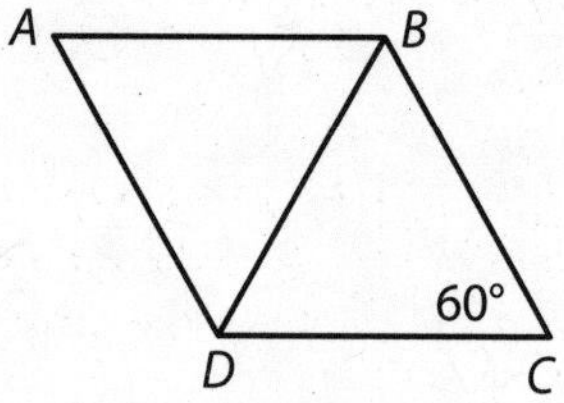

A. $\angle A \cong \angle C$ ○ True ○ False
B. $\angle A$ and $\angle B$ are complementary. ○ True ○ False
C. $\overline{AD} \parallel \overline{BC}$ ○ True ○ False

4. A line containing *D* bisects $\angle ABC$, $\angle ABD = 4x$, and $\angle DBC = x + 36$. Find m$\angle ABC$. Explain how you found your answer.

Coordinate Proof Using Slope and Distance

MODULE 2

Essential Question: How can you use coordinate proofs using slope and distance to solve real-world problems?

REAL WORLD VIDEO
Check out how workers use surveying tools and coordinate geometry to measure real-world distances and areas for the construction of roads and bridges.

MODULE PERFORMANCE TASK PREVIEW

How Do You Calculate the Containment of a Fire?

In this module, you will use concepts of perimeter and area to determine the percentage containment of a wildfire. To successfully complete this task, you'll need to master the skills of finding area and perimeter on the coordinate plane. So put on your safety gear and let's get started!

Are YOU Ready?

Complete these exercises to review the skills you will need for this module.

Personal Math Trainer
- Online Homework
- Hints and Help
- Extra Practice

Area of Composite Figures

Example 1

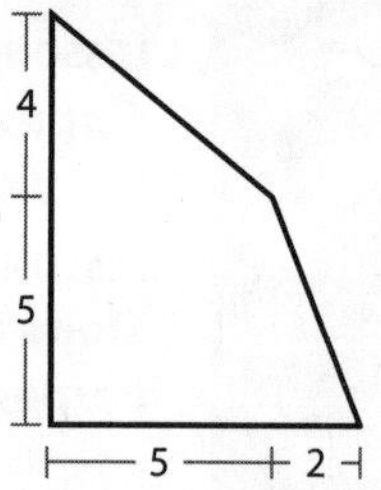

Find the area of the given figure.

Think of the shape as a square and two triangles. The square has sides of length 5 and an area of 25. The top triangle has a height of 4 and a base of 5, so its area is 10. The triangle on the right has a base of 2 and a height of 5, so its area will be 5. Altogether, the area will be 40.

Find the area of the given figure to the nearest hundredth as needed. Use 3.14 for pi.

1.

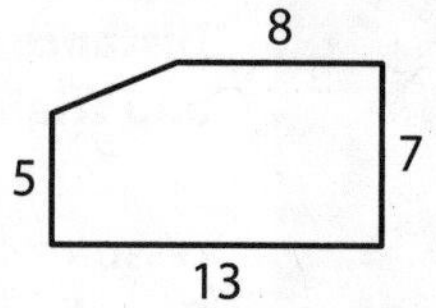

2.

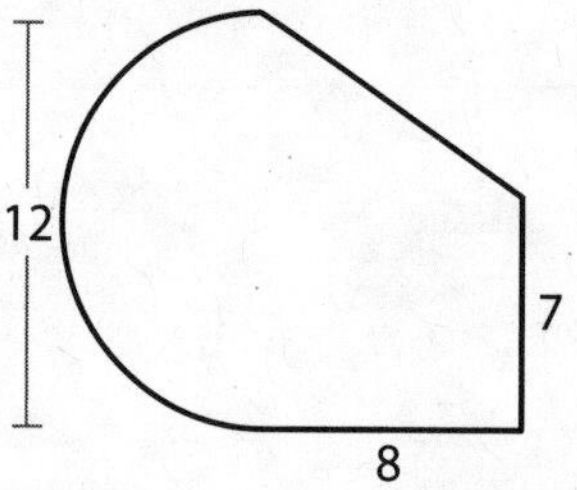

Distance and Midpoint Formula

Example 2 (3, 3) (5, 6)

Find the distance and midpoint for each set of ordered pairs.

$\sqrt{(5-3)^2 + (6-3)^2} = d$ Set up points in the distance formula.

$d = \sqrt{13}$ Simplify.

$M = \left(\frac{3+5}{2}, \frac{3+6}{2}\right)$ Set up points in the midpoint formula.

$M = (4, 4.5)$ Simplify.

Find the distance and midpoint for each set of ordered pairs, rounded to the nearest hundredth as needed.

3. (0, 9) (2, 5)

4. (2, 7) (4, 9)

5. (1, 8) (3, 8)

Writing Equations of Parallel, Perpendicular, Vertical, and Horizontal Lines

Example 3 Using the given *xy*-graph, find the equation of line *C* in slope-intercept form. The equation for this line is $y = 2$.

Using the given *xy*—graph, find the equation of the given line in slope-intercept form.

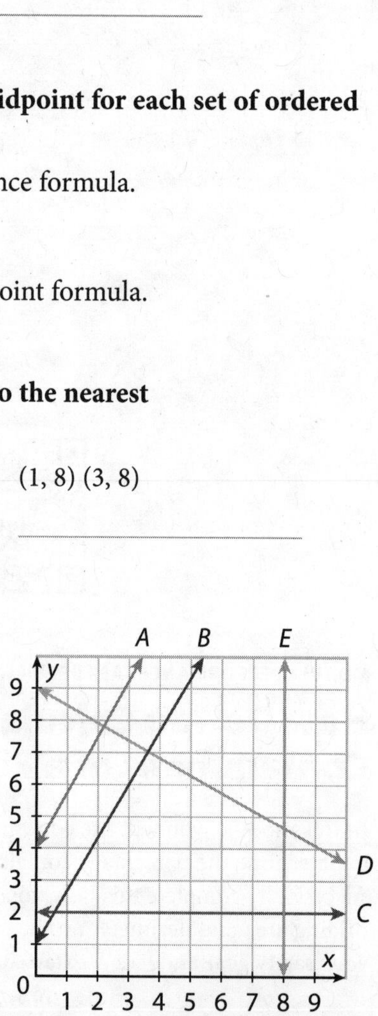

6. *E*

7. *B*

8. *A*

9. *D*

Name ____________________ Class ____________ Date ________

2.1 Slope and Parallel Lines

Essential Question: How can you use slope to solve problems involving parallel lines?

Resource Locker

Explore — Proving the Slope Criteria for Parallel Lines

The following theorem states an important connection between slope and parallel lines.

Theorem: Slope Criteria for Parallel Lines

Two nonvertical lines are parallel if and only if they have the same slope.

Follow these steps to prove the slope criteria for parallel lines.

(A) First prove that if two lines are parallel, then they have the same slope.

Suppose lines m and n are parallel lines that are neither vertical nor horizontal.

Let A and B be two points on line m, as shown. You can draw a horizontal line through A and a vertical line through B to create the "slope triangle," $\triangle ABC$.

You can extend $\overline{AC}$ to intersect line n at point D and then extend it to point F so that $AC = DF$. Finally, you can draw a vertical line through F intersecting line n at point E.

Mark the figure to show parallel lines, right angles, and congruent segments.

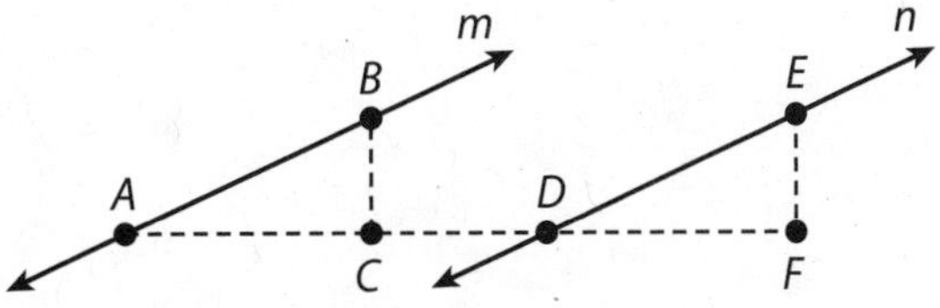

(B) When parallel lines are cut by a transversal, corresponding angles are congruent, so

$\angle BAC \cong$ ______.

$\triangle BAC \cong$ ______ by the ______ Triangle Congruence Theorem.

By CPCTC, $\overline{BC} \cong$ ____ and $BC =$ ____.

The slope of line $m = \frac{\square}{AC}$, and the slope of line $n = \frac{\square}{DF}$.

The slopes of the lines are equal because ______________________________

____

Ⓒ Now prove that if two lines have the same slope, then they are parallel.

Suppose lines m and n are two lines with the same nonzero slope. You can set up a figure in the same way as before.

Let A and B be two points on line m, as shown. You can draw a horizontal line through A and a vertical line through B to create the "slope triangle," $\triangle ABC$.

You can extend $\overline{AC}$ to intersect line n at point D and then extend it to point F so that $AC = DF$. Finally, you can draw a vertical line through F intersecting line n at point E.

Mark the figure to show right angles and congruent segments.

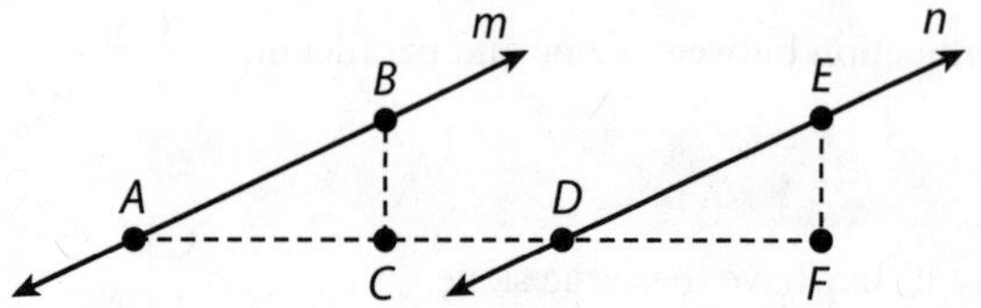

Ⓓ Since line m and line n have the same slope, $\frac{\square}{AC} = \frac{\square}{DF}$.

But $DF = AC$, so by substitution, $\frac{\square}{AC} = \frac{\square}{AC}$.

Multiplying both sides by AC shows that $BC =$ ____.

Now you can conclude that $\triangle BAC \cong$ ________ by the ________ Triangle Congruence Theorem.

By CPCTC, $\angle BAC \cong$ ________ .

Line m and line n are two lines that are cut by a transversal so that a pair of corresponding angles are congruent.

You can conclude that ______________________.

Reflect

1. Explain why the slope criteria can be applied to horizontal lines.

____

____

2. Explain why the slope criteria cannot be applied to vertical lines even though all vertical lines are parallel.

____

____

Explain 1 Using Slopes to Classify Quadrilaterals by Sides

You can use the slope criteria for parallel lines to analyze figures in the coordinate plane.

Example 1 **Show that each figure is the given type of quadrilateral.**

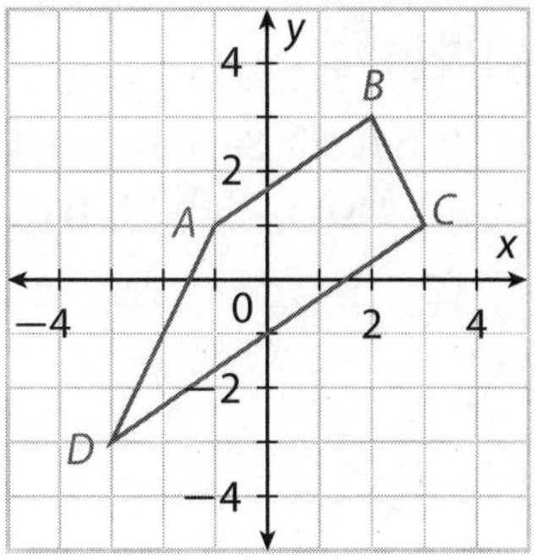

(A) Show that *ABCD* is a trapezoid.

Step 1 Find the coordinates of the vertices of quadrilateral *ABCD*.

$A(-1, 1), B(2, 3), C(3, 1), D(-3, -3)$

Step 2 Use the slope formula to find the slope of $\overline{AB}$ and the slope of $\overline{DC}$.

$$\text{slope of } \overline{AB} = \frac{y_2 - y_1}{x_2 - x_1} = \frac{3 - 1}{2 - (-1)} = \frac{2}{3}$$

$$\text{slope of } \overline{DC} = \frac{y_2 - y_1}{x_2 - x_1} = \frac{1 - (-3)}{3 - (-3)} = \frac{4}{6} = \frac{2}{3}$$

Step 3 Compare the slopes.

Since the slopes are the same, $\overline{AB}$ is parallel to $\overline{DC}$.

Quadrilateral *ABCD* is a trapezoid because it is a quadrilateral with at least one pair of parallel sides.

(B) Show that *PQRS* is a parallelogram.

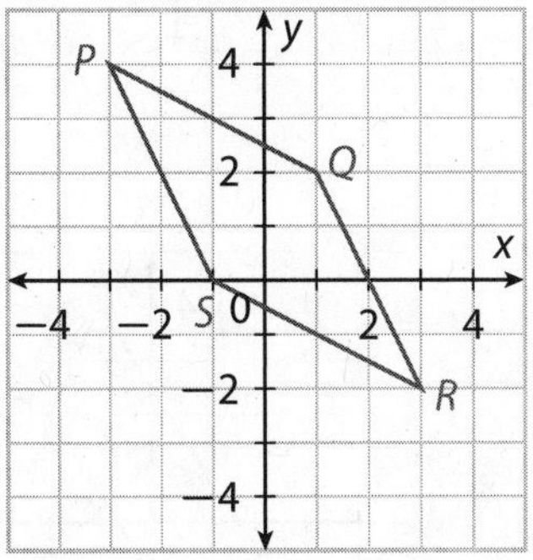

Step 1 Find the coordinates of the vertices of quadrilateral *PQRS*.

$P(-3, 4), Q(1, 2), R(\square, \square), S(\square, \square)$

Step 2 Use the slope formula to find the slope of each side.

$$PQ: \frac{y_2 - y_1}{x_2 - x_1} = \frac{2 - 4}{1 - (-3)} = \frac{-2}{4} = -\frac{1}{2}$$

$$QR: \frac{y_2 - y_1}{x_2 - x_1} = \frac{\square - 2}{\square - 1} = \frac{\square}{\square} = \square$$

$$RS: \frac{y_2 - y_1}{x_2 - x_1} = \frac{\square - \square}{\square - \square} = \frac{\square}{\square} = -\frac{\square}{\square}$$

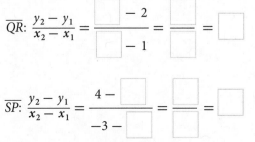

$$SP: \frac{y_2 - y_1}{x_2 - x_1} = \frac{4 - \square}{-3 - \square} = \frac{\square}{\square} = \square$$

Step 3 Compare the slopes.

Since the slope of $\overline{PQ}$ is the same as the slope of ______, $\overline{PQ}$ is parallel to ______.

Since the slope of $\overline{QR}$ is the same as the slope of ______, $\overline{QR}$ is parallel to ______.

Quadrilateral *PQRS* is a parallelogram because ________________________.

Reflect

3. **What If?** Suppose you know that the lengths of $\overline{PQ}$ and $\overline{QR}$ in the figure in Example 1B are each $\sqrt{20}$. What type of parallelogram is quadrilateral *PQRS*? Explain.

Your Turn

Show that each figure is the given type of quadrilateral.

4. Show that *JKLM* is a trapezoid.

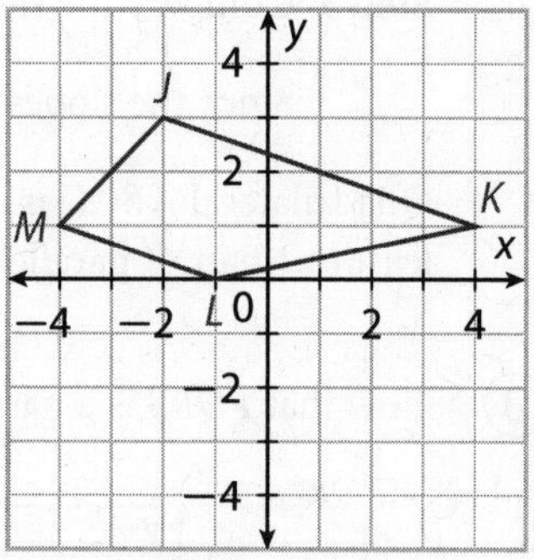

5. Show that *ABCD* is a parallelogram.

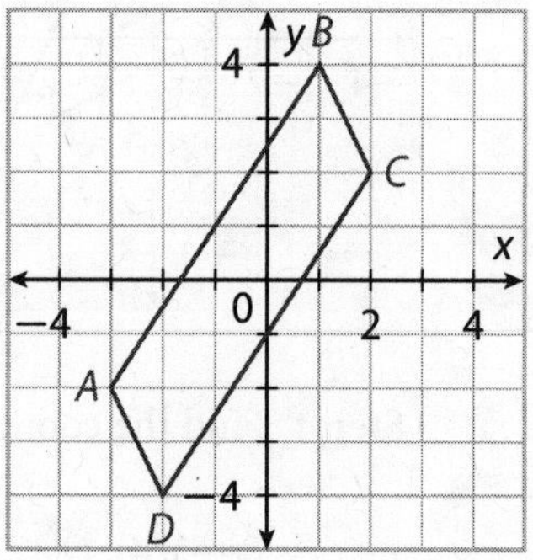

Explain 2 Using Slopes to Find Missing Vertices

Example 2 **Find the coordinates of the missing vertex in each parallelogram.**

(A) ▱$ABCD$ with vertices $A(1, -2)$, $B(-2, 3)$, and $D(5, -1)$

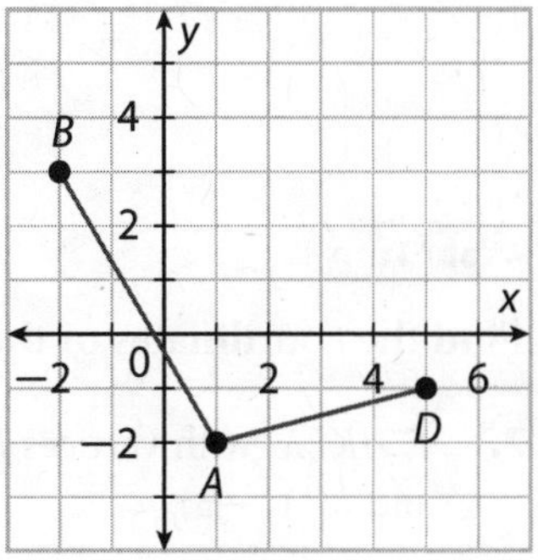

Step 1 Graph the given points.

Step 2 Find the slope of $\overline{AB}$ by counting units from A to B.

The rise from −2 to 3 is 5. The run from 1 to −2 is −3.

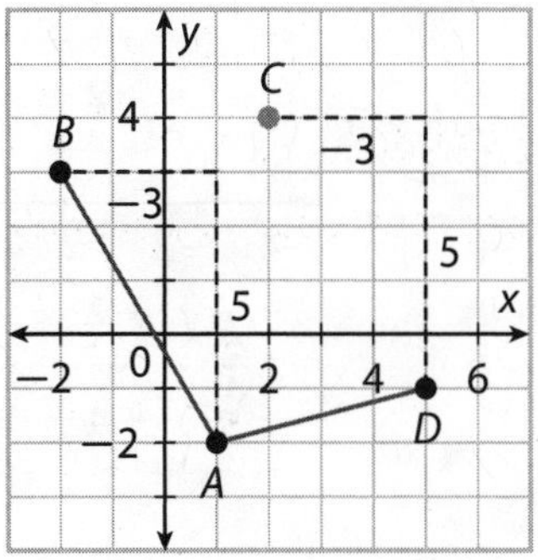

Step 3 Start at D and count the same number of units.

A rise of 5 from −1 is 4. A run of −3 from 5 is 2.

Label $(2, 4)$ as vertex C.

Step 4 Use the slope formula to verify that $\overline{BC} \parallel \overline{AD}$.

$$\text{slope of } \overline{BC} = \frac{4-3}{2-(-2)} = \frac{1}{4}$$

$$\text{slope of } \overline{AD} = \frac{-1-(-2)}{5-1} = \frac{1}{4}$$

The coordinates of vertex C are $(2, 4)$.

(B) ▱$PQRS$ with vertices $P(-3, 0)$, $Q(-2, 4)$, and $R(2, 2)$

Step 1 Graph the given points.

Step 2 Find the slope of $\overline{PQ}$ by counting units from Q to P.

The rise from 4 to 0 is $\square$. The run from −2 to −3 is $\square$.

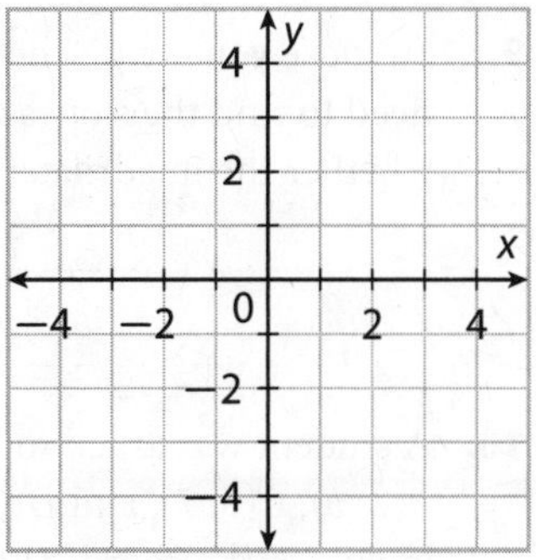

Step 3 Start at R and count the same number of units.

A rise of $\square$ from 2 is $\square$. A run of $\square$ from 2 is $\square$.

Label $(\square, \square)$ as vertex S.

Step 4 Use the slope formula to verify that $\overline{QR} \parallel \overline{PS}$.

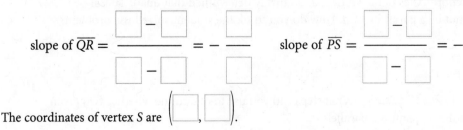

$$\text{slope of } \overline{QR} = \frac{\square - \square}{\square - \square} = -\frac{\square}{\square} \qquad \text{slope of } \overline{PS} = \frac{\square - \square}{\square - \square} = -\frac{\square}{\square}$$

The coordinates of vertex S are $(\square, \square)$.

Reflect

6. Discussion In Part A, you used the slope formula to verify that $\overline{BC} \parallel \overline{AD}$. Describe another way you can check that you found the correct coordinates of vertex C.

Your Turn

Find the coordinates of the missing vertex in each parallelogram.

7. ▱$JKLM$ with vertices $J(-3, -2)$, $K(0, 1)$, and $M(1, -3)$

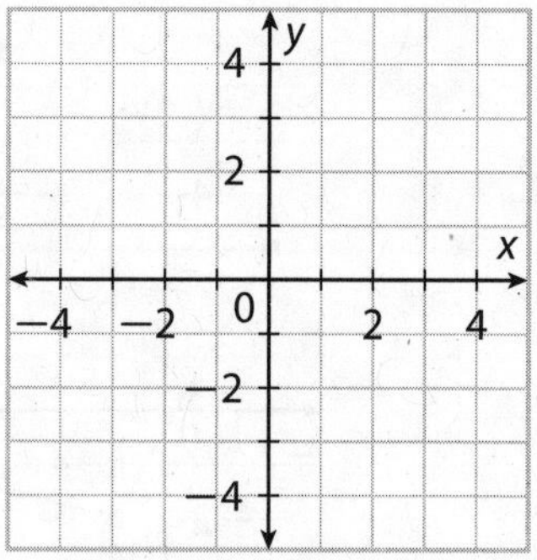

8. ▱$DEFG$ with vertices $E(-2, 2)$, $F(4, 1)$, and $G(3, -2)$

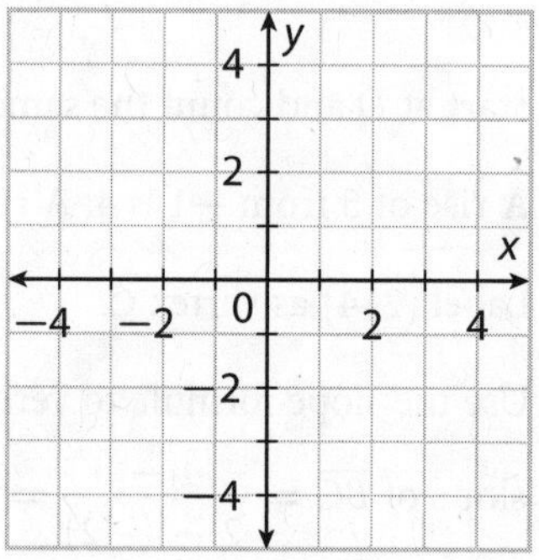

Elaborate

9. Suppose you are given the coordinates of the vertices of a quadrilateral. Do you always need to find the slopes of all four sides of the quadrilateral in order to determine whether the quadrilateral is a trapezoid? Explain.

10. A student was asked to determine whether quadrilateral $ABCD$ with vertices $A(0, 0)$, $B(2, 0)$, $C(5, 7)$, and $D(0, 2)$ was a parallelogram. Without plotting points, the student looked at the coordinates of the vertices and quickly determined that quadrilateral $ABCD$ could not be a parallelogram. How do you think the student solved the problem?

11. Essential Question Check-In What steps can you use to determine whether two given lines on a coordinate plane are parallel?

Evaluate: Homework and Practice

Personal Math Trainer
- Online Homework
- Hints and Help
- Extra Practice

1. Jodie draws parallel lines p and q. She sets up a figure as shown to prove that the lines must have the same slope. First she proves that $\triangle JKL \cong \triangle RST$ by the ASA Triangle Congruence Theorem. What should she do to complete the proof?

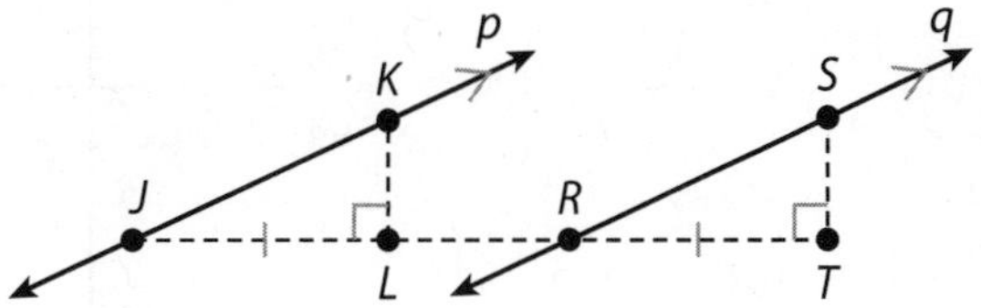

Show that each figure is the given type of quadrilateral.

2. Show that $ABCD$ is a trapezoid.

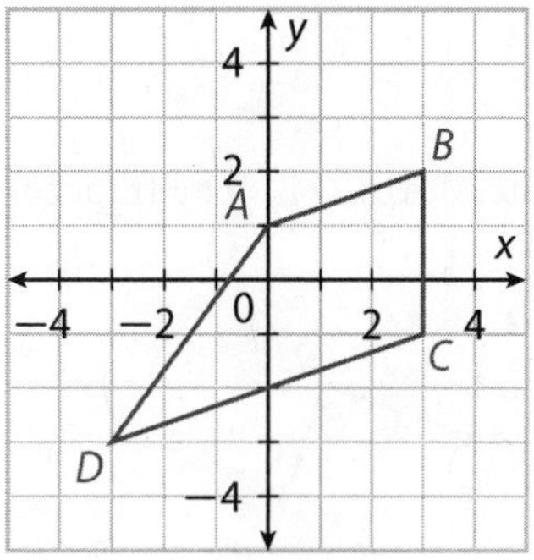

3. Show that $KLMN$ is a parallelogram.

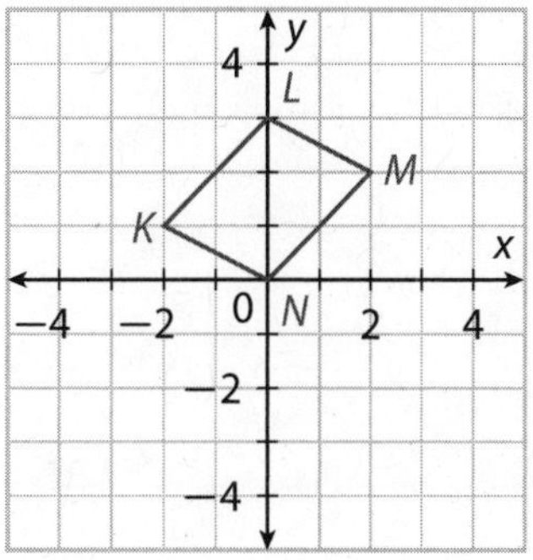

Find the coordinates of the missing vertex in each parallelogram. Use slopes to check your answer.

4. ▱$ABCD$ with vertices $A(3, -3)$, $B(-1, -2)$, and $D(5, -1)$

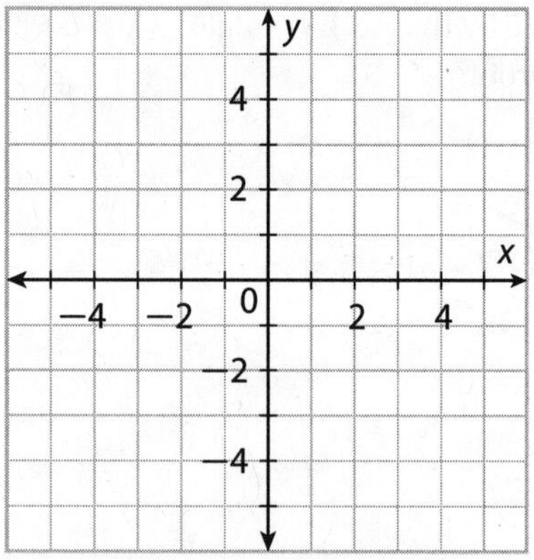

5. ▱$STUV$ with vertices $S(-3, -1)$, $T(-1, 1)$ and $V(0, 0)$

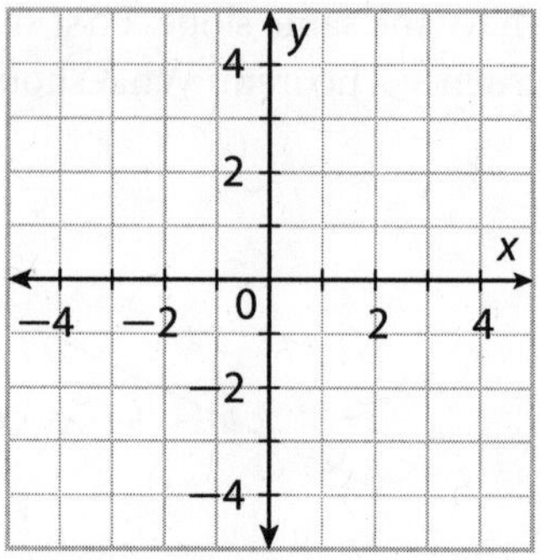

6. Show that quadrilateral $ABCD$ is *not* a trapezoid.

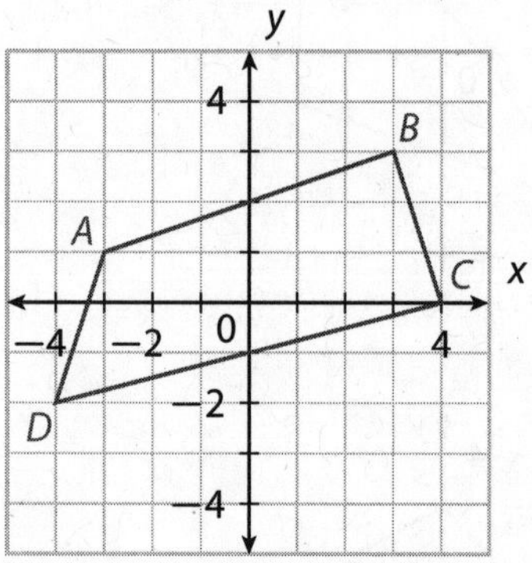

7. Show that quadrilateral $FGHJ$ is a trapezoid, but is not a parallelogram.

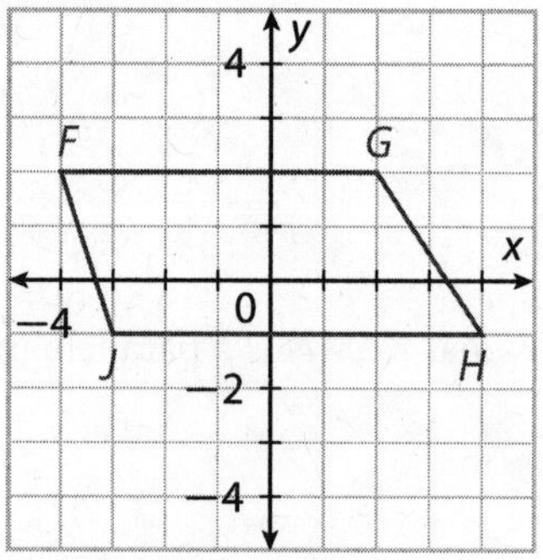

Determine whether each statement is always, sometimes, or never true. Explain your reasoning.

8. If quadrilateral $ABCD$ is a trapezoid and the slope of $\overline{AB}$ is 3, then the slope of $\overline{CD}$ is 3.

9. A parallelogram has vertices at $(0, 0)$, $(2, 0)$, $(0, 2)$, and at a point on the line $y = x$.

10. If the slope of $\overline{PQ}$ is $\frac{1}{3}$ and the slope of $\overline{RS}$ is $-\frac{1}{3}$, the quadrilateral $PQRS$ is a parallelogram.

11. If line m is parallel to line n and the slope of line m is greater than 1, then the slope of line n is greater than 1.

12. If trapezoid $JKLM$ has vertices $J(-4, 1)$, $K(-3, 3)$, and $L(-1, 4)$, then the coordinates of vertex M are $(2, 4)$.

Explain whether the quadrilateral determined by the intersections of the given lines is a trapezoid, a parallelogram, both, or neither.

13.

Line	Equation
Line ℓ	$y = 2x + 3$
Line m	$2y = -x + 6$
Line n	$y = x - 3$
Line p	$x + y = -3$

14.

Line	Equation
Line ℓ	$y = x + 3$
Line m	$y - x = 0$
Line n	$x + 2y = 6$
Line p	$y = -0.5x - 3$

15.

Line	Equation
Line ℓ	$2y = x + 4$
Line m	$y + 5 = 2x$
Line n	$-2x + y = 2$
Line p	$x + 2y = -6$

16.

Line	Equation
Line ℓ	$3x + y = 4$
Line m	$y + 3 = 0$
Line n	$y = 3x + 5$
Line p	$y = 3$

Algebra **Find the value of each variable in the parallelogram.**

17.

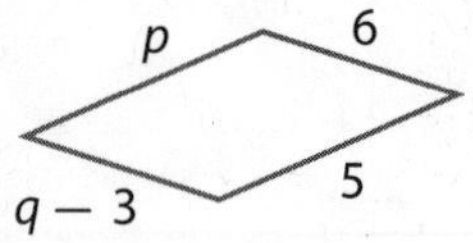

18.

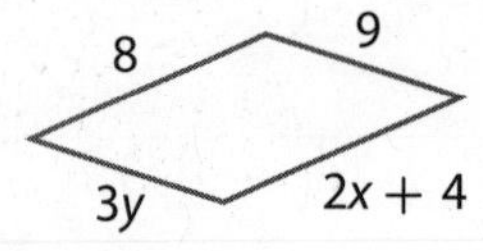

19.

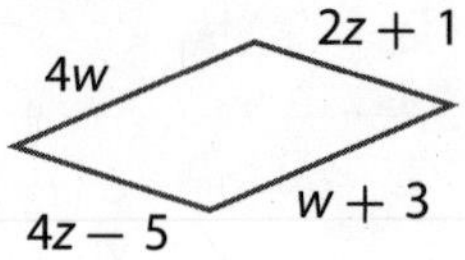

20. Use the slope-intercept form of a linear equation to prove that if two lines are parallel, then they have the same slope. (*Hint:* Use an indirect proof. Assume the lines have different slopes, m_1 and m_2. Write the equations of the lines and show that there must be a point of intersection.)

21. Critique Reasoning Mayumi was asked to determine whether quadrilateral *RSTU* is a trapezoid given the vertices $R(-2, 3)$, $S(1, 4)$, $T(1, -4)$, and $U(-2, 1)$. She noticed that the slopes of $\overline{RU}$ and $\overline{ST}$ are undefined, so she concluded that the quadrilateral could not be a trapezoid. Do you agree? Explain.

22. Kaitlyn is planning the diagonal spaces for the parking lot at a mall. Each space is a parallelogram. Kaitlyn has already planned the spaces shown in the figure and wants to continue the pattern to draw the next space to the right. What are the endpoints of the next line segment she should draw? Explain your reasoning.

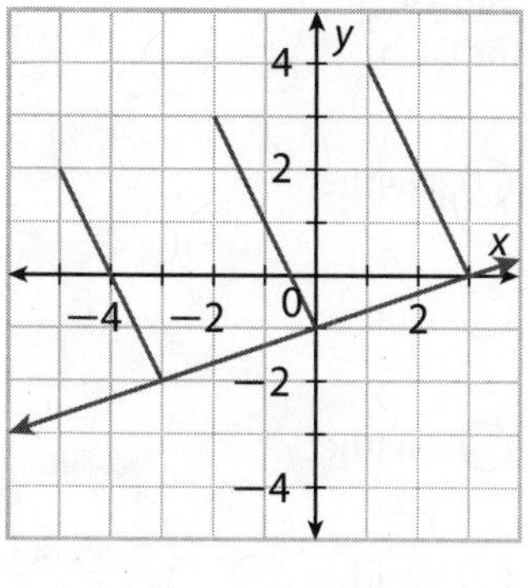

23. Multi-Step Two carpenters are using a coordinate plane to design a tabletop in the shape of a trapezoid. They have already drawn the two sides of the tabletop shown in the figure. They want side $\overline{AD}$ to lie on the line $x = -2$. What is the equation of the line on which side $\overline{CD}$ will lie? Explain your reasoning.

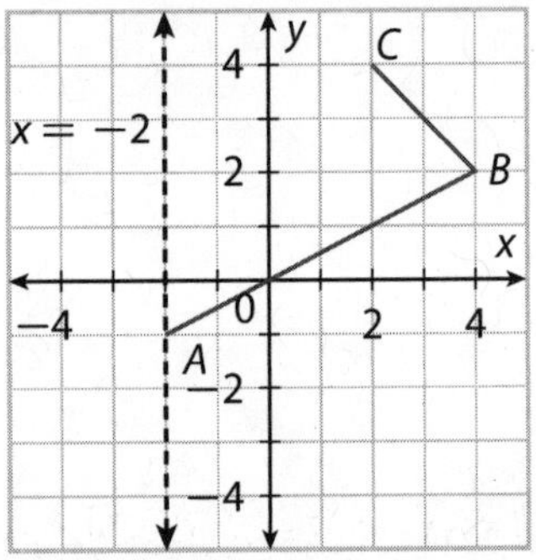

24. Quadrilateral *PQRS* has vertices *P*(−3, 2), *Q*(−1, 4), and *R*(5, 0). For each of the given coordinates of vertex *S*, determine whether the quadrilateral is a parallelogram, a trapezoid that is not a parallelogram, or neither. Select the correct answer for each lettered part.

a. *S*(0, 0) ○ Parallelogram ○ Trapezoid but not parallelogram ○ Neither

b. *S*(3, −2) ○ Parallelogram ○ Trapezoid but not parallelogram ○ Neither

c. *S*(2, −1) ○ Parallelogram ○ Trapezoid but not parallelogram ○ Neither

d. *S*(6, −4) ○ Parallelogram ○ Trapezoid but not parallelogram ○ Neither

e. *S*(5, −3) ○ Parallelogram ○ Trapezoid but not parallelogram ○ Neither

H.O.T. Focus on Higher Order Thinking

25. Explain the Error Tariq was given the points $P(0, 3)$, $Q(3, -3)$, $R(0, -4)$, and $S(-2, -1)$ and was asked to decide whether quadrilateral $PQRS$ is a trapezoid. Explain his error.

$$\text{slope of } \overline{SP} = \frac{3-(-1)}{0-(-2)} = \frac{4}{2} = 2$$

$$\text{slope of } \overline{QP} = \frac{3-(-3)}{3-0} = \frac{6}{3} = 2$$

Since at least two sides are parallel, the quadrilateral is a trapezoid.

26. Analyze Relationships Four members of a marching band are arranged to form the vertices of a parallelogram. The coordinates of three band members are $M(-3, 1)$, $G(1, 3)$, and $Q(2, -1)$. Find all possible coordinates for the fourth band member.

27. Make a Conjecture Plot any four points on the coordinate plane and connect them to form a quadrilateral. Find the midpoint of each side of the quadrilateral and connect consecutive midpoints to form a new quadrilateral. What type of quadrilateral is formed? Repeat the process by starting with a different set of four points. Do you get the same result? State a conjecture about your findings.

Lesson Performance Task

Suppose archeologists uncover an ancient city with the foundations of 16 houses. The locations of the houses are as follows:

$(2, 2)$ $(-5, 6)$ $(3, -6)$ $(-1, 0)$ $(5, -8)$ $(3, 5)$ $(-3, 3)$ $(0, 5)$

$(-8, 1)$ $(4, -1)$ $(1, -3)$ $(-4, -3)$ $(8, -7)$ $(-5, -4)$ $(-2, 8)$ $(6, -4)$

a. Besides graphing the points, how could you show that the streets are parallel? Explain.

b. Are the streets parallel?

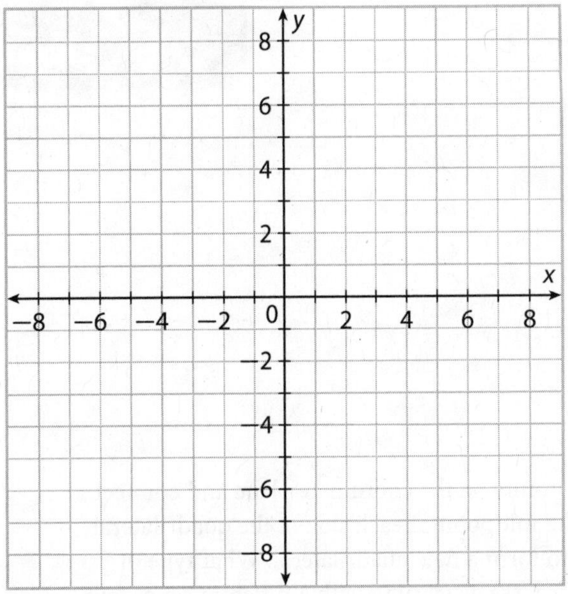

Name________________________________ Class________________ Date__________

2.2 Slope and Perpendicular Lines

Essential Question: How can you use slope to solve problems involving perpendicular lines?

Resource Locker

Explore — Proving the Slope Criteria for Perpendicular Lines

The following theorem states an important connection between slope and perpendicular lines.

Theorem: Slope Criteria for Perpendicular Lines

Two nonvertical lines are perpendicular if and only if the product of their slopes is −1.

Follow these steps to prove the slope criteria for perpendicular lines.

(A) First prove that if two lines are perpendicular, then the product of their slopes is −1.

Suppose lines m and n are perpendicular lines that intersect at point P, and that neither line is vertical. Assume the slope of line m is positive. (You can write a similar proof if the slope of line m is negative.)

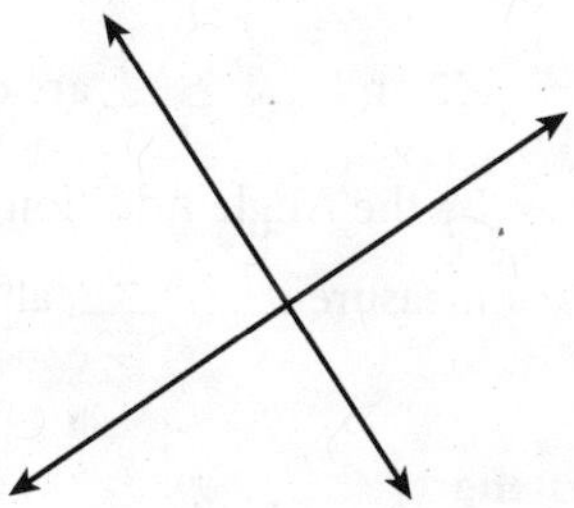

Copy the figure on a separate piece of paper. Mark your figure to show the perpendicular lines.

(B) Let Q be a point on line m, and draw a right triangle, $\triangle PQR$, as shown. Which line is this a "slope triangle" for?

____

Mark the figure to show the perpendicular segments.

(C) Assume that a and b are both positive. The slope of line m is $\frac{\square}{\square}$.

(D) Rotate $\triangle PQR$ 90° around point P. The image is $\triangle PQ'R'$, as shown.

Which line is $\triangle PQ'R'$ a slope triangle for? ______________

Let the coordinates of P be (x_1, y_1) and let the coordinates of Q' be (x_2, y_2).

Then the slope of line n is $\frac{y_2 - y_1}{x_2 - x_1} = \frac{b}{\square} = -\frac{\square}{\square}$.

(E) Now find the product of the slopes.

(slope of line m) · (slope of line n) $= \frac{\square}{\square} \cdot \left(-\frac{\square}{\square}\right) = \square$

(F) Now prove that if the product of the slopes of two lines is −1, then the lines are perpendicular.

Let the slope of line m be $\frac{a}{b}$, where a and b are both positive. Let line n have slope z. It is given that $z \cdot \frac{a}{b} = -1$. Solving for z gives the slope of line n.

$z = -\frac{\square}{\square}$

(G) Assume the lines intersect at P. Since the slope of m is positive and the slope of n is negative, you can set up slope triangles.

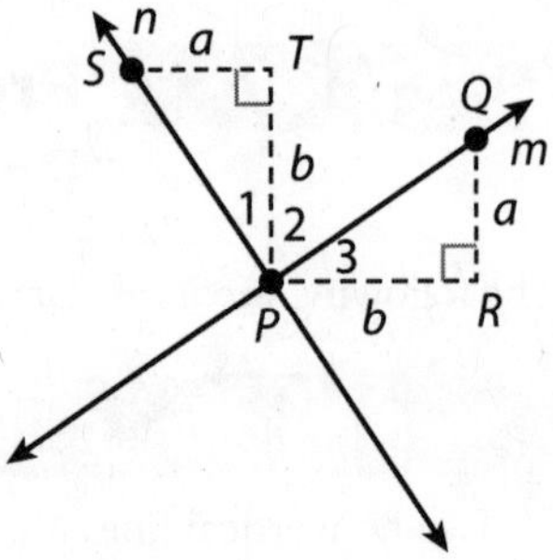

Based on the figure, $\overline{ST} \cong$ ________ and $\overline{PT} \cong$ ________.

Also, $\angle T \cong$ ________ because all right angles are congruent.

Therefore, ________ $\cong$ ________ by the SAS Triangle Congruence Theorem.

(H) By CPCTC, $\angle 1 \cong$ ________.

Since $\overline{TP}$ is vertical and $\overline{PR}$ is horizontal, $\angle TPR$ is a right angle.

So $\angle 2$ and ________ are complementary angles. You can conclude by substitution that

$\angle 2$ and ________ are complementary angles.

By the Angle Addition Postulate, $m\angle 1 + m\angle 2 = m\angle SPQ$, so $\angle SPQ$ must measure ________, and therefore line m is perpendicular to line n.

Reflect

1. In Step D, when you calculate the slope of line n, why is $x_2 - x_1$ negative?

2. The second half of the proof begins in Step F by assuming that line m has a positive slope. If the product of the slopes of two lines is −1, how do you know that one of the lines must have a positive slope?

3. Does this theorem apply when one of the lines is horizontal? Explain.

Explain 1 Using Slopes to Classify Figures by Right Angles

You can use the slope criteria for perpendicular lines to analyze figures in the coordinate plane.

Example 1 **Show that each figure is the given type of quadrilateral.**

(A) Show that *ABCD* is a rectangle.

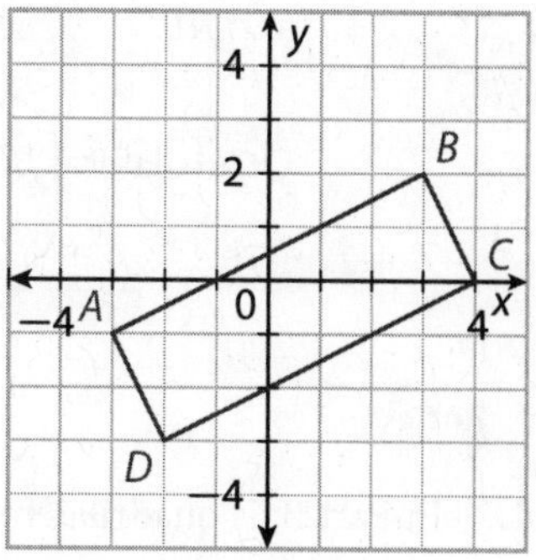

Step 1 Find the coordinates of the vertices of quadrilateral *ABCD*.

$A(-3, -1)$, $B(3, 2)$, $C(4, 0)$, $D(-2, -3)$

Step 2 Use the slope formula to find the slope of each side.

$\overline{AB}: \frac{2-(-1)}{3-(-3)} = \frac{1}{2}$ $\overline{BC}: \frac{0-2}{4-3} = -2$

$\overline{CD}: \frac{-3-0}{-2-4} = \frac{1}{2}$ $\overline{DA}: \frac{-1-(-3)}{-3-(-2)} = -2$

Step 3 Compare the slopes.

$$\left(\text{slope of } \overline{AB}\right) \cdot \left(\text{slope of } \overline{BC}\right) = \frac{1}{2} \cdot (-2) = -1$$

$$\left(\text{slope of } \overline{BC}\right) \cdot \left(\text{slope of } \overline{CD}\right) = -2 \cdot \frac{1}{2} = -1$$

$$\left(\text{slope of } \overline{CD}\right) \cdot \left(\text{slope of } \overline{DA}\right) = \frac{1}{2} \cdot (-2) = -1$$

$$\left(\text{slope of } \overline{DA}\right) \cdot \left(\text{slope of } \overline{AB}\right) = -2 \cdot \frac{1}{2} = -1$$

Consecutive sides are perpendicular since the product of the slopes is −1.

Quadrilateral *ABCD* is a rectangle because it is a quadrilateral with four right angles.

(B) Show that *JKLM* is a trapezoid with two right angles.

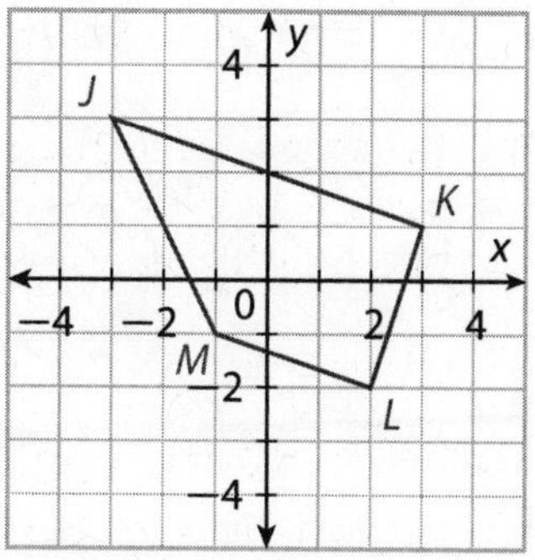

Step 1 Find the coordinates of the vertices of quadrilateral *JKLM*.

$J(-3, 3)$, $K(3, 1)$, $L(\square, \square)$, $M(\square, \square)$

Step 2 Use the slope formula to find the slope of each side.

$\overline{JK}: \frac{1-3}{3-(-3)} = \frac{-2}{6} = -\frac{1}{3}$

$\overline{KL}: \frac{\square - 1}{\square - 3} = \frac{\square}{\square} = \square$

$\overline{LM}: \frac{\square - \square}{\square - \square} = \frac{\square}{\square} = -\frac{\square}{\square}$

$\overline{MJ}: \frac{3 - \square}{-3 - \square} = \frac{\square}{\square} = \square$

Step 3 Compare the slopes.

Since the slope of $\overline{JK}$ is the same as the slope of ________, $\overline{JK}$ is parallel to ________.

Since the $\left(\text{slope of } \overline{JK}\right) \cdot \left(\text{slope of } \overline{KL}\right) = \frac{1}{3} \cdot \square = \square$ and

$\left(\text{slope of } \overline{KL}\right) \cdot \left(\text{slope of } \overline{LM}\right) = \square \cdot \left(-\frac{\square}{\square}\right) = \square$, $\overline{JK} \perp$ ________

and $\overline{KL} \perp$ ________.

Quadrilateral *JKLM* is a trapezoid with two right angles because ________________________________

____

Reflect

4. In Part B, is quadrilateral *JKLM* a parallelogram? Why or why not?

____

____

Your Turn

Show that each figure is the given type of quadrilateral.

5. Show that *DEFG* is a rectangle.

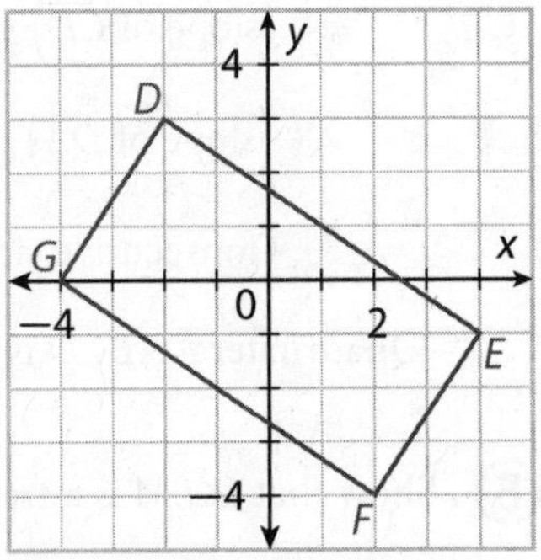

Explain 2 Using Slopes and Systems of Equations to Classify Figures

You can use slope to help you analyze a system of equations.

Example 2 **A city block is a quadrilateral bounded by four streets shown in the table. Classify the quadrilateral bounded by the streets.**

(A)

Street	Equation
Pine Street	$-x + 2y = 4$
Elm Road	$2x + y = 7$
Chestnut Street	$2y = x - 6$
Cedar Road	$y + 8 = -2x$

Step 1 Write each equation in slope-intercept form, $y = mx + b$.

Pine Street equation: $y = \frac{1}{2}x + 2$ Elm Road equation: $y = -2x + 7$

Chestnut Street equation: $y = \frac{1}{2}x - 3$ Cedar Road equation: $y = -2x - 8$

Step 2 Use the equations to determine the slope of each street.

Pine Street: $y = \frac{1}{2}x + 2$, so the slope is $\frac{1}{2}$.

Elm Road: $y = -2x + 7$, so the slope is -2.

Chestnut Street: $y = \frac{1}{2}x - 3$, so the slope is $\frac{1}{2}$.

Cedar Road: $y = -2x - 8$, so the slope is -2.

Step 3 Determine the type of quadrilateral bounded by the streets.

The product of the slopes of consecutive sides is -1.

So, the quadrilateral is a rectangle since it has four right angles.

Step 4 Check by graphing the equations.

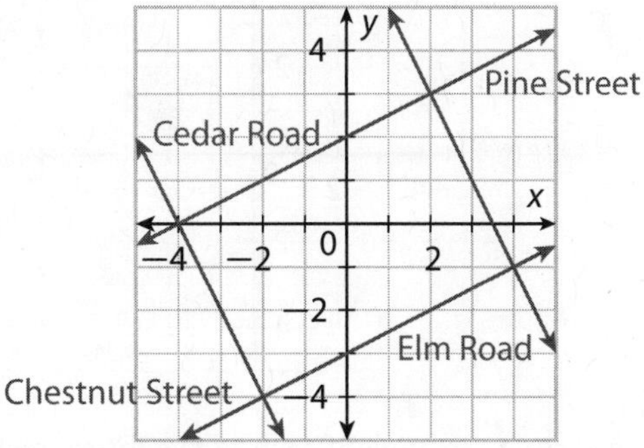

(B)

Street	Equation
Clay Avenue	$3y - 9 = x$
Fresno Road	$2x + y = 3$
Ward Street	$3y = x - 5$
Oakland Lane	$y + 4 = -2x$

Step 1 Write each equation in slope-intercept form, $y = mx + b$.

Clay Avenue equation: $y = \frac{\square}{\square}x + \square$

Fresno Road equation: $y =$ ____________

Ward Street equation: $y = \frac{\square}{\square}x - \frac{\square}{\square}$

Oakland Lane equation: $y =$ ____________

Step 2 Use the equations to determine the slope of each street.

Clay Avenue: ________________, so the slope is ____________.

Fresno Road ________________, so the slope is ____________.

Ward Street ________________, so the slope is ____________.

Oakland Lane: ________________, so the slope is ____________.

Step 3 Determine the type of quadrilateral bounded by the streets.

The slopes of opposite sides of the quadrilateral are ____________.

So, the quadrilateral is ________________ since ________________________________

Step 4 Check by graphing the equations.

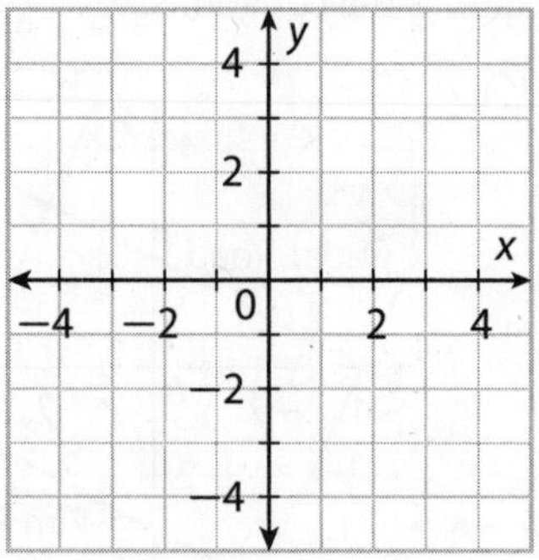

Reflect

6. **Discussion** Is it possible for four streets to form a rectangle if each of the four streets has a positive slope? Explain.

____

____

____

Your Turn

7. A farmers market is set up as a quadrilateral bounded by four streets shown in the table. Classify the quadrilateral bounded by the streets.

Street	Equation
Taft Road	$-2x + 3y = 13$
Harding Lane	$\frac{1}{3}y = -x - 1$
Wilson Avenue	$3y = 2x + 2$
Hoover Street	$3x + y = -14$

Elaborate

8. Suppose line ℓ has slope $\frac{a}{b}$ where $a \neq 0$ and $b \neq 0$, and suppose lines m and n are both perpendicular to line ℓ. Explain how you can use the slope criteria to show that line m must be parallel to line n.

9. **Essential Question Check-In** What steps can you use to determine whether two given lines on a coordinate plane are perpendicular?

Evaluate: Homework and Practice

Personal Math Trainer

- Online Homework
- Hints and Help
- Extra Practice

1. In the Explore, you proved that if two lines are perpendicular, then the product of their slopes is −1. You assumed that the slope of line m was positive. Follow these steps to complete the proof assuming that the slope of line m is negative.

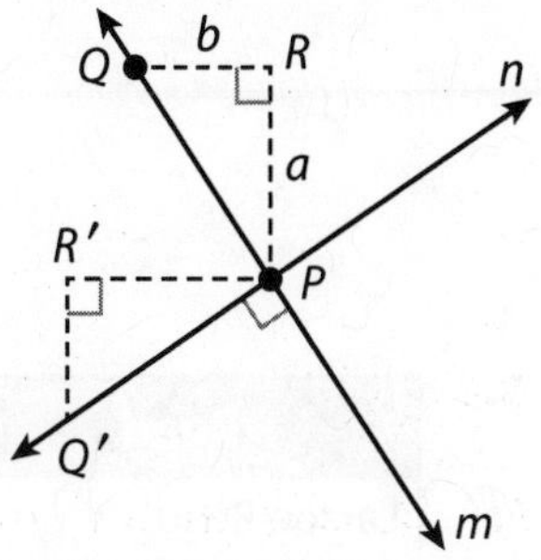

a. Suppose lines m and n are nonvertical perpendicular lines that intersect at point P. Let Q be a point on line m and draw a slope triangle, $\triangle PQR$, as shown. Write the slope of line m in terms of a and b, where a and b are both positive.

b. Rotate $\triangle PQR$ 90° around point P. The image is $\triangle PQ'R'$, as shown in the figure. Using $\triangle PQ'R'$, write the slope of line n in terms of a and b.

c. Explain how to complete the proof.

Show that each figure is the given type of quadrilateral.

2. Show that $QRST$ is a rectangle.

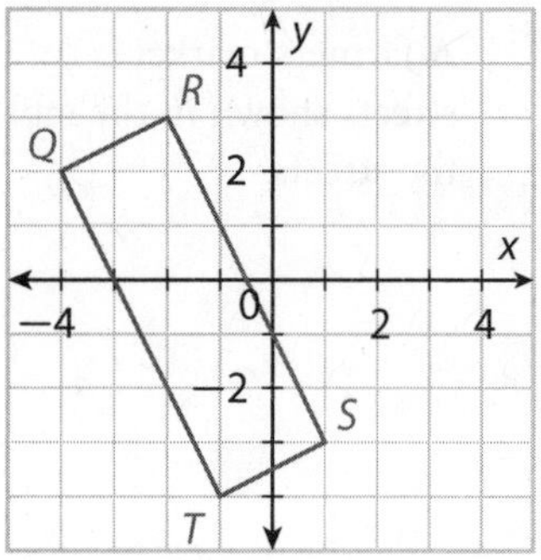

3. Show that $KLMN$ is a trapezoid with two right angles.

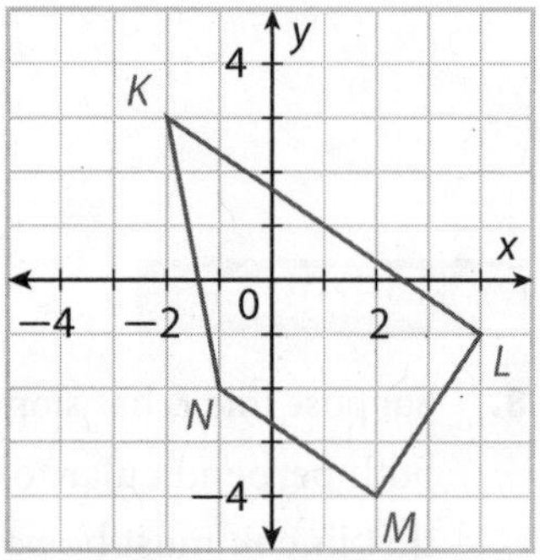

The boundary of a farm consists of four straight roads. Classify the quadrilateral bounded by the roads in each table.

4.

Road	Equation
Lewiston Road	$y - 8 = 2x$
Johnson Road	$2y = -x + 1$
Chavez Road	$-2x + y = -2$
Brannon Road	$x + 2y = -4$

5.

Road	Equation
Larson Road	$y + 1 = 2x$
Cortez Road	$2x + y = 3$
Madison Road	$2x = y + 5$
Jackson Road	$2x + y = -5$

Multi-Step Determine whether the quadrilateral with the given vertices is a parallelogram. If so, determine whether it is a rhombus, a rectangle, or neither. Justify your conclusions. (*Hint*: Recall that a parallelogram with perpendicular diagonals is a rhombus.)

6. Quadrilateral $ABCD$ with $A(-3, 0)$, $B(1, 2)$, $C(2, 0)$, and $D(-2, -2)$

7. Quadrilateral $KLMN$ with $K(-4, 2)$, $L(-1, 4)$, $M(3, 3)$, and $N(-3, -1)$

8. Quadrilateral $FGHJ$ with $F(-2, 3)$, $G(1, 2)$, $H(2, -1)$, and $J(-1, 0)$

Determine whether each statement is always, sometimes, or never true. Explain.

9. If quadrilateral $ABCD$ is a rectangle and the slope of $\overline{AB}$ is positive, then the slope of $\overline{BC}$ is negative.

10. If line m is perpendicular to line n, then the slope of line n is 0.

11. If quadrilateral $JKLM$ is a rhombus and one diagonal has a slope of 3, then the other diagonal has a slope of $\frac{1}{3}$.

12. If k is a real number, then the line $y = x + k$ is perpendicular to the line $y = -x + k$.

13. The slopes of two consecutive sides of a rectangle are $\frac{2}{3}$ and $\frac{3}{2}$.

Algebra The perimeter of ▱$PQRS$ is 84. Find the length of each side of ▱$PQRS$ under the given conditions.

14. $PQ = QR$

15. $QR = 3(RS)$

16. $RS = SP - 7$

17. $SP = RS^2$

18. **Multiple Representations** Line m has the equation $2x + 3y = 6$, line n passes through the points in the table, and line p has the graph shown in the figure. Which of these lines, if any, are perpendicular? Explain.

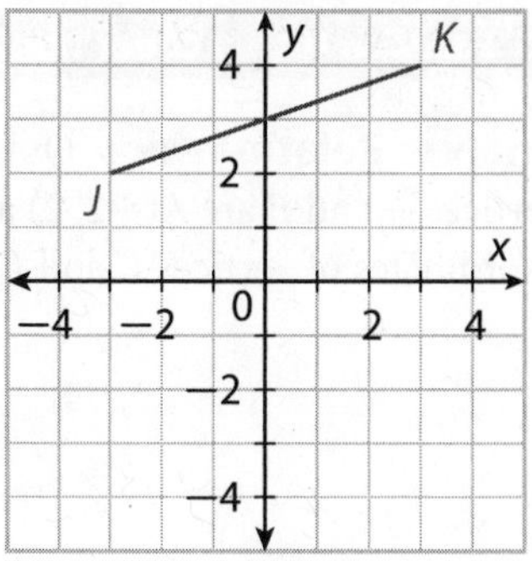

Line n	
x	y
4	5
6	8
8	11

19. Three subway lines run along straight tracks in the city. The equation for each subway line is given. City planners want to add a fourth subway line and want the tracks for the four lines to form a rectangle. What is a possible equation for the fourth subway line? Justify your answer.

Subway Line	Equation
B	$-2x + y = 4$
N	$2y = -x + 8$
S	$y + 11 = 2x$

20. Quadrilateral $JKLM$ is a rectangle. One side of the rectangle is shown in the figure. Which of the following are possible coordinates for vertices L and M? Select all that apply.

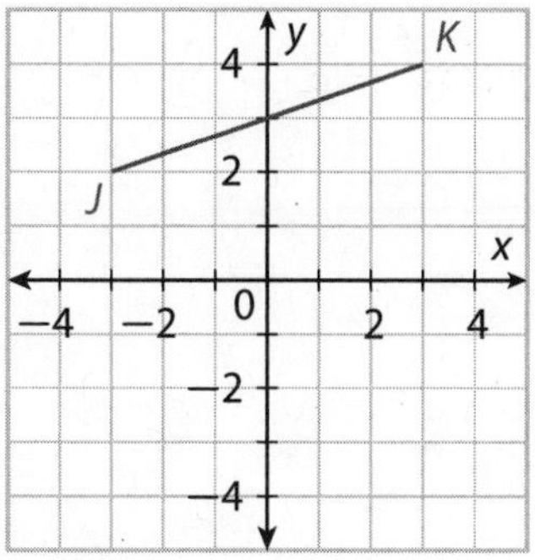

A. $L(4, 1)$ and $M(-2, -1)$

B. $L(5, -2)$ and $M(-1, -3)$

C. $L(4, 7)$ and $M(-2, 5)$

D. $L(5, -2)$ and $M(-1, -4)$

E. $L(3, 0)$ and $M(-3, 0)$

H.O.T. Focus on Higher Order Thinking

21. Analyze Relationships Quadrilateral *ABCD* is a rectangle. The coordinates of vertices *A* and *B* are $A(-2, 2)$ and $B(2, 0)$. Vertex *C* lies on the *y*-axis. What are the coordinates of vertices *C* and *D*? Explain.

22. Counterexamples A student said that any three noncollinear points can be three of the vertices of a rectangle because it is always possible to choose a fourth vertex that completes the rectangle. Give a counterexample to show that the student's statement is false and explain the counterexample.

Lesson Performance Task

Each unit on the grid represents 1 mile. A ship is in distress at the point shown. The navigator knows that the shortest distance from a point to a line is on a perpendicular to the line. So, the navigator directs the captain to head the ship on a perpendicular course toward the shoreline.

If the ship succeeds in staying on course, where will it hit land? Explain your method.

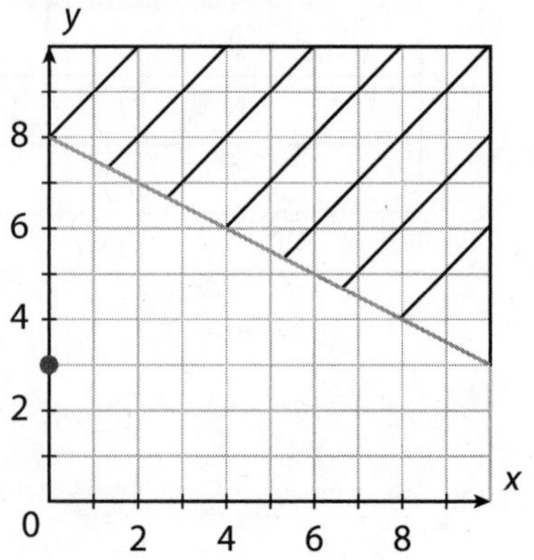

Name ____________________ Class ____________ Date ________

2.3 Coordinate Proof Using Distance with Segments and Triangles

Resource Locker

Essential Question: How do you write a coordinate proof?

Explore Deriving the Distance Formula and the Midpoint Formula

Complete the following steps to derive the Distance Formula and the Midpoint Formula.

(A) To derive the Distance Formula, start with points J and K as shown in the figure.

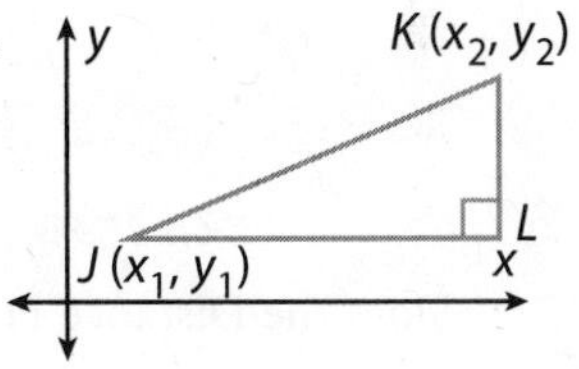

Given: $J(x_1, y_1)$ and $K(x_2, y_2)$ with $x_1 \neq x_2$ and $y_1 \neq y_2$

Prove: $JK = \sqrt{(x_2 - x_1)^2 + (y_2 - y_1)^2}$

Locate point L so that $\overline{JK}$ is the hypotenuse of right triangle JKL. What are the coordinates of L?

____

(B) Find JL and LK.

____

(C) By the Pythagorean Theorem, $JK^2 = JL^2 + LK^2$. Use this to find JK. Explain your steps.

____

____

(D) To derive the Midpoint Formula, start with points A and B as shown in the figure.

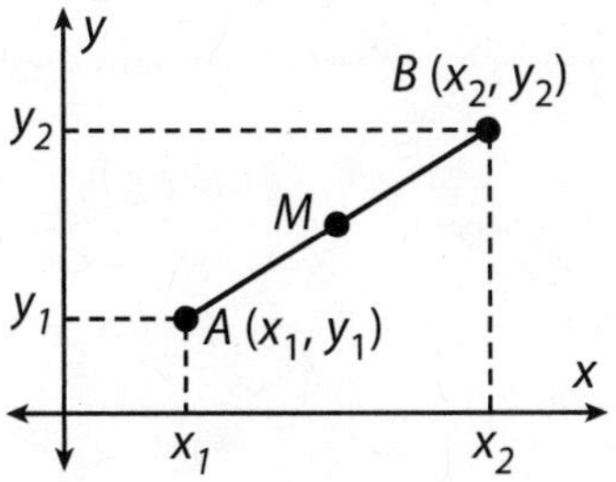

Given: $A(x_1, y_1)$ and $B(x_2, y_2)$

Prove: The midpoint of $\overline{AB}$ is $M\left(\frac{x_1 + x_2}{2}, \frac{y_1 + y_2}{2}\right)$.

What is the horizontal distance from point A to point B? What is the vertical distance from point A to point B?

____

(E) The horizontal and vertical distances from A to M must be half these distances.

What is the horizontal distance from point A to point M? ________

What is the vertical distance from point A to point M? ________

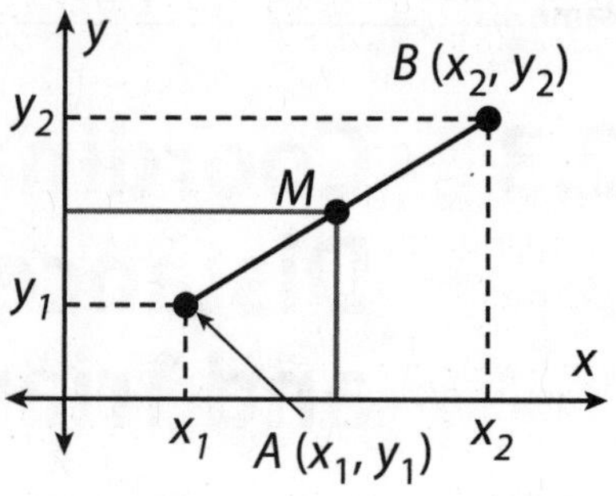

(F) To find the coordinates of point M, add the distances from Step E to the x- and y-coordinates of point A and simplify.

x-coordinate of point M: $x_1 + \frac{x_2 - x_1}{2} = \frac{2x_1}{2} + \frac{x_2 - x_1}{2} = \frac{2x_1 + x_2 - x_1}{2} = \frac{x_1 + x_2}{2}$

y-coordinate of point M: ________________________________

Reflect

1. In the proof of the Distance Formula, why do you assume that $x_1 \neq x_2$ and $y_1 \neq y_2$?

____

____

____

2. Does the Distance Formula still apply if $x_1 = x_2$ or $y_1 = y_2$? Explain.

____

____

____

3. Does the Midpoint Formula still apply if $x_1 = x_2$ or $y_1 = y_2$? Explain.

____

____

____

Explain 1 Positioning a Triangle on the Coordinate Plane

A **coordinate proof** is a style of proof that uses coordinate geometry and algebra. The first step of a coordinate proof is to position the given figure in the plane. You can use any position, but some strategies can make the steps of the proof simpler.

Strategies for Positioning Figures in the Coordinate Plane

- Use the origin as a vertex, keeping the figure in Quadrant I.
- Center the figure at the origin.
- Center a side of the figure at the origin.
- Use one or both axes as sides of the figure.

Example 1 Write each coordinate proof.

(A) **Given:** $\angle B$ is a right angle in $\triangle ABC$. D is the midpoint of $\overline{AC}$.

Prove: The area of $\triangle DBC$ is one half the area of $\triangle ABC$.

Step 1 Assign coordinates to each vertex. Since you will use the Midpoint Formula to find the coordinates of D, use multiples of 2 for the leg lengths.

The coordinates of A are $(0, 2j)$.

The coordinates of B are $(0, 0)$.

The coordinates of C are $(2n, 0)$.

Step 2 Position the figure on the coordinate plane.

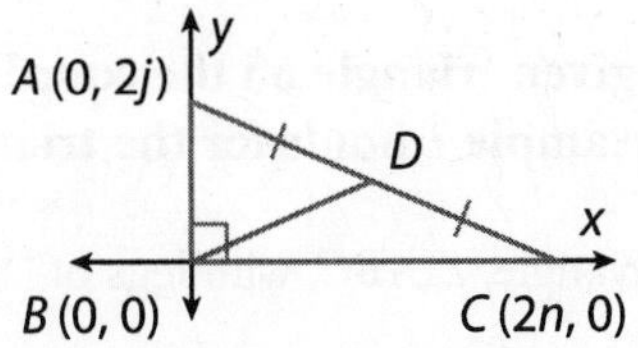

Step 3 Write a coordinate proof.

$\triangle ABC$ is a right triangle with height $2j$ and base $2n$.

$$\text{area of } \triangle ABC = \tfrac{1}{2}bh$$
$$= \tfrac{1}{2}(2n)(2j)$$
$$= 2nj \text{ square units}$$

By the Midpoint Formula, the coordinates of $D = \left(\frac{0 + 2n}{2}, \frac{2j + 0}{2}\right) = (n, j)$.

The height of $\triangle DBC$ is j units, and the base is $2n$ units.

$$\text{area of } \triangle DBC = \tfrac{1}{2}bh$$
$$= \tfrac{1}{2}(2n)(j)$$
$$= nj \text{ square units}$$

Since $nj = \frac{1}{2}(2nj)$, the area of $\triangle DBC$ is one half the area of $\triangle ABC$.

(B) **Given:** $\angle B$ is a right angle in $\triangle ABC$. D is the midpoint of $\overline{AC}$.

Prove: The area of $\triangle ADB$ is one half the area of $\triangle ABC$.

Assign coordinates and position the figure as in Example 1A.

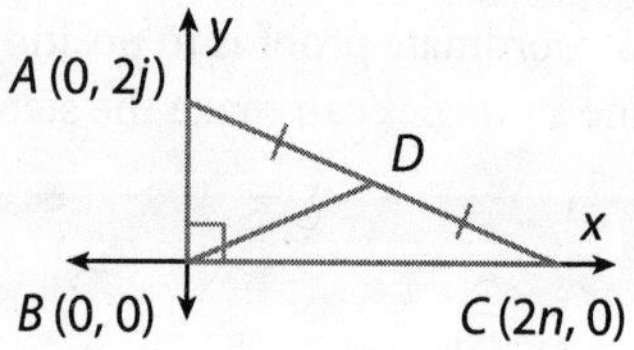

$\triangle ABC$ is a right triangle with height $\square$ and base $\square$.

area of $\triangle ABC = \frac{1}{2}bh$

$= \frac{1}{2}\square \cdot \square$

$= \square$ square units

By the Midpoint Formula, the coordinates of $D = \left(\frac{0 + \square}{2}, \frac{\square + 0}{2}\right) = \left(\square, \square\right)$.

The height of $\triangle ADB$ is $\square$ units, and the base is $\square$ units.

area of $\triangle ADB = \frac{1}{2}bh = \frac{1}{2}\square \cdot \square = \square$ square units

Since ______________, the area of $\triangle ADB$ is one half the area of $\triangle ABC$.

Reflect

4. Why is it possible to position $\triangle ABC$ so that two of its sides lie on the axes of the coordinate plane?

Your Turn

Position the given triangle on the coordinate plane. Then show that the result about areas from Example 1 holds for the triangle.

5. A right triangle, $\triangle ABC$, with legs of length 2 units and 4 units

6. A right triangle, $\triangle ABC$, with both legs of length 8 units

____

____

____

____

____

Explain 2 Proving the Triangle Midsegment Theorem

In Module 8, you learned that the Triangle Midsegment Theorem states that a midsegment of a triangle is parallel to the third side of the triangle and is half as long as the third side. You can now use a coordinate proof to show that the theorem is true.

Example 2 **Prove the Triangle Midsegment Theorem.**

Given: $\overline{XY}$ is a midsegment of $\triangle PQR$.

Prove: $\overline{XY} \parallel \overline{PQ}$ and $XY = \frac{1}{2}PQ$

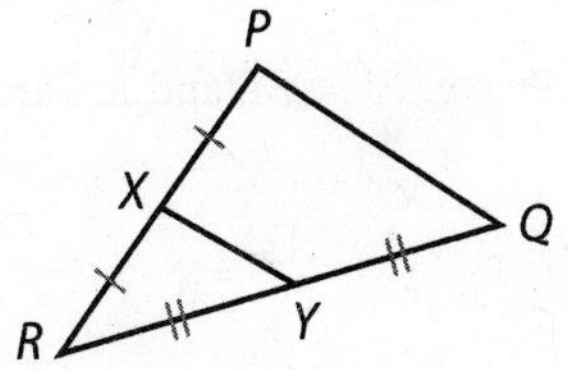

Place $\triangle PQR$ so that one vertex is at the origin. For convenience, assign vertex P the coordinates $(2a, 2b)$ and assign vertex Q the vertices $(2c, 2d)$.

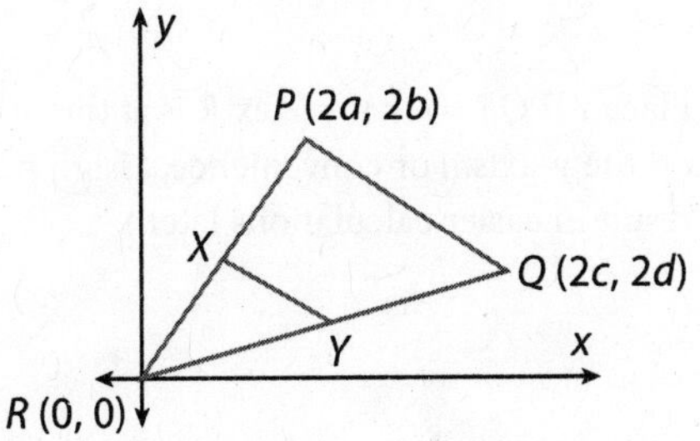

Use the Midpoint Formula to find the coordinates of X and Y.

The coordinates of X are $X\left(\frac{0+2a}{2}, \frac{0+2b}{2}\right) = X(a,b)$.

The coordinates of Y are $Y\left(\frac{\square + \square}{2}, \frac{\square + \square}{2}\right) = Y(\square, \square)$.

Find the slope of $\overline{PQ}$ and $\overline{XY}$.

slope of $\overline{PQ} = \frac{y_2 - y_1}{x_2 - x_1} = \frac{2d - 2b}{2c - 2a} = \frac{\square - \square}{\square - \square}$; slope of $\overline{XY} = \frac{y_2 - y_1}{x_2 - x_1} = \frac{\square - \square}{\square - \square}$

Therefore, $\overline{PQ} \parallel \overline{XY}$ since ______________________.

Use the Distance Formula to find PQ and XY.

$PQ = \sqrt{(x_2 - x_1)^2 + (y_2 - y_1)^2}$ $\quad = \sqrt{(2c - 2a)^2 + (2d - 2b)^2}$

$= \sqrt{\square \cdot (c - a)^2 + \square \cdot (d - b)^2}$ $\quad = \sqrt{\square \cdot \left((c - a)^2 + (d - b)^2\right)}$

$= \sqrt{\square} \cdot \sqrt{(c - a)^2 + (d - b)^2}$ $\quad = \square\sqrt{(c - a)^2 + (d - b)^2}$

$XY = \sqrt{(x_2 - x_1)^2 + (y_2 - y_1)^2}$ $\quad = \sqrt{(\square - \square)^2 + (\square - \square)^2}$

This shows that $XY = \frac{\square}{\square} PQ$.

Reflect

7. Discussion Why is it more convenient to assign vertex P the coordinates $(2a, 2b)$ and vertex Q the coordinates $(2c, 2d)$ rather than using the coordinates (a, b) and (c, d)?

____

____

____

Explain 3 Proving the Concurrency of Medians Theorem

You used the Concurrency of Medians Theorem in Module 8 and proved it in Module 9. Now you will prove the theorem again, this time using coordinate methods.

Example 3 **Prove the Concurrency of Medians Theorem.**

Given: $\triangle PQR$ with medians $\overline{PL}$, $\overline{QM}$, and $\overline{RN}$

Prove: $\overline{PL}$, $\overline{QM}$, and $\overline{RN}$ are concurrent.

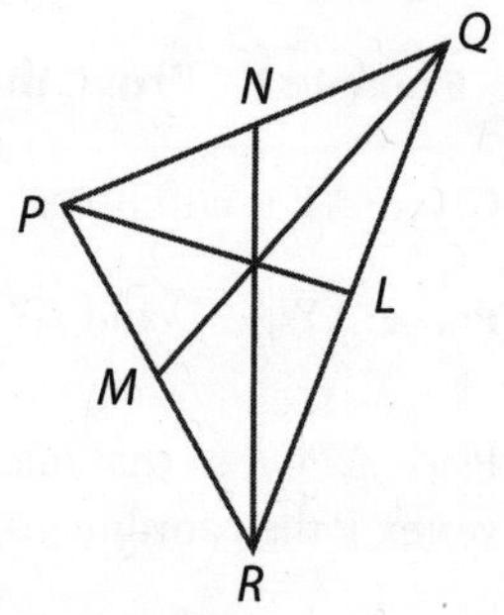

Place $\triangle PQR$ so that vertex R is at the origin. Also, place the triangle so that point N lies on the y-axis. For convenience, assign point N the vertices $(0, 6a)$. (The factor of 6 will result in easier calculations later.)

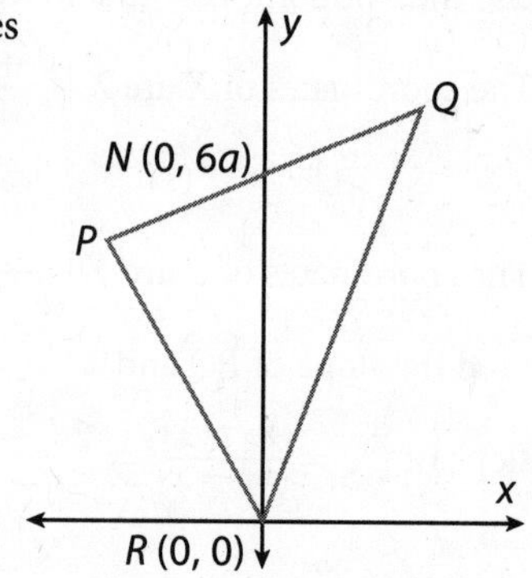

Since N is the midpoint of $\overline{PQ}$, assign coordinates to P and Q as follows.

The horizontal distance from N to P must be the same as the horizontal distance from N to Q. Let this distance be $2b$.

Then the x-coordinate of point P is $-2b$ and the x-coordinate of point Q is ______.

The vertical distance from N to P must be the same as the vertical distance from N to Q. Let this distance be $2c$.

Then the y-coordinate of point P is $6a - 2c$ and the y-coordinate of point Q is ______.

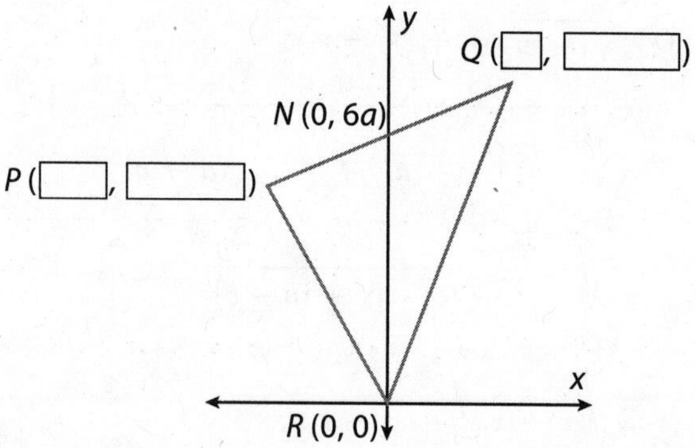

Complete the figure by writing the coordinates of points P and Q.

Now use the Midpoint Formula to find the coordinates of L and M.

The midpoint of $\overline{RQ}$ is $L\left(\frac{\square + \square}{2}, \frac{\square + \square}{2}\right) = L\left(\square, \square\right)$.

The midpoint of $\overline{RP}$ is $M\left(\frac{\square + \square}{2}, \frac{\square + \square}{2}\right) = M\left(\square, \square\right)$.

Complete the figure by writing the coordinates of points L and M.

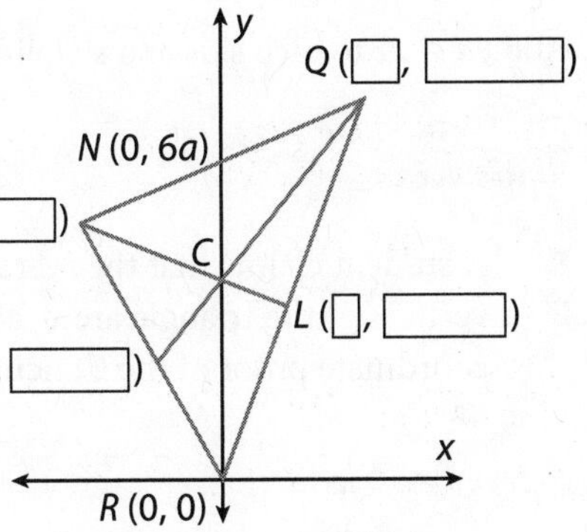

To complete the proof, write the equation of $\overleftrightarrow{QM}$ and use the equation to find the coordinates of point C, which is the intersection of the medians $\overline{QM}$ and $\overline{RN}$. Then show that point C lies on $\overleftrightarrow{PL}$.

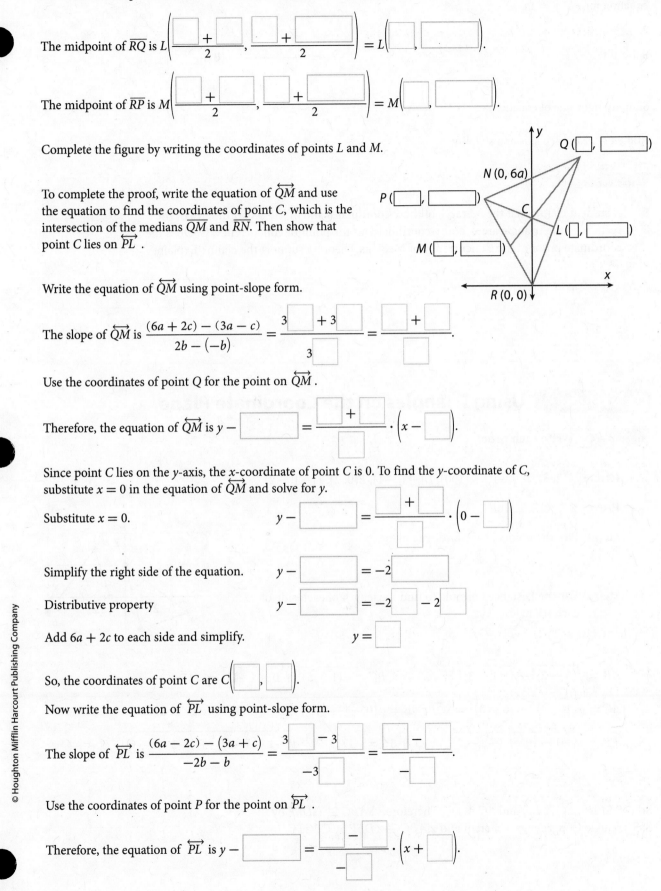

Write the equation of $\overleftrightarrow{QM}$ using point-slope form.

The slope of $\overleftrightarrow{QM}$ is $\frac{(6a + 2c) - (3a - c)}{2b - (-b)} = \frac{3\square + 3\square}{3\square} = \frac{\square + \square}{\square}$.

Use the coordinates of point Q for the point on $\overleftrightarrow{QM}$.

Therefore, the equation of $\overleftrightarrow{QM}$ is $y - \square = \frac{\square + \square}{\square} \cdot \left(x - \square\right)$.

Since point C lies on the y-axis, the x-coordinate of point C is 0. To find the y-coordinate of C, substitute $x = 0$ in the equation of $\overleftrightarrow{QM}$ and solve for y.

Substitute $x = 0$. $\quad y - \square = \frac{\square + \square}{\square} \cdot \left(0 - \square\right)$

Simplify the right side of the equation. $\quad y - \square = -2\square$

Distributive property $\quad y - \square = -2\square - 2\square$

Add $6a + 2c$ to each side and simplify. $\quad y = \square$

So, the coordinates of point C are $C\left(\square, \square\right)$.

Now write the equation of $\overleftrightarrow{PL}$ using point-slope form.

The slope of $\overleftrightarrow{PL}$ is $\frac{(6a - 2c) - (3a + c)}{-2b - b} = \frac{3\square - 3\square}{-3\square} = \frac{\square - \square}{-\square}$.

Use the coordinates of point P for the point on $\overleftrightarrow{PL}$.

Therefore, the equation of $\overleftrightarrow{PL}$ is $y - \square = \frac{\square - \square}{-\square} \cdot \left(x + \square\right)$.

Finally, show that point C lies on $\overleftrightarrow{PL}$. To do so, show that when $x = 0$ in the equation for $\overleftrightarrow{PL}$, $y = 4a$.

Substitute $x = 0$. $\qquad y - \square = \dfrac{\square - \square}{-\square} \cdot \left(0 + \square\right)$

Simplify right side of equation. $\qquad y - \square = -2\square + 2\square$

Add $6a - 2c$ to each side and simplify. $\qquad y = \square$

Reflect

8. A student claims that the averages of the x-coordinates and of the y-coordinates of the vertices of the triangle are x- and y-coordinates of the point of concurrency, C. Does the coordinate proof of the Concurrency of Medians Theorem support the claim? Explain.

____

____

____

____

Explain 4 Using Triangles on the Coordinate Plane

Example 4 **Write each proof.**

(A) **Given:** $A(2, 3)$, $B(5, -1)$, $C(1, 0)$, $D(-4, -1)$, $E(0, 2)$, $F(-1, -2)$

Prove: $\angle ABC \cong \angle DEF$

Step 1 Plot the points on a coordinate plane.

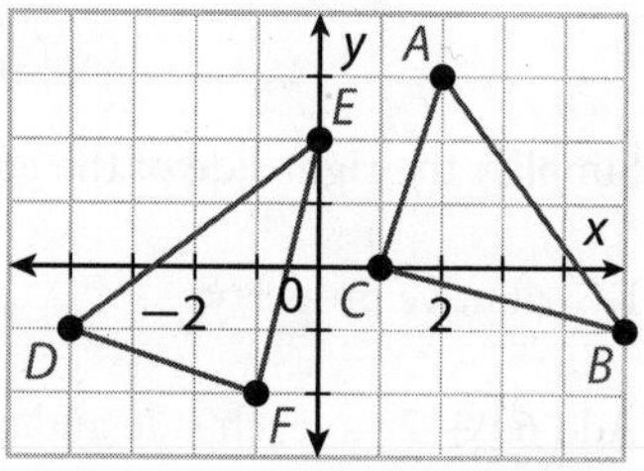

Step 2 Use the Distance Formula to find the length of each side of each triangle.

$AB = \sqrt{(5-2)^2 + (-1-3)^2} = \sqrt{25} = 5$; $BC = \sqrt{(1-5)^2 + 0 - (-1)^2} = \sqrt{17}$;

$AC = \sqrt{(1-2)^2 + (0-3)^2} = \sqrt{10}$; $DE = \sqrt{\left(0-(-4)\right)^2 + \left(2-(-1)\right)^2} = \sqrt{25} = 5$;

$EF = \sqrt{(-1-0)^2 + (-2-2)^2} = \sqrt{1+16} = \sqrt{17}$; $DF = \sqrt{\left(-1-(-4)\right)^2 + \left(-2-(-1)\right)^2}$

$= \sqrt{9+1} = \sqrt{10}$

So, $\overline{AB} \cong \overline{DE}$, $\overline{BC} \cong \overline{EF}$, and $\overline{AC} \cong \overline{DF}$. Therefore, $\triangle ABC \cong \triangle DEF$ by the SSS Triangle Congruence Theorem and $\angle ABC \cong \angle DEF$ by CPCTC.

Ⓑ **Given:** $J(-4, 1)$, $K(0, 5)$, $L(3, 1)$, $M(-1, -3)$, R is the midpoint of $\overline{JK}$, S is the midpoint of $\overline{LM}$.

Prove: $\angle JSK \cong \angle LRM$

Step 1 Plot the points on a coordinate plane.

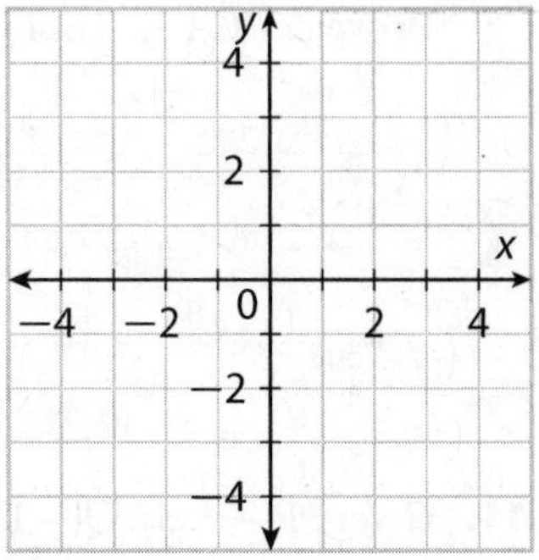

Step 2 Use the Midpoint Formula to find the coordinates of R and S.

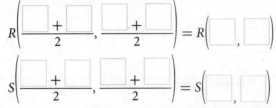

$$R\left(\frac{\square + \square}{2}, \frac{\square + \square}{2}\right) = R(\square, \square)$$

$$S\left(\frac{\square + \square}{2}, \frac{\square + \square}{2}\right) = S(\square, \square)$$

Step 3 Use the Distance Formula to find the length of each side of each triangle.

$$JK = \sqrt{(0 - (-4))^2 + (5 - 1)^2} = \sqrt{16 + 16} = \sqrt{32}$$

$$KS = \sqrt{(\square - 0)^2 + (\square - 5)^2} = \sqrt{\square + \square} = \sqrt{\square}$$

$$JS = \sqrt{(\square - (-4))^2 + (\square - 1)^2} = \sqrt{\square + \square} = \sqrt{\square}$$

$$LM = \sqrt{(-1 - 3)^2 + (-3 - 1)^2} = \sqrt{16 + 16} = \sqrt{32}$$

$$MR = \sqrt{(\square - (-1))^2 + (\square - (-3))^2} = \sqrt{\square + \square} = \sqrt{\square}$$

$$LR = \sqrt{(\square - 3)^2 + (\square - 1)^2} = \sqrt{\square + \square} = \sqrt{\square}$$

So, $\overline{JK} \cong$ $\square$, $\overline{KS} \cong$ $\square$, and $\overline{JS} \cong$ $\square$. Therefore, $\triangle JKS \cong$ $\square$ by the SSS Triangle Congruence Theorem and $\angle JSK \cong \angle LRM$

since ______________________________.

Reflect

9. In Part B, what other pairs of angles can you prove to be congruent? Why?

____

____

Your Turn

Write each proof.

10. **Given:** $A(-4, -2)$, $B(-3, 2)$, $C(-1, 3)$, $D(-5, 0)$, $E(-1, -1)$, $F(0, -3)$
Prove: $\angle BCA \cong \angle EFD$

11. **Given:** $P(-3, 5)$, $Q(-1, -1)$, $R(4, 5)$, $S(2, -1)$, M is the midpoint of $\overline{PQ}$, N is the midpoint of $\overline{RS}$.
Prove: $\angle PQN \cong \angle RSM$

Elaborate

12. When you write a coordinate proof, why might you assign $2p$ as a coordinate rather than p?

13. **Essential Question Check-In** What makes a coordinate proof different from the other types of proofs you have written so far?

Evaluate: Homework and Practice

Personal Math Trainer

- Online Homework
- Hints and Help
- Extra Practice

1. Explain how to derive the Distance Formula using $\triangle PQR$.

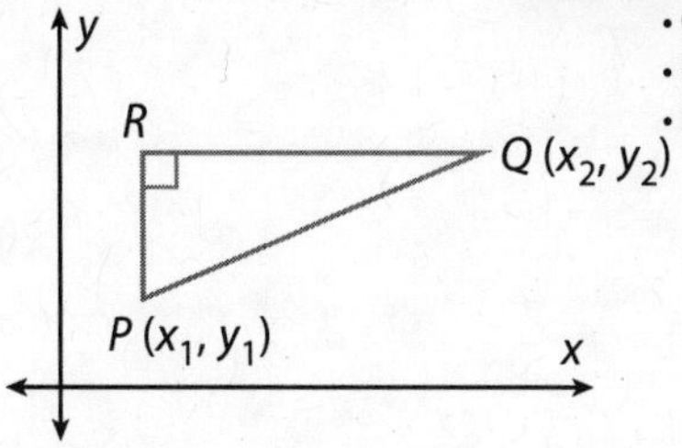

Write each coordinate proof.

2. **Given:** $\angle B$ is a right angle in $\triangle ABC$. M is the midpoint of $\overline{AC}$.

   Prove: M is equidistant from all three vertices of $\triangle ABC$.

   Use the coordinates that have been assigned in the figure.

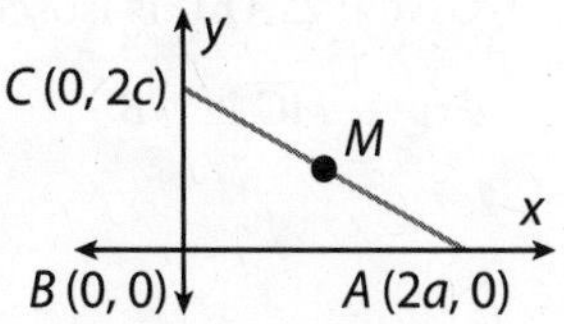

3. **Given:** $\triangle ABC$ is isosceles. X is the midpoint of $\overline{AB}$, Y is the midpoint of $\overline{AC}$, Z is the midpoint of $\overline{BC}$.

   Prove: $\triangle XYZ$ is isosceles.

   Use the coordinates that have been assigned in the figure.

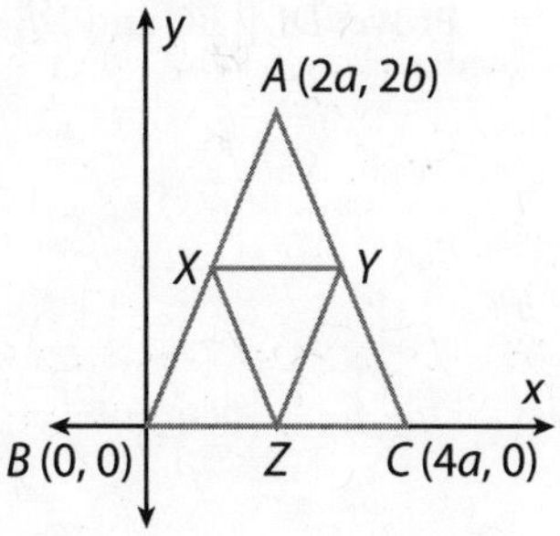

4. **Given:** $\angle R$ is a right angle in $\triangle PQR$. A is the midpoint of $\overline{PR}$. B is the midpoint of $\overline{QR}$.

Prove: $\overline{AB}$ is parallel to $\overline{PQ}$.

5. **Given:** $\triangle ABC$ is isosceles. M is the midpoint of $\overline{AB}$. N is the midpoint of $\overline{AC}$. $\overline{AB} \cong \overline{AC}$

Prove: $\overline{MC} \cong \overline{NB}$

6. Prove the Triangle Midsegment Theorem using the figure shown here.

Given: $\overline{DE}$ is a midsegment of $\triangle ABC$.

Prove: $\overline{DE} \parallel \overline{BC}$ and $DE = \frac{1}{2}BC$

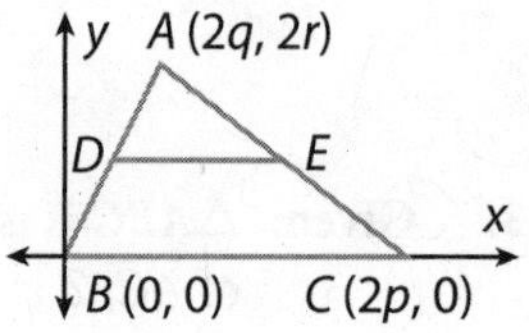

7. **Critique Reasoning** A student proves the Concurrency of Medians Theorem by first assigning coordinates to the vertices of $\triangle PQR$ as $P(0, 0)$, $Q(2a, 0)$, and $R(2a, 2c)$. The student says that this choice of coordinates makes the algebra in the proof a bit easier. Do you agree with the student's choice of coordinates? Explain.

Write each proof.

8. **Given:** $J(-2, 2)$, $K(0, 1)$, $L(-3, -1)$, $P(4, -2)$, $Q(3, -4)$, $R(1, -1)$

Prove: $\angle JKL \cong \angle PQR$

9. **Given:** $D(-3, 2)$, $E(3, 3)$, $F(1, 1)$, $S(9, -2)$, $T(3, -1)$, $U(5, -3)$

Prove: $\angle FDE \cong \angle UST$

10. **Given:** $A(-2, 2)$, $B(4, 4)$, $M(-2, -1)$, $N(4, -3)$, X is the midpoint of $\overline{AB}$, Y is the midpoint of $\overline{MN}$.

Prove: $\angle ABY \cong \angle MNX$

11. **Given:** $J(-1, 4)$, $K(3, 0)$, $P(3, -6)$, $Q(-1, -2)$, U is the midpoint of $\overline{JK}$, V is the midpoint of $\overline{PQ}$.

Prove: $\angle KVJ \cong \angle QUP$

Prove or disprove each statement.

12. The triangle with vertices $R(-2, -2)$, $S(1, 4)$, and $T(4, -5)$ is an equilateral triangle.

13. The triangle with vertices $J(-2, 2)$, $K(2, 3)$, and $L(-1, -2)$ is an isosceles triangle.

14. The triangle with vertices $A(-1, 3)$, $B(2, 1)$, and $C(0, -2)$ is a scalene triangle.

15. Two container ships depart from a port at $P(20, 10)$. The first ship travels to a location at $A(-30, 50)$, and the second ship travels to a location at $B(70, -30)$. Each unit represents one nautical mile. Find the distance between the ships to the nearest nautical mile. Verify that the port is the midpoint between the two ships.

16. The support structure for a hammock includes a triangle whose vertices have coordinates $G(-1, 3)$, $H(-3, -2)$, and $J(1, -2)$.

a. Classify the triangle and justify your answer.

b. **Algebra** Each unit of the coordinate plane represents one foot. To the nearest tenth of a foot, how much metal is needed to make one of the triangular parts for the support structure?

17. Communicate Mathematical Ideas Explain how the perimeter of $\triangle JKL$ compares to the perimeter of $\triangle MNP$.

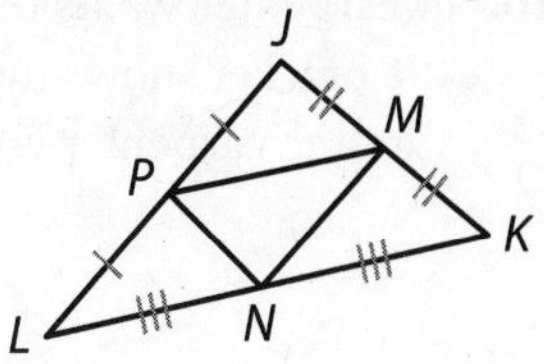

18. The coordinates of the vertices of $\triangle LMN$ are shown in the figure. Determine whether each statement is true or false. Select the correct answer for each lettered part.

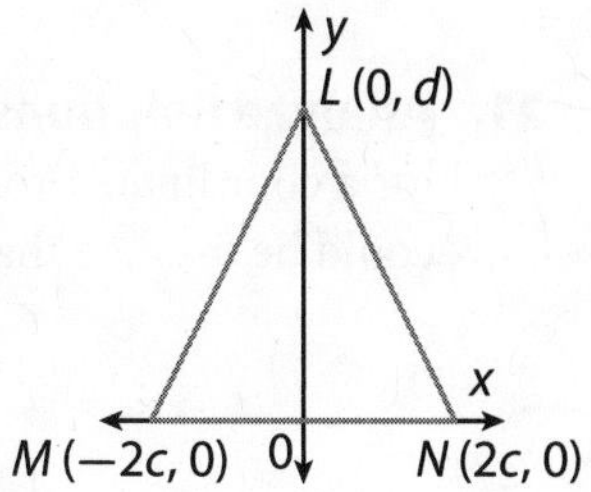

a. $\triangle LMN$ is isosceles. ○ True ○ False

b. One side of $\triangle LMN$ has a length of $2c$ units. ○ True ○ False

c. If P is the midpoint of $\overline{LN}$, then $\overline{OP}$ is parallel to $\overline{LM}$. ○ True ○ False

d. The area of $\triangle LMN$ is $4cd$ square units. ○ True ○ False

e. The midpoint of $\overline{MN}$ is the origin. ○ True ○ False

H.O.T. Focus on Higher Order Thinking

19. Explain the Error A student assigns coordinates to a right triangle as shown in the figure. Then he uses the Distance Formula to show that $PQ = a$ and $RQ = a$. Since $PQ = RQ$, the student says he has proved that every right triangle is isosceles. Explain the error in the student's proof.

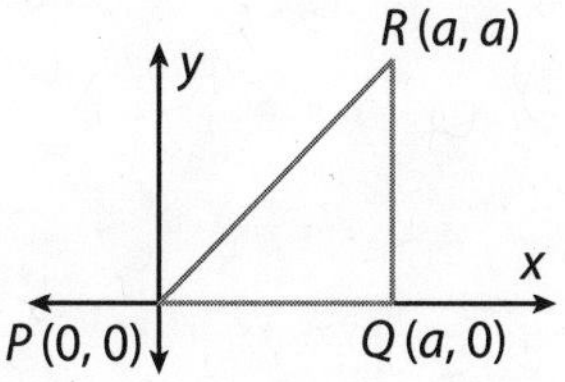

20. A carpenter wants to make a triangular bracket to hold up a bookshelf. The plan for the bracket shows that the vertices of the triangle are $R(-2, 2)$, $S(1, 4)$, and $T(1, -2)$. Can the carpenter conclude that the bracket is a right triangle? Explain.

21. Analyze Relationships The vertices chosen to represent an isosceles right triangle for a coordinate proof are at $(-2s, 2s)$, $(0, 2s)$, and $(0, 0)$. What other coordinates could be used so that the coordinate proof would be easier to complete? Explain.

Lesson Performance Task

A triathlon course was mapped on a coordinate grid marked in 1-kilometer units. The starting point was (0, 0). The triathlon was broken into three stages:

- Stage 1: Contestants swim from (0, 0) to (0.6, 0.8).
- Stage 2: Contestants bicycle from the previous stopping point to (30.6, 16.8).
- Stage 3: Contestants run from the previous stopping point to (25.6, 28.8).

The winner averaged 4 kilometers per hour for Stage 1, 50 kilometers per hour for Stage 2, and 13 kilometers per hour for Stage 3. What was the winner's time for the entire race? (Assume that no time elapsed between stages.) Explain how you found the answer.

Name________________________ Class______________ Date________

2.4 Coordinate Proof Using Distance with Quadrilaterals

Essential Question: How can you use slope and the distance formula in coordinate proofs?

Resource Locker

Explore Positioning a Quadrilateral on the Coordinate Plane

You have used coordinate geometry to find the midpoint of a line segment and to find the distance between two points. Coordinate geometry can also be used to prove conjectures.

Remember that you previously learned several strategies that make using a coordinate proof simpler. They are:

- Use the origin as a vertex, keeping the figure in Quadrant I.
- Center the figure at the origin.
- Center a side of the figure at the origin.
- Use one or both axes as sides of the figure.

Position a rectangle with a length of 8 units and a width of 3 units in the coordinate plane as described.

(A) **Method 1** Center the longer side of the rectangle at the origin.

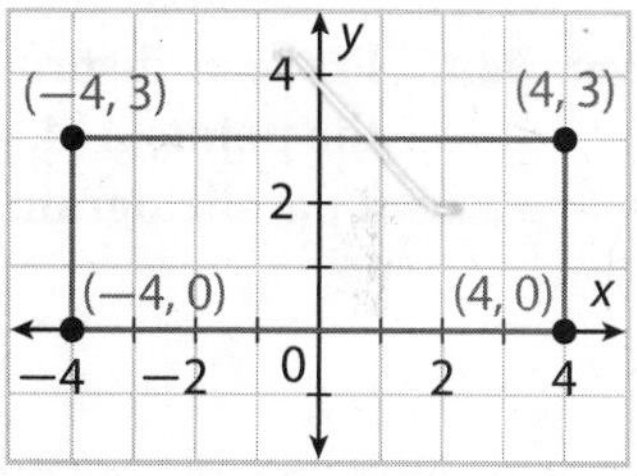

(B) **Method 2** Use the origin as a vertex of the rectangle.
Depending on what you are using the figure to prove, one method may be better than the other. For example, if you need to find the midpoint of the longer side, use the first method.

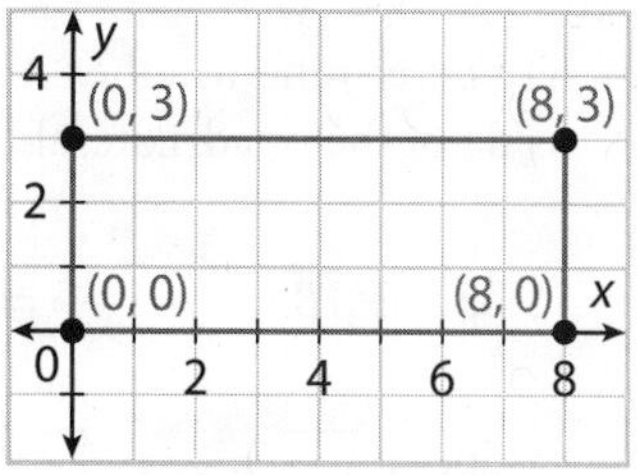

A coordinate proof can also be used to prove that a certain relationship is always true. You can prove that a statement is true for all right triangles without knowing the side lengths. To do this, assign variables as the coordinates of the vertices.

Position a square, with side lengths $2a$, on a coordinate plane and give the coordinates of each vertex.

(C) Sketch the square. Label the side lengths.

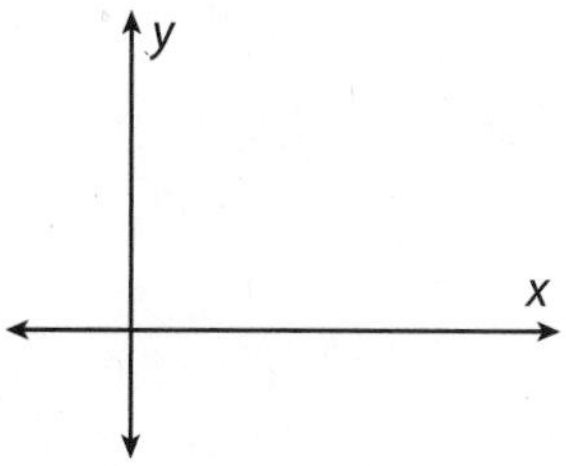

Ⓓ What are the coordinates of each vertex?

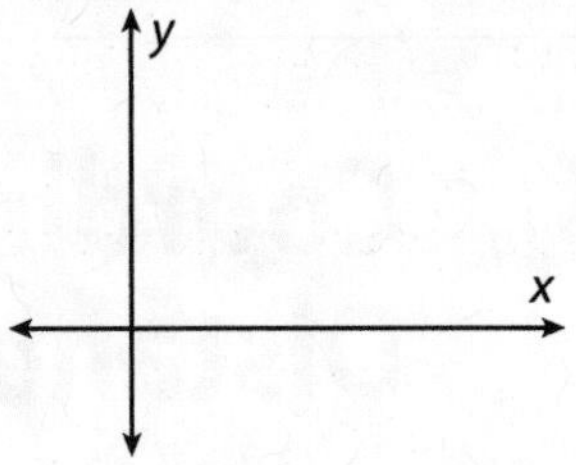

Reflect

1. **Discussion** Describe another way you could have positioned the square and give the coordinates of its vertices.

2. When writing a coordinate proof why are variables used instead of numbers as coordinates for the vertices of a figure?

Explain 1 Proving Conditions for a Parallelogram

You have already used the Distance Formula and the Midpoint Formula in coordinate proofs. As you will see, slope is useful in coordinate proofs whenever you need to show that lines are parallel or perpendicular.

Example 1 **Prove or disprove that the quadrilateral determined by the points $A(4, 4)$, $B(3, 1)$, $C(-2, -1)$, and $D(-1, 2)$ is a parallelogram.**

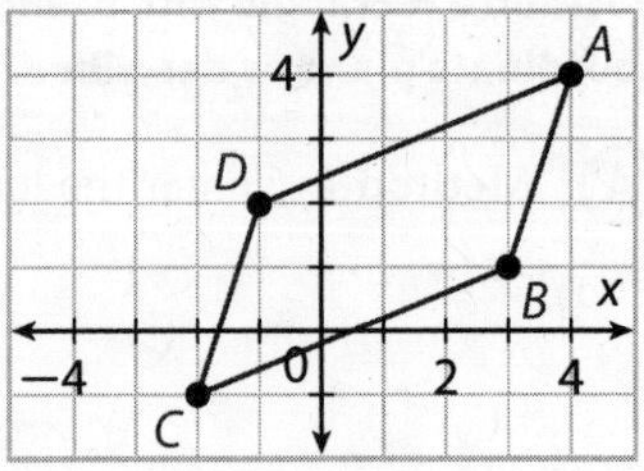

Ⓐ Use slopes to write the coordinate proof.

To determine whether $ABCD$ is a parallelogram, find the slope of each side of the quadrilateral.

Slope of $\overline{AB} = \frac{y_2 - y_1}{x_2 - x_1} = \frac{1 - 4}{3 - 4} = \frac{-3}{-1} = 3$; Slope of $\overline{BC} = \frac{y_2 - y_1}{x_2 - x_1} = \frac{-1 - 1}{-2 - 3} = \frac{-2}{-5} = \frac{2}{5}$;

Slope of $\overline{CD} = \frac{y_2 - y_1}{x_2 - x_1} = \frac{2 - (-1)}{-1 - (-2)} = \frac{3}{1} = 3$; Slope of $\overline{DA} = \frac{y_2 - y_1}{x_2 - x_1} = \frac{4 - 2}{4 - (-1)} = \frac{2}{5}$

Compare slopes. The slopes of opposite sides are equal. This means opposite sides are parallel. So, quadrilateral $ABCD$ is a parallelogram.

(B) Use the Distance Formula to write the coordinate proof.

To determine whether *ABCD* is a parallelogram, find the length of each side of the quadrilateral. Remember that the Distance Formula is length $= \sqrt{(x_2 - x_1)^2 + (y_2 - y_1)^2}$.

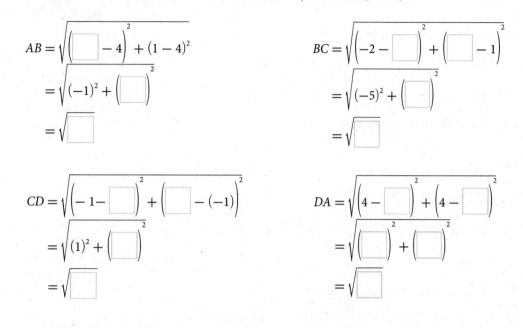

$$AB = \sqrt{(\square - 4)^2 + (1 - 4)^2} = \sqrt{(-1)^2 + (\square)^2} = \sqrt{\square}$$

$$BC = \sqrt{(-2 - \square)^2 + (\square - 1)^2} = \sqrt{(-5)^2 + (\square)^2} = \sqrt{\square}$$

$$CD = \sqrt{(-1 - \square)^2 + (\square - (-1))^2} = \sqrt{(1)^2 + (\square)^2} = \sqrt{\square}$$

$$DA = \sqrt{(4 - \square)^2 + (4 - \square)^2} = \sqrt{(\square)^2 + (\square)^2} = \sqrt{\square}$$

Compare the side lengths. The lengths of the opposite sides are ________. By the ________________________, we can conclude that *ABCD* is a ____________.

Reflect

3. Suppose you want to prove that a general parallelogram *WXYZ* has diagonals that bisect each other. Why is it convenient to use general vertex coefficients, such as $2a$ and $2b$?

____

____

____

Your Turn

Write a coordinate proof given quadrilateral *ABCD* with vertices $A(3, 2)$, $B(8, 2)$, $C(5, 0)$, and $D(0, 0)$.

4. Prove that *ABCD* is a parallelogram.

5. Prove that the diagonals of *ABCD* bisect each other.

Explain 2 Proving Conditions for Special Parallelograms

Example 2 **Prove or disprove each statement about the quadrilateral determined by the points $Q(2, -3)$, $R(-4, 0)$, $S(-2, 4)$, and $T(4, 1)$.**

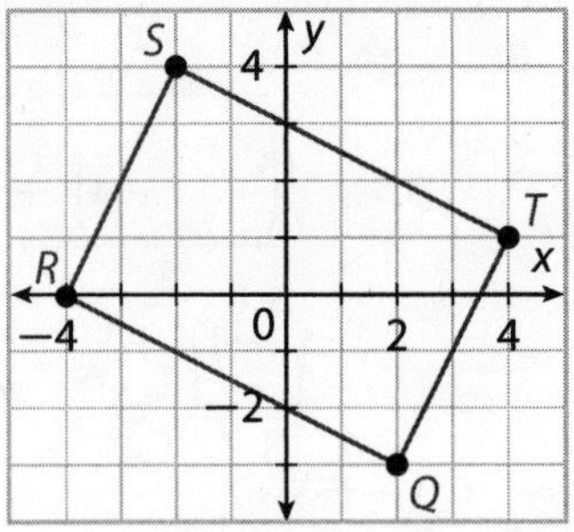

Ⓐ The diagonals of $QRST$ are congruent.

The length of $\overline{SQ} = \sqrt{(2-(-2))^2 + (-3-4)^2} = \sqrt{65}$.

The length of $\overline{RT} = \sqrt{(-4-4)^2 + (0-1)^2} = \sqrt{65}$.

So, the diagonals of $QRST$ are congruent.

Ⓑ $QRST$ is a rectangle.

Find the slope of each side of the quadrilateral.

Slope of $\overline{QR} = \frac{y_2 - y_1}{x_2 - x_1} = \frac{0-(-3)}{-4-2} = \frac{3}{-6} = -\frac{1}{2}$; Slope of $\overline{RS} = \frac{y_2 - y_1}{x_2 - x_1} = \frac{\square - \square}{\square - \square} = \frac{\square}{\square} = \square$;

Slope of $\overline{ST} = \frac{y_2 - y_1}{x_2 - x_1} = \frac{\square - \square}{\square - \square} = \frac{\square}{\square} = \square$;

Slope of $\overline{TQ} = \frac{y_2 - y_1}{x_2 - x_1} = \frac{\square - \square}{\square - \square} = \frac{\square}{\square} = \square$

Find the products of the slopes of adjacent sides.

$\left(\text{slope of } \overline{QR}\right)\left(\text{slope of } \overline{RS}\right) = \square \cdot \square = \square$; $\left(\text{slope of } \overline{RS}\right)\left(\text{slope of } \overline{ST}\right) = \square \cdot \square = \square$;

$\left(\text{slope of } \overline{ST}\right)\left(\text{slope of } \overline{TQ}\right) = \square \cdot \square = \square$; $\left(\text{slope of } \overline{TQ}\right)\left(\text{slope of } \overline{QR}\right) = \square \cdot \square = \square$

You can conclude that adjacent sides are ______________. So, quadrilateral $QRST$ is a ____________.

Reflect

6. Explain how to prove that $QRST$ is not a square.

____

____

Your Turn

Prove or disprove each statement about quadrilateral *WXYZ* determined by the points $W(0, 0)$, $X(4, 3)$, $Y(9, 3)$, and $Z(5, 0)$.

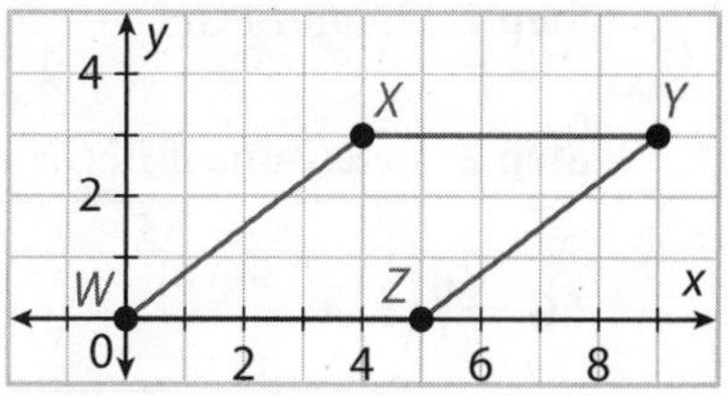

7. *WXYZ* is a rhombus.

8. The diagonals of *WXYZ* are perpendicular.

Explain 3 Identifying Figures on the Coordinate Plane

Example 3 **Use the diagonals to determine whether a parallelogram with the given vertices is a rectangle, rhombus, or square. Give all the names that apply.**

(A) $A(0, 2)$, $B(3, 6)$, $C(8, 6)$, $D(5, 2)$

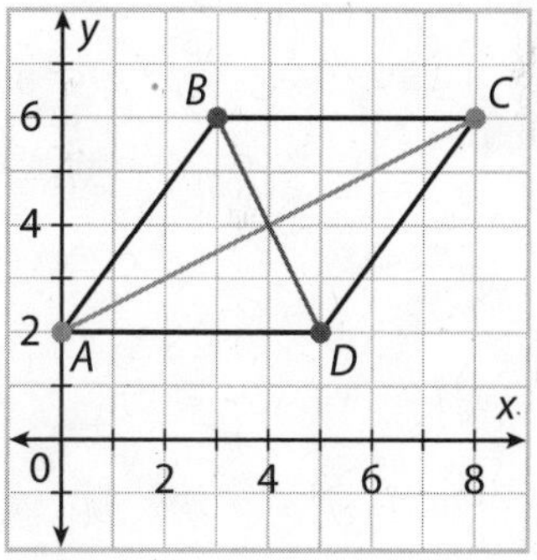

Step 1 Graph *ABCD*.

Step 2 Determine if *ABCD* is a rectangle.

$AC = \sqrt{(8-0)^2 + (6-2)^2} = \sqrt{80} = 4\sqrt{5}$

$BD = \sqrt{(5-3)^2 + (2-6)^2} = \sqrt{20} = 2\sqrt{5}$

Since $4\sqrt{5} \neq 2\sqrt{5}$, *ABCD* is not a rectangle. Thus, *ABCD* is not a square.

Step 3 Determine if *ABCD* is a rhombus.

Slope of $\overline{AC} = \frac{6-2}{8-0} = \frac{1}{2}$

Slope of $\overline{BD} = \frac{2-6}{5-3} = -2$

Since $\left(\frac{1}{2}\right)(-2) = -1$, $\overline{AC} \perp \overline{BD}$. *ABCD* is a rhombus.

(B) $E(-4, -1), F(-3, 2), G(3, 0), H(2, -3)$

Step 1 Graph *EFGH*.

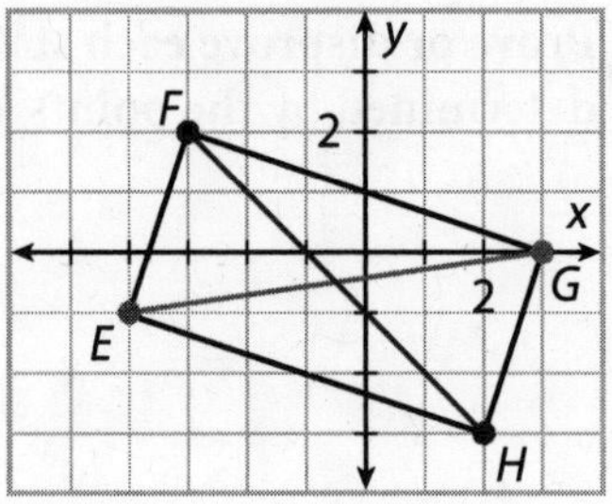

Step 2 Determine if *EFGH* is a rectangle.

$$EG = \sqrt{\left(3 - \square\right)^2 + \left(0 - \square\right)^2} = \sqrt{\square} = \square$$

$$FH = \sqrt{\left(\square - (-3)\right)^2 + \left(\square - 2\right)^2} = \sqrt{\square} = 5\sqrt{\square}$$

Since $\square = 5\sqrt{\square}$, the diagonals are ________. *EFGH* ________ a rectangle.

Step 3 Determine if *EFGH* is a rhombus.

Slope of ______ $= \dfrac{0-(-1)}{3-(-4)} = \dfrac{1}{7}$; Slope of ______ $= \dfrac{-3-2}{2-(-3)} = \dfrac{-5}{5} = -1$

Since $\left(\frac{1}{7}\right)(-1) \neq -1$, $\overline{EG}$ is ________________ to $\overline{FH}$. So, *EFGH* is not a rhombus and cannot be a ________.

Your Turn

Use the diagonals to determine whether a parallelogram with the given vertices is a rectangle, rhombus, or square. Give all the names that apply.

9. $K(-5, -1), L(-2, 4), M(3, 1), N(0, -4)$

10. $P(-4, 6), Q(2, 5), R(3, -1), S(-3, 0)$

Elaborate

11. How can you use slopes to show that two line segments are parallel? Perpendicular?

____

____

12. When you use the Distance Formula, you find the square root of a value. When finding the square root of a value, you must consider both the positive and negative outcomes. Explain why the negative outcome is not used in the coordinate proofs in the lesson.

____

____

13. **Essential Question Check-In** How can you use slope in coordinate proofs?

Evaluate: Homework and Practice

Personal Math Trainer
- Online Homework
- Hints and Help
- Extra Practice

1. Suppose you have a right triangle. If you want to write a proof about the midpoints of the legs of the triangle, which placement of the triangle would be most helpful? Explain.

   A. Use the origin as a vertex, keeping the figure in Quadrant I with vertices $(0, 2b)$, $(2a, 0)$, and $(0, 0)$.

   B. Center the triangle at the origin.

   C. Use the origin as a vertex, keeping the figure in Quadrant I with vertices $(0, b)$, $(a, 0)$, and $(0, 0)$.

   D. Center one leg of the triangle on the y-axis with vertices $(0, a)$, $(0, -a)$, and $(b, -a)$.

   E. Use the x-axis as one leg of the triangle with vertices $(a, 0)$, (a, b), and $(a + c, 0)$.

2. Describe the position of a general isosceles trapezoid $WXYZ$ determined by the points $W(0, 0)$, $X(a, 0)$, $Y(a - c, b)$, and $Z(c, b)$. Then sketch the trapezoid.

Write a coordinate proof for the quadrilateral determined by the points $A(2, 4)$, $B(4, -1)$, $C(-1, -3)$, and $D(-3, 2)$.

3. Prove that $ABCD$ is a parallelogram.

4. Prove that $ABCD$ is a rectangle.

5. Prove that *ABCD* is a rhombus.

6. Prove that *ABCD* is a square.

Prove or disprove each statement about the quadrilateral determined by the points $W(-2, 5)$, $X(5, 5)$, $Y(5, 0)$, and $Z(-2, 0)$.

7. Prove that the diagonals are congruent.

8. Prove that the diagonals are perpendicular.

9. Prove that the diagonals bisect each other.

10. Prove that *WXYZ* is a square.

Algebra Use the diagonals to determine whether a parallelogram with the given vertices is a rectangle, rhombus, or square. Give all the names that apply.

11. $A(-10, 4)$, $B(-2, 10)$, $C(4, 2)$, $D(-4, -4)$

12. $J(-9, -7)$, $K(-4, -2)$, $L(3, -3)$, $M(-2, -8)$

Analyze Relationships **The coordinates of three vertices of parallelogram *ABCD* are given. Find the coordinates of the fourth point so that the given type of figure is formed.**

13. $A(4, -2), B(-5, -2), D(4, 4)$, rectangle

14. $A(-5, 5), B(0, 0), C(7, 1)$, rhombus

15. $A(0, 2), B(4, -2), C(0, -6)$, square

16. $A(2, 1), B(-1, 5), C(-5, 2)$, square

Paul designed a doghouse to fit against the side of his house. His plan consisted of a right triangle on top of a rectangle. Use the drawing for Exercises 17–18.

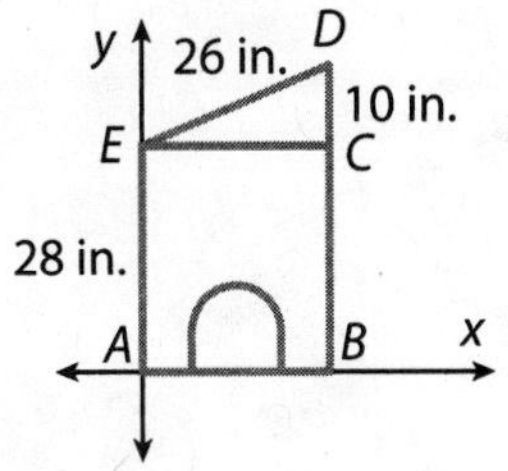

17. Find *BD*, *CE*, and *BE*.

18. Before building the doghouse, Paul sketched his plan on a coordinate plane. He placed *A* at the origin and $\overline{AB}$ on the *x*-axis. Find the coordinates of *B*, *C*, *D*, and *E*, assuming that each unit of the coordinate plane represents one inch.

19. Critical Thinking On the National Mall in Washington, D.C., a reflecting pool lies between the Lincoln Memorial and the World War II Memorial. The pool has two 2300-foot-long sides and two 150-foot-long sides. Tell what additional information you need to know in order to determine whether the reflecting pool is a rectangle. (*Hint*: Remember that you have to show it is a parallelogram first.)

Algebra Write a coordinate proof.

20. The Bushmen in South Africa use the Global Positioning System to transmit data about endangered animals to conservationists. The Bushmen have sighted animals at the following coordinates: $(-25, 31.5)$, $(-23.2, 31.4)$, and $(-24, 31.1)$. Prove that the distance between two of these locations is approximately twice the distance between two other locations.

21. Two cruise ships leave a port located at $P(10, 50)$. One ship sails to an island located at $A(-40, -10)$, and the other sails to an island located at $B(60, 110)$. Suppose that each unit represents one nautical mile. Find the distance between the ships rounded to the nearest nautical mile. Then show that the triangle formed by using the locations of the 2 ships and the port as its vertices is an isosceles triangle.

22. A parallelogram has vertices at $(0, 0)$, $(5, 6)$, and $(10, 0)$. Which could be the fourth vertex of the parallelogram? Choose all that apply.

A. $(5, -6)$

B. $(15, 6)$

C. $(0, -6)$

D. $(10, 6)$

E. $(-5, 6)$

H.O.T. Focus on Higher Order Thinking

23. **Draw Conclusions** The diagonals of a parallelogram intersect at $(-2, 1.5)$. Two vertices are located at $(-7, 2)$ and $(2, 6.5)$. Find the coordinates of the other two vertices.

24. **Analyze Relationships** Consider points $L(3, -4)$, $M(1, -2)$, and $N(5, 2)$.

a. Find coordinates for point P so that the quadrilateral determined by points L, M, N, and P is a parallelogram. Is there more than one possibility? Explain.

b. Are any of the parallelograms a rectangle? Why?

25. **Critical Thinking** Rhombus $OPQR$ has vertices $O(0, 0)$, $P(a, b)$, $Q(a + b, a + b)$, and $R(b, a)$. Prove the diagonals of the rhombus are perpendicular.

26. Multi-Step Use coordinates to verify the Trapezoid Midsegment Theorem which states "The midsegment of a trapezoid is parallel to each base, and its length is one half the sum of the lengths of the bases."

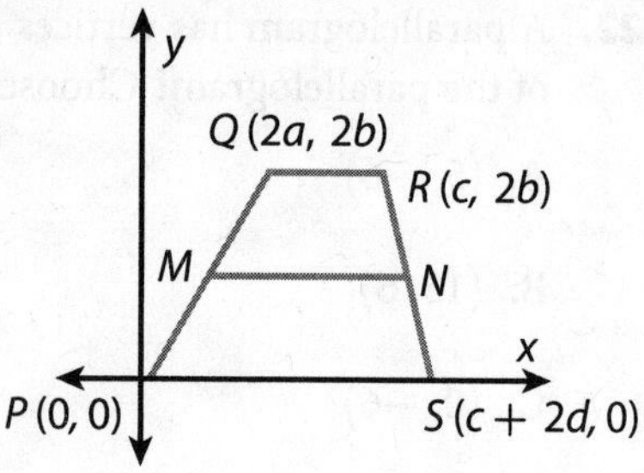

a. M is the midpoint of $\overline{QP}$. What are its coordinates?

b. N is the midpoint of $\overline{RS}$. What are its coordinates?

c. Find the slopes of $\overline{QR}$, $\overline{PS}$, $\overline{MN}$. What can you conclude?

d. Find $\overline{QR}$, $\overline{PS}$, $\overline{MN}$. Show that $MN = \frac{1}{2}(PS + QR)$.

Lesson Performance Task

According to the new mayor, the shape of City Park is downright ugly. While the parks in all of the other towns in the vicinity have nice, regular polygonal shapes, City Park is the shape of an irregular quadrilateral. On a coordinate map of the park, the four corners are located at $(-3, 4)$, $(5, 2)$, $(1, -2)$, and $(-5, -4)$. The mayor's chief assistant knows a little mathematics and proposes that a special "inner park" be created by joining the midpoints of the sides of City Park. The assistant claims that the boundaries of the inner park will create a nice, regular polygonal shape, just like the parks in all the other towns. The mayor thinks the idea is ridiculous, saying, "You can't create order out of chaos."

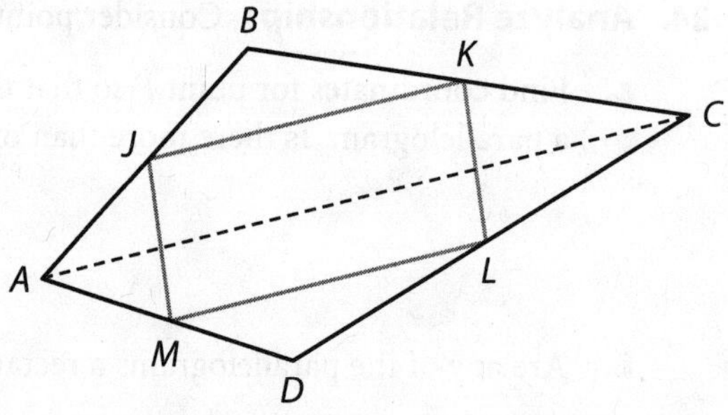

1. Who was right? Explain your reasoning in detail.

2. Irregular quadrilateral *ABCD* is shown here. Points *J*, *K*, *L*, and *M* are midpoints.

a. What must you show to prove that quadrilateral *JKLM* is a parallelogram?

b. How can you show this?

c. If the adjacent sides of *JKLM* are perpendicular, what type of figure does that make *JKLM*?

Name________________ Class________________ Date________

2.5 Perimeter and Area on the Coordinate Plane

Resource Locker

Essential Question: How do you find the perimeter and area of polygons in the coordinate plane?

Explore Finding Perimeters of Figures on the Coordinate Plane

Recall that the perimeter of a polygon is the sum of the lengths of the polygon's sides. You can use the Distance Formula to find perimeters of polygons in a coordinate plane.

Follow these steps to find the perimeter of a pentagon with vertices $A(-1, 4)$, $B(4, 4)$, $C(3, -2)$, $D(-1, -4)$, and $E(-4, 1)$. Round to the nearest tenth.

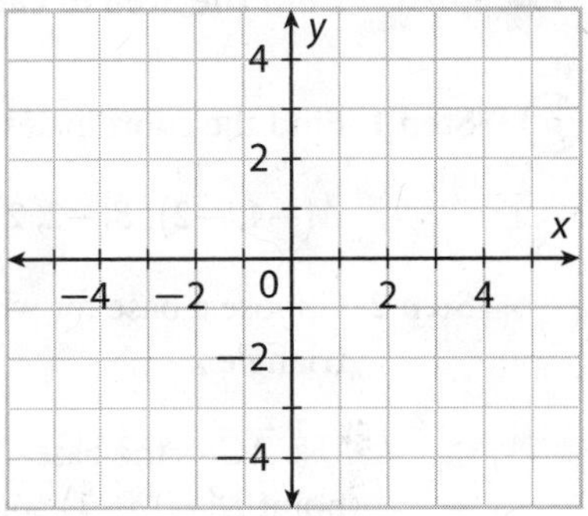

(A) Plot the points. Then use a straightedge to draw the pentagon that is determined by the points.

(B) Are there any sides for which you do not need to use the Distance Formula? Explain, and give their length(s). ________________

____

(C) Use the Distance Formula to find the remaining side lengths. Round your answers to the nearest tenth.

(D) Find the sum of the side lengths.

____

Reflect

1. Explain how you can find the perimeter of a rectangle to check that your answer is reasonable.

____

____

____

Explain 1 Finding Areas of Figures on the Coordinate Plane

You can use area formulas together with the Distance Formula to determine areas of figures such as triangles, rectangles and parallelograms.

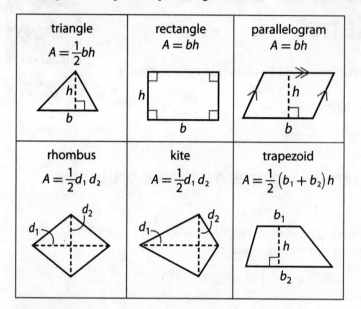

triangle	rectangle	parallelogram
$A = \frac{1}{2}bh$	$A = bh$	$A = bh$
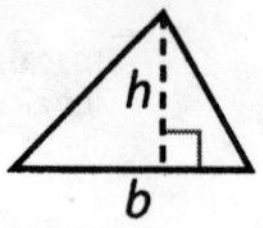	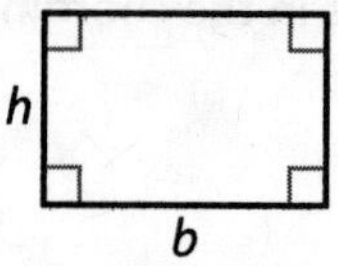	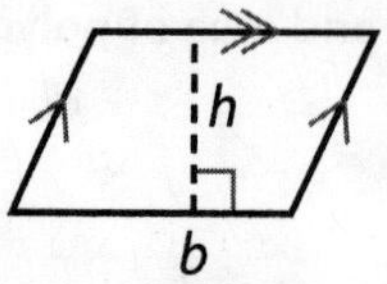
rhombus	**kite**	**trapezoid**
$A = \frac{1}{2}d_1 d_2$	$A = \frac{1}{2}d_1 d_2$	$A = \frac{1}{2}(b_1 + b_2)h$
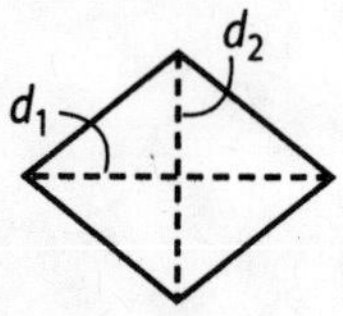	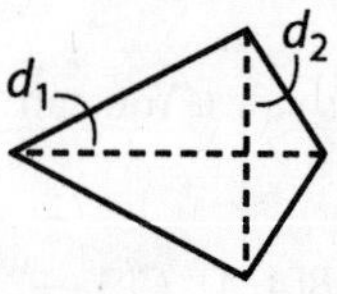	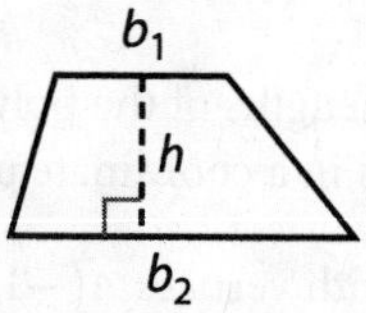

Example 1 **Find the area of each figure.**

(A) **Step 1** Find the coordinates of the vertices of $\triangle ABC$.

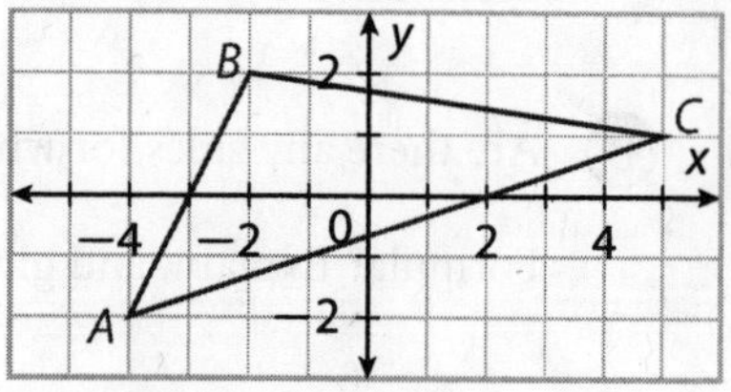

$A(-4, -2)$, $B(-2, 2)$, $C(5, 1)$

Step 2 Choose a base for which you can easily find the height of the triangle.

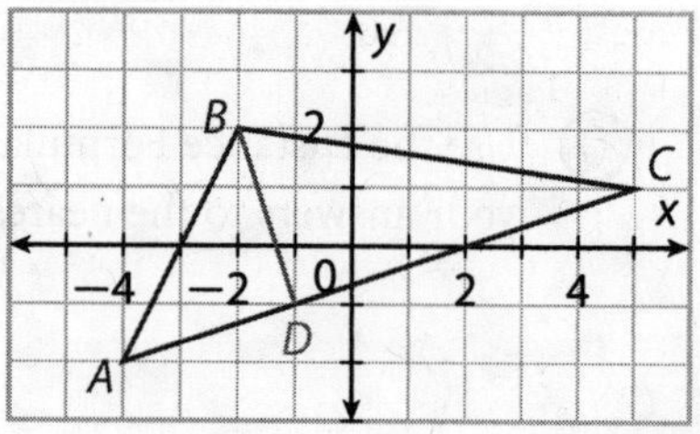

Use $\overline{AC}$ as the base. A segment from the opposite vertex, B, to point $D(-1, -1)$ appears to be perpendicular to the base $\overline{AC}$. Use slopes to check.

slope of $\overline{AC} = \frac{1-(-2)}{5-(-4)} = \frac{1}{3}$; slope of $\overline{BD} = \frac{-1-2}{-1-(-2)} = -3$

The product of the slopes is $\frac{1}{3} \cdot (-3) = -1$. $\overline{BD}$ is perpendicular to $\overline{AC}$, so $\overline{BD}$ is the height for the base $\overline{AC}$.

Find the length of the base and the height.

$AC = \sqrt{(5-(-4))^2 + (1-(-2))^2} = \sqrt{90} = 3\sqrt{10}$; $BD = \sqrt{(-1-(-2))^2 + (-1-2)^2} = \sqrt{10}$

Step 3 Determine the area of $\triangle ABC$.

$\text{Area} = \frac{1}{2}bh = \frac{1}{2}(AC)(BD) = \frac{1}{2} \cdot (3\sqrt{10})(\sqrt{10}) = \frac{1}{2} \cdot 30 = 15$ square units

(B) **Step 1** Find the coordinates of the vertices of *DEFG*.

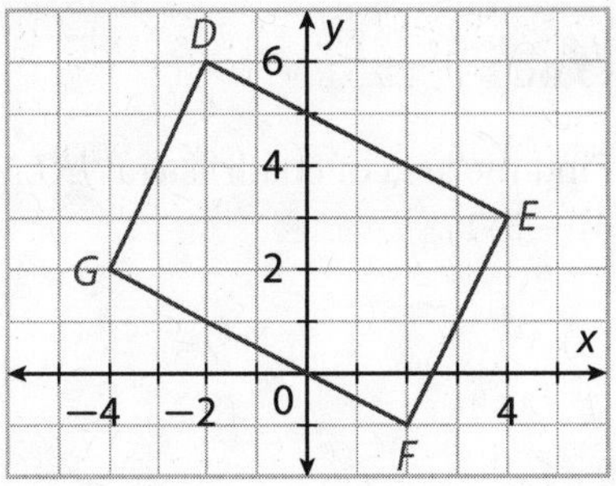

$D(-2, 6), E(4, 3), F(2, -1), G(-4, 2)$

Step 2 *DEFG* appears to be a rectangle. Use slopes to check that adjacent sides are perpendicular.

slope of $\overline{DE}$: $\dfrac{\square - \square}{4-(-2)} = \dfrac{\square}{6} = \square$; slope of $\overline{EF}$: $\dfrac{\square - 3}{2 - \square} = \dfrac{\square}{\square} = \square$

slope of $\overline{FG}$: $\dfrac{2 - \square}{-4 - \square} = \dfrac{\square}{\square} = \square$; slope of $\overline{DG}$: $\dfrac{2 - \square}{\square - \square} = \dfrac{\square}{\square} = \square$

so *DEFG* is a ______________.

Step 3 Find the area of *DEFG*.

$b = FG = \sqrt{\left(2 - \square\right)^2 + \left(\square - 2\right)^2} = \sqrt{\square} = \square\sqrt{\square}$

$h = GD = \sqrt{\left(\square - (-4)\right)^2 + \left(6 - \square\right)^2} = \sqrt{\square} = \square\sqrt{\square}$

Area of *DEFG*: $A = bh = \left(\square\sqrt{\square}\right)\left(\square\sqrt{\square}\right) = \square$ square units

Reflect

2. In Part A, is it possible to use another side of $\triangle ABC$ as the base? If so, what length represents the height of the triangle?

____

____

____

3. **Discussion** In Part B, why was it necessary to find the slopes of the sides?

____

____

Your Turn

4. Find the area of quadrilateral $JKLM$ with vertices $J(-4, -2)$, $K(2, 1)$, $L(3, 4)$, $M(-3, 1)$.

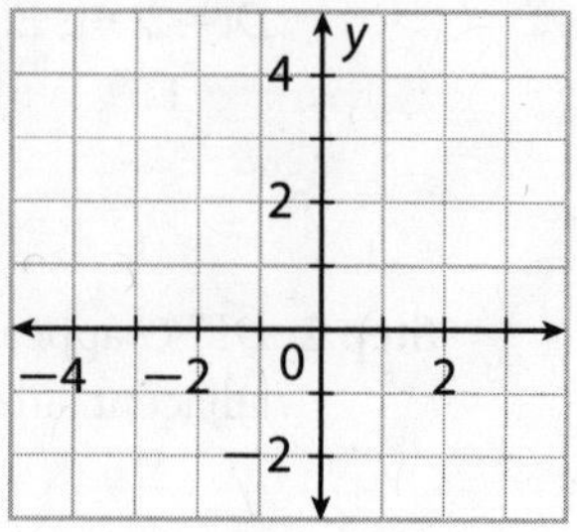

Explain 2 Finding Areas of Composite Figures

A **composite figure** is made up of simple shapes, such as triangles, rectangles, and parallelograms. To find the area of a composite figure, find the areas of the simple shapes and then use the Area Addition Postulate. You can use the Area Addition Postulate to find the area of a composite figure.

Area Addition Postulate

The area of a region is equal to the sum of the areas of its nonoverlapping parts.

Example 2 **Find the area of each figure.**

(A) Possible solution: $ABCDE$ can be divided up into a rectangle and two triangles, each with horizontal bases.

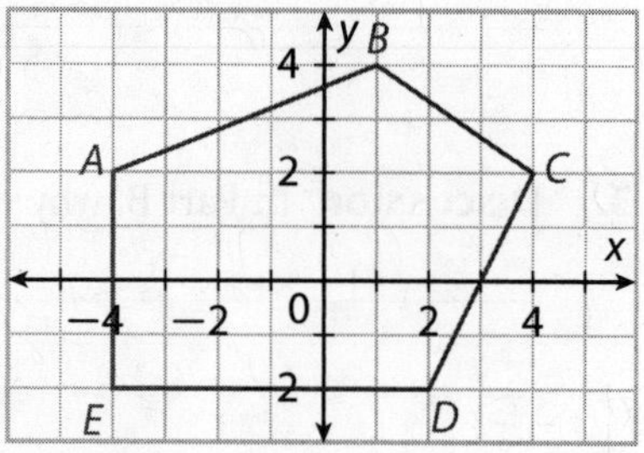

area of rectangle $AGDE$: $A = bh = (DE)(AE) = (6)(4) = 24$

area of $\triangle ABC$: $A = \frac{1}{2}bh = \frac{1}{2}(AC)(BF) = \frac{1}{2}(8)(2) = 8$

area of $\triangle CDG$: $A = \frac{1}{2}bh = \frac{1}{2}(CG)(DG) = \frac{1}{2}(2)(4) = 4$

area of $ABCDE$: $A = 24 + 8 + 4 = 36$ square units

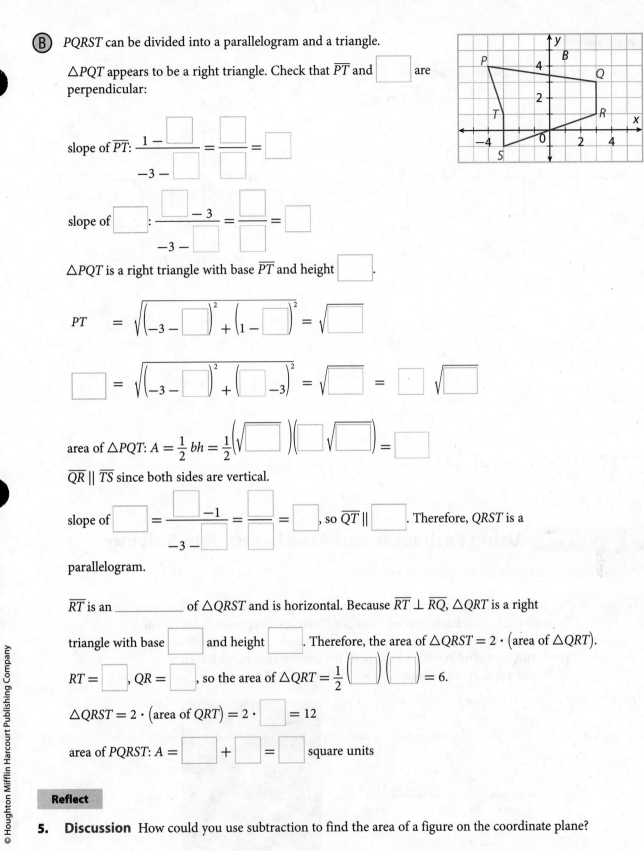

(B) *PQRST* can be divided into a parallelogram and a triangle.

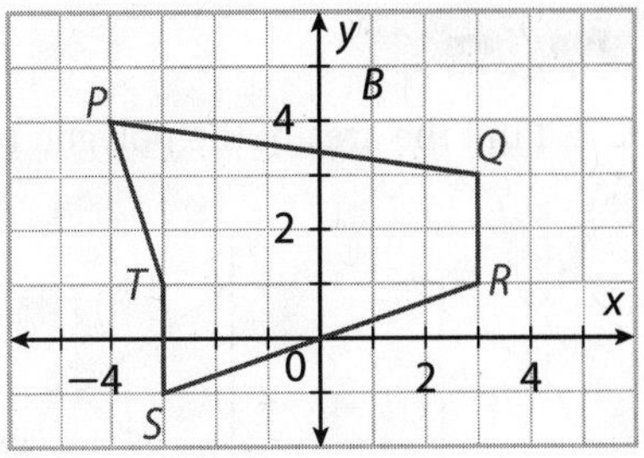

$\triangle PQT$ appears to be a right triangle. Check that $\overline{PT}$ and $\square$ are perpendicular:

slope of $\overline{PT}$: $\dfrac{1-\square}{-3-\square} = \dfrac{\square}{\square} = \square$

slope of $\square$: $\dfrac{\square - 3}{-3-\square} = \dfrac{\square}{\square} = \square$

$\triangle PQT$ is a right triangle with base $\overline{PT}$ and height $\square$.

$PT = \sqrt{\left(-3-\square\right)^2 + \left(1-\square\right)^2} = \sqrt{\square}$

$\square = \sqrt{\left(-3-\square\right)^2 + \left(\square-3\right)^2} = \sqrt{\square} = \square\sqrt{\square}$

area of $\triangle PQT$: $A = \frac{1}{2}bh = \frac{1}{2}\left(\sqrt{\square}\right)\left(\square\sqrt{\square}\right) = \square$

$\overline{QR} \parallel \overline{TS}$ since both sides are vertical.

slope of $\square = \dfrac{\square - 1}{-3-\square} = \dfrac{\square}{\square} = \square$, so $\overline{QT} \parallel \square$. Therefore, *QRST* is a parallelogram.

$\overline{RT}$ is an __________ of $\triangle QRST$ and is horizontal. Because $\overline{RT} \perp \overline{RQ}$, $\triangle QRT$ is a right triangle with base $\square$ and height $\square$. Therefore, the area of $\triangle QRST = 2 \cdot (\text{area of } \triangle QRT)$.

$RT = \square$, $QR = \square$, so the area of $\triangle QRT = \frac{1}{2}\left(\square\right)\left(\square\right) = 6$.

$\triangle QRST = 2 \cdot (\text{area of } QRT) = 2 \cdot \square = 12$

area of *PQRST*: $A = \square + \square = \square$ square units

Reflect

5. Discussion How could you use subtraction to find the area of a figure on the coordinate plane?

____

____

____

Your Turn

6. Find the area of the polygon by addition.

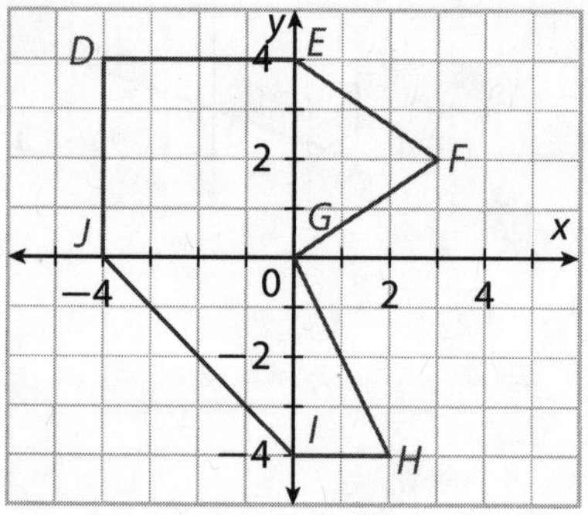

7. Find the area of polygon by subtraction.

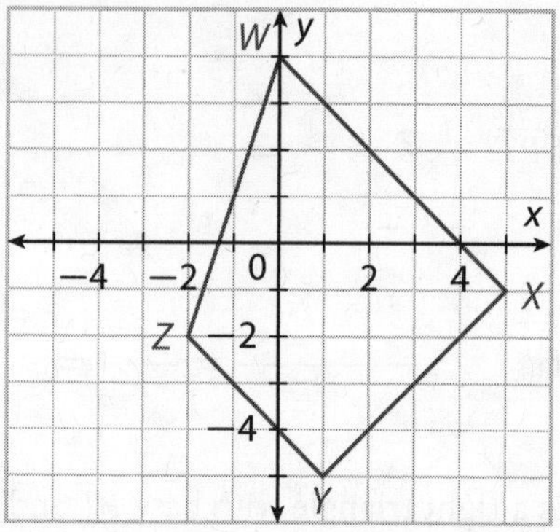

Explain 3 Using Perimeter and Area in Problem Solving

You can use perimeter and area techniques to solve problems.

Example 3 **Miguel is planning and costing an ornamental garden in the a shape of an irregular octagon. Each unit on the coordinate grid represents one yard. He wants to lay the whole garden with turf, which costs \$3.25 per square yard, and surround it with a border of decorative stones, which cost \$7.95 per yard. What is the total cost of the turf and stones?**

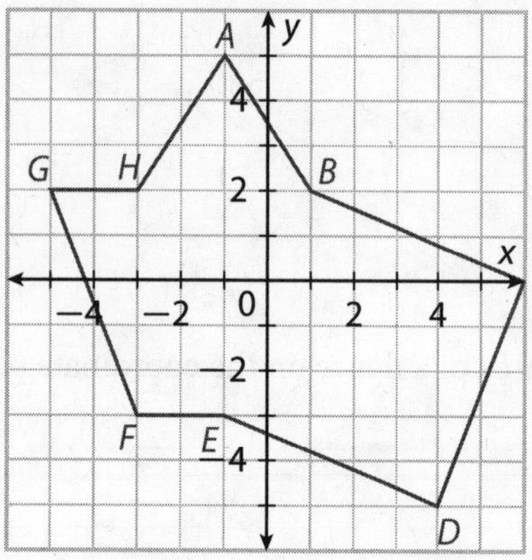

Analyze Information

Identify the important information.

- The vertices are $A(\square, 5)$, $B(1, \square)$, $C(6, \square)$, $D(4, \square)$, $E(-1, -3)$, $F(\square, -3)$, $G(-5, \square)$, and $H(\square, 2)$.
- The cost of turf is $\square per square yard.
- The cost of the ornamental stones is $\square per yard.

Formulate a Plan

- Divide the garden up into ________.
- Add up the ________ of the smaller figures.
- Find the cost of turf by ________ the total area by the cost per square yard.
- Find the perimeter of the garden by adding the ________ of the sides.
- Find the cost of the border by ________ the perimeter by the cost per yard.
- Find total cost by adding the ________ and ________.

Solve

Divide the garden into smaller figures.
The garden can be divided into square *BCDE*, kite *ABEH*, and parallelogram *EFGH*.

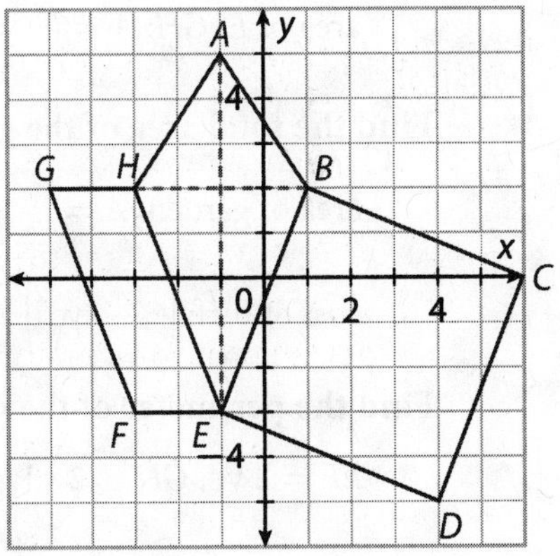

Find the area of each smaller figure.

area of *BCDE*:

slope of $\overline{BC}$: $\dfrac{\square - 2}{6 - \square} = \square$

slope of $\square$: $\dfrac{\square - 0}{4 - \square} = \square$

Also, $BC = \sqrt{\left(\square - 1\right)^2 + \left(0 - \square\right)^2} = \sqrt{\square}$ and

$CD = \sqrt{\left(4 - \square\right)^2 + \left(\square - \square\right)^2} = \sqrt{\square}$.

So *BCDE* is a square, with area $A = s^2 = \left(\sqrt{\square}\ \text{yd}\right)^2 = \square\ \text{yd}^2$.

area of kite *ABEH*:

$$HA = \sqrt{\left(-1-\left(\square\right)\right)^2 + \left(\square - 2\right)^2} = \sqrt{4+\square} = \sqrt{\square} \approx \square;$$

$$AB = \sqrt{\left(\square - (-1)\right)^2 + \left(2 - \square\right)^2} = \sqrt{\square + 9} = \sqrt{\square} \approx \square;$$

$$HE = \sqrt{\left(-1-\left(\square\right)\right)^2 + \left(\square - 2\right)^2} = \sqrt{\square + 25} = \sqrt{\square} \approx \square;$$

$$BE = \sqrt{\left(\square - 1\right)^2 + \left(-3 - \square\right)^2} = \sqrt{4+\square} = \sqrt{\square} \approx \square$$

So, $\square \cong \square$ and $\square \cong \square$. Therefore *ABEH* is a kite.

$b = d_1 = 8,\ h = d_2 = 4$

$$A = \frac{1}{2}d_1d_2 = \frac{1}{2}\left(\square\right)\left(\square\right) = \square \text{ yd}^2$$

area of parallelogram *EFGH*:

$\square$ and $\overline{GH}$ are both horizontal, so are parallel;

slope of $\overline{EH}$: $\dfrac{2-\square}{-3-\square} = \dfrac{\square}{\square} = \square$; slope of $\square$: $\dfrac{2-\square}{\square - \square} = \dfrac{\square}{\square} = \square$

So *EFGH* is a parallelogram, with base $\square = \square$ and height. $FH = \square$.

area of *EFGH*: $A = bh = \left(\square\ yd\right)\left(\square\ yd\right) = \square \text{ yd}^2$

Find the total area of the garden and the cost of turf.

area of garden: $A = \square \text{ yd}^2 + \square \text{ yd}^2 + \square \text{ yd}^2 = \square \text{ yd}^2$

cost of turf: $\left(\square \text{ yd}^2\right)\left(\$\square/\text{yd}^2\right) = \$\square$

Find the perimeter of the garden.

$EF = 2$ yd, $GH = 2$ yd

From area calculations, $BC = CD = DE = \sqrt{\square} \approx \square$ yd, and $AB = AH = \square$ yd

$$FG = \sqrt{\left(\square - \square\right)^2 + \left(\square - (-3)\right)^2} = \sqrt{\square},$$

perimeter of garden $= GH + HA + AB + BC + CD + DE + EF + FG$

$$= \square + \square + \square + \square + \square + \square + \square + \square = \square \text{ yd}$$

Find the cost of the stones for the border.

cost of stones: $\left(\square \text{ yd}\right)\left(\$\square \text{ per yd}\right) = \$\square$

Find the total cost.

total cost: $\$\square + \$\square = \$\square$

Justify and Evaluate

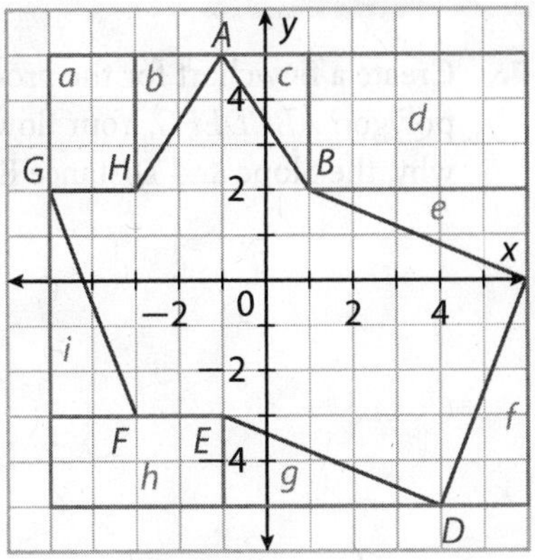

The area can be checked by subtraction:

area of large rectangle = (11)(10) = 110 square units

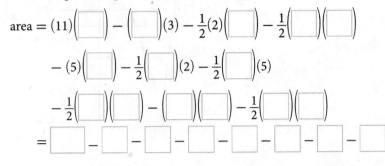

$$\text{area} = (11)(\square) - (\square)(3) - \frac{1}{2}(2)(\square) - \frac{1}{2}(\square)(\square)$$

$$- (5)(\square) - \frac{1}{2}(\square)(2) - \frac{1}{2}(\square)(5)$$

$$- \frac{1}{2}(\square)(\square) - (\square)(\square) - \frac{1}{2}(\square)(\square)$$

$$= \square - \square - \square - \square - \square - \square - \square - \square - \square - \square = \square$$

The perimeter is approximately the perimeter of the polygon shown:

The perimeter of the polygon shown is $\square$,

so the answer is reasonable.

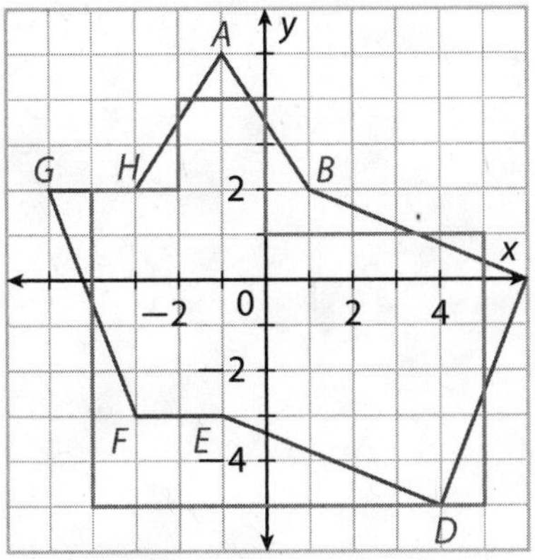

Your Turn

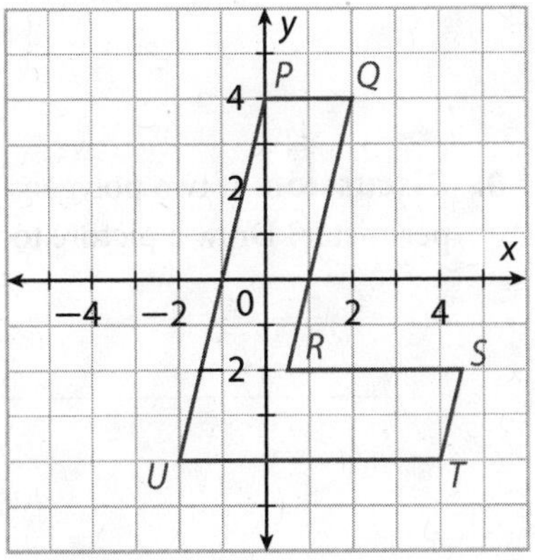

8. A designer is making a medallion in the shape of the letter "L." Each unit on the coordinate grid represents an eighth of an inch, and the medallion is to be cut from a 1-in. square of metal. How much metal is wasted to make each medallion? Write your answer as a decimal.

Elaborate

9. Create a flowchart for the process of finding the area of the polygon *ABCDEFG*. Your flowchart should show when, and why, the Slope and Distance Formulas are used.

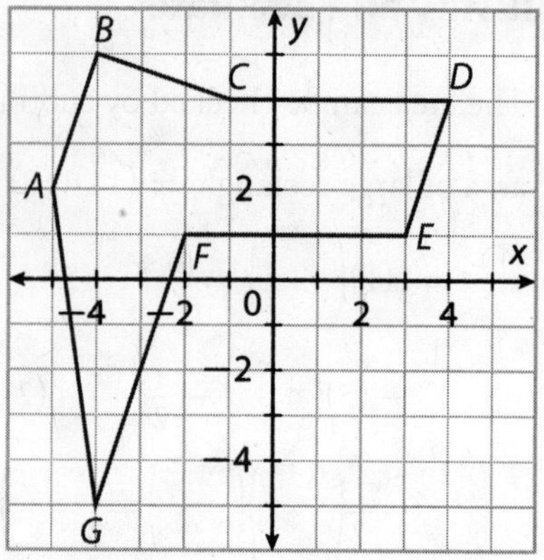

10. Discussion If two polygons have approximately the same area, do they have approximately the same perimeter? Draw a picture to justify your answer.

11. Essential Question Check-In What formulas might you need to solve problems involving the perimeter and area of triangles and quadrilaterals in the coordinate plane?

Evaluate: Homework and Practice

Personal Math Trainer

- Online Homework
- Hints and Help
- Extra Practice

Find the perimeter of the figure with the given vertices. Round to the nearest tenth.

1. $D(0, 1)$, $E(5, 4)$, and $F(2, 6)$

2. $P(2, 5)$, $Q(-3, 0)$, $R(2, -5)$, and $S(6, 0)$

3. $M(-3, 4)$, $N(1, 4)$, $P(4, 2)$, $Q(4, -1)$, and $R(2, 2)$

4. $A(-5, 1)$, $B(0, 3)$, $C(5, 1)$, $D(4, -2)$, $E(0, -4)$, and $F(-2, -4)$

Find the area of each figure.

5.

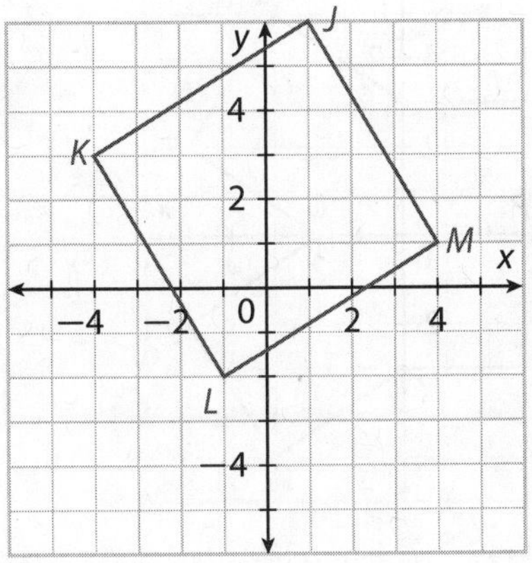

6.

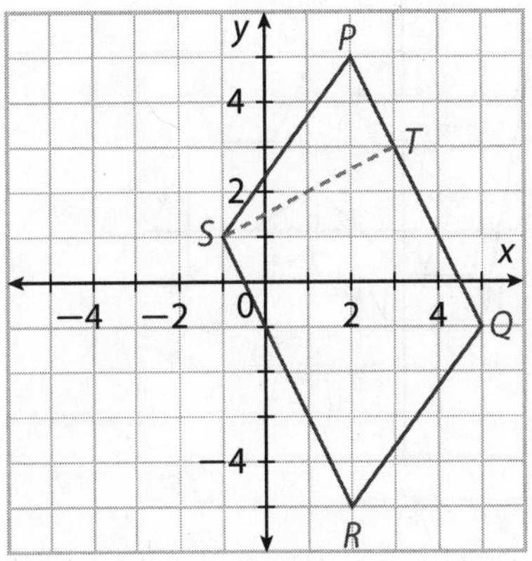

Find the area of each figure by addition.

7.

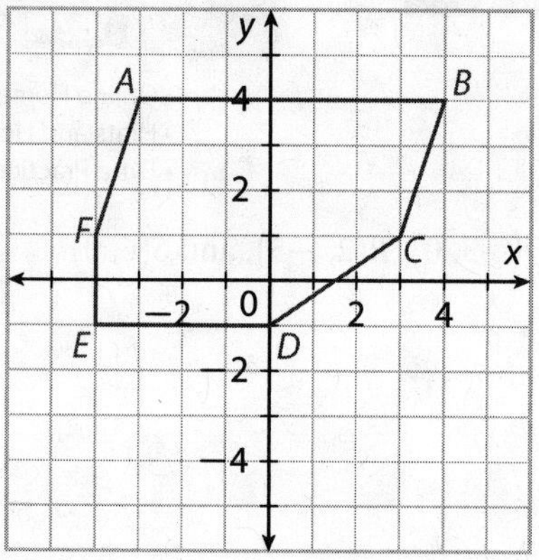

8.

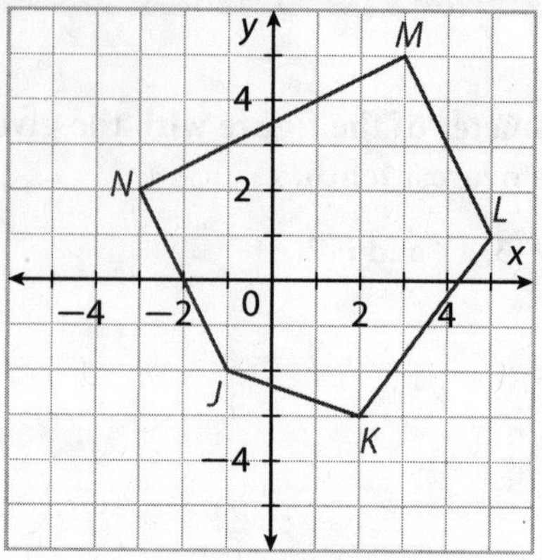

Find the area of each figure by subtraction.

9.

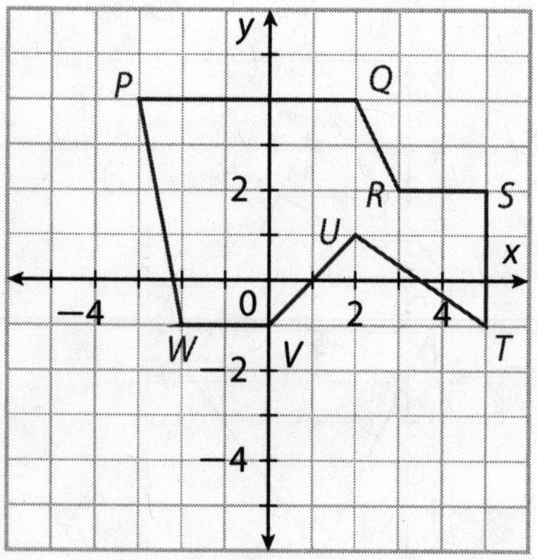

10.

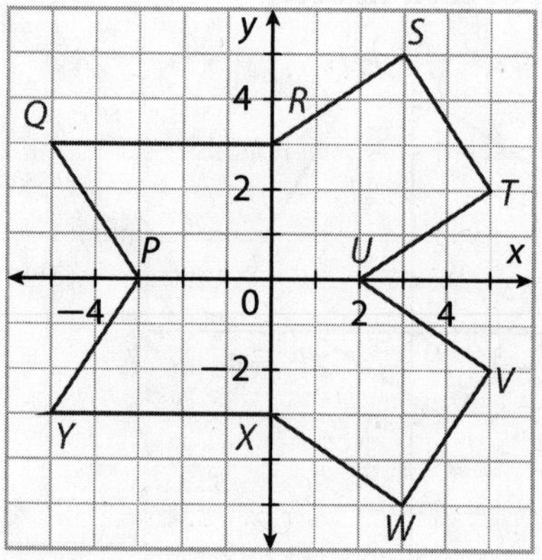

11. Fencing costs \$1.45 per yard, and each unit on the grid represents 50 yd. How much will it cost to fence the plot of land represented by the polygon *ABCDEF*?

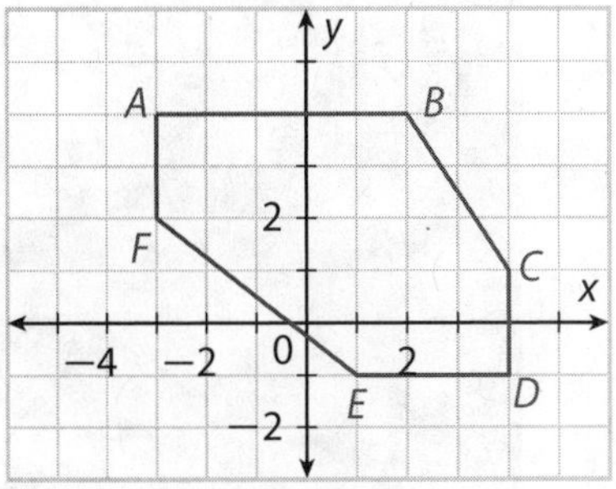

12. A machine component has a geometric shaped plate, represented on the coordinate grid. Each unit on the grid represents 1 cm. Each plate is punched from an 8-cm square of alloy. The cost of the alloy is $\$0.43/\text{cm}^2$, but $\$0.28/\text{cm}^2$ can be recovered on wasted scraps of alloy. What is the net cost of alloy for each component?

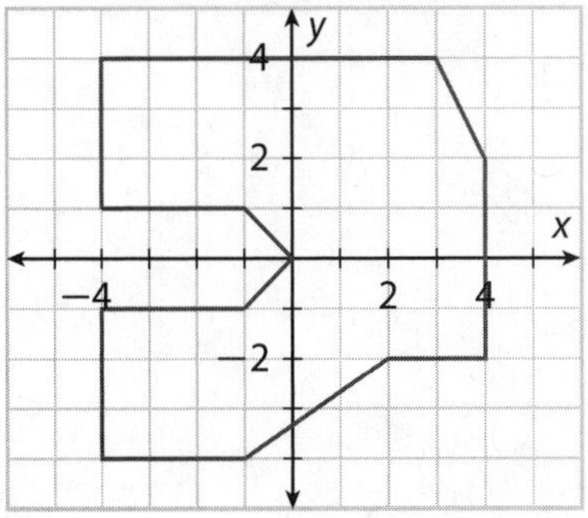

13. $\triangle ABC$ with vertices $A(1, 1)$ and $B(3, 5)$ has an area of 10 units^2. What is the location of the third vertex? Select all that apply.

A. $C(-5, 5)$

B. $C(3, -5)$

C. $C(-2, 5)$

D. $C(6, 1)$

E. $C(3, -3)$

14. Pentagon *ABCDE* shows the path of an obstacle course, where each unit of the coordinate plane represents 10 meters. Find the length of the course to the nearest meter.

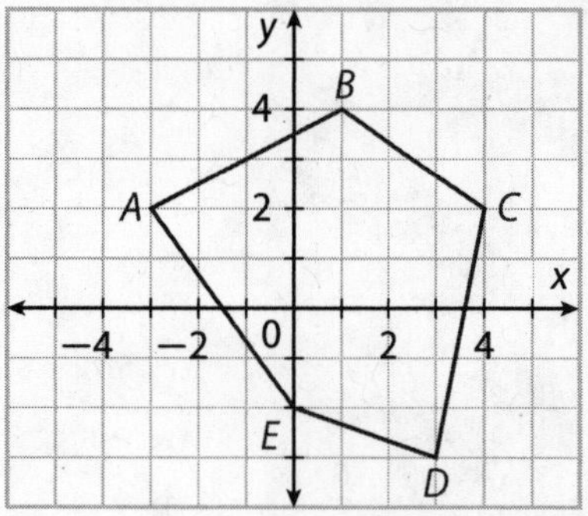

Algebra Graph each set of lines to form a triangle. Find the area and perimeter.

15. $y = 2$, $x = 5$, and $y = x$

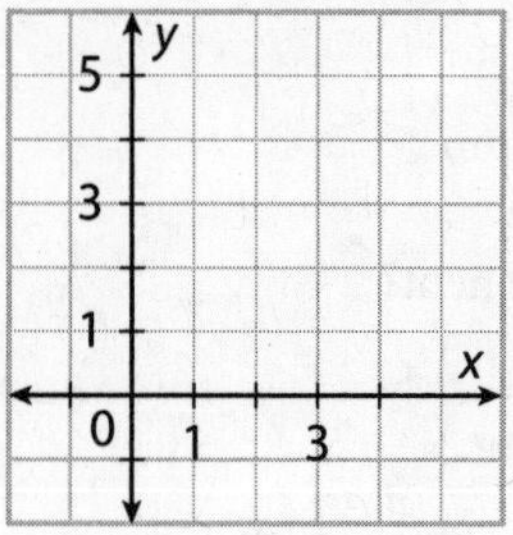

16. $y = -5$, $x = 2$, and $y = -2x + 7$

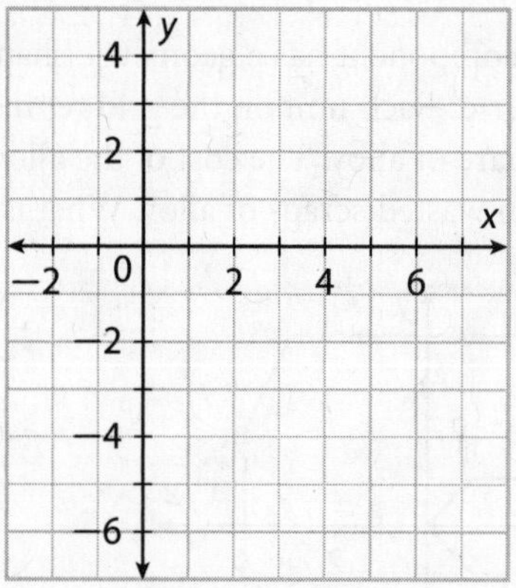

17. Prove that quadrilateral *JKLM* with vertices $J(1, 5)$, $K(4, 2)$, $L(1, -4)$, and $M(-2, 2)$ is a kite, and find its area.

H.O.T. Focus on Higher Order Thinking

18. Explain the Error Wendell is trying to prove that *ABCD* is a rhombus and to find its area. Identify and correct his error. (*Hint:* A rhombus is a quadrilateral with four congruent sides.)

$AB = \sqrt{(2-(-2))^2 + (5-2)^2} = \sqrt{25} = 5,$

$BC = \sqrt{(6-2)^2 + (2-5)^2} = \sqrt{25} = 5$

$CD = \sqrt{(2-6)^2 + (-1-2)^2} = \sqrt{25} = 5,$

$AD = \sqrt{(2-(-2))^2 + (-1-(-2))^2} = \sqrt{25} = 5$

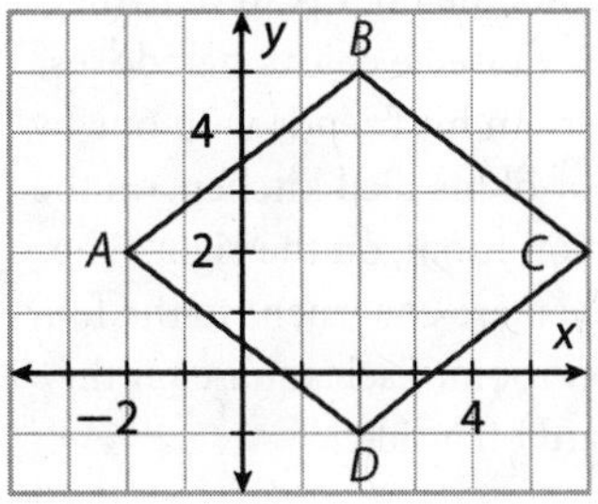

So $\overline{AB} \cong \overline{BC} \cong \overline{CD} \cong \overline{AD}$, and therefore *ABCD* is a rhombus.

area of *ABCD*: $b = AB = 5$ and $h = BC = 5$, so $A = bh = (5)(5) = 25$

19. Communicate Mathematical Ideas Using the figure, prove that the area of a kite is half the product of its diagonals. (Do not make numerical calculations.)

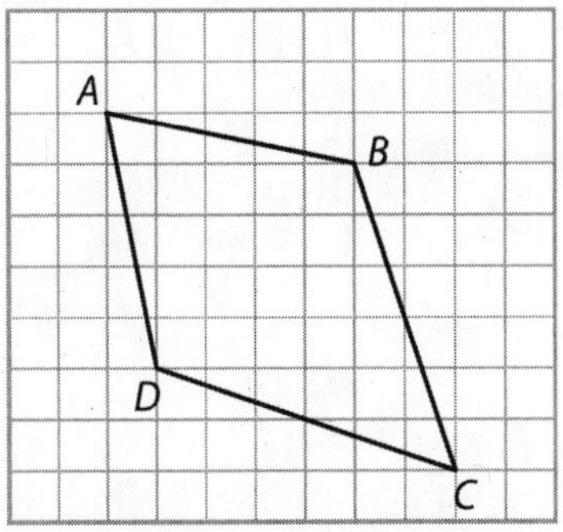

20. Justify Reasoning Use the figure to derive the formula for the area of a trapezoid. Then use the Trapezoid Midsegment Theorem to show that the area of a trapezoid is the product of the length of its midsegment and its height.

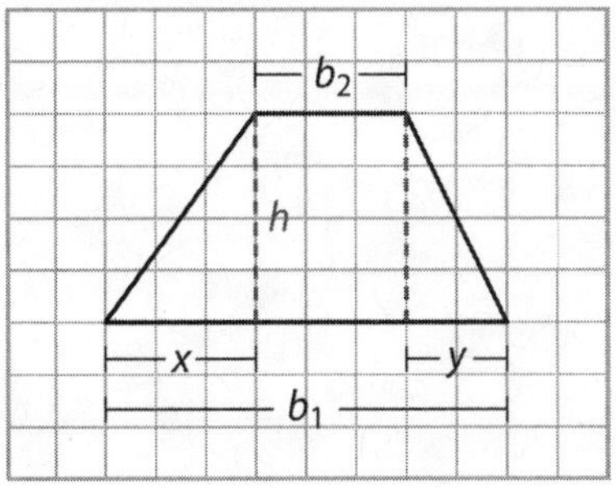

Lesson Performance Task

The coordinate plane shows the floor plan of two rooms in Fritz's house. Because he enjoys paradoxes, Fritz has decided to entertain his friends with one by drawing lines on the floor of his tiled kitchen, on the left, and his tiled recreation room, on the right. The four sections in the kitchen are congruent to the four sections in the recreation room. Each square on the floor plan measures 1 yard on a side.

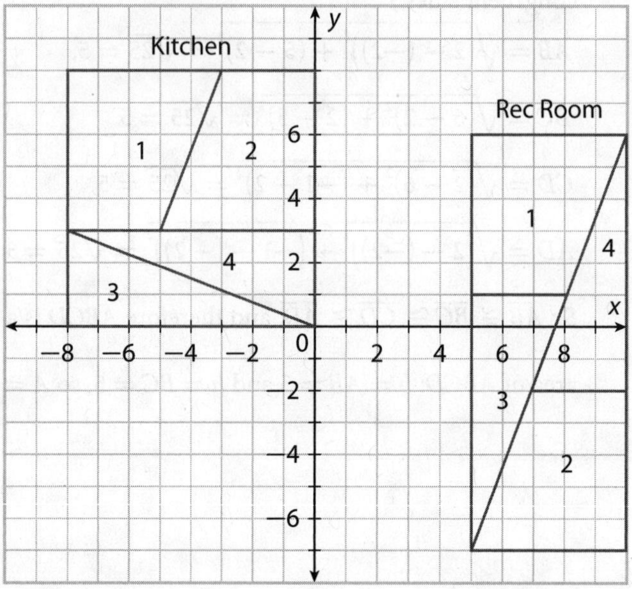

1. Find the area of each of the four sections of the kitchen. Add the four areas to find the total area of the kitchen.

2. Find the area of the kitchen by finding the product of the length and the width.

3. Find the area of the recreation room by finding the product of the length and the width.

4. Describe the paradox.

5. Explain the paradox.

Name ____________ Class ____________ Date ____________

2.6 Subdividing a Segment in a Given Ratio

Essential Question: How do you find the point on a directed line segment that partitions the given segment in a given ratio?

Resource Locker

Explore — Partitioning a Segment in a One-Dimensional Coordinate System

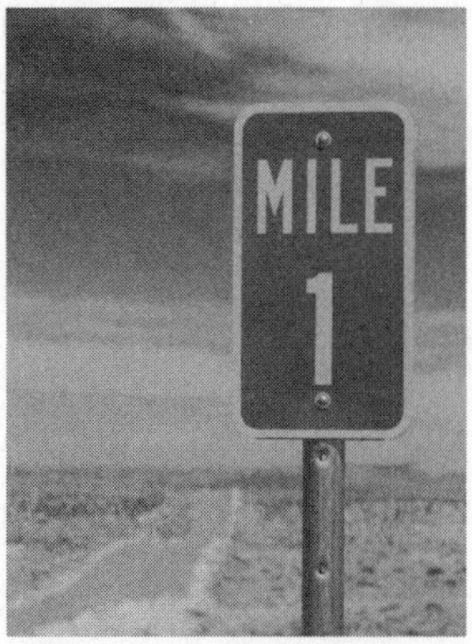

It takes just one number to specify an exact location on a number line. For this reason, a number line is sometimes called a one-dimensional coordinate system. The mile markers on a straight stretch of a highway turn that part of the highway into a one-dimensional coordinate system.

On a straight highway, the exit for Arthur Avenue is at mile marker 14. The exit for Collingwood Road is at mile marker 44. The state highway administration plans to put an exit for Briar Street at a point that is $\frac{2}{3}$ of the distance from Arthur Avenue to Collingwood Road. Follow these steps to determine where the new exit should be placed.

(A) Mark Arthur Avenue (point A) and Collingwood Road (point C) on the number line.

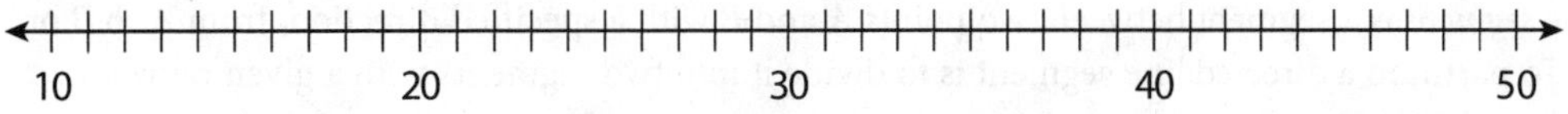

(B) What is the distance from Arthur Avenue to Collingwood Road? Explain.

____

(C) How far will the Briar Street exit be from Arthur Avenue? Explain.

____

(D) What is the mile marker number for the Briar Street exit? Why?

____

(E) Plot and label the Briar Street exit (point B) on the number line.

____

Ⓕ The highway administration also plans to put an exit for Dakota Lane at a point that divides the highway from Arthur Avenue to Collingwood Road in a ratio of 2 to 3. What is the mile marker number for Dakota Lane? Why? (*Hint*: Let the distance from Arthur Avenue to Dakota Lane be $2x$ and let the distance from Dakota Lane to Collingwood Road be $3x$.)

Ⓖ Plot and label the Dakota Lane exit (point D) on the number line.

Reflect

1. How can you tell that the location at which you plotted point B is reasonable?

2. Would your answer in Step F be different if the exit for Dakota Avenue divided the highway from Arthur Avenue to Collingwood Road in a ratio of 3 to 2? Explain.

Explain 1 Partitioning a Segment in a Two-Dimensional Coordinate System

A *directed line segment* is a segment between two points A and B with a specified direction, from A to B or from B to A. To partition a directed line segment is to divide it into two segments with a given ratio.

Example 1 **Find the coordinates of the point P that divides the directed line segment from A to B in the given ratio.**

Ⓐ $A(-8, -7)$, $B(8, 5)$; 3 to 1

Step 1 Write a ratio that expresses the distance of point P along the segment from A to B.

Point P is $\frac{3}{3+1} = \frac{3}{4}$ of the distance from A to B.

Step 2 Find the run and the rise of the directed line segment.

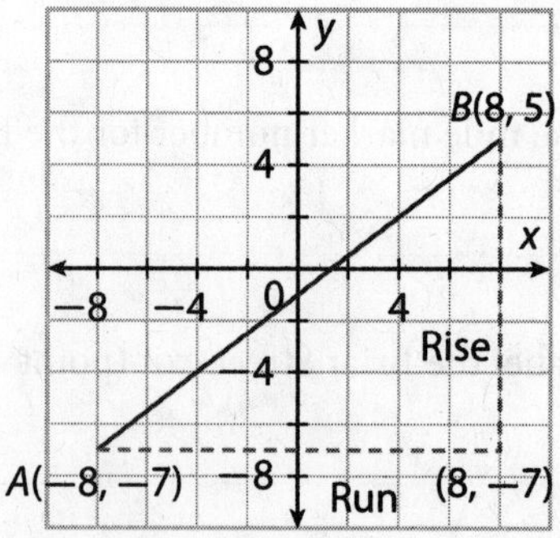

$\text{run} = 8 - (-8) = 16$

$\text{rise} = 5 - (-7) = 12$

Step 3 Point P is $\frac{3}{4}$ of the distance from point A to point B, so find $\frac{3}{4}$ of both the rise and the run.

$\frac{3}{4}$ of run $= \frac{3}{4}(16) = 12$ $\qquad$ $\frac{3}{4}$ of rise $= \frac{3}{4}(12) = 9$

Step 4 To find the coordinates of point P, add the values from Step 3 to the coordinates of point A.

x-coordinate of point $P = -8 + 12 = 4$

y-coordinate of point $P = -7 + 9 = 2$

The coordinates of point P are $(4, 2)$.

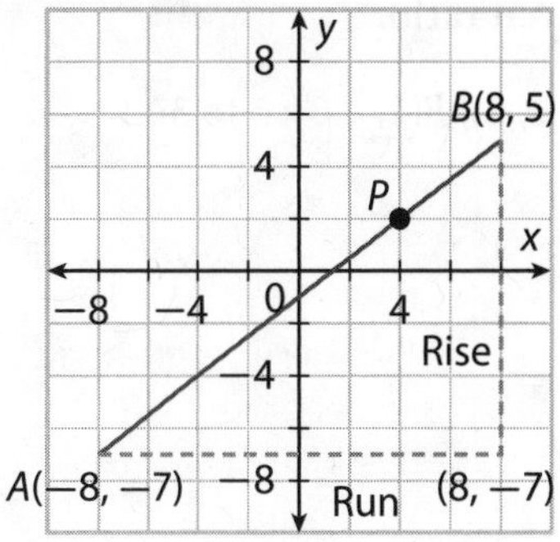

(B) $A(-4, 4)$, $B(2, 1)$; 1 to 2

Step 1 Write a ratio that expresses the distance of point P along the segment from A to B.

Point P is $\frac{\square}{\square + \square} = \frac{\square}{\square}$ of the distance from A to B.

Step 2 Graph the directed line segment. Find the rise and the run of the directed line segment.

run $= 2 - (-4) = 6$

rise $= \square - \square = \square$

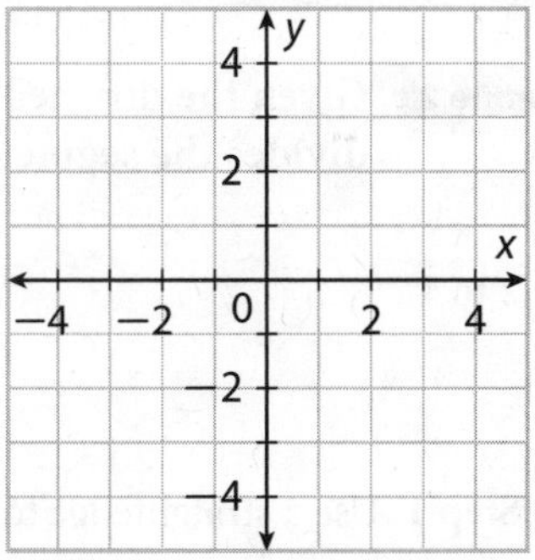

Step 3 Point P is $\frac{\square}{\square}$ of the distance from point A to point B.

$\frac{\square}{\square}$ of run $= \frac{\square}{\square}(6) = \square$ $\qquad$ $\frac{\square}{\square}$ of run $= \frac{\square}{\square}(\square) = \square$

Step 4 To find the coordinates of point P, add the values from Step 3 to the coordinates of point A.

x-coordinate of point $P = -4 + \square = \square$ $\qquad$ y-coordinate of point $P = 4 + \square = \square$

The coordinates of point P are $(\square, \square)$. Plot point P on the above graph.

Reflect

3. In Part A, show how you can use the Distance Formula to check that point P partitions the directed line segment in the correct ratio.

4. **Discussion** What can you conclude about a point that partitions a segment in the ratio 1 to 1? How can you find the coordinates of such a point?

Your Turn

Find the coordinates of the point P that divides the directed line segment from A to B in the given ratio.

5. $A(-6, 5), B(2, -3)$; 5 to 3

6. $A(4, 2), B(-6, -13)$; 3 to 2

Explain 2 Constructing a Partition of a Segment

Example 2 **Given the directed line segment from A to B, construct the point P that divides the segment in the given ratio from A to B.**

(A) 2 to 1

Step 1 Use a straightedge to draw $\overrightarrow{AC}$. The exact measure of the angle is not important, but the construction is easiest for angles from about 30° to 60°.

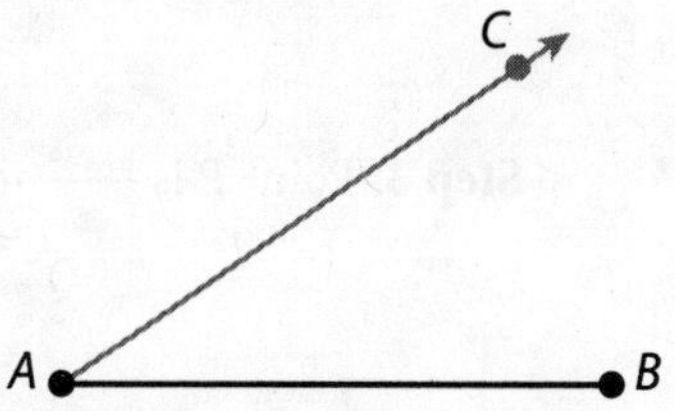

Step 2 Place the compass point on A and draw an arc through $\overrightarrow{AC}$. Label the intersection D. Using the same compass setting, draw an arc centered on D and label the intersection E. Using the same compass setting, draw an arc centered on E and label the intersection F.

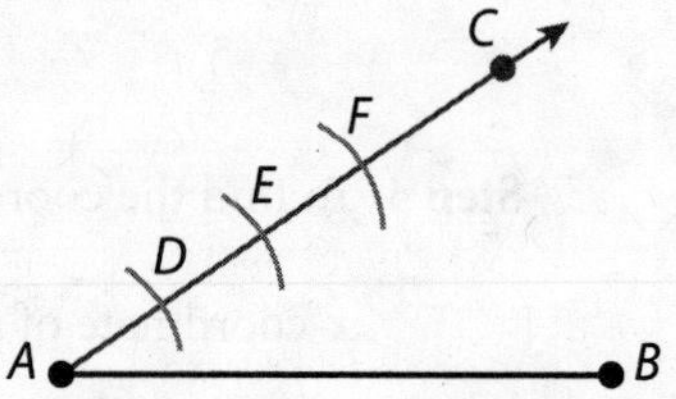

Step 3 Use the straightedge to connect points B and F. Construct an angle congruent to $\angle AFB$ with D as its vertex. Construct an angle congruent to $\angle AFB$ with E as its vertex.

Step 4 The construction partitions $\overline{AB}$ into 3 equal parts. Label point P at the point that divides the segment in the ratio 2 to 1 from A to B.

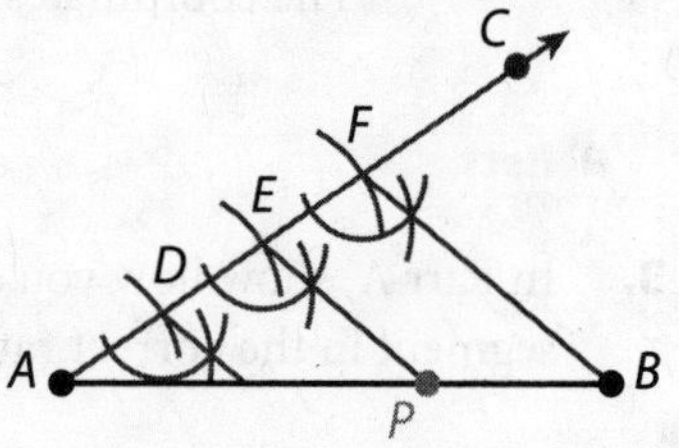

(B) 1 to 3

Step 1 Use a straightedge to draw $\overrightarrow{AC}$.

Step 2 Place the compass point on *A* and draw an arc through $\overrightarrow{AC}$. Label the intersection *D*. Using the same compass setting, draw an arc centered on *D* and label the intersection *E*. Using the same compass setting, draw an arc centered on *E* and label the intersection *F*. Using the same compass setting, draw an arc centered on *F* and label the intersection *G*.

Step 3 Use the straightedge to connect points *B* and *G*. Construct angles congruent to $\angle AGB$ with *D*, *E*, and *F* as the vertices.

Step 4 The construction partitions $\overline{AB}$ into ___ equal parts. Label point *P* at the point that divides the segment in the ratio ___ to ___ from *A* to *B*.

Reflect

7. In Part A, why is $\overline{EP}$ is parallel to $\overline{FB}$?

8. How can you use the Triangle Proportionality Theorem to explain why this construction method works?

Your Turn

Given the directed line segment from *A* to *B*, construct the point *P* that divides the segment in the given ratio from *A* to *B*.

9. 1 to 2

10. 3 to 2

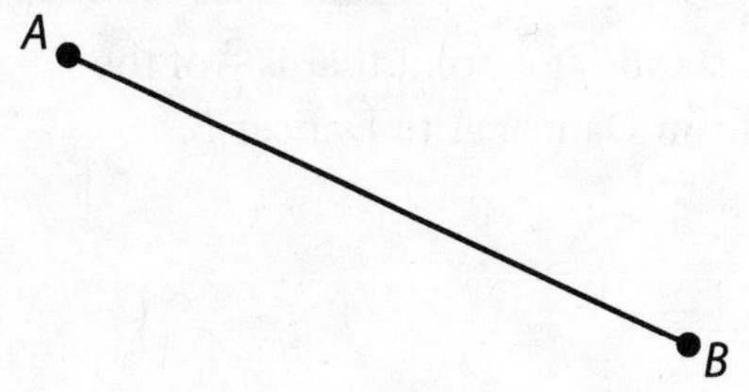

Elaborate

11. How is a one-dimensional coordinate system similar to a two-dimensional coordinate system? How is it different?

12. Is finding a point that is $\frac{4}{5}$ of the distance from point A to point B the same as finding a point that divides $\overline{AB}$ in the ratio 4 to 5? Explain.

13. **Essential Question Check-In** What are some different ways to divide a segment in the ratio 2 to 1?

Evaluate: Homework and Practice

Personal Math Trainer
- Online Homework
- Hints and Help
- Extra Practice

A choreographer uses a number line to position dancers for a ballet. Dancers A and B have coordinates 5 and 23, respectively. In Exercises 1–4, find the coordinate for each of the following dancers based on the given locations.

1. Dancer C stands at a point that is $\frac{5}{6}$ of the distance from Dancer A to Dancer B.

2. Dancer D stands at a point that is $\frac{1}{3}$ of the distance from Dancer A to Dancer B.

3. Dancer E stands at a point that divides the line segment from Dancer A to Dancer B in a ratio of 2 to 1.

4. Dancer F stands at a point that divides the line segment from Dancer A to Dancer B in a ratio of 1 to 5.

Find the coordinates of the point P that divides the directed line segment from A to B in the given ratio.

5. $A(-3, -2)$, $B(12, 3)$; 3 to 2

6. $A(-1, 5)$, $B(7, -3)$; 7 to 1

7. $A(-1, 4)$, $(B-9, 0)$; 1 to 3

8. $A(7, -3)$, $B(-7, 4)$; 3 to 4

Given the directed line segment from A to B, construct the point P that divides the segment in the given ratio from A to B.

9. 3 to 1

10. 2 to 3

Given the directed line segment from A to B, construct the point P that divides the segment in the given ratio from A to B.

11. 1 to 4

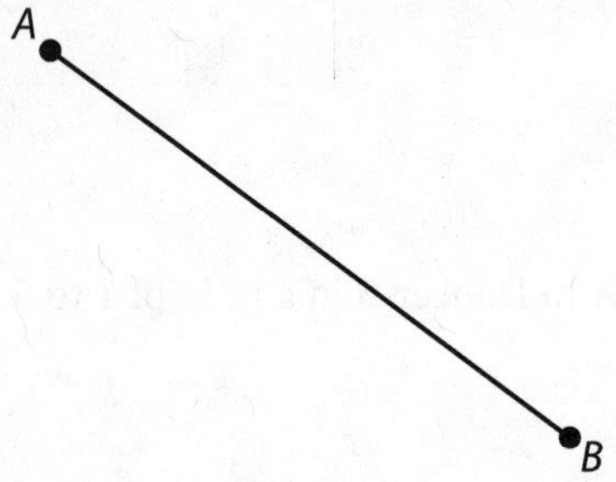

12. 4 to 1

Find the coordinate of the point *P* that divides each directed line segment in the given ratio.

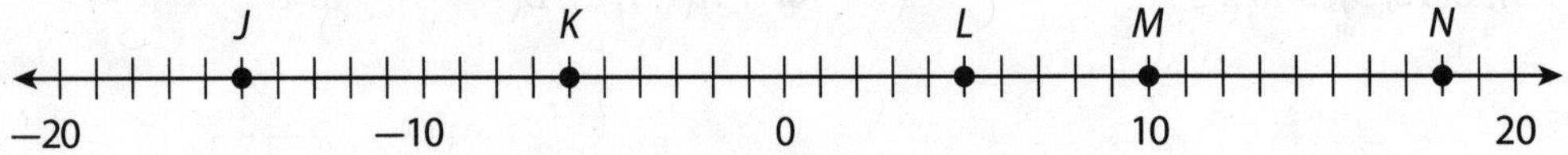

13. from *J* to *M*; 1 to 9

14. from *K* to *L*; 1 to 1

15. from *N* to *K*; 3 to 5

16. from *K* to *J*; 7 to 11

17. Communicate Mathematical Ideas Leon constructed a point *P* that divides the directed segment from *A* to *B* in the ratio 2 to 1. Chelsea constructed a point *Q* that divides the directed segment from *B* to *A* in the ratio 1 to 2. How are points *P* and *Q* related? Explain.

18. City planners use a number line to place landmarks along a new street. Each unit of the number line represents 100 feet. A fountain F is located at coordinate -3 and a plaza P is located at coordinate 21. The city planners place two benches along the street at points that divide the segment from F to P in the ratios 1 to 2 and 3 to 1. What is the distance between the benches?

19. The course for a marathon includes a straight segment from city hall to the main library. The planning committee wants to put water stations along this part of the course so that the stations divide the segment into three equal parts. Find the coordinates of the points at the which the water stations should be placed.

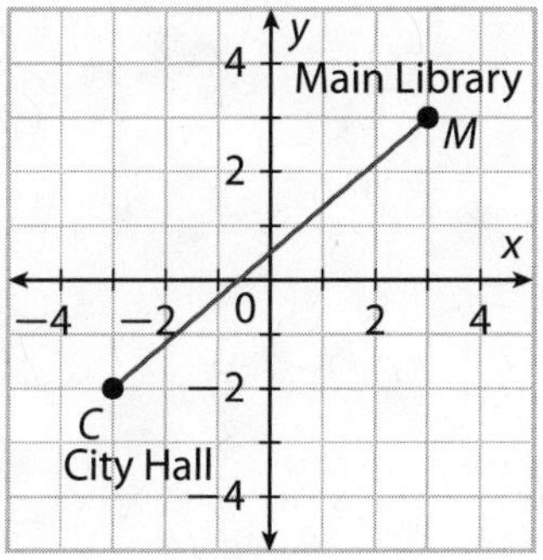

20. Multi-Step Carlos is driving on a straight section of highway from Ashford to Lincoln. Ashford is at mile marker 433 and Lincoln is at mile marker 553. A rest stop is located along the highway $\frac{2}{3}$ of the distance from Ashford to Lincoln. Assuming Carlos drives at a constant rate of 60 miles per hour, how long will it take him to drive from Ashford to the rest stop?

21. The directed segment from J to K is shown in the figure.

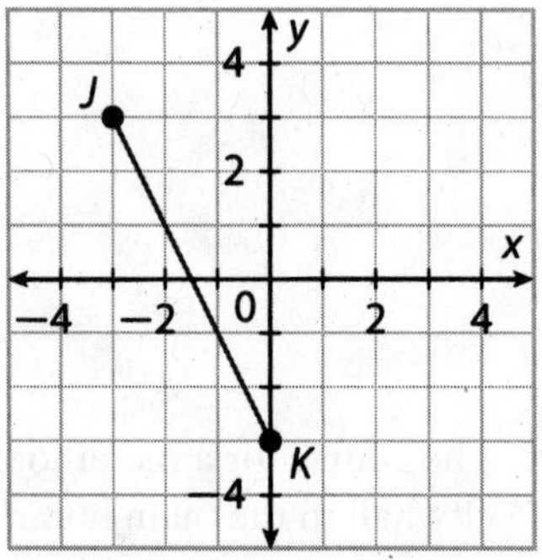

Points divide the segment from J to K in the each of the following ratios. Which points have integer coordinates? Select all that apply

A. 1 to 1

B. 2 to 1

C. 2 to 3

D. 1 to 3

E. 1 to 2

H.O.T. Focus on Higher Order Thinking

22. Critique Reasoning Jeffrey was given a directed line segment and was asked to use a compass and straightedge to construct the point that divides the segment in the ratio 4 to 2. He said he would have to draw a ray and then construct 6 congruent segments along the ray. Tamara said it is not necessary to construct 6 congruent segments along the ray. Do you agree? If so, explain Tamara's shortcut. If not, explain why not.

23. Explain the Error Point A has coordinate -9 and point B has coordinate 9. A student was asked to find the coordinate of the point P that is $\frac{2}{3}$ of the distance from A to B. The student said the coordinate of point P is -3.

a. Without doing any calculations, how can you tell that the student made an error?

b. What error do you think the student made?

24. Analyze Relationships Point P divides the directed segment from A to B in the ratio 3 to 2. The coordinates of point A are $(-4, -2)$ and the coordinates of point P are $(2, 1)$. Find the coordinates of point B.

25. Critical Thinking $\overline{RS}$ passes through $R(-3, 1)$ and $S(4, 3)$. Find a point P on $\overline{RS}$ such that the ratio of RP to SP is 5 to 4. Is there more than one possibility? Explain.

Lesson Performance Task

In this lesson you will subdivide line segments in given ratios. The diagram shows a line segment divided into two parts in such a way that the longer part divided by the shorter part equals the entire length divided by the longer part:

$$\frac{a}{b} = \frac{a+b}{a}$$

Each of these ratios is called the Golden Ratio. To find the point on a line segment that divides the segment this way, study this figure:

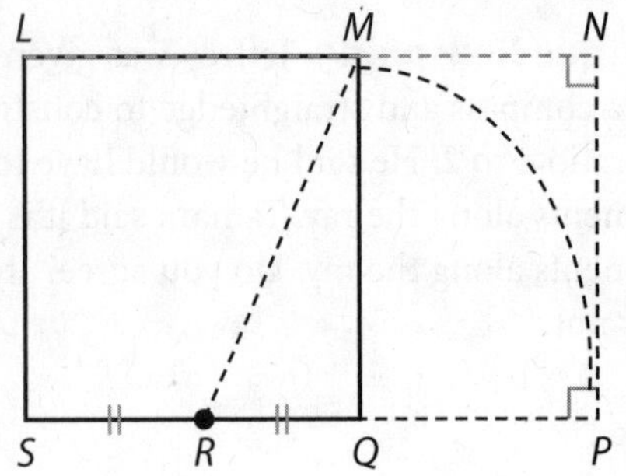

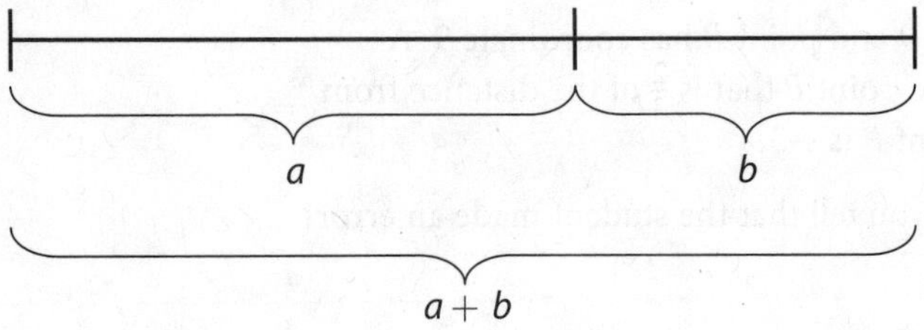

In the figure, *LMQS* is a square. $\frac{LN}{LM}$ equals the Golden Ratio (the entire segment length divided by the longer part).

1. Describe how, starting with line segment $\overline{LM}$, you can find the location of point *N*.

2. Letting *LM* equal 1, find $\frac{LN}{LM} = \frac{LN}{1} = LN$, the Golden Ratio. Describe your method.

STUDY GUIDE REVIEW

Coordinate Proof Using Slope and Distance

MODULE 2

Essential Question: How can you use coordinate proofs using slope and distance to solve real-world problems?

Key Vocabulary
coordinate proof
(prueba coordenada)
composite figure
(figura compuesta)

KEY EXAMPLE (Lesson 2.1)

Show that the figure given by the points $A(2, 4)$, $B(3, 2)$, $C(2, 1)$, and $D(0, 5)$ is a trapezoid.

Determine whether the slopes of $\overline{AB}$ and $\overline{CD}$ are equal to determine whether they are parallel, and whether the figure is a trapezoid.

$$\text{slope of } \overline{AB} = \frac{4-2}{2-3} = \frac{2}{-1} = -2$$

$$\text{slope of } \overline{CD} = \frac{5-1}{0-2} = \frac{4}{-2} = -2$$

Thus, the figure $ABCD$ is a trapezoid.

KEY EXAMPLE (Lesson 2.2)

Show that $\triangle ABC$ with points $A(-2, 1)$, $B(-3, 3)$, and $C(2, 3)$ is a right triangle.

A right triangle should have a pair of sides that are perpendicular.

$$\text{slope of } \overline{AB} = \frac{1-3}{-2-(-3)} = \frac{-2}{1} = -2$$

$$\text{slope of } \overline{BC} = \frac{3-3}{-3-2} = \frac{0}{-5} = 0$$

$$\text{slope of } \overline{CA} = \frac{3-1}{2-(-2)} = \frac{2}{4} = \frac{1}{2}$$

One pair of slopes has a product of -1, so the triangle is right.

KEY EXAMPLE (Lesson 2.3)

Prove the triangles $\triangle ABC$ and $\triangle DCB$ are congruent given $A(1, 1)$, $B(3, 1)$, $C(1, 4)$, and $D(3, 4)$.

Note that the triangles share a side. Find the length of each other side.

$$AC = \sqrt{(1-1)^2 + (4-1)^2} = \sqrt{0+9} = 3$$

$$AB = \sqrt{(3-1)^2 + (1-1)^2} = \sqrt{4+0} = 2$$

$$DC = \sqrt{(3-1)^2 + (4-4)^2} = \sqrt{4+0} = 2$$

$$DB = \sqrt{(3-3)^2 + (4-1)^2} = \sqrt{0+9} = 3$$

$AC = DB$, so $\overline{AC} \cong \overline{DB}$, and $AB = DC$, so $\overline{AB} \cong \overline{DC}$. Additionally, $\overline{CB} \cong \overline{CB}$ is congruent to itself by the Reflexive Property.

The triangles have three congruent sides, so are congruent by SSS.

EXERCISES

Determine whether the statement is True or False. *(Lesson 2.1)*

1. The figure given by the points $A(0, -1)$, $B(3, -2)$, $C(5, -4)$, and $D(-1, -2)$ is a trapezoid.
2. The figure given by the points $A(0, 3)$, $B(5, 3)$, and $C(2, 0)$ is a right triangle.

Prove or disprove the statement.

3. $\triangle ABC$ and $\triangle DEF$ are congruent, given $A(-4, 4)$, $B(-2, 5)$, $C(-3, 1)$, $D(-2, -1)$, $E(-1, -3)$, and $F(-5, -2)$. *(Lesson 2.2)*

Find the area of the polygon. *(Lesson 2.3)*

4. $ABCDE$ defined by the points $A(-3, 4)$, $B(-1, 4)$, $C(1, 1)$, $D(-1, 1)$, and $E(-4, -1)$

MODULE PERFORMANCE TASK

How Do You Calculate the Containment of a Fire?

Most news stories about large wildfires report some level of "containment" reached by firefighters. To prevent a blaze from spreading, firefighters dig a "fire line" around its perimeter. For example, if 3 miles of fire line have been dug around a fire that is 10 miles in perimeter, then the fire is said to be 30 percent contained.

The image shows a forest fire, the forest is shown in light grey while the fire is in dark grey. The darker lines show where fire lines have been dug. What is the percentage containment of the fire as well as the total area that has been burned?

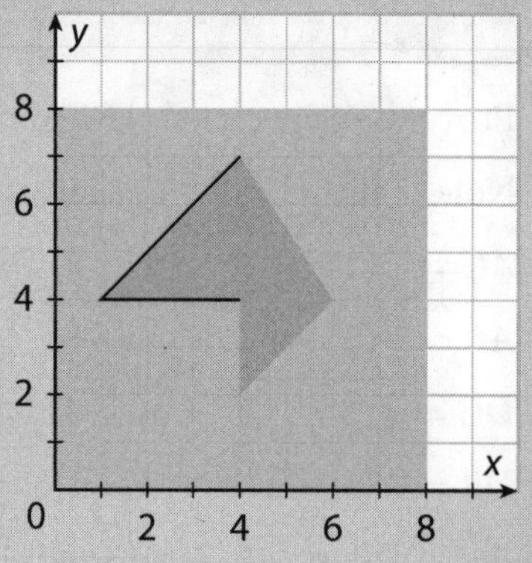

Use your own paper to complete the task. Be sure to write down all your data and assumptions. Then use graphs, numbers, words, or algebra to explain how you reached your conclusions.

Ready to Go On?

2.1–2.6 Coordinate Proof Using Slope and Distance

Personal Math Trainer
- Online Homework
- Hints and Help
- Extra Practice

Determine and prove what shaped is formed for the given coordinates for *ABCD*, and then find the perimeter and area as an exact value and rounded to the nearest tenth. *(Lessons 2.1, 2.3, 2.4, 2.5)*

1. $A(10, -6), B(-7, 2), C(1, 8), D(-6, 9)$

2. $A(10, -6), B(6, -9), C(3, -5), D(7, -2)$

ESSENTIAL QUESTION

3. When is a quadrilateral both a trapezoid and a parallelogram? Is a quadrilateral ever a parallelogram but not a trapezoid?

MODULE 2

MIXED REVIEW

Assessment Readiness

1. Does the name correctly describe the shape given by the points $A(2, 2)$, $B(3, 4)$, $C(6, 4)$, and $D(5, 2)$?

A. Rectangle ○ Yes ○ No

B. Parallelogram ○ Yes ○ No

C. Square ○ Yes ○ No

2. Triangle ABC is given by the points $A(3, 2)$, $B(4, 4)$, and $C(5, 1)$. Choose True or False for each statement.

A. The perimeter of $\triangle ABC$ is 9.9 units. ○ True ○ False

B. $\triangle ABC$ is an equilateral triangle. ○ True ○ False

C. The perimeter of $\triangle ABC$ is 7.6 units. ○ True ○ False

3. Triangle DEF is given by the points $D(1, 1)$, $E(3, 8)$, and $F(8, 0)$. Choose True or False for each statement.

A. The area of $\triangle DEF$ is 25.5 square units. ○ True ○ False

B. $\triangle DEF$ is a scalene triangle. ○ True ○ False

C. The area of $\triangle DEF$ is 30 square units. ○ True ○ False

4. What type of triangle is given by the points $D(1, 1)$, $E(3, 8)$, and $F(5, 1)$? Explain how you could find the perimeter of the triangle.

5. For the polygon shown, specify how to find its area using triangles, parallelograms, and rectangles.

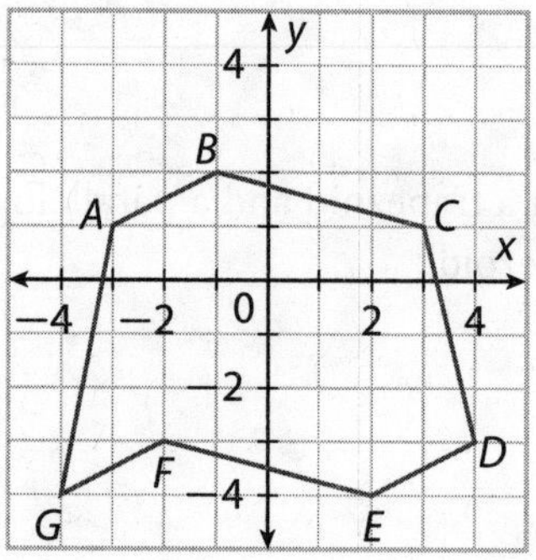

Assessment Readiness

Personal Math Trainer
- Online Homework
- Hints and Help
- Extra Practice

1. Using known properties, determine if the statements are true or not. Select True or False for each statement.

A. If one pair of consecutive sides of a parallelogram is congruent, then the parallelogram is a rectangle. ○ True ○ False

B. If all angles of a quadrilateral measure 90°, the quadrilateral is a parallelogram. ○ True ○ False

C. If a quadrilateral has one pair of parallel sides then it is a parallelogram. ○ True ○ False

2. Given the line $y = -\frac{2}{5}x + 3$, determine if the given line is parallel, perpendicular, or neither. Select the correct answer for each lettered part.

A. $y = \frac{2}{5}x + 7$ ○ Parallel ○ Perpendicular ○ Neither

B. $5y + 2x = -10$ ○ Parallel ○ Perpendicular ○ Neither

C. $-5x + 2y = 4$ ○ Parallel ○ Perpendicular ○ Neither

3. Is $\overline{AB}$ parallel to $\overline{CD}$?

Select Yes or No for each statement.

A. $A(-5, 12)$, $B(7, 18)$, $C(0, -4)$, and $D(-8, 0)$ ○ Yes ○ No

B. $A(-6, 2)$, $B(4, 6)$, $C(7, -4)$, and $D(-3, -8)$ ○ Yes ○ No

C. $A(-6, 2)$, $B(4, 6)$, $C(7, -4)$, and $D(-4, -8)$ ○ Yes ○ No

4. Is $\overline{RS}$ perpendicular to $\overline{DF}$?

Select Yes or No for each statement.

A. $R(6, -2)$ $S(-1, 8)$ and $D(-1, 11)$ $F(11, 4)$ ○ Yes ○ No

B. $R(1, 3)$ $S(4, 7)$ and $D(3, 9)$ $F(15, 0)$ ○ Yes ○ No

C. $R(-5, -5)$ $S(0, 2)$ and $D(8, 3)$ $F(1, 8)$ ○ Yes ○ No

5. Use the distance formula to determine if $\angle ABC \cong \angle DEF$.

Select Yes or No for each statement.

A. $A(-5, -7)$, $B(0, 0)$, $C(4, -7)$, $D(-6, -6)$, $E(-1, 1)$, $F(5, -8)$ ○ Yes ○ No

B. $A(-3, 1)$, $B(1, 1)$, $C(-4, -8)$, $D(1, 1)$, $E(-3, 1)$, $F(4, 8)$ ○ Yes ○ No

C. $A(-8, 8)$, $B(-4, 6)$, $C(-10, 2)$, $D(4, -4)$, $E(8, -2)$, $F(2, 2)$ ○ Yes ○ No

6. Is Point M the midpoint of $\overline{AB}$? Select Yes or No for each statement.

Select True or False for each statement.

A. $A(1, 2), B(3,4), M(2, 3)$ ○ Yes ○ No

B. $A(0, 8), B(10,-1), M(5, 3.5)$ ○ Yes ○ No

C. $A(-7, -5), B(6, 4), M(-1, -1)$ ○ Yes ○ No

D. $A(4, -2), B(6, -8), M(5, -5)$ ○ Yes ○ No

7. Determine whether the statement about *QRST* is true or false using the given image.

Select True or False for each statement.

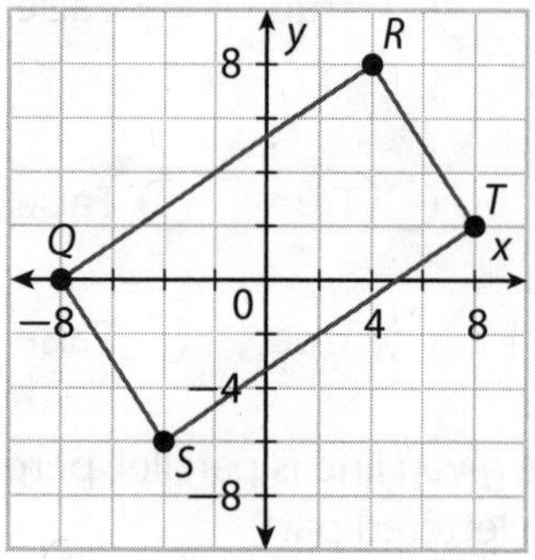

A. The diagonals of *QRST* are congruent. ○ True ○ False

B. *QRST* is a square. ○ True ○ False

C. *QRST* is a rectangle. ○ True ○ False

D. The diagonals of *QRST* are perpendicular. ○ True ○ False

8. A city has a walkway between the middle school and the library that can be represented in the image given. The city decides it wants to place three trash cans, equally spaced along the walkway, to help reduce any littering. Find the coordinates of the points at which the trash cans should be placed, and then plot them on the graph.

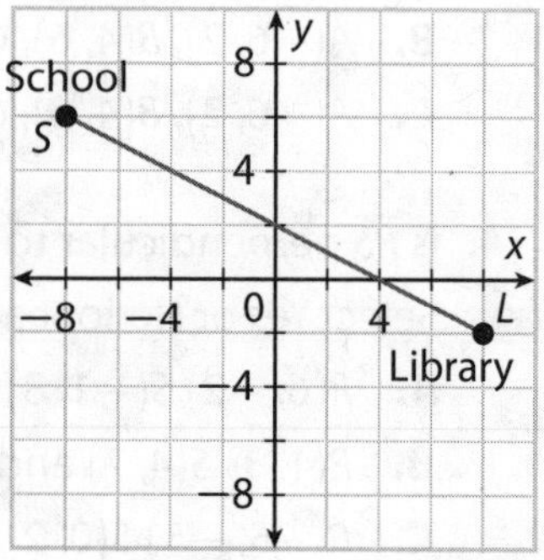

Performance Tasks

★ **9.** Jasmine is putting up a fence around her rectangular property. She drew a scale model on a coordinate grid, and the corners of her property are at $(-3, 4)$, $(5, 4)$, $(5, -3)$, and $(-3, -3)$. Each square on the coordinate grid corresponds to 25 square meters.

A. How much fencing does Jasmine need completely enclose her property?

B. If fencing costs \$6.50/meter, how much will it cost? Show your work.

★★**10.** A quadrilateral has vertices at $G(3, 0)$, $H(4, 4)$, $J(7, 6)$, and $K(9, 4)$. Prove $GHJK$ is a trapezoid. Show your work and explain your reasoning.

★★★**11.** The equation $5x - 2y = 2$ describes a line. Consider the additional line $ax + by = 0$.

A. What are the smallest (in absolute value) integer values of a and b such that the line $ax + by = 0$ is parallel to $5x - 2y = 2$? Explain your answer.

B. What are the smallest (in absolute value) integer values of a and b such that the line $ax + by = 0$ is perpendicular to $5x - 2y = 2$? Explain your answer.

MATH IN CAREERS

Landscape Architect A landscape architect is creating a plan for a flower garden. She wants to have a circular path with six small fountains equally spaced along the circular path.

a. Draw a plan for the path and show where the fountains should be placed using a compass and straightedge. Explain how you constructed the figure.

b. She decides to include a path across the circle from point A to point D. and a row of hedges parallel to this path and tangent to the circular path. Include these features on your drawing and explain how you constructed the parallel path.

UNIT 2

Measurement and Modeling in Two and Three Dimensions

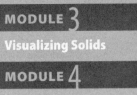

MODULE 3
Visualizing Solids

MODULE 4
Modeling and Problem Solving

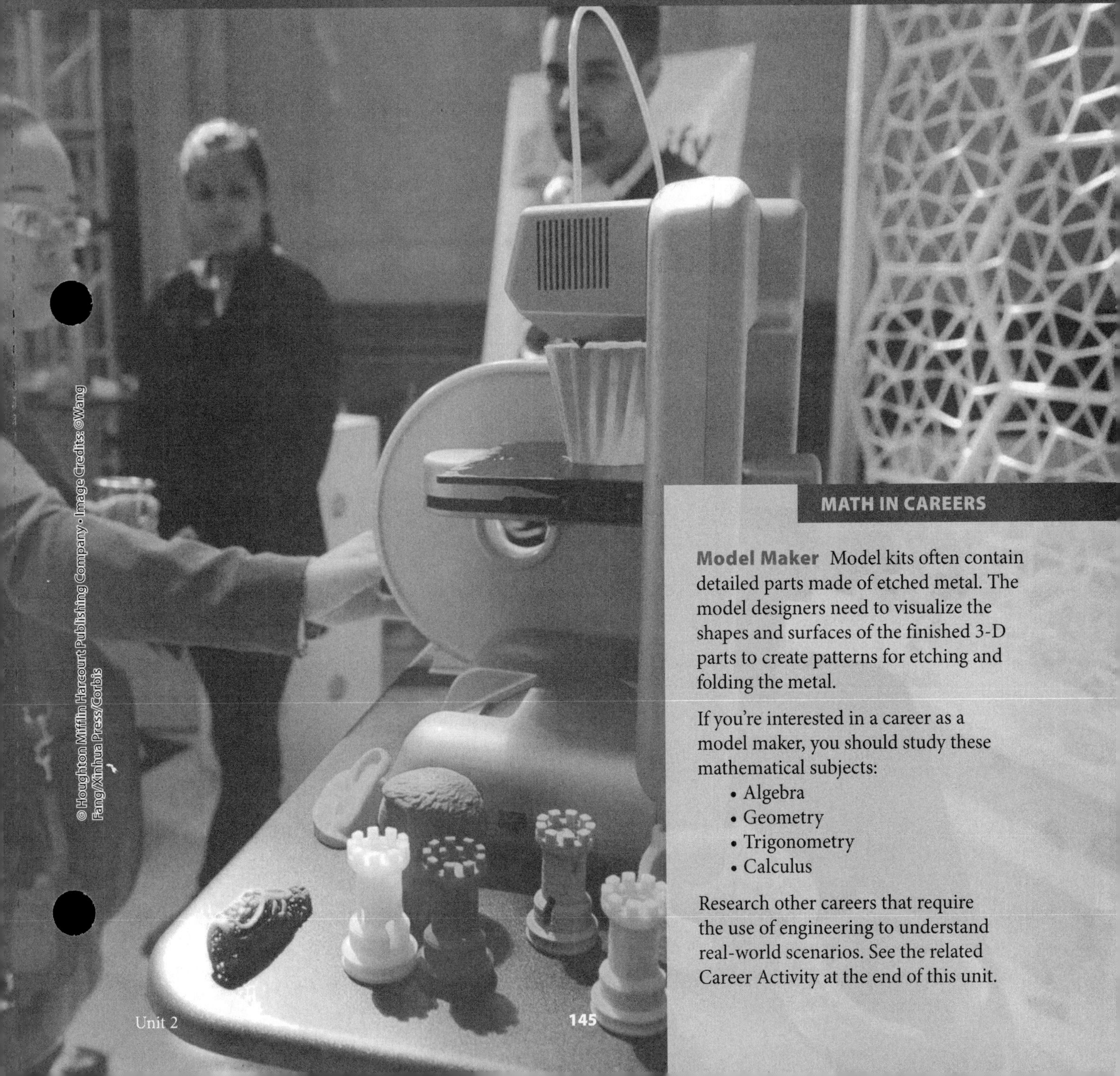

MATH IN CAREERS

Model Maker Model kits often contain detailed parts made of etched metal. The model designers need to visualize the shapes and surfaces of the finished 3-D parts to create patterns for etching and folding the metal.

If you're interested in a career as a model maker, you should study these mathematical subjects:

- Algebra
- Geometry
- Trigonometry
- Calculus

Research other careers that require the use of engineering to understand real-world scenarios. See the related Career Activity at the end of this unit.

Reading Start-Up

Vocabulary

Review Words

✔ area (*área*)
✔ composite figure (*figura compuesta*)
✔ cone (*cono*)
✔ cylinder (*cilindro*)
✔ pyramid (*pirámide*)
✔ sphere (*esfera*)

Preview Words

apothem (*apotema*)
cross section (*sección transversal*)
great circle (*gran círculo*)
net (*neto*)
oblique cylinder (*cilindro oblicuo*)
oblique prism (*prisma oblicuo*)
regular pyramid (*pirámide regular*)
right cone (*cono recto*)
right cylinder (*cilindro recto*)
right prism (*prisma recto*)
surface area (*área de la superficie*)

Visualize Vocabulary

Use the ✔ words and draw examples to complete the chart.

Object	Example

Understand Vocabulary

Complete the sentences using the preview words.

1. A(n) ____________ is the region of a plane that intersects a solid figure.

2. A cross section of a sphere with the same radius as the sphere is called a ____________.

3. The ____________ of a right prism is a two-dimensional image containing six rectangles.

Active Reading

Pyramid Create a Pyramid and organize the adjectives used to describe different objects—right, regular, oblique—on each of its faces. When listening to descriptions of objects, look for these words and associate them with the object that follows.

Visualizing Solids

MODULE 3

Essential Question: How can visualizing solids and surface area help you to solve real-world problems?

REAL WORLD VIDEO
Check out how visualization of solids and surface area can be used to determine critical dimensions of the Space Shuttle and other spacecraft.

MODULE PERFORMANCE TASK PREVIEW

How Much Does the Paint on the Space Shuttle Weigh?

At some point, NASA stopped painting the fuel tanks for the Space Shuttle because of the extra weight it added. In this module, you will be challenged to use surface area to come up with an estimate for the weight of that paint. Let's start the countdown!

Are YOU Ready?

Complete these exercises to review skills you will need for this module.

Personal Math Trainer
- Online Homework
- Hints and Help
- Extra Practice

Cross Sections

Example 1 What is the cross section of a plane that passes through (but not tangent to) a sphere?

No matter how or where the plane passes, the cross section will always be a circle with radius less than or equal to the radius of the sphere.

Find the cross section of the following.

1. A plane passing through a cylinder parallel to the bases.

____

Volume

Example 2 Find the exact volume of a right cylinder with a radius 9 and height 5.

$V = Bh$	Volume of a cylinder
$B = \pi r^2$	Area of base equals the area of a circle.
$B = \pi(9)^2 = 81\pi$	Substitute and solve.
$V = (81\pi)(5) = 405\pi$	Substitute and solve to find the volume.

Find the volume of the following. Give exact values.

2. A sphere with radius 6 ________

3. A pyramid whose base is a square with a base having sides of length 17 and whose height is 9 ________

Surface Area

Example 3 Given a cube with a side of length 5, find the surface area.

Since the surface area of a cube is 6 squares of equal area, find the area of one face of the cube and then multiply by 6.

$A = s^2$	Area of a square
$A = (5)^2 = 25$	Substitute and solve.
$SA = 25 \cdot 6 = 150$	Multiply by 6, the number of faces of a cube.

Find the surface area of a cube with the following side lengths.

4. 7 ________

5. 10 ________

Name_________________________ Class_____________ Date________

3.1 Cross Sections and Solids of Rotation

Resource Locker

Essential Question: What tools can you use to visualize solid figures accurately?

Explore Exploring Nets

A **net** is a diagram of the surfaces of a three-dimensional figure that can be folded to form the three-dimensional figure. To identify a three-dimensional figure from a net, look at the number of faces and the shape of each face.

(A) Complete each row of the table. Express the circumference of the cylinder as a multiple of π.

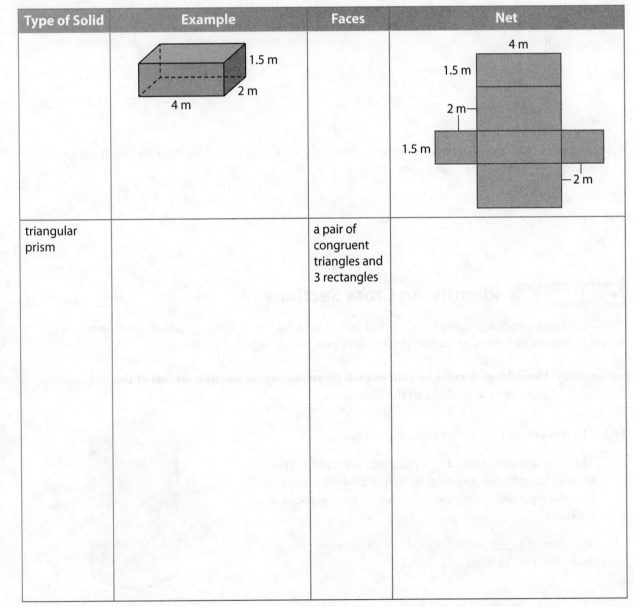

Type of Solid	Example	Faces	Net
	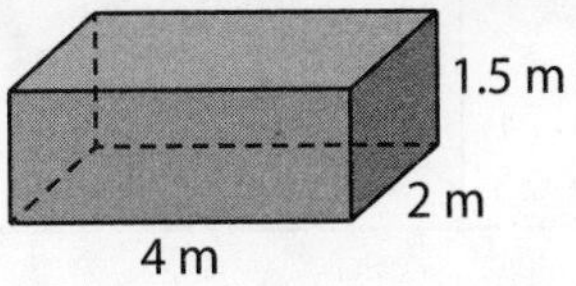		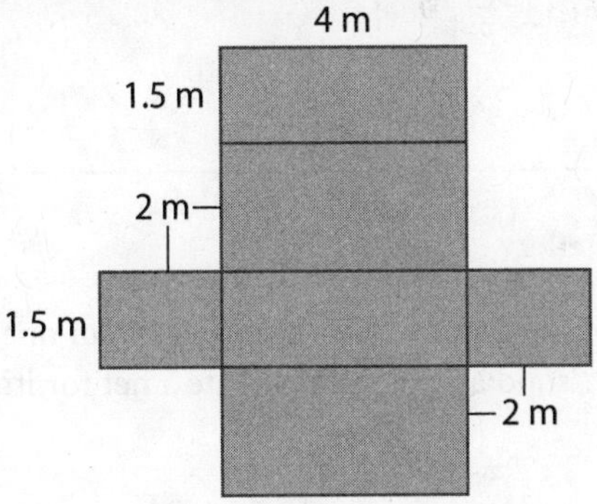
triangular prism		a pair of congruent triangles and 3 rectangles	

Type of Solid	Example	Faces	Net
		a rectangle and 2 pairs of congruent isosceles triangles	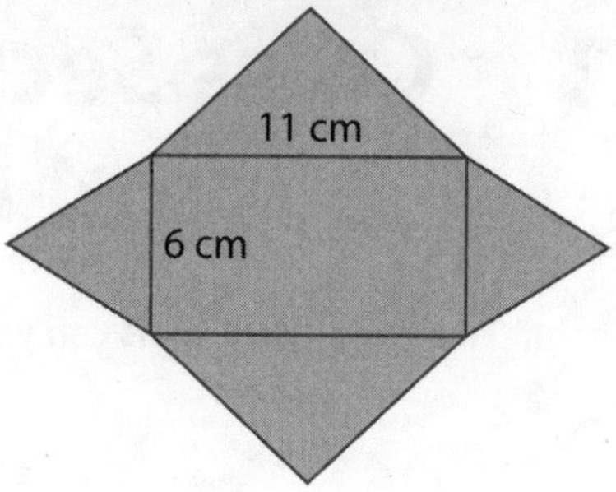
cylinder	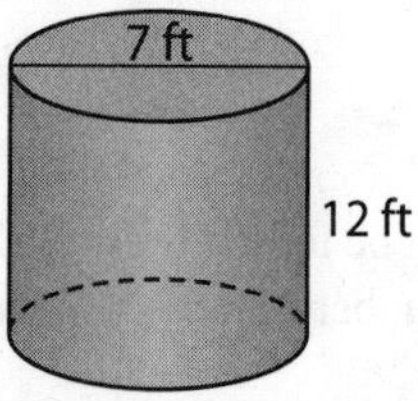		

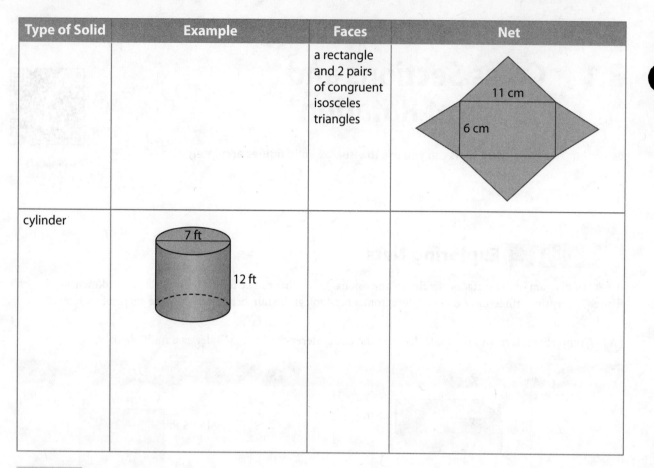

Reflect

1. **Discussion** Is there more than one way to draw a net for a solid? Are there rules for how the faces of a solid are joined to create a net for it?

____

____

____

Explain 1 Identifying Cross Sections

Recall that a *cross section* is a region of a plane that intersects a solid figure. Cross sections of three-dimensional figures sometimes turn out to be simple figures such as triangles, rectangles, or circles.

Example 1 **Describe each cross section of each figure. Compare the dimensions of the cross section to those of the figure.**

Ⓐ The bases of the cylinder are congruent circles.

The cross section is formed by a plane that is parallel to the bases of the cylinder. Any cross section of a cylinder made by a plane parallel to the bases will have the same shape as the bases.

Therefore, the cross section is a circle with the same radius or diameter as the bases.

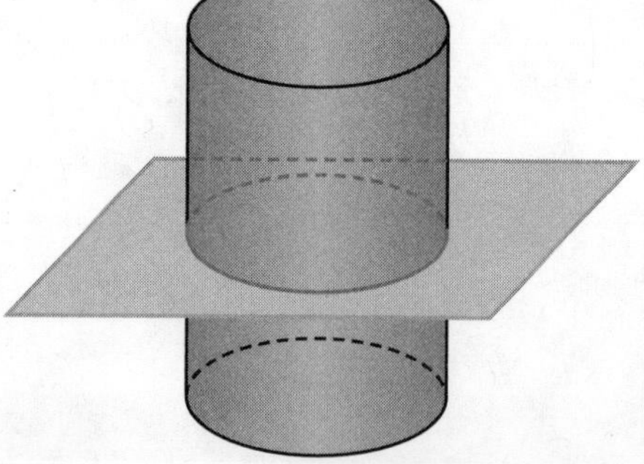

(B) The lateral surface of the cone curves in the horizontal direction, but not the vertical direction. Therefore the two sides of the cross section along this surface are straight line segments with equal lengths.

The third side is a diameter of the base of the cone. Therefore, the cross section is a(n) ______ triangle. Its base is the ______ of the cone and its leg length is the ______ height of the cone.

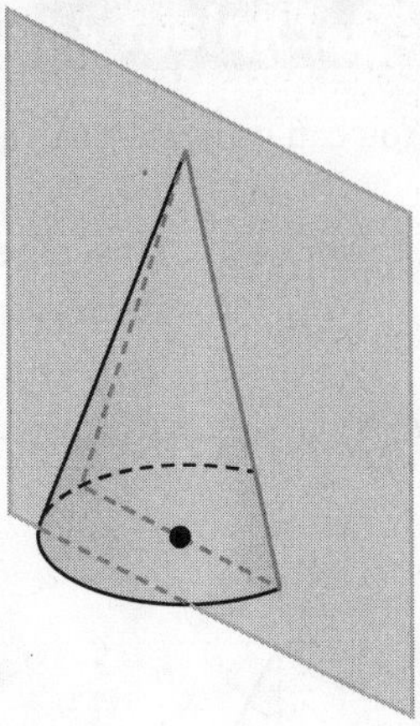

Reflect

2. A plane intersects a sphere. Make a conjecture about the resulting cross section.

______

Your Turn

Describe each cross section of each figure. Compare the dimensions of the cross section to those of the figure.

3.

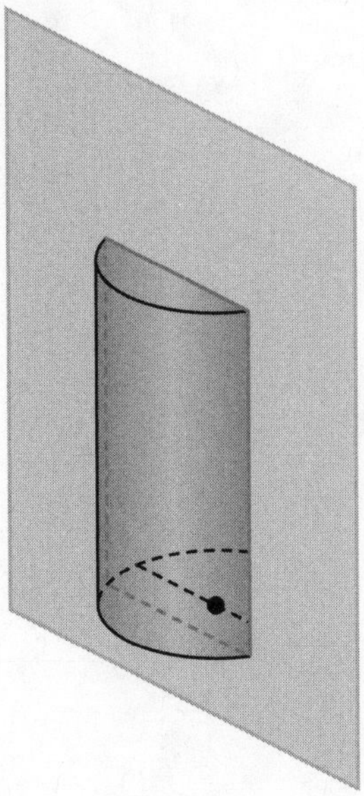

Explain 2 Generating Three-Dimensional Figures

You can generate a three-dimensional figure by rotating a two-dimensional figure around an appropriate axis.

Example 2 **Describe and then sketch the figure that is generated by each rotation in three-dimensional space.**

(A) A right triangle rotated around a line containing one of its legs

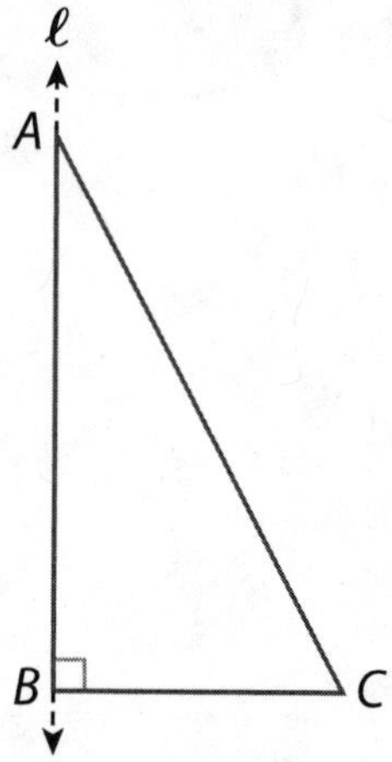

Leg $\overline{BC}$ is perpendicular to ℓ, so vertex C traces out a circle as it rotates about ℓ, and therefore $\overline{BC}$ traces out a circular base. The hypotenuse, $\overline{AC}$, traces out the curving surface of the cone whose base is formed by $\overline{BC}$. The figure formed by the rotation is a cone.

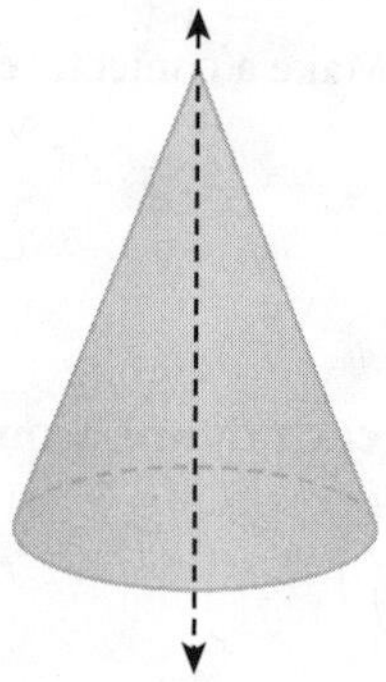

(B) A rectangle rotated around a line containing one of its sides

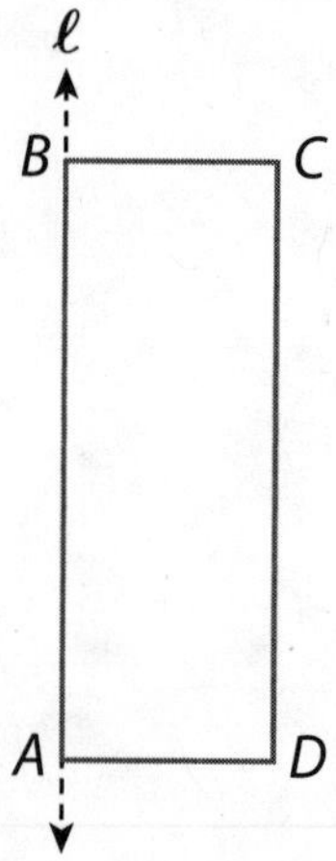

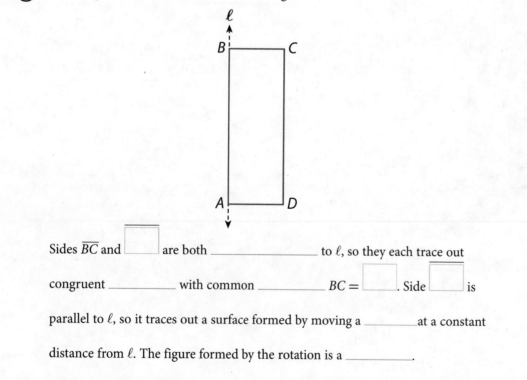

Sides $\overline{BC}$ and ____ are both ____ to ℓ, so they each trace out congruent ____ with common ____ $BC =$ ____. Side ____ is parallel to ℓ, so it traces out a surface formed by moving a ____ at a constant distance from ℓ. The figure formed by the rotation is a ____.

Reflect

4. **Discussion** What principles can you identify for generating a solid by rotation of a two-dimensional figure?

Your Turn

Describe and then sketch the figure that is generated by each rotation in three-dimensional space.

5. A trapezoid with two adjacent acute angles rotated around a line containing the side adjacent to these angles

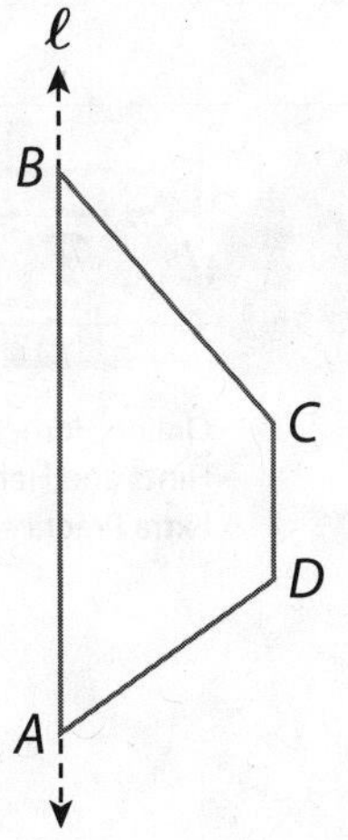

6. A semicircle rotated around a line containing its diameter

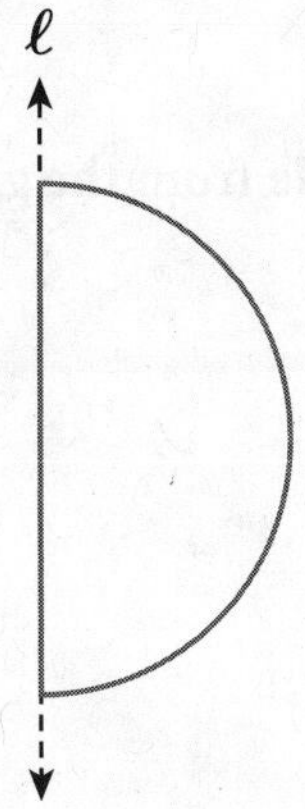

Elaborate

7. Discussion If a solid has been generated by rotating a plane figure around an axis, will the solid always have cross-sections that are circles? Will it always have cross sections that are not circles? Explain.

8. Essential Question Check-In What tools can you use to visualize solid figures? Explain how each tool is helpful.

Evaluate: Homework and Practice

Personal Math Trainer

- Online Homework
- Hints and Help
- Extra Practice

1. Which of the figures is not a net for a cube? Explain.

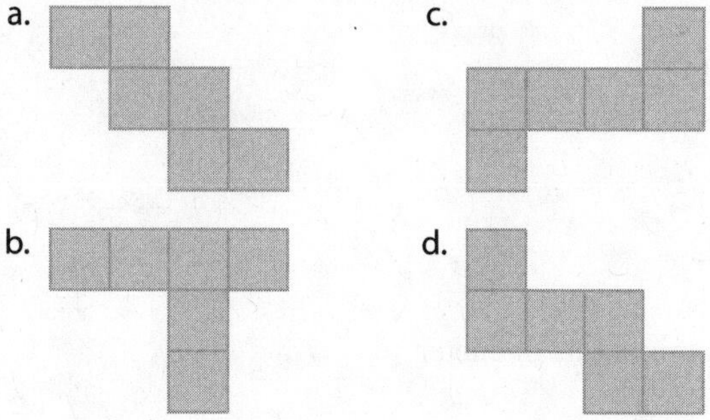

Describe the three-dimensional figure that can be made from the given net.

2.

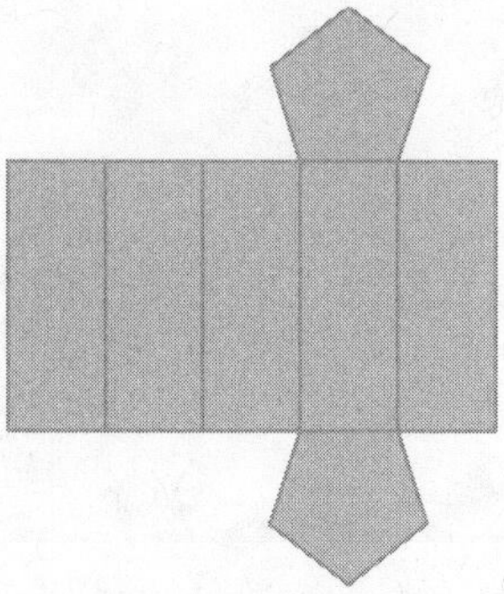

3.

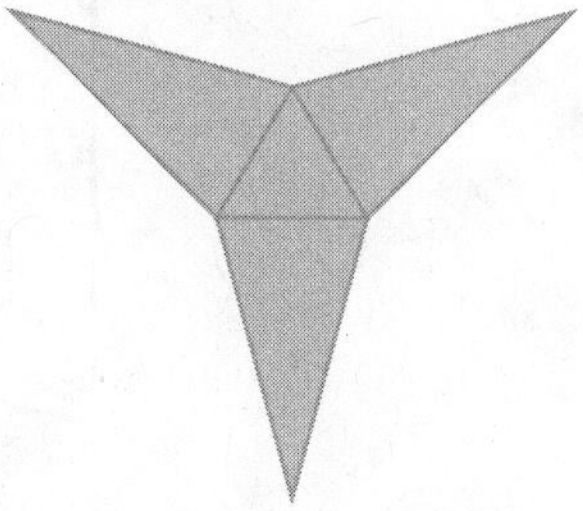

Describe the cross-section.

4.

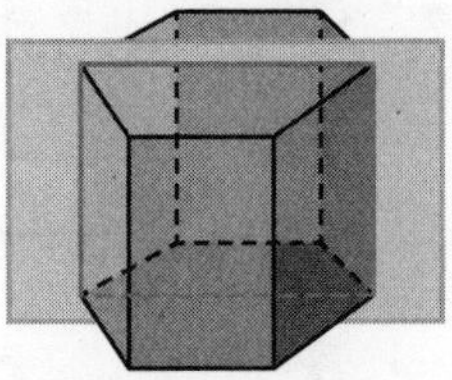

5.

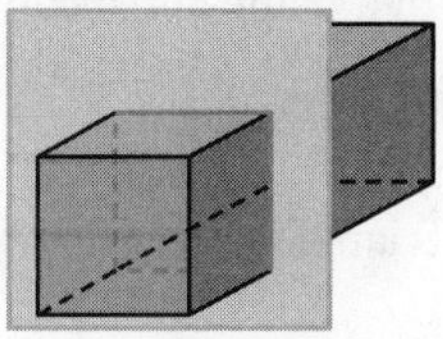

6.

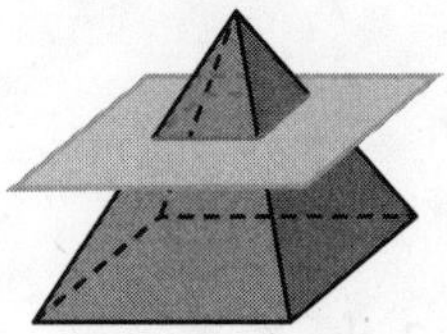

7.

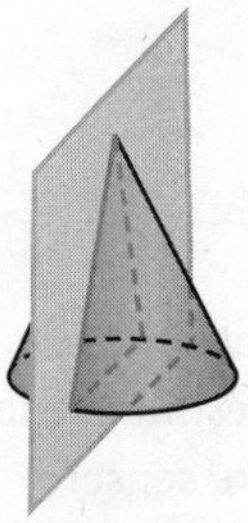

8.

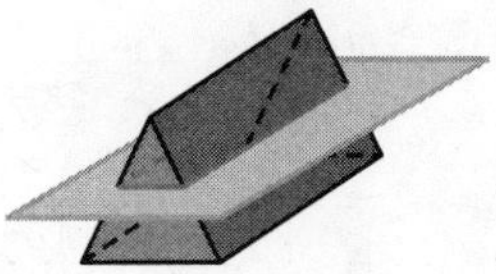

9.

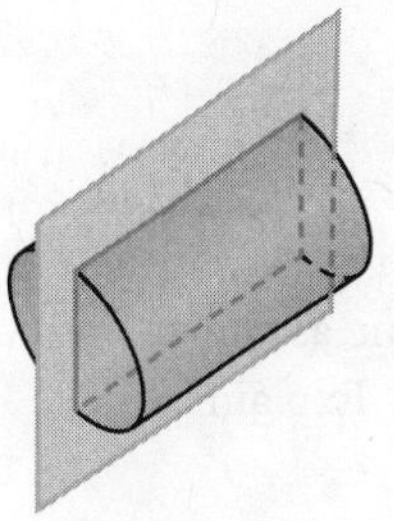

10. Describe the cross section formed by the intersection of a cone and a plane parallel to the base of the cone.

11. Describe the cross section formed by the intersection of a sphere and a plane that passes through the center of the sphere.

Sketch and describe the figure that is generated by each rotation in three-dimensional space.

12. Rotate a semicircle around a line through the endpoints of the semicircle.

13. Rotate an isosceles triangle around the triangle's line of symmetry.

14. Rotate an isosceles right triangle around a line that contains the triangle's hypotenuse

15. Rotate a line segment around a line that is perpendicular to the segment that passes through an endpoint to the segment.

16. **Multiple Response** Which of the following shapes could be formed by the intersection of a plane and a cube? Select all that apply.

A. Equilateral Triangle

B. Scalene Triangle

C. Square

D. Rectangle

E. Circle

17. A student claims that if you dilate the net for a cube using a scale factor of 2, the surface area of the resulting cube is multiplied by 4 and the volume is multiplied by 8. Does this claim make sense?

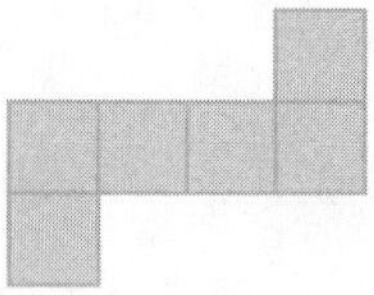

18. **Find the Error** A regular hexagonal prism is intersected by a plane as shown. Which cross section is incorrect? Explain.

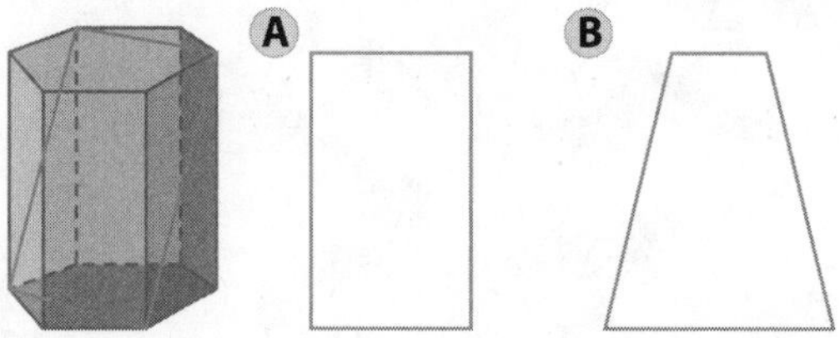

H.O.T. Focus on Higher Order Thinking

19. **Architecture** An architect is drawing plans for a building that is a hexagonal prism. Describe how the architect could draw a cutaway of the building that shows a cross section in the shape of a hexagon, and a cross section in the shape of a rectangle.

20. **Draw Conclusions** Is it possible for a cross section of a cube to be an octagon? Explain.

21. Communicate Mathematical Ideas A cube with sides of length *s* is intersected by a plane that passes through three of the cube's vertices, forming the cross section shown. What type of triangle is in the cross section? Explain.

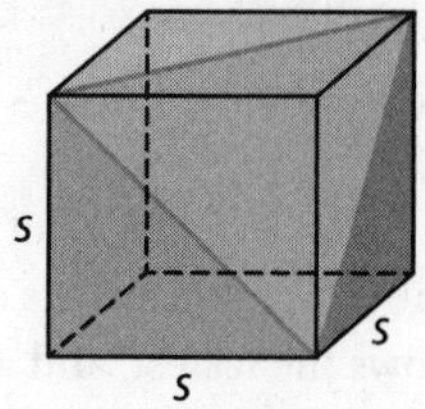

22. The three triangles all have the same area because each base and each height are congruent. Make and test a conjecture about the volume of the solids generated by rotating these triangles around the base.

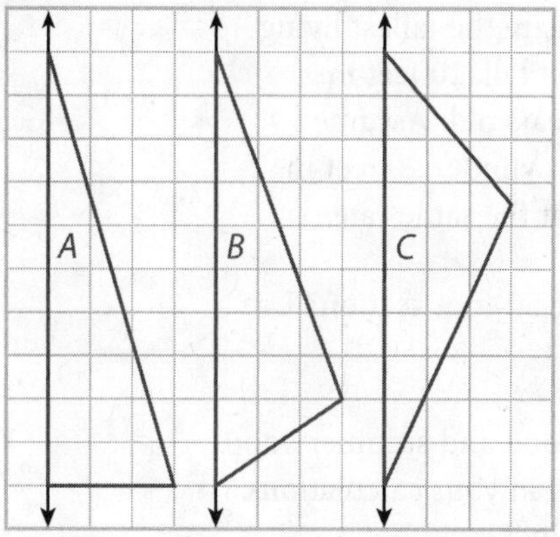

Lesson Performance Task

Each year of its life, a tree grows a new ring just under the outside bark. The new ring consists of two parts, light-colored *springwood*, when the tree grows the fastest, and a darker-colored *summerwood*, when growth slows. When conditions are good and there is lots of sun and rain, the new ring is thicker than the rings formed when there is drought or excessive cold. At the center of the tree is a dark circle called *pith* that is not connected to the age of the tree.

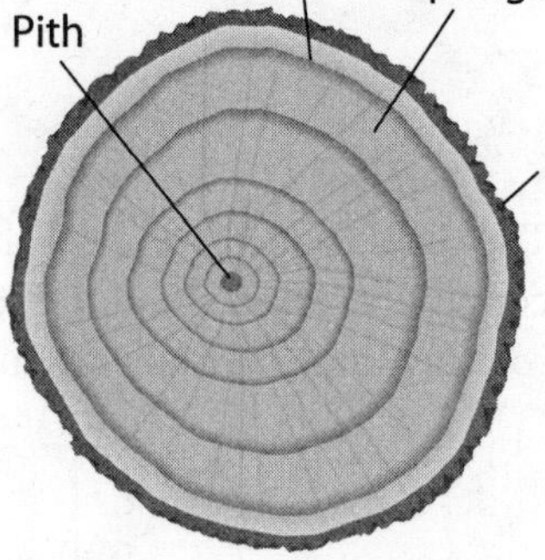

1. Describe the history of the tree in the diagram.

2. The redwood trees of coastal California are the tallest living things on earth. One redwood is 350 feet tall, 20 feet in diameter at its base, and around 2000 years old. Assume that the lower 50 feet of the tree form a cylinder 20 feet in diameter and that all of the rings grew at the same rate.

a. What is the total volume of wood in the 50-foot section? Use 3.14 for π.

b. How wide is each annual ring (springwood and summerwood combined)? Disregard the bark and pith in your calculations. Show your work. Write your answer in inches.

Name ________________ Class ________________ Date ________

3.2 Surface Area of Prisms and Cylinders

Resource Locker

Essential Question: How can you find the surface area of a prism or cylinder?

Explore Developing a Surface Area Formula

Surface area is the total area of all the faces and curved surfaces of a three-dimensional figure. The *lateral area* of a prism is the sum of the areas of the lateral faces.

(A) Consider the right prism shown here and the net for the right prism. Complete the figure by labeling the dimensions of the net.

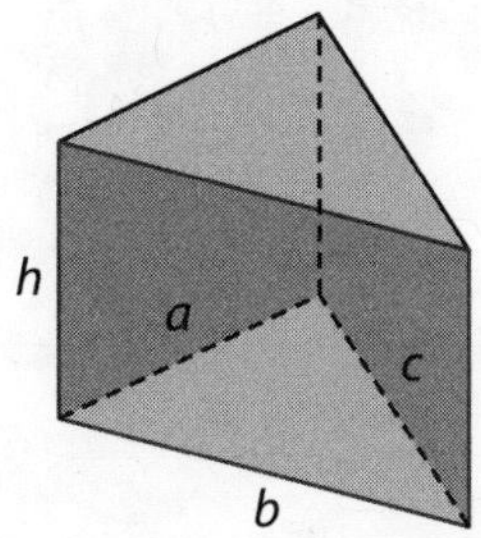

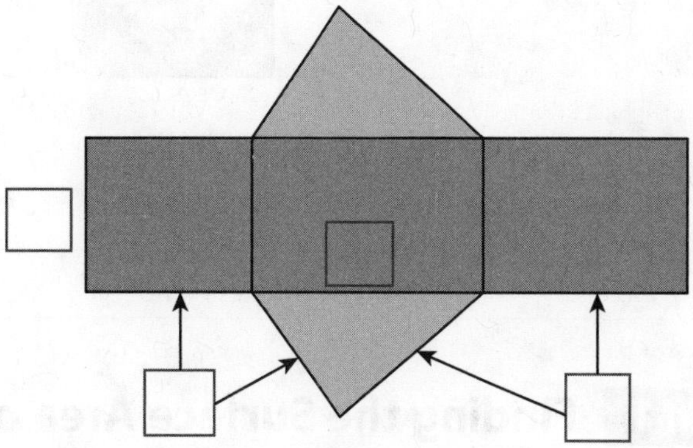

(B) In the net, what type of figure is formed by the lateral faces of the prism?

____

(C) Write an expression for the length of the base of the rectangle.

____

(D) How is the base of the rectangle related to the perimeter of the base of the prism?

____

(E) The lateral area L of the prism is the area of the rectangle. Write a formula for L in terms of h, a, b, and c.

____

(F) Write the formula for L in terms of P, where P is the perimeter of the base of the prism.

____

Ⓖ Let B be the area of the base of the prism. Write a formula for the surface area S of the prism in terms of B and L. Then write the formula in terms of B, P, and h.

Reflect

1. Explain why the net of the lateral surface of any right prism will always be a rectangle.

2. Suppose a rectangular prism has length ℓ, width w, and height h, as shown. Explain how you can write a formula for the surface area of the prism in terms of ℓ, w, and h.

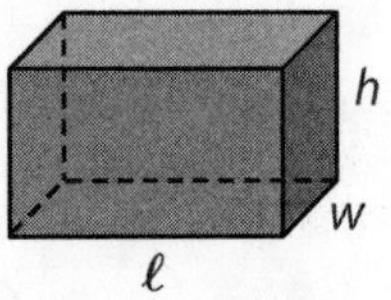

Explain 1 Finding the Surface Area of a Prism

Lateral Area and Surface Area of Right Prisms

The lateral area of a right prism with height h and base perimeter P is $L = Ph$.

The surface area of a right prism with lateral area L and base area B is $S = L + 2B$, or $S = Ph + 2B$.

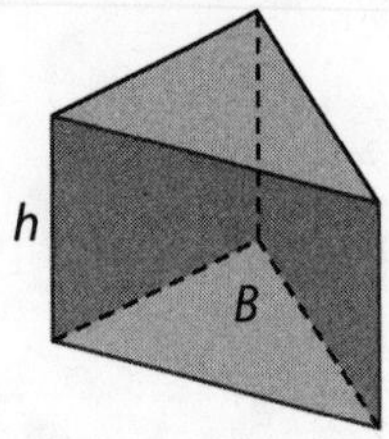

Example 1 **Each gift box is a right prism. Find the total amount of paper needed to wrap each box, not counting overlap.**

(A) **Step 1** Find the lateral area.

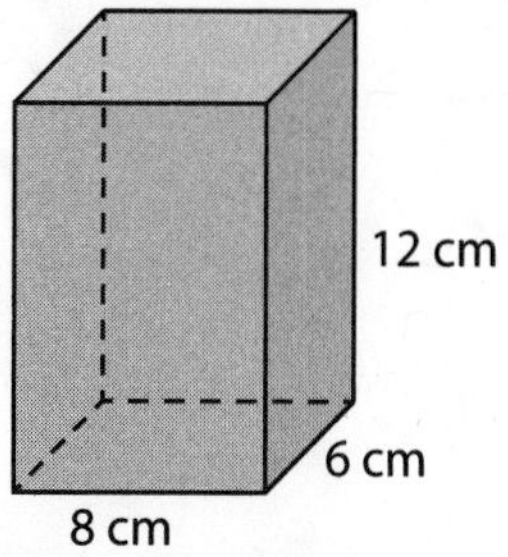

Lateral area formula	$L = Ph$
$P = 2(8) + 2(6) = 28$ cm	$= 28(12)$
Multiply.	$= 336 \text{ cm}^2$

Step 2 Find the surface area.

Surface area formula	$S = L + 2B$
Substitute the lateral area.	$= 336 + 2(6)(8)$
Simplify.	$= 432 \text{ cm}^2$

(B) **Step 1** Find the length *c* of the hypotenuse of the base.

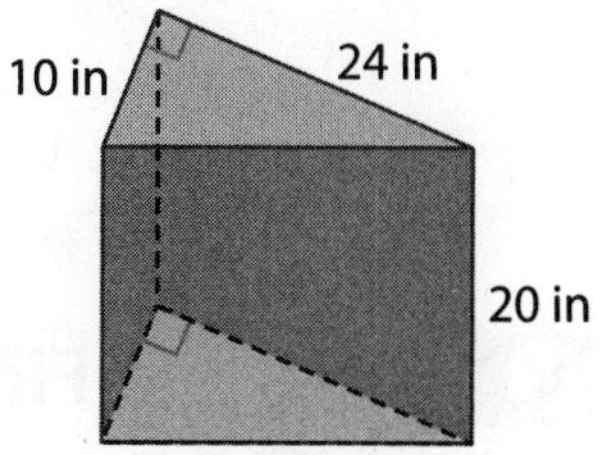

Pythagorean Theorem	$c^2 = a^2 + b^2$
Substitute.	$= \square^2 + \square^2$
Simplify.	$= \square$
Take the square root of each side.	$c = \square$

Step 2 Find the lateral area.

Lateral area formula	$L = Ph$
Substitute.	$= \square(\square)$
Multiply.	$= \square \text{ in}^2$

Step 3 Find the surface area.

Surface area formula	$S = L + 2B$
Substitute.	$= \square + 2 \cdot \frac{1}{2} \square \cdot \square$
Simplify.	$= \square \text{ in}^2$

Reflect

3. A gift box is a rectangular prism with length 9.8 cm, width 10.2 cm, and height 9.7 cm. Explain how to estimate the amount of paper needed to wrap the box, not counting overlap.

Your Turn

Each gift box is a right prism. Find the total amount of paper needed to wrap each box, not counting overlap.

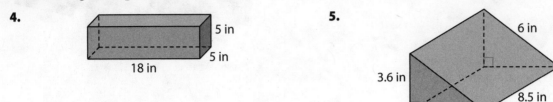

4.

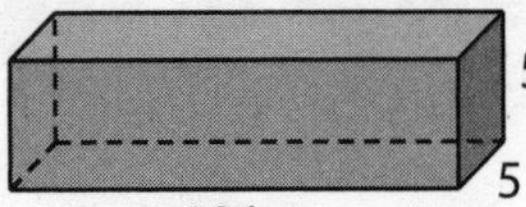

5.

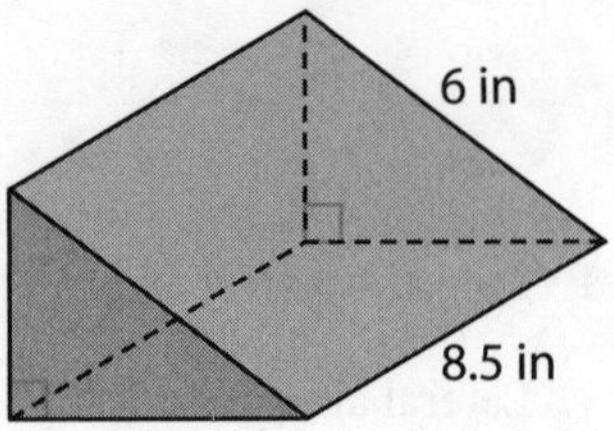

Explain 2 Finding the Surface Area of a Cylinder

Lateral Area and Surface Area of Right Cylinders

The *lateral area* of a cylinder is the area of the curved surface that connects the two bases.

The lateral area of a right cylinder with radius r and height h is $L = 2\pi rh$.

The surface area of a right cylinder with lateral area L and base area B is $S = L + 2B$, or $S = 2\pi rh + 2\pi r^2$.

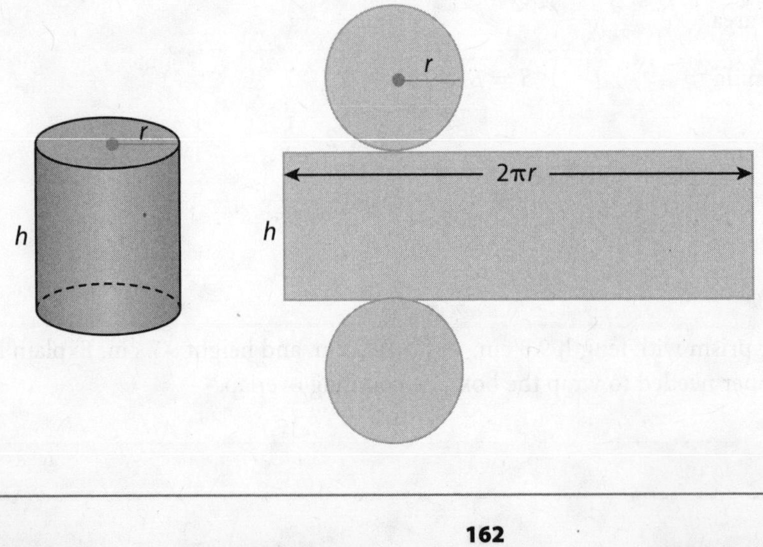

Example 2 **Each aluminum can is a right cylinder. Find the amount of paper needed for the can's label and the total amount of aluminum needed to make the can. Round to the nearest tenth.**

Ⓐ **Step 1** Find the lateral area.

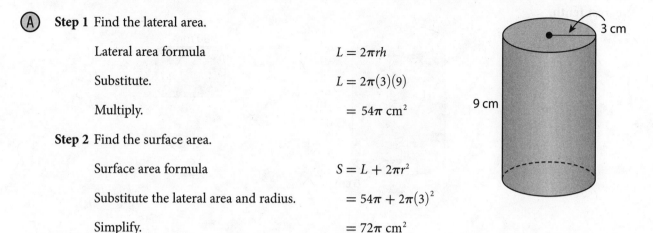

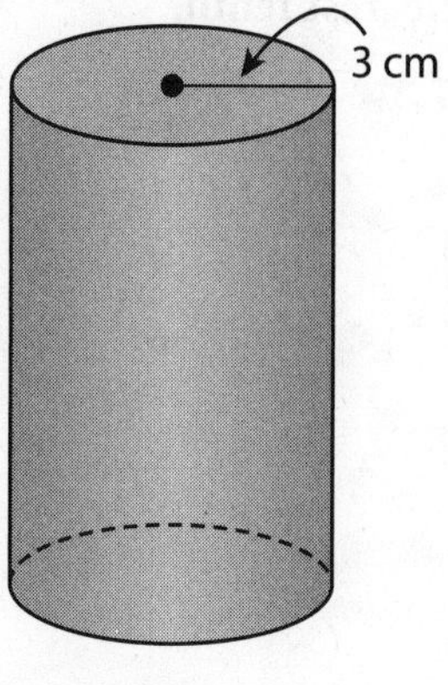

Lateral area formula $L = 2\pi rh$

Substitute. $L = 2\pi(3)(9)$

Multiply. $= 54\pi \text{ cm}^2$

Step 2 Find the surface area.

Surface area formula $S = L + 2\pi r^2$

Substitute the lateral area and radius. $= 54\pi + 2\pi(3)^2$

Simplify. $= 72\pi \text{ cm}^2$

Step 3 Use a calculator and round to the nearest tenth.

The amount of paper needed for the label is the lateral area, $54\pi \approx 169.6 \text{ cm}^2$.

The amount of aluminum needed for the can is the surface area, $72\pi \approx 226.2 \text{ cm}^2$.

Ⓑ **Step 1** Find the lateral area.

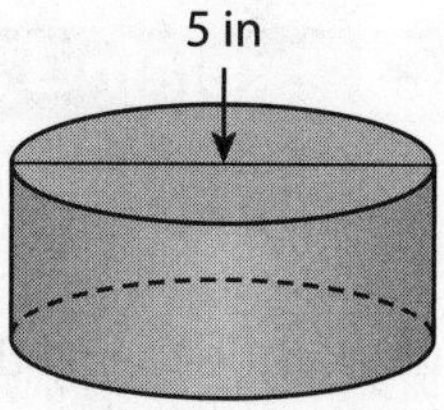

Lateral area formula $L = 2\pi rh$

Substitute; the radius is half the diameter. $= 2\pi(\square)(\square)$

Multiply. $= \square\pi \text{ in}^2$

Step 2 Find the surface area.

Surface area formula $S = L + 2\pi r^2$

Substitute the lateral area and radius. $= \square\pi + 2\pi(\square)^2$

Simplify. $= \square\pi \text{ in}^2$

Step 3 Use a calculator and round to the nearest tenth.

The amount of paper needed for the label is the lateral area, $\square\pi \approx \square \text{ in}^2$.

The amount of aluminum needed for the can is the surface area, $\square\pi \approx \square \text{ in}^2$.

Reflect

6. In these problems, why is it best to round only in the final step of the solution?

Your Turn

Each aluminum can is a right cylinder. Find the amount of paper needed for the can's label and the total amount of aluminum needed to make the can. Round to the nearest tenth.

7.

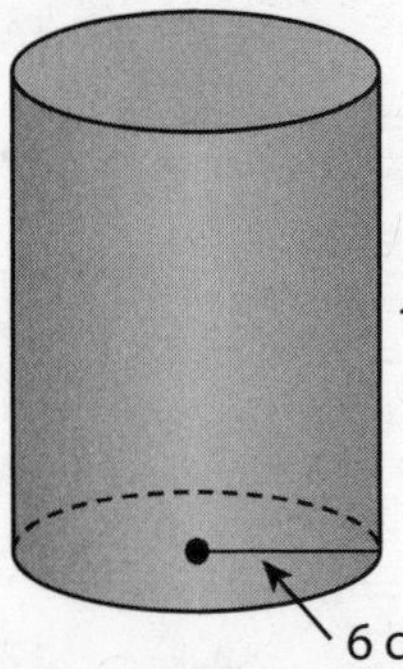

8.

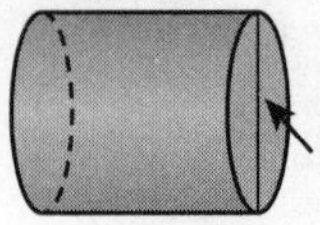

Explain 3 Finding the Surface Area of a Composite Figure

Example 3 **Find the surface area of each composite figure. Round to the nearest tenth.**

Ⓐ **Step 1** Find the surface area of the right rectangular prism.

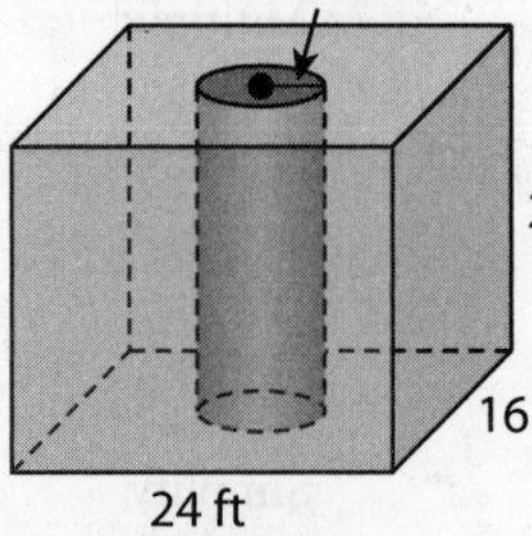

Surface area formula $S = Ph + 2B$

Substitute. $= 80(20) + 2(24)(16)$

Simplify. $= 2368 \text{ ft}^2$

Step 2 A cylinder is removed from the prism. Find the lateral area of the cylinder and the area of its bases.

Lateral area formula $L = 2\pi rh$

Substitute. $= 2\pi(4)(20)$

Simplify. $= 160\pi \text{ ft}^2$

Base area formula $B = \pi r^2$

Substitute. $= \pi(4)^2$

Simplify. $= 16\pi \text{ ft}^2$

Step 3 Find the surface area of the composite figure. The surface area is the sum of the areas of all surfaces on the exterior of the figure.

$S =$ (prism surface area) $+$ (cylinder lateral area) $-$ (cylinder base areas)

$= 2368 + 160\pi - 2(16\pi)$

$= 2368 + 128\pi \approx 2770.1 \text{ ft}^2$

Ⓑ Step 1 Find the surface area of the right rectangular prism.

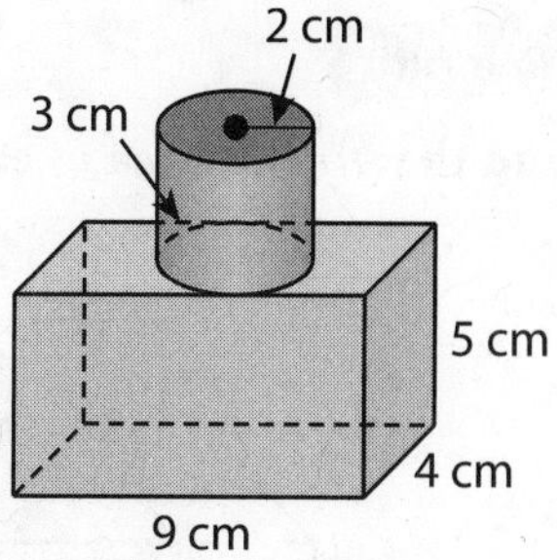

Surface area formula $S = Ph + 2B$

Substitute. $= \square(\square) + 2(\square)(\square)$

Simplify. $= \square$ cm^2

Step 2 Find the surface area of the cylinder.

Lateral area formula $L = 2\pi rh$

Substitute. $= 2\pi(\square)(\square)$

Simplify. $= \square \pi$ cm^2

Surface area formula $S = L + 2\pi r^2$

Substitute. $= \square \pi + 2\pi(\square)^2$

Simplify. $= \square \pi$ cm^2

Step 3 Find the surface area of the composite figure. The surface area is the sum of the areas of all surfaces on the exterior of the figure.

$S =$ (prism surface area) + (cylinder surface area) − 2(area of one cylinder base)

$= \square + \square \pi - 2\pi(\square)^2$

$= \square + \square \pi \approx \square$ cm^2

Reflect

9. **Discussion** A student said the answer in Part A must be incorrect since a part of the rectangular prism is removed, yet the surface area of the composite figure is greater than the surface area of the rectangular prism. Do you agree with the student? Explain.

Your Turn

Find the surface area of each composite figure. Round to the nearest tenth.

10.

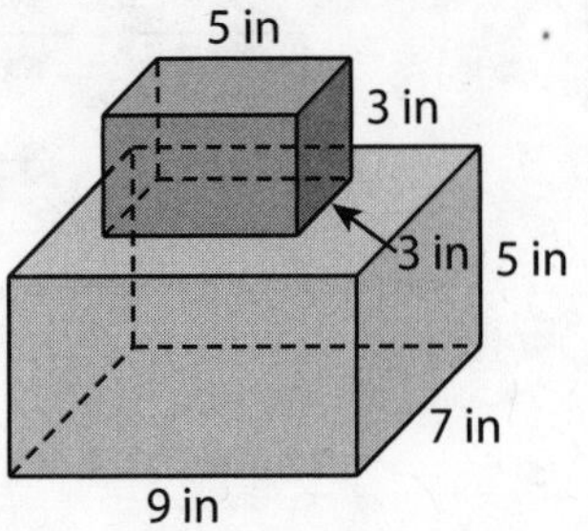

11.

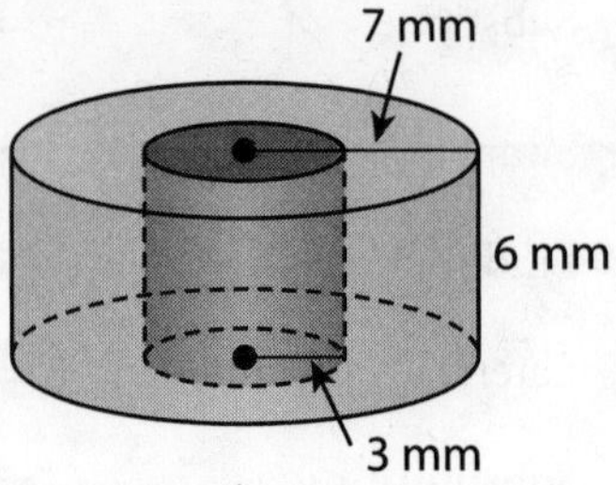

Elaborate

12. Can the surface area of a cylinder ever be less than the lateral area of the cylinder? Explain.

13. Is it possible to find the surface area of a cylinder if you know the height and the circumference of the base? Explain.

14. **Essential Question Check-In** How is finding the surface area of a right prism similar to finding the surface area of a right cylinder?

Evaluate: Homework and Practice

Personal Math Trainer

- Online Homework
- Hints and Help
- Extra Practice

Find the lateral area and surface area of each prism.

1.

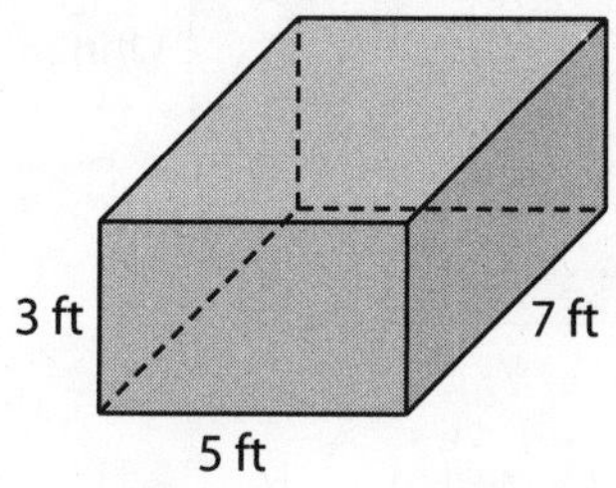

2.

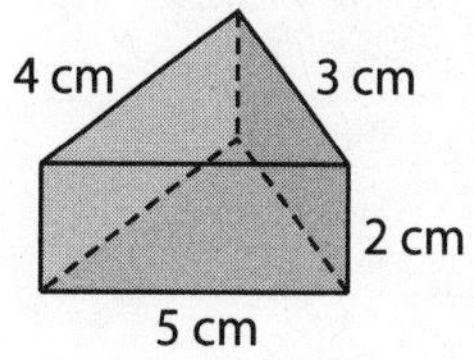

3.

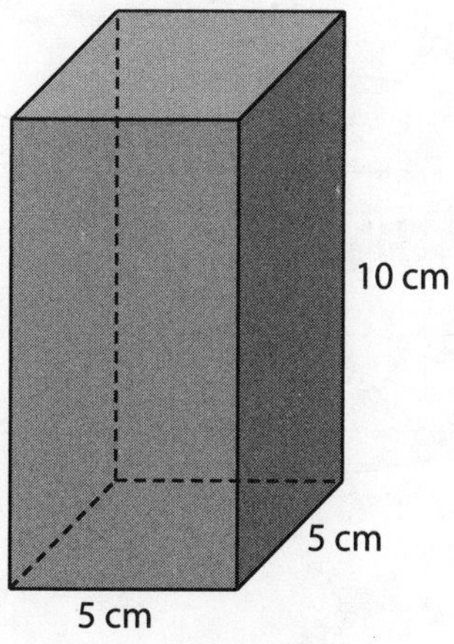

4.

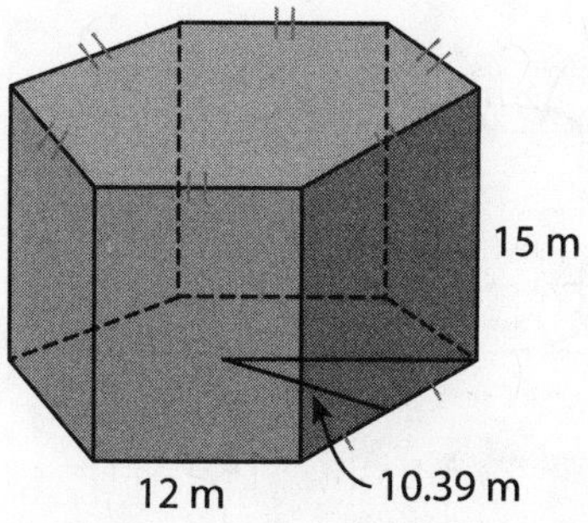

Find the lateral area and surface area of the cylinder. Leave your answer in terms of π.

5.

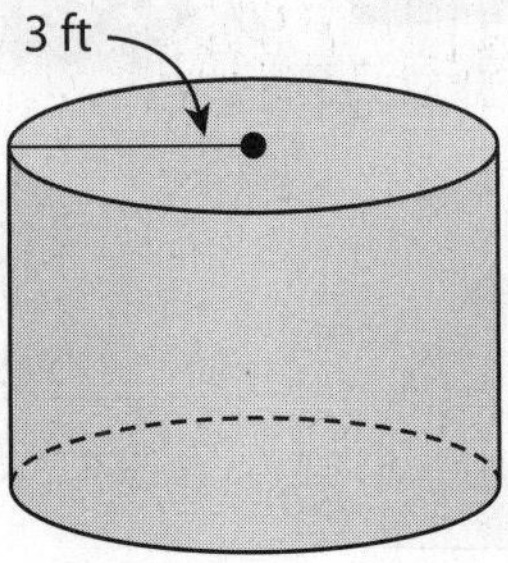

6.

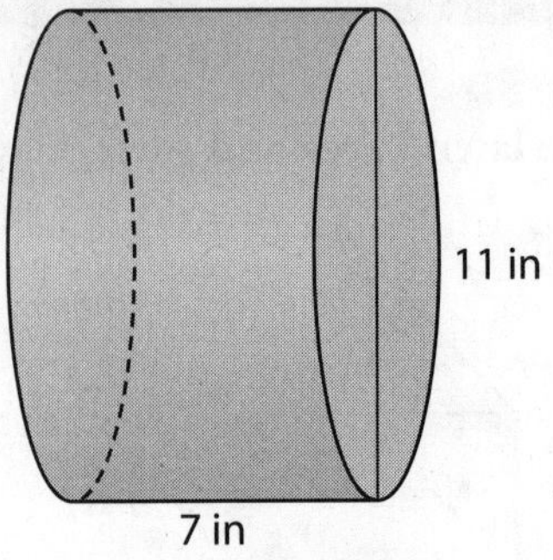

Find the total surface area of the composite figure. Round to the nearest tenth.

7.

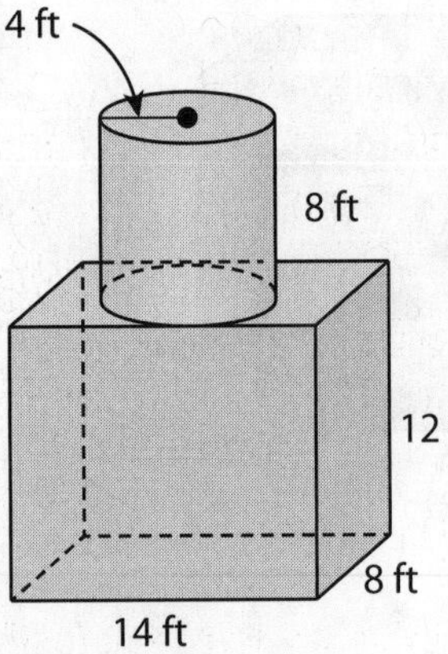

8.

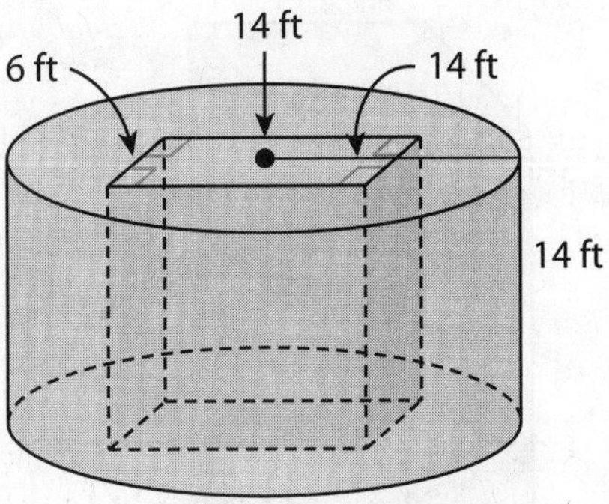

Find the total surface area of the composite figure. Round to the nearest tenth.

9.

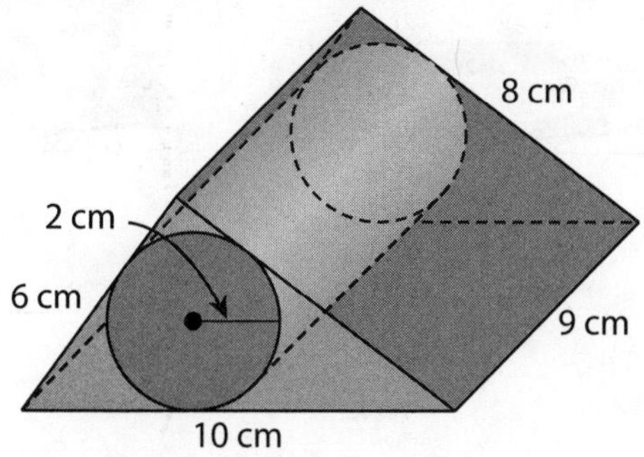

10.

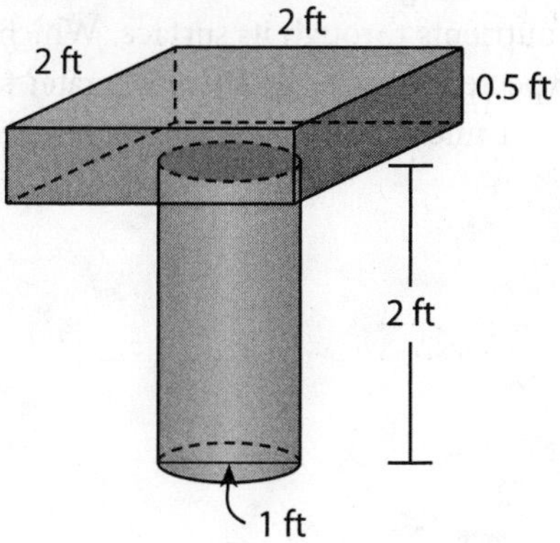

11. The greater the lateral area of a florescent light bulb, the more light the bulb produces. One cylindrical light bulb is 16 inches long with a 1-inch radius. Another cylindrical bulb is 23 inches long with a $\frac{3}{4}$-inch radius. Which bulb will produce more light?

12. Find the lateral and surface area of a cube with edge length 9 inches.

13. Find the lateral and surface area of a cylinder with base area 64π m^2 and a height 3 meters less than the radius.

14. Biology Plant cells are shaped approximately like a right rectangular prism. Each cell absorbs oxygen and nutrients through its surface. Which cell can be expected to absorb at a greater rate? (*Hint:* 1 μm = 1 micrometer = 0.000001 meter)

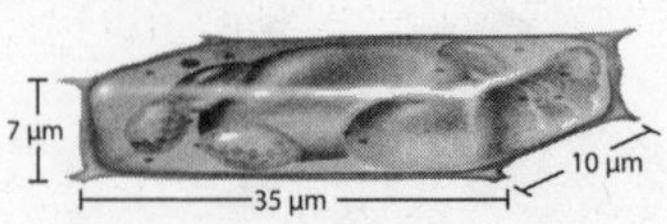

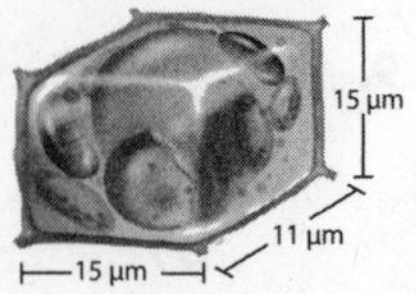

15. Find the height of a right cylinder with surface area 160π ft^2 and radius 5 ft.

16. Find the height of a right rectangular prism with surface area 286 m^2, length 10 m, and width 8 m.

17. Represent Real-World Problems If one gallon of paint covers 250 square feet, how many gallons of paint will be needed to cover the shed, not including the roof? If a gallon of paint costs $25, about how much will it cost to paint the walls of the shed?

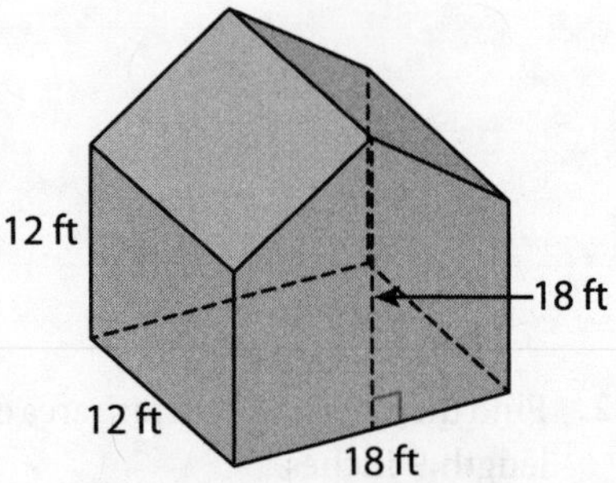

18. Match the Surface Area with the appropriate coin in the table.

Coin	Diameter (mm)	Thickness (mm)	Surface Area (mm^2)
Penny	19.05	1.55	
Nickel	21.21	1.95	
Dime	17.91	1.35	
Quarter	24.26	1.75	

A. 836.58

B. 579.82

C. 662.81

D. 1057.86

19. Algebra The lateral area of a right rectangular prism is 144 cm^2. Its length is three times its width, and its height is twice its width. Find its surface area.

20. A cylinder has a radius of 8 cm and a height of 3 cm. Find the height of another cylinder that has a radius of 4 cm and the same surface area as the first cylinder.

H.O.T. Focus on Higher Order Thinking

21. Analyze Relationships Ingrid is building a shelter to protect her plants from freezing. She is planning to stretch plastic sheeting over the top and the ends of the frame. Assume that the triangles in the frame on the left are equilateral. Which of the frames shown will require more plastic? Explain how finding the surface area of these figures is different from finding the lateral surface area of a figure.

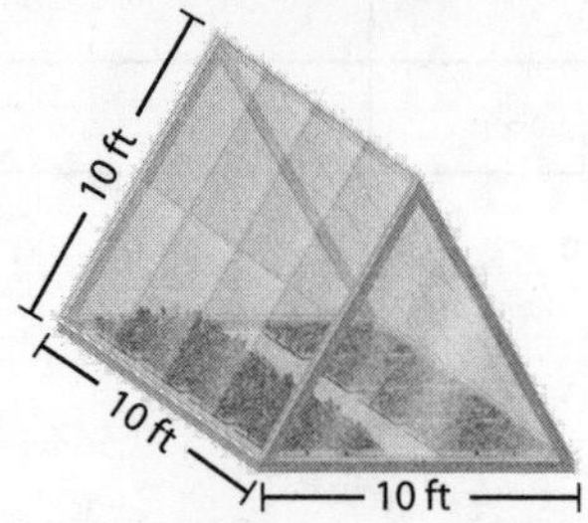

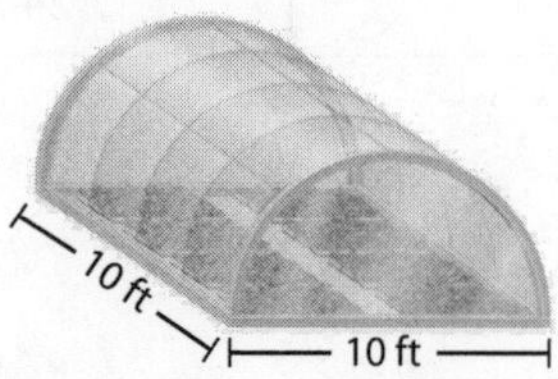

22. Draw Conclusions Explain how the edge lengths of a rectangular prism can be changed so that the surface area is multiplied by 9.

Lesson Performance Task

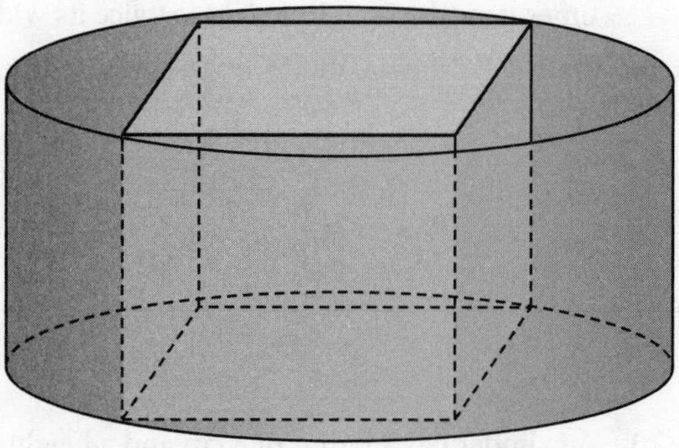

A manufacturer of number cubes has the bright idea of packaging them individually in cylindrical boxes. Each number cube measures 2 inches on a side.

1. What is the surface area of each cube?

2. What is the surface area of the cylindrical box? Assume the cube fits snugly in the box and that the box includes a top. Use 3.14 for π.

Name _______________ Class _______ Date _______

3.3 Surface Area of Pyramids and Cones

Resource Locker

Essential Question: How is the formula for the lateral area of a regular pyramid similar to the formula for the lateral area of a right cone?

Explore Developing a Surface Area Formula

The base of a **regular pyramid** is a regular polygon, and the lateral faces are congruent isosceles triangles.

(A) The lateral faces of a regular pyramid can be arranged to cover half of a rectangle whose height is equal to the slant height of the pyramid. Complete the figure by labeling the missing dimensions.

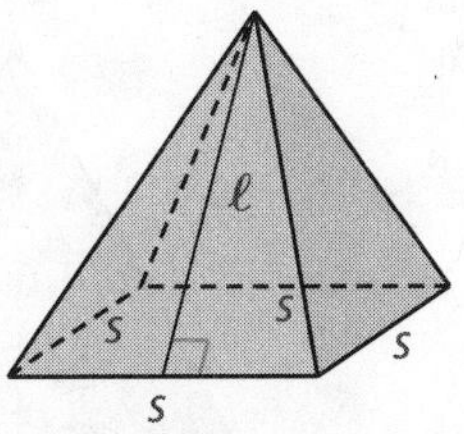

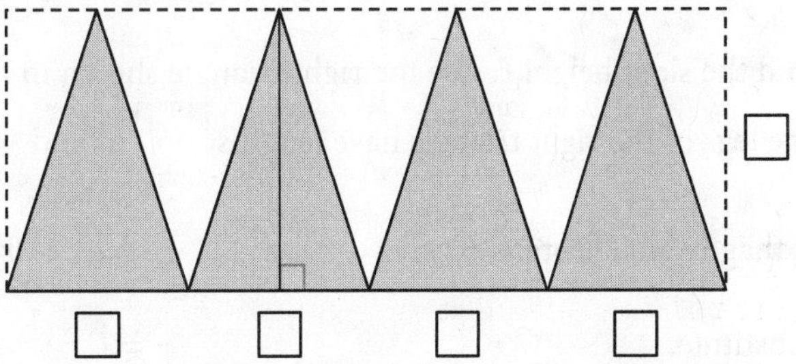

(B) Write an expression for the length of the rectangle in terms of s.

____

(C) How does the length of the rectangle compare to P, the perimeter of the base of the pyramid?

____

(D) Write an expression for the area of the rectangle in terms of P and ℓ.

____

(E) Write a formula for the lateral area L of the pyramid. (*Hint*: Use the fact that the lateral faces of the pyramid cover half of the rectangle.)

____

(F) Let B be the base area of the pyramid. Write a formula for the surface area S of the pyramid in terms of B and L. Then write the formula in terms of B, P, and ℓ.

____

Reflect

1. Discussion The pyramid in the above figure has a square base. Do your formulas only hold for square pyramids or do they hold for other pyramids as well? Explain.

____

____

Explain 1 Finding the Surface Area of a Pyramid

Lateral Area and Surface Area of a Regular Pyramid

The lateral area of a regular pyramid with perimeter P and slant height ℓ is $L = \frac{1}{2}P\ell$.

The surface area of a regular pyramid with lateral area L and base area B is $S = L + B$, or $S = \frac{1}{2}P\ell + B$.

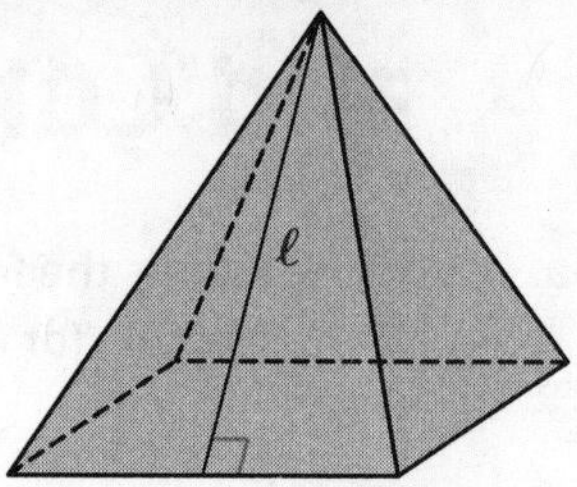

Example 1 **Find the lateral area and surface area of each regular pyramid.**

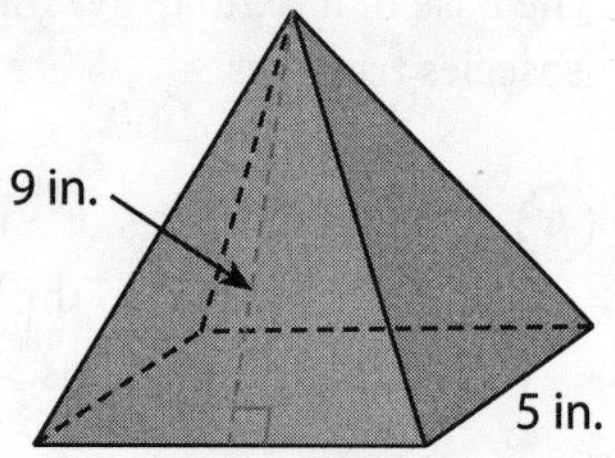

(A) **Step 1** Find the lateral area.

Lateral area formula $L = \frac{1}{2}P\ell$

$P = 4(5) = 20$ in. $= \frac{1}{2}(20)(9)$

Multiply. $= 90 \text{ in}^2$

Step 2 Find the surface area.

Surface area formula $S = L + B$

Substitute the lateral area; $B = 5^2 = 25$ in. $= 90 + 25$

Add. $= 115 \text{ in}^2$

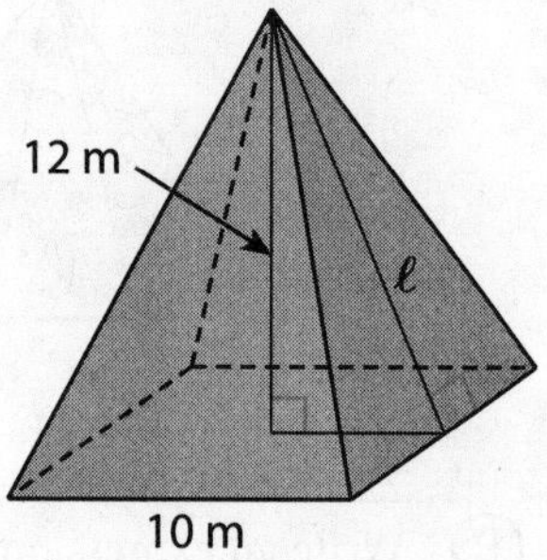

(B) **Step 1** Find the slant height ℓ. Use the right triangle shown in the figure.

The legs of the right triangle have lengths ___ m and ___ m.

Pythagorean Theorem $\ell^2 = a^2 + b^2$

Substitute. $= \underline{\quad}^2 + \underline{\quad}^2$

Simplify. $= \underline{\quad}$

Take the square root of each side. $\ell = \underline{\quad}$

Step 2 Find the lateral area.

Lateral area formula $L = \frac{1}{2}P\ell$

Substitute. $= \frac{1}{2}(\underline{\quad})(\underline{\quad})$

Multiply. $= \underline{\quad}\ \text{m}^2$

Step 3 Find the surface area.

Surface area formula $S = L + B$

Substitute. $= \underline{\quad} + \underline{\quad}^2$

Simplify. $= \underline{\quad}\ \text{m}^2$

Reflect

2. Can you use the formula $L = \frac{1}{2}P\ell$ to find the lateral area of a pyramid whose base is a scalene triangle? If so, describe the dimensions that you need to know. If not, explain why not.

Your Turn

Find the lateral area and surface area of each regular pyramid. Round to the nearest tenth, if necessary.

3.

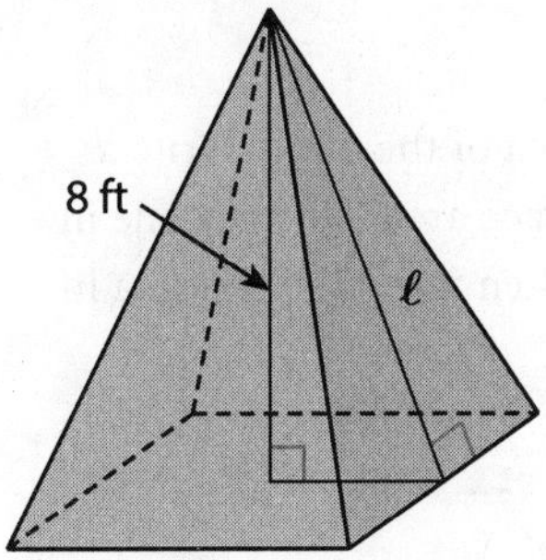

4.

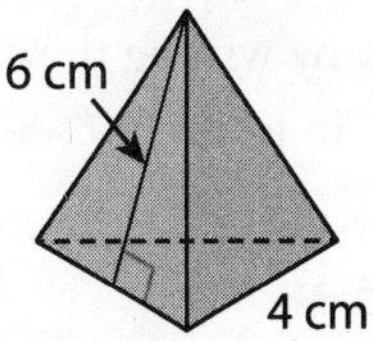

Explain 2 Developing Another Surface Area Formula

The axis of a cone is a segment with endpoints at the vertex and the center of the base. A **right cone** is a cone whose axis is perpendicular to the base.

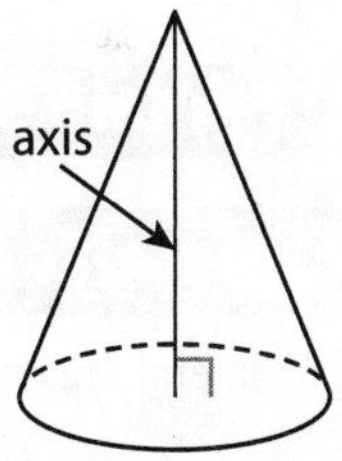

Right Cone

Example 2 **Justify a formula for the surface area of a cone.**

(A) A net for a right cone consists of a circle and a sector of a circle, as shown. Complete the figure by labeling the missing dimensions.

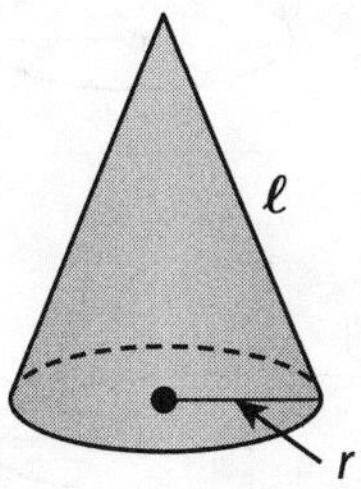

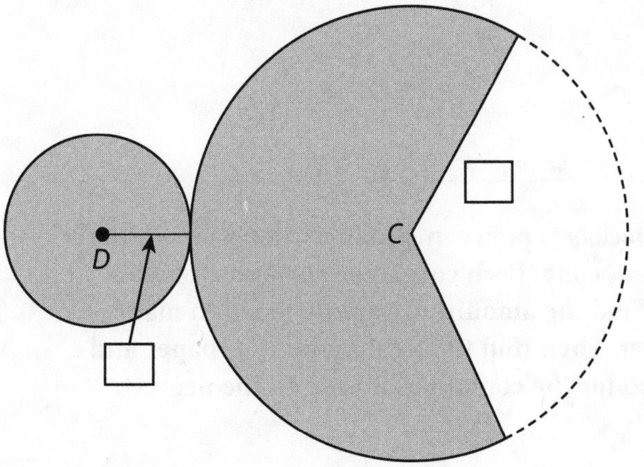

(B) Consider the shaded sector in the net. Complete the proportion.

$$\frac{\text{Area of sector}}{\text{Area of} \odot C} = \frac{\text{Arc length of sector}}{\boxed{}}$$

(C) Multiply both sides of the proportion by the area of $\odot$ C. Complete the equation.

$$\text{Area of sector} = \frac{\text{Arc length of sector}}{\boxed{}} \cdot \text{Area of} \odot C$$

(D) The arc length of the sector is equal to the circumference of $\odot D$. Therefore, the arc length of the sector equals $2\pi r$. Complete the equation by substituting this expression for the arc length of the sector and by writing the circumference and area of $\odot C$ in terms of ℓ.

Area of sector $= \frac{\square}{\square} \cdot \square$

(E) Simplify the right side of the equation as much as possible.

Area of sector $= \square$

(F) The area of the sector in Step E is the lateral area L of the cone. Complete the formula.

$L = \square$

(G) Let B be the base area of the cone. Write a formula for the surface area S of the cone in terms of B and L. Then write the formula in terms of r and ℓ.

____

Reflect

5. In Step D, why is the arc length of the sector equal to the circumference of $\odot D$?

____

____

Explain 3 Finding the Surface Area of a Cone

Lateral Area and Surface Area of a Right Cone

The lateral area of a right cone with radius r and slant height ℓ is $L = \pi r \ell$.

The surface area of a right cone with lateral area L and base area B is $S = L + B$, or $S = \pi r \ell + \pi r^2$.

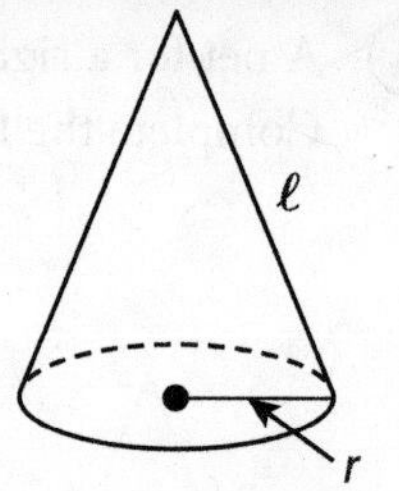

Example 3 **A company packages popcorn in paper containers in the shape of a right cone. Each container also has a plastic circular lid. Find the amount of paper needed to make each container. Then find the total amount of paper and plastic needed for the container. Round to the nearest tenth.**

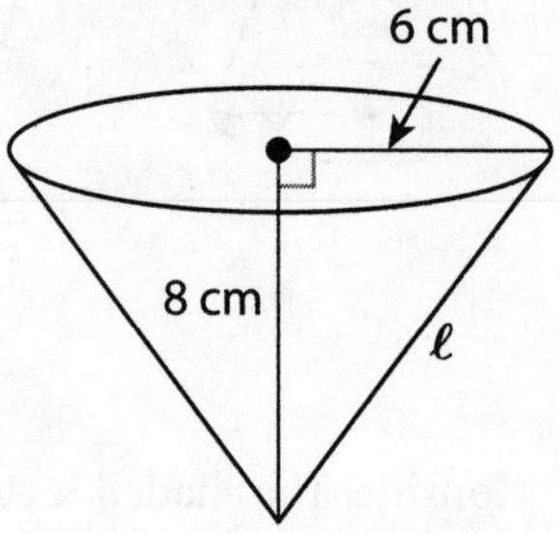

(A) **Step 1** Find the slant height.

Pythagorean Theorem	$\ell^2 = 6^2 + 8^2$
Simplify.	$= 100$
Take the square root of each side.	$\ell = 10$

Step 2 Find the lateral area.

Lateral area formula	$L = \pi r \ell$
Substitute.	$= \pi(6)(10)$
Multiply.	$= 60\pi \text{ cm}^2$

Step 3 Find the surface area.

Surface area formula	$S = L + \pi r^2$
Substitute.	$= 60\pi + \pi(6)^2$
Simplify.	$= 96\pi \text{ cm}^2$

Step 4 Use a calculator and round to the nearest tenth.

The amount of paper needed for the container is the lateral area, $60\pi \approx 188.5$ cm². The amount of paper and plastic needed for the container is the surface area, $96\pi \approx 301.6$ cm².

(B) **Step 1** Find the radius.

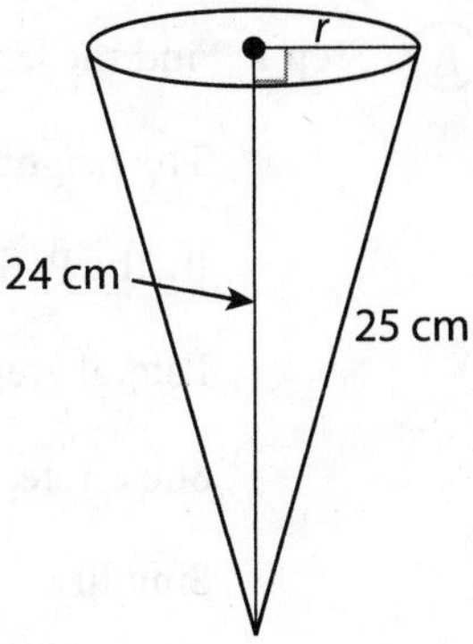

Pythagorean Theorem $\square^2 = r^2 + \square^2$

Simplify. $\square = r^2 + \square$

Subtract $\square$ from each side. $\square = r^2$

Take the square root of each side. $\square = r$

Step 2 Find the lateral area. $L = \pi r\ell$

Substitute and simplify. $= \pi(\square)(\square) = \square\,\pi$ cm²

Step 3 Find the surface area. $S = L + \pi r^2$

Substitute and simplify. $= \square\,\pi + \pi(\square)^2 = \square\,\pi$ cm²

Step 4 Use a calculator and round to the nearest tenth.

The amount of paper needed for the container is the lateral area, $\square\,\pi \approx \square$ cm².

The amount of paper and plastic needed for the container is $\square\,\pi \approx \square$ cm².

Reflect

6. Two right cones have the same radius. A student said that the cone with the greater slant height must have the greater lateral area. Do you agree? Explain.

____

____

Your Turn

A company makes candles in the shape of a right cone. The lateral surface of each candle is covered with paper for shipping and each candle also has a plastic circular base. Find the amount of paper needed to cover the lateral surface of each candle. Then find the total amount of paper and plastic needed. Round to the nearest tenth.

7.

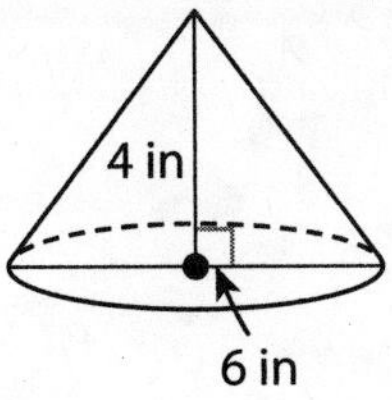

8.

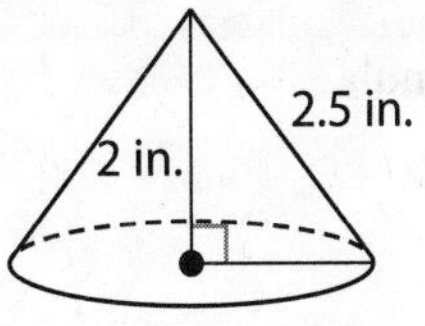

Explain 4 Finding the Surface Area of a Composite Figure

Example 4 **Find the surface area of each composite figure. Round to the nearest tenth.**

Ⓐ **Step 1** Find the lateral area of the cone.

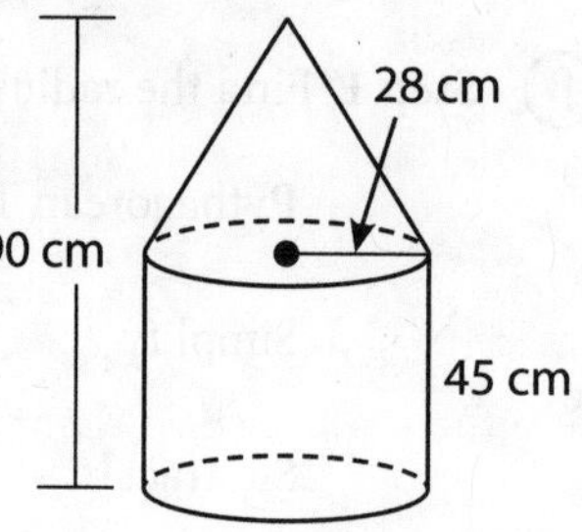

The height of the cone is $90 - 45 = 45$ cm.

By the Pythagorean Theorem, $\ell = \sqrt{28^2 + 45^2} = 53$ cm.

Lateral area formula	$L = \pi r \ell$
Substitute.	$= \pi(28)(53)$
Simplify.	$= 1484\pi \text{ cm}^2$

Step 2 Find the lateral area of the cylinder.

Lateral area	$L = 2\pi rh$
Substitute.	$= 2\pi(28)(45)$
Simplify.	$= 2520\pi \text{ cm}^2$

Step 3 Find the area of the base of the cylinder.

Area of circle	$B = \pi r^2$
Substitute.	$= \pi(28)^2$
Simplify.	$= 784\pi \text{ cm}^2$

Step 4 Find the surface area of the composite figure.

$S =$ (cone lateral area) + (cylinder lateral area) + (base area)

$= 1484\pi + 2520\pi + 784\pi$

$= 4788\pi \approx 15,041.9 \text{ cm}^2$

Ⓑ **Step 1** Find the slant height of the pyramid.

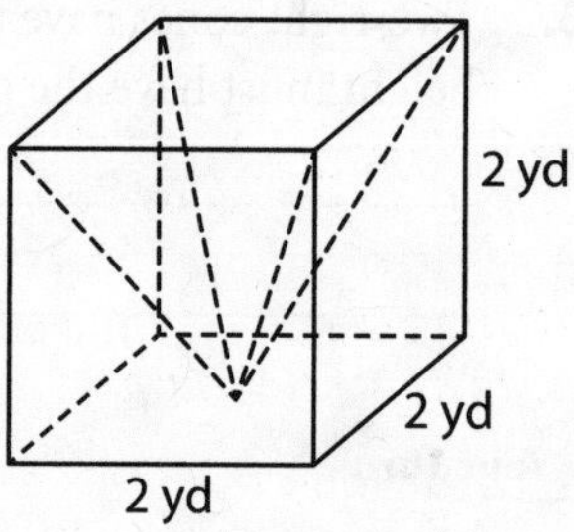

By the Pythagorean Theorem, $\ell = \sqrt{\square^2 + \square^2} = \square$ yd.

Step 2 Find the lateral area of the pyramid.

Lateral area formula	$L = \frac{1}{2}P\ell$
Substitute.	$= \frac{1}{2}(\square)(\square)$
Simplify.	$= \square \text{ yd}^2$

Step 3 Find the lateral area of the rectangular prism.

Lateral area formula	$L = Ph$
Substitute.	$= (\square)(\square)$
Simplify.	$= \square \text{ yd}^2$

Step 4 Find the surface area of the composite figure.

$S =$ (pyramid lateral area) + (prism lateral area) + (base area)

$= \square + \square + \square$

$= \square \approx \square \text{ yd}^2$

Reflect

9. How can you check that your answer in Part B is reasonable?

Your Turn

Find the surface area of each composite figure. Round to the nearest tenth.

10.

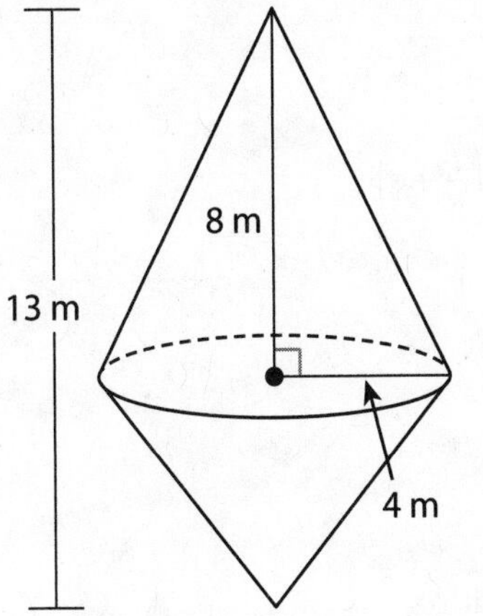

11.

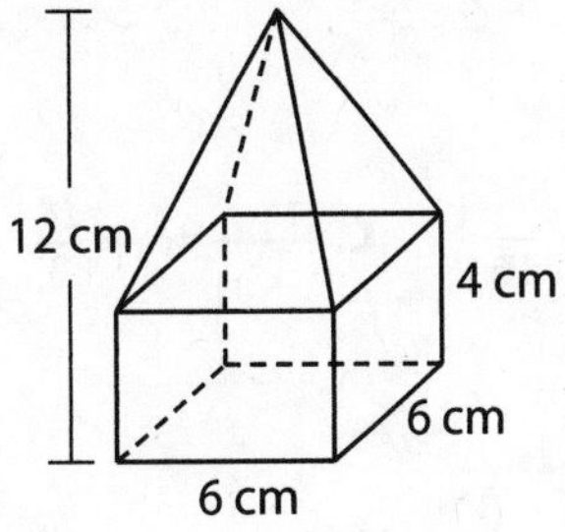

Elaborate

12. A regular pyramid has a base that is an equilateral triangle with sides 16 inches long. Is it possible to determine the surface area of the pyramid? If not, what additional information do you need?

13. Explain how to estimate the lateral area of a right cone with radius 5 cm and slant height 6 cm. Is your estimate an underestimate or overestimate? Explain.

14. **Essential Question Check-In** How is the formula for the lateral area of a regular pyramid similar to the formula for the lateral area of a right cone?

Evaluate: Homework and Practice

- Online Homework
- Hints and Help
- Extra Practice

1. **Multiple Response** Which expression represents the surface area of the regular square pyramid shown? Select all that apply.

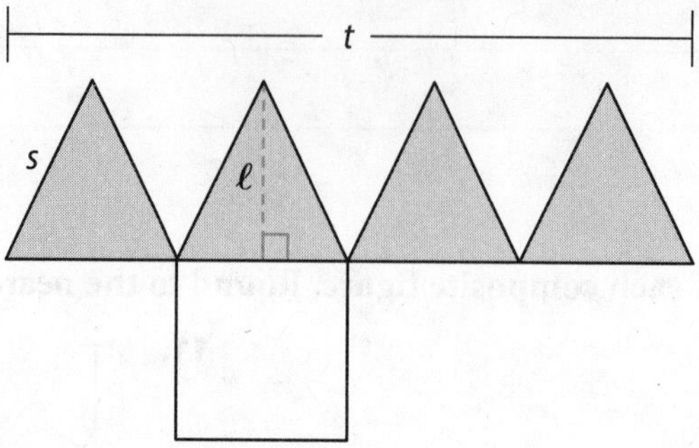

A. $\frac{t^2}{16} + \frac{ts}{2}$ **B.** $\frac{t^2}{16}$ **C.** $\frac{t^2}{4} + t\ell + \frac{t\ell}{2}$ **D.** $\frac{t}{2}\left(\frac{t}{8} + \ell\right)$ **E.** $\frac{t}{2}\left(\frac{t}{8} + s\right)$

2. **Justify Reasoning** A frustum of a pyramid is a part of the pyramid with two parallel bases. The lateral faces of the frustum are trapezoids. Use the area formula for a trapezoid to derive a formula for the lateral area of a frustum of a regular square pyramid with base edge lengths b_1 and b_2 and slant height ℓ. Show all of your steps.

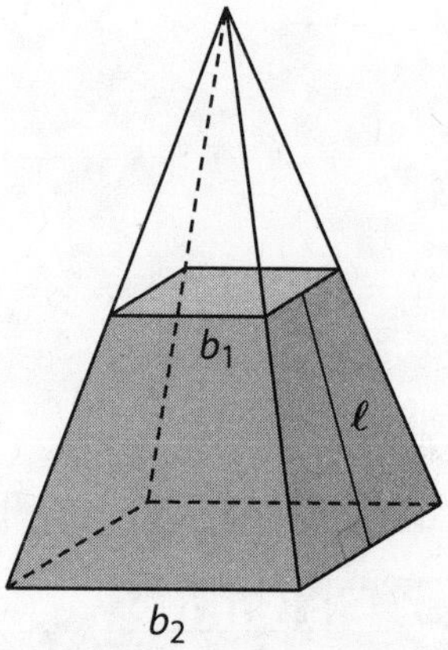

3. **Draw Conclusions** Explain why slant height is not defined for an oblique cone.

Find the lateral and surface area for each pyramid with a regular base. Where necessary, round to the nearest tenth.

4.

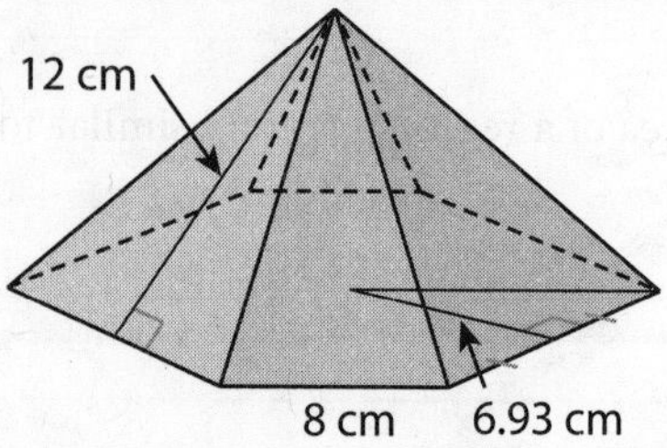

5.

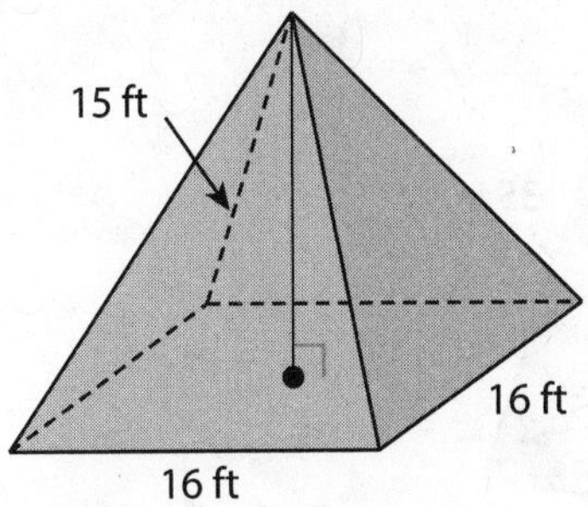

6.

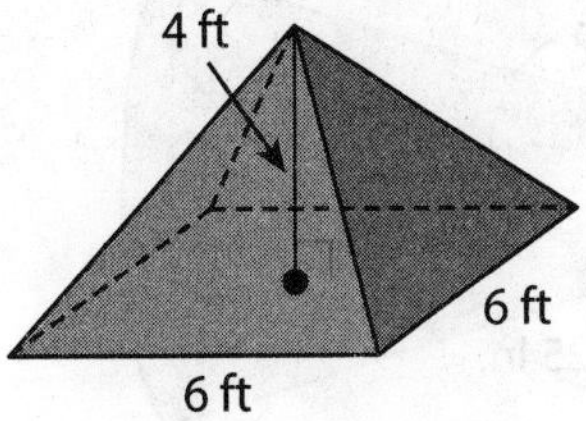

7.

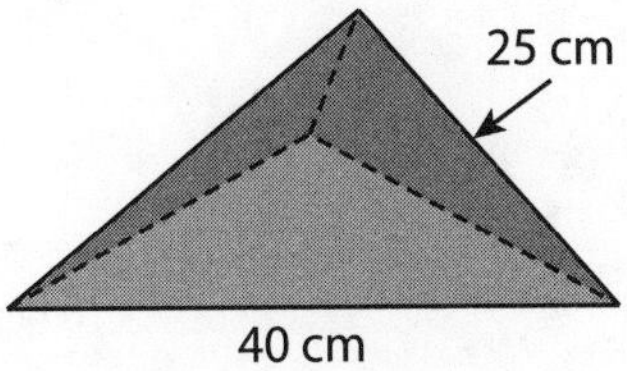

Find the lateral and total surface area for each cone. Leave the answer in terms of π.

8.

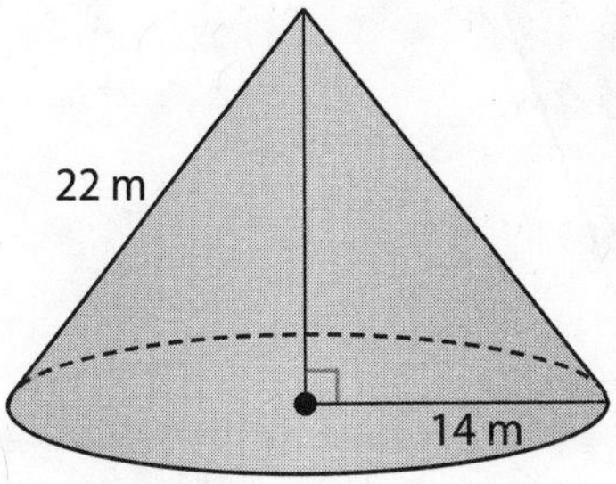

9.

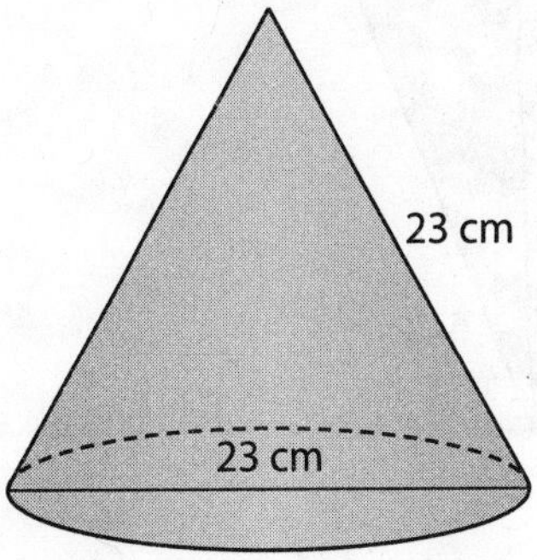

10.

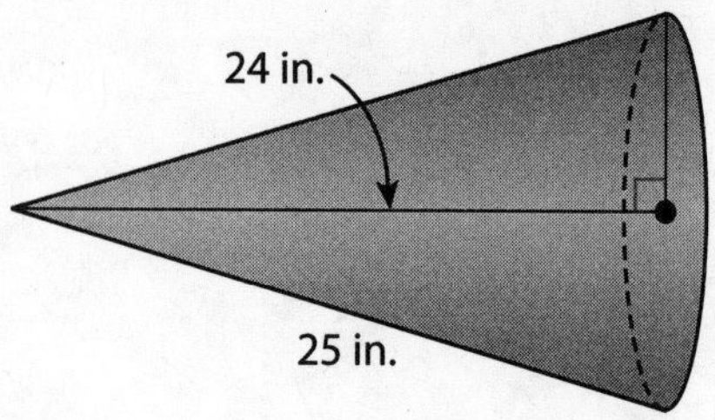

11.

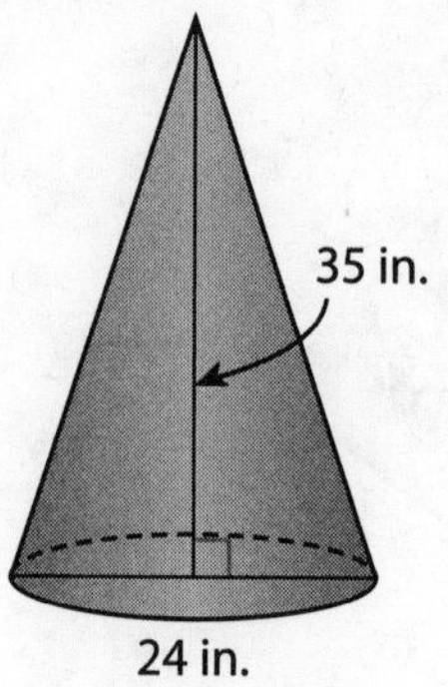

Find the surface area for the composite shape. Where appropriate, leave in terms of π. When necessary, round to nearest tenth.

12.

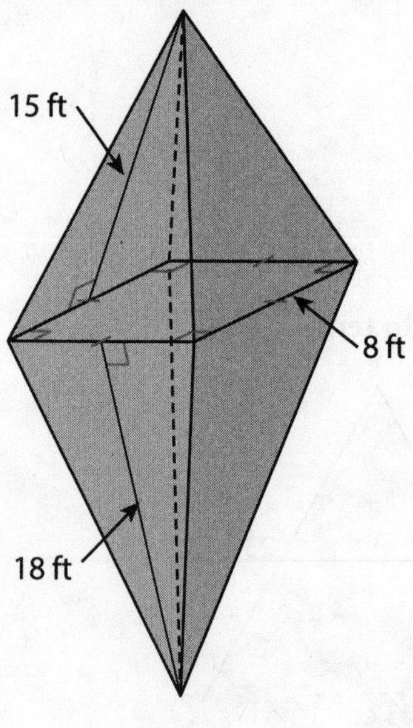

13.

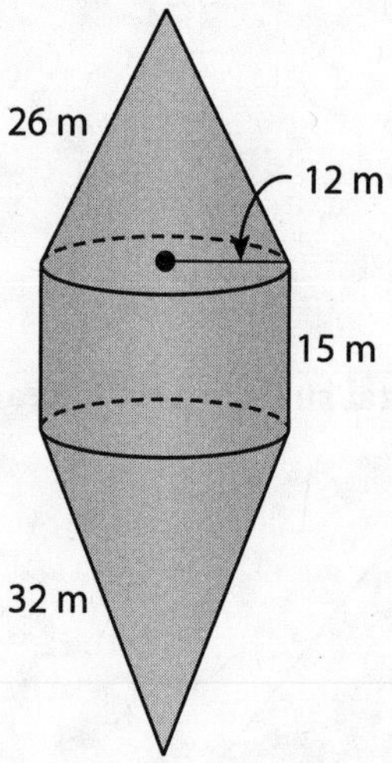

14.

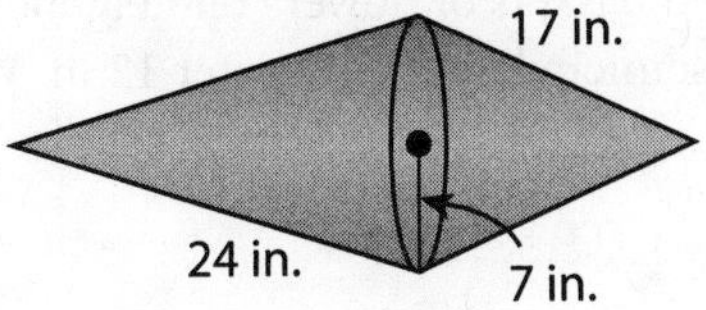

15.

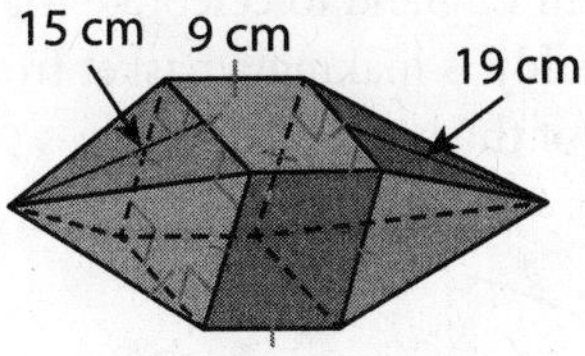

16.

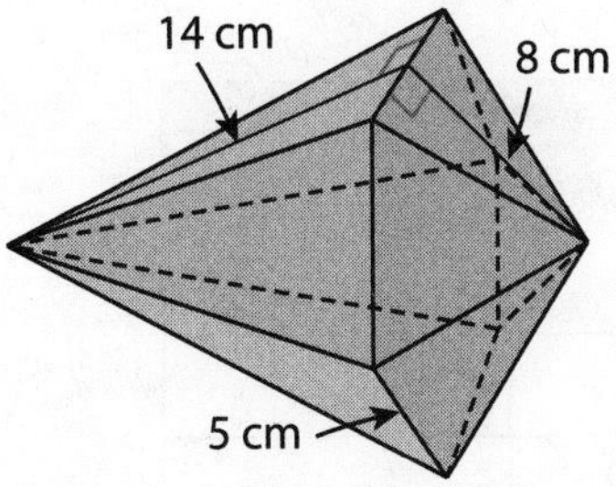

17.

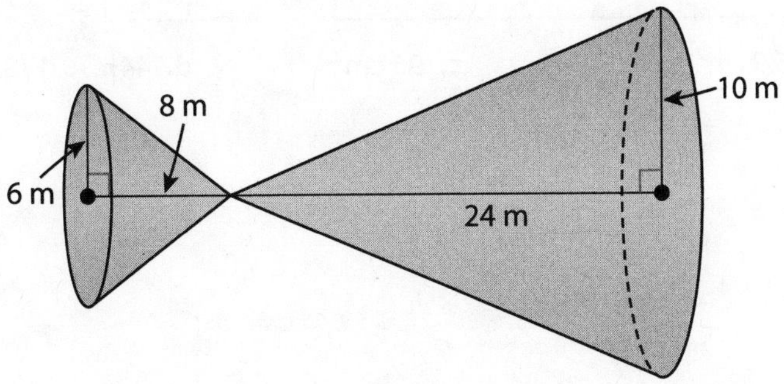

18. Anna is making a birthday hat from a pattern that is $\frac{3}{4}$ of a circle of colored paper. If Anna's head is 7 inches in diameter, will the hat fit her? Explain.

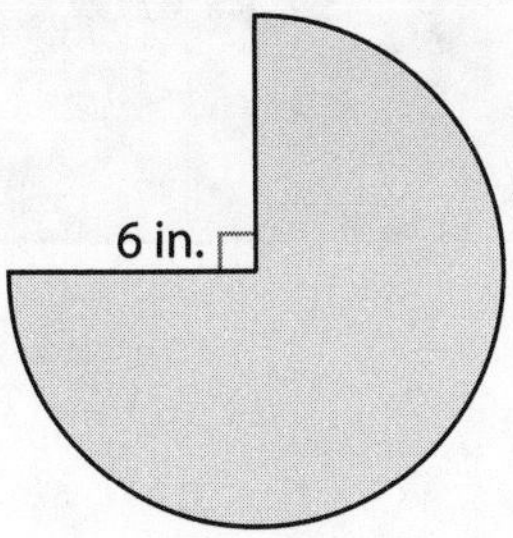

19. It is a tradition in England to celebrate May 1st by hanging cone-shaped baskets of flowers on neighbors' door handles. Addy is making a basket from a piece of paper that is a semicircle with diameter 12 in. What is the diameter of the basket?

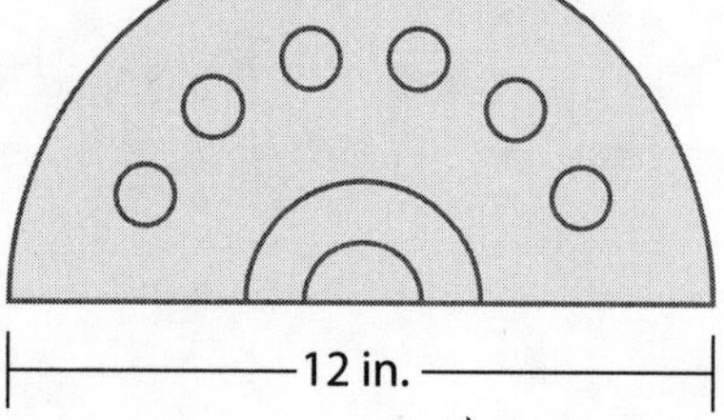

20. Match the figure with the correct surface area.

Shape	Base Area	Slant Height	Surface Area
Regular square pyramid	36 cm^2	5 cm	
Regular triangular pyramid	$\sqrt{3}$ cm^2	$\sqrt{3}$ cm	
Right cone	16π cm^2	7 cm	
Right cone	π cm^2	2 cm	

a. $3\pi \approx 9.4$ cm^2 **b.** $4\sqrt{3} \approx 6.9$ cm^2 **c.** 96 cm^2 **d.** $44\pi \approx 138.2$ cm^2

21. The Pyramid Arena in Memphis, Tennessee, is a square pyramid with base edge lengths of 200 yd and a height of 32 stories. Estimate the area of the glass on the sides of the pyramid. (*Hint:* 1 story $\approx$ 10 ft)

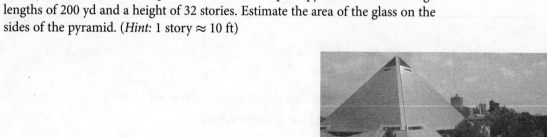

22. A juice container is a regular square pyramid with the dimensions shown.

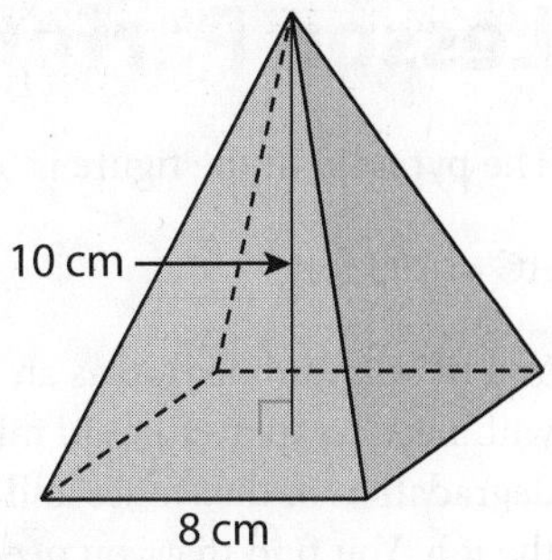

a. Find the surface area of the container to the nearest tenth.

b. The manufacturer decides to make a container in the shape of a right cone that requires the same amount of material. The base diameter must be 9 cm. Find the slant height of the container to the nearest tenth.

23. Persevere in Problem Solving A *frustum* of a cone is a part of the cone with two parallel bases. The height of the frustum of the cone that is shown is half the height of the original cone.

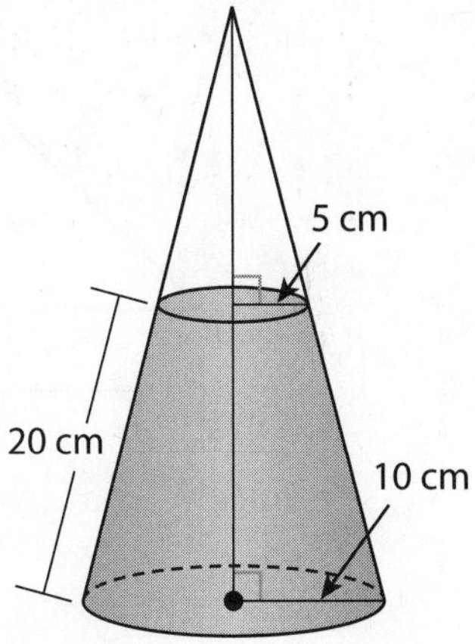

a. Find the surface area of the original cone.

b. Find the lateral area of the top of the cone.

c. Find the area of the top base of the frustum.

d. Use your results from parts a, b, and c to find the surface area of the frustum of the cone.

H.O.T. Focus on Higher Order Thinking

24. Communicate Mathematical Ideas Explain how you would find the volume of a cone, given the radius and the surface area.

25. Draw Conclusions Explain why the slant height of a regular square pyramid must be greater than half the base edge length.

Lesson Performance Task

The pyramid in the figure is built in two levels.

$AC = 200$ feet

You have a summer job as an intern archaeologist. The archaeologists you are working with need to apply a liquid microbial biofilm inhibitor to the pyramid to prevent bacterial degradation of the stones and have asked you to calculate the volume of inhibitor needed for the job. You find that you need 36,000 gallons of inhibitor for the top level. How many gallons will you need for the bottom level? (Keep in mind that you won't be treating the square bases of the levels.) Explain how you found the answer.

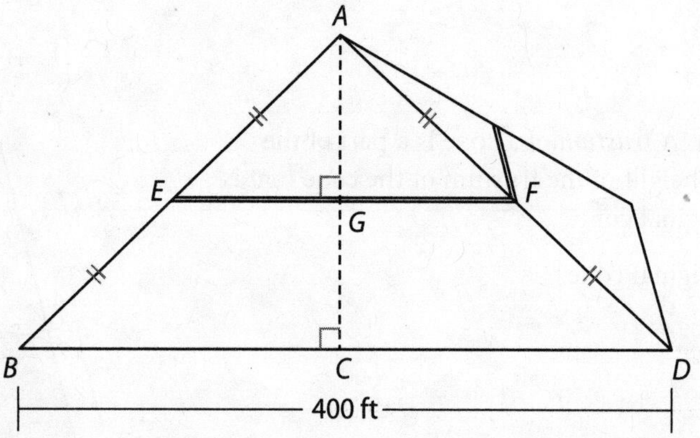

Name________________ Class__________ Date________

3.4 Surface Area of Spheres

Essential Question: How can you use the formula for the surface area of a sphere to calculate the surface areas of composite figures?

Resource Locker

Explore Developing a Surface Area Formula

You can derive the formula for the surface area of a sphere with radius r by imagining that it is filled with a large number of pyramids, whose apexes all meet at the center of the sphere and whose bases rest against the sphere's surface. It does not matter exactly what shape each base is, as long as all the bases have the same area, B, and they are not too far from regular polygons in shape. The figure shows a sphere with the first three pyramids inscribed.

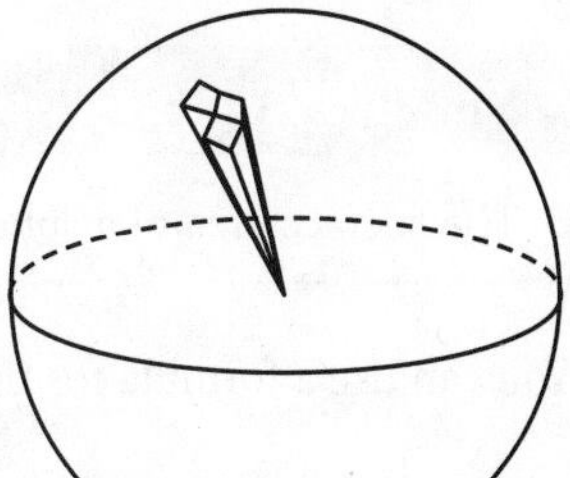

(A) What is the approximate volume of each pyramid?

(B) Express the approximate volume of the sphere in terms of the n pyramids.

(C) Use the formula for the volume of a sphere to write an approximate equation that can be solved for B, and solve it.

(D) Write an approximate expression for the sphere's surface area S in terms of the pyramid bases.

(E) Substitute your expression for the base area B of each pyramid from step C into your expression from step D. This gives you an approximate expression for the surface area S that does not involve the pyramids.

Reflect

1. As n gets larger and larger, what do you think will happen to the closeness of the approximations in steps A, B, C, and E? Explain.

2. As a conjecture, write the formula for the surface area S of a sphere with radius r.

Explain 1 Finding the Surface Area of a Sphere

Surface Area of a Sphere

The surface area of a sphere with radius r is given by $S = 4\pi r^2$.

You can use a formula for the surface area of a sphere to solve real-world problems.

Example 1 **A spherical water tank is 21.5 ft in diameter. The corrosion-resistant alloy skin of the tank is $\frac{1}{8}$ in thick. How much alloy is used to make the tank, to the nearest cubic inch?**

(A) Find the radius of the tank in inches.

The radius of the tank is $\frac{1}{2}(21.5 \text{ ft}) = 10.75 \text{ ft} \times \frac{12 \text{ in.}}{1 \text{ ft}} = 129 \text{ in.}$

(B) Find the surface area of the tank.

$S = 4\pi r^2 = 4\pi\left(\boxed{}\right)^2 = \boxed{}$ ... in^2

(C) Find the amount of alloy, to the nearest cubic inch.

Amount of alloy = surface area × thickness

$= \left(\boxed{} \text{... in}^2\right) \times \left(\boxed{} \text{ in.}\right) \approx \boxed{} \text{ in}^3$

Your Turn

A basketball is a sphere 29.5 in. in circumference. A baseball is a sphere of circumference 9.0 in. How much material is needed to make each ball, and how does the ratio of these amounts compare to the ratio of the circumferences?

3. How much material is needed to make a basketball, to the nearest tenth of a square inch?

4. How much material is needed to make a baseball, to the nearest tenth?

5. Compare the ratio of the amounts of material to the ratio of the circumferences. What do you notice?

____

____

Explain 2 Finding the Surface Area of a Composite Figure

You can find the surface area of a composite figure using appropriate formulas for the areas of the different surfaces of the figure.

Example 2 **Find the surface area of the composite figure, in terms of π and to the nearest tenth.**

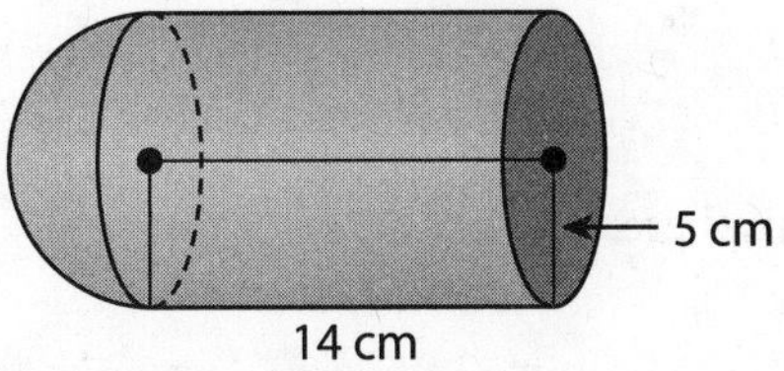

(A) Find the area of the base of the cylinder.

$A_1 = \pi r^2 = \pi(5)^2 = 25\pi \text{ cm}^2$

(B) Find the area of the curved surface of the cylinder.

$A_2 = 2\pi rh = 2\pi(\square)(\square) = \square\,\pi \text{ cm}^2$

(C) Find the surface area of the hemisphere.

$A_3 = \frac{1}{2}(4\pi r^2) = 2\pi(\square)^2 = \square\,\pi \text{ cm}^2$

(D) Find the surface area of the composite figure.

$S = A_1 + A_2 + A_3$

$= \square\,\pi \text{ cm}^2 + \square\,\pi \text{ cm}^2 + \square\,\pi \text{ cm}^2$

$= \square\,\pi \text{ cm}^2 \approx \square \text{ cm}^2$

Reflect

6. **Discussion** Could you have used the formula for the surface area of a cylinder? Explain.

____

____

Your Turn

Find the surface area of the composite figure, in terms of π and to the nearest tenth.

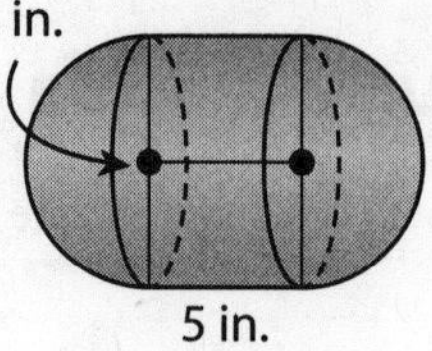

7. Find the lateral area of the cylinder.

8. Find the surface area of each hemisphere.

9. Find the surface area of the composite figure.

Elaborate

10. How does deriving the formula for the surface area of a sphere depend on knowing the formula for its volume?

11. Essential Question Check-In How can you use the formula for the surface area of a sphere to calculate the surface areas of composite figures?

Evaluate: Homework and Practice

- Online Homework
- Hints and Help
- Extra Practice

1. Using your knowledge of surface area and area, create a formula that will work to find the total surface area of the closed hemisphere for any value of r.

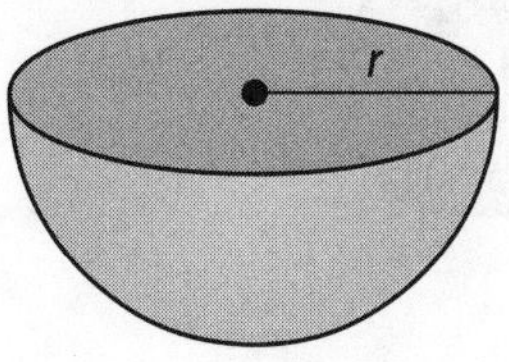

Find the surface area of the sphere. Leave the answer in terms of π.

2.

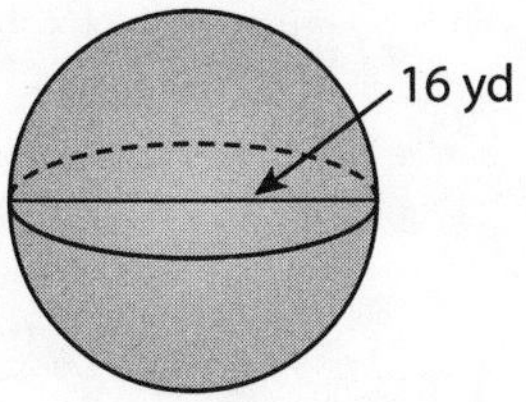

3.

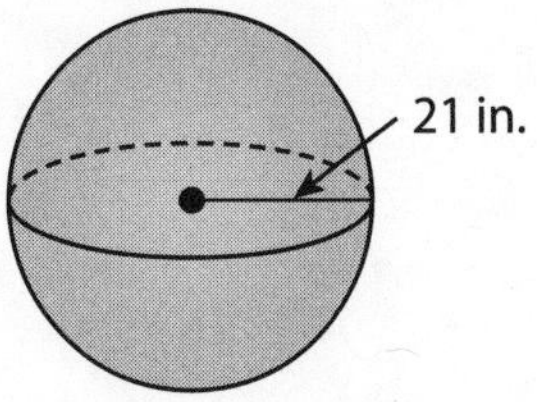

4.

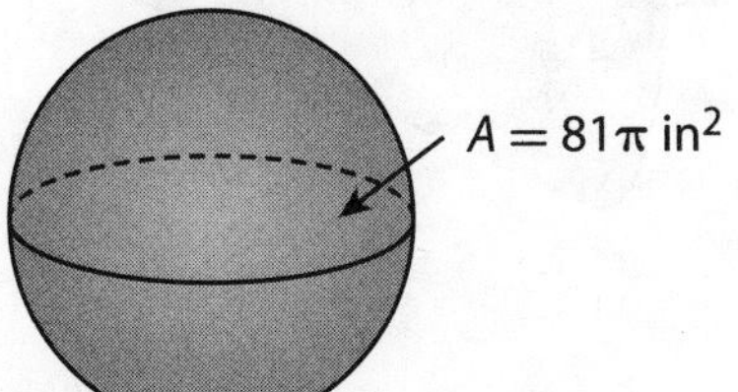

5.

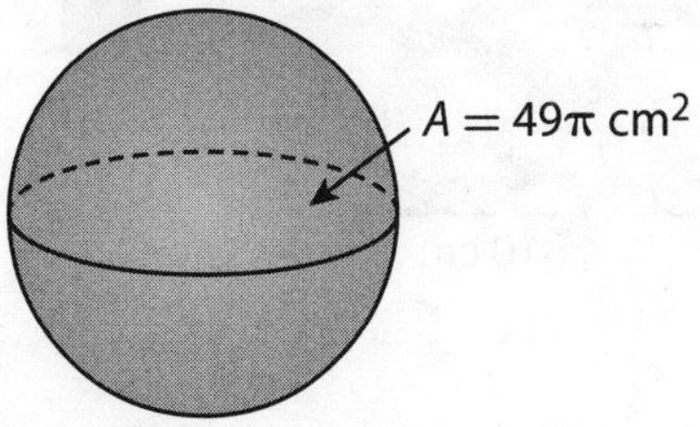

Find the surface area of the composite figure. Leave the answer in terms of π.

6.

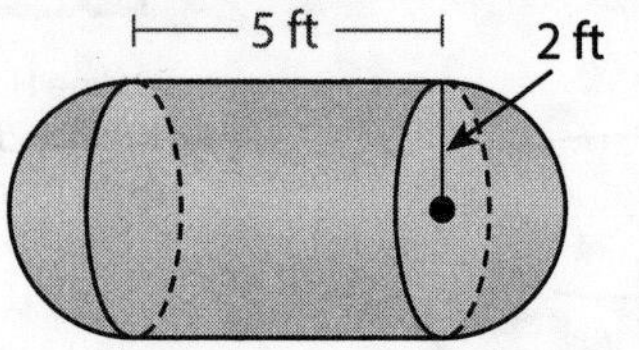

7.

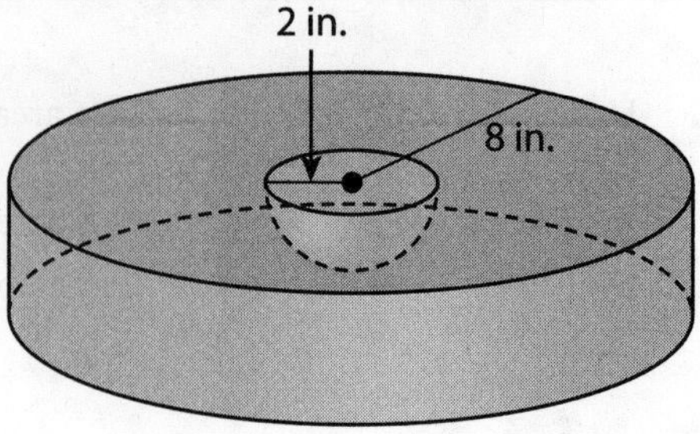

8.

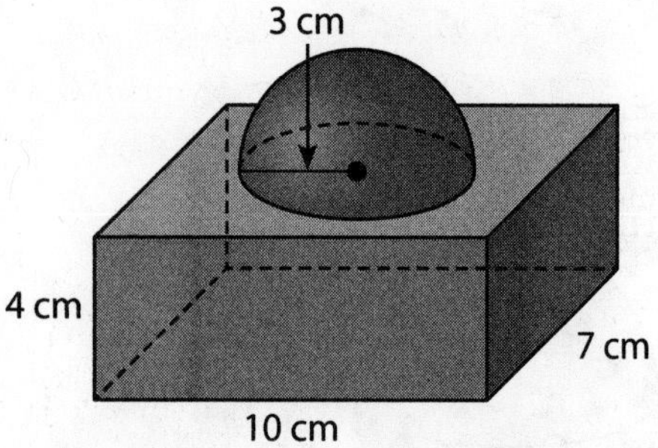

9.

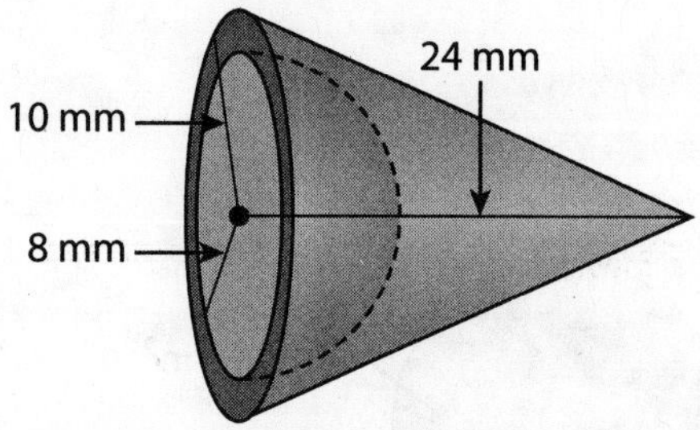

10. Find the surface area of the closed hemisphere.

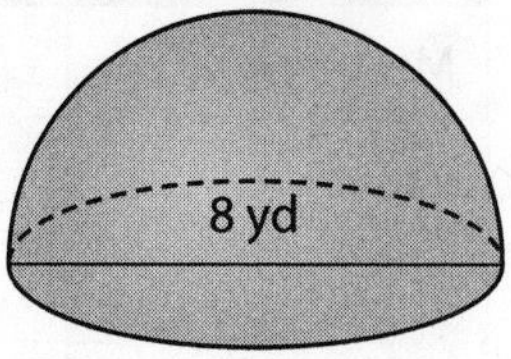

11. Find the circumference of the sphere with a surface area of 60π in^2. Leave the answer in terms of π.

12. Geography Earth's radius is approximately 4000 mi. About two-thirds of Earth's surface is covered by water. Estimate the land area on Earth.

13. A baseball has a radius of approximately 1.5 inches. Estimate the amount of leather used to cover the baseball. Leave the answer in terms of π.

14. Which of the following expressions represents the ratio of the surface area of a cylinder to the surface area of a sphere with the same radius, r?

A. $\frac{1}{2} + \frac{h}{r}$

B. $\frac{\pi + h}{r^2}$

C. $\frac{h}{4\pi}$

D. $\frac{r + h}{4r}$

E. $\frac{r + h}{2r}$

15. Explain the Error Susana solved for the surface area of the sphere using the following method:

$$S = \frac{4}{3}\pi r^2$$
$$= \frac{4}{3}\pi(10)^2$$
$$= \frac{4}{3}\pi 100$$
$$= \frac{400}{3}\pi \text{ m}^2$$

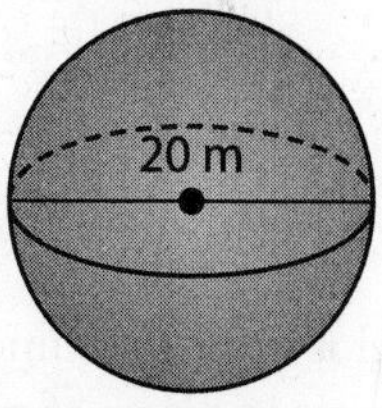

Find her error, and explain how to fix it.

16. Use the table to answer the question.

Planet	Diameter (mi)
Mercury	3,032
Venus	7,521
Earth	7,926
Mars	4,222
Jupiter	88,846
Saturn	74,898
Uranus	31,763
Neptune	30,775

a. Which is greater, the sum of the surface areas of Uranus and Neptune or the surface area of Saturn?

b. About how many times as great is the surface area of Earth as the surface area of Mars?

17. A globe has a volume of 288π in^3. What is the surface area of the globe? Give your answer in terms of π.

18. A bead is formed by drilling a cylindrical hole, with a 2 mm diameter, through a sphere with an 8 mm diameter. Estimate the surface area of the bead.

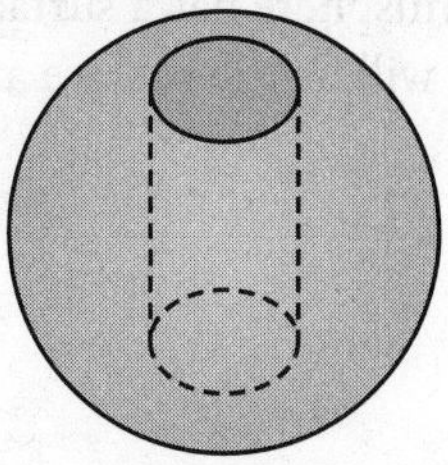

19. The size of a cultured pearl is typically indicated by its diameter in mm. About how many times as great is the surface area of the 9 mm pearl compared to the surface area of the 6 mm pearl?

20. The diameter of an orange is 10 cm and the diameter of a lime is 5 cm. About how many times as great is the surface area of a half of the orange when compared to the surface area of a half of the lime?

21. A hemisphere has a surface area of $972\pi \text{ cm}^2$. If the radius is multiplied by $\frac{1}{3}$, what will be the surface area of the new hemisphere?

H.O.T. Focus on Higher Order Thinking

22. Communicate Mathematical Ideas Describe the effect on the surface area if the dimension on the sphere is doubled.

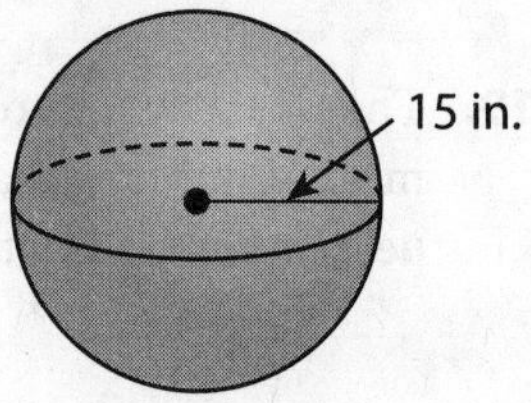

23. Analyze Relationships What is the relationship between the surface area of the sphere and the lateral area of the cylinder?

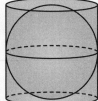

24. Persevere in Problem Solving A company sells orange juice in spherical containers that look like oranges. Each container has a surface area of approximately 50.3 in^2.

a. What is the volume of the container? Round to the nearest tenth.†

b. The company decides to increase the radius of the container by 10%. What is the surface area of the new container?

25. Draw Conclusions Suppose a sphere and a cube have equal surface areas. Using r for the radius of the sphere and s for the side of a cube, write an equation to show the relationship between r and s.

Lesson Performance Task

Locations on Earth are measured in relation to longitude and latitude lines. Longitude lines run north and south through the North and South poles. The 0° longitude line is called the Prime Meridian and runs through Greenwich, England. Latitude lines circle the Earth parallel to the Equator, which is designated 0° latitude. Longitude and latitude lines intersect one another at right angles.

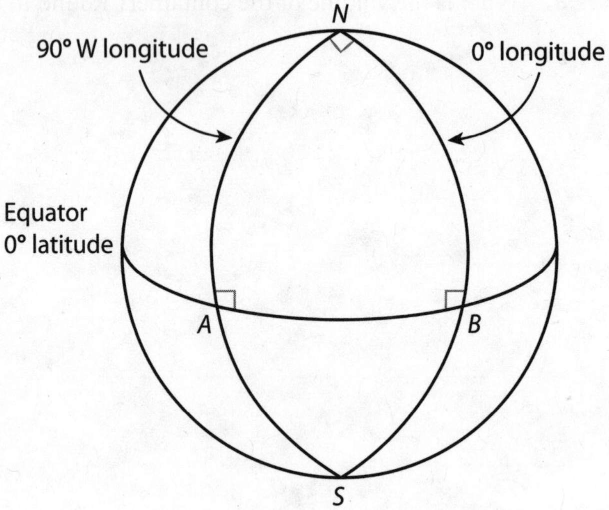

1. Triangle *ABN* is formed by the Equator and two lines of longitude. It is called a spherical triangle. Describe the ways that it is similar to a plane triangle and the ways that it differs.

2. Find the area of spherical triangle *ABN*. Explain how you found the area. Use 7912 miles as the diameter of the Earth. Use 3.14 for π.

Visualizing Solids

Essential Question: How can you use visualizing solids to solve real-world problems?

Key Vocabulary
net *(red)*
surface area *(área de la superficie)*
regular pyramid *(pirámide regular)*
right cone *(cono recto)*

KEY EXAMPLE (Lesson 3.1)

Describe the cross section formed when a plane cuts through the center of a sphere. Compare the dimensions of the cross section to those of the figure.

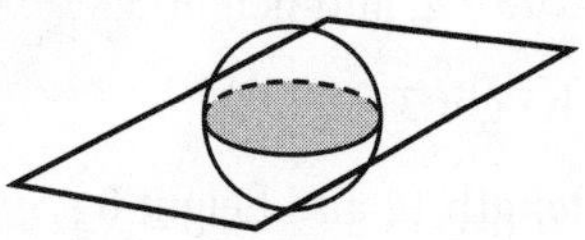

Since the sphere and the plane are both rotationally symmetric about the perpendicular axis, the cross section is also rotationally symmetric and is therefore a circle. Since it passes through the sphere's widest part, the circle's radius is equal to the radius of the circle.

KEY EXAMPLE (Lesson 3.2)

Find the surface area of a right prism with length of 10, width of 5, and height of 4.

$L = Ph$	Apply the lateral area formula.
$L = (2 \cdot 10 + 2 \cdot 5)4 = 120$	Substitute and solve.
$S = L + 2B$	Apply the surface area formula.
$S = 120 + 2 \cdot 10 \cdot 5 = 220$	Substitute and solve.

KEY EXAMPLE (Lesson 3.3)

Find the surface area of a right cone with radius 12 and height 16.

$l^2 = 12^2 + 16^2$	Use the Pythagorean Theorem to find the slant height.
$l = 20$	Solve.
$L = \pi r l$	Find the lateral area.
$L = \pi(12)(20) = 240\pi$	Substitute and multiply.
$S = L + \pi r^2$	Find the surface area.
$S = 240\pi + \pi(12)^2 = 384\pi$	Substitute and solve.

KEY EXAMPLE (Lesson 3.4)

Find the surface area of a sphere with radius 14.

$S = 4\pi r^2$	Use the formula for surface area of a sphere.
$S = 4\pi(14)^2 = 784\pi$	Substitute and solve.

EXERCISES

Determine if it is possible to form the following shapes by rotating a two-dimensional shape around the *y*-axis. If so, state the shape needed to do so. *(Lesson 3.1)*

1. sphere ________________
2. right prism ________________
3. cylinder ________________

Find the exact surface area of the following shapes. *(Lessons 3.2, 3.3, 3.4)*

4. right prism with length 3, width 4, and height 5 ________
5. cylinder with radius 8 and height 3 ________
6. regular pyramid with side length 12 and height 8 ________
7. right cone with diameter 8 and height 3 ________
8. sphere with radius 8 ________
9. hemisphere with radius 9 ________

MODULE PERFORMANCE TASK

How Much Does the Paint on a Space Shuttle Weigh?

NASA used to paint the fuel tanks for the Space Shuttle with white latex paint, but they decided to stop painting them because of the extra weight that the paint added. Just how much could that paint weigh?

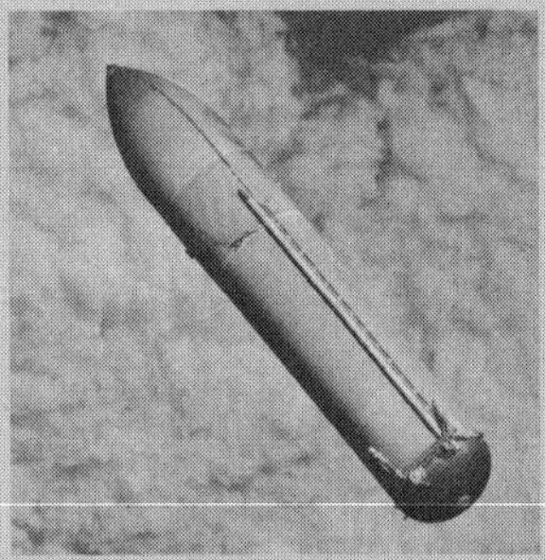

The photo gives you a good sense of the shape of the fuel tank. According to NASA, the tank has a height of 153.8 feet and a diameter of 27.6 feet. Use one or more of the formulas you have learned to find the surface area of the tank. Then use your calculation to come up with your best estimate of the weight of the paint required to cover the fuel tank.

Start by listing in the space below any additional information you will need to solve the problem. Then use your own paper to complete the task. Be sure to write down all of your assumptions and data. Use tables, diagrams, words, or numbers to explain how you came to your conclusion.

Ready to Go On?

3.1–3.4 Visualizing Solids

Personal Math Trainer
- Online Homework
- Hints and Help
- Extra Practice

State the figure obtained when rotating the figure about an axis along its largest side, and find the exact surface area of the resulting figure.

1. A rectangle with length 18 and width 14. *(Lesson 3.1)*

Find the exact surface area of the following. *(Lessons 3.3, 3.4)*

2.

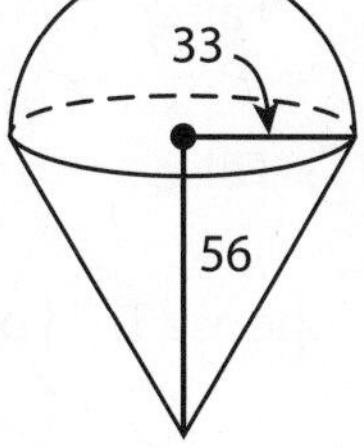

ESSENTIAL QUESTION

3. When finding the surface area of a composite figure, why is it often necessary to subtract sides common to each individual shape?

MODULE 3
MIXED REVIEW

Assessment Readiness

1. A rectangular prism has a surface area of 922 square units. Consider each set of dimensions. Could these be the dimensions of the right prism?
Select Yes or No for A–C.

A. length = 23, width = 7, height = 10 ○ Yes ○ No
B. length = 17, width = 8, height = 13 ○ Yes ○ No
C. length = 10, width = 9, height = 12 ○ Yes ○ No

2. A sphere has a radius of 27. Choose True or False for each statement.

A. The surface area of the sphere is 729π square units. ○ True ○ False
B. The volume of the sphere is 26,244π cubic units. ○ True ○ False
C. The surface area of the sphere is 2916π square units. ○ True ○ False

3. $\triangle ABC$ maps to $\triangle DEF$ with the transformation $(x, y) \rightarrow \left(\frac{1}{4}x, \frac{1}{4}y\right)$. Choose True or False for each statement.

A. If $BC = 8$, $EF = 2$. ○ Yes ○ No
B. If $BC = 4$, $EF = 16$. ○ Yes ○ No
C. If $BC = 20$, $EF = 5$. ○ Yes ○ No

4. What solid is formed when rotating a square about a horizontal or vertical axis through the center of the square? Does this solid have a square for a base? Does this solid have a square for a cross-section?

5. Draw the net of a right cylinder with a radius of 2 and a height of 6, and then explain if this answer is the only possible net for this cylinder.

MODULE 4

Modeling and Problem Solving

Essential Question: How can you use modeling to solve real-world problems?

REAL WORLD VIDEO
Check out how GPS coordinates can be used to calculate the area of a region of the Earth's surface.

MODULE PERFORMANCE TASK PREVIEW

Population Density

It's easy to find the population density of a region once you know the population and the area. What's not always so easy is counting the population (New York City, 8,336,697 in 2012) and calculating the area (New York City, 302.64 square miles). Of course, there are some regions whose populations are much smaller than that of New York City and whose areas are easier to calculate. You'll find the population density of one of them after you complete this module.

Are YOU Ready?

Complete these exercises to review skills you will need for this module.

Personal Math Trainer

- Online Homework
- Hints and Help
- Extra Practice

Scale Factor and Scale Drawings

Example 1 The width on an architectural plan for a rectangular room is 8 cm. The actual room will be 12 ft wide and 18 ft long. How long is the length of the room on the plan?

$$\frac{\text{plan width}}{\text{actual width}} = \frac{\text{plan length}}{\text{actual length}} \rightarrow \frac{8}{12} = \frac{x}{18}$$

$$x = \frac{18 \cdot 8}{12} = 12 \quad \text{Multiply and simplify.}$$

The plan length is 12 cm.

Find the missing length for a rectangular room.

1. plan length: 4 in.
actual width: 28 ft
actual length: 32 ft
Find the plan width.

______

2. plan width: 6 in.
plan length: 8 in.
actual length: 24 yd
Find the actual width.

______

3. plan width: 2.4 cm
plan length: 9 cm
actual width: 3.6 m
Find the actual length.

______

Volume

Example 2 The volume of a cylinder is 42 cm^3. Its height is 3.5 cm. Find the diameter of the cylinder.

$V = \pi r^2 h$ — Write the formula.

$42 = \pi r^2(3.5)$ — Substitute.

$r^2 = \frac{42}{3.5\pi} = \frac{12}{\pi}$ — Solve for r^2.

$r \approx 1.954$ — Solve for r to the nearest thousandth.

$2r \approx 3.91$ — Find the diameter.

The diameter of the cylinder is about 3.91 cm.

Find the missing measure of the cylinder to the nearest hundredth.

4. diameter: 7 ft
height: 2 ft
Find the volume.

______

5. radius: 10 in.
volume: 490 $in.^3$
Find the height.

______

6. diameter: 1.2 m
volume: 4.8 m^3
Find the height.

______

Name ______________________ Class ____________ Date ________

4.1 Scale Factor

Essential Question: How does multiplying one or more of the dimensions of a figure affect its attributes?

Resource Locker

Explore — Exploring Effects of Changing Dimensions on Perimeter and Area

Changes made to the dimensions of a figure can affect the perimeter and the area.

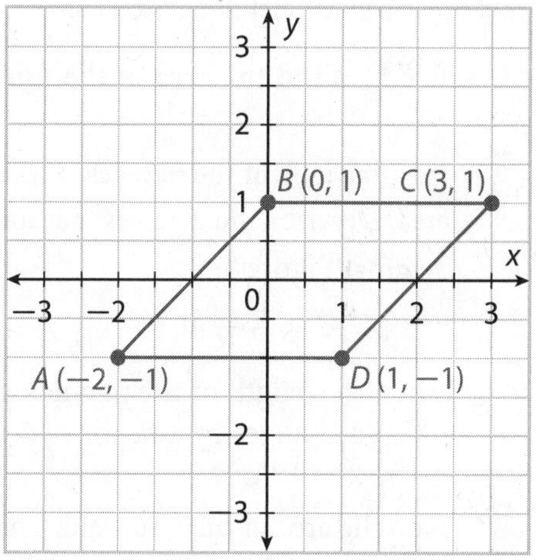

Use the figure to investigate how changing one or more dimensions of the figure affect its perimeter and area.

(A) Apply the transformation $(x, y) \to (3x, y)$. Find the perimeter and the area.

Original Dimensions	Dimensions after $(x, y) \to (3x, y)$
$P = 6 + 4\sqrt{2}$	$P =$
$A = 6$	$A =$

(B) Apply the transformation $(x, y) \to (x, 3y)$. Find the perimeter and the area.

Original Dimensions	Dimensions after $(x, y) \to (x, 3y)$
$P = 6 + 4\sqrt{2}$	$P =$
$A = 6$	$A =$

(C) Apply the transformation $(x, y) \to (3x, 3y)$. Find the perimeter and the area.

Original Dimensions	Dimensions after $(x, y) \to (3x, 3y)$
$P = 6 + 4\sqrt{2}$	$P =$
$A = 6$	$A =$

Reflect

1. Describe the changes that occurred in Steps A and B. Did the perimeter or area change by a constant factor?

2. Describe the changes that occurred in Step C. Did the perimeter or area change by a constant factor?

Explain 1 Describe a Non-Proportional Dimension Change

In a non-proportional dimension change, you do not use the same factor to change each dimension of a figure.

Example 1 **Find the area of the figure.**

(A) Find the area of the parallelogram. Then multiply the length by 2 and determine the new area. Describe the changes that took place.

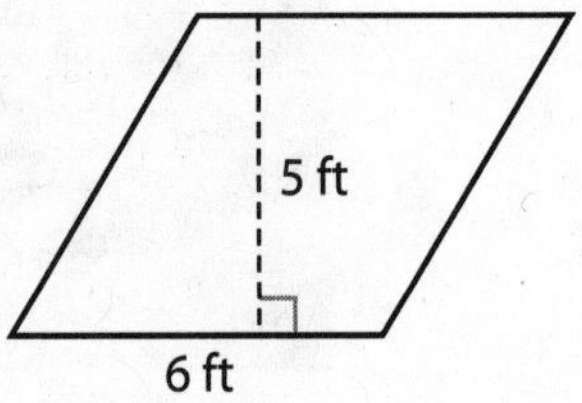

Original Figure | Transformed Figure

$A = bh = 6 \cdot 5 = 30 \text{ ft}^2$ | $A = bh = 12 \cdot 5 = 60 \text{ ft}^2$

When the length of the parallelogram changes by a factor of 2, the area changes by a factor of 2.

(B) Find the area of the trapezoid. Then multiply the height by 0.5 and determine the new area. Describe the changes that took place.

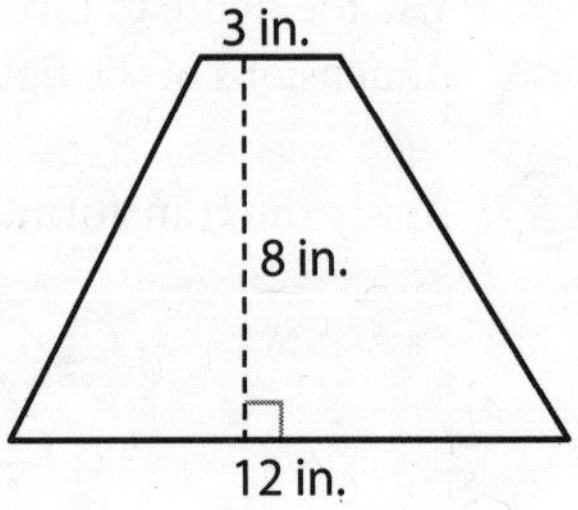

Original Figure $A = \frac{1}{2}(b_1 + b_2)h =$ ☐

Transformed Figure $A = \frac{1}{2}(b_1 + b_2)h =$ ☐

When the height of the trapezoid changes by a factor of ______, the area of the trapezoid changes by a factor of ______.

Reflect

3. **Discussion** When a non-proportional change is applied to the dimensions of a figure, does the perimeter change in a predictable way?

Your Turn

4. Find the area of a triangle with vertices $(-5, -2)$, $(-5, 7)$, and $(3, 1)$. Then apply the transformation $(x, y) \rightarrow (x, 4y)$ and determine the new area. Describe the changes that took place.

5. Find the area of the figure. Then multiply the width by 5 and determine the new area. Describe the changes that took place.

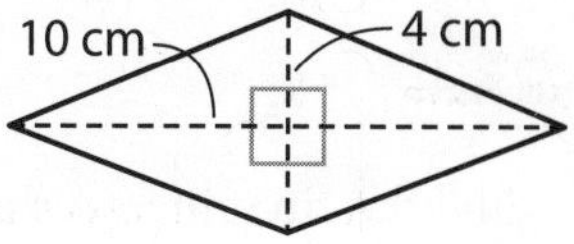

Explain 2 Describe a Proportional Dimension Change

In a proportional dimension change, you use the same factor to change each dimension of a figure.

Example 2 **Find the area and perimeter of a circle.**

Ⓐ Find the circumference and area of the circle. Then multiply the radius by 3 and find the new circumference and area. Describe the changes that took place.

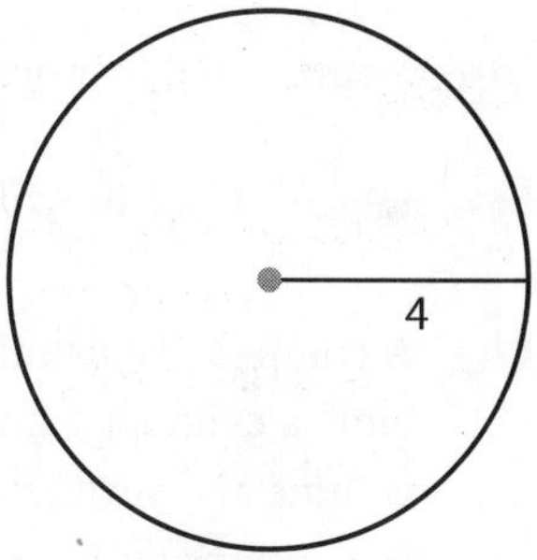

Original Figure $C = 2\pi(4) = 8\pi$

$A = \pi(4)^2 = 16\pi$

Transformed Figure $C = 2\pi(12) = 24\pi$

$A = \pi(12)^2 = 144\pi$

The circumference changes by a factor of 3, and the area changes by a factor of 9 or 3^2.

Ⓑ Find the perimeter and area of the figure. Then multiply the length and height by $\frac{1}{3}$ and find the new perimeter and area. Describe the changes that took place.

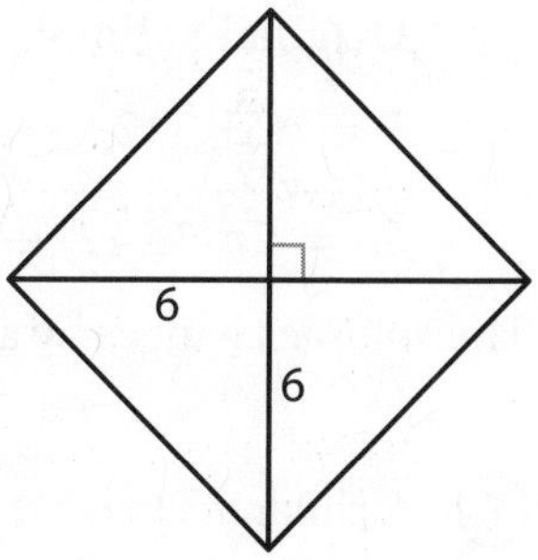

Original Figure

$P =$ ______

$A =$ ______

Transformed Figure

$P =$ ______

$A =$ ______

The perimeter changes by a factor of ______, and the area changes by a factor of ______.

Reflect

6. Fill in the table to describe the effect on perimeter (or circumference) and area when the dimensions of a figure are changed proportionally.

Effects of Changing Dimensions Proportionally		
Change in Dimensions	**Perimeter or Circumference**	**Area**
All dimensions multiplied by a		

Your Turn

7. Find the circumference and area of the circle. Then multiply the radius by 0.25 and find the new circumference and area. Describe the changes that took place.

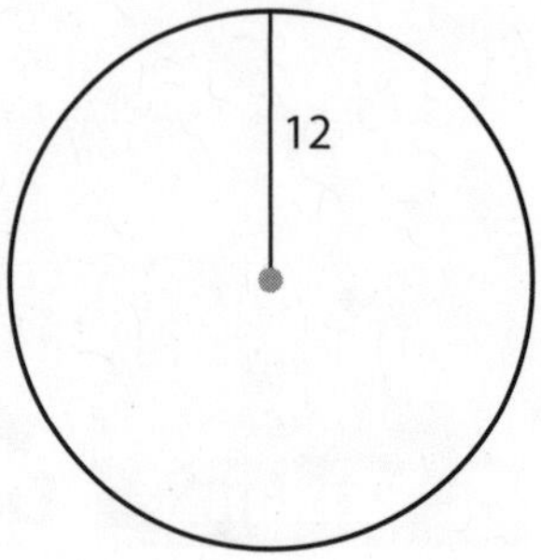

Explain 3 Describe a Proportional Dimension Change for a Solid

In a proportional dimension change to a solid, you use the same factor to change each dimension of a figure.

Example 3 **Find the volume of the composite solid.**

(A) A company is planning to create a similar version of this storage tank, a cylinder with hemispherical caps at each end. Find the volume and surface area of the original tank. Then multiply all the dimensions by 2 and find the new volume and surface area. Describe the changes that took place.

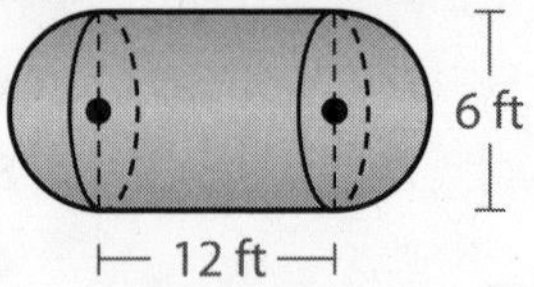

The volume of the solid is $V = \pi r^2 h + \frac{4}{3}\pi r^3$, and the surface area is $A = 2\pi rh + 4\pi r^2$.

Original Solid

$V = \pi(3)^2(12) + \frac{4}{3}\pi(3)^3 = 144\pi$ cu. ft.

$SA = 2\pi(3 \cdot 12) + 4\pi(3)^2 = 108\pi$ sq. ft.

Transformed Solid

$V = \pi(6)^2(24) + \frac{4}{3}\pi(6)^3 = 1152\pi$ cu. ft.

$SA = 2\pi(6 \cdot 24) + 4\pi(6)^2 = 432\pi$ sq. ft.

The volume changes by a factor of 8, and the surface area changes by a factor of 4.

(B) A children's toy is shaped like a hemisphere with a conical top. A company decides to create a smaller version of the toy. Find the volume and surface area of the original toy. Then multiply all dimensions by $\frac{2}{3}$ and find the new volume and surface area. Describe the changes that took place.

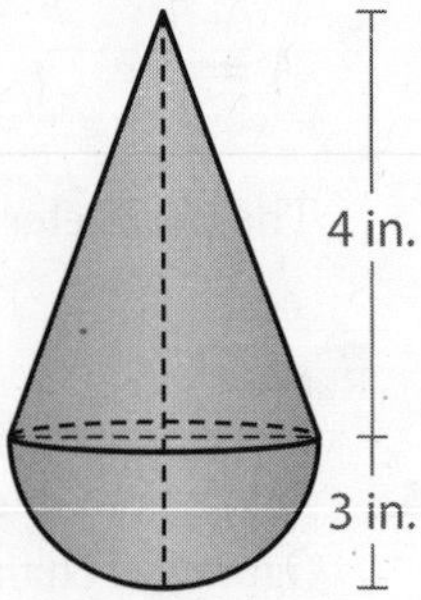

The volume of the solid is $V = \frac{1}{3}\pi r^2 h + \frac{2}{3}\pi r^3$,

and the surface area is $A = \pi r\sqrt{r^2 + h^2} + 2\pi r^2$.

Original Solid

$V =$ ______ cu. in.

$A =$ ______ sq. in.

Transformed Solid

$V =$ ______ cu. in.

$A =$ ______ sq. in.

The volume changes by a factor of ______, and the surface area changes by a factor of ______.

Reflect

8. Fill in the table to describe the effect on surface area and volume when the dimensions of a figure are changed proportionally.

Effects of Changing Dimensions Proportionally		
Change in Dimensions	**Surface Area**	**Volume**
All dimensions multiplied by a		

Your Turn

9. A farmer has made a scale model of a new grain silo. Find the volume and surface area of the model. Use the scale ratio 1 : 36 to find the volume and surface area of the silo. Compare the volumes and surface areas relative to the scale ratio. Be consistent with units of measurement.

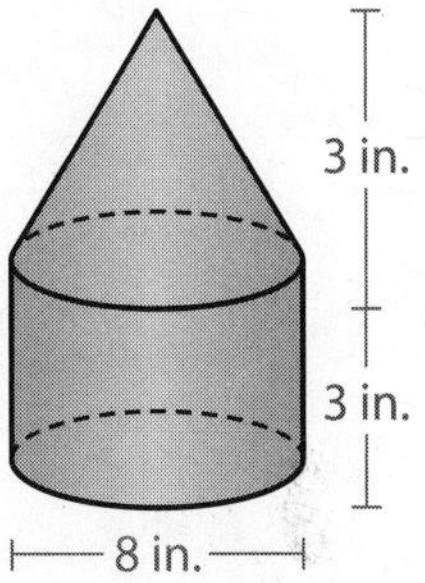

Elaborate

10. Two square pyramids are similar. If the ratio of a pair of corresponding edges is $a : b$, what is the ratio of their volumes? What is the ratio of their surface areas?

11. **Essential Question Check-In** How is a non-proportional dimension change different from a proportional dimension change?

Evaluate: Homework and Practice

Personal Math Trainer

- Online Homework
- Hints and Help
- Extra Practice

A trapezoid has the vertices $(0, 0)$, $(4, 0)$, $(4, 4)$, and $(-3, 4)$.

1. Describe the effect on the area if only the x-coordinates of the vertices are multiplied by $\frac{1}{2}$.

2. Describe the effect on the area if only the y-coordinates of the vertices are multiplied by $\frac{1}{2}$.

3. Describe the effect on the area if both the x- and y-coordinates of the vertices are multiplied by $\frac{1}{2}$.

4. Describe the effect on the area if the x-coordinates are multiplied by 2 and y-coordinates are multiplied by $\frac{1}{2}$.

Describe the effect of the change on the area of the given figure.

5. The height of the triangle is doubled.

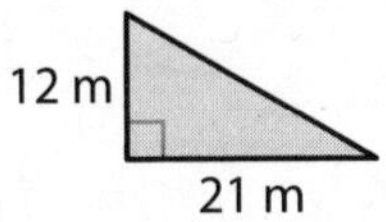

6. The height of a trapezoid with base lengths 12 cm and 8 cm and height 5 cm is multiplied by $\frac{1}{3}$.

7. The base of the parallelogram is multiplied by $\frac{2}{3}$.

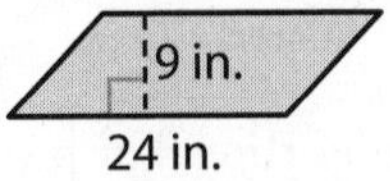

8. **Communicate Mathematical Ideas**
A triangle has vertices (1, 5), (2, 3), and (−1, −6). Find the effect that multiplying the height of the triangle by 4 has on the area of the triangle, without doing any calculations. Explain.

Describe the effect of each change on the perimeter or circumference and the area of the given figure.

9. The base and height of an isosceles triangle with base 12 in. and height 6 in. are both tripled.

10. The base and height of the rectangle are both multiplied by $\frac{1}{2}$.

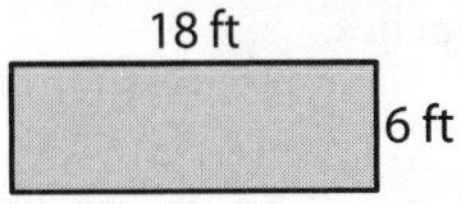

11. The dimensions are multiplied by 5.

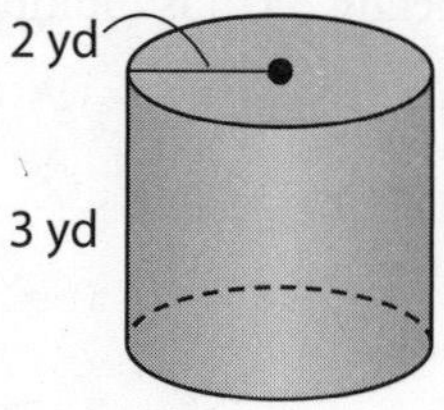

12. The dimensions are multiplied by $\frac{3}{5}$.

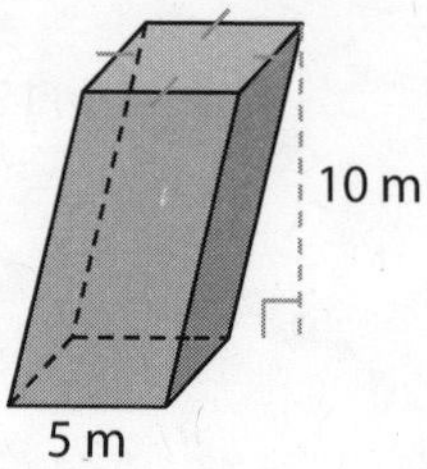

13. For each change, check whether the change is non-proportional or proportional.

A. The height of a triangle is doubled. ○ proportional ○ non-proportional

B. All sides of a square are quadrupled. ○ proportional ○ non-proportional

C. The length of a rectangle is multiplied by $\frac{3}{4}$. ○ proportional ○ non-proportional

D. The height of a triangular prism is tripled. ○ proportional ○ non-proportional

E. The radius of a sphere is multiplied by $\sqrt{5}$. ○ proportional ○ non-proportional

14. Tina and Kleu built rectangular play areas for their dogs. The play area for Tina's dog is 1.5 times as long and 1.5 times as wide as the play area for Kleu's dog. If the play area for Kleu's dog is 60 square feet, how big is the play area for Tina's dog?

15. A map has the scale 1 inch = 10 miles. On the map, the area of Big Bend National Park in Texas is about 12.5 square inches. Estimate the actual area of the park in acres. (*Hint:* 1 square mile = 640 acres)

16. A restaurant has a weekly ad in a local newspaper that is 2 inches wide and 4 inches high and costs $36.75 per week. The cost of each ad is based on its area. If the owner of the restaurant decided to double the width and height of the ad, how much will the new ad cost?

17. Suppose the dimensions of a triangle with a perimeter of 18 inches are doubled. Find the perimeter of the new triangle in inches.

A rectangular prism has vertices (0, 0, 0), (0, 3, 0), (7, 0, 0), (7, 3, 0), (0, 0, 6), (0, 3, 6), (7, 0, 6) and (7, 3, 6).

18. Suppose all the dimensions are tripled. Find the new vertices.

19. Find the effect of the change on the volume of the prism.

20. How would the effect of the change be different if only the height had been tripled?

21. **Analyze Relationships** How could you change the dimensions of a parallelogram to increase the area by a factor of 5 if the parallelogram does not have to be similar to the original parallelogram? if the parallelogram does have to be similar to the original parallelogram?

H.O.T. Focus on Higher Order Thinking

22. **Algebra** A square has a side length of $(2x + 5)$ cm.

    a. If the side length is mulitplied by 5, what is the area of the new square?

    b. Use your answer to part (a) to find the area of the original square without using the area formula. Justify your answer.

23. **Algebra** A circle has a diameter of 6 in. If the circumference is multiplied by $(x + 3)$, what is the area of the new circle? Justify your answer.

24. **Communicate Mathematical Ideas** The dimensions of a prism with volume V and surface area S are multiplied by a scale factor of k to form a similar prism. Make a conjecture about the ratio of the surface area of the new prism to its volume. Test your conjecture using a cube with an edge length of 1 and a scale factor of 2.

Lesson Performance Task

On a computer screen, lengths and widths are measured not in inches or millimeters but in **pixels**. A pixel is the smallest visual element that a computer is capable of processing. A common size for a large computer screen is 1024 × 768 pixels. (Widths rather than heights are conventionally listed first.) For the following, assume you're working on a 1024 × 768 screen.

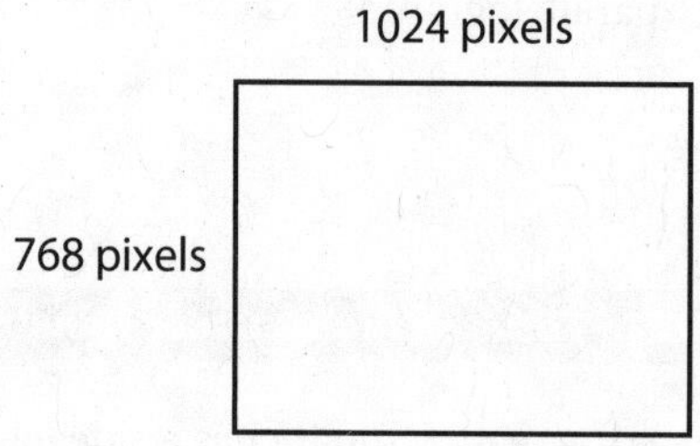

1. You have a photo measuring 640 × 300 pixels and you want to enlarge it proportionally so that it is as wide as the computer screen. Find the measurements of the photo after it has been scaled up. Explain how you found the answer.

2. **a.** Explain why you can't enlarge the photo proportionally so that it is as tall as the computer screen.

   b. Why can't you correct the difficulty in (a) by scaling the width of the photo by a factor of 1024 ÷ 640 and the height by a factor of 768 ÷ 300?

3. You have some square photos and you would like to fill the screen with them, so there is no overlap and there are no gaps between photos. Find the dimensions of the largest such photos you can use (all of them the same size), and find the number of photos. Explain your reasoning.

Name ______________________ Class ______________ Date ________

4.2 Modeling and Density

Essential Question: How can you model real-world situations involving density?

Resource Locker

Explore Comparing Density

Density is the amount of matter that an object has in a given unit of volume. The density of an object is calculated by dividing its mass by its volume.

$$\text{density} = \frac{\text{mass}}{\text{volume}}$$

Density can be used to help distinguish between similar materials, like identifying different types of wood.

Data about two approximately cylindrical wood logs is shown in the table. Determine which wood is denser.

Type of wood	Diameter (cm)	Height (cm)	Mass (kg)
Douglas fir	6	17	254
American redwood	8	12	271

(A) Make a prediction, based on the data but without calculating, about which wood is denser. Describe your reasoning

____

____

(B) Determine the volume of each log.

(C) Determine the density of each log. Identify the denser wood.

Reflect

1. What do your results tell you about the two types of wood?

____

____

Explain 1 Calculating a Population Density

You can define density in other situations that involve area or volume besides mass per unit volume. For example, the population density of a region, or the population per unit area, can be found by using the density formula.

Example 1 **Find the approximate population density.**

(A) Burlington, Vermont has an area of about 160 km^2 and a population of 109,000 people. What is the approximate population density of Burlington?

$$\text{Population density} = \frac{\text{population}}{\text{area}} = \frac{\mathbf{109{,}000}}{\mathbf{160}} \approx \mathbf{681}\ \text{persons/km}^2$$

(B) The state of Vermont has a population of 626,000. Vermont's territory can be modeled as a trapezoid, as shown in the figure. Each unit on the coordinate grid represents one mile. Find the approximate population density of Vermont.

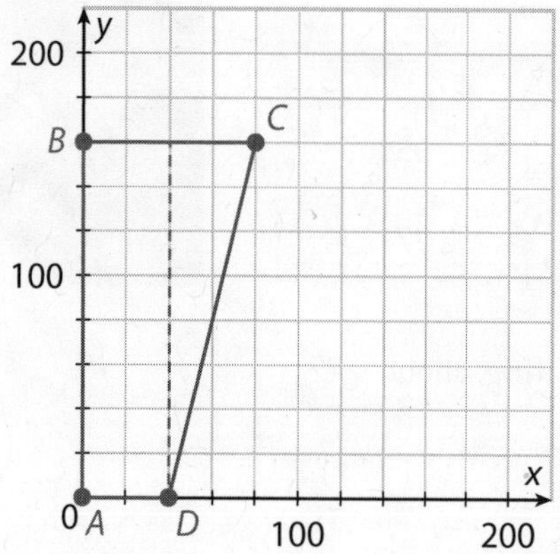

$$\text{Area} = \frac{1}{2}(b_1+b_2)h = \frac{1}{2}\left(40 + \boxed{}\right)\left(\boxed{}\right) = \boxed{}\ \text{mi}^2$$

$$\text{Population density} = \frac{\text{population}}{\text{area}} = \frac{\boxed{}}{\boxed{}} \approx \boxed{}\ \text{persons/mi}^2$$

Reflect

2. **Discussion** The actual area of Vermont is 9,620 mi^2. Is your approximation an overestimate or underestimate? Explain.

3. How would the population density of Vermont change if its given population doubled by 2100? Why?

4. **Critique Reasoning** Marya claims that Burlington is about 10 times more densely populated than the state average. Is she correct? Explain your reasoning.

Your Turn

5. Chicago has a population of about 2,715,000. Its territory can be modeled as a parallelogram, as shown in the figure. Each unit on the coordinate grid represents one mile. Find the approximate population density of Chicago.

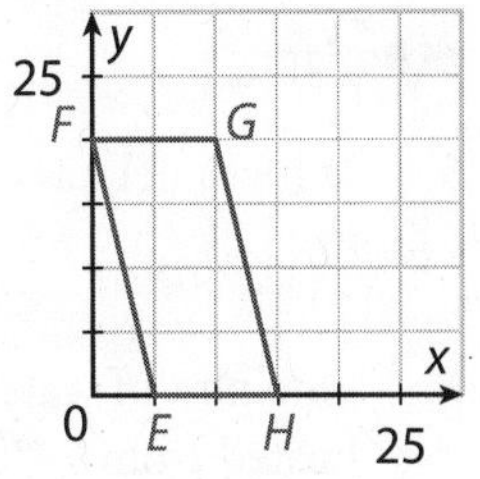

Explain 2 Calculating Measures of Energy

A British thermal unit (BTU), a unit of energy, is approximately the amount of energy needed to increase the temperature of one pound of water by one degree Fahrenheit. The energy content of a fuel may be measured in BTUs per unit of volume.

Example 2 **A spherical tank is filled with a gas and it has the dimensions shown. Find the number of BTUs produced by one cubic foot of the gas. Round to the nearest BTU.**

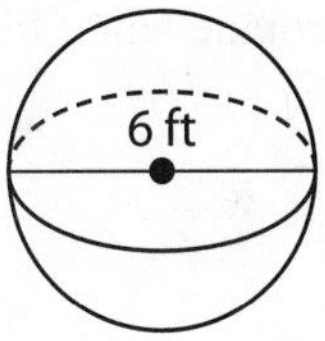

(A) When the tank is filled with natural gas, it provides 116,151 BTUs.

Find the volume of the spherical tank.

$$r = \frac{1}{2}(6 \text{ ft}) = 3 \text{ ft}$$

$$V = \frac{4}{3}\pi r^3 = \frac{4}{3}\pi(3)^3 = 36\pi \text{ ft}^3$$

Divide to find the number of BTUs in one cubic foot of natural gas.

$$\frac{\text{BTUs}}{1 \text{ ft}^3} = \frac{\text{BTUs in tank}}{\text{volume of tank}}$$

$$= \frac{116{,}151 \text{ BTUs}}{36\pi \text{ ft}^3}$$

$$\approx 1{,}027 \text{ BTUs}$$

(B) When the tank is filled with kerosene, it provides about 114,206,000 BTUs.

The volume of the tank is ________.

$$\frac{\text{BTUs}}{1\text{ ft}^3} = \frac{\text{BTUs in tank}}{\text{volume of tank}}$$

$$= \frac{\boxed{}\text{ BTUs}}{\boxed{}\text{ ft}^3}$$

$$\approx \boxed{}\text{ BTUs}$$

Reflect

6. Which fuel has a higher energy density?

7. One pint of water weighs approximately one pound. How many pints of water can be heated from 74°F to 75°F by one cubic foot of natural gas? How many pints of water can be heated from 75°F to 85°F by one cubic foot of natural gas?

Your Turn

8. A cylindrical tank has the dimensions shown. How many BTUs will the tank provide when filled with natural gas?

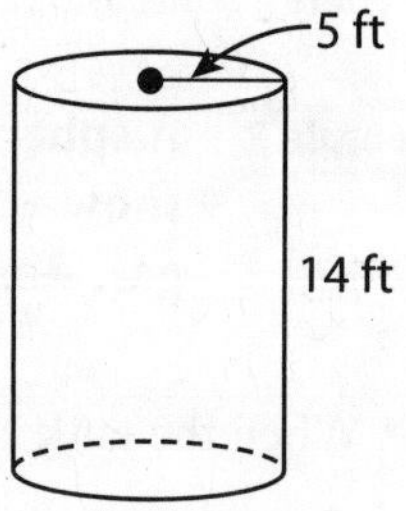

Elaborate

9. Pressure is defined in terms of force per unit area. Is pressure an example of a density?

10. **Essential Question Check-In** Describe the general concept of *density* and give two real-world examples.

Evaluate: Homework and Practice

Personal Math Trainer

- Online Homework
- Hints and Help
- Extra Practice

Determine which is denser.

1. Cylindrical logs of wood

Type of wood	Diameter (ft)	Height (ft)	Mass (lb)
Aspen	3.6	4.5	1,195
Juniper	3.0	6.0	1,487

2. Cylindrical bars of alloy

Alloy	Radius (cm)	Height (cm)	Mass (g)
Nichrome	3.9	27.2	10,800
Mild steel	4.6	18.8	9,840

3. Spherical tanks of liquefied gases

Liquefied Gas	Radius (m)	Mass (kg)
Oxygen (O_2), at −186°C	0.8	2477
Hydrogen (H_2), at −256°C	1.2	514

4. Colorado has a population of 5,268,367. Its territory can be modeled by a rectangle approximately 280 mi by 380 mi. Find the approximate population density of Colorado.

5. Tennessee has a population of 6,495,978. Its territory can be modeled by a trapezoid, as shown in the figure. Each unit on the coordinate grid represents one mile. Find the approximate population density of Tennessee.

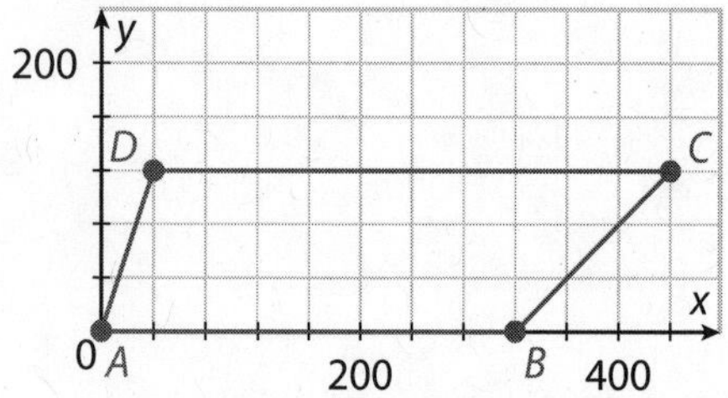

6. New Hampshire has a population of 1,323,459. Its territory can be modeled by a triangle, as shown in the figure. Each unit on the coordinate grid represents one mile. Find the approximate population density of New Hampshire.

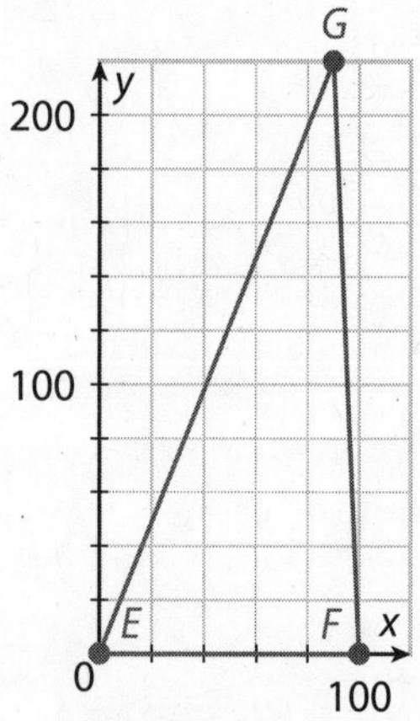

7. A spherical gas tank has a 10 foot diameter. When filled with propane, it provides 358,000,000 BTUs. How many BTUs does 1 cubic foot of propane yield? Round to the nearest thousand.

8. Ethan has collected information about the energy content of various fuels. Order the fuels by their energy density from greatest to least. (1 barrel = 42 gallons; 1 gallon = 8 pints)

Fuel	Heat Content
Jet fuel	5,670,000 BTUs/barrel
Gasoline	160,937 BTUs/gallon
Home fuel	138,690 BTUs/gallon
Propane	11,417 BTUs/pint

9. A fuel tank has a volume of 32 gallons. When filled with biodiesel, it provides 4,000,000 BTUs. How many BTUs does 1 gallon of biodiesel yield?

10. A piece of marble has been machine-carved into the shape of a cone with the dimensions shown. It has a mass of 169 kg. What is the density of the marble, to the nearest kilogram per cubic meter?

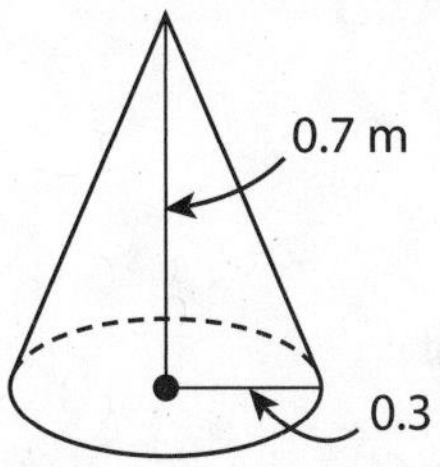

11. **Metallurgy** The purity of gold is measured in carats. 24-carat gold is pure gold, and has a density of 19.3 g/cm^3. 18-carat gold is often used for jewelry because it holds its shape better than pure gold. An 18-carat gold ring, which is 75% pure gold, has a mass of 18 g. What volume of pure gold was used to make the ring, to the nearest hundredth?

12. Agriculture The maximum grain yield for corn is achieved by planting at a density of 38,000 plants per acre. A farmer wants to maximize the yield for the field represented on the coordinate grid. Each unit on the coordinate grid represents one foot. How many corn plants, to the nearest thousand, does the farmer need? (*Hint:* 1 acre = 43,560 ft^2)

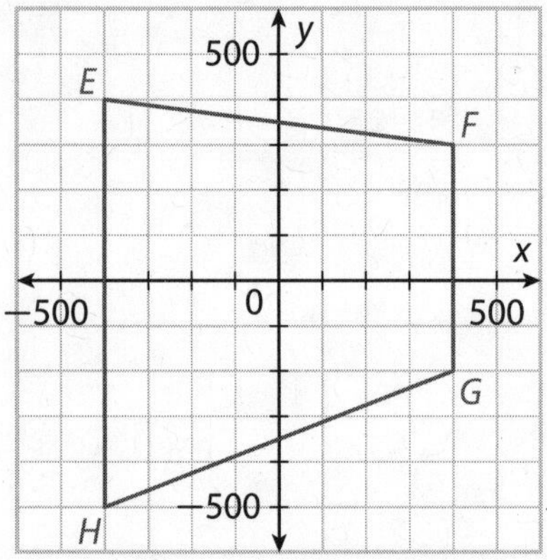

13. The density of water at 4°C is 1000 kg/m^3. A cubic meter of water, when frozen to −20°C, has a volume of 1.0065 m^3. What is the density of ice at this temperature, to the nearest tenth?

14. Space A launch vehicle is designed to carry up to 35 tons of payload into orbit. When fully fueled, it will contain 1,216,000 kg of liquid oxygen (LO_2) at a density of 1155 kg/m^3 and 102,000 kg of liquid hydrogen (LH_2) at a density of 71 kg/m^3. What is the total volume of liquefied gases carried by the launch vehicle, to the nearest tenth?

15. Manila, Philippines, has one of the highest population densities in the world with 111,002 people/mi^2. Manila's total population is 1,652,171. How large is Manilla, to the nearest tenth of a square mile?

16. Multistep A building has apartments on 67 floors and each floor measures 110 feet by 85 feet. Currently, 2340 people live in the building. Find the population density of the building to the nearest person per square mile, in terms of the area occupied by the building at street level. Also find the population density of the building in terms of its total floor area. (*Hint*: 1 mi^2 = 27,878,400 ft^2)

17. The caloric density of foods is a useful tool when comparing calorie counts. The table shows typical serving sizes for several foods and the number of calories per serving. Complete the fourth column. Then use the final column to number the foods from the lowest caloric density to the highest. Round to the nearest calorie per gram.

Food	Grams (g)	Calories (Cal)	Cal per 100 g	
1 cubic inch cheddar cheese	17	69		
1 large hard boiled egg	50	78		
1 medium apple	138	72		
1.5 ounces raisins	43	129		

H.O.T. Focus on Higher Order Thinking

18. Analyze Relationships The graph shows the relationship between mass and volume for pure silver. Use the graph to determine the density of pure silver to the nearest tenth and explain your method.

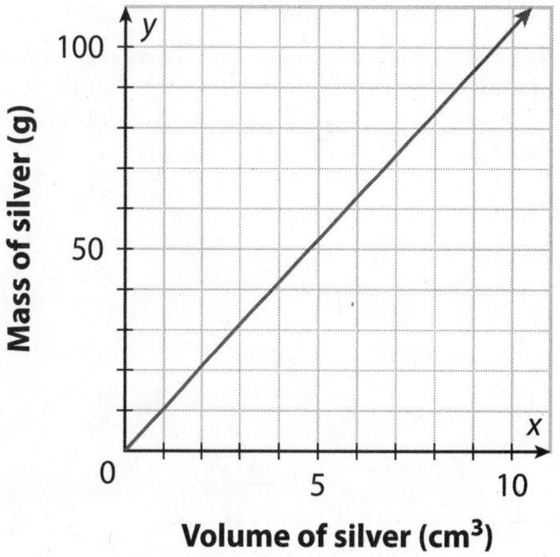

19. Communicate Mathematical Ideas According to Archimedes' Principle, an object placed in water will experience an upward force equal to the weight of water the object displaces. It is this upward force that causes objects less dense than water to float. For example, a cork floats when it is displacing a weight of water exactly equal to its own weight. When placed in water, what percent of a cork's volume will remain above the surface? Explain your answer.

	Density
Cork	0.24 g/cm^3
Water	1.00 g/cm^3

Lesson Performance Task

A regular pyramid made of pure gold with the dimensions shown has a mass of 160.5 grams. Find the density of gold. Round to the nearest tenth. If the dimensions of the pyramid doubled, what would change about the mass and density?

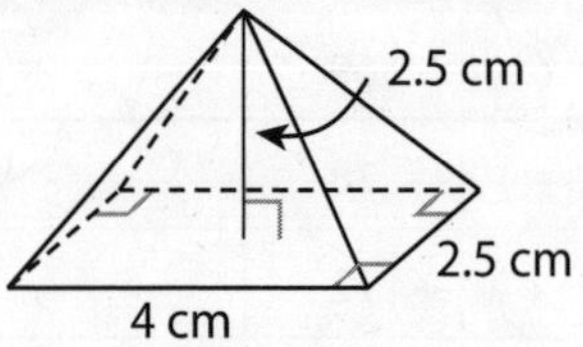

Name________________________ Class______________ Date________

4.3 Problem Solving with Constraints

Resource Locker

Essential Question: How can you model situations to meet real-world constraints?

Explore Maximizing Volume

Real-world problems often involve constraints. For example, for a given surface area, a sphere maximizes volume, but this is not usually the best shape for a package design.

Suppose you want to build a storage box from a rectangular piece of plywood that measures 4 ft by 8 ft. You must use six pieces, for the top, bottom, and sides of the box, and you can only make cuts perpendicular to the edges of the plywood. Given these constraints, what design appears to give the maximum possible volume for the box?

(A) Consider the top, bottom, front, and back of the box. Which dimensions must these rectangular pieces have in common?

____

____

(B) Sketch two possible sets of cuts of the plywood. You do not have to use all the plywood in your design. Label your sketch with all the dimension information you have, using variable expressions if necessary.

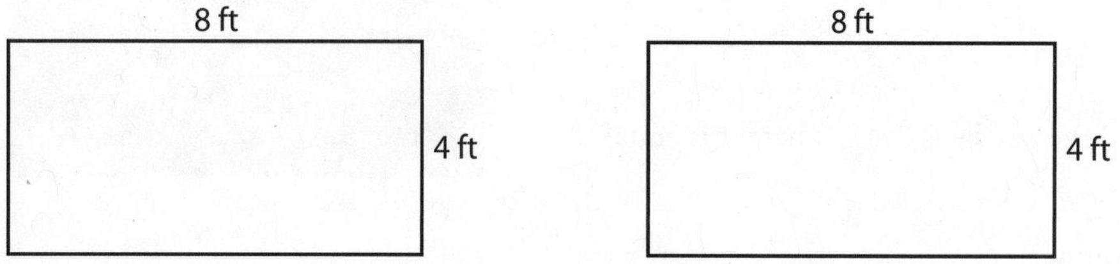

(C) Calculate the volume of the resulting box for each of your designs.

(D) Which design is better? Do you think one of your designs provides the greatest possible volume given the constraints of the problem?

____

____

Reflect

1. How effective is this design in maximizing the volume? Explain.

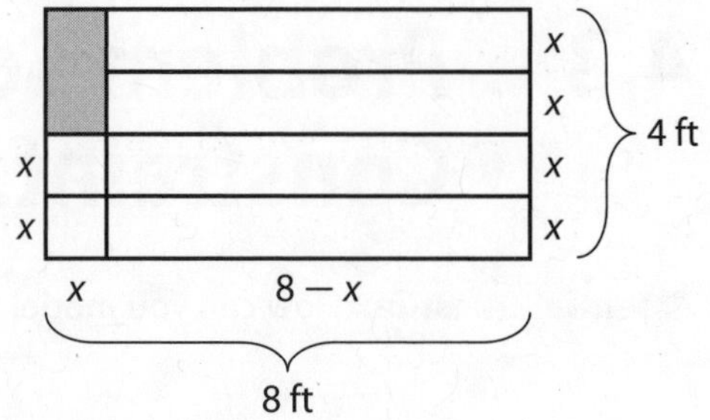

2. **Discussion** Compare results with others in your class. What seems to be a good strategy?

Explain 1 Determining Dimensions Given a Volume

Volume formulas are useful for solving problems where the constraint is to use a given volume of material for a given shape. For instance, suppose you want to make a cylindrical candle using a given amount of wax. You can use the formula for the volume of a cylinder to determine the candle's dimensions.

Example 1 **Determine the necessary dimensions.**

(A) You have 150 cm^3 of wax and want to make a cylindrical candle. If you want the candle's height and diameter to be equal, what radius and height should it have, to the nearest tenth?

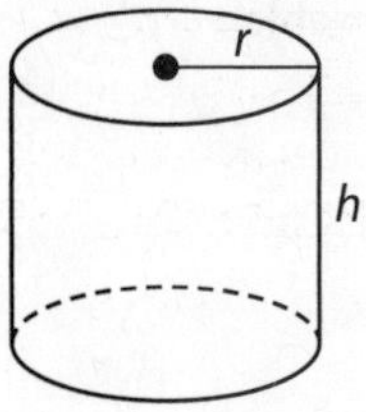

The diameter of the candle is $2r$. The height is equal to the diameter, so $h = 2r$.

The candle's volume is: $V = \pi r^2 h$

Substitute $2r$ for h: $V = \pi r^2(2r)$

Simplify: $V = 2\pi r^3$

Substitute the given volume of wax: $150 = 2\pi r^3$

Solve for r^3. $r^3 = \frac{150}{2\pi} \approx 23.9$

Use a graphing calculator to graph each side of the equation as a separate function.

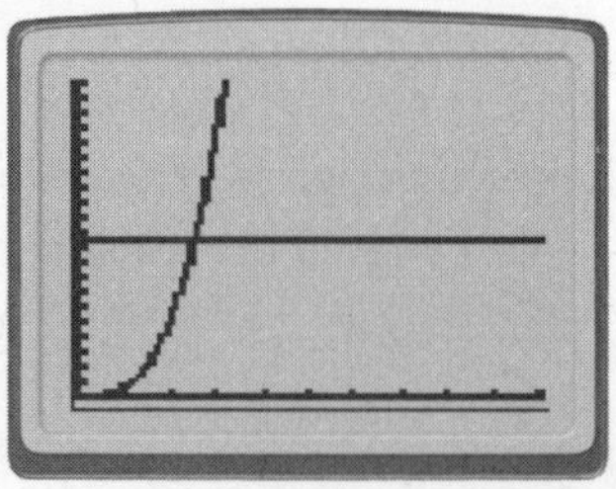

Graph $y = r^3$ and $y = 23.9$. The coordinates of the intersection are $(2.879..., 23.9)$.

The radius of the candle should be 2.9 cm. The height of the candle should be twice the radius or 5.8 cm.

(B) You have 300 cm^3 of wax and want to make a candle in the shape of a square prism. If you want the candle to be twice as tall as it is wide, what side lengths should it have, to the nearest tenth?

Let the length of the base be b. The height h is twice the base or ______________.

The candle's volume is: ______________

Substitute $2b$ for h: ______________

Simplify: ______________

Substitute the given volume of wax: ______________

Solve for b^3. ______________

Graph $y = b^3$ and $y =$ ______________. The coordinates of the intersection are ______________.

The side lengths of the square base of the candle should be ______________. The height of the candle should be twice the base or ______________.

Reflect

3. How can you check that your answer to Example 1B is reasonable?

____

____

Your Turn

4. You want to make a conical candle using 15 $in.^3$ of wax. If the candle's height is twice its diameter, what radius and height should it have, to the nearest tenth?

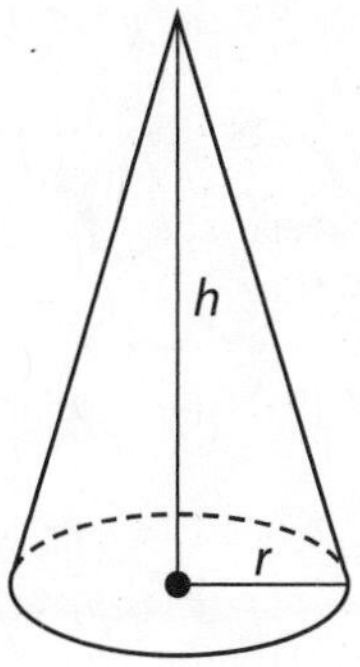

5. You have an octagonal candle mold that has a base that is three inches across and has side length 1.2 inches. If you use this mold to make a candle using 50 $in.^3$ of wax, how tall will the candle be?

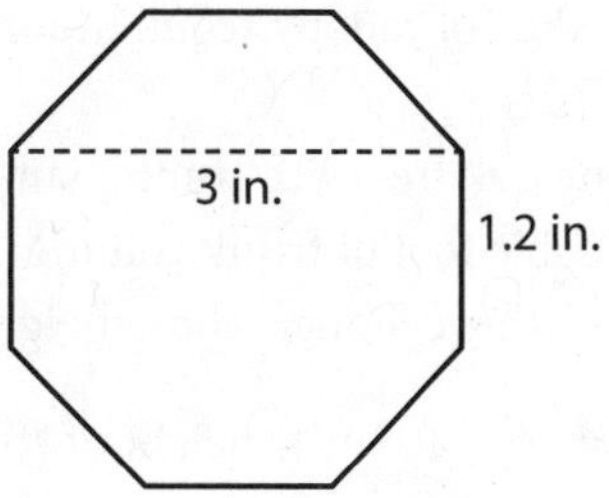

Explain 2 Modeling to Meet Constraints

A full-grown tree needs to have a minimum size canopy to photosynthesize enough sugar to feed the tree's bulk. This constraint can be modeled by relating the tree's canopy surface area to the volume of its trunk. By making some simplifying assumptions, you can explore this relationship.

Example 2 **What is the minimum radius for the described tree, to the nearest foot?**

(A) Suppose a full-grown oak tree with trunk diameter 6 ft requires at least 8 ft^2 of exterior canopy area per cubic foot of trunk volume. Model the canopy with a hemisphere, and model the trunk with a cylinder whose height is three times its diameter.

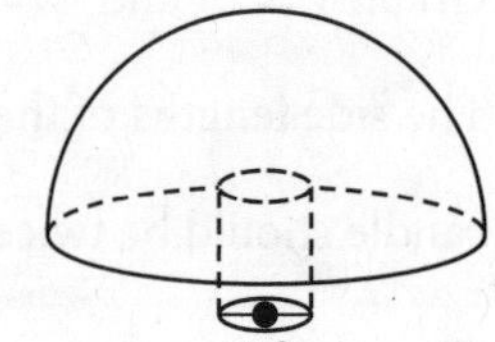

Find the volume of the trunk.

Radius of trunk $= \frac{1}{2}(6 \text{ ft}) = 3$ ft   Height of trunk $= 3(6 \text{ ft}) = 18$ ft

Volume of trunk $= \pi r^2 h = \pi(3)^2(18) = 162\pi \text{ ft}^3$

Find the minimum exterior canopy area for this size of trunk.

Minimum exterior canopy area $= \frac{8 \text{ ft}^2}{1 \text{ ft}^3} \times \left(162\pi \text{ ft}^3\right) = 1{,}296\pi \text{ ft}^2$

Write an expression for the curved surface area of a hemisphere with radius r.

Surface area $= \frac{1}{2}\left(4\pi r^2\right) = 2\pi r^2$

Write an equation that shows the relation between the surface area and the canopy area.

Surface area = Minimum canopy area

$2\pi r^2 = 1{,}296\pi$

$r^2 = \frac{1{,}296\pi}{2\pi} = 648$ $r = \sqrt{648} \approx 25\text{ft}$

The minimum radius of canopy required for this oak tree is 25 feet.

(B) Suppose a growing oak tree with trunk diameter 12 inches requires at least 12 ft^2 of exterior canopy area per cubic foot of trunk volume. Model the canopy with a hemisphere, and model the trunk with a cylinder whose height is 24 times its diameter.

radius of trunk = ☐ ft   height of trunk = ☐

Volume of trunk $= \pi r^2 h = \pi(\square)^2(\square) = \square \pi \text{ ft}^3$

Curved surface area = Minimum canopy area

$\frac{1}{2}(4\pi r^2) = \frac{\square \text{ ft}^2}{1 \text{ ft}^3} \times \left(\square \pi \text{ ft}^3\right)$

$2\pi r^2 = \square \pi \text{ ft}^2$

$r^2 = \frac{\square}{\square} = \square$ $r = \square = \square$

The minimum radius of canopy required for this oak tree is 6 feet.

Reflect

6. **Discussion** How could you use this model to make decisions about planting trees?

Your Turn

7. Assume a mature sequoia tree requires at least 0.6 m^2 of exterior canopy area per cubic meter of trunk volume. Also assume that the canopy can be modeled by a cone whose slant height is 4 times its radius, and that the trunk of the tree can be modeled by a cone whose height is 12 times its diameter. The formula for the lateral surface area of a cone is $A = \pi$(radius) (slant height). What is the minimum base radius of canopy required for a sequoia with trunk diameter 5 m? Round your answer to the nearest tenth.

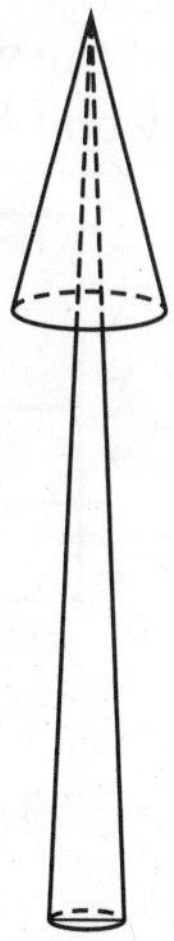

Elaborate

8. What is the role of a constraint in solving a real-world problem?

9. **Essential Question Check-In** How can you model situations to meet real-world constraints?

Evaluate: Homework and Practice

- Online Homework
- Hints and Help
- Extra Practice

Find the volume of each design for a box built from a piece of plywood measuring 60 cm by 180 cm.

1.

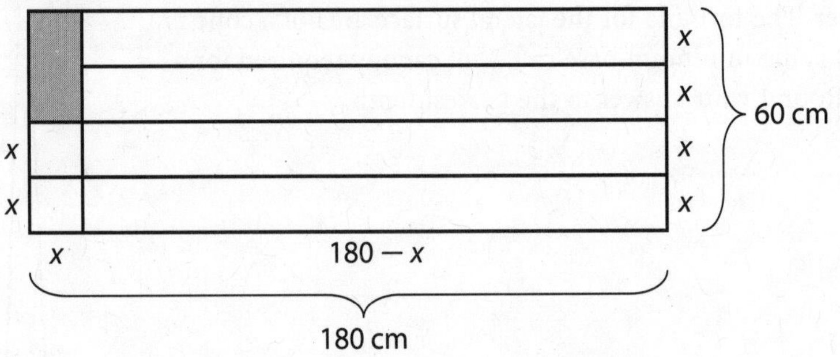

2.

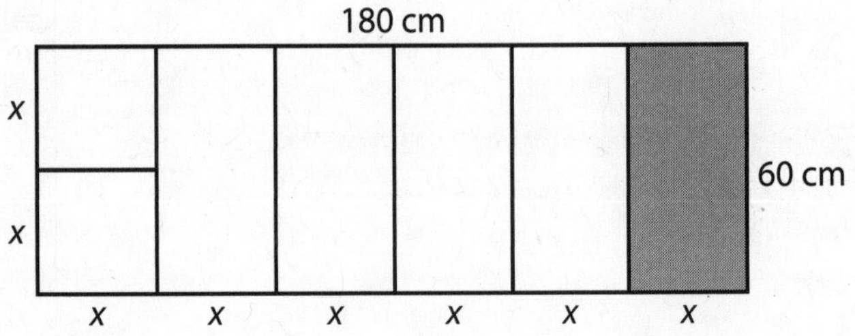

3.

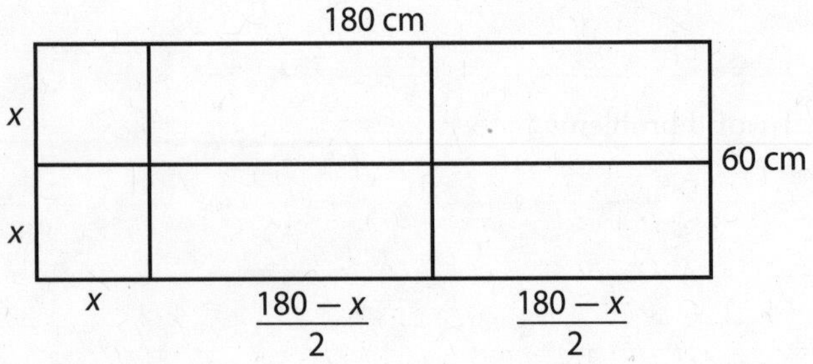

4.

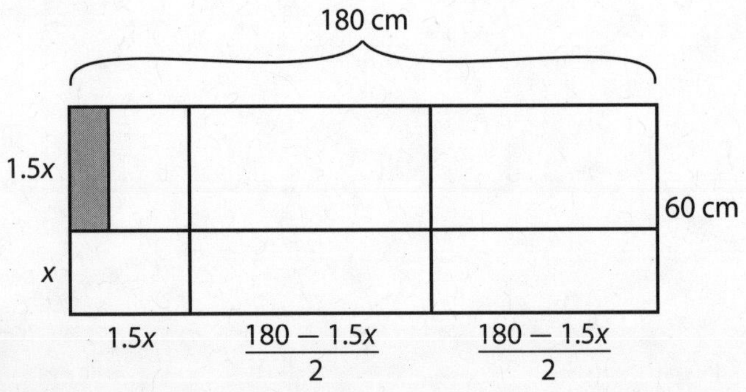

5. A cylindrical candle is to be made from 18 in^3 of wax. If the candle's height is twice its diameter, what radius and height should it have, to the nearest tenth?

6. A conical candle is to be made from 240 cm^3 of wax. If the candle's height is three times its diameter, what radius and height should it have, to the nearest tenth?

7. The design specifications for a coffee mug state that it should be cylindrical, with height 1.5 times its diameter, and with a capacity of 450 mL when filled to the brim. What interior radius and height should the coffee mug have, to the nearest tenth of a centimeter? (*Hint:* 1 mL = 1 cm^3)

8. A bob for a pendulum clock will be a cone of equal height and diameter, made from 3 in^3 of metal. What radius and height should the bob have, to the nearest tenth?

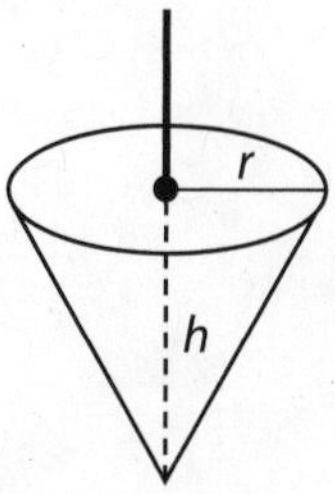

9. Assume a full-grown oak tree requires at least 8 ft^2 of exterior canopy area per cubic foot of trunk volume. Model the canopy with a hemisphere, and model the trunk using a cylinder whose height is three times its diameter. What is the minimum radius of canopy required for an oak with trunk diameter 9 ft? Round your answer to the nearest foot.

10. A mature beech tree requires at least 20 m^2 of exterior canopy area per cubic meter of trunk volume. Model the canopy with a hemisphere, and model the trunk using a cylinder whose height is three times its diameter. What is the minimum radius of canopy required for a beech with trunk diameter 2 m? Round your answer to the nearest foot.

11. Assume a mature sequoia tree requires at least 0.6 m^2 of exterior canopy area per cubic meter of trunk volume. Model the canopy with a cone whose slant height is 4 times its radius. Model the trunk with a cone whose height is 12 times its diameter. What is the minimum base radius of canopy required for a sequoia with trunk diameter 8 m? Round your answer to the nearest tenth.

12. Assume a mature Douglas fir requires at least 2 ft^2 of exterior canopy area per cubic foot of trunk volume. Model the canopy with a cone whose slant height is 4 times its diameter, and model the trunk with a cone whose height is 12 times its diameter. What is the minimum base radius of canopy required for a Douglas fir with trunk diameter 4 ft? Round your answer to the nearest tenth.

13. None of the designs in Questions 1–4 actually maximize the volume of a box made from a 60 cm by 180 cm plywood sheet. Find a design that does maximize the volume. (*Hint:* Use two variables, x and y, for the dimensions of the two side pieces.)

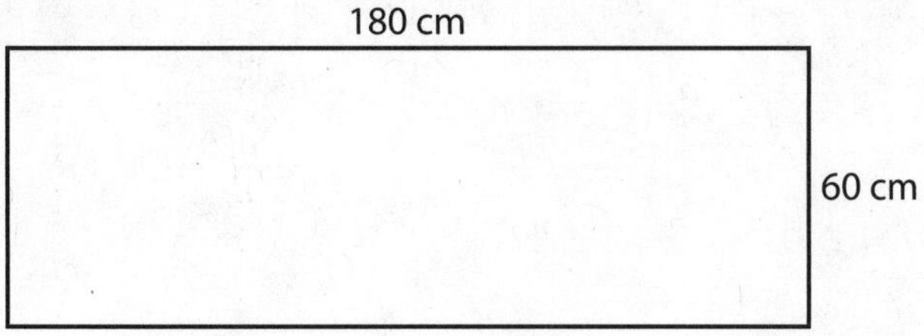

14. Jack is planning to build an aquarium in the shape of a rectangular prism. He wants the base to measure 90 cm by 40 cm. The maximum safe weight this type of aquarium can support is 150 kg. Given that the density of water is 0.001 kg/cm^3 and that Jack estimates he will have 5 kg of rocks, sand, and fish to put in the aquarium, what is the aquarium's maximum height, to the nearest centimeter?

15. Rita is making a box from a 2 ft by 5 ft piece of plywood. The box does not need a top, so only five pieces are needed. Suggest two designs to maximize the volume of the box. Check your designs by calculating the volume.

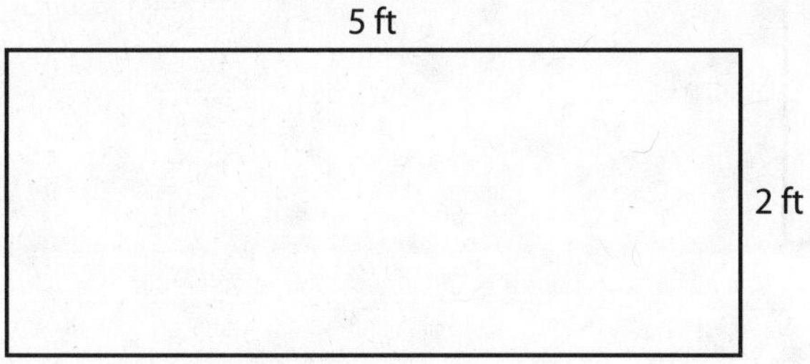

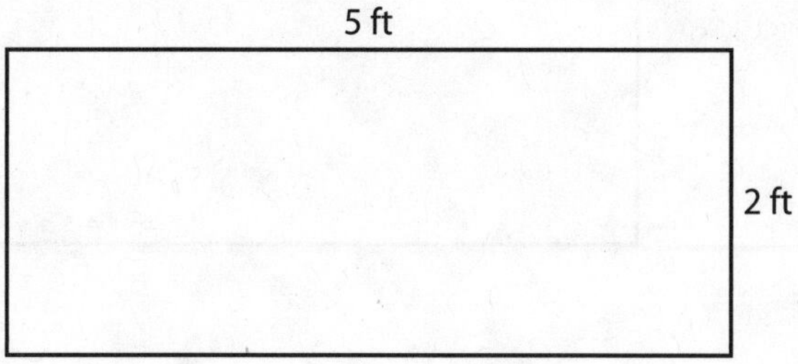

16. Multi-step A propane tank is designed in the shape of a cylinder with two hemispherical ends. The cylinder's height is twice its diameter, and the tank's capacity is 1,000 gal. What is the radius of the tank, to the nearest tenth of a foot? (*Hint:* 1 ft^3 = 7.48 gal)

17. A cylindrical space station is 5 m in diameter and 12 m long, and it requires 0.2 m^2 of solar panels per cubic meter of volume to provide power. If it has two sets of rectangular solar panels, each 2 m wide, how long should each set of panels be? Round your answer to the nearest tenth.

18. Create a design to make a cylinder, including both circular ends, from a sheet of metal that measures 150 cm by 60 cm. Calculate the volume of your design, to the nearest thousand cubic centimeters.

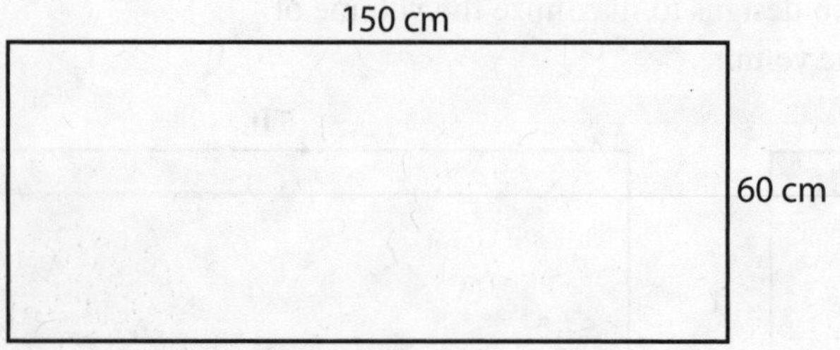

19. A roll of aluminum foil is 15 in. wide. It has an interior diameter of 1.2 in. and an exterior diameter of 1.6 in. If the foil is 0.001 in. thick, what length of foil is rolled up, to the nearest foot? (*Hint:* Start by finding the volume of a 1-ft length of foil 15 in. wide.)

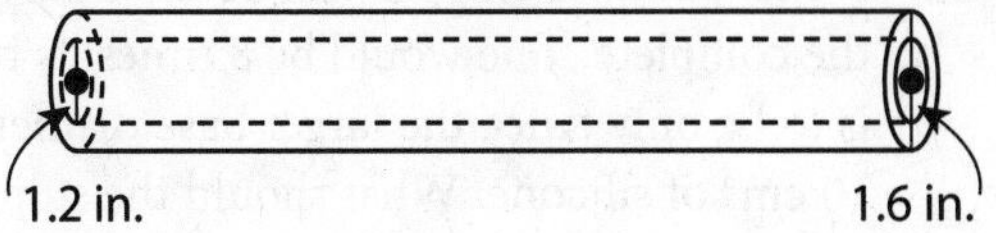

20. Assume a full-grown oak tree requires at least 8 ft^2 of exterior canopy area per cubic foot of trunk volume. Model the canopy with a hemisphere. Model the trunk with a cylinder whose height is three times its diameter. Develop a formula for the minimum radius R of canopy required for an oak with trunk radius r, in feet.

H.O.T. Focus on Higher Order Thinking

21. What If? An animal's weight is proportional to its volume. The strength in its legs to support its weight is proportional to their cross-sectional area. Imagine magnifying a mouse to the size of an elephant. If its length is multiplied by 50, and its density and proportions stay the same, what are the multipliers for its weight and the cross-sectional areas for its legs? Would a mouse this size be able to support itself?

22. Multi-step A stopper will be the shape of the frustum of a cone. The height of the complete cone would be 8 times its base diameter, but the stopper's height is to be only twice the larger base diameter. The stopper is to be made from 10 cm^3 of silicone. What should the stopper's base radius R, base radius r, and height be, to the nearest tenth?

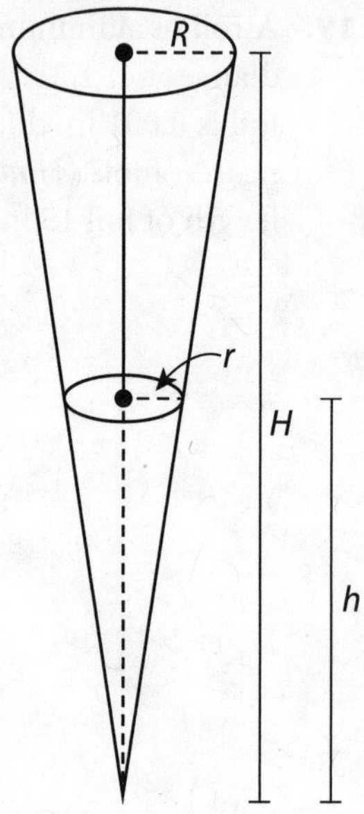

23. Look for a Pattern An aluminum soda can holds 12 fl oz. Investigate the least amount of aluminum needed to make the can: Use the given volume to find a formula for the can's height h in terms of its radius r, substitute into a formula for the can's surface area, and use trial values to determine the values of r and h, to the nearest tenth of an inch, that minimize the can's surface area. (*Hint*: 1 fl oz $= 1.73$ in^3)

24. Persevere in Problem Solving People have a wide variety of body plans, from endomorphic (short and stocky) to ectormorphic (tall and slender). These body plans represent adaptations to cold or hot climates from earlier in human history. A higher surface area to volume ratio allows body heat to be shed more easily in a hot climate, while a lower ratio helps to retain body heat in very cold conditions. Complete the table. Find the ratio of surface area to volume for each body plan. How much greater is the ratio for the ectomorphic body plan than for the endomorphic one? (For each cylindrical form, count only one circular base in addition to the curved surface.)

Endomorphic body plan			
Part of Body	**Form and Dimensions**	**Volume**	**Exterior Surface Area**
Head	sphere, $d = 6$ in.		
Torso	cylinder, $d = 15$ in., $h = 30$ in.		
Arms	cylinder, $d = 3$ in., $h = 24$ in.		
Legs	cylinder, $d = 6$ in., $h = 28$ in.		
Whole body			

Ectomorphic body plan			
Part of Body	**Form and Dimensions**	**Volume**	**Exterior Surface Area**
Head	sphere, $d = 6$ in.		
Torso	cylinder, $d = 10$ in., $h = 32$ in.		
Arms	cylinder, $d = 2$ in., $h = 34$ in.		
Legs	cylinder, $d = 4$ in., $h = 36$ in.		
Whole body			

Lesson Performance Task

In trying to disguise a gift, Henry decides to put a box of blocks into a cylindrical box. The set of blocks is a cube that measures 4 inches on each side. About how much extra wrapping paper will Henry use as a result of this decision?

Modeling and Problem Solving

Essential Question: How can you use modeling to solve real-world problems?

Key Vocabulary

density *(densidad)*

scale factor *(factor de escala)*

KEY EXAMPLE *(Lesson 4.1)*

Find the surface area and volume of a rectangular prism-shaped box measuring 6 inches by 8 inches by 12 inches. Then multiply the dimensions by 2 and find the new surface area and volume. Describe the changes that took place.

$2(6 \times 8) + 2(6 \times 12) + 2(8 \times 12) = 96 + 144 + 192$ Find the original surface area.

$= 432 \text{ in}^2$

$6 \times 8 \times 12 = 576 \text{ in}^3$ Find the original volume.

$2(12 \times 16) + 2(12 \times 24) + 2(16 \times 24) = 384 + 576 + 768$ Find the new surface area.

$= 1{,}728 \text{ in}^2$

$12 \times 16 \times 24 = 4608 \text{ in}^3$ Find the new volume

$\frac{1728}{432} = 4$ Compare the surface areas. $\frac{4608}{576} = 8$ Compare the volumes.

The surface area is multiplied by 4. The volume is multiplied by 8.

KEY EXAMPLE *(Lesson 4.2)*

Logan County, Kansas, has a population of 2,784. Its border can be modeled by a rectangle with vertices $A(-18, 15)$, $B(18, 15)$, $C(18, -15)$, and $D(-18, -15)$, where each unit on the coordinate plane represents 1 mile. Find the approximate population density of Logan County. Round to the nearest tenth.

$18 - (-18) = 36$ mi The width of Logan County is the difference of the x-coordinates.

$15 - (-15) = 30$ mi The height of Logan County is the difference of the y-coordinates.

$36 \times 30 = 1080 \text{ mi}^2$ area = length × width

$\frac{2784}{1080} \approx 2.6$ Population density $= \frac{\text{population}}{\text{area}}$

The population density is about 2.6 persons per square mile.

KEY EXAMPLE *(Lesson 4.3)*

The height of a filing cabinet is 1.5 times the width. The depth is twice the width. The volume of the cabinet is 12,288 in³. What are the cabinet's dimensions?

$\text{Volume} = l \times w \times h$ Write the formula for the volume.

$12{,}288 = x \times 1.5x \times 2x$ Substitute for the volume, width, height, and depth.

$x = \sqrt[3]{4096}$ Simplify.

$x = 16$ Evaluate the cube root.

Width: 16 inches. Height: $1.5 \times 16 = 24$ inches. Depth: $2 \times 16 = 32$ inches.

EXERCISES

1. One side of a rhombus measures 12 inches. Two angles measure 60°. Find the perimeter and area of the rhombus. Then multiply the side lengths by 3. Find the new perimeter and area. Describe the changes that took place. *(Lesson 4.1)*

2. A box of cereal measures 2.25 inches by 7.5 inches by 10 inches. The box contains 16 ounces of cereal. Find the cereal density, to the nearest thousandth. *(Lesson 4.2)*

3. The height and diameter of a cylindrical water tank are equal. The tank has a volume of 1200 cubic feet. Find the height of the tank to the nearest tenth. *(Lesson 4.3)*

MODULE PERFORMANCE TASK

Population Density

Unlike most geographical regions, the Canadian province of Saskatchewan has a shape that is almost exactly a regular geometric figure. That figure is an isosceles trapezoid. Here are the lengths of the province's four borders:

North: 277 miles South: 390 miles East: 761 miles West: 761 miles

- Saskatchewan's population in the 2011 census was 1,033,381. What was its population density?
- Saskatchewan is divided into 18 census divisions. Division 18, which makes up the northern half of the province (actually 49.3% of the area), has a population of 36,557. How does the population density of Division 18 compare with that of the southern half of the province?

Start by listing on your own paper the information you will need to solve the problem. Then complete the task. Use numbers, words, or algebra to explain how you reached your conclusion.

Ready to Go On?

4.1–4.3 Modeling and Problem Solving

Personal Math Trainer
- Online Homework
- Hints and Help
- Extra Practice

Solve. Round answers to the nearest tenth. *(Lessons 4.1, 4.2, 4.3)*

1. A circle containing the point $(4, -2)$ has its center at $(1, 2)$. Describe the changes in the circumference and area of the circle if the radius is multiplied by 2.

2. Seven hundred people are gathered in a trapezoidal park with bases measuring 60 yards and 80 yards and a height of 50 yards.

a. Find the population density of the park.

b. Find the population density if the bases and height are halved.

3. An aquarium in the shape of a rectangular prism has a bottom, no top, two square sides, and two sides the same height as the square sides but twice their length. The total area of the five sides is 1800 in^2. Find the volume of the aquarium. Explain your reasoning.

4. A triangle has base b and height h. The base is doubled. Describe how the height must change so that the area remains the same. Explain your reasoning.

ESSENTIAL QUESTION

5. How can you use mathematics to model real-world situations?

MODULE 4
MIXED REVIEW

Assessment Readiness

1. The dimensions of a cube are tripled. Choose True or False for each statement.

A. The perimeter of each face is tripled. ◯ True ◯ False

B. The surface area of the cube is multiplied by 6. ◯ True ◯ False

C. The volume of the cube is multiplied by 27. ◯ True ◯ False

2. A solid figure has a volume of 300 cubic centimeters. The radius and the height of the figure are equal. Select Yes or No for A–C.

A. The figure could be a cylinder with a radius of $\sqrt{\frac{300}{\pi}}$. ◯ Yes ◯ No

B. The figure could be a cone with a radius of $\sqrt[3]{\frac{900}{\pi}}$. ◯ Yes ◯ No

C. The figure could be a cylinder with a height of $\sqrt[3]{\frac{300}{\pi}}$. ◯ Yes ◯ No

3. A 4-square-mile community of prairie dogs in South Dakota has a total population of 12,000. Over a 3-year period, the total population increases at an average rate of 2% per year. Describe the change in the population density, assuming the total area of the community remains unchanged.

4. A city park in the shape of a right triangle has an area of $450\sqrt{3}$ square yards. One leg of the triangle measures half the length of the hypotenuse. What are the dimensions of the park? Explain your reasoning.

Assessment Readiness

Personal Math Trainer
- Online Homework
- Hints and Help
- Extra Practice

Consider each congruence theorem below. Can you use the theorem to determine whether $\triangle ABC \cong \triangle ABD$?

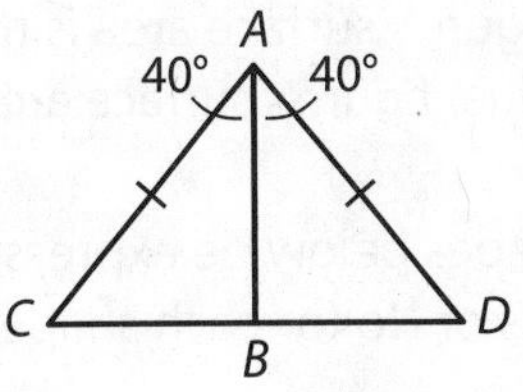

Select Yes or No for A–C.

A. ASA Triangle Congruence Theorem ○ Yes ○ No

B. SAS Triangle Congruence Theorem ○ Yes ○ No

C. SSS Triangle Congruence Theorem ○ Yes ○ No

1. For each pyramid, determine whether the statement regarding its surface area is true.

Select True or False for each statement.

A. A square pyramid with $s = 10$ m and $h = 12$ m has surface area 240 m^2. ○ True ○ False

B. A triangular pyramid with perimeter $P = 14$ ft and $\ell = 5$ ft has surface area 70 ft^2. ○ True ○ False

C. A pyramid with the same base and height of a prism has less surface area. ○ True ○ False

2. For each shape, determine whether the statement regarding its surface area is true.

Select True or False for each statement.

A. A cone with base radius $r = 5$ in. and $\ell = 12$ in. has surface area 85π in^2. ○ True ○ False

B. A sphere with radius $r = \frac{6}{\pi}$ m has surface area $\frac{144}{\pi}$ m^2. ○ True ○ False

C. The surface areas of a sphere with $r = 3$ in. and a cylinder with $r = 3$ in. and $h = 3$ in. are the same. ○ True ○ False

3. DeMarcus draws $\triangle ABC$. Then he translates it along the vector $\langle -4, -3 \rangle$, rotates it 180°, and reflects it across the x-axis.

Choose True or False for each statement.

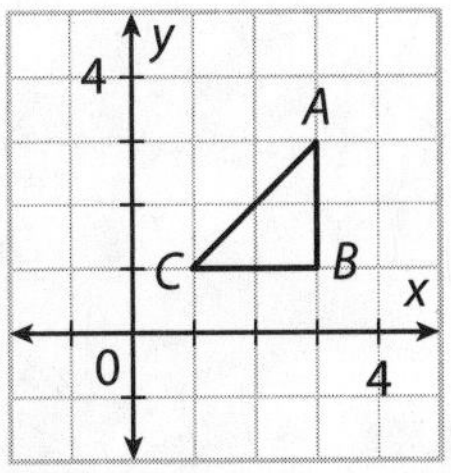

A. The final image of $\triangle ABC$ is in Quadrant IV. ○ True ○ False

B. The final image of $\triangle ABC$ is a right triangle. ○ True ○ False

C. DeMarcus will get the same result if he performs the reflection followed by the translation and rotation. ○ True ○ False

5. Determine whether each statement regarding surface area is true. Select True or False for each statement.

A. The surface area of a cone is the sum of the areas of a circle and sector of a circle. ○ True ○ False

B. The surface area of a sphere is greater than a cube's with $s = r$. ○ True ○ False

C. A composite figure's surface area is the sum of each individual figure's surface area. ○ True ○ False

6. Can each of the shapes below be expressed as a composite figure of equilateral triangles? Select Yes or No for each shape.

A. A pyramid ○ Yes ○ No

B. A hexagon ○ Yes ○ No

C. A pentagon ○ Yes ○ No

7. The figure shows a composite figure formed by two right triangles, a square, and a circle. Determine whether the probability of throwing a dart into each shape is correct, assuming that the dart will always land in one of the shapes. Select True or False for each statement.

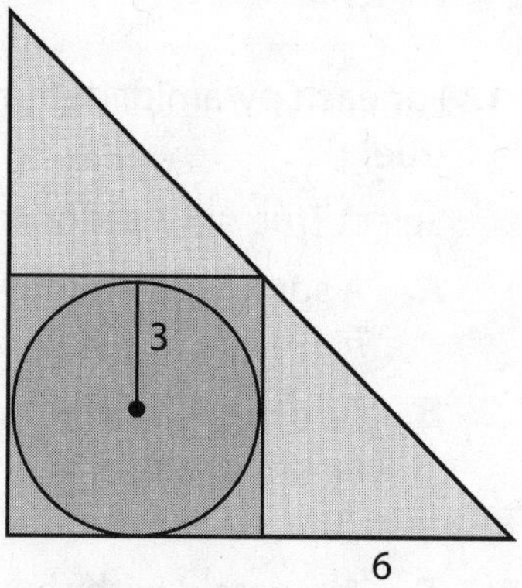

A. The probability of landing in the circle is $\frac{\pi}{8}$. ○ True ○ False

B. The probability of landing in one of the tan triangles is $\frac{1}{4}$. ○ True ○ False

C. The probability of landing in the square is $\frac{1}{2}$. ○ True ○ False

8. A cube is dilated by a factor of 4. By what factor does its volume increase? Explain your reasoning.

9. The perimeter of $\triangle PQR$ is 44 cm, and $\triangle PQR \sim \triangle WXY$. If $PQ = 12$ and $XY + WY = 24$, what is the perimeter of WXY?

Performance Tasks

★10. A scientist wants to compare the densities of two cylinders, but one is twice as high and has a diameter two times as long as the other. How should the scientist compare the two densities of the cylinders if he doesn't know the volume of the larger cylinder? If the volume of the smaller cylinder is 30 cm^3, what is the volume of the larger cylinder?

★★11. You are trying to pack in preparation for a trip and need to fit a collection of children's toys in a box. Each individual toy is a composite figure of four cubes, and all of the toys are shown in the figure. Arrange the toys in an orderly fashion so that they will fit in the smallest box possible. Draw the arrangement. What is the volume of the box if each of the cubes have side lengths of 10 cm?

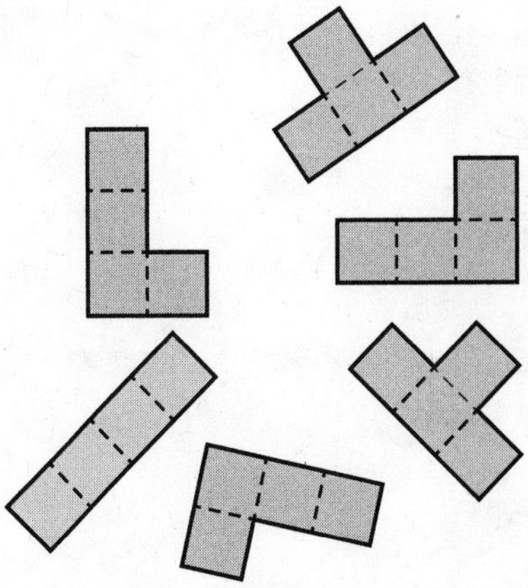

★★★12. A carpenter has a wooden cone with a slant height of 16 inches and a diameter of 12 inches. The vertex of the cone is directly above the center of its base. He measures halfway down the slant height and makes a cut parallel to the base. He now has a truncated cone and a cone half the height of the original.

A. He expected the two parts to weigh about the same, but they don't. Which is heavier? Why?

B. Find the ratio of the weight of the small cone to that of the truncated cone. Show your work.

MATH IN CAREERS

Model Maker A model maker wants to create a scale model of a sphere with a volume of 1000 m^3. The model should have a volume of 1000 cm^3. What scale factor should the model maker use? If a triangle drawn on the model has three right angles, what is its area?

UNIT 3

Polynomial Functions, Expressions, and Equations

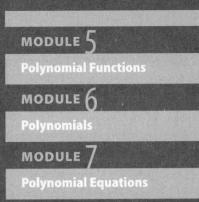

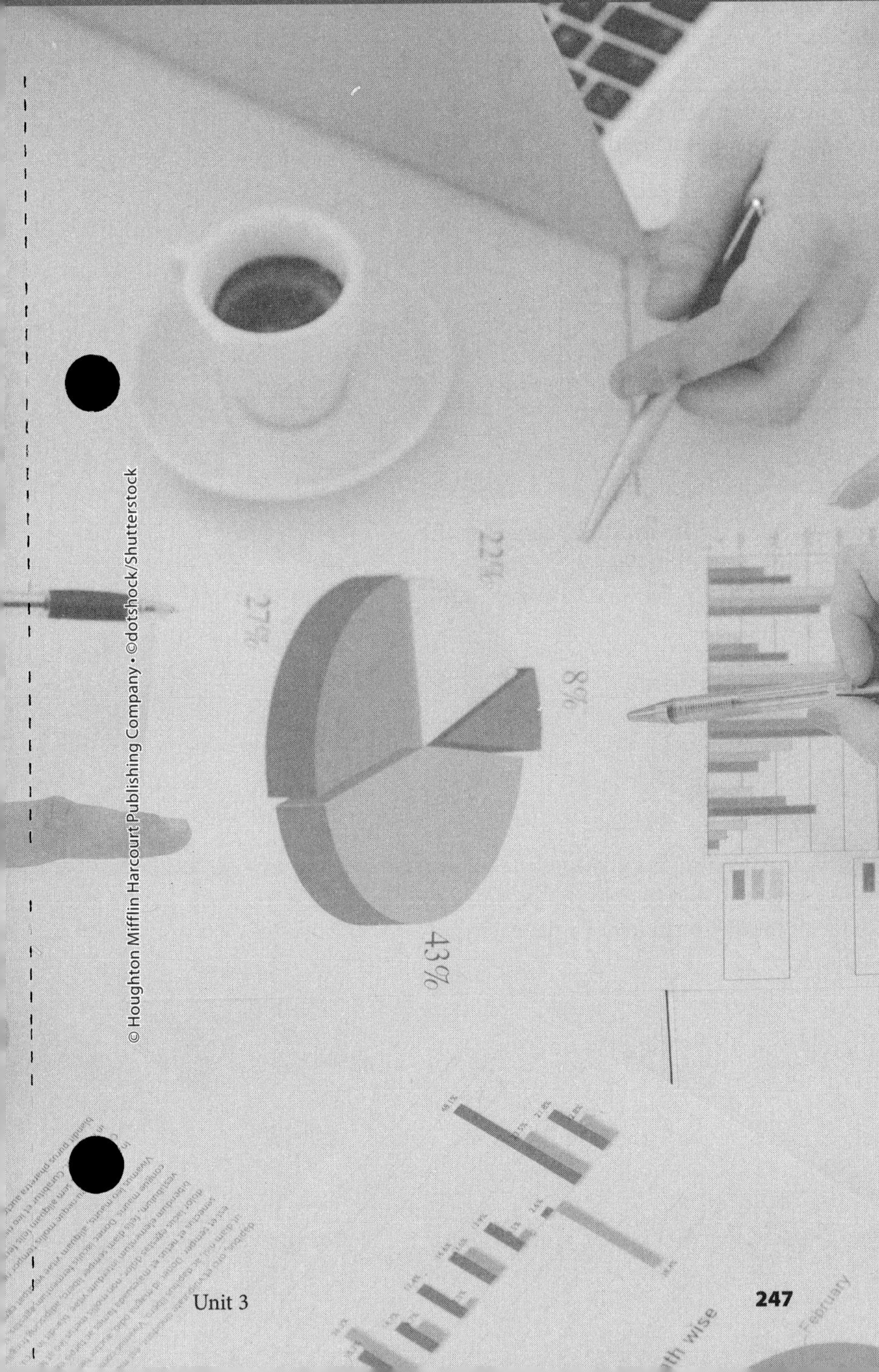

MATH IN CAREERS

Statistician Statisticians use math to describe patterns and relationships. Statisticians design surveys and collect data, and rely on mathematical modeling and computational methods to analyze their findings. They use these findings and analyses to help solve problems in various fields, such as business, engineering, the sciences, and government.

If you are interested in a career as a statistician, you should study these mathematical subjects:

- Algebra
- Geometry
- Calculus
- Differential Equations
- Probability
- Statistics

Research other careers that require understanding and analyzing data. Check out the career activity at the end of the unit to find out how **Statisticians** use math.

Reading Start-Up

Vocabulary

Review Words

✔ coefficient *(coeficiente)*
✔ factor *(factor)*
✔ parameter *(parámetro)*
✔ real number *(número real)*
✔ term *(término)*
✔ transformation *(transformación)*

Preview Words

binomial *(binomio)*
cubic function *(función cúbica)*
inverse function *(función inversa)*
monomial *(monomio)*
polynomial *(polinomio)*
root *(raíz)*
trinomial *(trinomio)*

Visualize Vocabulary

Use the review words to complete the chart.

	a number or expression that divides a product exactly
	a rational or irrational number
	a number, variable, product, or quotient in an expression
	one of the constants in a function or equation that may be changed
	a change in the size, position, or shape of a figure or graph
	a numerical factor in a term of an algebraic expression

Understand Vocabulary

To become familiar with some of the vocabulary terms in the module, consider the following. You may refer to the module, the glossary, or a dictionary.

1. A polynomial with two terms is a ___________________.

2. A polynomial function of degree 3 is a ___________________.

3. A ___________________ of a polynomial is a zero of the function associated with that polynomial.

Active Reading

Key-Term Fold Before beginning the unit, create a key-term fold to help you organize what you learn. Write a vocabulary term on each tab of the key-term fold. Under each tab, write the definition of the term and an example.

MODULE 5

Polynomial Functions

Essential Question: How can polynomial functions help to solve real-world problems?

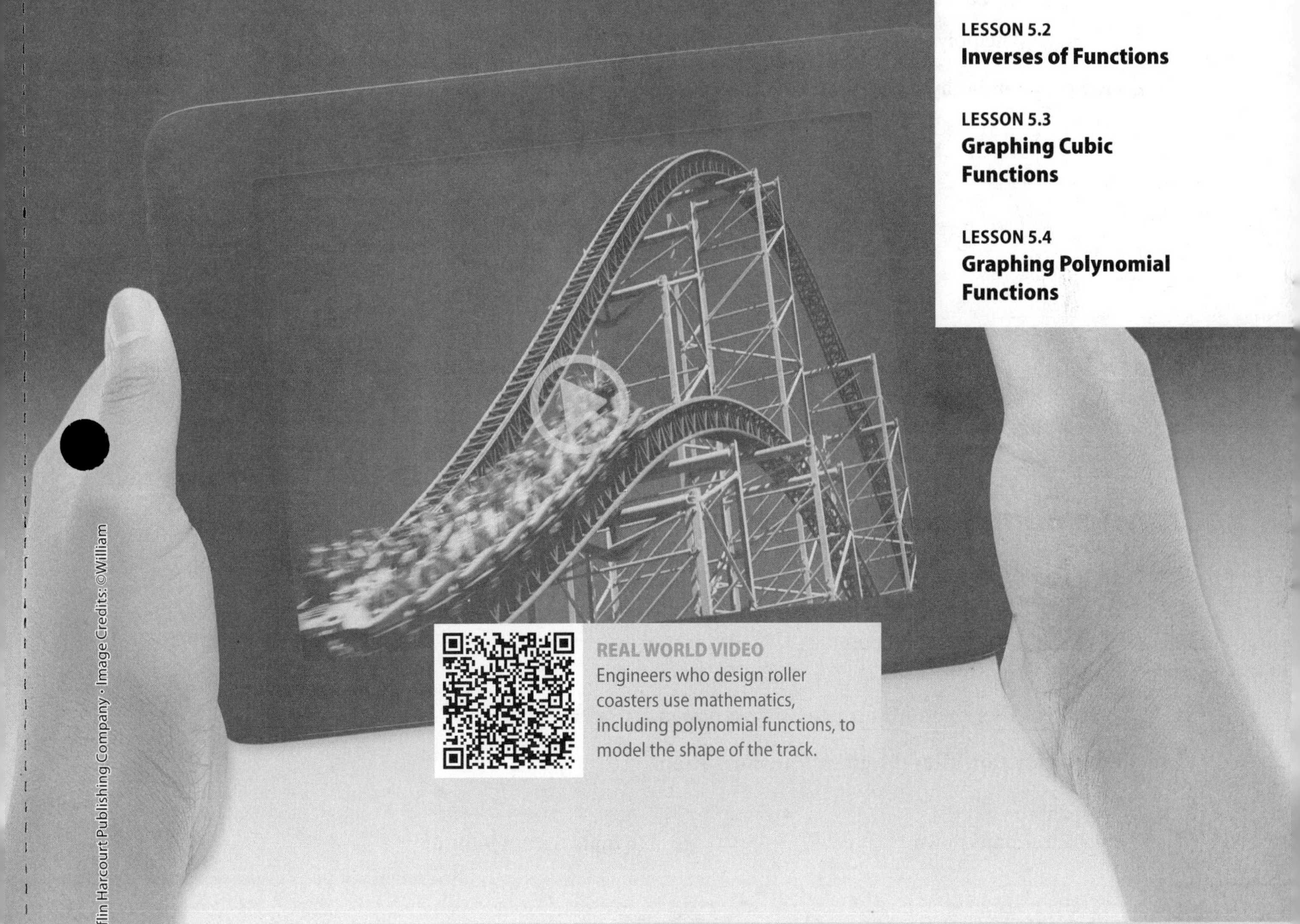

REAL WORLD VIDEO
Engineers who design roller coasters use mathematics, including polynomial functions, to model the shape of the track.

MODULE PERFORMANCE TASK PREVIEW

What's the Function of a Roller Coaster?

Nothing compares with riding a roller coaster. The thrill of a steep drop, the breathtaking speed, and the wind in your face make the ride unforgettable. How can a polynomial function model the path of a roller coaster? Hang on to your seat and let's find out!

Are YOU Ready?

Complete these exercises to review skills you will need for this module.

Personal Math Trainer

- Online Homework
- Hints and Help
- Extra Practice

Classifying Polynomials

Example 1 Classify the polynomial $2x^4 + x^3 - 1$ by its degree and number of terms.

Because the greatest exponent is 4, this is a quartic polynomial.

Because the polynomial has three terms, it is a trinomial.

The polynomial $2x^4 + x^3 - 1$ is a quartic trinomial.

Classify the polynomial by its degree and number of terms.

1. $3x^3$

2. $9x - 3y + 7$

3. $x^2 - 4$

4. $x^5 + x^4$

5. $5x^3 - 7y^2 + 2$

6. x

Transforming Cubic Functions

Example 2 The graph of $f(x) = 0.5(x - 3)^3 + 2$ is transformed 4 units right and 5 units down. Write the new function.

The inflection point is $(3, 2)$. Its location after the transformation is $(3 + 4, 2 - 5)$, or $(7, -3)$.

After the transformation, the function is $f'(x) = 0.5(x - 7)^3 - 3$.

Write the new function after the given transformation.

7. $g(x) = 0.25(x - 6)^3 - 1$
10 units left, 7 units down

8. $h(x) = (x + 9)^3 - 5$
6 units right, 4 units up

9. $f(x) = -0.5(x + 8)^3 + 12$
1 unit left, 3 units up

10. $f(x) = x^3$
3 units right, 2 units up

11. $g(x) = 5(x + 1)^3 - 4$
1 unit right, 4 units up

12. $h(x) = (x - 5)^3 + 5$
0.5 unit right, 1.5 units down

Name________________________ Class______________ Date__________

5.1 Transformations of Function Graphs

Resource Locker

Essential Question: What are the ways you can transform the graph of the function f(x)?

Explore 1 Investigating Translations of Function Graphs

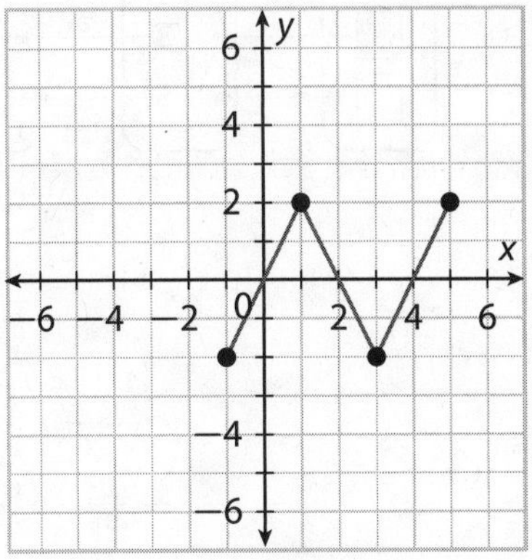

You can transform the graph of a function in various ways. You can translate the graph horizontally or vertically, you can stretch or compress the graph horizontally or vertically, and you can reflect the graph across the x-axis or the y-axis. How the graph of a given function is transformed is determined by the way certain numbers, called **parameters**, are introduced in the function. The graph of f(x) is shown. Use this graph for the exploration.

(A) First graph $g(x) = f(x) + k$ where k is the parameter. Let $k = 4$ so that $g(x) = f(x) + 4$. Complete the input-output table and then graph $g(x)$. In general, how is the graph of $g(x) = f(x) + k$ related to the graph of $f(x)$ when k is a positive number?

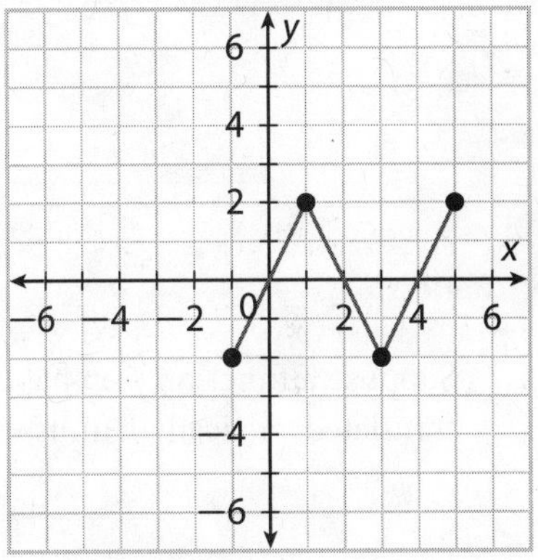

x	$f(x)$	$f(x) + 4$
−1	−2	2
1	2	6
3	−2	
5	2	

____

(B) Now try a negative value of k in $g(x) = f(x) + k$. Let $k = -3$ so that $g(x) = f(x) - 3$. Complete the input-output table and then graph $g(x)$ on the same grid. In general, how is the graph of $g(x) = f(x) + k$ related to the graph of $f(x)$ when k is a negative number?

x	$f(x)$	$f(x) - 3$
−1	−2	−5
1	2	−1
3	−2	
5	2	

____

Ⓒ Now graph $g(x) = f(x - h)$ where h is the parameter. Let $h = 2$ so that $g(x) = f(x - 2)$. Complete the mapping diagram and then graph $g(x)$. (To complete the mapping diagram, you need to find the inputs for g that produce the inputs for f after you subtract 2. Work backward from the inputs for f to the missing inputs for g by adding 2.) In general, how is the graph of $g(x) = f(x - h)$ related to the graph of $f(x)$ when h is a positive number?

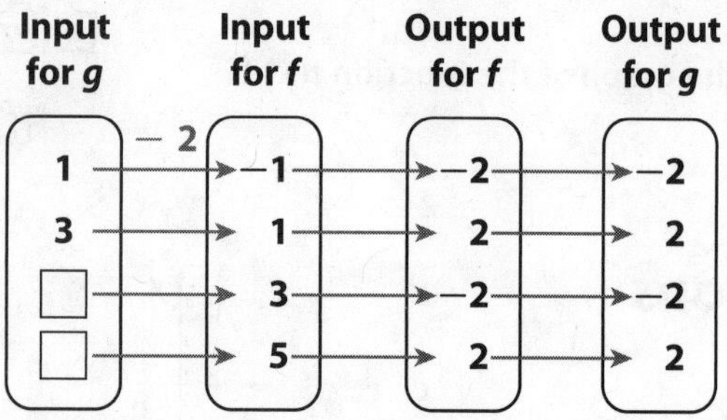

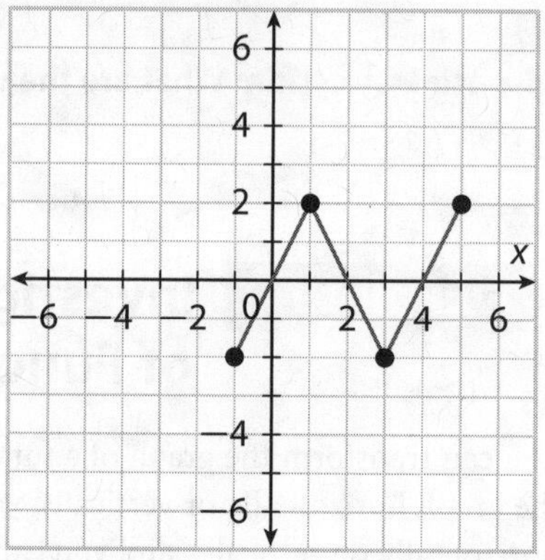

Ⓓ **Make a Conjecture** How would you expect the graph of $g(x) = f(x - h)$ to be related to the graph of $f(x)$ when h is a negative number?

Reflect

1. Suppose a function $f(x)$ has a domain of $[x_1, x_2]$ and a range of $[y_1, y_2]$. When the graph of $f(x)$ is translated vertically k units where k is either positive or negative, how do the domain and range change?

2. Suppose a function $f(x)$ has a domain of $[x_1, x_2]$ and a range of $[y_1, y_2]$. When the graph of $f(x)$ is translated horizontally h units where h is either positive or negative, how do the domain and range change?

3. You can transform the graph of $f(x)$ to obtain the graph of $g(x) = f(x - h) + k$ by combining transformations. Predict what will happen by completing the table.

Sign of h	Sign of k	Transformations of the Graph of $f(x)$
+	+	Translate right h units and up k units.
+	−	
−	+	
−	−	

Explore 2 Investigating Stretches and Compressions of Function Graphs

In this activity, you will consider what happens when you multiply by a positive parameter inside or outside a function. Throughout, you will use the same function $f(x)$ that you used in the previous activity.

(A) First graph $g(x) = a \cdot f(x)$ where a is the parameter. Let $a = 2$ so that $g(x) = 2f(x)$. Complete the input-output table and then graph $g(x)$. In general, how is the graph of $g(x) = a \cdot f(x)$ related to the graph of $f(x)$ when a is greater than 1?

x	$f(x)$	$2f(x)$
−1	−2	−4
1	2	4
3	−2	
5	2	

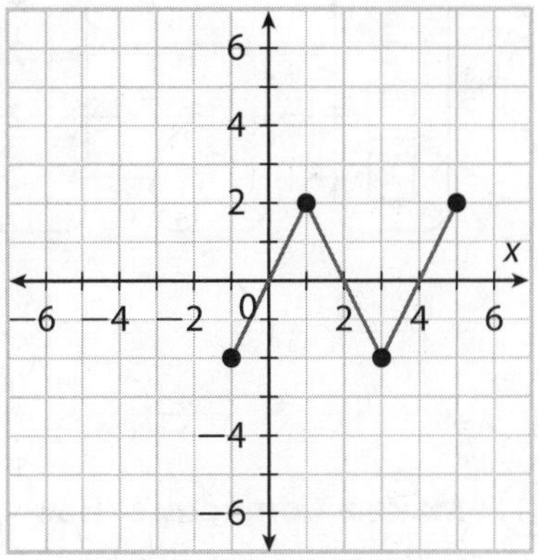

(B) Now try a value of a between 0 and 1 in $g(x) = a \cdot f(x)$. Let $a = \frac{1}{2}$ so that $g(x) = \frac{1}{2}f(x)$. Complete the input-output table and then graph $g(x)$. In general, how is the graph of $g(x) = a \cdot f(x)$ related to the graph of $f(x)$ when a is a number between 0 and 1?

x	$f(x)$	$\frac{1}{2}f(x)$
−1	−2	−1
1	2	1
3	−2	
5	2	

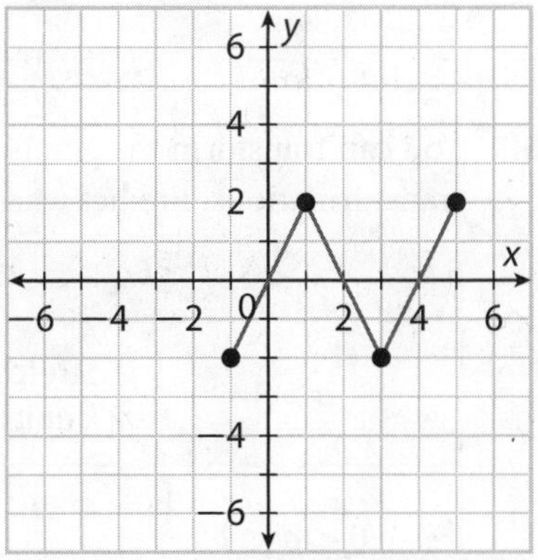

Ⓒ Now graph $g(x) = f\left(\frac{1}{b} \cdot x\right)$ where b is the parameter. Let $b = 2$ so that $g(x) = f\left(\frac{1}{2}x\right)$. Complete the mapping diagram and then graph $g(x)$. (To complete the mapping diagram, you need to find the inputs for g that produce the inputs for f after you multiply by $\frac{1}{2}$. Work backward from the inputs for f to the missing inputs for g by multiplying by 2.) In general, how is the graph of $g(x) = f\left(\frac{1}{b}x\right)$ related to the graph of $f(x)$ when b is a number greater than 1?

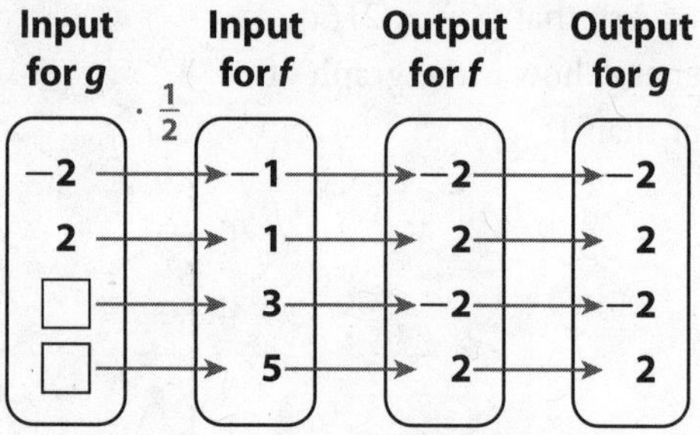

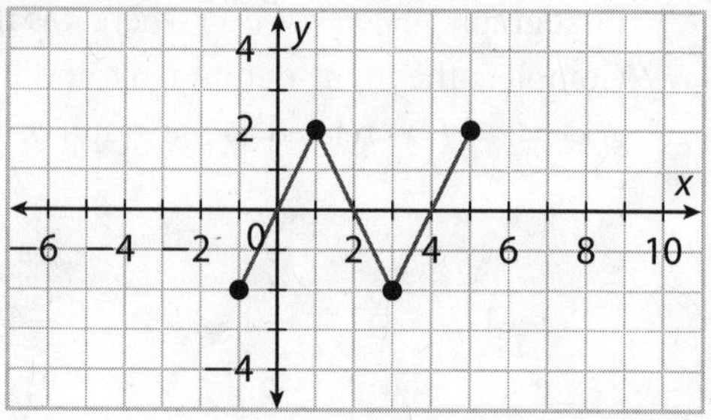

Ⓓ **Make a Conjecture** How would you expect the graph of $g(x) = f\left(\frac{1}{b} \cdot x\right)$ to be related to the graph of $f(x)$ when b is a number between 0 and 1?

Reflect

4. Suppose a function $f(x)$ has a domain of $[x_1, x_2]$ and a range of $[y_1, y_2]$. When the graph of $f(x)$ is stretched or compressed vertically by a factor of a, how do the domain and range change?

5. You can transform the graph of $f(x)$ to obtain the graph of $g(x) = a \cdot f(x - h) + k$ by combining transformations. Predict what will happen by completing the table.

Value of a	Transformations of the Graph of $f(x)$
$a > 1$	Stretch vertically by a factor of a, and translate h units horizontally and k units vertically.
$0 < a < 1$	

6. You can transform the graph of $f(x)$ to obtain the graph of $g(x) = f\left(\frac{1}{b}(x - h)\right) + k$ by combining transformations. Predict what will happen by completing the table.

Value of b	Transformations of the Graph of $f(x)$
$b > 1$	Stretch horizontally by a factor of b, and translate h units horizontally and k units vertically.
$0 < b < 1$	

Explore 3 Investigating Reflections of Function Graphs

When the parameter in a stretch or compression is negative, another transformation called a *reflection* is introduced. Examining reflections will also tell you whether a function is an *even function* or an *odd function*. An **even function** is one for which $f(-x) = f(x)$ for all x in the domain of the function, while an **odd function** is one for which $f(-x) = -f(x)$ for all x in the domain of the function. A function is not necessarily even or odd; it can be neither.

(A) First graph $g(x) = a \cdot f(x)$ where $a = -1$. Complete the input-output table and then graph $g(x) = -f(x)$. In general, how is the graph of $g(x) = -f(x)$ related to the graph of $f(x)$?

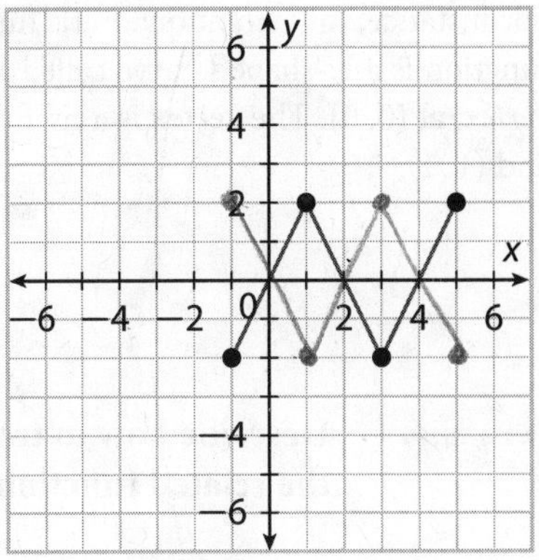

x	$f(x)$	$-f(x)$
−1	−2	2
1	2	−2
3	−2	2
5	2	−2

____

(B) Now graph $g(x) = f\left(\frac{1}{b} \cdot x\right)$ where $b = -1$. Complete the input-output table and then graph $g(x) = f(-x)$. In general, how is the graph of $g(x) = f(-x)$ related to the graph of $f(x)$?

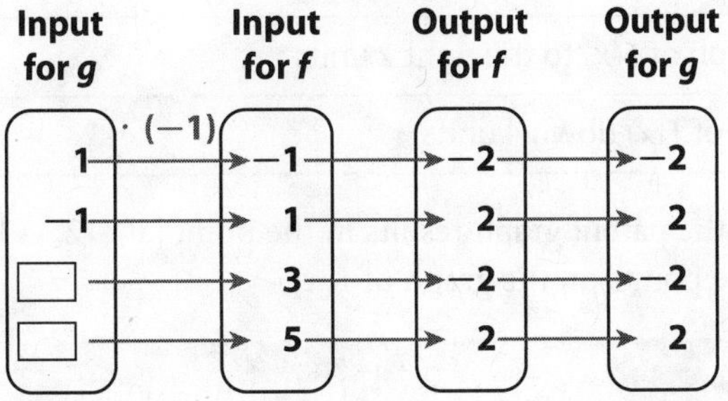

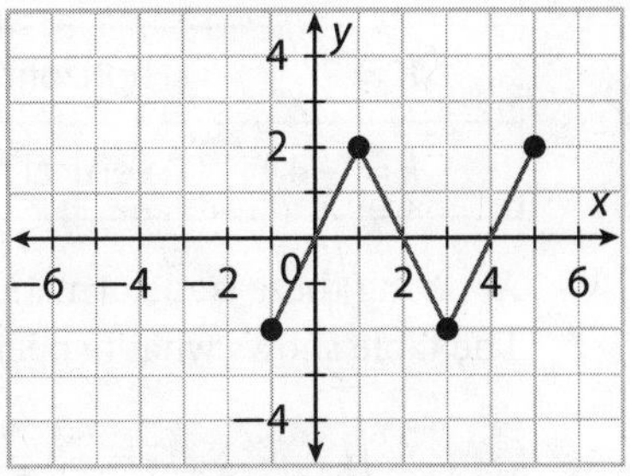

____

Reflect

7. **Discussion** Suppose a function $f(x)$ has a domain of $[x_1, x_2]$ and a range of $[y_1, y_2]$. When the graph of $f(x)$ is reflected across the x-axis, how do the domain and range change?

____

8. For a function $f(x)$, suppose the graph of $f(-x)$, the reflection of the graph of $f(x)$ across the y-axis, is identical to the graph of $f(x)$. What does this tell you about $f(x)$? Explain.

____

9. Is the function whose graph you reflected across the axes in Steps A and B an even function, an odd function, or neither? Explain.

____

____

Explain 1 Transforming the Graph of the Parent Quadratic Function

You can use transformations of the graph of a basic function, called a *parent function*, to obtain the graph of a related function. To do so, focus on how the transformations affect reference points on the graph of the parent function.

For instance, the parent quadratic function is $f(x) = x^2$. The graph of this function is a U-shaped curve called a *parabola* with a turning point, called a *vertex*, at (0, 0). The vertex is a useful reference point, as are the points (−1, 1) and (1, 1).

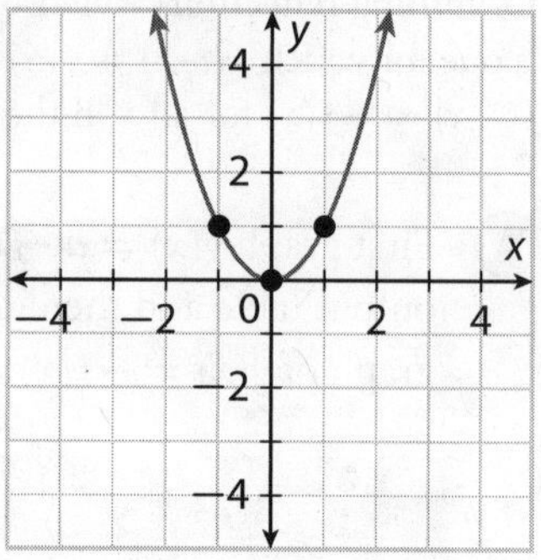

Example 1 **Describe how to transform the graph of $f(x) = x^2$ to obtain the graph of the related function $g(x)$. Then draw the graph of $g(x)$.**

(A) $g(x) = -3f(x - 2) - 4$

Parameter and Its Value	Effect on the Parent Graph
$a = -3$	vertical stretch of the graph of $f(x)$ by a factor of 3 and a reflection across the x-axis
$b = 1$	Since $b = 1$, there is no horizontal stretch or compression.
$h = 2$	horizontal translation of the graph of $f(x)$ to the right 2 units
$k = -4$	vertical translation of the graph of $f(x)$ down 4 units

Applying these transformations to a point (x, y) on the parent graph results in the point $(x + 2, -3y - 4)$. The table shows what happens to the three reference points on the graph of $f(x)$.

Point on the Graph of $f(x)$	Corresponding Point on $g(x)$
$(-1, 1)$	$(-1 + 2, -3(1) - 4) = (1, -7)$
$(0, 0)$	$(0 + 2, -3(0) - 4) = (2, -4)$
$(1, 1)$	$(1 + 2, -3(1) - 4) = (3, -7)$

Use the transformed reference points to graph $g(x)$.

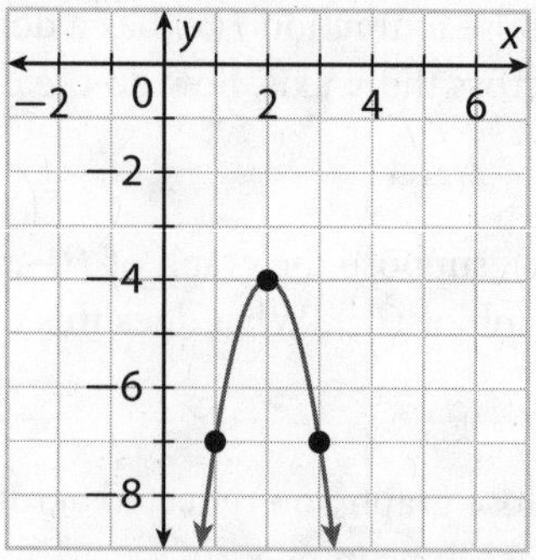

(B) $g(x) = f\left(\frac{1}{2}(x+5)\right) + 2$

Parameter and Its Value	Effect on the Parent Graph
$a =$ ☐	There is no vertical stretch, no vertical compression, and no reflection across the *x*-axis.
$b =$ ☐	The parent graph is stretched/compressed horizontally by a factor of ________. There is no reflection across the y-axis.
$h =$ ☐	The parent graph is translated ________ units horizontally/vertically.
$k =$ ☐	The parent graph is translated ________ units horizontally/vertically.

Applying these transformations to a point on the parent graph results in the point $(2x - 5, y + 2)$. The table shows what happens to the three reference points on the graph of $f(x)$.

Point on the Graph of $f(x)$	Corresponding Point on the Graph of $g(x)$
$(-1, 1)$	$(2(-1) - 5, 1 + 2) = (\square, \square)$
$(0, 0)$	$(2(0) - 5, 0 + 2) = (\square, \square)$
$(1, 1)$	$(2(1) - 5, 1 + 2) = (\square, \square)$

Use the transformed reference points to graph $g(x)$.

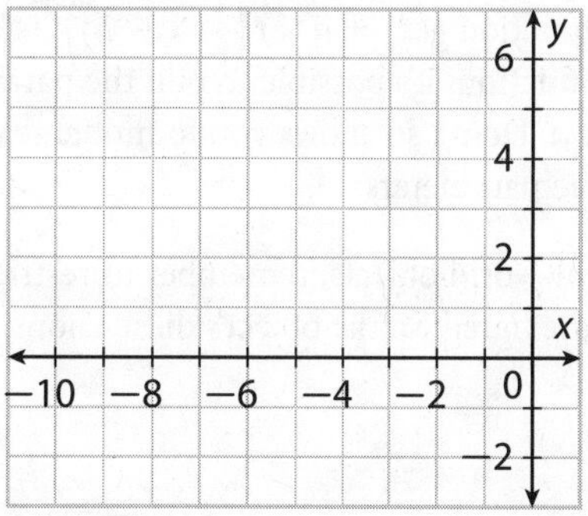

Reflect

10. Is the function $f(x) = x^2$ an even function, an odd function, or neither? Explain.

____

____

11. The graph of the parent quadratic function $f(x) = x^2$ has the vertical line $x = 0$ as its axis of symmetry. Identify the axis of symmetry for each of the graphs of $g(x)$ in Parts A and B. Which transformation(s) affect the location of the axis of symmetry?

____

____

Your Turn

12. Describe how to transform the graph of $f(x) = x^2$ to obtain the graph of the related function $g(x) = f\left(-4(x - 3)\right) + 1$. Then draw the graph of $g(x)$.

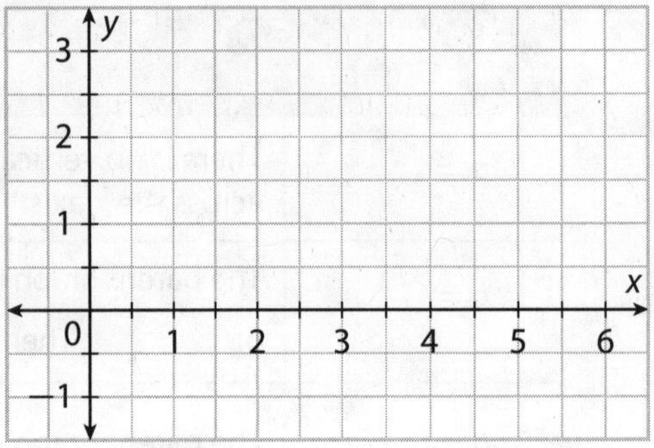

Explain 2 Modeling with a Quadratic Function

You can model real-world objects that have a parabolic shape using a quadratic function. In order to fit the function's graph to the shape of the object, you will need to determine the values of the parameters in the function $g(x) = a \cdot f\left(\frac{1}{b}(x - h)\right) + k$ where $f(x) = x^2$. Note that because $f(x)$ is simply a squaring function, it's possible to pull the parameter b outside the function and combine it with the parameter a. Doing so allows you to model real-objects using $g(x) = a \cdot f(x - h) + k$, which has only three parameters.

When modeling real-world objects, remember to restrict the domain of $g(x) = a \cdot f(x - h) + k$ to values of x that are based on the object's dimensions.

Example 2

An old stone bridge over a river uses a parabolic arch for support. In the illustration shown, the unit of measurement for both axes is feet, and the vertex of the arch is point C. Find a quadratic function that models the arch, and state the function's domain.

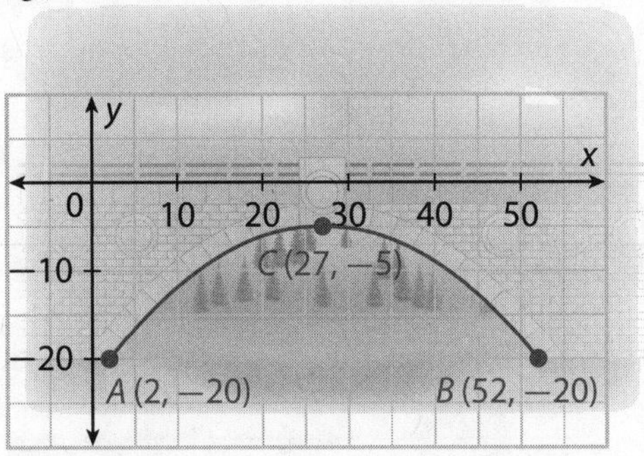

Analyze Information

Identify the important information.

- The shape of the arch is a ________________.
- The vertex of the parabola is ________________.
- Two other points on the parabola are ________________ and ________________.

Formulate a Plan

You want to find the values of the parameters a, h, and k in $g(x) = a \cdot f(x - h) + k$ where $f(x) = x^2$. You can use the coordinates of point ______ to find the values of h and k. Then you can use the coordinates of one of the other points to find the value of a.

Solve

The vertex of the graph of $g(x)$ is point C, and the vertex of the graph of $f(x)$ is the origin. Point C is the result of translating the origin 27 units to the right and 5 units down. This means that $h = 27$ and $k = -5$. Substituting these values into $g(x)$ gives $g(x) = a \cdot f(x - 27) - 5$. Now substitute the coordinates of point B into $g(x)$ and solve for a.

$g(x) = a \cdot f(x - 27) - 5$	Write the general function.
$g(\boxed{}) = a \cdot f(52 - 27) - 5$	Substitute 52 for x.
$-20 = a \cdot f(52 - 27) - 5$	Replace $g(52)$ with -20, the y-value of B.
$-20 = a \cdot f(\boxed{}) - 5$	Simplify.
$-20 = a(625) - 5$	Evaluate $f(25)$ for $f(x) = x^2$.
$a = \boxed{}$	Solve for a.

Substitute the value of a into $g(x)$.

$$g(x) = -\frac{3}{125} f(x - 27) - 5$$

The arch exists only between points A and B, so the domain of $g(x)$ is $\{x | 2 \leq x \leq 52\}$.

Justify and Evaluate

To justify the answer, verify that $g(2) = -20$.

$g(x) = -\frac{3}{125} f(x - 27) - 5$	Write the function.
$g(\boxed{}) = -\frac{3}{125} f(\boxed{} - 27) - 5$	Substitute 2 for x.
$= -\frac{3}{125} f(\boxed{}) - 5$	Subtract.
$= -\frac{3}{125} \cdot (\boxed{}) - 5$	Evaluate $f(-25)$.
$= -20$ ✓	Simplify.

Your Turn

13. The netting of an empty hammock hangs between its supports along a curve that can be modeled by a parabola. In the illustration shown, the unit of measurement for both axes is feet, and the vertex of the curve is point C. Find a quadratic function that models the hammock's netting, and state the function's domain.

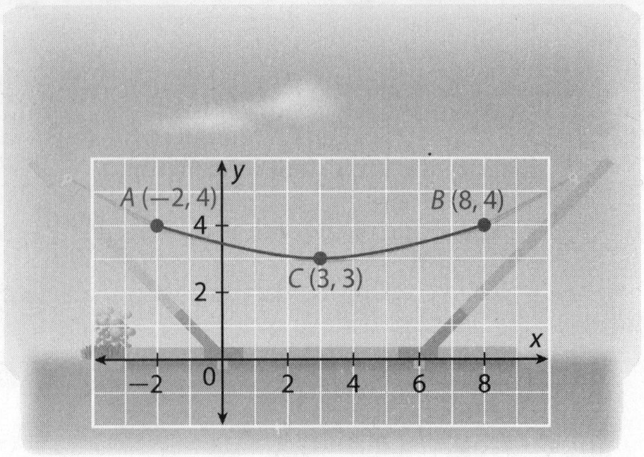

Elaborate

14. What is the general procedure to follow when graphing a function of the form $g(x) = a \cdot f(x - h) + k$ given the graph of $f(x)$?

15. What are the general steps to follow when determining the values of the parameters a, h, and k in $f(x) = a(x - h)^2 + k$ when modeling a parabolic real-world object?

16. Essential Question Check-In How can the graph of a function $f(x)$ be transformed?

Evaluate: Homework and Practice

Personal Math Trainer

- Online Homework
- Hints and Help
- Extra Practice

Write $g(x)$ in terms of $f(x)$ after performing the given transformation of the graph of $f(x)$.

1. Translate the graph of $f(x)$ to the left 3 units.

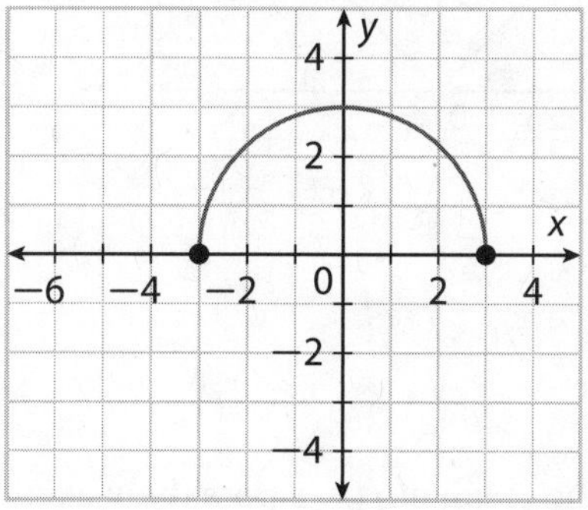

2. Translate the graph of $f(x)$ up 2 units.

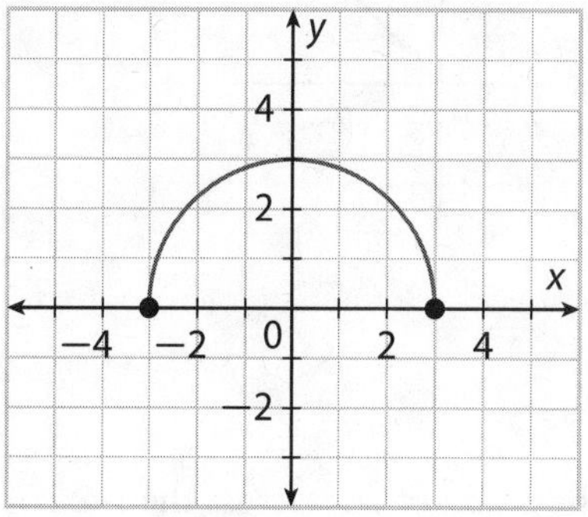

3. Translate the graph of $f(x)$ to the right 4 units.

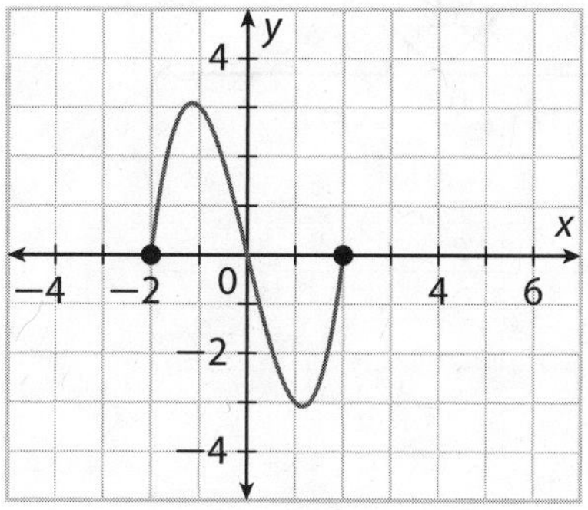

4. Translate the graph of $f(x)$ down 3 units.

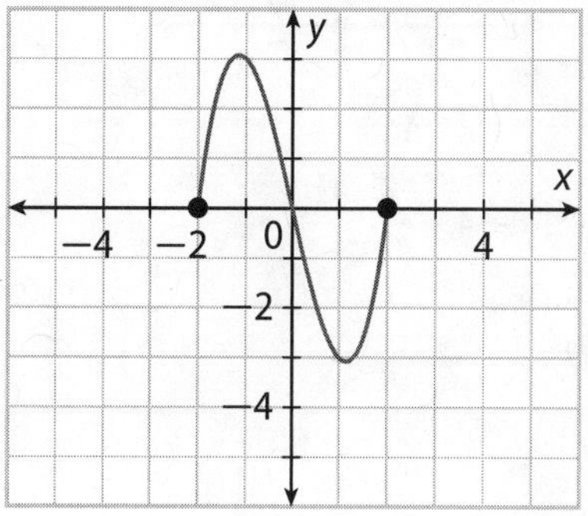

5. Stretch the graph of $f(x)$ horizontally by a factor of 3.

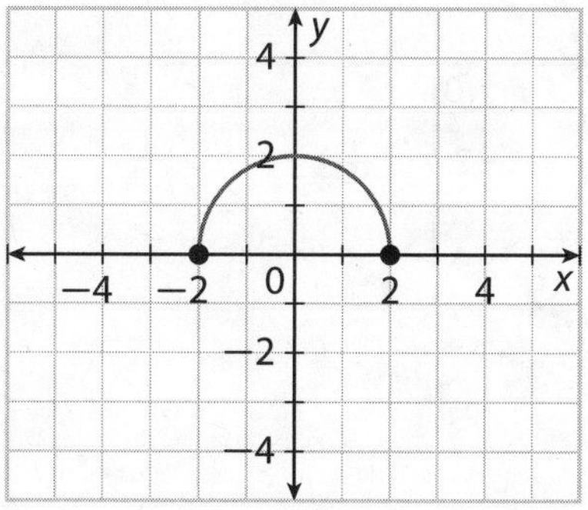

6. Stretch the graph of $f(x)$ vertically by a factor of 2.

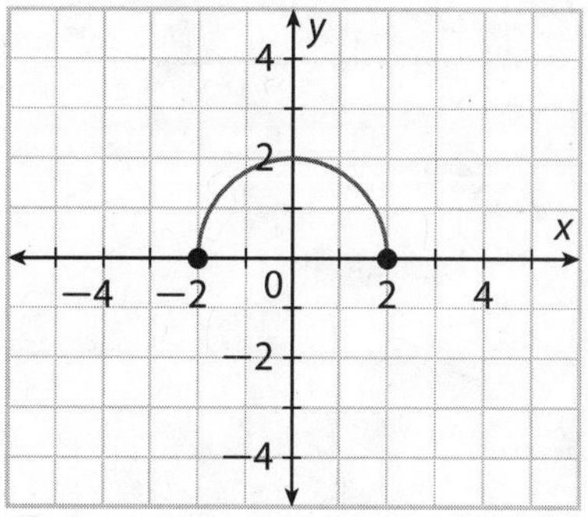

7. Compress the graph of $f(x)$ horizontally by a factor of $\frac{1}{3}$.

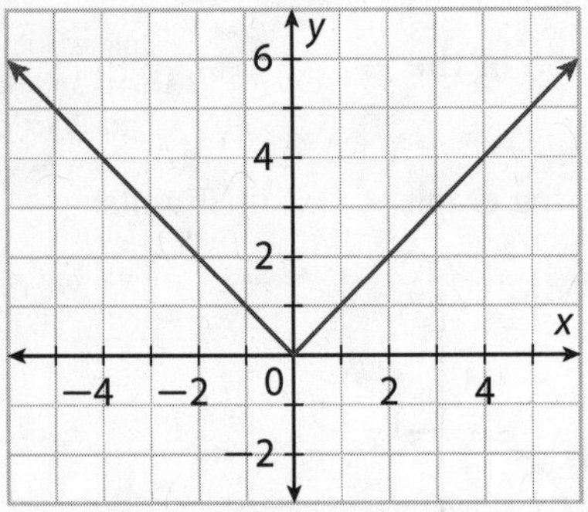

8. Compress the graph of $f(x)$ vertically by a factor of $\frac{1}{2}$.

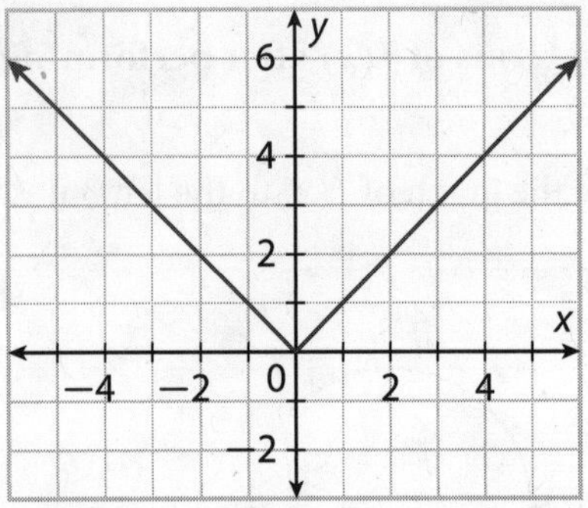

9. Reflect the graph of $f(x)$ across the y-axis.

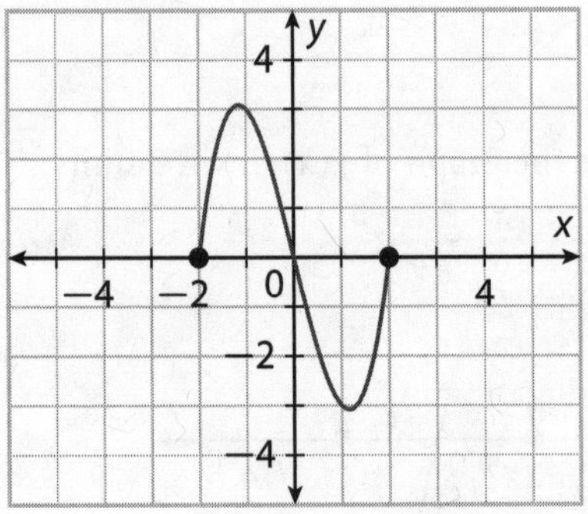

10. Reflect the graph of $f(x)$ across the x-axis.

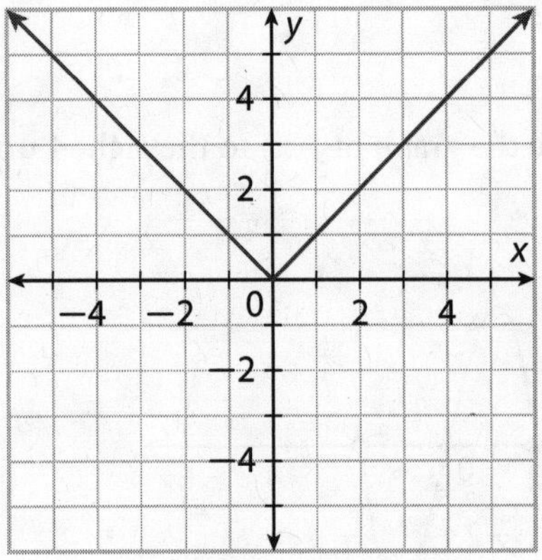

11. Reflect the graph of $f(x)$ across the y-axis.

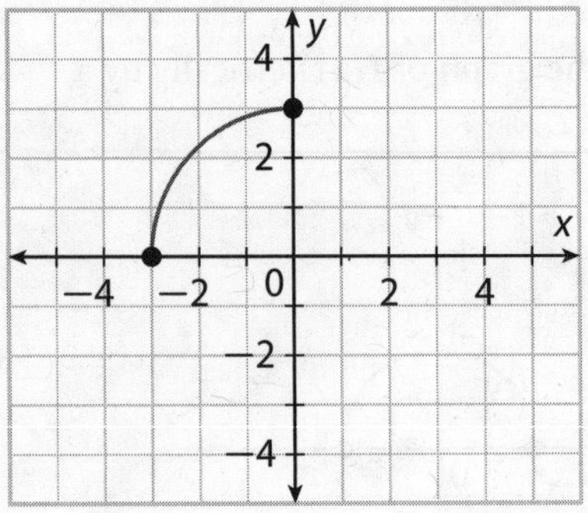

12. Reflect the graph of $f(x)$ across the x-axis.

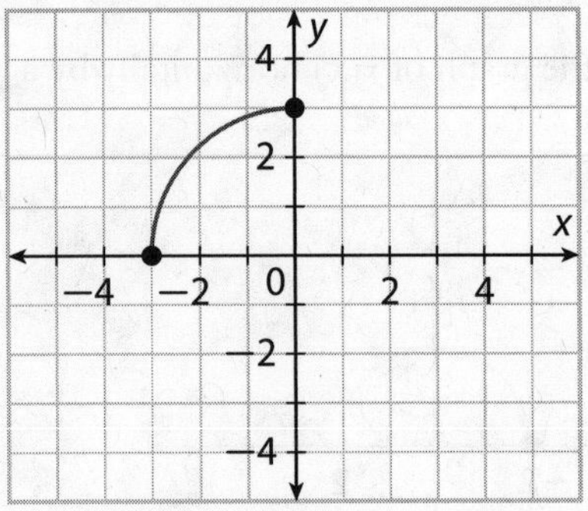

13. Determine if each function is an even function, an odd function, or neither.

a.

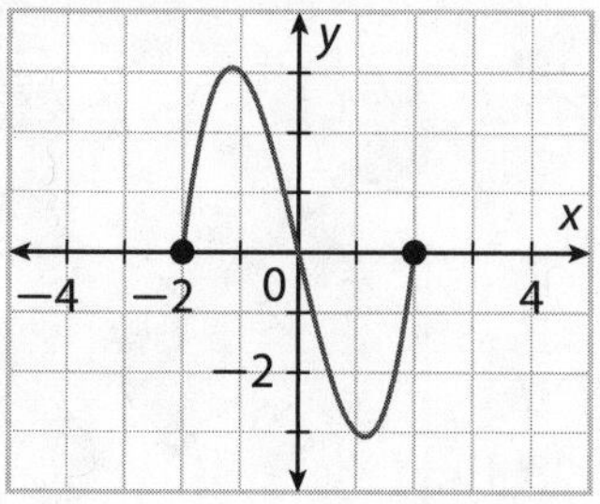

b.

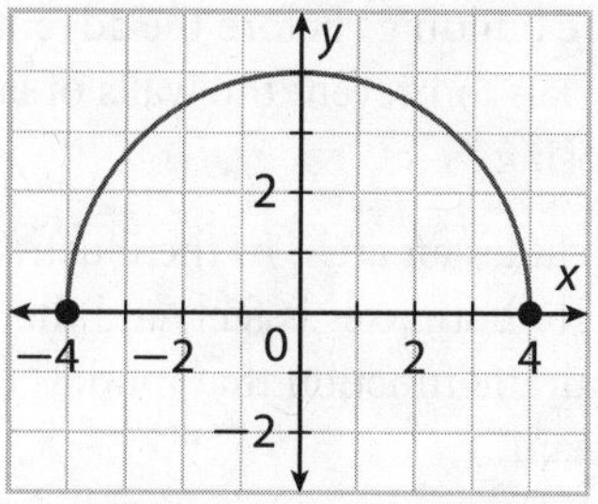

c.

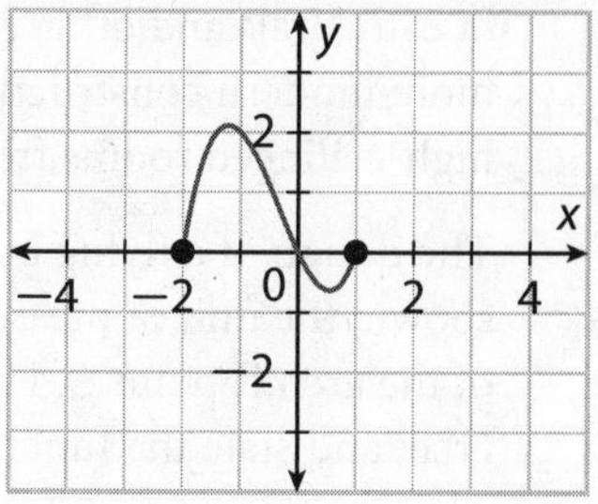

______________ ______________ ______________

14. Determine whether each quadratic function is an even function. Answer *yes* or *no*.

a. $f(x) = 5x^2$ ______________

b. $f(x) = (x - 2)^2$ ______________

c. $f(x) = \left(\frac{x}{3}\right)^2$ ______________

d. $f(x) = x^2 + 6$ ______________

Describe how to transform the graph of $f(x) = x^2$ to obtain the graph of the related function $g(x)$. Then draw the graph of $g(x)$.

15. $g(x) = -\dfrac{f(x+4)}{3}$

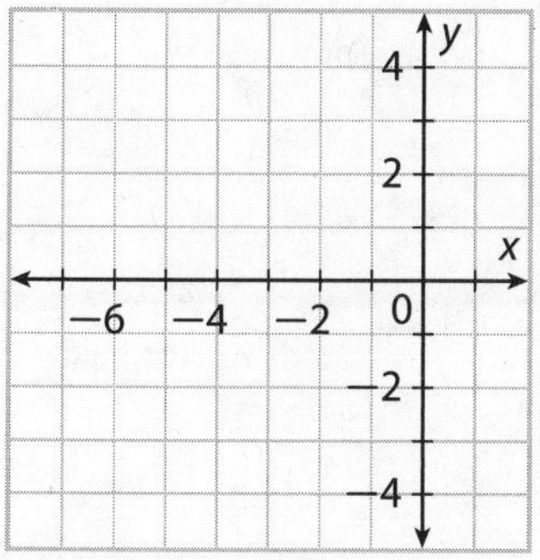

16. $g(x) = f(2x) + 2$

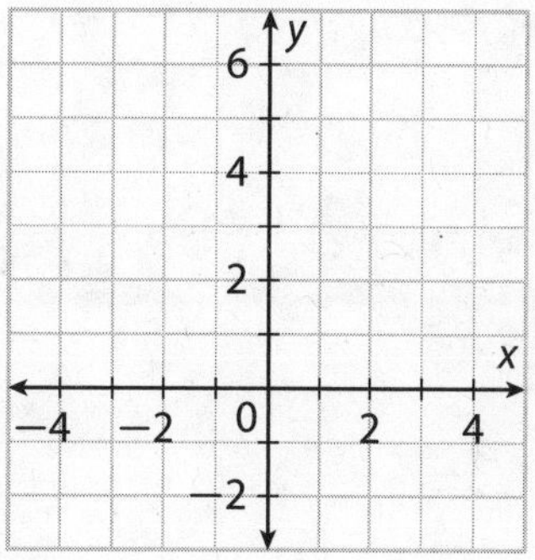

17. Architecture Flying buttresses were used in the construction of cathedrals and other large stone buildings before the advent of more modern construction materials to prevent the walls of large, high-ceilinged rooms from collapsing.

The design of a flying buttress includes an arch. In the illustration shown, the unit of measurement for both axes is feet, and the vertex of the arch is point C. Find a quadratic function that models the arch, and state the function's domain.

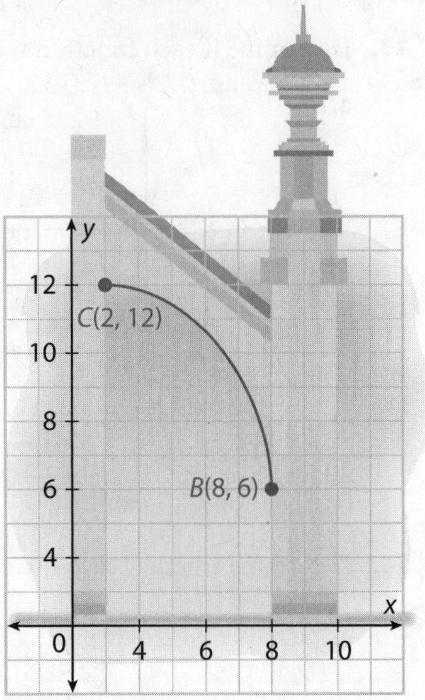

18. A red velvet rope hangs between two stanchions and forms a curve that can be modeled by a parabola. In the illustration shown, the unit of measurement for both axes is feet, and the vertex of the curve is point C. Find a quadratic function that models the rope, and state the function's domain.

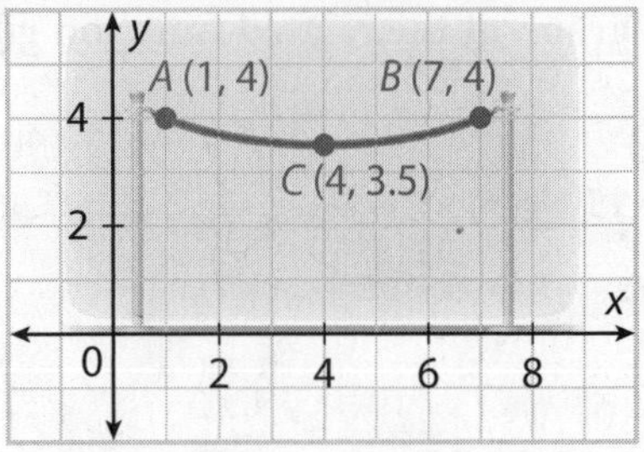

H.O.T. Focus on Higher Order Thinking

19. Multiple Representations The graph of the function $g(x) = \left(\frac{1}{2}x + 2\right)^2$ is shown.

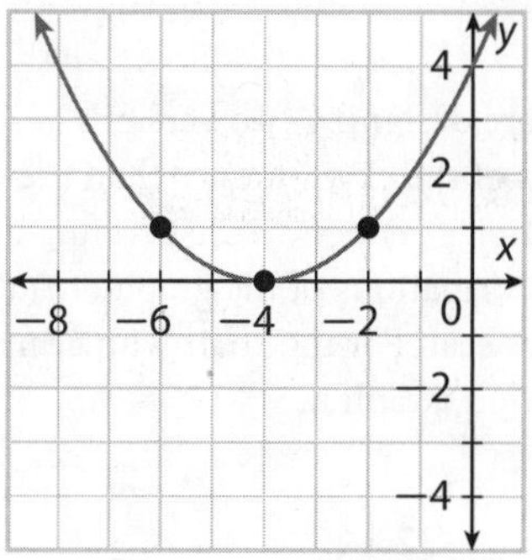

Use the graph to identify the transformations of the graph of $f(x) = x^2$ needed to produce the graph of $g(x)$. (If a stretch or compression is involved, give it in terms of a horizontal stretch or compression rather than a vertical one.) Use your list of transformations to write $g(x)$ in the form $g(x) = f\left(\frac{1}{b}(x - h)\right) + k$. Then show why the new form of $g(x)$ is algebraically equivalent to the given form.

20. Represent Real-World Situations The graph of the ceiling function, $f(x) = \lceil x \rceil$, is shown. This function accepts any real number x as input and delivers the least integer greater than or equal to x as output. For instance, $f(1.3) = 2$ because 2 is the least integer greater than or equal to 1.3. The ceiling function is a type of *step function*, so named because its graph looks like a set of steps.

Write a function $g(x)$ whose graph is a transformation of the graph of $f(x)$ based on this situation: A parking garage charges \$4 for the first hour or less and \$2 for every additional hour or fraction of an hour. Then graph $g(x)$.

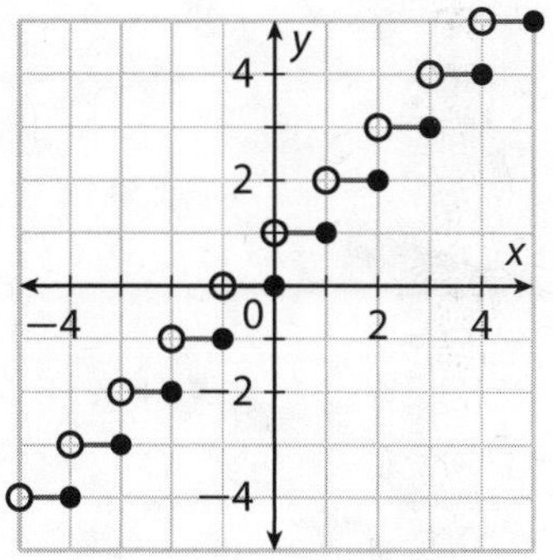

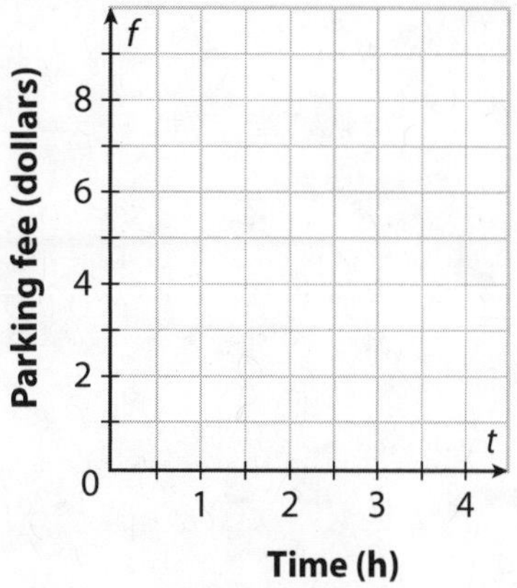

Lesson Performance Task

You are designing two versions of a chair, one without armrests and one with armrests. The diagrams show side views of the chair. Rather than use traditional straight legs for your chair, you decide to use parabolic legs. Given the function $f(x) = x^2$, write two functions, $g(x)$ and $h(x)$, whose graphs represent the legs of the two chairs and involve transformations of the graph of $f(x)$. For the chair without armrests, the graph of $g(x)$ must touch the bottom of the chair's seat. For the chair with armrests, the graph of $h(x)$ must touch the bottom of the armrest. After writing each function, graph it.

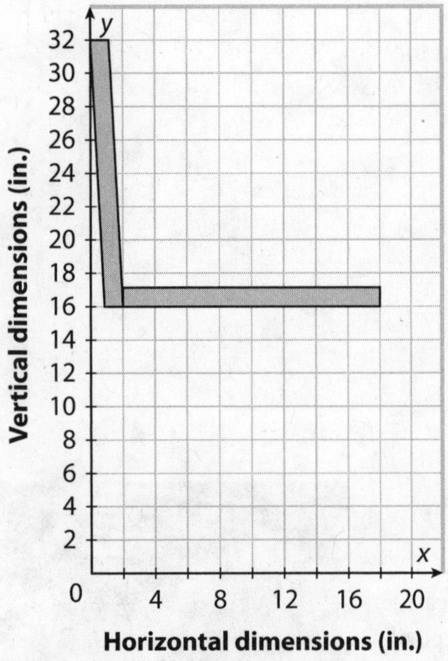

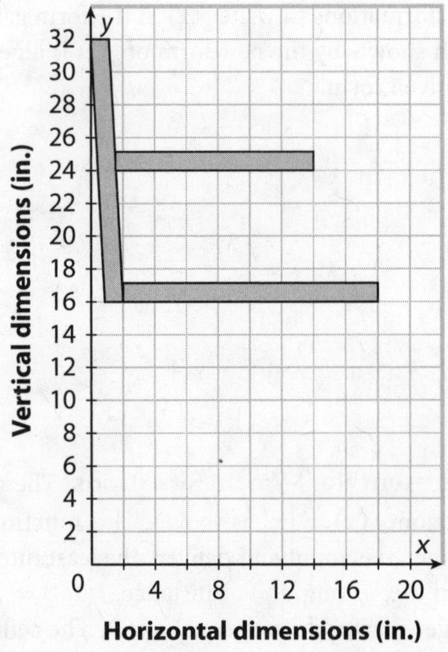

Name ______________________ Class ____________ Date ____________

5.2 Inverses of Functions

Essential Question: What is an inverse function, and how do you know it's an inverse function?

Resource Locker

Explore Understanding Inverses of Functions

Recall that a *relation* is any pairing of the elements of one set (the domain) with the elements of a second set (the range). The elements of the domain are called inputs, while the elements of the range are called outputs. A function is a special type of relation that pairs every input with exactly one output. In a *one-to-one function*, no output is ever used more than once in the function's pairings. In a *many-to-one function*, at least one output is used more than once.

An **inverse relation** reverses the pairings of a relation. If a relation pairs an input x with an output y, then the inverse relation pairs an input y with an output x. The inverse of a function may or may not be another function. If the inverse of a function $f(x)$ is also a function, it is called the **inverse function** and is written $f^{-1}(x)$. If the inverse of a function is not a function, then it is simply an inverse relation.

(A) The mapping diagrams show a function and its inverse. Complete the diagram for the inverse of the function.

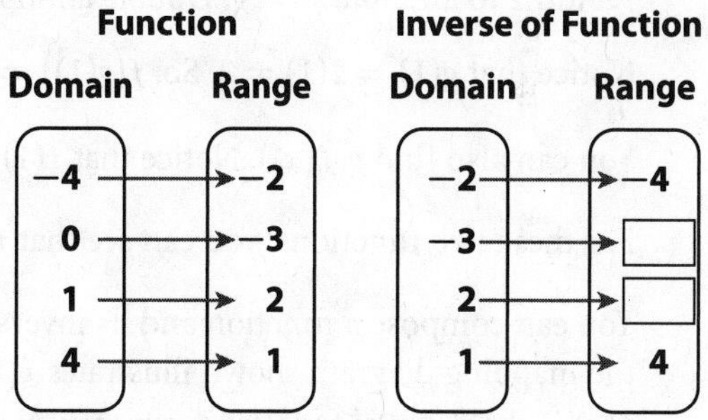

Is the function one-to-one or many-to-one? Explain.

____

____

Is the inverse of the function also a function? Explain.

____

(B) The mapping diagrams show a function and its inverse. Complete the diagram for the inverse of the function.

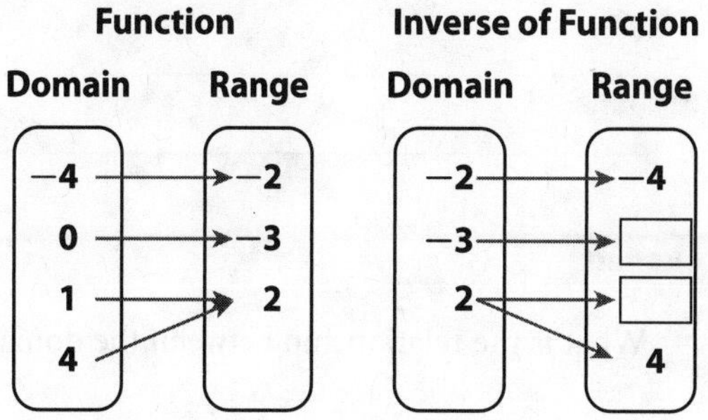

Is the function one-to-one or many-to-one? Explain.

____

____

Is the inverse of the function also a function? Explain.

____

Ⓒ The graph of the original function in Step A is shown. Note that the graph also shows the dashed line $y = x$. Write the inverse of the function as a set of ordered pairs and graph them.

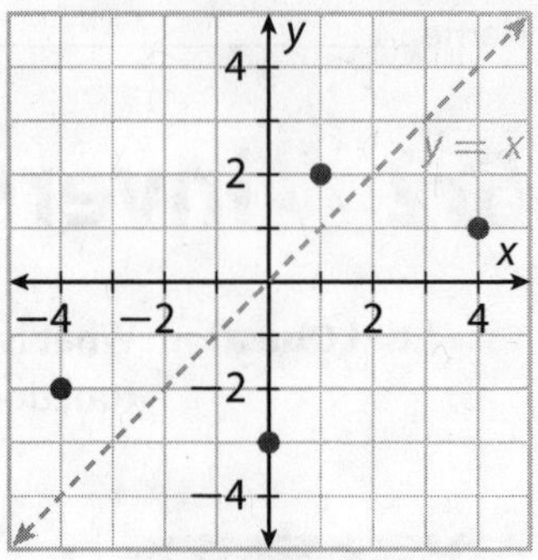

Function: $\{(-4, -2), (0, -3), (1, 2), (4, 1)\}$

Inverse of function:

$\{(\square, \square), (\square, \square), (\square, \square), (\square, \square)\}$

What do you observe about the graphs of the function and its inverse in relationship to the line $y = x$? Why does this make sense?

Ⓓ The **composition of two functions** $f(x)$ and $g(x)$, written $f(g(x))$ and read as "f of g of x," is a new function that uses the output of $g(x)$ as the input of $f(x)$. For example, consider the functions f and g with the following rules.

f: Add 1 to an input. g: Double an input.

Notice that $g(1) = 2(1) = 2$. So, $f(g(1)) = f(2) = 2 + 1 = 3$.

You can also find $g(f(x))$. Notice that $f(1) = 1 + 1 = 2$. So, $g(f(1)) = g(2) = 2(2) = 4$.

For these two functions, you can see that $f(g(1)) \neq g(f(1))$.

You can compose a function and its inverse. For instance, the mapping diagram shown illustrates $f^{-1}(f(x))$ where $f(x)$ is the original function from Step A and $f^{-1}(x)$ is its inverse. Notice that the range of $f(x)$ serves as the domain of $f^{-1}(x)$. Complete the diagram. What do you notice about the outputs of $f^{-1}(f(x))$? Explain why this makes sense.

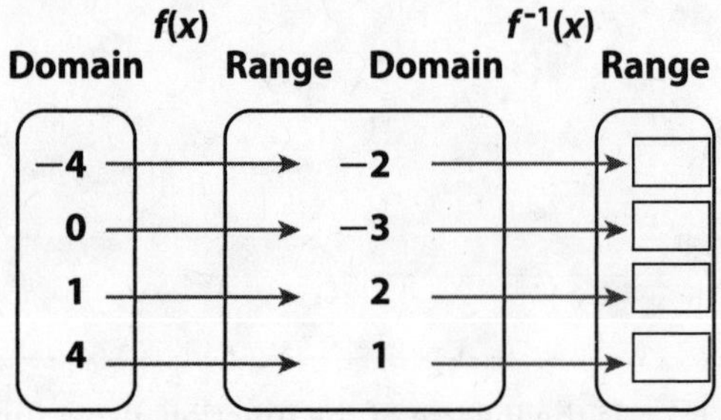

Reflect

1. What is the relationship between the domain and range of a relation and its inverse?

2. **Discussion** In Step D, you saw that for inverse functions, $f^{-1}(f(x)) = x$. What do you expect $f(f^{-1}(x))$ to equal? Explain.

Explain 1 Finding the Inverse of a Linear Function

Every linear function $f(x) = mx + b$ where $m \neq 0$ is a one-to-one function. So, its inverse is also a function. To find the inverse function, use the fact that inverse functions undo each other's pairings.

To find the inverse of a function $f(x)$:

1. Substitute y for $f(x)$.
2. Solve for x in terms of y.
3. Switch x and y (since the inverse switches inputs and outputs).
4. Replace y with $f^{-1}(x)$.

To check your work and verify that the functions are inverses, show that $f\left(f^{-1}(x)\right) = x$ and that $f^{-1}\left(f(x)\right) = x$.

Example 1 **Find the inverse function $f^{-1}(x)$ for the given function $f(x)$. Use composition to verify that the functions are inverses. Then graph the function and its inverse.**

(A) $f(x) = 3x + 4$

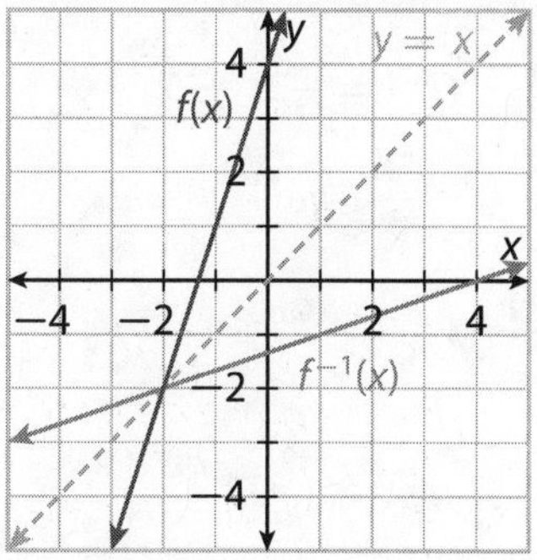

Replace $f(x)$ with y. $y = 3x + 4$

Solve for x. $y - 4 = 3x$

$\frac{y - 4}{3} = x$

Switch x and y. $y = \frac{x - 4}{3}$

Replace y with $f^{-1}(x)$. $f^{-1}(x) = \frac{x - 4}{3}$

Check: Verify that $f^{-1}\left(f(x)\right) = x$ and $f\left(f^{-1}(x)\right) = x$.

$$f^{-1}\left(f(x)\right) = f^{-1}(3x + 4) = \frac{(3x + 4) - 4}{3} = \frac{3x}{3} = x$$

$$f\left(f^{-1}(x)\right) = f\left(\frac{x - 4}{3}\right) = 3\left(\frac{x - 4}{3}\right) + 4 = (x - 4) + 4 = x$$

(B) $f(x) = 2x - 2$

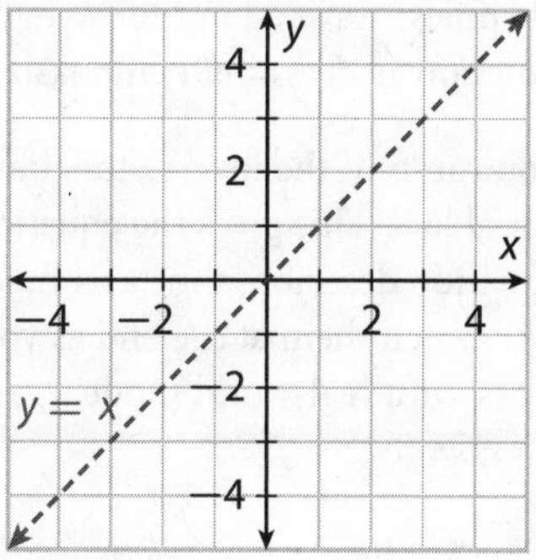

Replace $f(x)$ with y. $y = \square$

Solve for x. $y \square = 2x$

$\frac{y + 2}{2} = x$

Switch x and y. $y = \square$

Replace y with $f^{-1}(x)$. $\square = \frac{x + 2}{2}$

Check: Verify that $f^{-1}\left(f(x)\right) = x$ and $f\left(f^{-1}(x)\right) = x$.

$$f^{-1}\left(f(x)\right) = f^{-1}\left(\square\right) = \frac{(2x - 2) + \square}{\square} = \frac{\square}{2} = \square$$

$$f\left(f^{-1}(x)\right) = f\left(\square\right) = \square\left(\frac{x + 2}{2}\right) - \square = \left(\square\right) - 2 = \square$$

Reflect

3. What is the significance of the point where the graph of a linear function and its inverse intersect?

4. The graph of a constant function $f(x) = c$ for any constant c is a horizontal line through the point $(0, c)$. Does a constant function have an inverse? Does it have an inverse function? Explain.

Your Turn

Find the inverse function $f^{-1}(x)$ for the given function $f(x)$. Use composition to verify that the functions are inverses. Then graph the function and its inverse.

5. $f(x) = -2x + 3$

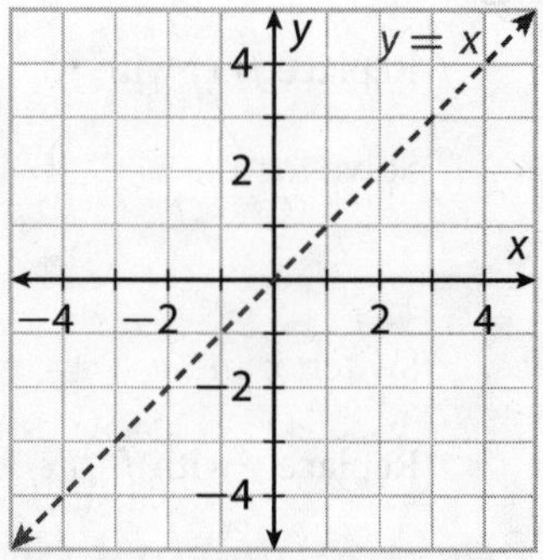

Explain 2 Modeling with the Inverse of a Linear Function

In a model for a real-world situation, the variables have specific real-world meanings. For example, the distance d (in miles) traveled in time t (in hours) at a constant speed of 60 miles per hour is $d = 60t$. Writing this in function notation as $d(t) = 60t$ emphasizes that this equation describes distance as a function of time.

You can find the inverse function for $d = 60t$ by solving for the independent variable t in terms of the dependent variable d. This gives the equation $t = \frac{d}{60}$. Writing this in function notation as $t(d) = \frac{d}{60}$ emphasizes that this equation describes time as a function of distance. Because the meanings of the variables can't be interchanged, you do not switch them at the end as you would switch x and y when working with purely mathematical functions. As you work with real-world models, you may have to restrict the domain and range.

Example 2 **For the given function, state the domain of the inverse function using set notation. Then find an equation for the inverse function, and graph it. Interpret the meaning of the inverse function.**

(A) The equation $C = 3.5g$ gives the cost C (in dollars) as a function of the number of gallons of gasoline g when the price is \$3.50 per gallon.

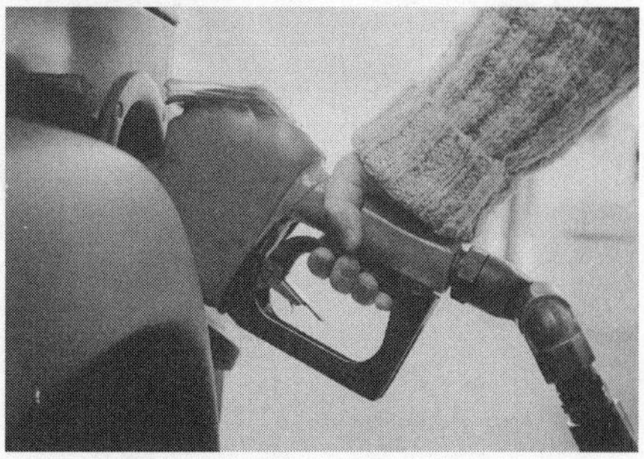

The domain of the function $C = 3.5g$ is restricted to nonnegative numbers to make real-world sense, so the range of the function also consists of nonnegative numbers. This means that the domain of the inverse function is $\{C \mid C \geq 0\}$

Solve the given equation for g to find the inverse function.

Write the equation. $C = 3.5g$

Divide both sides by 3.5. $\frac{C}{3.5} = g$

So, the inverse function is $g = \frac{C}{3.5}$.

Graph the inverse function.

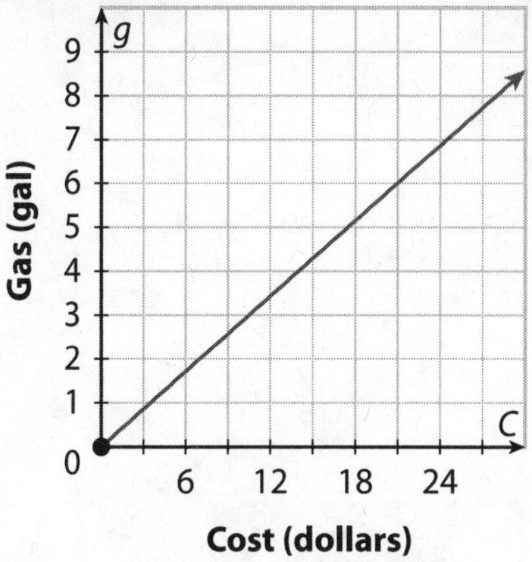

The inverse function gives the number of gallons of gasoline as a function of the cost (in dollars) when the price of gas is \$3.50 per gallon.

(B) A car's gas tank, which can hold 14 gallons of gas, contains 4 gallons of gas when the driver stops at a gas station to fill the tank. The gas pump dispenses gas at a rate of 5 gallons per minute. The equation $g = 5t + 4$ gives the number of gallons of gasoline g in the tank as a function of the pumping time t(in minutes).

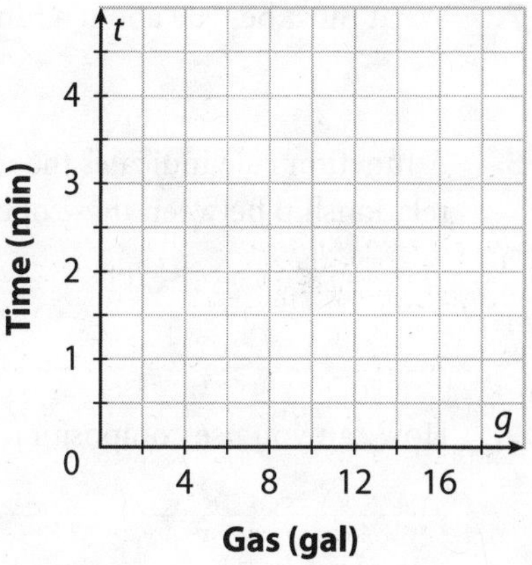

The range of the function $g = 5t + 4$ is the number of gallons of gas in the tank, which varies from ______ gallons to ______ gallons. So, the domain of the inverse function is $\{g \mid \square \leq g \leq \square\}$.

Solve the given equation for g to find the inverse function.

Write the equation. $g = \square t + \square$

Solve for t. $\frac{\square}{5} = t$

So, the inverse function is $t = \square$.

Graph the inverse function.

The inverse function gives ______________________________ as a function of ______________________________.

Your Turn

For the given function, determine the domain of the inverse function. Then find an equation for the inverse function, and graph it. Interpret the meaning of the inverse function.

6. A municipal swimming pool containing 600,000 gallons of water is drained. The amount of water w (in thousands of gallons) remaining in the pool at time t (in hours) after the draining begins is $w = 600 - 20t$.

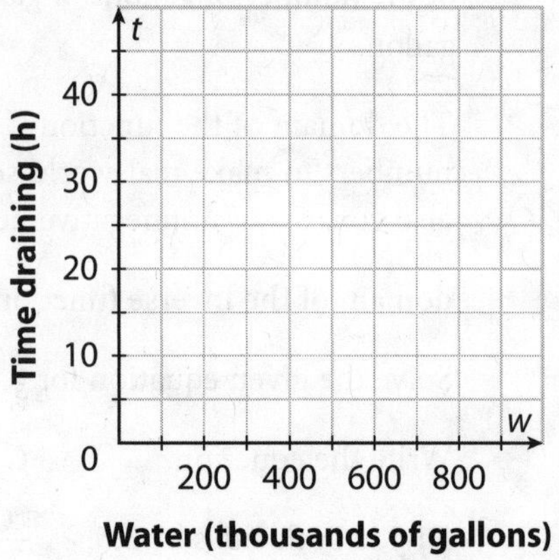

Elaborate

7. What must be true about a function for its inverse to be a function?

8. A function rule indicates the operations to perform on an input to produce an output. What is the relationship between these operations and the operations indicated by the inverse function?

9. How can you use composition to verify that two functions $f(x)$ and $g(x)$ are inverse functions?

10. Describe a real-world situation modeled by a linear function for which it makes sense to find an inverse function. Give an example of how the inverse function might also be useful.

11. Essential Question Check-In What is an inverse relation?

Evaluate: Homework and Practice

Personal Math Trainer

- Online Homework
- Hints and Help
- Extra Practice

The mapping diagrams show a function and its inverse. Complete the diagram for the inverse of the function. Then tell whether the inverse is a function, and explain your reasoning.

1.

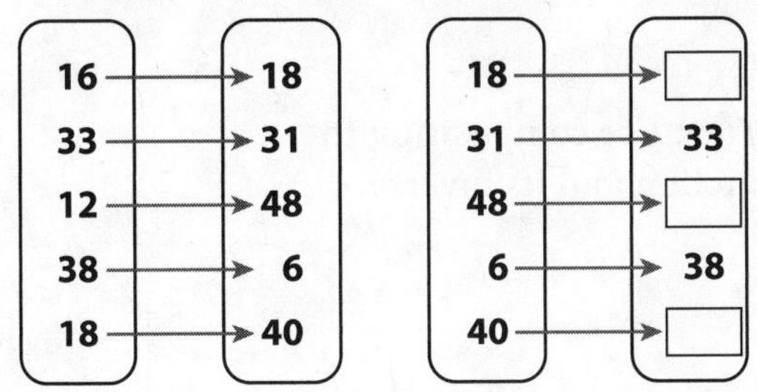

2.

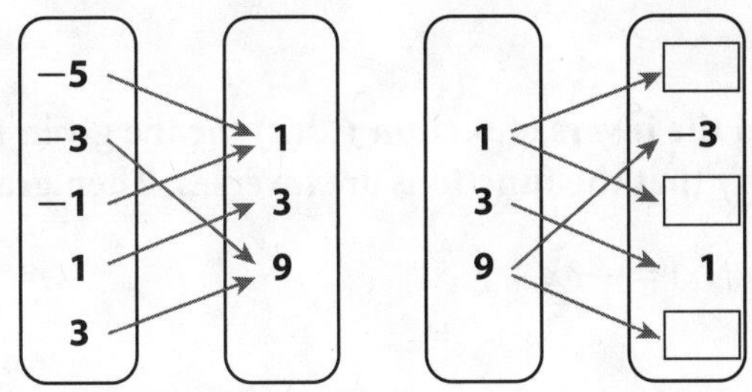

Write the inverse of the given function as a set of ordered pairs and then graph the inverse on the coordinate plane.

3. Function:

$\{(-4, -3), (-2, -4), (0, -2), (1, 0), (2, 3)\}$

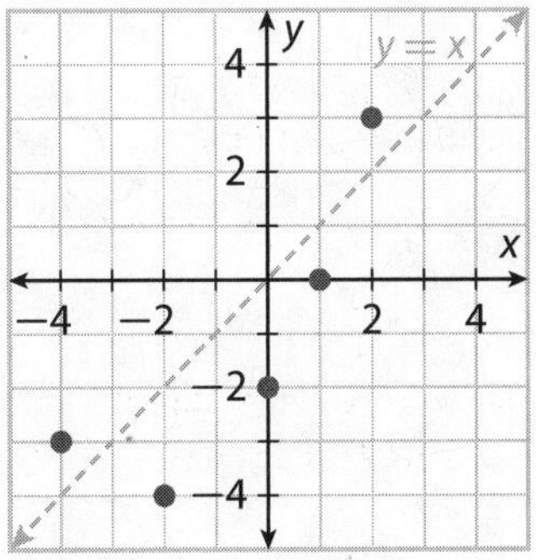

4. Function:

$\{(-3, -4), (-2, -3), (-1, 2), (1, 2), (2, 4), (3, 4)\}$

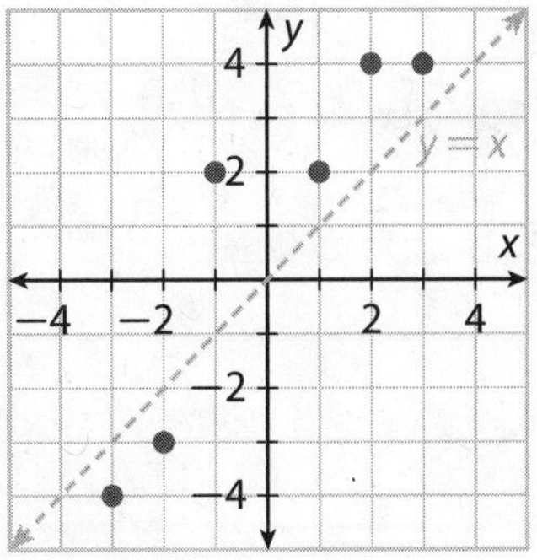

Find the inverse function $f^{-1}(x)$ for the given function $f(x)$.

5. $f(x) = 4x - 8$

6. $f(x) = \frac{x}{3}$

7. $f(x) = \dfrac{x+1}{6}$

8. $f(x) = -0.75x$

Find the inverse function $f^{-1}(x)$ for the given function $f(x)$. Use composition to verify that the functions are inverses. Then graph the function and its inverse.

9. $f(x) = -3x + 3$

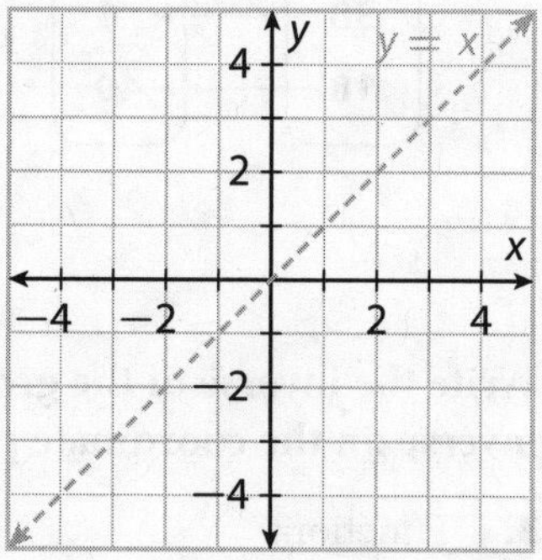

10. $f(x) = \frac{2}{5}x - 2$

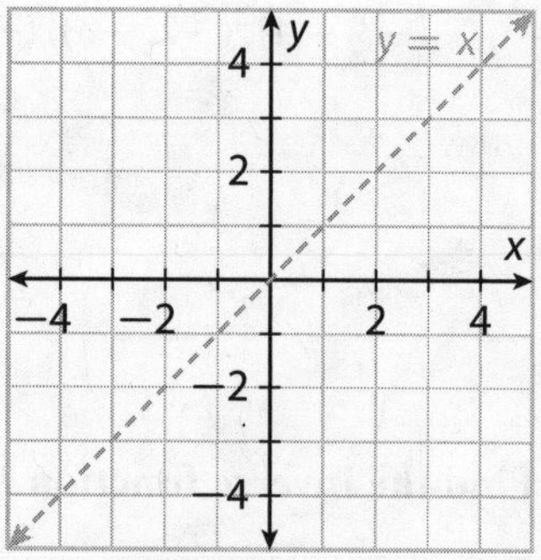

For the given function, determine the domain of the inverse function. Then find an equation for the inverse function, and graph it. Interpret the meaning of the inverse function.

11. **Geometry** The equation $A = \frac{1}{2}(20)h$ gives the area A (in square inches) of a triangle with a base of 20 inches as a function of its height h (in inches).

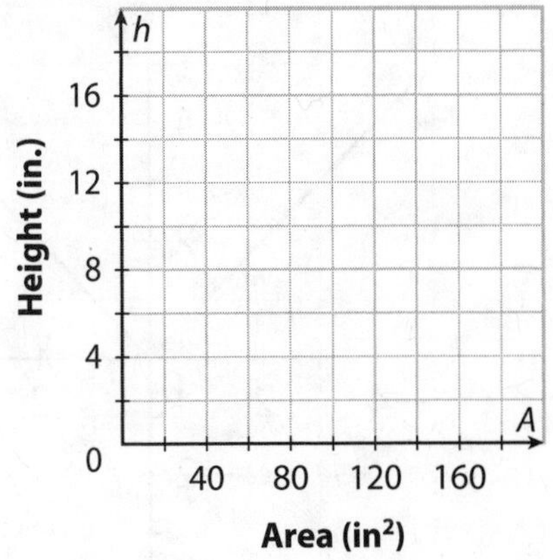

12. The label on a gallon of paint says that it will cover from 250 square feet to 450 square feet depending on the surface that is being painted. A painter has 12 gallons of paint on hand. The equation $A = 12c$ gives the area A (in square feet) that the 12 gallons of paint will cover if applied at a coverage rate c (in square feet per gallon).

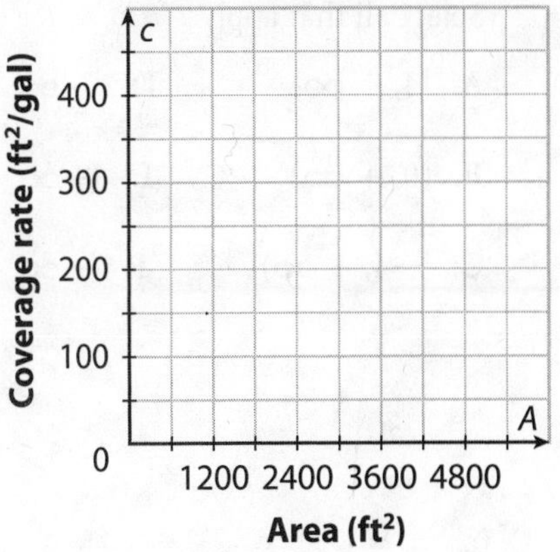

The graph of a function is given. Tell whether the function's inverse is a function, and explain your reasoning. If the inverse is not a function, tell how can you restrict the domain of the function so that its inverse is a function.

13.

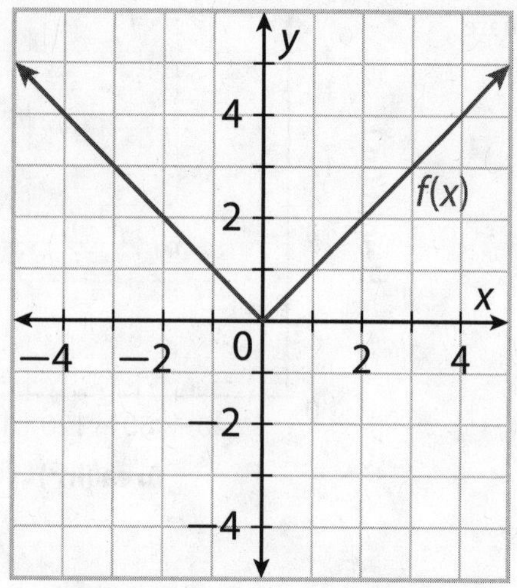

14.

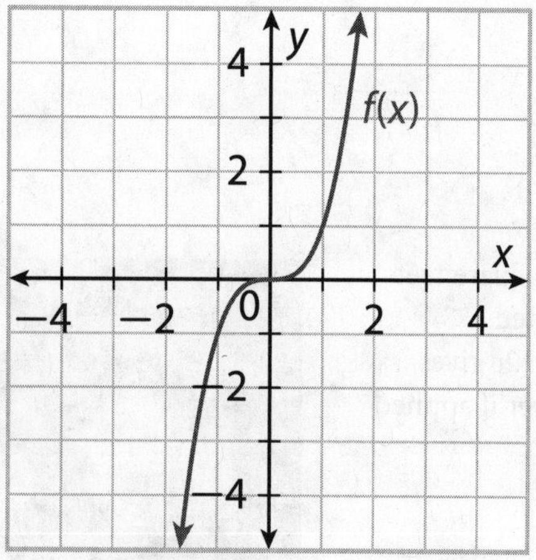

15. Multiple Response Identify the domain intervals over which the inverse of the graphed function is also a function. Select all that apply.

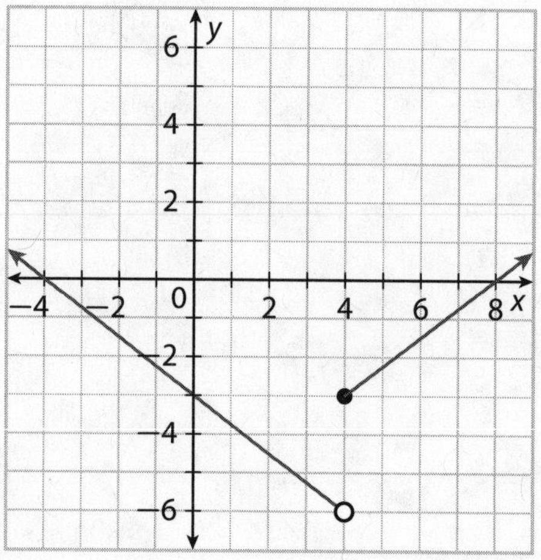

A. $[4, +\infty)$

B. $(0, +\infty)$

C. $[-4, +\infty)$

D. $(-\infty, +\infty)$

E. $(-\infty, 4]$

F. $(-\infty, 4)$

G. $(4, 8)$

H. $(8, +\infty)$

I. $(0, 8]$

H.O.T. Focus on Higher Order Thinking

16. Draw Conclusions Identify all linear functions that are their own inverse.

17. Make a Conjecture Among linear functions (excluding constant functions), quadratic functions, absolute value functions, and exponential functions, which types of function do you have to restrict the domain for the inverse to be a function? Explain.

18. Find the Error A student was asked to find the inverse of $f(x) = 2x + 1$. The student's work is shown. Explain why the student is incorrect and what the student should have done to get the correct answer.

> The function $f(x) = 2x + 1$ involves two operations: multiplying by 2 and adding 1. The inverse operations are dividing by 2 and subtracting 1. So, the inverse function is $f^{-1}(x) = \frac{x}{2} - 1$.

Lesson Performance Task

In an anatomy class, a student measures the femur of an adult male and finds the length of the femur to be 50.0 cm. The student is then asked to estimate the height of the male that the femur came from.

The table shows the femur lengths and heights of some adult males and females. Using a graphing calculator, perform linear regression on the data to obtain femur length as a function of height (one function for adult males, one for adult females). Then find the inverse of each function. Use the appropriate inverse function to find the height of the adult male and explain how the inverse functions would be helpful to a forensic scientist.

Femur Length (cm)	30	38	46	54	62
Male Height (cm)	138	153	168	183	198
Female Height (cm)	132	147	163	179	194

Name________________________ Class______________ Date________

5.3 Graphing Cubic Functions

Essential Question: How are the graphs of $f(x) = a(x - h)^3 + k$ and $f(x) = \left(\frac{1}{b}(x - h)\right)^3 + k$ related to the graph of $f(x) = x^3$?

Resource Locker

Explore 1 Graphing and Analyzing $f(x) = x^3$

You know that a quadratic function has the standard form $f(x) = ax^2 + bx + c$ where a, b, and c are real numbers and $a \neq 0$. Similarly, a **cubic function** has the standard form $f(x) = ax^3 + bx^2 + cx + d$ where a, b, c and d are all real numbers and $a \neq 0$. You can use the basic cubic function, $f(x) = x^3$, as the parent function for a family of cubic functions related through transformations of the graph of $f(x) = x^3$.

(A) Complete the table, graph the ordered pairs, and then draw a smooth curve through the plotted points to obtain the graph of $f(x) = x^3$.

x	$y = x^3$
−2	
−1	
0	
1	
2	

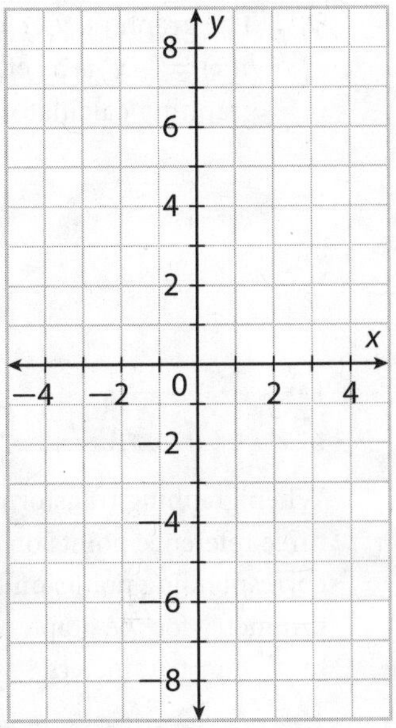

(B) Use the graph to analyze the function and complete the table.

Attributes of $f(x) = x^3$	
Domain	$\mathbb{R}$
Range	
End behavior	As $x \to +\infty$, $f(x) \to$ ☐. As $x \to -\infty$, $f(x) \to$ ☐.
Zeros of the function	$x = 0$
Where the function has positive values	$x > 0$
Where the function has negative values	
Where the function is increasing	
Where the function is decreasing	The function never decreases.
Is the function even $(f(-x) = f(x))$, odd $(f(-x) = -f(x))$, or neither?	______, because $(x)^3 =$ ☐.

Reflect

1. How would you characterize the rate of change of the function on the intervals $[-1, 0]$ and $[0, 1]$ compared with the rate of change on the intervals $[-2, -1]$ and $[1, 2]$? Explain.

2. A graph is said to be *symmetric about the origin* (and the origin is called the graph's *point of symmetry*) if for every point (x, y) on the graph, the point $(-x, -y)$ is also on the graph. Is the graph of $f(x) = x^3$ symmetric about the origin? Explain.

3. The graph of $g(x) = (-x)^3$ is a reflection of the graph of $f(x) = x^3$ across the y-axis, while the graph of $h(x) = -x^3$ is a reflection of the graph of $f(x) = x^3$ across the x-axis. If you graph $g(x)$ and $h(x)$ on a graphing calculator, what do you notice? Explain why this happens.

Explain 1 Graphing Combined Transformations of $f(x) = x^3$

When graphing transformations of $f(x) = x^3$, it helps to consider the effect of the transformations on the three reference points on the graph of $f(x)$: $(-1, -1)$, $(0, 0)$, and $(1,1)$. The table lists the three points and the corresponding points on the graph of $g(x) = a\left(\frac{1}{b}(x - h)\right)^3 + k$. Notice that the point $(0, 0)$, which is the point of symmetry for the graph of $f(x)$, is affected only by the parameters h and k. The other two reference points are affected by all four parameters.

$f(x) = x^3$		$g(x) = a\left(\frac{1}{b}(x - h)\right)^3 + k$	
x	y	x	y
-1	-1	$-b + h$	$-a + k$
0	0	h	k
1	1	$b + h$	$a + k$

Example 1 **Identify the transformations of the graph of $f(x) = x^3$ that produce the graph of the given function $g(x)$. Then graph $g(x)$ on the same coordinate plane as the graph of $f(x)$ by applying the transformations to the reference points $(-1, -1)$, $(0, 0)$, and $(1, 1)$.**

Ⓐ $g(x) = 2(x - 1)^3 - 1$

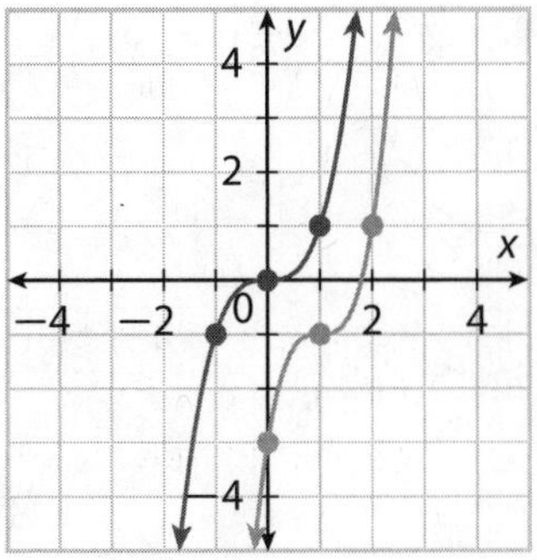

The transformations of the graph of $f(x)$ that produce the graph of $g(x)$ are:

- a vertical stretch by a factor of 2
- a translation of 1 unit to the right and 1 unit down

Note that the translation of 1 unit to the right affects only the x-coordinates of points on the graph of $f(x)$, while the vertical stretch by a factor of 2 and the translation of 1 unit down affect only the y-coordinates.

$f(x) = x^3$		$g(x) = 2(x-1)^3 - 1$	
x	y	x	y
−1	−1	$-1 + 1 = 0$	$2(-1) - 1 = -3$
0	0	$0 + 1 = 1$	$2(0) - 1 = -1$
1	1	$1 + 1 = 2$	$2(1) - 1 = 1$

Ⓑ $g(x) = \left(2(x + 3)\right)^3 + 4$

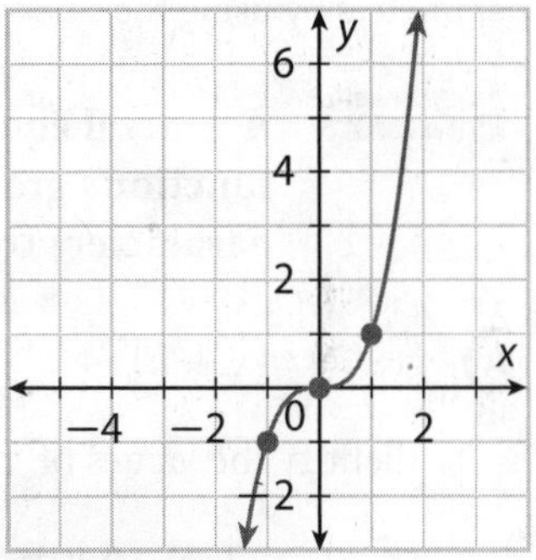

The transformations of the graph of $f(x)$ that produce the graph of $g(x)$ are:

- a horizontal compression by a factor of $\frac{1}{2}$
- a translation of 3 units to the left and 4 units up

Note that the horizontal compression by a factor of $\frac{1}{2}$ and the translation of 3 units to the left affect only the x-coordinates of points on the graph of $f(x)$, while the translation of 4 units up affects only the y-coordinates.

$f(x) = x^3$		$g(x) = \left(2(x+3)\right)^3 + 4$	
x	y	x	y
−1	−1	$\square(-1) + \square = \square$	$-1 + \square = \square$
0	0	$\square(0) + \square = \square$	$0 + \square = \square$
1	1	$\square(1) + \square = \square$	$1 + \square = \square$

Your Turn

Identify the transformations of the graph of $f(x) = x^3$ that produce the graph of the given function $g(x)$. Then graph $g(x)$ on the same coordinate plane as the graph of $f(x)$ by applying the transformations to the reference points $(-1, -1)$, $(0, 0)$, and $(1, 1)$.

4. $g(x) = -\frac{1}{2}(x - 3)^3$

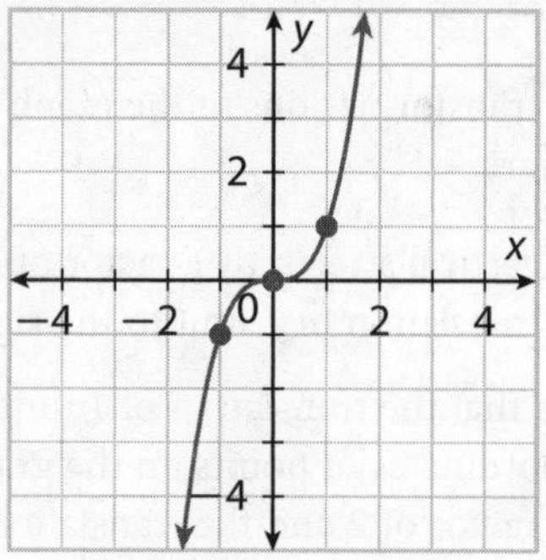

Explain 2 Writing Equations for Combined Transformations of $f(x) = x^3$

Given the graph of the transformed function $g(x) = a\left(\frac{1}{b}(x - h)\right)^3 + k$, you can determine the values of the parameters by using the same reference points that you used to graph $g(x)$ in the previous example.

Example 2 **A general equation for a cubic function $g(x)$ is given along with the function's graph. Write a specific equation by identifying the values of the parameters from the reference points shown on the graph.**

3=h+1

Ⓐ $g(x) = a(x - h)^3 + k$

Identify the values of h and k from the point of symmetry.

$(h, k) = (2, 1)$, so $h = 2$ and $k = 1$.

Identify the value of a from either of the other two reference points.

The rightmost reference point has general coordinates $(h + 1, a + k)$. Substituting 2 for h and 1 for k and setting the general coordinates equal to the actual coordinates gives this result:

$(h + 1, a + k) = (3, a + 1) = (3, 4)$, so $a = 3$.

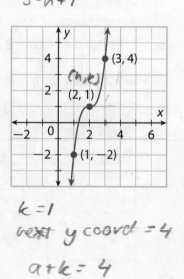

Write the function using the values of the parameters: $g(x) = 3(x - 2)^3 + 1$

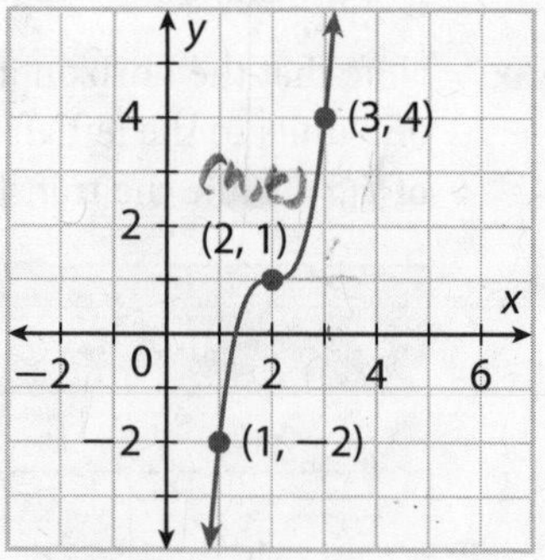

k=1
next y coord = 4
a+k= 4

(B) $g(x) = \left(\frac{1}{b}(x - h)\right)^3 + k$

Identify the values of h and k from the point of symmetry.

$(h, k) = \left(-4, \square\right)$, so $h = -4$ and $k = \square$.

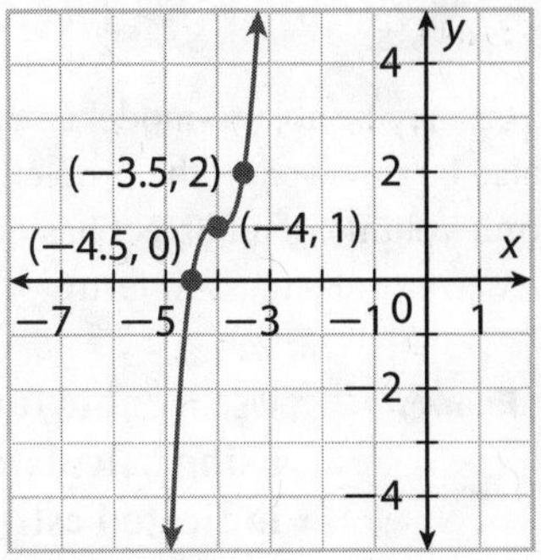

Identify the value of b from either of the other two reference points.

The rightmost reference point has general coordinates

$(b + h, 1 + k)$. Substituting -4 for h and ______ for k and setting the general coordinates equal to the actual coordinates gives this result:

$$\left(b + h, 1 + \square\right) = \left(b - 4, \square\right) = (-3.5, 2), \text{ so } b = \square.$$

Write the function using the values of the parameters, and then simplify.

$$g(x) = \left(\frac{1}{\square}\left(x - \square\right)\right)^3 + \square$$

or

$$g(x) = \left(\square\left(x + \square\right)\right)^3 + \square$$

Your Turn

A general equation for a cubic function $g(x)$ is given along with the function's graph. Write a specific equation by identifying the values of the parameters from the reference points shown on the graph.

5. $g(x) = a(x - h)^3 + k$

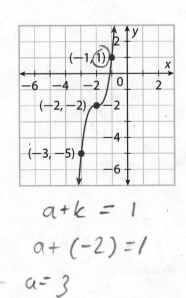

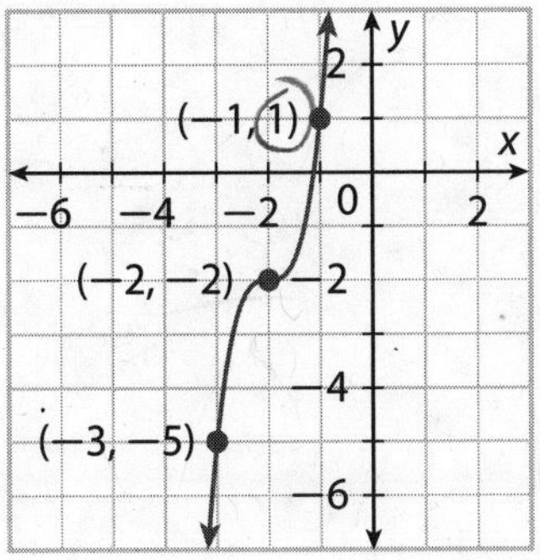

a+k = 1

a+ (−2) = 1

a = 3

6. $g(x) = \left(\frac{1}{b}(x - h)\right)^3 + k$

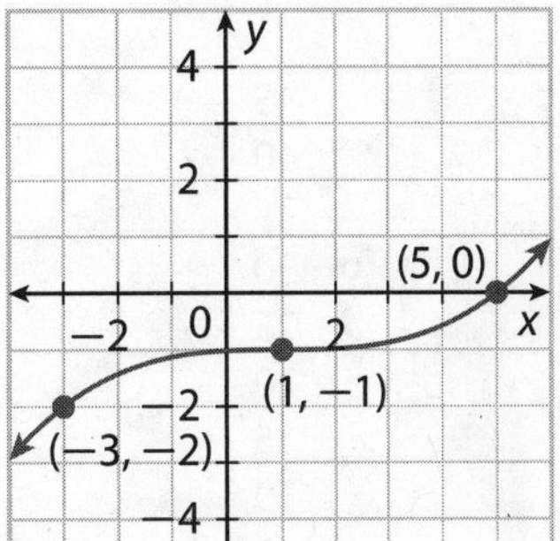

1 = a(−1+2)^3 −2

1 = a(1)^3 −2

1 = 1a −2
+2 +2

3 = 1a   a = 3

Explain 3 Modeling with a Transformation of $f(x) = x^3$

You may be able to model a real-world situation that involves volume with a cubic function. Sometimes mass may also be involved in the problem. Mass and volume are related through *density*, which is defined as an object's mass per unit volume. If an object has mass m and volume V, then its density d is $d = \frac{m}{V}$. You can rewrite the formula as $m = dV$ to express mass in terms of density and volume.

Example 3 **Use a cubic function to model the situation, and graph the function using calculated values of the function. Then use the graph to obtain the indicated estimate.**

(A) Estimate the length of an edge of a child's alphabet block (a cube) that has a mass of 23 g and is made from oak with a density of 0.72 g/cm³.

Let ℓ represent the length (in centimeters) of an edge of the block. Since the block is a cube, the volume V (in cubic centimeters) is $V(\ell) = \ell^3$. The mass m (in grams) of the block is $m(\ell) = 0.72 \cdot V(\ell) = 0.72\ell^3$. Make a table of values for this function.

Length (cm)	Mass (g)
0	0
1	0.72
2	5.76
3	19.44
4	46.08

Draw the graph of the mass function, recognizing that the graph is a vertical compression of the graph of the parent cubic function by a factor of 0.72. Then draw the horizontal line $m = 23$ and estimate the value of ℓ where the graphs intersect.

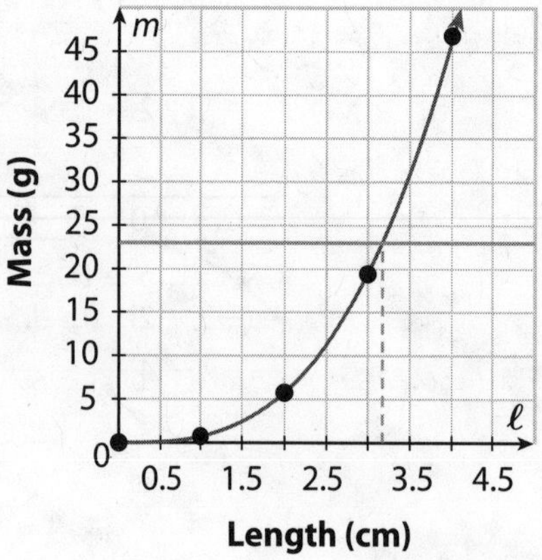

The graphs intersect where $\ell \approx 3.2$, so the edge length of the child's block is about 3.2 cm.

(B) Estimate the radius of a steel ball bearing with a mass of 75 grams and a density of 7.82 g/cm³.

Let r represent the radius (in centimeters) of the ball bearing.
The volume V (in cubic centimeters) of the ball bearing is

$V(r) =$ ☐ r^3. The mass m (in grams) of the ball

bearing is $m(r) = 7.82 \cdot V(r) =$ ☐ r^3.

Radius (cm)	Mass (g)
0	
0.5	
1	
1.5	
2	

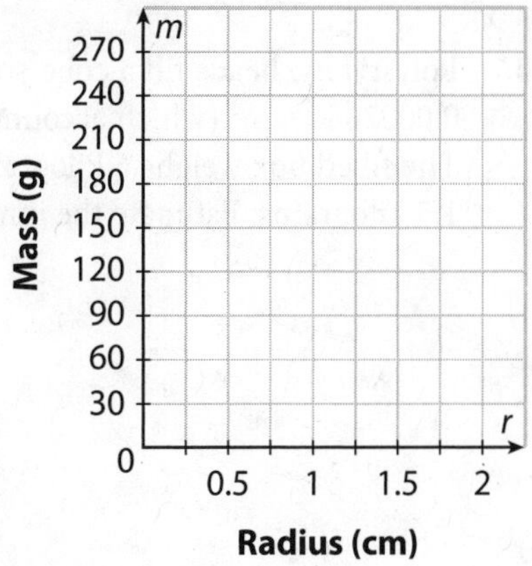

Draw the graph of the mass function, recognizing that the graph is a vertical ________

of the graph of the parent cubic function by a factor of ________. Then draw the

horizontal line $m =$ ☐ and estimate the value of r where the graphs intersect.

The graphs intersect where $r \approx$ ☐, so the radius of the steel ball bearing is about

________ cm.

Reflect

7. Discussion Why is it important to plot multiple points on the graph of the volume function.

Your Turn

Use a cubic function to model the situation, and graph the function using calculated values of the function. Then use the graph to obtain the indicated estimate.

8. Polystyrene beads fill a cube-shaped box with an effective density of 0.00076 kg/cm³ (which accounts for the space between the beads). The filled box weighs 6 kilograms while the empty box had weighed 1.5 kilograms. Estimate the inner edge length of the box.

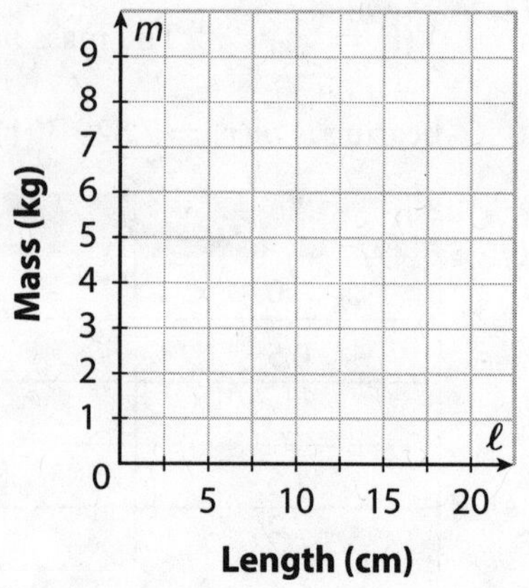

Elaborate

9. Identify which transformations (stretches or compressions, reflections, and translations) of $f(x) = x^3$ change the following attributes of the function.

a. End behavior

b. Location of the point of symmetry

c. Symmetry about a point

10. **Essential Question Check-In** Describe the transformations you must perform on the graph of $f(x) = x^3$ to obtain the graph of $f(x) = a(x - h)^3 + k$.

Evaluate: Homework and Practice

Personal Math Trainer

- Online Homework
- Hints and Help
- Extra Practice

1. Graph the parent cubic function $f(x) = x^3$ and use the graph to answer each question.

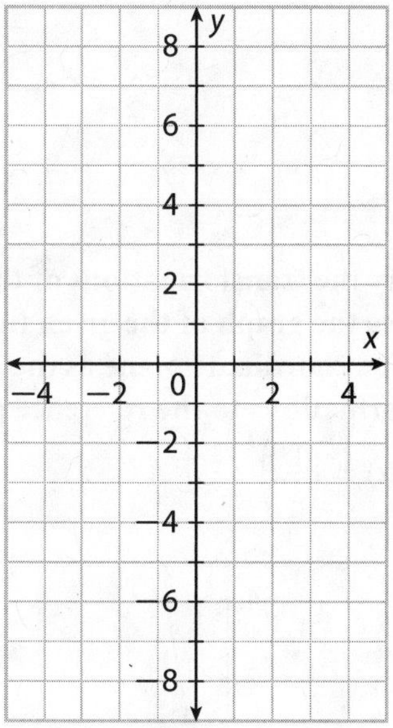

a. State the function's domain and range.

b. Identify the function's end behavior.

c. Identify the graph's x- and y-intercepts.

d. Identify the intervals where the function has positive values and where it has negative values.

e. Identify the intervals where the function is increasing and where it is decreasing.

f. Tell whether the function is even, odd, or neither. Explain.

g. Describe the graph's symmetry.

Describe how the graph of $g(x)$ is related to the graph of $f(x) = x^3$.

2. $g(x) = (x - 4)^3$

3. $g(x) = -5x^3$

4. $g(x) = x^3 + 2$

5. $g(x) = (3x)^3$

6. $g(x) = (x + 1)^3$

7. $g(x) = \frac{1}{4}x^3$

8. $g(x) = x^3 - 3$

9. $g(x) = \left(-\frac{2}{3}x\right)^3$

Identify the transformations of the graph of $f(x) = x^3$ that produce the graph of the given function $g(x)$. Then graph $g(x)$ on the same coordinate plane as the graph of $f(x)$ by applying the transformations to the reference points $(-1, -1)$, $(0, 0)$, and $(1, 1)$.

10. $g(x) = \left(\frac{1}{3}x\right)^3$

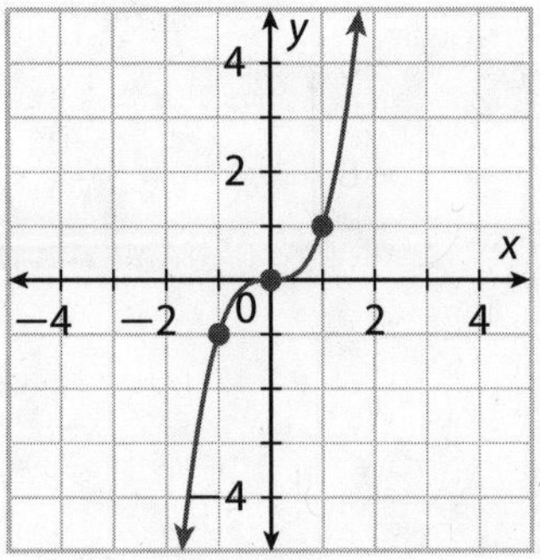

11. $g(x) = \frac{1}{3}x^3$

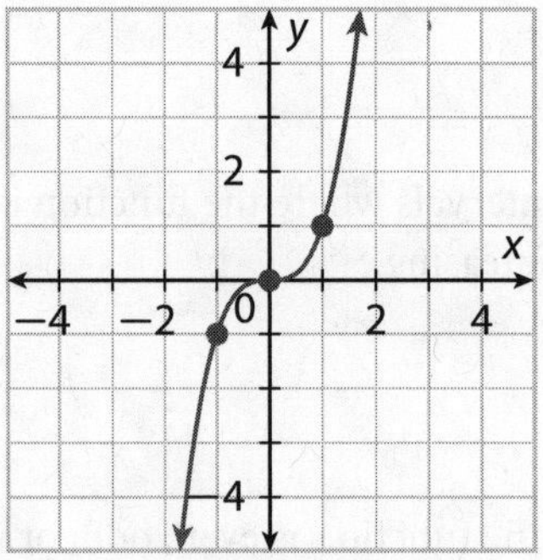

12. $g(x) = (x - 4)^3 - 3$

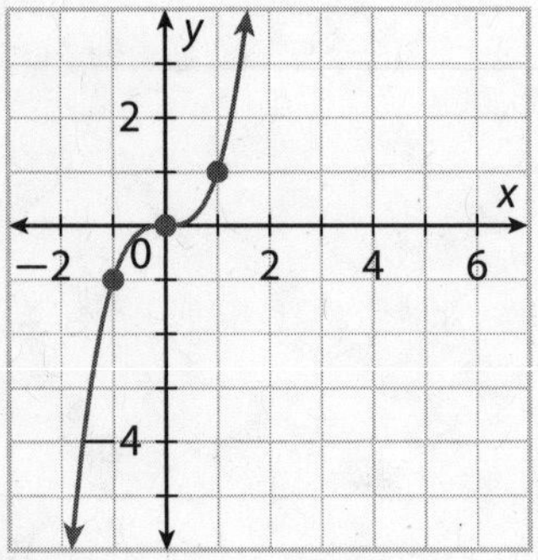

13. $g(x) = (x + 1)^3 + 2$

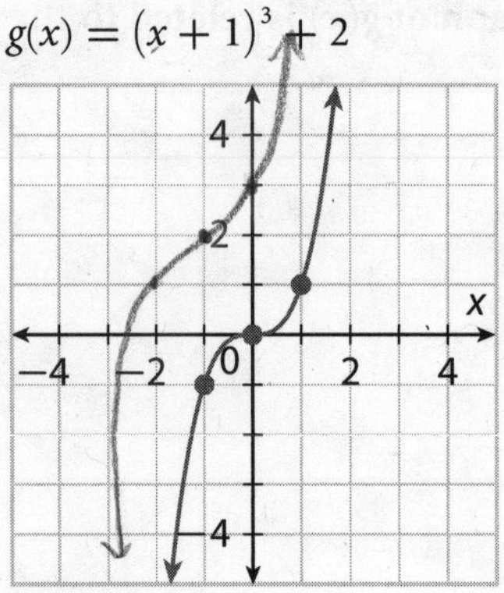

A general equation for a cubic function $g(x)$ is given along with the function's graph. Write a specific equation by identifying the values of the parameters from the reference points shown on the graph.

14. $g(x) = \left(\frac{1}{b}(x - h)\right)^3 + k$

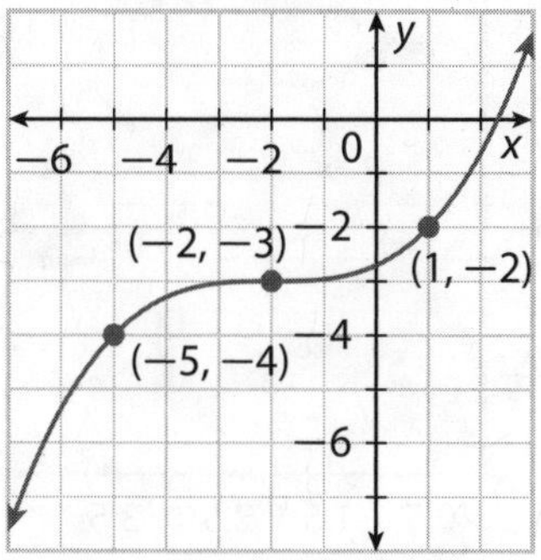

15. $g(x) = a(x - h)^3 + k$

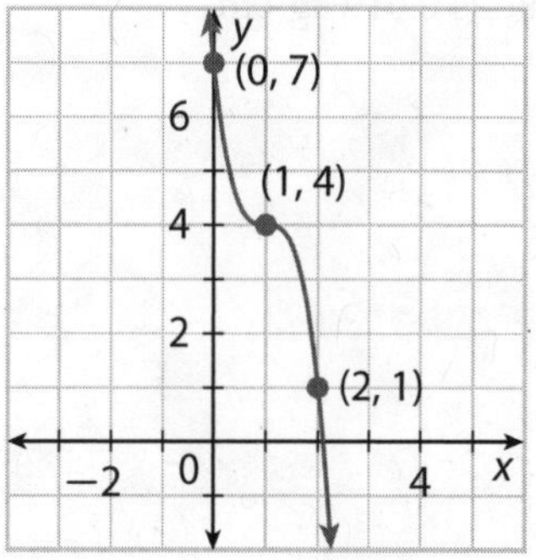

16. $g(x) = \left(\frac{1}{b}(x - h)\right)^3 + k$

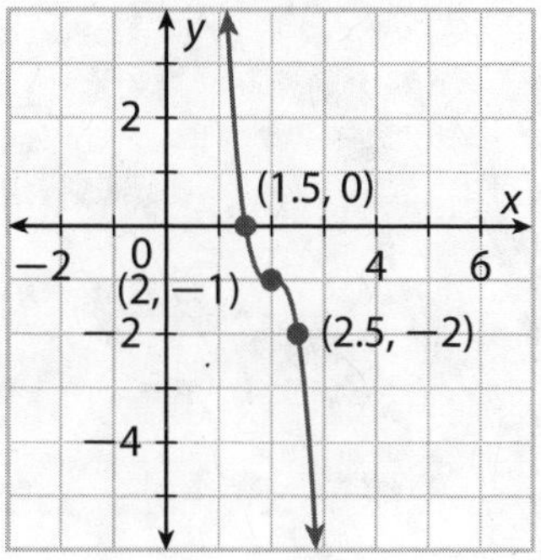

17. $g(x) = a(x - h)^3 + k$

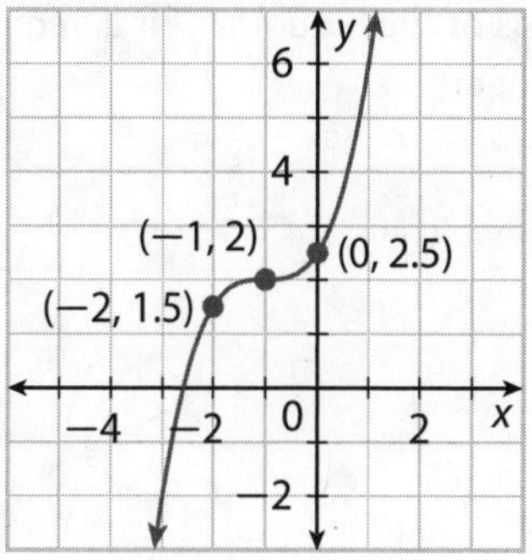

$g(x) = 0.5(x+1)^3 + 2$

Use a cubic function to model the situation, and graph the function using calculated values of the function. Then use the graph to obtain the indicated estimate.

18. Estimate the edge length of a cube of gold with a mass of 1 kg. The density of gold is 0.019 kg/cm^3.

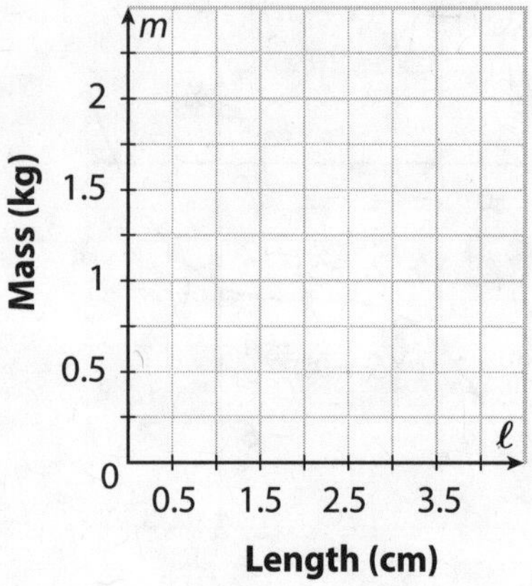

19. A proposed design for a habitable Mars colony is a hemispherical biodome used to maintain a breathable atmosphere for the colonists. Estimate the radius of the biodome if it is required to contain 5.5 billion cubic feet of air.

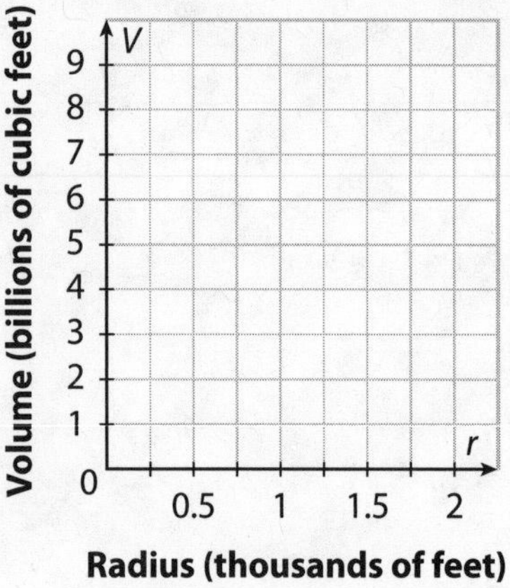

20. Multiple Response Select the transformations of the graph of the parent cubic function that result in the graph of $g(x) = \left(3(x - 2)\right)^3 + 1$.

A. Horizontal stretch by a factor of 3

B. Horizontal compression by a factor of $\frac{1}{3}$

C. Vertical stretch by a factor of 3

D. Vertical compression by a factor of $\frac{1}{3}$

E. Translation 1 unit up

F. Translation 1 unit down

G. Translation 2 units left

H. Translation 2 units right

H.O.T. Focus on Higher Order Thinking

21. Justify Reasoning Explain how horizontally stretching (or compressing) the graph of $f(x) = x^3$ by a factor of b can be equivalent to vertically compressing (or stretching) the graph of $f(x) = x^3$ by a factor of a.

22. Critique Reasoning A student reasoned that $g(x) = (x - h)^3$ can be rewritten as $g(x) = x^3 - h^3$, so a horizontal translation of h units is equivalent to a vertical translation of $-h^3$ units. Is the student correct? Explain.

Lesson Performance Task

Julio wants to purchase a spherical aquarium and fill it with salt water, which has an average density of 1.027 g/cm^3. He has found a company that sells four sizes of spherical aquariums.

Aquarium Size	Diameter (cm)
Small	15
Medium	30
Large	45
Extra large	60

a. If the stand for Julio's aquarium will support a maximum of 50 kg, what is the largest size tank that he should buy? Explain your reasoning.

b. Julio's friend suggests that he could buy a larger tank if he uses fresh water, which has a density of 1.0 g/cm^3. Do you agree with the friend? Why or why not?

Name ______________________ Class ____________ Date ________

5.4 Graphing Polynomial Functions

Essential Question: How do you sketch the graph of a polynomial function in intercept form?

Resource Locker

Explore 1 Investigating the End Behavior of the Graphs of Simple Polynomial Functions

Linear, quadratic, and cubic functions belong to a more general class of functions called *polynomial functions*, which are categorized by their degree. Linear functions are polynomial functions of degree 1, quadratic functions are polynomial functions of degree 2, and cubic functions are polynomial functions of degree 3. In general, a **polynomial function of degree *n*** has the standard form $p(x) = a_nx^n + a_{n-1}x^{n-1} + \ldots + a_2x^2 + a_1x + a_0$, where $a_n, a_{n-1}, \ldots, a_2, a_1$, and a_0 are real numbers called the *coefficients* of the expressions $a_nx^n, a_{n-1}x^{n-1}, \ldots, a_2x^2, a_1x$, and a_0, which are the *terms* of the polynomial function. (Note that the constant term, a_0, appears to have no power of x associated with it, but since $x^0 = 1$, you can write a_0 as a_0x^0 and treat a_0 as the coefficient of the term.)

A polynomial function of degree 4 is called a *quartic* function, while a polynomial function of degree 5 is called a *quintic* function. After degree 5, polynomial functions are generally referred to by their degree, as in "a sixth-degree polynomial function."

(A) Use a graphing calculator to graph the polynomial functions $f(x) = x$, $f(x) = x^2$, $f(x) = x^3$, $f(x) = x^4$, $f(x) = x^5$, and $f(x) = x^6$. Then use the graph of each function to determine the function's domain, range, and end behavior. (Use interval notation for the domain and range.)

Function	Domain	Range	End Behavior
$f(x) = x$	$\mathbb{R}$	$\mathbb{R}$	As $x \to +\infty$, $f(x) \to$ ∞. As $x \to -\infty$, $f(x) \to$ $-\infty$.
$f(x) = x^2$	$\mathbb{R}$	$(0, \infty)$	As $x \to +\infty$, $f(x) \to$ ∞. As $x \to -\infty$, $f(x) \to$ $-\infty$.
$f(x) = x^3$	$\mathbb{R}$	$\mathbb{R}$	As $x \to +\infty$, $f(x) \to$ ∞. As $x \to -\infty$, $f(x) \to$ $-\infty$.
$f(x) = x^4$	$\mathbb{R}$	$(0, \infty)$	As $x \to +\infty$, $f(x) \to$ ∞. As $x \to -\infty$, $f(x) \to$ $-\infty$.
$f(x) = x^5$	$\mathbb{R}$	$\mathbb{R}$	As $x \to +\infty$, $f(x) \to$ ∞. As $x \to -\infty$, $f(x) \to$ $-\infty$.
$f(x) = x^6$	$\mathbb{R}$	$(0, \infty)$	As $x \to +\infty$, $f(x) \to$ ∞. As $x \to -\infty$, $f(x) \to$ $-\infty$.

(B) Use a graphing calculator to graph the polynomial functions $f(x) = -x$, $f(x) = -x^2$, $f(x) = -x^3$, $f(x) = -x^4$, $f(x) = -x^5$, and $f(x) = -x^6$. Then use the graph of each function to determine the function's domain, range, and end behavior. (Use interval notation for the domain and range.)

Function	Domain	Range	End Behavior
$f(x) = -x$			As $x \to +\infty$, $f(x) \to$ ☐. As $x \to -\infty$, $f(x) \to$ ☐.
$f(x) = -x^2$	ℝ	(0, -∞)	As $x \to +\infty$, $f(x) \to$ -∞. As $x \to -\infty$, $f(x) \to$ -∞.
$f(x) = -x^3$	ℝ	ℝ	As $x \to +\infty$, $f(x) \to$ -∞. As $x \to -\infty$, $f(x) \to$ ∞.
$f(x) = -x^4$			As $x \to +\infty$, $f(x) \to$ ☐. As $x \to -\infty$, $f(x) \to$ ☐.
$f(x) = -x^5$			As $x \to +\infty$, $f(x) \to$ ☐. As $x \to -\infty$, $f(x) \to$ ☐.
$f(x) = -x^6$			As $x \to +\infty$, $f(x) \to$ ☐. As $x \to -\infty$, $f(x) \to$ ☐.

Reflect

1. How can you generalize the results of this Explore for $f(x) = x^n$ and $f(x) = -x^n$ where n is positive whole number?

Explore 2 Investigating the *x*-intercepts and Turning Points of the Graphs of Polynomial Functions

The cubic function $f(x) = x^3$ has three factors, all of which happen to be x. One or more of the x's can be replaced with other linear factors in x, such as $x - 2$, without changing the fact that the function is cubic. In general, a polynomial function of the form $p(x) = a(x - x_1)(x - x_2)...(x - x_n)$ where $a, x_1, x_2, ...,$ and x_n are real numbers (that are not necessarily distinct) has degree n where n is the number of variable factors.

The graph of $p(x) = a(x - x_1)(x - x_2)...(x - x_n)$ has $x_1, x_2, ...,$ and x_n as its x-intercepts, which is why the polynomial is said to be in *intercept form*. Since the graph of $p(x)$ intersects the x-axis only at its x-intercepts, the graph must move away from and then move back toward the x-axis between each pair of successive x-intercepts, which means that the graph has a *turning point* between those x-intercepts. Also, instead of crossing the x-axis at an x-intercept, the graph can be *tangent* to the x-axis, and the point of tangency becomes a turning point because the graph must move toward the x-axis and then away from it near the point of tangency.

The y-coordinate of each turning point is a maximum or minimum value of the function at least near that turning point. A maximum or minimum value is called *global* or *absolute* if the function never takes on a value that is greater than the maximum or less than the minimum. A *local maximum* or *local minimum,* also called a *relative maximum* or *relative minimum,* is a maximum or minimum within some interval around the turning point that need not be (but may be) a global maximum or global minimum.

(A) Use a graphing calculator to graph the cubic functions $f(x) = x^3$, $f(x) = x^2(x - 2)$, and $f(x) = x(x - 2)(x + 2)$. Then use the graph of each function to answer the questions in the table.

Function	$f(x) = x^3$	$f(x) = x^2(x - 2)$	$f(x) = x(x - 2)(x + 2)$
How many distinct factors does $f(x)$ have?	1	2	3
What are the graph's x-intercepts?	0	2, 0	0, 2, -2
Is the graph tangent to the x-axis or does it cross the x-axis at each x-intercept?	no	yes (con)	no
How many turning points does the graph have?	1	2	2
How many global maximum values? How many local maximum values that are not global?	0	1, 0	1, 0
How many global minimum values? How many local minimum values that are not global?			

(B) Use a graphing calculator to graph the quartic functions $f(x) = x^4$, $f(x) = x^3(x - 2)$, $f(x) = x^2(x - 2)(x + 2)$, and $f(x) = x(x - 2)(x + 2)(x + 3)$. Then use the graph of each function to answer the questions in the table.

Function	$f(x) = x^4$	$f(x) = x^3(x - 2)$	$f(x) = x^2(x - 2)(x + 2)$	$f(x) = x(x - 2)(x + 2)(x + 3)$
How many distinct factors?				
What are the x-intercepts?				
Tangent to or cross the x-axis at x-intercepts?				
How many turning points?				
How many global maximum values? How many local maximum values that are not global?				
How many global minimum values? How many local minimum values that are not global?				

Reflect

2. What determines how many x-intercepts the graph of a polynomial function in intercept form has?

3. What determines whether the graph of a polynomial function in intercept form crosses the x-axis or is tangent to it at an x-intercept?

4. Suppose you introduced a factor of -1 into each of the quartic functions in Step B. (For instance, $f(x) = x^4$ becomes $f(x) = -x^4$.) How would your answers to the questions about the functions and their graphs change?

Explain 1 Sketching the Graph of Polynomial Functions in Intercept Form

Given a polynomial function in intercept form, you can sketch the function's graph by using the end behavior, the x-intercepts, and the sign of the function values on intervals determined by the x-intercepts. The sign of the function values tells you whether the graph is above or below the x-axis on a particular interval. You can find the sign of the function values by determining the sign of each factor and recognizing what the sign of the product of those factors is.

Example 1 **Sketch the graph of the polynomial function.**

(A) $f(x) = x(x + 2)(x - 3)$

Identify the end behavior. For the function $p(x) = a(x - x_1)(x - x_2)\dots(x - x_n)$, the end behavior is determined by whether the degree n is even or odd and whether the constant factor a is positive or negative. For the given function $f(x)$, the degree is 3 and the constant factor a, which is 1, is positive, so $f(x)$ has the following end behavior:

As $x \to +\infty$, $f(x) \to +\infty$.

As $x \to -\infty$, $f(x) \to -\infty$.

Identify the graph's x-intercepts, and then use the sign of $f(x)$ on intervals determined by the x-intercepts to find where the graph is above the x-axis and where it's below the x-axis.

The x-intercepts are $x = 0$, $x = -2$, and $x = 3$. These three x-intercepts divide the x-axis into four intervals: $x < -2$, $-2 < x < 0$, $0 < x < 3$, and $x > 3$.

Interval	Sign of the Constant Factor	Sign of x	Sign of $x + 2$	Sign of $x - 3$	Sign of $f(x) = x(x+2)(x-3)$
$x < -2$	+	−	−	−	−
$-2 < x < 0$	+	−	+	−	+
$0 < x < 3$	+	+	+	−	−
$x > 3$	+	+	+	+	+

So, the graph of $f(x)$ is above the x-axis on the intervals $-2 < x < 0$ and $x > 3$, and it's below the x-axis on the intervals $x < -2$ and $0 < x < 3$.

Sketch the graph.

While you should be precise about where the graph crosses the x-axis, you do not need to be precise about the y-coordinates of points on the graph that aren't on the x-axis. Your sketch should simply show where the graph lies above the x-axis and where it lies below the x-axis.

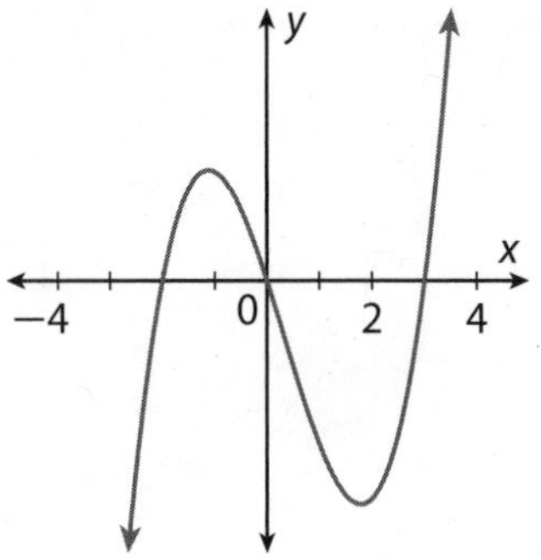

(B) $f(x) = -(x - 4)(x - 1)(x + 1)(x + 2)$

Identify the end behavior.

As $x \to +\infty$, $f(x) \to$ ☐.

As $x \to -\infty$, $f(x) \to$ ☐.

Identify the graph's x-intercepts, and then use the sign of $f(x)$ on intervals determined by the x-intercepts to find where the graph is above the x-axis and where it's below the x-axis.

The x-intercepts are $x =$ ☐, $x =$ ☐, $x =$ ☐, $x =$ ☐.

Interval	Sign of the Constant Factor	Sign of $x - 4$	Sign of $x - 1$	Sign of $x + 1$	Sign of $x + 2$	Sign of $f(x) = -(x - 4)(x - 1)(x + 1)(x + 2)$
$x <$ ☐	−		−		−	
☐ $< x <$ ☐	−		−		+	
☐ $< x <$ ☐	−		+		+	
☐ $< x <$ ☐	−		+		+	
$x >$ ☐	−		+		+	

So, the graph of $f(x)$ is above the x-axis on the intervals

☐ $< x <$ ☐ and ☐ $< x <$ ☐, and

it's below the x-axis on the intervals $x <$ ☐, ☐ $< x <$ ☐,

and $x >$ ☐.

Sketch the graph.

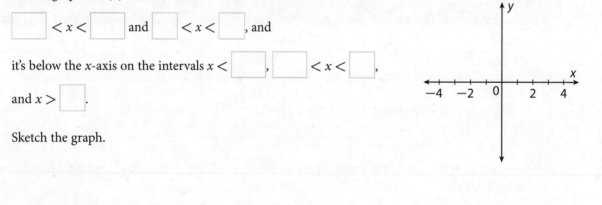

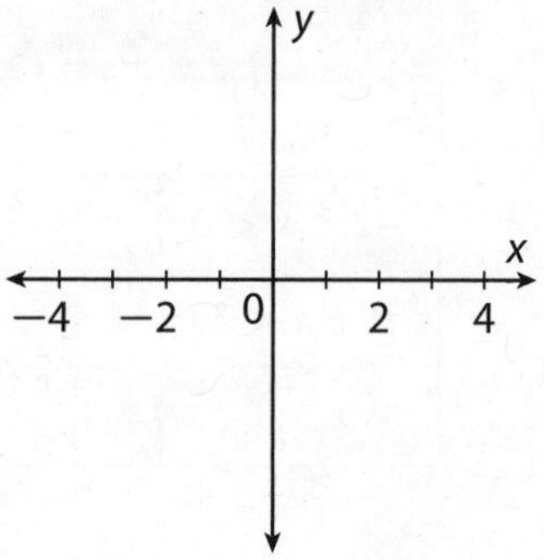

Your Turn

Sketch the graph of the polynomial function.

5. $f(x) = -x^2(x - 4)$

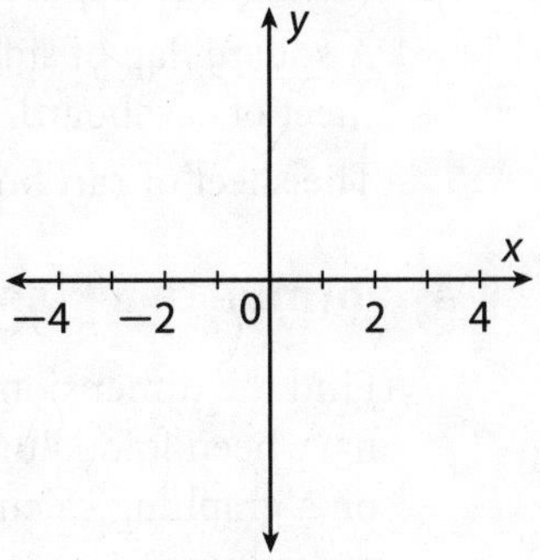

Explain 2 Modeling with a Polynomial Function

You can use cubic functions to model real-world situations. For example, you find the volume of a box (a rectangular prism) by multiplying the length, width, and height. If each dimension of the box is given in terms of x, then the volume is a cubic function of x.

Example 2

To create an open-top box out of a sheet of cardboard that is 9 inches long and 5 inches wide, you make a square flap of side length x inches in each corner by cutting along one of the flap's sides and folding along the other side. (In the first diagram, a solid line segment in the interior of the rectangle indicates a cut, while a dashed line segment indicates a fold.) After you fold up the four sides of the box (see the second diagram), you glue each flap to the side it overlaps. To the nearest tenth, find the value of x that maximizes the volume of the box.

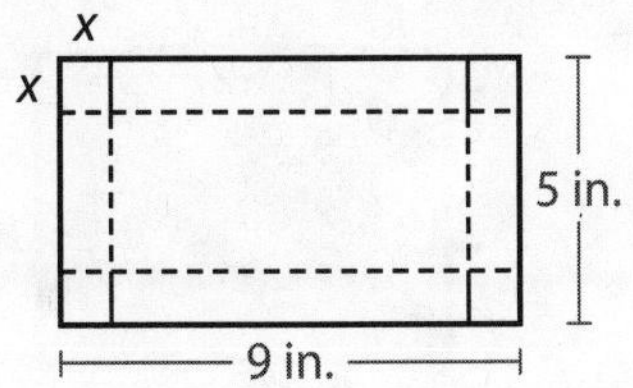

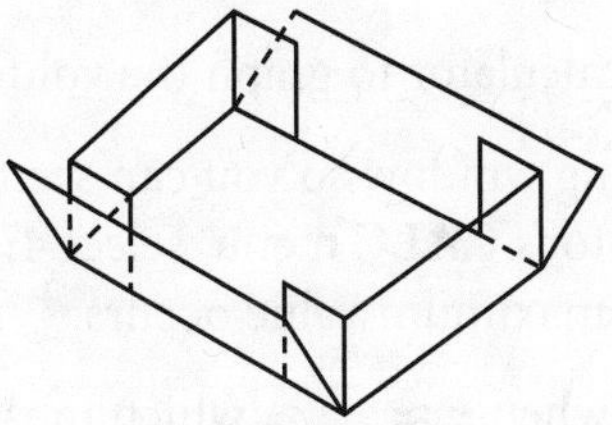

Analyze Information

Identify the important information.

A square flap of side length x inches is made in each corner of a rectangular sheet of cardboard.

The sheet of cardboard measures 9 inches by 5 inches.

Formulate a Plan

Find the dimensions of the box once the flaps have been made and the sides have been folded up. Create a volume function for the box, graph the function on a graphing calculator, and use the graph to find the value of x that maximizes the volume.

Solve

1. Write expressions for the dimensions of the box.

Length of box: $9 - \square$

Width of box: $5 - \square$

Height of box: $\square$

2. Write the volume function and determine its domain.

$V(x) = \left(9 - \square\right)\left(5 - \square\right)\square$

Because the length, width, and height of the box must all be positive, the volume function's domain is determined by the following three constraints:

$9 - 2x > 0$, or $x < \square$

$5 - 2x > 0$, or $x < \square$

$x > 0$

Taken together, these constraints give a domain of $0 < x < \square$.

3. Use a graphing calculator to graph the volume function on its domain.

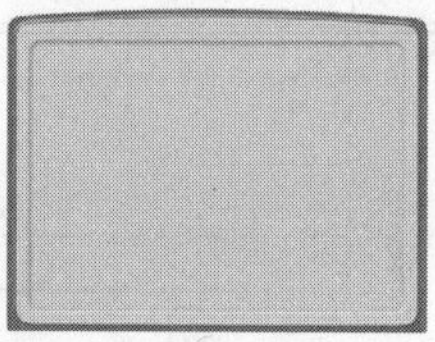

Adjust the viewing window so you can see the maximum. From the graphing calculator's **CALC** menu, select **4: maximum** to locate the point where the maximum value occurs.

So, $V(x) \approx 21.0$ when $x \approx \square$, which means that the box has a maximum volume of about 21 cubic inches when square flaps with a side length of 1 inch are made in the corners of the sheet of cardboard.

Justify and Evaluate

Making square flaps with a side length of 1 inch means that the box will be 7 inches long, 3 inches wide, and 1 inch high, so the volume is 21 cubic inches. As a check on this result, consider making square flaps with a side length of 0.9 inch and 1.1 inches:

$V(0.9) = (9 - 1.8)(5 - 1.8)(0.9) =$ ______

$V(1.1) = (9 - 2.2)(5 - 2.2)(1.1) =$ ______

Both volumes are slightly less than 21 cubic inches, which suggests that 21 cubic inches is the maximum volume.

Reflect

6. **Discussion** Although the volume function has three constraints on its domain, the domain involves only two of them. Why?

Your Turn

7. To create an open-top box out of a sheet of cardboard that is 25 inches long and 13 inches wide, you make a square flap of side length x inches in each corner by cutting along one of the flap's sides and folding along the other. (In the diagram, a solid line segment in the interior of the rectangle indicates a cut, while a dashed line segment indicates a fold.) Once you fold up the four sides of the box, you glue each flap to the side it overlaps. To the nearest tenth, find the value of x that maximizes the volume of the box.

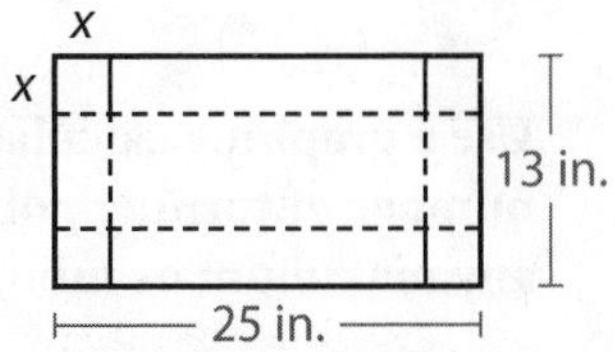

Elaborate

8. Compare and contrast the domain, range, and end behavior of $f(x) = x^n$ when n is even and when n is odd.

9. **Essential Question Check-In** For a polynomial function in intercept form, why is the constant factor important when graphing the function?

Evaluate: Homework and Practice

Personal Math Trainer

- Online Homework
- Hints and Help
- Extra Practice

Use a graphing calculator to graph the polynomial function. Then use the graph to determine the function's domain, range, and end behavior. (Use interval notation for the domain and range.)

1. $f(x) = x^7$

2. $f(x) = -x^9$

3. $f(x) = x^{10}$

4. $f(x) = -x^8$

Use a graphing calculator to graph the function. Then use the graph to determine the number of turning points and the number and type (global, or local but not global) of any maximum or minimum values.

5. $f(x) = x(x+1)(x+3)$

6. $f(x) = (x+1)^2(x-1)(x-2)$

7. $f(x) = -x(x-2)^2$

8. $f(x) = -(x-1)(x+2)^3$

Sketch the graph the polynomial function.

9. $f(x) = x^2(x - 2)$

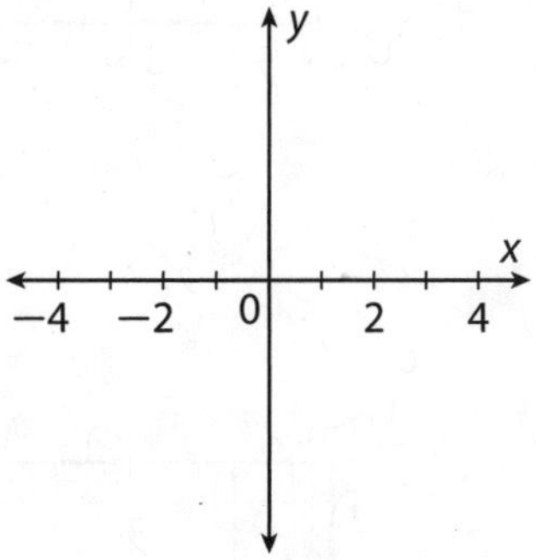

10. $f(x) = -(x + 1)(x - 2)(x - 3)$

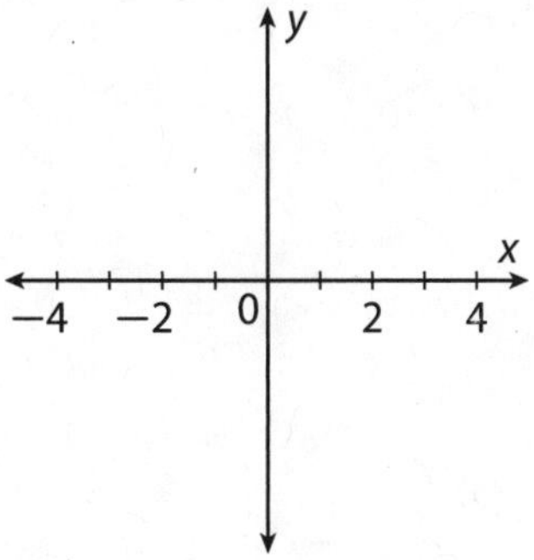

11. $f(x) = x(x + 2)^2(x - 1)$

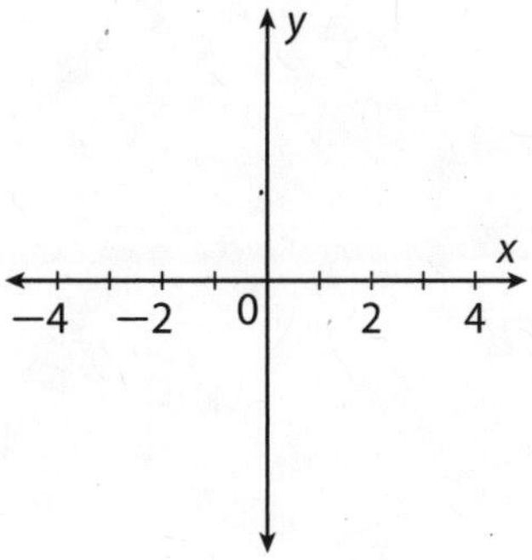

12. To create an open-top box out of a sheet of cardboard that is 6 inches long and 3 inches wide, you make a square flap of side length x inches in each corner by cutting along one of the flap's sides and folding along the other. Once you fold up the four sides of the box, you glue each flap to the side it overlaps. To the nearest tenth, find the value of x that maximizes the volume of the box.

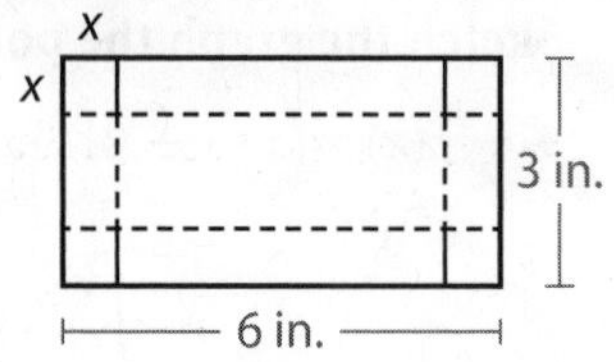

13. The template shows how to create a box from a square sheet of cardboard that has a side length of 36 inches. In the template, solid line segments indicate cuts, dashed line segments indicate folds, and grayed rectangles indicate pieces removed. The vertical strip that is 2 inches wide on the left side of the template is a flap that will be glued to the side of the box that it overlaps when the box is folded up. The horizontal strips that are $\frac{x}{2}$ inches wide at the top and bottom of the template are also flaps that will overlap to form the top and bottom of the box when the box is folded up. Write a volume function for the box in terms of x only. (You will need to determine a relationship between x and y first.) Then, to the nearest tenth, find the dimensions of the box with maximum volume.

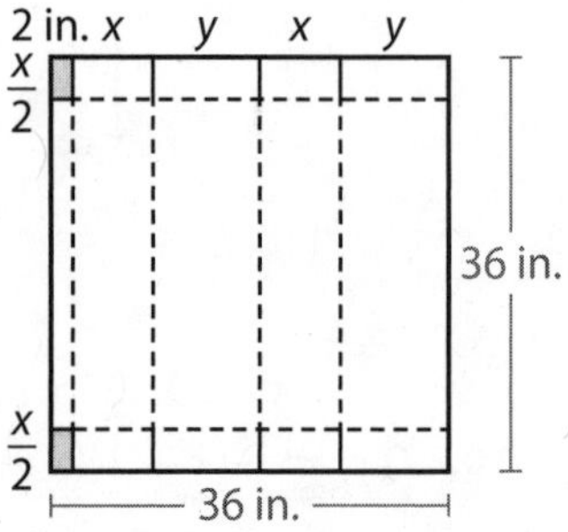

20. Make a Prediction Knowing the characteristics of the graphs of cubic and quartic functions in intercept form, sketch the graph of the quintic function $f(x) = x^2(x + 2)(x - 2)^2$.

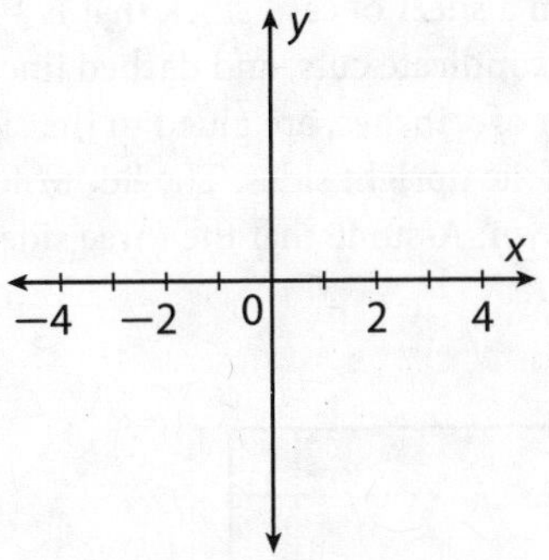

21. Represent Real-World Situations A rectangular piece of sheet metal is rolled and riveted to form a circular tube that is open at both ends, as shown. The sheet metal has a perimeter of 36 inches. Each of the two sides of the rectangle that form the two ends of the tube has a length of x inches, and the tube has a circumference of $x - 1$ inches because an overlap of 1 inch is needed for the rivets. Write a volume function for the tube in terms of x. Then, to the nearest tenth, find the value of x that maximizes the volume of the tube.

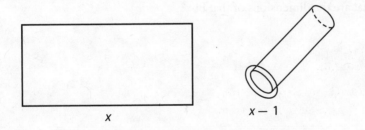

Lesson Performance Task

The template shows how to create a box with a lid from a sheet of card stock that is 10 inches wide and 24 inches long. In the template, solid line segments indicate cuts, and dashed line segments indicate folds. The square flaps, each with a side length of x inches, are glued to the sides they overlap when the box is folded up. The box has a bottom and four upright sides. The lid, which is attached to one of the upright sides, has three upright sides of its own. Assume that the three sides of the lid can be tucked inside the box when the lid is closed.

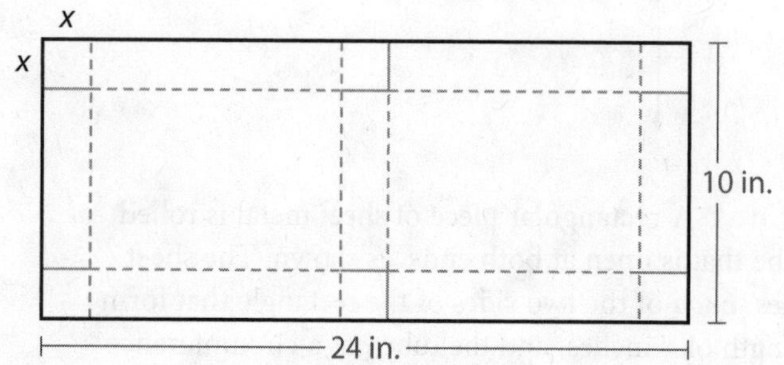

a. Write a polynomial function that represents the volume of the box, and state its domain.

b. Use a graphing calculator to find the value of x that will produce the box with maximum volume. What are the dimensions of that box?

Polynomial Functions

Essential Question: How can polynomial functions help to solve real-world problems?

Key Vocabulary
cubic function (*función cúbica*)
domain (*dominio*)
end behavior (*comportamiento final*)
finite interval (*intervalo finito*)
infinite interval (*intervalo infinito*)
polynomial function (*función polinomial*)
range (*rango*)

KEY EXAMPLE (*Lesson 5.1*)

Describe how to transform the graph of $f(x) = x^2$ to obtain the graph of the related function $g(x) = 2f(x-1)+3$.

Parameter	Effect on the Parent Graph
$a = 2$	vertical stretch of the graph of $f(x)$ by a factor of 2
$h = 1$	translation of the graph of $f(x)$ to the right 1 unit
$k = 3$	translation of the graph of $f(x)$ up 3 units

A point (x, y) on the graph of $f(x) = x^2$ becomes the point $(x+1, 2y+3)$.

KEY EXAMPLE (*Lesson 5.2*)

Find the inverse function $f^{-1}(x)$ for $f(x) = -2x + 3$.

$y = -2x + 3$ Replace $f(x)$ with y.

$\frac{y-3}{-2} = x$ Solve for x.

$y = \frac{x-3}{-2}$ Switch x and y.

$f^{-1}(x) = \frac{x-3}{-2}$ Replace y with $f^{-1}(x)$.

KEY EXAMPLE (*Lesson 5.3*)

Identify the transformations of the graph $f(x) = x^3$ that produce the graph of the function $g(x) = \frac{1}{3}(x+2)^3$. Then create a table with the corresponding input and output values.

- a vertical compression by a factor of $\frac{1}{3}$
- a translation of 2 units to the left

x	$f(x) = x^3$	$g(x) = \frac{1}{3}(x+2)^3$
-2	-8	$\frac{1}{3}(-2+2)^3 = 0$
-1	-1	$\frac{1}{3}(-1+2)^3 = \frac{1}{3}$
0	0	$\frac{1}{3}(0+2)^3 = \frac{8}{3}$
1	1	$\frac{1}{3}(1+2)^3 = 9$
2	8	$\frac{1}{3}(2+2)^3 = \frac{64}{3}$

EXERCISES

Identify the transformations of the graph $f(x) = x^3$ that produce the graph of the function. (Lesson 5.3)

1. $g(x) = \left(-\frac{1}{4}(x+2)\right)^3 + 3$

2. $h(x) = \frac{1}{3}(x-4)^3$

Use a graphing calculator to graph each function, then use the graph to determine the number of turning points, global maximums and minimums, and local maximums and minimums that are not global. (Lesson 5.4)

3. $s(x) = x(x+2)(x+1)^2$

4. $h(x) = x^2(x-3)(x+2)(x-2)$

5. Explain how to transform the graph of the function $f(x) = x^2$ to obtain the graph of the related function $g(x) = -2f(x+1) - 3$. (Lesson 5.1)

MODULE PERFORMANCE TASK

What's the Function of a Roller Coaster?

An engineer is designing part of a roller coaster track that can be modeled by the polynomial function

$$f(x) = 2.0 \times 10^{-6}x^4 - 0.0011x^3 + 0.195x^2 - 12.25x + 250$$

where $f(x)$ is the height in feet of a roller coaster car above ground level, and x is the horizontal distance in feet. For this section of track, the domain is $0 \le x \le 250$.

The factored form of this function is

$$f(x) = 2.0 \times 10^{-6}(x-200)(x-250)(x-50)^2.$$

Describe the experience of a rider who is riding a roller coaster on this track.

Use your own paper to complete the task. Be sure to write down all your data and assumptions. Then use graphs, numbers, words, or algebra to explain how you reached your conclusion.

Ready to Go On?

5.1–5.4 Polynomial Functions

Personal Math Trainer

- Online Homework
- Hints and Help
- Extra Practice

Identify the transformations of the graph of $f(x) = x^3$ that produce the graph of $g(x) = -\frac{1}{4}(x + 4)^3$. *(Lesson 5.3)*

1. Changes to x.

2. Changes to y.

Find the inverse for each linear function. *(Lesson 5.2)*

3. $f(x) = -2x + 4$

4. $g(x) = \frac{x}{4} - 3$

5. $h(x) = \frac{3}{4}x + 1$

6. $j(x) = 5x - 6$

Graph the given function on your graphing calculator. Use the graph to state the number of turning points in the graph and the x-intercepts. *(Lesson 5.4)*

7. $g(x) = x^2(x - 3)$

8. $h(x) = (x - 4)(x - 3)(x + 2)^2$

ESSENTIAL QUESTION

9. Give a real world example of a cubic function.

MODULE 5
MIXED REVIEW

Assessment Readiness

1. Look at each equation. Is the vertex of the graph translated to the right and up when compared to $f(x) = x^3$?
Select Yes or No for A–C.

A. $y = (x + 6)^3 + 2$ ○ Yes ○ No
B. $y = 5x^3 + 7$ ○ Yes ○ No
C. $y = (x - 4)^3 + 2$ ○ Yes ○ No

2. Consider the function $g(x) = -f(x + 3) - 2$. Choose True or False for each statement.

A. When compared to $f(x) = x^2$, $g(x)$ will have a vertical stretch of 3. ○ True ○ False
B. When compared to $f(x) = x^2$, $g(x)$ will be reflected over the x-axis. ○ True ○ False
C. When compared to $f(x) = x^2$, $g(x)$ will be translated left 3 units. ○ True ○ False

3. Consider the linear equation $f(x) = 3x + 5$. Choose True or False for each statement.

A. The line $g(x) = 3x - 4$ is perpendicular to $f(x)$. ○ True ○ False
B. The line $h(x) = 3x + 10$ is parallel to $f(x)$. ○ True ○ False
C. The line $j(x) = -\frac{1}{3}x - 4$ is perpendicular to $f(x)$. ○ True ○ False

4. Consider a parallelogram with vertices at (1, 1), (2, 5), (6, 3), and (7, 7). Explain how to find the perimeter and area of the parallelogram.

Polynomials

MODULE 6

Essential Question: How can you use polynomials to solve real-world problems?

REAL WORLD VIDEO
Meteorologists use mathematics and computer models to analyze climate patterns and forecast weather. For example, polynomial functions can be used to model temperature patterns.

MODULE PERFORMANCE TASK PREVIEW

What's the Temperature?

The weather is always a topic for conversation. Is it hot or cold outside? Is it T-shirt and shorts weather, or should you bundle up? What were the high and low temperatures for a particular day? You might suspect that the outdoor temperature follows a pattern. How can you use a polynomial to model the temperature? Let's find out!

Are YOU Ready?

Complete these exercises to review skills you will need for this module.

Personal Math Trainer
- Online Homework
- Hints and Help
- Extra Practice

Adding and Subtracting Polynomials

Example 1 Subtract.

$(7a^3 - 4a^2 + 11) - (3a^2 - 2a + 5)$

$7a^3 - 4a^2 + 11 - 3a^2 + 2a - 5$ Multiply by -1.

$7a^3 - 7a^2 + 2a + 6$ Combine like terms.

Add or subtract the polynomials.

1. $(m^5 + 4m^2 + 6) - (3m^5 - 8m^2)$

2. $(k^2 + 3k + 1) + (k^2 - 8)$

Algebraic Expressions

Example 2 Simplify the expression $5x^3 - 10x^2 + x^3 + 10$.

$6x^3 - 10x^2 + 10$ Combine like terms.

Simplify each expression.

3. $6x - 2x^2 - 2x$

4. $(5x)(2x^2) - x^2$

5. $4(2x - 3y) + 2(x + y)$

6. $4(a + b) - 7(a + 2b)$

Multiplying Polynomials

Example 3 Multiply. $(2a - b)(a + ab + b)$

$(2a - b)(a + ab + b) = 2a(a + ab + b) - b(a + ab + b)$

$= 2a \cdot a + 2a \cdot ab + 2a \cdot b - b \cdot a - b \cdot ab - b \cdot b$

$= 2a^2 + 2a^2b + 2ab - ab - ab^2 - b^2$

$= 2a^2 + 2a^2b + ab - ab^2 - b^2$

Multiply the polynomials.

7. $(x^2 - 4)(x + y)$

8. $(3m + 2)(3m^2 - 2m + 1)$

Name ________________ Class ________ Date ________

6.1 Adding and Subtracting Polynomials

Resource Locker

Essential Question: How do you add or subtract two polynomials, and what type of expression is the result?

Explore Identifying and Analyzing Monomials and Polynomials

A polynomial function of degree n has the *standard form* $p(x) = a_nx^n + a_{n-1}x^{n-1} + \ldots + a_2x^2 + a_1x + a_0$, where $a_n, a_{n-1}, \ldots, a_2, a_1$, and a_0 are real numbers and $a_n \neq 0$. The expression $a_nx^n + a_{n-1}x^{n-1} + \ldots a_2x^2 + a_1x + a_0$ is called a **polynomial**, and each term of a polynomial is called a **monomial**. A monomial is the product of a number and one or more variables with whole-number exponents. A polynomial is a monomial or a sum of monomials. The *degree of a monomial* is the sum of the exponents of the variables, and the *degree of a polynomial* is the degree of the monomial term with the greatest degree. The *leading coefficient* of a polynomial is the coefficient of the term with the greatest degree.

(A) Identify the monomials: x^3, $y + 3y^2 - 5y^3 + 10$, a^2bc^{12}, 76

Monomials: ________________

Not monomials: ________________

(B) Identify the degree of each monomial.

Monomial	x^3	a^2bc^{12}	76
Degree			

(C) Identify the terms of the polynomial $y + 3y^2 - 5y^3 + 10$. ________________

(D) Identify the coefficient of each term.

Term	y	$3y^2$	$-5y^3$	10
Coefficient				

(E) Identify the degree of each term.

Term	y	$3y^2$	$-5y^3$	10
Degree				

(F) Write the polynomial in standard form. ________________

(G) What is the leading coefficient of the polynomial? ________________

Reflect

1. **Discussion** How can you find the degree of a polynomial with multiple variables in each term?

____

____

Explain 1 Adding Polynomials

To add polynomials, combine like terms.

Example 1 **Add the polynomials.**

(A) $(4x^2 - x^3 + 2 + 5x^4) + (-x + 6x^2 + 3x^4)$

$5x^4$	$-x^3$	$+4x^2$		$+2$	Write in standard form.
$+3x^4$		$+6x^2$	$-x$		Align like terms.
$8x^4$	$-x^3$	$+10x^2$	$-x$	$+2$	Add.

(B) $(10x - 18x^3 + 6x^4 - 2) + (-7x^4 + 5 + x + 2x^3)$

$(6x^4 - 18x^3 + 10x - 2) + (-7x^4 + 2x^3 + x + 5)$ Write in standard form.

$= (6x^4 - \square) + (\square + 2x^3) + (\square + x) + (-2 + \square)$ Group like terms.

$= \square - 16x^3 + \square + 3$ Add.

Reflect

2. Is the sum of two polynomials always a polynomial? Explain.

____

____

Your Turn

Add the polynomials.

3. $(17x^4 + 8x^2 - 9x^7 + 4 - 2x^3) + (11x^3 - 8x^2 + 12)$

4. $(-8x + 3x^{11} + x^6) + (4x^4 - x + 17)$

Explain 2 Subtracting Polynomials

To subtract polynomials, combine like terms.

Example 2 **Subtract the polynomials.**

(A) $(12x^3 + 5x - 8x^2 + 19) - (6x^2 - 9x + 3 - 18x^3)$

Write in standard form.	$12x^3$	$-8x^2$	$+5x$	$+19$
Align like terms and add the opposite.	$+18x^3$	$-6x^2$	$+9x$	-3
Add.	$30x^3$	$-14x^2$	$+14x$	$+16$

(B) $(-4x^2 + 8x^3 + 19 - 5x^5) - (9 + 2x^2 + 10x^5)$

Write in standard form and add the opposite. $(-5x^5 + 8x^3 - 4x^2 + 19) + (-10x^5 - 2x^2 - 9)$

Group like terms $= \left(-5x^5 - \square\right) + \left(\square\right) + \left(\square - 2x^2\right) + \left(\square - 9\right)$

Add $= \square + 8x^3 - \square + 10$

Reflect

5. Is the difference of two polynomials always a polynomial? Explain.

____

____

____

Your Turn

Subtract the polynomials.

6. $(23x^7 - 9x^4 + 1) - (-9x^4 + 6x^2 - 31)$

7. $(7x^3 + 13x - 8x^5 + 20x^2) - (-2x^5 + 9x^2)$

Explain 3 Modeling with Polynomial Addition and Subtraction

Polynomial functions can be used to model real-world quantities. If two polynomial functions model quantities that are two parts of a whole, the functions can be added to find a function that models the quantity as a whole. If the polynomial function for the whole and a polynomial function for a part are given, subtraction can be used to find the polynomial function that models the other part of the whole.

Example 3 **Find the polynomial that models the problem and use it to estimate the quantity.**

(A) The data from the U.S. Census Bureau for 2005–2009 shows that the number of male students enrolled in high school in the United States can be modeled by the function $M(x) = -10.4x^3 + 74.2x^2 - 3.4x + 8320.2$, where x is the number of years after 2005 and $M(x)$ is the number of male students in thousands. The number of female students enrolled in high school in the United States can be modeled by the function $F(x) = -13.8x^3 + 55.3x^2 + 141x + 7880$, where x is the number of years after 2005 and $F(x)$ is the number of female students in thousands. Estimate the total number of students enrolled in high school in the United States in 2009.

In the equation $T(x) = M(x) + F(x)$, $T(x)$ is the total number of students in thousands.

Add the polynomials.

$$\left(-10.4x^3 + 74.2x^2 - 3.4x + 8320.2\right) + \left(-13.8x^3 + 55.3x^2 + 141x + 7880\right)$$

$$= \left(-10.4x^3 - 13.8x^3\right) + \left(74.2x^2 + 55.3x^2\right) + \left(-3.4x + 141x\right) + \left(8320.2 + 7880\right)$$

$$= -24.2x^3 + 129.5x^2 + 137.6x + 16{,}200.2$$

The year 2009 is 4 years after 2005, so substitute 4 for x.

$$-24.2(4)^3 + 129.5(4)^2 + 137.6(4) + 16{,}200.2 \approx 17{,}274$$

About 17,274 thousand students were enrolled in high school in the United States in 2009.

(B) The data from the U.S. Census Bureau for 2000–2010 shows that the total number of overseas travelers visiting New York and Florida can be modeled by the function $T(x) = 41.5x^3 - 689.1x^2 + 4323.3x + 2796.6$, where x is the number of years after 2000 and $T(x)$ is the total number of travelers in thousands. The number of overseas travelers visiting New York can be modeled by the function $N(x) = -41.6x^3 + 560.9x^2 - 1632.7x + 6837.4$, where x is the number of years after 2000 and $N(x)$ is the number of travelers in thousands. Estimate the total number of overseas travelers to Florida in 2008.

In the equation $F(x) = T(x)$ ☐ $N(x)$, $F(x)$ is the number of travelers to Florida in thousands.

Subtract the polynomials.

$$\left(41.5x^3 - 689.1x^2 + 4323.3x + 2796.6\right) \ \square \ \left(-41.6x^3 + 560.9x^2 - 1632.7x + 6837.4\right)$$

$$= \left(41.5x^3 - 689.1x^2 + 4323.3x + 2796.6\right) + \left(41.6x^3 - 560.9x^2 + 1632.7x - 6837.4\right)$$

$= \left(41.5x^3 + \boxed{}\right) + \left(\boxed{} - 560.9x^2\right) + \left(\boxed{} + 1632.7x\right) + \left(2796.6 - \boxed{}\right)$

$= \boxed{}\, x^3 - \boxed{}\, x^2 + \boxed{}\, x - \boxed{}$

The year 2008 is 8 years after 2000, so substitute $\boxed{}$ for x.

$83.1(8)^3 - 1250(8)^2 + 5956(8) - 4040.8 \approx \boxed{}$

About $\boxed{}$ thousand overseas travelers visited Florida in 2008.

Your Turn

8. According to the data from the U.S. Census Bureau for 1990–2009, the number of commercially owned automobiles in the United States can be modeled by the function $A(x) = 1.4x^3 - 130.6x^2 + 1831.3x + 128{,}141$, where x is the number of years after 1990 and $A(x)$ is the number of automobiles in thousands. The number of privately-owned automobiles in the United States can be modeled by the function $P(x) = -x^3 + 24.9x^2 - 177.9x + 1709.5$, where x is the number of years after 1990 and $P(x)$ is the number of automobiles in thousands. Estimate the total number of automobiles owned in 2005.

Elaborate

9. How is the degree of a polynomial related to the degrees of the monomials that comprise the polynomial?

10. How is polynomial subtraction based on polynomial addition?

11. How would you find the model for a whole if you have polynomial functions that are models for the two distinct parts that make up that whole?

12. **Essential Question Check-In** What is the result of adding or subtracting polynomials?

Evaluate: Homework and Practice

Personal Math Trainer

- Online Homework
- Hints and Help
- Extra Practice

1. Write the polynomial $-23x^7 + x^9 - 6x^3 + 10 + 2x^2$ in standard form, and then identify the degree and leading coefficient.

Add the polynomials.

2. $(82x^8 + 21x^2 - 6) + (18x + 7x^8 - 42x^2 + 3)$

3. $(15x - 121x^{12} + x^9 - x^7 + 3x^2) + (x^7 - 68x^2 - x^9)$

4. $(16 - x^2) + (-18x^2 + 7x^5 - 10x^4 + 5)$

5. $(x + 1 - 3x^2) + (8x + 21x^2 - 1)$

6. $(64 + x^3 - 8x^2) + (7x + 3 - x^2) + (19x^2 - 7x - 2)$

7. $(x^4 - 7x^3 + 2 - x) + (2x^3 - 3) + (1 - 5x^3 - x^4 + x)$

Subtract the polynomials.

8. $(-2x + 23x^5 + 11) - (5 - 9x^3 + x)$

9. $\left(7x^3 + 68x^4 - 14x + 1\right) - \left(-10x^3 + 8x + 23\right)$

10. $\left(57x^{18} - x^2\right) - \left(6x - 71x^3 + 5x^2 + 2\right)$

11. $\left(9x - 12x^3\right) - \left(5x^3 + 7x - 2\right)$

12. $\left(3x^5 - 9\right) - \left(11 + 13x^2 - x^4\right) - \left(10x^2 + x^4\right)$

13. $\left(10x^2 - x + 4\right) - (5x + 7) + (6x - 11)$

Find the polynomial that models the problem and use it to estimate the quantity.

14. A rectangle has a length of x and a width of $5x^3 + 4 - x^2$. Find the perimeter of the rectangle when the length is 5 feet.

15. A rectangle has a perimeter of $6x^3 + 9x^2 - 10x + 5$ and a length of x. Find the width of the rectangle when the length is 21 inches.

16. Cho is making a rectangular garden, where the length is x feet and the width is $4x - 1$ feet. He wants to add garden stones around the perimeter of the garden once he is done. If the garden is 4 feet long, how many feet will Cho need to cover with garden stones?

17. Employment The data from the U.S. Census Bureau for 1980–2010 shows that the median weekly earnings of full-time male employees who have at least a bachelor's degree can be modeled by the function $M(x) = 0.009x^3 - 0.29x^2 + 30.7x + 439.6$, where x is the number of years after 1980 and $M(x)$ is the median weekly earnings in dollars. The median weekly earnings of all full-time employees who have at least a bachelor's degree can be modeled by the function $T(x) = 0.012x^3 - 0.46x^2 + 56.1x + 732.3$, where x is the number of years after 1980 and $T(x)$ is the median weekly earnings in dollars. Estimate the median weekly earnings of a full-time female employee with at least a bachelor's degree in 2010.

18. Business From data gathered in the period 2008–2012, the yearly value of U.S. exports can be modeled by the function $E(x) = -228x^3 + 2552.8x^2 - 6098.5x + 11{,}425.8$, where x is the number of years after 2008 and $E(x)$ is the value of exports in billions of dollars. The yearly value of U.S. imports can be modeled by the function $I(x) = -400.4x^3 + 3954.4x^2 - 11{,}128.8x + 17{,}749.6$, where x is the number of years after 2008 and $I(x)$ is the value of imports in billions of dollars. Estimate the total amount the United States imported and exported in 2012.

19. Education From data gathered in the period 1970–2010, the number of full-time students enrolled in a degree-granting institution can be modeled by the function $F(x) = 8.7x^3 - 213.3x^2 + 2015.5x + 3874.9$, where x is the number of years after 1970 and $F(x)$ is the number of students in thousands. The number of part-time students enrolled in a degree-granting institution can be modeled by the function $P(x) = 12x^3 - 285.3x^2 + 2217x + 1230$, where x is the number of years after 1970 and $P(x)$ is the number of students in thousands. Estimate the total number of students enrolled in a degree-granting institution in 2000.

20. Geography The data from the U.S. Census Bureau for 1982–2003 shows that the surface area of the United States that is covered by rural land can be modeled by the function $R(x) = 0.003x^3 - 0.086x^2 - 1.2x + 1417.4$, where x is the number of years after 1982 and $R(x)$ is the surface area in millions of acres. The total surface area of the United States can be modeled by the function $T(x) = 0.0023x^3 + 0.034x^2 - 5.9x + 1839.4$, where x is the number of years after 1982 and $T(x)$ is the surface area in millions of acres. Estimate the surface area of the United States that is not covered by rural land in 2001.

21. Determine which polynomials are monomials. Choose all that apply.

a. $4x^3y$

b. $12 - x^2 + 5x$

c. $152 + x$

d. 783

e. x

f. $19x^{-2}$

g. $4x^4x^2$

H.O.T. Focus on Higher Order Thinking

22. Explain the Error Colin simplified $(16x + 8x^2y - 7xy^2 + 9y - 2xy) - (-9xy + 8xy^2 + 10x^2y + x - 7y)$. His work is shown below. Find and correct Colin's mistake.

$$(16x + 8x^2y - 7xy^2 + 9y - 2xy) - (-9xy + 8xy^2 + 10x^2y + x - 7y)$$
$$= (16x + 8x^2y - 7xy^2 + 9y - 2xy) + (9xy - 8xy^2 - 10x^2y - x + 7y)$$
$$= (16x - x) + (8x^2y - 7xy^2 - 8xy^2 - 10x^2y) + (9y + 7y) + (-2xy + 9xy)$$
$$= 15x - 17x^2y^2 + 16y + 7xy$$

23. Critical Reasoning Janice is building a fence around a portion of her rectangular yard. The length of yard she will enclose is x, and the width is $2x^2 - 98x + 5$, where the measurements are in feet. If the length of the enclosed yard is 50 feet and the cost of fencing is \$13 per foot, how much will Janice need to spend on fencing?

24. Multi-Step Find a polynomial expression for the perimeter of a trapezoid with legs of length x and bases of lengths $0.1x^3 + 2x$ and $x^2 + 3x - 10$ where each is measured in inches.

a. Find the perimeter of the trapezoid if the length of one leg is 6 inches.

b. If the leg length is increased by 5 inches, will the perimeter also increase? By how much?

25. Communicate Mathematical Ideas Present a formal argument for why the set of polynomials is closed under addition and subtraction. Use the polynomials $ax^m + bx^m$ and $ax^m - bx^m$, for real numbers a and b and whole number m, to justify your reasoning.

Lesson Performance Task

The table shows the average monthly maximum and minimum temperatures for Death Valley throughout one year.

Month	Maximum Temperature	Minimum Temperature
January	67	40
February	73	46
March	82	55
April	91	62
May	101	73
June	110	81
July	116	88
August	115	86
September	107	76
October	93	62
November	77	48
December	65	38

Use a graphing calculator to find a good fourth-degree polynomial regression model for both the maximum and minimum temperatures. Then find a function that models the range in monthly temperatures and use the model to estimate the range during September. How does the range predicted by your model compare with the range shown in the table?

Name ______________________ Class ______________ Date ________

6.2 Multiplying Polynomials

Essential Question: How do you multiply polynomials, and what type of expression is the result?

Resource Locker

Explore Analyzing a Visual Model for Polynomial Multiplication

The volume of a rectangular prism is the product of the length, width, and height of that prism. If the dimensions are all known, then the volume is a simple calculation. What if some of the dimensions are given as *binomials*? A **binomial** is a polynomial with two terms. How would you find the volume of a rectangular prism that is $x + 3$ units long, $x + 2$ units wide, and x units high? The images below show two methods for finding the solution.

$V = \text{length} \times \text{width} \times \text{height}$
$= (x + 3)(x + 2)x$

$V = V_1 + V_2 + V_3 + V_4$

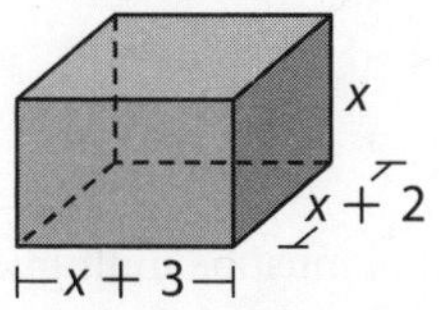

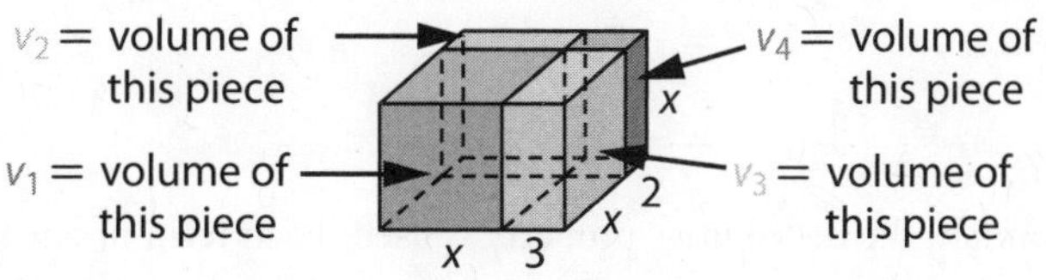

(A) The first model shows the rectangular prism, and its volume is calculated directly as the product of two binomials and a monomial.

(B) The second image divides the rectangular prism into ____________ smaller prisms, the dimensions of which are each ____________.

(C) The volume of a cube (V_1) where all sides have a length of x, is ____________.

(D) The volume of a rectangular prism (V_2) with dimensions x by x by 2 is ____________.

(E) The volume of a rectangular prism (V_3) with dimensions x by x by 3 is ____________.

(F) The volume of a rectangular prism (V_4) with dimensions x by 3 by 2 is ____________.

(G) So the volume of the rectangular prism is the sum of the volumes of the four smaller regions.

$V_1 + V_2 + V_3 + V_4 = \square + \square + \square + \square$

$= \square$

Reflect

1. If all three dimensions were binomials, how many regions would the rectangular prism be divided into?

2. **Discussion** Can this method be applied to finding the volume of other simple solids? Are there solids that this process would be difficult to apply to? Are there any solids that this method cannot be applied to?

Explain 1 Multiplying Polynomials

Multiplying polynomials involves using the product rule for exponents and the distributive property. The product of two monomials is the product of the coefficients and the sum of the exponents of each variable.

$$5x \cdot 6x^3 = 30x^{1+3} \qquad -2x^2y^4z \cdot 5y^2z = -10x^2y^{4+2}z^{1+1}$$

$$= 30x^4 \qquad = -10x^2y^6z^2$$

When multiplying two binomials, the distributive property is used. Each term of one polynomial must be multiplied by each term of the other.

$$\begin{aligned}(2+3x)(1+x) &= 2(1+x) + 3x(x+1)\\ &= 2(1) + 2(x) + 3x(x) + 3x(1)\\ &= 2 + 2x + 3x^{1+1} + 3x\\ &= 2 + 5x + 3x^2\end{aligned}$$

The polynomial $2 + 5x + 3x^2$ is called a **trinomial** because it has three terms.

Example 1 **Perform the following polynomial multiplications.**

(A) $(x+2)(1-4x+2x^2)$

Find the product by multiplying horizontally.

$(x+2)(2x^2-4x+1)$	Write the polynomials in standard form.
$x(2x^2) + x(-4x) + x(1) + 2(2x^2) + 2(-4x) + 2(1)$	Distribute the x and the 2.
$2x^3 - 4x^2 + x + 4x^2 - 8x + 2$	Simplify.
$2x^3 - 7x + 2$	Combine like terms.

Therefore, $(x+2)(2x^2-4x+1) = 2x^3 - 7x + 2$.

Ⓑ $(3x - 4)(2 + x - 7x^2)$

Find the product by multiplying vertically.

$-7x^2 + \square + 2$ $3x - 4$	Write each polynomial in standard form.
$\square - 4x - 8$	Multipy -4 and $(-7x^2 + x + 2)$.
$\square + 3x^2 + 6x$	Multipy $\square$ and $(-7x^2 + x + 2)$.
$-21x^3 + \square + 2x - 8$	Combine like terms.

Therefore, $(3x - 4)(2 + x - 7x^2) =$ ______________________.

Your Turn

3. $(3 + 2x)(4 - 7x + 5x^2)$

4. $(x - 6)(3 - 8x - 4x^2)$

Explain 2 Modeling with Polynomial Multiplication

Many real-world situations can be modeled with polynomial functions. Sometimes, a situation will arise in which a model is needed that combines two quantities modeled by polynomial functions. In this case, the desired model would be the product of the two known models.

Example 2 **Find the polynomial function modeling the desired relationship.**

Ⓐ Mr. Silva manages a manufacturing plant. From 1990 through 2005, the number of units produced (in thousands) can be modeled by $N(x) = 0.02x^2 + 0.2x + 3$, where x is the number of years since 1990. The average cost per unit (in dollars) can be modeled by $C(x) = -0.002x^2 - 0.1x + 2$, where x is the number of years since 1990. Write a polynomial $T(x)$ that can be used to model Mr. Silva's total manufacturing cost for those years.

The total manufacturing cost is the product of the number of units made and the cost per unit.

$T(x) = N(x) \cdot C(x)$

Multiply the two polynomials.

$$
\begin{array}{rrrrr}
 & & 0.02x^2 & +\,0.2x & +\,3 \\
 & \times & -\,0.002x^2 & -\,0.1x & +\,2 \\
\hline
 & & 0.04x^2 & +\,0.4x & +\,6 \\
 & -0.002x^3 & -\,0.02x^2 & -\,0.3x & \\
-0.00004x^4 & -\,0.0004x^3 & -\,0.006x^2 & & \\
\hline
-0.00004x^4 & -\,0.0024x^3 & +\,0.014x^2 & +\,0.1x & +\,6
\end{array}
$$

Therefore, the total manufacturing cost can be modeled by the following polynomial, where x is the number of years since 1990.

$T(x) = -0.00004x^4 - 0.0024x^3 + 0.014x^2 + 0.1x + 6$

(B) Ms. Liao runs a small dress company. From 1995 through 2005, the number of dresses she made can be modeled by $N(x) = 0.3x^2 - 1.6x + 14$, and the average cost to make each dress can be modeled by $C(x) = -0.001x^2 - 0.06x + 8.3$, where x is the number of years since 1995. Write a polynomial that can be used to model Ms. Liao's total dressmaking costs, $T(x)$, for those years.

The total dressmaking cost is the product of the number of dresses made and the cost per dress.

$T(x) = N(x) \cdot C(x)$

Multiply the two polynomials.

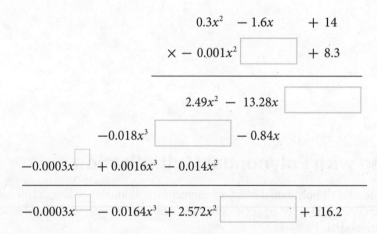

$$
\begin{array}{rrrrr}
 & & 0.3x^2 & -\,1.6x & +\,14 \\
 & \times & -\,0.001x^2 & \square & +\,8.3 \\
\hline
 & & 2.49x^2 & -\,13.28x & \square \\
 & -0.018x^3 & \square & -\,0.84x & \\
-0.0003x^{\square} & +\,0.0016x^3 & -\,0.014x^2 & & \\
\hline
-0.0003x^{\square} & -\,0.0164x^3 & +\,2.572x^2 & \square & +\,116.2
\end{array}
$$

Therefore, the total dressmaking cost can be modeled by the following polynomial, where x is the number of years since 1995.

$T(x) =$ ________________________________

Your Turn

5. Brent runs a small toy store specializing in wooden toys. From 2000 through 2012, the number of toys Brent made can be modeled by $N(x) = 0.7x^2 - 2x + 23$, and the average cost to make each toy can be modeled by $C(x) = -0.004x^2 - 0.08x + 25$, where x is the number of years since 2000. Write a polynomial that can be used to model Brent's total cost for making the toys, $T(x)$, for those years.

Explain 3 Verifying Polynomial Identities

You have already seen certain special polynomial relationships. For example, a difference of two squares can be easily factored: $x^2 - a^2 = (x + a)(x - a)$. This equation is an example of a **polynomial identity**, a mathematical relationship equating one polynomial quantity to another. Another example of a polynomial identity is

$$(x + a)^2 - (x - a)^2 = 4ax.$$

The identity can be verified by simplifying one side of the equation to match the other.

Example 3 **Verify the given polynomial identity.**

(A) $(x + a)^2 - (x - a)^2 = 4ax$

The right side of the identity is already fully simplified. Simplify the left-hand side.

$$(x + a)^2 - (x - a)^2 = 4ax$$

$x^2 + 2ax + a^2 - (x^2 - 2ax + a^2) = 4ax$ Square each binomial.

$x^2 + 2ax + a^2 - x^2 + 2ax - a^2 = 4ax$ Distribute the negative.

$\cancel{x^2 - x^2} + 2ax + 2ax + \cancel{a^2 - a^2} = 4ax$ Rearrange terms.

$4ax = 4ax$ Simplify.

Therefore, $(x + a)^2 - (x - a)^2 = 4ax$ is a true statement.

(B) $(a+b)(a^2-ab+b^2)=a^3+b^3$

The right side of the identity is already fully simplified. Simplify the left-hand side.

$$(a+b)(a^2-ab+b^2)=a^3+b^3$$

$a(a^2)+a(\boxed{})+a(b^2)+b(a^2)+\boxed{}(-ab)+b(b^2)=a^3+b^3$ Distribute a and b.

$a^3-a^2b+ab^2+\boxed{}-ab^2+\boxed{}=a^3+b^3$ ______

$a^3-\boxed{}+a^2b+ab^2-\boxed{}+b^3=a^3+b^3$ Rearrange terms.

$a^3\boxed{}b^3=a^3+b^3$ Combine like terms.

Therefore, $(a+b)(a^2-ab+b^2)=a^3+b^3$ is a ______ statement.

Your Turn

6. Show that $a^5-b^5=(a-b)(a^4+a^3b+a^2b^2+ab^3+b^4)$.

7. Show that $(a-b)(a^2+ab+b^2)=a^3-b^3$.

Explain 4 Using Polynomial Identities

The most obvious use for polynomial identities is simplifying algebraic expressions, but polynomial identities often turn out to have nonintuitive uses as well.

Example 4 **For each situation, find the solution using the given polynomial identity.**

(A) The polynomial identity $(x^2+y^2)^2=(x^2-y^2)^2+(2xy)^2$ can be used to identify Pythagorean triples. Generate a Pythagorean triple using $x=4$ and $y=3$.

Substitute the given values into the identity.

$$(4^2+3^2)^2=(4^2-3^2)^2+(2\cdot4\cdot3)^2$$
$$(16+9)^2=(16-9)^2+(24)^2$$
$$(25)^2=(7)^2+(24)^2$$
$$625=49+576$$
$$625=625$$

Therefore, 7, 24, 25 is a Pythagorean triple.

(B) The identity $(x + y)^2 = x^2 + 2xy + y^2$ can be used for mental-math calculations to quickly square numbers.

Find the square of 27.

Find two numbers whose sum is equal to 27.

Let $x = \square$ and $y = 7$

Evaluate

$$(20 + \square)^2 = 20^2 + \square + 7^2$$

$$27^2 = 400 + \square + 49$$

$$27^2 = \square$$

Verify by using a calculator to find 27^2.

$27^2 = \square$

Your Turn

8. The identity $(x + y)(x - y) = x^2 - y^2$ can be used for mental-math calculations to quickly multiply two numbers in specific situations.

Find the product of 37 and 43. (Hint: What values should you choose for x and y so the equation calculates the product of 37 and 43?)

9. The identity $(x - y)^2 = x^2 - 2xy + y^2$ can also be used for mental-math calculations to quickly square numbers.

Find the square of 18. (Hint: What values should you choose for x and y so the equation calculates the square of 18?)

Elaborate

10. What property is employed in the process of polynomial multiplication?

11. How can you use unit analysis to justify multiplying two polynomial models of real-world quantities?

12. Give an example of a polynomial identity and how it's useful.

13. **Essential Question Check-In** When multiplying polynomials, what type of expression is the product?

Evaluate: Homework and Practice

Personal Math Trainer

- Online Homework
- Hints and Help
- Extra Practice

1. The dimensions for a rectangular prism are $x + 5$ for the length, $x + 1$ for the width, and x for the height. What is the volume of the prism?

Perform the following polynomial multiplications.

2. $(3x - 2)(2x^2 + 3x - 1)$

3. $(x^3 + 3x^2 + 1)(3x^2 + 6x - 2)$

4. $(x^2 + 9x + 7)(3x^2 + 9x + 5)$

5. $(2x + 5y)(3x^2 - 4xy + 2y^2)$

6. $(x^3 + x^2 + 1)(x^2 - x - 5)$

7. $(4x^2 + 3x + 2)(3x^2 + 2x - 1)$

Write a polynomial function to represent the new value.

8. The volume of a stock, or number of shares traded, is modeled over time during a given day by $S(x) = x^5 - 3x^4 + 10x^2 - 6x + 30$. The cost per share of that stock during that day is modeled by $C(x) = 0.004x^4 - 0.02x^2 + 0.3x + 4$. Write a polynomial function $V(x)$ to model the changing value during that day of the trades made of shares of that stock.

9. A businessman models the number of items (in thousands) that his company sold from 1998 through 2004 as $N(x) = -0.1x^3 + x^2 - 3x + 4$ and the average price per item (in dollars) as $P(x) = 0.2x + 5$, where x represents the number of years since 1998. Write a polynomial $R(x)$ that can be used to model the total revenue for this company.

10. **Biology** A biologist has found that the number of branches on a certain rare tree can be modeled by the polynomial $b(y) = 4y^2 + y$ where y is the number of years after the tree reaches a height of 6 feet. The number of leaves on each branch can be modeled by the polynomial $l(y) = 2y^3 + 3y^2 + y$. Write a polynomial describing the total number of leaves on the tree.

11. **Physics** An object thrown in the air has a velocity after t seconds that can be described by $v(t) = -9.8t + 24$ (in meters/second) and a height $h(t) = -4.9t^2 + 24t + 60$ (in meters). The object has mass $m = 2$ kilograms. The kinetic energy of the object is given by $K = \frac{1}{2}mv^2$, and the potential energy is given by $U = 9.8mh$. Find an expression for the total kinetic and potential energy $K + U$ as a function of time. What does this expression tell you about the energy of the falling object?

Verify the given polynomial identity.

12. $(x + y + z)^2 = x^2 + y^2 + z^2 + 2xy + 2xz + 2yz$

13. $a^5 + b^5 = (a + b)(a^4 - a^3b + a^2b^2 - ab^3 + b^4)$

14. $x^4 - y^4 = (x - y)(x + y)(x^2 + y^2)$

15. $\left(a^2 + b^2\right)\left(x^2 + y^2\right) = \left(ax - by\right)^2 + \left(bx + ay\right)^2$

Find the square of the number or the product of the numbers using one or more of these identities.

$(x + y)^2 = x^2 + 2xy + y^2$, $(x + y)(x - y) = x^2 - y^2$, or $(x - y)^2 = x^2 - 2xy + y^2$.

16. 43^2

17. 32^2

18. 89^2

19. 47^2

20. $54 \cdot 38$

21. $58 \cdot 68$

22. Explain the Error A polynomial identity for the difference of two cubes is $a^3 - b^3 = (a - b)(a^2 + ab + b^2)$. A student uses the identity to factor $64 - 27x^6$. Identity the error the student made, and then correct it.

Each term of $64 - 27x^6$ is a perfect cube. Let $a = 4$ and $b = 3x^2$. Then:

$$64 - 27x^6 = 4^3 - \left(3x^2\right)^3$$
$$= \left(4 - 3x^2\right)\left(4^2 + 4\left(-3x^2\right) + \left(-3x^2\right)^2\right)$$
$$= \left(4 - 3x^2\right)\left(16 - 12x^2 + 9x^4\right)$$

23. Determine how many terms there will be after performing the polynomial multiplication.

a. $(5x)(3x)$ ☐ 1 ☐ 2 ☐ 3 ☐ 4

b. $(3x)(2x + 1)$ ☐ 1 ☐ 2 ☐ 3 ☐ 4

c. $(x + 1)(x - 1)$ ☐ 1 ☐ 2 ☐ 3 ☐ 4

d. $(x + 2)(3x^2 - 2x + 1)$ ☐ 1 ☐ 2 ☐ 3 ☐ 4

H.O.T. Focus on Higher Order Thinking

24. Multi-Step Given the polynomial identity: $x^6 + y^6 = (x^2 + y^2)(x^4 - x^2y^2 + y^4)$

a. Verify directly by expanding the right hand side.

b. Use another polynomial identity to verify this identity. (Note that $a^6 = (a^2)^3 = (a^3)^2$)

25. Communicate Mathematical Ideas Explain why the set of polynomials is closed under multiplication.

26. Critical Thinking Explain why every other term of the polynomial product $(x - y)^5$ written in standard form is subtracted when $(x - y)$ is raised to the fifth power.

Lesson Performance Task

The table presents data about oil wells in the state of Oklahoma from 1992 through 2008.

Year	Number of Wells	Average Daily Oil Production per Well (Barrels)
2008	83,443	2.178
2007	82,832	2.053
2006	82,284	2.108
2005	82,551	2.006
2004	83,222	2.10
2003	83,415	2.12
2002	83,730	2.16
2001	84,160	2.24
2000	84,432	2.24
1999	85,043	2.29
1998	85,691	2.49
1997	86,765	2.62
1996	88,144	2.66
1995	90,557	2.65
1994	91,289	2.73
1993	92,377	2.87
1992	93,192	2.99

a. Given the data in this table, use regression to find models for the number of producing wells (cubic regression) and average daily well output (quadratic regression) in terms of t years since 1992.

b. Find a function modeling the total daily oil output for the state of Oklahoma.

Name _______________ Class _______________ Date _______________

6.3 The Binomial Theorem

Essential Question: How is the Binomial Theorem useful?

Resource Locker

Explore 1 Generating Pascal's Triangle

Pascal's Triangle is a famous number pattern named after the French mathematician Blaise Pascal (1623–1662). You can use Pascal's Triangle to help you expand a power of a binomial of the form $(a + b)^n$.

Use the tree diagram shown to generate Pascal's Triangle. Notice that from each node in the diagram to the nodes immediately below it there are two paths, a left path (L) and a right path (R). You can describe a path from the single node in row 0 to any other node in the diagram using a string of Ls and Rs.

First, notice that there is only one possible path to each node in row 1, which is why a 1 appears in those nodes. In row 2, there is only one possible path, LL, to the first node and only one possible path, RR, to the last node, but there are two possible paths, LR and RL, to the center node.

(A) Complete only rows 3 and 4 of Pascal's Triangle. (You will complete rows 5 and 6 in Step C.) In each node, write the number of possible paths from the top down to that node.

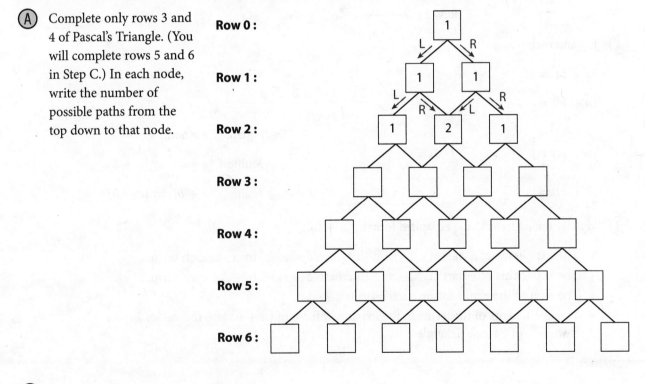

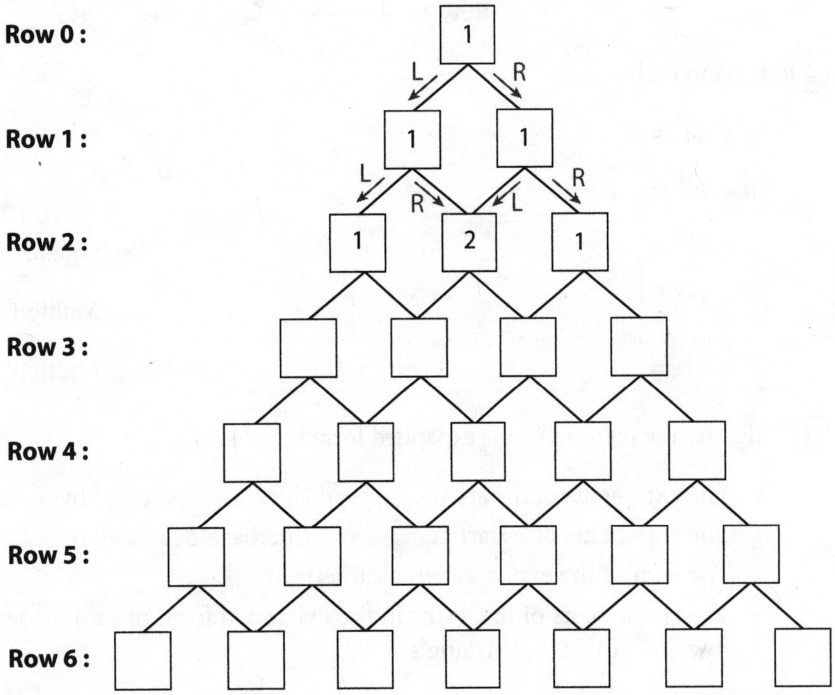

(B) Look for patterns in the tree diagram.

What is the value in the first and last node in each row? _______

For every other node, the value in the node is the _______ of the two values above it.

(C) Using the patterns in Step B, go back to Pascal's Triangle in Step A and complete rows 5 and 6.

Reflect

1. Using strings of Ls and Rs, write the paths that lead to the second node in row 3 of Pascal's Triangle. How are the paths alike, and how are they different?

2. The path LLRLR leads to which node in which row of Pascal's Triangle? What is the value of that node?

Explore 2 Relating Pascal's Triangle to Powers of Binomials

As shown, the value in position r of row n of Pascal's Triangle is written as ${}_nC_r$ where the position numbers in each row start with 0. In this Explore, you will see how the values in Pascal's Triangle are related to powers of a binomial.

Row 0: ⟶ ${}_0C_0$

Row 1: ⟶ ${}_1C_0$ ${}_1C_1$

Row 2: ⟶ ${}_2C_0$ ${}_2C_1$ ${}_2C_2$

Row 3: ⟶ ${}_3C_0$ ${}_3C_1$ ${}_3C_2$ ${}_3C_3$

(A) Expand each power.

$(a+b)^0 = \square$

$(a+b)^1 = \square$

$(a+b)^2 = \square$ Square of a binomial

$(a+b)^3 = \square$ Multiply $(a+b)^2$ by $(a+b)$.

$(a+b)^4 = \square$ Multiply $(a+b)^3$ by $(a+b)$.

(B) Identify the patterns in the expanded form of $(a+b)^n$.

- The exponents of a start at ____ and [increase/decrease] by ____ each term.
- The exponents of b start at ____ and [increase/decrease] by ____ each term.
- The sum of the exponents in each term is ____.
- The coefficients of the terms in the expanded form of $(a+b)^n$ are the values in row ____ of Pascal's Triangle.

Reflect

3. How many terms are in the expanded form of $(a+b)^n$?

4. Without expanding the power, determine the middle term of $(a+b)^6$. Explain how you found your answer.

5. Without expanding the power, determine the first term of $(a+b)^{15}$. Explain how you found your answer.

Explain 1 Expanding Powers of Binomials Using the Binomial Theorem

The **Binomial Theorem** states the connection between the terms of the expanded form of $(a + b)^n$ and Pascal's Triangle.

Binomial Theorem

For any whole number n, the binomial expansion of $(a + b)^n$ is given by
$(a+b)^n = {}_nC_0a^nb^0 + {}_nC_1a^{n-1}b^1 + {}_nC_2a^{n-2}b^2 + \ldots + {}_nC_{n-1}a^1b^{n-1} + {}_nC_na^0b^n$
where ${}_nC_r$ is the value in position r (where r starts at 0) of the nth row of Pascal's Triangle.

Since it can be cumbersome to look up numbers from Pascal's Triangle each time you want to expand a power of a binomial, you can use a calculator instead. To do so, enter the value of n, press **MATH**, go to the **PRB** menu, select **3:nCr**, and then enter the value of r. The calculator screen shows the values for ${}_6C_1$, ${}_6C_2$, and ${}_6C_3$.

Example 1 **Use the Binomial Theorem to expand each power of a binomial.**

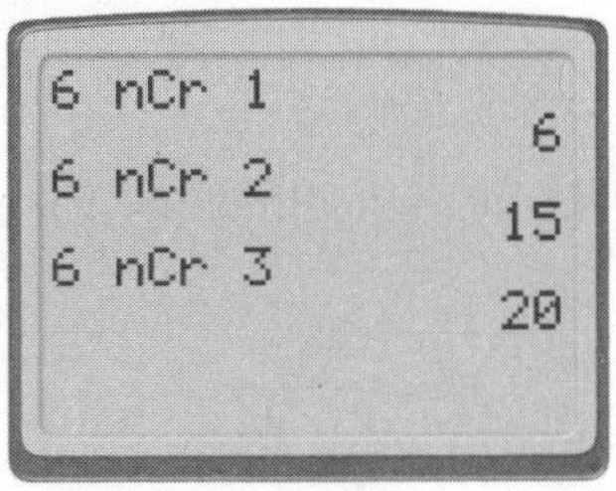

(A) $(x - 2)^3$

Step 1 Identify the values in row 3 of Pascal's Triangle.

1, 3, 3, and 1

Step 2 Expand the power as described by the Binomial Theorem, using the values from Pascal's Triangle as coefficients.

$(x - 2)^3 = 1x^3(-2)^0 + 3x^2(-2)^1 + 3x^1(-2)^2 + 1x^0(-2)^3$

Step 3 Simplify.

$(x - 2)^3 = x^3 - 6x^2 + 12x - 8$

(B) $(x + y)^7$

Step 1 Use a calculator to determine the values of ${}_7C_0$, ${}_7C_1$, ${}_7C_2$, ${}_7C_3$, ${}_7C_4$, ${}_7C_5$, ${}_7C_6$, and ${}_7C_7$.

____

Step 2 Expand the power as described by the Binomial Theorem, using the values of ${}_7C_0$, ${}_7C_1$, ${}_7C_2$, ${}_7C_3$, ${}_7C_4$, ${}_7C_5$, ${}_7C_6$, and ${}_7C_7$ as coefficients.

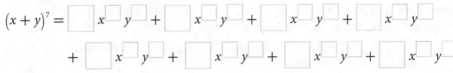

$(x+y)^7 = \square x^{\square}y^{\square} + \square x^{\square}y^{\square} + \square x^{\square}y^{\square} + \square x^{\square}y^{\square}$
$+ \square x^{\square}y^{\square} + \square x^{\square}y^{\square} + \square x^{\square}y^{\square} + \square x^{\square}y^{\square}$

Step 3 Simplify.

$(x+y)^7 = x^{\square} + \square x^{\square}y + \square x^{\square}y^{\square} + \square x^{\square}y^{\square} + \square x^{\square}y^{\square}$
$+ \square x^{\square}y^{\square} + \square xy^{\square} + y^{\square}$

Reflect

6. What happens to the signs of the terms in the expanded form of $(x - 2)^3$? Why does this happen?

7. If the number 11 is written as the binomial $(10 + 1)$, how can you use the Binomial Theorem to find 11^2, 11^3, and 11^4? What is the pattern in the digits?

Your Turn

8. Use the Binomial Theorem to expand $(x - y)^4$.

Explain 2 Solving a Real-World Problem Using Binomial Probabilities

Recall that the probability of an event A is written as $P(A)$ and is expressed as a number between 0 and 1, where 0 represents impossibility and 1 represents certainty.

When dealing with probabilities, you will find these two rules helpful.

1. **Addition Rule for Mutually Exclusive Events:** If events A and B are *mutually exclusive* (that is, they cannot occur together), then $P(A \text{ or } B) = P(A) + P(B)$. For example, when rolling a die, getting a 1 and getting a 2 are mutually exclusive events, so $P(1 \text{ or } 2) = P(1) + P(2) = \frac{1}{6} + \frac{1}{6} = \frac{1}{3}$.

2. **Complement Rule:** The *complement* of event A consists of all of the possible outcomes that are not part of A, and the probability that A does not occur is $P(\text{not } A) = 1 - P(A)$. For example, when rolling a die, the probability of not getting a 2 is $P(\text{not } 2) = 1 - P(2) = 1 - \frac{1}{6} = \frac{5}{6}$.

A **binomial experiment** involves many trials where each trial has only two possible outcomes: success or failure. If the probability of success in each trial is p and the probability of failure in each trial is $q = 1 - p$, the **binomial probability** of exactly r successes in n trials is given by $P(r) = {}_nC_r p^r q^{n-r}$. Since ${}_nC_r = {}_nC_{n-r}$, you can rewrite $P(r)$ as $P(r) = {}_nC_{n-r} p^r q^{n-r}$, which represents the $(n - r)$th term in the expanded form of $(p + q)^n$.

Example 2 **One in 5 boats traveling down a river bypass a harbor at the mouth of the river and head out to sea. Currently, 4 boats are traveling down the river and approaching the mouth of the river.**

(A) What is the probability that exactly 2 of the 4 boats head out to sea?

The probability that a boat will head out to sea is $\frac{1}{5}$, or 0.2.

Substitute 4 for n, 2 for r, 0.2 for p, and 0.8 for q.

$$P(2) = {}_4C_2(0.2)^2(0.8)^{4-2}$$
$$= 6(0.2)^2(0.8)^2$$
$$= 6(0.04)(0.64)$$
$$= 0.1536$$

So, the probability that exactly 2 of the 4 boats will head out to sea is 0.1536, or 15.36%.

(B) What is the probability that at least 2 of the 4 boats will head out to sea?

To find the probability that at least 2 of the 4 boats will head out to sea, find the probability that 2, ____, or ____ boats will head out to sea and add the probabilities.

From Part A, you know that $P(2) = 0.1536$.

$$P(3) = {}_4C_{\square}(0.2)^{\square}(0.8)^{\square}$$
$$= 4(\square)(\square)$$
$$= \square$$

$$P(4) = {}_4C_{\square}(0.2)^{\square}(0.8)^{\square}$$
$$= 1(\square)(\square)$$
$$= \square$$

$$P(\text{at least } 2) = P(2 \text{ or } 3 \text{ or } 4)$$
$$= P(2) + P(3) + P(4)$$
$$= 0.1536 + \square + \square$$
$$= \square$$

So, the probability that at least 2 of the 4 boats will head out to sea is 0.1808, or 18.08%.

Reflect

9. In words, state the complement of the event that at least 2 of the 4 boats will head out to sea. Then find the probability of the complement.

Your Turn

10. Students are assigned randomly to 1 of 3 guidance counselors at a school. What is the probability that Ms. Banks, one of the school's guidance counselors, will get exactly 2 of the next 3 students assigned?

Elaborate

11. How do the numbers in one row of Pascal's Triangle relate to the numbers in the previous row?

12. How does Pascal's Triangle relate to the power of a binomial?

13. The expanded form of $(p + q)^3$ is $p^3 + 3p^2q + 3pq^2 + q^3$. In terms of a binomial experiment with a probability p of success and a probability q of failure on each trial, what do each of the terms p^3, $3p^2q$, $3pq^2$, and q^3 represent?

14. **Essential Question Check-In** The Binomial Theorem says that the expanded form of $(a + b)^n$ is a sum of terms of the form ${}_nC_r a^{n-r} b^r$ for what values of r?

Evaluate: Homework and Practice

Personal Math Trainer

- Online Homework
- Hints and Help
- Extra Practice

1. The path LLRRLLR leads to which node in which row of Pascal's Triangle? What is the value of that node?

2. Without expanding the power, determine the middle term of $(a+b)^8$. Explain how you found your answer.

Use the Binomial Theorem to expand each power of a binomial.

3. $(x+6)^3$

4. $(x-5)^4$

5. $(x+3)^6$

6. $(2x-1)^3$

7. $(3x+4)^5$

8. $(2x-3)^7$

9. $(x + 2y)^5$

10. $(3x - y)^4$

11. $(5x + y)^4$

12. $(x - 6y)^5$

13. $(5x - 4y)^3$

14. $(4x + 3y)^6$

Use the Binomial Theorem to find the specified term of the given power of a binomial. (Remember that *r* starts at 0 in the Binomial Theorem, so finding, say, the second term means that $r = 1$.)

15. Find the fourth term in the expanded form of $(x - 1)^6$.

16. Find the second term in the expanded form of $(2x + 1)^4$.

17. Find the third term in the expanded form of $(3x - 2y)^5$.

18. Find the fifth term in the expanded form of $(6x + 8y)^7$.

Ellen takes a multiple-choice quiz that has 5 questions, with 4 answer choices for each question.

19. What is the probability that she will get exactly 2 answers correct by guessing?

20. What is the probability that Ellen will get at least 3 answers correct by guessing?

Manufacturing **A machine that makes a part used in cars has a 98% probability of producing the part within acceptable tolerance levels. The machine makes 25 parts per hour.**

21. What is the probability that the machine will make exactly 20 acceptable parts in an hour?

22. What is the probability that the machine makes 23 or fewer acceptable parts?

23. Match each term of an expanded power of a binomial on the right with the corresponding description of the term on the left. (Remember that r starts at 0 in the Binomial Theorem, so finding, say, the second term means that $r = 1$.)

A. Fifth term in the expanded form of $(x + 2)^6$ ________ $640x^2$

B. Fourth term in the expanded form of $(x + 4)^5$ ________ $48x^2$

C. Third term in the expanded form of $(x + 8)^4$ ________ $240x^2$

D. Second term in the expanded form of $(x + 16)^3$ ________ $384x^2$

H.O.T. Focus on Higher Order Thinking

24. Construct Arguments Identify the symmetry in the rows of Pascal's Triangle and give an argument based on strings of Ls and Rs to explain why the symmetry exists.

25. Communicate Mathematical Ideas Explain why the numbers from Pascal's Triangle show up in the Binomial Theorem.

26. Represent Real-World Situations A small airline overbooks flights on the assumption that some passengers will not show up. The probability that a passenger shows up is 0.8. What number of tickets can the airline sell for a 20-seat flight and still have a probability of seating everyone that is at least 90%? Explain your reasoning.

Lesson Performance Task

Suppose that a basketball player has just been fouled while attempting a 3-point shot and is awarded three free throws. Given that the player is 85% successful at making free throws, calculate the probability that the player successfully makes zero, one, two, or all three of the free throws. Which situation is most likely to occur?

Name ______________________ Class ______________ Date __________

6.4 Factoring Polynomials

Essential Question: What are some ways to factor a polynomial, and how is factoring useful?

Resource Locker

Explore Analyzing a Visual Model for Polynomial Factorization

Factoring a polynomial of degree n involves finding factors of a lesser degree that can be multiplied together to produce the polynomial. When a polynomial has degree 3, for example, you can think of it as the volume of a rectangular prism whose dimensions you need to determine.

(A) The volumes of the parts of the rectangular prism are as follows:

Red (R): $V = x^3$

Green (G): $V = 2x^2$

Yellow (Y): $V = 8x$

Blue (B): $V = 4x^2$

Total volume: $V = x^3 + 6x^2 + 8x$

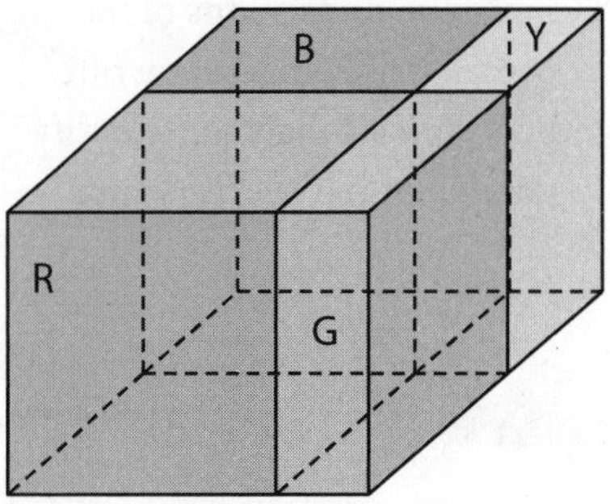

(B) The volume of the red piece is found by cubing the length of one edge. What is the height of this piece?

____

(C) The volume of a rectangular prism is $V = lwh$, where l is the length, w is the width, and h is the height of the prism. Notice that the green prism shares two dimensions with the cube. What are these dimensions?

____

(D) What is the length of the third edge of the green prism?

____

(E) You showed that the width of the cube is ______ and the width of the green prism is ______. What is the width of the entire prism?

____

Ⓕ You determined that the length of the green piece is x. Use the volume of the yellow piece and the information you have derived to find the length of the prism.

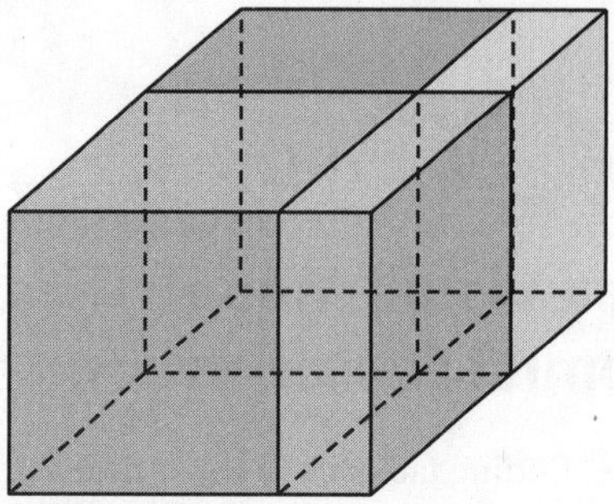

Ⓖ Since the dimensions of the overall prism are x, $x + 2$, and $x + 4$, the volume of the overall prism can be rewritten in factored form as $V = (x)(x + 2)(x + 4)$. Multiply these polynomials together to verify that this is equal to the original given expression for the volume of the overall figure.

Reflect

1. **Discussion** What is one way to double the volume of the prism?

Explain 1 Factoring Out the Greatest Common Monomial First

Most polynomials cannot be *factored over the integers*, which means to find factors that use only integer coefficients. But when a polynomial can be factored, each factor has a degree less than the polynomial's degree. While the goal is to write the polynomial as a product of linear factors, this is not always possible. When a factor of degree 2 or greater cannot be factored further, it is called an **irreducible factor**.

Example 1 **Factor each polynomial over the integers.**

Ⓐ $6x^3 + 15x^2 + 6x$

$6x^3 + 15x^2 + 6x$	Write out the polynomial.
$x(6x^2 + 15x + 6)$	Factor out a common monomial, an x.
$3x(2x^2 + 5x + 2)$	Factor out a common monomial, a 3.
$3x(2x + 1)(x + 2)$	Factor into simplest terms.

Note: The second and third steps can be combined into one step by factoring out the greatest common monomial.

(B) $2x^3 - 20x$

$\_\_\_\_^3 - \_\_\_\_x$ Write out the polynomial.

$\_\_\_\_(x^2 - 10)$ Factor out the greatest common monomial.

Reflect

2. Why wasn't the factor $x^2 - 10$ further factored?

3. Consider what happens when you factor $x^2 - 10$ over the real numbers and not merely the integers. Find a such that $x^2 - 10 = (x - a)(x + a)$.

Your Turn

4. $3x^3 + 7x^2 + 4x$

Explain 2 Recognizing Special Factoring Patterns

Remember the factoring patterns you already know:

Difference of two squares: $a^2 - b^2 = (a + b)(a - b)$

Perfect square trinomials: $a^2 + 2ab + b^2 = (a + b)^2$ and $a^2 - 2ab + b^2 = (a - b)^2$

There are two other factoring patterns that will prove useful:

Sum of two cubes: $a^3 + b^3 = (a + b)(a^2 - ab + b^2)$

Difference of two cubes: $a^3 - b^3 = (a - b)(a^2 + ab + b^2)$

Notice that in each of the new factoring patterns, the quadratic factor is irreducible over the integers.

Example 2 **Factor the polynomial using a factoring pattern.**

(A) $27x^3 + 64$

$27x^3 + 64$ Write out the polynomial.

$27x^3 = (3x)^3$ Check if $27x^3$ is a perfect cube.

$64 = (4)^3$ Check if 64 is a perfect cube.

$a^3 + b^3 = (a + b)(a^2 - ab + b^2)$ Use the sum of two cubes formula to factor.

$(3x)^3 + 4^3 = (3x + 4)((3x)^2 - (3x)(4) + 4^2)$

$27x^3 + 64 = (3x + 4)(9x^2 - 12x + 16)$

Ⓑ $8x^3 - 27$

$8\underline{\quad}^3 - 27$ Write out the polynomial.

$8x^3 = (\underline{\quad} x)^3$ Check if $8x^3$ is a perfect cube.

$27 = (\underline{\quad})^3$ Check if 27 is a perfect cube.

$a^3 - b^3 = (a - b)(a^2 + ab + b^2)$ Use the difference of two cubes formula to factor.

$8x^3 - 27 = (\underline{\quad} x - \underline{\quad})(\underline{\quad} x^2 + \underline{\quad} x + \underline{\quad})$

Reflect

5. The equation $8x^3 - 27 = 0$ has three roots. How many of them are real, what are they, and how many are nonreal?

Your Turn

6. $40x^4 + 5x$

Explain 3 Factoring by Grouping

Another technique for factoring a polynomial is grouping. If the polynomial has pairs of terms with common factors, factor by grouping terms with common factors and then factoring out the common factor from each group. Then look for a common factor of the groups in order to complete the factorization of the polynomial.

Example 3 **Factor the polynomial by grouping.**

(A) $x^3 - x^2 + x - 1$

Write out the polynomial.	$x^3 - x^2 + x - 1$
Group by common factor.	$(x^3 - x^2) + (x - 1)$
Factor.	$x^2(x - 1) + 1(x - 1)$
Regroup.	$(x^2 + 1)(x - 1)$

(B) $x^4 + x^3 + x + 1$

Write out the polynomial.	$x^4 + x^3 + x + 1$
Group by common factor.	$(\_\_\_ + \_\_\_) + (x + 1)$
Factor.	$\_\_\_(x + 1) + \_\_\_(x + 1)$
Regroup.	$(\_\_\_ + \_\_\_)(x + 1)$
Apply sum of two cubes to the first term.	$(\_\_\_ - \_\_\_ + 1)(x + 1)(x + 1)$
Substitute this into the expression and simplify.	$(\_\_\_)^2(\_\_\_^2 - \_\_\_ + 1)$

Your Turn

7. $x^3 + 3x^2 + 3x + 2$

Explain 4 Solving a Real-World Problem by Factoring a Polynomial

Remember that the zero-product property is used in solving factorable quadratic equations. It can also be used in solving factorable polynomial equations.

Example 4 **Write and solve a polynomial equation for the situation described.**

(A) A water park is designing a new pool in the shape of a rectangular prism. The sides and bottom of the pool are made of material 5 feet thick. The interior length must be twice the interior height (depth), and the interior width must be three times the interior height. The volume of water that the pool holds must be 6000 cubic feet. What are the exterior dimensions of the pool?

Let x represent the exterior height of the pool, that is, including its bottom. Let h, l, and w represent the interior dimensions. Then the dimensions of the interior of the pool are the following:

$h = x - 5$

$l = 2x - 10$

$w = 3x - 15$

The formula for the volume of a rectangular prism is $V = lwh$. Plug the values into the volume equation.

$V = (2x - 10)(3x - 15)(x - 5)$

$V = (6x^2 - 60x + 150)(x - 5)$

$V = 6x^3 - 90x^2 + 450x - 750$

Now solve for $V = 6000$.

$6000 = 6x^3 - 90x^2 + 450x - 750$

$0 = 6x^3 - 90x^2 + 450x - 6750$

Factor the resulting new polynomial.

$6x^3 - 90x^2 + 450x - 6750$

$= 6x^2(x - 15) + 450(x - 15)$

$= (6x^2 + 450)(x - 15)$

The only real root is $x = 15$. This is the exterior height of the pool.

The interior height of the pool will be 10 feet, the interior length 20 feet, and the interior width 30 feet. Because each side wall of the pool is 5 feet thick, the exterior length is 30 feet and the exterior width is 40 feet.

(B) **Engineering** To build a hefty wooden feeding trough for a zoo, its sides and bottom should be 2 feet thick, and its outer length should be twice its outer width and height.

What should the outer dimensions of the trough be if it is to hold 288 cubic feet of water?

Volume = Interior Length(feet) · Interior Width(feet) · Interior Height(feet)

$288 = (\_\_\_ - 4)(\_\_\_ - 4)(\_\_\_ - 2)$

$288 = \_\_\_x^3 - \_\_\_x^2 + \_\_\_x - \_\_\_$

$0 = \_\_\_x^3 - \_\_\_x^2 + \_\_\_x - \_\_\_$

$0 = \_\_\_(x - \_\_\_) + \_\_\_(x - \_\_\_)$

$0 = \_\_\_(x^2 + \_\_\_)(x - \_\_\_)$

The only real solution is $x =$ ___. The trough is ___ feet long, ___ feet wide, and ___ feet high.

Your Turn

8. **Engineering** A small bank vault is being designed in the shape of a rectangular prism. The vault's sides and top should all be 3 feet thick. The outer length of the vault should be twice the outer width. The outer height should be the same as the outer width. What should the outer dimensions of the vault be if it is to have 972 cubic feet of space?

Elaborate

9. Describe how the method of grouping incorporates the method of factoring out the greatest common monomial.

10. How do you decide if an equation fits in the sum of two cubes pattern?

11. How can factoring be used to solve a polynomial equation of the form $p(x) = a$, where a is a nonzero constant?

12. **Essential Question Check-In** What are two ways to factor a polynomial?

Evaluate: Homework and Practice

Personal Math Trainer

- Online Homework
- Hints and Help
- Extra Practice

Factor the polynomial, or identify it as irreducible.

1. $x^3 + x^2 - 12x$

2. $x^3 + 5$

3. $x^3 - 125$

4. $x^3 + 5x^2 + 6x$

5. $8x^3 + 125$

6. $2x^3 + 6x$

7. $216x^3 + 64$

8. $8x^3 - 64$

9. $10x^3 - 80$

10. $2x^4 + 7x^3 + 5x^2$

11. $x^3 + 10x^2 + 16x$

12. $x^3 + 9769$

Factor the polynomial by grouping.

13. $x^3 + 8x^2 + 6x + 48$

14. $x^3 + 4x^2 - x - 4$

15. $8x^4 + 8x^3 + 27x + 27$

16. $27x^4 + 54x^3 - 64x - 128$

17. $x^3 + 2x^2 + 3x + 6$

18. $4x^4 - 4x^3 - x + 1$

Write and solve a polynomial equation for the situation described.

19. Engineering A rectangular two-story horse barn is being designed for a farm. The upper floor will be used for storing hay, and the lower floor will have horse stalls that extend 5 feet from both of the longer walls. The barn's length is twice the barn's width, and the lower floor's ceiling height is 6 feet less than the barn's width. What should the dimensions of the lower floor be if the space not used for stalls is to have a volume of 1920 cubic feet?

20. Arts A piece of rectangular crafting supply is being cut for a new sculpture. You want its length to be 4 times its height and its width to be 2 times its height. If you want the wood to have a volume of 64 cubic centimeters, what will its length, width, and height be?

21. Engineering A new rectangular holding tank is being built. The tank's sides and bottom should be 1 foot thick. Its outer length should be twice its outer width and height.

What should the outer dimensions of the tank be if it is to hold 36 cubic feet?

22. Construction A piece of granite is being cut for a building foundation. You want its length to be 8 times its height and its width to be 3 times its height. If you want the granite to have a volume of 648 cubic yards, what will its length, width, and height be?

23. State which, if any, special factoring pattern each of the following polynomial expressions follows:

a. $x^2 - 4$

b. $3x^3 + 5$

c. $4x^2 + 25$

d. $27x^3 + 1000$

e. $64x^3 - x^2 + 1$

H.O.T. Focus on Higher Order Thinking

24. Communicate Mathematical Ideas What is the relationship between the degree of a polynomial and the degree of its factors?

25. Critical Thinking Why is there no sum-of-two-squares factoring pattern?

26. **Explain the Error** Jim was trying to factor a polynomial and produced the following result:

$3x^3 + x^2 + 3x + 1$	Write out the polynomial.
$3x^2(x + 1) + 3(x + 1)$	Group by common factor.
$3(x^2 + 1)(x + 1)$	Regroup.

Explain Jim's error.

27. Factoring can also be done over the complex numbers. This allows you to find all the roots of an equation, not just the real ones.

Complete the steps showing how to use a special factor identity to factor $x^2 + 4$ over the complex numbers.

$x^2 + 4$	Write out the polynomial.
$x^2 - (-4)$	____________________
$(x +$ ______$)$ $(x -$ ______$)$	Factor.
$(x + 2i)$ (______)	Simplify.

28. Find all the imaginary roots of the equation $x^4 - 16 = 0$.

29. Factor $x^3 + x^2 + x + 1$ over the complex numbers.

Lesson Performance Task

Sabrina is building a rectangular raised flower bed. The boards on the two shorter sides are 6 inches thick, and the boards on the two longer sides are 4 inches thick. Sabrina wants the outer length of her bed to be 4 times its height and the outer width to be 2 times its height. She also wants the boards to rise 4 inches above the level of the soil in the bed. What should the outer dimensions of the bed be if she wants it to hold 3136 cubic inches of soil?

Name ______________________ Class ____________ Date ________

6.5 Dividing Polynomials

Essential Question: What are some ways to divide polynomials, and how do you know when the divisor is a factor of the dividend?

Resource Locker

Explore Evaluating a Polynomial Function Using Synthetic Substitution

Polynomials can be written in something called nested form. A polynomial in nested form is written in such a way that evaluating it involves an alternating sequence of additions and multiplications. For instance, the nested form of $p(x) = 4x^3 + 3x^2 + 2x + 1$ is $p(x) = x(x(4x + 3) + 2) + 1$, which you evaluate by starting with 4, multiplying by the value of x, adding 3, multiplying by x, adding 2, multiplying by x, and adding 1.

(A) Given $p(x) = 4x^3 + 3x^2 + 2x + 1$, find $p(-2)$.

You can set up an array of numbers that captures the sequence of multiplications and additions needed to find $p(a)$. Using this array to find $p(a)$ is called **synthetic substitution**.

Given $p(x) = 4x^3 + 3x^2 + 2x + 1$, find $p(-2)$ by using synthetic substitution. The dashed arrow indicates bringing down, the diagonal arrows represent multiplication by –2, and the solid down arrows indicate adding.

The first two steps are to bring down the leading number, 4, then multiply by the value you are evaluating at, –2.

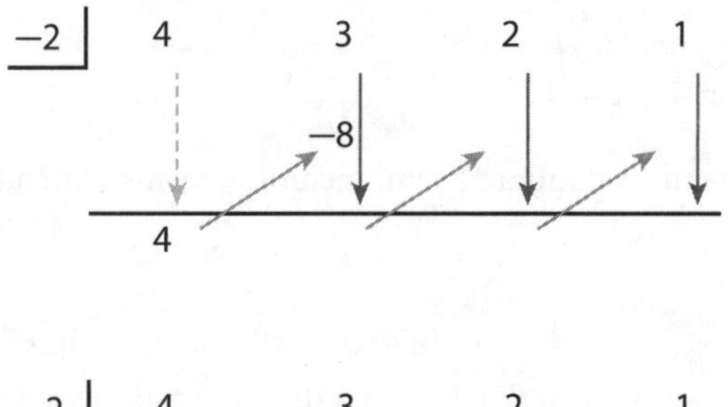

(B) Add 3 and –8.

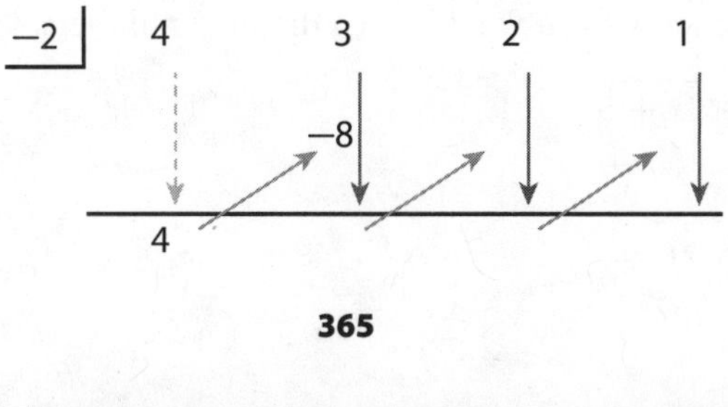

Ⓒ Multiply the previous answer by −2.

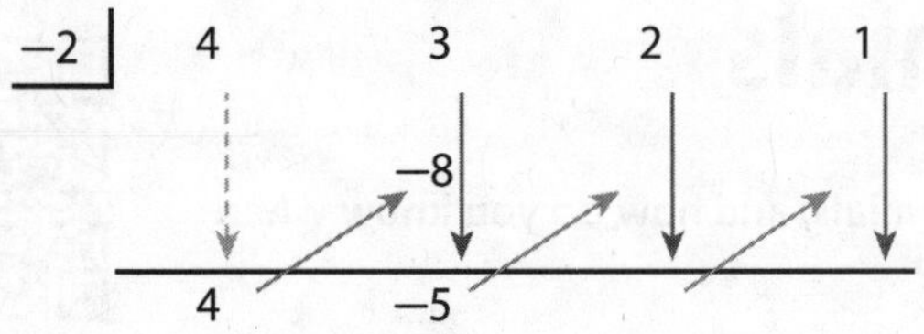

Ⓓ Continue this sequence of steps until you reach the last addition.

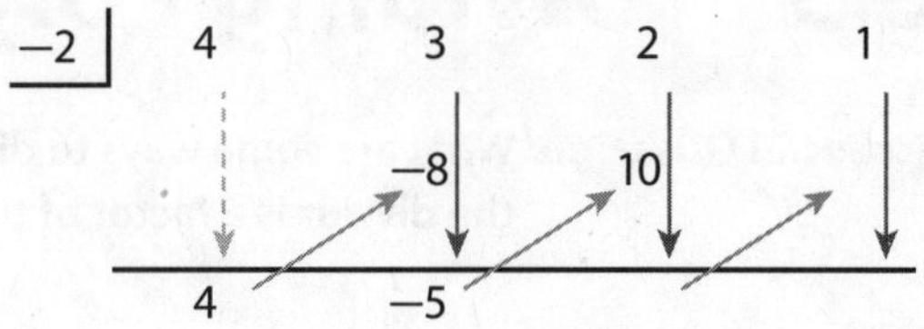

Ⓔ $p(-2) = \square$

Reflect

1. Discussion After the final addition, what does this sum correspond to?

____

____

Explain 1 Dividing Polynomials Using Long Division

Recall that arithmetic long division proceeds as follows.

```
Divisor      23 ← Quotient
         12) 277 ← Dividend
             24
             ---
              37
              36
             ---
               1 ← Remainder
```

Notice that the long division leads to the result $\frac{dividend}{divisor} = quotient + \frac{remainder}{divisor}$. Using the numbers from above, the arithmetic long division leads to $\frac{277}{12} = 23 + \frac{1}{12}$. Multiplying through by the divisor yields the result $dividend = (divisor)(quotient) + remainder$. (This can be used as a means of checking your work.)

Example 1 **Given a polynomial divisor and dividend, use long division to find the quotient and remainder. Write the result in the form *dividend* = *(divisor)(quotient)* + *remainder* and then carry out the multiplication and addition as a check.**

Ⓐ $(4x^3 + 2x^2 + 3x + 5) \div (x^2 + 3x + 1)$

Begin by writing the dividend in standard form, including terms with a coefficient of 0 (if any).

$4x^3 + 2x^2 + 3x + 5$

Write division in the same way as you would when dividing numbers.

$x^2 + 3x + 1\overline{)\,4x^3 + 2x^2 + 3x + 5}$

Find the value you need to multiply the divisor by so that the first term matches with the first term of the dividend. In this case, in order to get $4x^2$, we must multiply x^2 by $4x$. This will be the first term of the quotient.

$$\begin{array}{r l} & 4x \\ x^2 + 3x + 1 \big) & \overline{4x^3 + 2x^2 + 3x + 5} \end{array}$$

Next, multiply the divisor through by the term of the quotient you just found and subtract that value from the dividend. $(x^2 + 3x + 1)(4x) = 4x^3 + 12x^2 + 4x$, so subtract $4x^3 + 12x^2 + 4x$ from $4x^3 + 2x^2 + 3x + 5$.

$$\begin{array}{r l} & 4x \\ x^2 + 3x + 1 \big) & \overline{4x^3 + 2x^2 + 3x + 5} \\ & \underline{-(4x^3 + 12x^2 + 4x)} \\ & \quad -10x^2 - x + 5 \end{array}$$

Taking this difference as the new dividend, continue in this fashion until the largest term of the remaining dividend is of lower degree than the divisor.

$$\begin{array}{r l} & 4x - 10 \\ x^2 + 3x + 1 \big) & \overline{4x^3 + 2x^2 + 3x + 5} \\ & \underline{-(4x^3 + 12x^2 + 4x)} \\ & -10x^2 - x + 5 \\ & \underline{-(-10x^2 - 30x - 10)} \\ & \qquad 29x + 15 \end{array}$$

Since $29x + 5$ is of lower degree than $x^2 + 3x + 1$, stop. $29x + 15$ is the remainder.

Write the final answer.

$$4x^3 + 2x^2 + 3x + 5 = (x^2 + 3x + 1)(4x - 10) + 29x + 15$$

Check.

$$\begin{aligned} 4x^3 + 2x^2 + 3x + 5 &= (x^2 + 3x + 1)(4x - 10) + 29x + 15 \\ &= 4x^3 + 12x^2 + 4x - 10x^2 - 30x - 10 + 29x + 15 \\ &= 4x^3 + 2x^2 + 3x + 5 \end{aligned}$$

(B) $(6x^4 + 5x^3 + 2x + 8) \div (x^2 + 2x - 5)$

Write the dividend in standard form, including terms with a coefficient of 0.

Write the division in the same way as you would when dividing numbers.

$$x^2 + 2x - 5 \big) \overline{6x^4 + 5x^3 + 0x^2 + 2x + 8}$$

Divide.

$$
\begin{array}{r}
6x^2 - \square + \square \\
x^2 + 2x - 5 \overline{) 6x^4 + 5x^3 + 0x^2 + 2x + 8} \\
-\left(6x^4 + 12x^3 - 30x^2\right) \\
\hline
-7x^3 + 30x^2 + 2x \\
-\left(-7x^3 \quad \square \right) \\
\hline
\square \quad + 8 \\
-\left(\square \right) \\
\hline
\square
\end{array}
$$

Write the final answer.

$6x^4 + 5x^3 + 2x + 8 =$ $\square$

Check.

Reflect

2. How do you include the terms with coefficients of 0?

____

____

Your Turn

Use long division to find the quotient and remainder. Write the result in the form *dividend* = (*divisor*)(*quotient*) + *remainder* and then carry out a check.

3. $(15x^3 + 8x - 12) \div (3x^2 + 6x + 1)$

4. $(9x^4 + x^3 + 11x^2 - 4) \div (x^2 + 16)$

Explain 2 Dividing $p(x)$ by $x - a$ Using Synthetic Division

Compare long division with synthetic substitution. There are two important things to notice. The first is that $p(a)$ is equal to the remainder when $p(x)$ is divided by $x - a$. The second is that the numbers to the left of $p(a)$ in the bottom row of the synthetic substitution array give the coefficients of the quotient. For this reason, synthetic substitution is also called **synthetic division**.

Long Division	Synthetic Substitution
$\begin{array}{r} 3x^2 + 10x + 20 \\ x - 2\overline{)\,3x^3 + 4x^2 + 0x + 10} \\ -(3x^3 - 6x^2) \\ \hline 10x^2 + 0x \\ -(10x^2 - 20x) \\ \hline 20x + 10 \\ -20x - 40 \\ \hline 50 \end{array}$	$\begin{array}{r\|rrrr} 2 & 3 & 4 & 0 & 10 \\ & & 6 & 20 & 40 \\ \hline & 3 & 10 & 20 & 50 \end{array}$

Example 2 **Given a polynomial $p(x)$, use synthetic division to divide by $x - a$ and obtain the quotient and the (nonzero) remainder. Write the result in the form $p(x) = (x - a)$ *(quotient)* $+ p(a)$ then carry out the multiplication and addition as a check.**

Ⓐ $(7x^3 - 6x + 9) \div (x + 5)$

By inspection, $a = -5$. Write the coefficients and a in the synthetic division format.

$$\begin{array}{r|rrrr} -5 & 7 & 0 & -6 & 9 \\ & & & & \\ \hline & & & & \end{array}$$

Bring down the first coefficient. Then multiply and add for each column.

$$\begin{array}{r|rrrr} -5 & 7 & 0 & -6 & 9 \\ & & -35 & 175 & -845 \\ \hline & 7 & -35 & 169 & -836 \end{array}$$

Write the result, using the non-remainder entries of the bottom row as the coefficients.

$$(7x^3 - 6x + 9) = (x + 5)(7x^2 - 35x + 169) - 836$$

Check.

$$(7x^3 - 6x + 9) = (x + 5)(7x^2 - 35x + 169) - 836$$

$$= 7x^3 - 35x^2 - 35x^2 - 175x + 169x + 845 - 836$$

$$= 7x^3 - 6x + 9$$

(B) $\left(4x^4 - 3x^2 + 7x + 2\right) \div \left(x - \frac{1}{2}\right)$

Find a. Then write the coefficients and a in the synthetic division format.

Find a = ☐

$\underline{\quad}\big|\ 4 \quad 0 \quad -3 \quad 7 \quad 2$

Bring down the first coefficient. Then multiply and add for each column.

$\big|\ 4 \quad 0 \quad -3 \quad 7 \quad 2$

4

Write the result.

$\left(4x^4 - 3x^2 + 7x + 2\right) =$ ☐

Check.

Reflect

5. Can you use synthetic division to divide a polynomial by $x^2 + 3$? Explain.

Your Turn

Given a polynomial $p(x)$, use synthetic division to divide by $x - a$ and obtain the quotient and the (nonzero) remainder. Write the result in the form $p(x) = (x - a)(\textit{quotient}) + p(a)$. You may wish to perform a check.

6. $\left(2x^3 + 5x^2 - x + 7\right) \div (x - 2)$

7. $\left(6x^4 - 25x^3 - 3x + 5\right) \div \left(x + \frac{1}{3}\right)$

Explain 3 Using the Remainder Theorem and Factor Theorem

When $p(x)$ is divided by $x - a$, the result can be written in the form $p(x) = (x - a)q(x) + r$ where $q(x)$ is the quotient and r is a number. Substituting a for x in this equation gives $p(a) = (a - a)q(a) + r$. Since $a - a = 0$, this simplifies to $p(a) = r$. This is known as the **Remainder Theorem**.

If the remainder $p(a)$ in $p(x) = (x - a)q(x) + p(a)$ is 0, then $p(x) = (x - a)q(x)$, which tells you that $x - a$ is a factor of $p(x)$. Conversely, if $x - a$ is a factor of $p(x)$, then you can write $p(x)$ as $p(x) = (x - a)q(x)$, and when you divide $p(x)$ by $x - a$, you get the quotient $q(x)$ with a remainder of 0. These facts are known as the **Factor Theorem**.

Example 3 **Determine whether the given binomial is a factor of the polynomial $p(x)$. If so, find the remaining factors of $p(x)$.**

(A) $p(x) = x^3 + 3x^2 - 4x - 12$; $(x + 3)$

Use synthetic division.

$$\begin{array}{r|rrrr} -3 & 1 & 3 & -4 & -12 \\ & & -3 & 0 & 12 \\ \hline & 1 & 0 & -4 & \boxed{0} \end{array}$$

Since the remainder is 0, $x + 3$ is a factor.

Write $q(x)$ and then factor it.

$q(x) = x^2 - 4 = (x + 2)(x - 2)$

So, $p(x) = x^3 + 3x^2 - 4x - 12 = (x + 2)(x - 2)(x + 3)$.

(B) $p(x) = x^4 - 4x^3 - 6x^2 + 4x + 5$; $(x + 1)$

Use synthetic division.

$$\begin{array}{r|rrrrr} -1 & 1 & -4 & -6 & 4 & 5 \\ & & & & & \\ \hline & 1 & & & & \boxed{} \end{array}$$

Since the remainder is ______, $(x + 1)$ ______ a factor. Write $q(x)$.

$q(x) =$ ______

Now factor $q(x)$ by grouping.

$q(x) =$ ______

$=$ ______

$=$ ______

$=$ ______

So, $p(x) = x^4 - 4x^3 - 6x^2 + 4x + 5 =$ ______.

Your Turn

Determine whether the given binomial is a factor of the polynomial $p(x)$. If it is, find the remaining factors of $p(x)$.

8. $p(x) = 2x^4 + 8x^3 + 2x + 8$; $(x + 4)$

9. $p(x) = 3x^3 - 2x + 5$; $(x - 1)$

Elaborate

10. Compare long division and synthetic division of polynomials.

11. How does knowing one linear factor of a polynomial help find the other factors?

12. What conditions must be met in order to use synthetic division?

13. **Essential Question Check-In** How do you know when the divisor is a factor of the dividend?

Evaluate: Homework and Practice

Personal Math Trainer

- Online Homework
- Hints and Help
- Extra Practice

Given $p(x)$, find $p(-3)$ by using synthetic substitution.

1. $p(x) = 8x^3 + 7x^2 + 2x + 4$

2. $p(x) = x^3 + 6x^2 + 7x - 25$

3. $p(x) = 2x^3 + 5x^2 - 3x$

4. $p(x) = -x^4 + 5x^3 - 8x + 45$

Given a polynomial divisor and dividend, use long division to find the quotient and remainder. Write the result in the form *dividend* $=$ (*divisor*)(*quotient*) $+$ *remainder*. You may wish to carry out a check.

5. $(18x^3 - 3x^2 + x - 1) \div (x^2 - 4)$

6. $(6x^4 + x^3 - 9x + 13) \div (x^2 + 8)$

7. $(x^4 + 6x - 2.5) \div (x^2 + 3x + 0.5)$

8. $(x^3 + 250x^2 + 100x) \div \left(\frac{1}{2}x^2 + 25x + 9\right)$

Given a polynomial $p(x)$, use synthetic division to divide by $x - a$ and obtain the quotient and the (nonzero) remainder. Write the result in the form $p(x) = (x - a)(\text{quotient}) + p(a)$. You may wish to carry out a check.

9. $(7x^3 - 4x^2 - 400x - 100) \div (x - 8)$

10. $(8x^4 - 28.5x^2 - 9x + 10) \div (x + 0.25)$

11. $(2.5x^3 + 6x^2 - 5.5x - 10) \div (x + 1)$

Determine whether the given binomial is a factor of the polynomial $p(x)$. If so, find the remaining factors of $p(x)$.

12. $p(x) = x^3 + 2x^2 - x - 2;\ (x + 2)$

13. $p(x) = 2x^4 + 6x^3 - 5x - 10;\ (x + 2)$

14. $p(x) = x^3 - 22x^2 + 157x - 360;\ (x - 8)$

15. $p(x) = 4x^3 - 12x^2 + 2x - 5;\ (x - 3)$

16. The volume of a rectangular prism whose dimensions are binomials with integer coefficients is modeled by the function $V(x) = x^3 - 8x^2 + 19x - 12$. Given that $x - 1$ and $x - 3$ are two of the dimensions, find the missing dimension of the prism.

3	1	0	1	0	2	-0	-828
	↓	3	9	30	90	276	828
	1	3	10	30	92	276	0

$x^4 + 3x^4 + 10x^3 + 30x^2 + 92x + 276$

17. Given that the height of a rectangular prism is $x + 2$ and the volume is $x^3 - x^2 - 6x$, write an expression that represents the area of the base of the prism.

18. Physics A Van de Graaff generator is a machine that produces very high voltages by using small, safe levels of electric current. One machine has a current that can be modeled by $I(t) = t + 2$, where $t > 0$ represents time in seconds. The power of the system can be modeled by $P(t) = 0.5t^3 + 6t^2 + 10t$. Write an expression that represents the voltage of the system. Recall that $V = \frac{P}{I}$.

19. Geometry The volume of a hexagonal pyramid is modeled by the function $V(x) = \frac{1}{3}x^3 + \frac{4}{3}x^2 + \frac{2}{3}x - \frac{1}{3}$. Given the height $x + 1$, use polynomial division to find an expression for the area of the base.

(Hint: For a pyramid, $V = \frac{1}{3}Bh$.)

20. Explain the Error Two students used synthetic division to divide $3x^3 - 2x - 8$ by $x - 2$. Determine which solution is correct. Find the error in the other solution.

A.	B.
$\begin{array}{r\|rrrr} 2 & 3 & 0 & -2 & -8 \\ & & 6 & 12 & 20 \\ \hline & 3 & 6 & 10 & 12 \end{array}$	$\begin{array}{r\|rrrr} -2 & 3 & 0 & -2 & -8 \\ & & -6 & 12 & -20 \\ \hline & 3 & -6 & 10 & -28 \end{array}$

H.O.T. Focus on Higher Order Thinking

21. Multi-Step Use synthetic division to divide $p(x) = 3x^3 - 11x^2 - 56x - 50$ by $(3x + 4)$. Then check the solution.

22. Critical Thinking The polynomial $ax^3 + bx^2 + cx + d$ is factored as $3(x - 2)(x + 3)(x - 4)$. What are the values of a and d? Explain.

23. Analyze Relationships Investigate whether the set of whole numbers, the set of integers, and the set of rational numbers are closed under each of the four basic operations. Then consider whether the set of polynomials in one variable is closed under the four basic operations, and determine whether polynomials are like whole numbers, integers, or rational numbers with respect to closure. Use the table to organize.

	Whole Numbers	Integers	Rational Numbers	Polynomials
Addition				
Subtraction				
Multiplication				
Division (by nonzero)				

Lesson Performance Task

The table gives the attendance data for all divisions of NCAA Women's Basketball.

NCAA Women's Basketball Attendance			
Season	**Years since 2006–2007**	**Number of teams in all 3 divisions**	**Attendance (in thousands) for all 3 divisions**
2006–2007	0	1003	10,878.3
2007–2008	1	1013	11,120.8
2008–2009	2	1032	11,160.3
2009–2010	3	1037	11,134.7
2010–2011	4	1048	11,160.0
2011–2012	5	1055	11,201.8

Enter the data from the second, third, and fourth columns of the table and perform linear regression on the data pairs (t, T) and cubic regression on the data pairs (t, A) where $t =$ years since the 2006–2007 season, $T =$ number of teams, and $A =$ attendance (in thousands).

Then create a model for the average attendance per team: $A_{avg}(t) = \frac{A(t)}{T(t)}$. Carry out the division to write $A_{avg}(t)$ in the form $\textit{quadratic quotient} + \frac{\textit{remainder}}{T(t)}$.

Use an online computer algebra system to carry out the division of $A(t)$ by $T(t)$.

STUDY GUIDE REVIEW

Polynomials

MODULE 6

Essential Question: How can you use polynomials to solve real-world problems?

Key Vocabulary

binomial *(binomio)*
monomial *(monomio)*
polynomial *(polinomio)*
synthetic division *(división sintética)*
trinomial *(trinomio)*

KEY EXAMPLE (Lesson 6.1)

Subtract: $\left(5x^4 - x^3 + 2x + 1\right) - \left(2x^3 + 3x^2 - 4x - 7\right)$

$$\begin{array}{rrrrr} 5x^4 & -\;x^3 & 0x^2 & 2x & 1 \\ + & -2x^3 & -3x^2 & 4x & 7 \\ \hline 5x^4 & -\;3x^3 & -3x^2 & +\;6x & +\;8 \end{array}$$

Write in standard form.

Align like terms and add the opposite.

Add.

Therefore, $\left(5x^4 - x^3 + 2x + 1\right) - \left(2x^3 + 3x^2 - 4x - 7\right) = 5x^4 - 3x^3 - 3x^2 + 6x + 8.$

KEY EXAMPLE (Lesson 6.2)

Multiply: $(3x - 2)\left(2x^2 - 5x + 1\right)$

$(3x - 2)\left(2x^2 - 5x + 1\right)$	Write in standard form.
$3x\left(2x^2\right) + 3x(-5x) + 3x(1) + (-2)\left(2x^2\right) + (-2)(-5x) + (-2)(1)$	Distribute the $3x$ and the -2.
$6x^3 - 15x^2 + 3x - 4x^2 + 10x - 2$	Simplify.
$6x^3 - 19x^2 + 13x - 2$	Combine like terms.

Therefore, $(3x - 2)\left(2x^2 - 5x + 1\right) = 6x^3 - 19x^2 + 13x - 2.$

KEY EXAMPLE (Lesson 6.5)

Divide: $\left(x^3 + 10x^2 + 13x + 36\right) \div (x + 9)$

$$\begin{array}{r|l} & x^2 + x + 4 \\ \hline x + 9 & x^3 + 10x^2 + 13x + 36 \\ & -\left(x^3 + 9x^2\right) \\ \hline & x^2 + 13x \\ & -\left(x^2 + 9x\right) \\ \hline & 4x + 36 \\ & -(4x + 36) \\ \hline & 0 \end{array}$$

In order to get x^3, multiply by x^2.

Multiply the divisor through by x^2, then subtract.

In order to get x^2, multiply by x.

Multiply the divisor through by x, then subtract.

In order to get $4x$, multiply by 4.

Multiply the divisor through by 4, then subtract.

Therefore, $\left(x^3 + 10x^2 + 13x + 36\right) \div (x + 9) = x^2 + x + 4.$

EXERCISES

Solve. *(Lessons 6.1, 6.2, 6.5)*

1. $(9x^2 + 2x + 12) + (7x^2 + 10x - 13)$

2. $(6x^6 - 4x^5) - (10x^5 - 15x^4 + 8)$

3. $(x - 3)(4x^2 - 2x + 3)$

4. $(9x^4 + 27x^3 + 23x^2 + 10x) \div (x^2 + 2x)$

5. Mr. Alonzo runs a car repair garage. The average income from repairing a car can be modeled by $C(x) = 45x + 150$. If, for one year, the number of cars repaired can be modeled by $N(x) = 9x^2 + 7x + 6$, write a polynomial that can be used to model Mr. Alonzo's business income for that year. Explain. *(Lesson 6.2)*

MODULE PERFORMANCE TASK

What's the Temperature?

A meteorologist studying the temperature patterns for Redding, California, found the average of the daily minimum and maximum temperatures for each month, but the August temperatures are missing.

Month	Jan	Feb	Mar	Apr	May	June	July	Aug	Sep	Oct	Nov	Dec
Average Max Temperature (°F)	55.3	61.3	62.5	69.6	80.5	90.4	98.3	?	89.3	77.6	62.1	54.7
Average Min Temperature (°F)	35.7	40	41.7	46	52.3	61.8	64.7	?	58.8	49.2	41.4	35.2

How can she find the averages for August? She began by fitting the polynomial function shown below to the data for the average maximum temperature, where x is the month, with $x = 1$ corresponding to January, and the temperature is in degrees Fahrenheit.

$$T_{max}(x) = 0.0095x^5 - 0.2719x^4 + 2.5477x^3 - 9.1882x^2 + 17.272x + 45.468$$

She also thinks that a vertical compression of this function will create a function that fits the average minimum temperature data for Redding.

Use this information to find the average high and low temperature for August. Use graphs, numbers, words, or algebra to explain how you reached your conclusion.

Ready to Go On?

6.1–6.5 Polynomials

Personal Math Trainer

- Online Homework
- Hints and Help
- Extra Practice

Factor the polynomial. *(Lesson 6.4)*

1. $3x^2 + 4x - 4$

2. $2x^3 + 4x^2 - 30x$

3. $9x^2 - 25$

4. $4x^2 - 16x + 16$

Complete the polynomial operation. *(Lesson 6.1, 6.2, 6.3, 6.5)*

5. $(8x^3 - 2x^2 - 4x + 8) + (5x^2 + 6x - 4)$

6. $(-4x^2 - 2x + 8) - (x^2 + 8x - 5)$

7. $5x(x + 2)(3x - 7)$

8. $(3x^3 + 12x^2 + 11x - 2) \div (x + 2)$

9. $(x + y)^6$

ESSENTIAL QUESTION

10. Write a real-world situation that would require adding polynomials. *(Lesson 6.1)*

MODULE 6
MIXED REVIEW

Assessment Readiness

1. Look at each polynomial division problem. Can the polynomials be divided without a remainder?
Select Yes or No for A–C.

A. $(3x^3 - 5x^2 + 10x + 4) \div (3x + 1)$ ○ Yes ○ No

B. $(2x^2 - 5x - 1) \div (x - 3)$ ○ Yes ○ No

C. $(x^3 - 4x^2 + 2x - 3) \div (x + 2)$ ○ Yes ○ No

2. Consider the polynomial $x^3 - x^2 - 6x$.
Select True or False for each statement.

A. $6x$ can be factored out of every term. ○ True ○ False

B. The completely factored polynomial is $x(x + 2)(x - 3)$. ○ True ○ False

C. $f(x) = x^3 - x^2 - 6x$ has a global minimum. ○ True ○ False

3. Alana completed a problem where she had to find the sum of the polynomials $(3x^2 + 8x - 4)$ and $(-8x^3 - 3x + 4)$. Her answer is 0. Describe and correct her mistake. When graphed, how many times does the sum change directions?

4. A rectangular plot of land has a length of $(2x^2 + 5x - 20)$ and a width of $(3x + 4)$. What polynomial represents the area of the plot of land? Explain how you got your answer.

Polynomial Equations

MODULE 7

Essential Question: How can you use polynomial equations to solve real-world problems?

LESSON 7.1
Finding Rational Solutions of Polynomial Equations

LESSON 7.2
Finding Complex Solutions of Polynomial Equations

REAL WORLD VIDEO
The population of the Texas horned lizard has decreased rapidly, and the species is now considered threatened. Biologists use polynomials and other mathematical models to study threatened and endangered species.

MODULE PERFORMANCE TASK PREVIEW

What Do Polynomials Have to Do with Endangered Species?

A species is considered to be endangered when the population is so low that the species is at risk of becoming extinct. Biologists use mathematics to model the population of species, and they use their models to help them predict the future population and to determine whether or not a species is at risk of extinction. How can a polynomial be used to model a species population? Let's find out!

Are YOU Ready?

Complete these exercises to review skills you will need for this module.

Personal Math Trainer

- Online Homework
- Hints and Help
- Extra Practice

Real Numbers

Example 1 Compare $2\sqrt{64}$ and $\sqrt{225}$.

$2\sqrt{64} = 2 \cdot 8$ and $\sqrt{225} = 15$ — Evaluate the radicals.

$16 > 15$ — Multiply and compare.

Since $16 > 15$, $2\sqrt{64} > \sqrt{225}$.

Compare. Use > or <.

1. $4\sqrt{25}$ ______ $25\sqrt{4}$

2. $0.75\sqrt{144}$ ______ $8\sqrt{16}$

3. $2.2\sqrt{100}$ ______ $3\sqrt{36}$

Add and Subtract Rational Numbers

Example 2 Add $\frac{3}{4} + \frac{5}{6}$.

$\left(\frac{3}{3}\right) \cdot \frac{3}{4} + \left(\frac{2}{2}\right) \cdot \frac{5}{6}$ — The LCM is 12. Multiply by 1.

$\frac{9}{12} + \frac{10}{12}$ — Add.

$\frac{19}{12}$

Add or subtract.

4. $\frac{1}{3} + \frac{5}{8}$ ______

5. $\frac{7}{12} - \frac{4}{9}$ ______

6. $\frac{9}{8} - \frac{5}{6}$ ______

Solving Quadratic Equations by Factoring

Example 3 Solve $x^2 + 3x - 10 = 0$ for x.

$(x - 2)(x + 5) = 0$ — Factor.

Either $(x - 2) = 0$ or $(x + 5) = 0$

$x = 2$ or $x = -5$ — Solve.

The solutions for x are 2 and –5.

Solve for x.

7. $x^2 - 5x + 4 = 0$ ______

8. $x^2 + 11x + 30 = 0$ ______

9. $x^2 + 6x = 16$ ______

Name_____________________ Class_____________ Date________

7.1 Finding Rational Solutions of Polynomial Equations

Resource Locker

Essential Question: How do you find the rational roots of a polynomial equation?

Explore Relating Zeros and Coefficients of Polynomial Functions

The zeros of a polynomial function and the coefficients of the function are related. Consider the polynomial function $f(x) = (x + 2)(x - 1)(x + 3)$.

(A) Identify the zeros of the polynomial function. ______________________

(B) Multiply the factors to write the function in standard form.

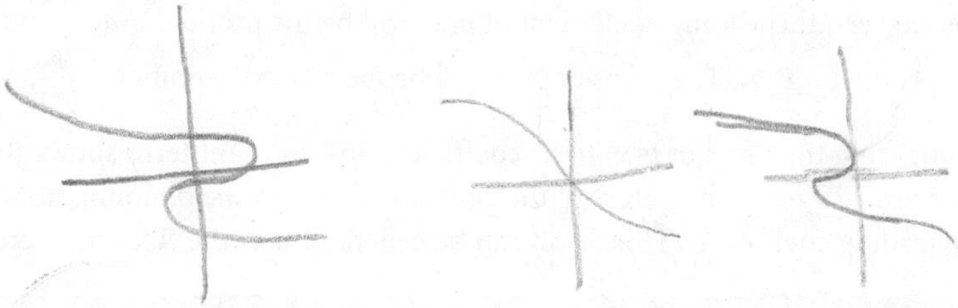

(C) How are the zeros of $f(x)$ related to the standard form of the function? ______________________

____

(D) Now consider the polynomial function $g(x) = (2x + 3)(4x - 5)(6x - 1)$. Identify the zeros of this function.

____

(E) Multiply the factors to write the function in standard form.

$(x+2)(x-1)(x+3)$

$x^2 - x + 2x - 2$

$(x^2 + x - 2)(x + 3)$

$\rightarrow x^3 + x^2 - 2x + 3x^2 + 3x - 6$

(F) How are the zeros of $g(x)$ related to the standard form of the function? $\rightarrow x^3 + 4x^2 + x - 6$

____

____

Reflect

1. In general, how are the zeros of a polynomial function related to the function written in standard form?

2. **Discussion** Does the relationship from the first Reflect question hold if the zeros are all integers? Explain.

3. If you use the zeros, you can write the factored form of $g(x)$ as $g(x) = \left(x + \frac{3}{2}\right)\left(x - \frac{5}{4}\right)\left(x - \frac{1}{6}\right)$, rather than as $g(x) = (2x + 3)(4x - 5)(6x - 1)$. What is the relationship of the factors between the two forms? Give this relationship in a general form.

Explain 1 Finding Zeros Using the Rational Zero Theorem

If a polynomial function $p(x)$ is equal to $(a_1x + b_1)(a_2x + b_2)(a_3x + b_3)$, where a_1, a_2, a_3, b_1, b_2, and b_3 are integers, the leading coefficient of $p(x)$ will be the product $a_1a_2a_3$ and the constant term will be the product $b_1b_2b_3$. The zeros of $p(x)$ will be the rational numbers $-\frac{b_1}{a_1}$, $-\frac{b_2}{a_2}$, $-\frac{b_3}{a_3}$.

Comparing the zeros of $p(x)$ to its coefficient and constant term shows that the numerators of the polynomial's zeros are factors of the constant term and the denominators of the zeros are factors of the leading coefficient. This result can be generalized as the Rational Zero Theorem.

Rational Zero Theorem

If $p(x)$ is a polynomial function with integer coefficients, and if $\frac{m}{n}$ is a zero of $p(x)$ $\left(p\left(\frac{m}{n}\right) = 0\right)$, then m is a factor of the constant term of $p(x)$ and n is a factor of the leading coefficient of $p(x)$.

Example 1 **Find the rational zeros of the polynomial function; then write the function as a product of factors. Make sure to test the possible zeros to find the actual zeros of the function.**

Ⓐ $f(x) = x^3 + 2x^2 - 19x - 20$

a. Use the Rational Zero Theorem to find all possible rational zeros.
Factors of -20: $\pm1, \pm2, \pm4, \pm5, \pm10, \pm20$

b. Test the possible zeros. Use a synthetic division table to organize the work. In this table, the first row (shaded) represents the coefficients of the polynomial, the first column represents the divisors, and the last column represents the remainders.

$\frac{m}{n}$	1	2	−19	−20
1	1	3	−16	−36
2	1	4	−11	−42
4	1	6	5	0
5	1	7	16	60

c. Factor the polynomial. The synthetic division by 4 results in a remainder of 0, so 4 is a zero and the polynomial in factored form is given as follows:

$$(x - 4)(x^2 + 6x + 5) = 0$$

$$(x - 4)(x + 5)(x + 1) = 0$$

$$x = 4, x = -5, \text{ or } x = -1$$

The zeros are $x = 4$, $x = -5$, and $x = -1$.

(B) $f(x) = x^4 - 4x^3 - 7x^2 + 22x + 24$

a. Use the Rational Zero Theorem to find all possible rational zeros.

Factors of 24: ±____, ±____, ±____, ±____, ±____, ±____, ±____, ±____

b. Test the possible zeros. Use a synthetic division table.

$\frac{m}{n}$	1	−4	−7	22	24
1					
2					
3					

c. Factor the polynomial. The synthetic division by ____ results in a remainder of 0, so ____ is a zero and the polynomial in factored form is given as follows:

$(x - \_\_\_\_)(x^3 - x^2 - \_\_\_\_ x - \_\_\_\_) = 0$

d. Use the Rational Zero Theorem again to find all possible rational zeros of

$g(x) = x^3 - x^2 - \_\_\_\_ x - \_\_\_\_$.

Factors of −8: ±____, ±____, ±____, ±____

e. Test the possible zeros. Use a synthetic division table.

$\frac{m}{n}$	1	−1	−10	−8
1				
2				
4				

f. Factor the polynomial. The synthetic division by ____ results in a remainder of 0, so ____ is a zero and the polynomial in factored form is:

$(x - \_\_\_\_)(x - \_\_\_\_)(\_\_\_\_ x^2 + \_\_\_\_ x + \_\_\_\_) = 0$

$(x - \_\_\_\_)(x - \_\_\_\_)(x + \_\_\_\_)(x + \_\_\_\_) = 0$

$x = \_\_\_\_$, $x = \_\_\_\_$, $x = \_\_\_\_$, or $x = \_\_\_\_$

The zeros are ________.

Reflect

4. How is using synthetic division on a 4th degree polynomial to find its zeros different than using synthetic division on a 3rd degree polynomial to find its zeros?

5. Suppose you are trying to find the zeros the function $f(x) = x^2 + 1$. Would it be possible to use synthetic division on this polynomial? Why or why not?

6. Using synthetic division, you find that $\frac{1}{2}$ is a zero of $f(x) = 2x^3 + x^2 - 13x + 6$. The quotient from the synthetic division array for $f\left(\frac{1}{2}\right)$ is $2x^2 + 2x - 12$. Show how to write the factored form of $f(x) = 2x^3 + x^2 - 13x + 6$ using integer coefficients.

Your Turn

7. Find the zeros of $f(x) = x^3 - 2x^2 - 8x$.

Explain 2 Solving a Real-World Problem Using the Rational Root Theorem

Since a zero of a function $f(x)$ is a value of x for which $f(x) = 0$, finding the zeros of a polynomial function $p(x)$ is the same thing as find the solutions of the polynomial equation $p(x) = 0$. Because a solution of a polynomial equation is known as a **root**, the Rational Zero Theorem can be also expressed as the Rational Root Theorem.

Rational Root Theorem

If the polynomial $p(x)$ has integer coefficients, then every rational root of the polynomial equation $p(x) = 0$ can be written in the form $\frac{m}{n}$, where m is a factor of the constant term of $p(x)$ and n is a factor of the leading coefficient of $p(x)$.

Example 2

Engineering A pen company is designing a gift container for their new premium pen. The marketing department has designed a pyramidal box with a rectangular base. The base width is 1 inch shorter than its base length and the height is 3 inches taller than 3 times the base length. The volume of the box must be 6 cubic inches. What are the dimensions of the box? Graph the volume function and the line $y = 6$ on a graphing calculator to check your solution.

A. Analyze Information

The important information is that the base width must be _____ inch shorter than

the base length, the height must be _____ inches taller than 3 times the base length,

and the box must have a volume of _____ cubic inches.

B. Formulate a Plan

Write an equation to model the volume of the box.

Let x represent the base length in inches. The base width is _______ and the height is _________, or _________.

$$\frac{1}{3}\ell w h = V$$

$$\frac{1}{3}(\_\_\_)(x - \_\_\_)(3)(x + \_\_\_) = \_\_\_$$

$$\_\_\_x^3 - \_\_\_x - \_\_\_ = 0$$

C. Solve

Use the Rational Root Theorem to find all possible rational roots.

Factors of −6: ±______, ±______, ±______, ±______

Test the possible roots. Use a synthetic division table.

$\frac{m}{n}$	1	0	−1	−6
1	1	1	0	−6
2	1	2	3	0
3	1	3	8	18

Factor the polynomial. The synthetic division by ______ results in a remainder of 0,

so ______ is a root and the polynomial in factored form is as follows:

$(\_\_\_\_ x - \_\_\_\_)(\_\_\_\_ x^2 + \_\_\_\_ x + \_\_\_\_) = 0$

The quadratic polynomial produces only ______ roots, so the only possible answer for the base length is ______ inches. The base width is ______ inch and the height is ______ inches.

D. Justify and Evaluate

The x-coordinates of the points where the graphs of two functions, f and g, intersect is the solution of the equation $f(x) = g(x)$. Using a graphing calculator to graph the volume function and $y = 6$ results in the graphs intersecting at the point ______. Since the x-coordinate is ______, the answer is correct.

Your Turn

8. **Engineering** A box company is designing a new rectangular gift container. The marketing department has designed a box with a width 2 inches shorter than its length and a height 3 inches taller than its length. The volume of the box must be 56 cubic inches. What are the dimensions of the box?

Elaborate

9. For a polynomial function with integer coefficients, how are the function's coefficients and rational zeros related?

10. Describe the process for finding the rational zeros of a polynomial function with integer coefficients.

11. How is the Rational Root Theorem useful when solving a real-world problem about the volume of an object when the volume function is a polynomial and a specific value of the function is given?

12. **Essential Question Check-In** What does the Rational Root Theorem find?

Evaluate: Homework and Practice

Personal Math Trainer

- Online Homework
- Hints and Help
- Extra Practice

Find the rational zeros of each polynomial function. Then write each function in factored form.

1. $f(x) = x^3 - x^2 - 10x - 8$

2. $f(x) = x^3 + 2x^2 - 23x - 60$

3. $j(x) = 2x^3 - x^2 - 13x - 6$

4. $g(x) = x^3 - 9x^2 + 23x - 15$

5. $h(x) = x^3 - 5x^2 + 2x + 8$

6. $h(x) = 6x^3 - 7x^2 - 9x - 2$

7. $s(x) = x^3 - x^2 - x + 1$

8. $t(x) = x^3 + x^2 - 8x - 12$

9. $k(x) = x^4 + 5x^3 - x^2 - 17x + 12$

10. $g(x) = x^4 - 6x^3 + 11x^2 - 6x$

11. $h(x) = x^4 - 2x^3 - 3x^2 + 4x + 4$

12. $f(x) = x^4 - 5x^2 + 4$

13. **Manufacturing** A laboratory supply company is designing a new rectangular box in which to ship glass pipes. The company has created a box with a width 2 inches shorter than its length and a height 9 inches taller than twice its length. The volume of each box must be 45 cubic inches. What are the dimensions?

14. **Engineering** A natural history museum is building a pyramidal glass structure for its tree snake exhibit. Its research team has designed a pyramid with a square base and with a height that is 2 yards more than a side of its base. The volume of the pyramid must be 147 cubic yards. What are the dimensions?

15. **Engineering** A paper company is designing a new, pyramid-shaped paperweight. Its development team has decided that to make the length of the paperweight 4 inches less than the height and the width of the paperweight 3 inches less than the height. The paperweight must have a volume of 12 cubic inches. What are the dimensions of the paperweight?

16. Match each set of roots with its polynomial function.

A. $x = 2, x = 3, x = 4$ ______ $f(x) = (x + 2)(x + 4)\left(x - \frac{3}{2}\right)$

B. $x = -2, x = -4, x = \frac{3}{2}$ ______ $f(x) = \left(x - \frac{1}{2}\right)\left(x - \frac{5}{4}\right)\left(x + \frac{7}{3}\right)$

C. $x = \frac{1}{2}, x = \frac{5}{4}, x = \frac{-7}{3}$ ______ $f(x) = (x - 2)(x - 3)(x - 4)$

D. $x = \frac{-4}{5}, x = \frac{6}{7}, x = 4$ ______ $f(x) = \left(x + \frac{4}{5}\right)\left(x - \frac{6}{7}\right)(x - 4)$

17. Identify the zeros of $f(x) = (x + 3)(x - 4)(x - 3)$, write the function in standard form, and state how the zeros are related to the standard form.

H.O.T. Focus on Higher Order Thinking

18. **Critical Thinking** Consider the polynomial function $g(x) = 2x^3 - 6x^2 + \pi x + 5$. Is it possible to use the Rational Zero Theorem and synthetic division to factor this polynomial? Explain.

19. **Explain the Error** Sabrina was told to find the zeros of the polynomial function $h(x) = x(x - 4)(x + 2)$. She stated that the zeros of this polynomial are $x = 0$, $x = -4$, and $x = 2$. Explain her error.

20. **Justify Reasoning** If $\frac{c}{b}$ is a rational zero of a polynomial function $p(x)$, explain why $bx - c$ must be a factor of the polynomial.

21. **Justify Reasoning** A polynomial function $p(x)$ has degree 3, and its zeros are -3, 4, and 6. What do you think is the equation of $p(x)$? Do you think there could be more than one possibility? Explain.

Lesson Performance Task

For the years from 2001–2010, the number of Americans traveling to other countries by plane can be represented by the polynomial function $A(t) = 20t^4 - 428t^3 + 2760t^2 - 4320t + 33{,}600$, where A is the number of thousands of Americans traveling abroad by airplane and t is the number of years since 2001. In which year were there 40,000,000 Americans traveling abroad? Use the Rational Root Theorem to find your answer.
[Hint: consider the function's domain and range before finding all possible rational roots.]

Name ______________________ Class ______________ Date ________

7.2 Finding Complex Solutions of Polynomial Equations

Resource Locker

Essential Question: What do the Fundamental Theorem of Algebra and its corollary tell you about the roots of the polynomial equation $p(x) = 0$ where $p(x)$ has degree n?

Explore Investigating the Number of Complex Zeros of a Polynomial Function

You have used various algebraic and graphical methods to find the roots of a polynomial equation $p(x) = 0$ or the zeros of a polynomial function $p(x)$. Because a polynomial can have a factor that repeats, a zero or a root can occur multiple times.

The polynomial $p(x) = x^3 + 8x^2 + 21x + 18 = (x + 2)(x + 3)^2$ has -2 as a zero once and -3 as a zero twice, or *with multiplicity 2*. The **multiplicity** of a zero of $p(x)$ or a root of $p(x) = 0$ is the number of times that the related factor occurs in the factorization.

In this Explore, you will use algebraic methods to investigate the relationship between the degree of a polynomial function and the number of zeros that it has.

Ⓐ Find all zeros of $p(x) = x^3 + 7x^2$. Include any multiplicities greater than 1.

$$p(x) = x^3 + 7x^2$$

Factor out the GCF. $p(x) = \square(x + 7)$

What are all the zeros of $p(x)$? ______________

Ⓑ Find all zeros of $p(x) = x^3 - 64$. Include any multiplicities greater than 1.

$$p(x) = x^3 - 64$$

Factor the difference of two cubes. $p(x) = (x \square 4)(x^2 + \square + \square)$

What are the real zeros of $p(x)$? ______________

Solve $x^2 + 4x + 16 = 0$ using the quadratic formula.

$$x = \frac{-b \pm \sqrt{b^2 - 4ac}}{2a}$$

$$x = \frac{\square \pm \sqrt{4^2 - 4 \cdot 1 \cdot \square}}{2 \cdot \square} \quad x = \frac{-4 \pm \sqrt{\square}}{2} \quad x = \frac{-4 \pm \square\sqrt{3}}{2}$$

$$x = -2 \pm 2i\sqrt{3}$$

What are the non-real zeros of $p(x)$? ______________

(C) Find all zeros of $p(x) = x^4 + 3x^3 - 4x^2 - 12x$. Include any multiplicities greater than 1.

$$p(x) = x^4 + 3x^3 - 4x^2 - 12x$$

Factor out the GCF. $p(x) = x(\square)$

Group terms to begin factoring by grouping. $p(x) = x\left((x^3 + 3x^2) - (\square)\right)$

Factor out common monomials. $p(x) = x\left(\square(x + 3) - \square(x + 3)\right)$

Factor out the common binomial. $p(x) = x(x + 3)(x^2 - 4)$

Factor the difference of squares. $p(x) = x(x + 3)(\square)(\square)$

What are all the zeros of $p(x)$? ______

(D) Find all zeros of $p(x) = x^4 - 16$. Include any multiplicities greater than 1.

$$p(x) = x^4 - 16$$

Factor the difference of squares. $p(x) = (\square)(x^2 + 4)$

Factor the difference of squares. $p(x) = (\square)(\square)(x^2 + 4)$

What are the real zeros of $p(x)$? ______

Solve $x^2 + 4 = 0$ by taking square roots.

$x^2 + 4 = 0$

$x^2 = -4$

$x = \pm\sqrt{-4}$

$x = \pm\square$

What are the non-real zeros of $p(x)$? ______

Ⓔ Find all zeros of $p(x) = x^4 + 5x^3 + 6x^2 - 4x - 8$. Include multiplicities greater than 1.

By the Rational Zero Theorem, possible rational zeros are ±1, ±2, ±4, and ±8. Use a synthetic division table to test possible zeros.

$\frac{m}{n}$	1	5	6	−4	−8
1	1	6	12	8	0

The remainder is 0, so 1 is/is not a zero.

$p(x)$ factors as $(x - 1)(\quad)$.

Test for zeros in the cubic polynomial.

$\frac{m}{n}$	1	6	12	8
1	1	7	19	27
−1	1	5	7	1
2	1	8	28	64
−2	1	4	4	0

_____ a zero.

$p(x)$ factors as $(x - 1)(x + 2)(\quad)$. The quadratic is a perfect square trinomial.

So, $p(x)$ factors completely as $p(x) = (x - 1)$ ______.

What are all the zeros of $p(x)$? ______________

Ⓕ Complete the table to summarize your results from Steps A–E.

Polynomial Function in Standard Form	Polynomial Function Factored over the Integers	Real Zeros and Their Multiplicities	Non-real Zeros and Their Multiplicities
$p(x) = x^3 + 7x^2$			
$p(x) = x^3 - 64$			
$p(x) = x^4 + 3x^3 - 4x^2 - 12x$			
$p(x) = x^4 - 16$			
$p(x) = x^4 + 5x^3 + 6x^2 - 4x - 8$			

Reflect

1. Examine the table. For each function, count the number of unique zeros, both real and non-real. How does the number of unique zeros compare with the degree?

2. Examine the table again. This time, count the total number of zeros for each function, where a zero of multiplicity m is counted as m zeros. How does the total number of zeros compare with the degree?

3. **Discussion** Describe the apparent relationship between the degree of a polynomial function and the number of zeros it has.

Explain 1 Applying the Fundamental Theorem of Algebra to Solving Polynomial Equations

The Fundamental Theorem of Algebra and its corollary summarize what you have observed earlier while finding rational zeros of polynomial functions and in completing the Explore.

The Fundamental Theorem of Algebra
Every polynomial function of degree $n \geq 1$ has at least one zero, where a zero may be a complex number.
Corollary: Every polynomial function of degree $n \geq 1$ has exactly n zeros, including multiplicities.

Because the zeros of a polynomial function $p(x)$ give the roots of the equation $p(x) = 0$, the theorem and its corollary also extend to finding all roots of a polynomial equation.

Example 1 **Solve the polynomial equation by finding all roots.**

Ⓐ $2x^3 - 12x^2 - 34x + 204 = 0$

The polynomial has degree 3, so the equation has exactly 3 roots.

$$2x^3 - 12x^2 - 34x + 204 = 0$$

Divide both sides by 2. $\quad x^3 - 6x^2 - 17x + 102 = 0$

Group terms. $\quad (x^3 - 6x^2) - (17x - 102) = 0$

Factor out common monomials. $\quad x^2(x - 6) - 17(x - 6) = 0$

Factor out the common binomial. $\quad (x^2 - 17)(x - 6) = 0$

One root is $x = 6$. Solving $x^2 - 17 = 0$ gives $x^2 = 17$, or $x = \pm\sqrt{17}$.

The roots are $-\sqrt{17}$, $\sqrt{17}$, and 6.

(B) $x^4 - 6x^2 - 27 = 0$

The polynomial has degree ____, so the equation has exactly ____ roots.

Notice that $x^4 - 6x^2 - 27$ has the form $u^2 - 6u - 27$, where $u = x^2$. So, you can factor it like a quadratic trinomial.

$$x^4 - 6x^2 - 27 = 0$$

Factor the trinomial. $\left(x^2 - \square\right)\left(x^2 + \square\right) = 0$

Factor the difference of squares. $\left(x + \square\right)\left(x - \square\right)\left(x^2 + 3\right) = 0$

The real roots are ______ and ______. Solving $x^2 + 3 = 0$ gives $x^2 = -3$, or

$x = \pm\sqrt{-3} = \pm \square \sqrt{\square}$.

The roots are ____________________.

Reflect

4. Restate the Fundamental Theorem of Algebra and its corollary in terms of the roots of equations.

____

____

____

____

Your Turn

Solve the polynomial equation by finding all roots.

5. $8x^3 - 27 = 0$

6. $p(x) = x^4 - 13x^3 + 55x^2 - 91x$

Explain 2 Writing a Polynomial Function From Its Zeros

You may have noticed in finding roots of quadratic and polynomial equations that any irrational or complex roots come in pairs. These pairs reflect the "±" in the quadratic formula. For example, for any of the following number pairs, you will never have a polynomial equation for which only one number in the pair is a root.

$$\sqrt{5} \text{ and } -\sqrt{5};\ 1 + \sqrt{7} \text{ and } 1 - \sqrt{7};\ i \text{ and } -i;\ 2 + 14i \text{ and } 2 - 14i;\ \frac{11}{6} + \frac{1}{6}i\sqrt{3} \text{ and } \frac{11}{6} - \frac{1}{6}i\sqrt{3}$$

The irrational root pairs $a + b\sqrt{c}$ and $a - b\sqrt{c}$ are called *irrational conjugates.* The complex root pairs $a + bi$ and $a - bi$ are called *complex conjugates.*

Irrational Root Theorem

If a polynomial $p(x)$ has rational coefficients and $a + b\sqrt{c}$ is a root of the equation $p(x) = 0$, where a and b are rational and $\sqrt{c}$ is irrational, then $a - b\sqrt{c}$ is also a root of $p(x) = 0$.

Complex Conjugate Root Theorem

If $a + bi$ is an imaginary root of a polynomial equation with real-number coefficients, then $a - bi$ is also a root.

Because the roots of the equation $p(x) = 0$ give the zeros of a polynomial function, corresponding theorems apply to the zeros of a polynomial function. You can use this fact to write a polynomial function from its zeros. Because irrational and complex conjugate pairs are a sum and difference of terms, the product of irrational conjugates is always a rational number and the product of complex conjugates is always a real number.

$$\left(2 - \sqrt{10}\right)\left(2 + \sqrt{10}\right) = 2^2 - \left(\sqrt{10}\right)^2 = 4 - 10 = -6$$
$$\left(1 - i\sqrt{2}\right)\left(1 + i\sqrt{2}\right) = 1^2 - \left(i\sqrt{2}\right)^2 = 1 - (-1)(2) = 3$$

Example 2 **Write the polynomial function with least degree and a leading coefficient of 1 that has the given zeros.**

(A) 5 and $3 + 2\sqrt{7}$

Because irrational zeros come in conjugate pairs, $3 - 2\sqrt{7}$ must also be a zero of the function. Use the 3 zeros to write a function in factored form, then multiply to write it in standard form.

$$p(x) = \left[x - \left(3 + 2\sqrt{7}\right)\right]\left[x - \left(3 - 2\sqrt{7}\right)\right](x - 5)$$

Multiply the first two factors using FOIL. $= \left[x^2 - \left(3 - 2\sqrt{7}\right)x - \left(3 + 2\sqrt{7}\right)x + \left(3 + 2\sqrt{7}\right)\left(3 - 2\sqrt{7}\right)\right](x - 5)$

Multipy the conjugates. $= \left[x^2 - \left(3 - 2\sqrt{7}\right)x - \left(3 + 2\sqrt{7}\right)x + (9 - 4 \cdot 7)\right](x - 5)$

Combine like terms. $= \left[x^2 + \left(-3 + 2\sqrt{7} - 3 - 2\sqrt{7}\right)x + (-19)\right](x - 5)$

Simplify. $= \left[x^2 - 6x - 19\right](x - 5)$

Distributive property $= x\left(x^2 - 6x - 19\right) - 5\left(x^2 - 6x - 19\right)$

Multiply. $= x^3 - 6x^2 - 19x - 5x^2 + 30x + 95$

Combine like terms. $= x^3 - 11x^2 + 11x + 95$

The polynomial function is $p(x) = x^3 - 11x^2 + 11x + 95$.

(B) 2, 3 and $1-i$

Because complex zeros come in conjugate pairs, ______ must also be a zero of the function.

Use the 4 zeros to write a function in factored form, then multiply to write it in standard form.

$$p(x) = \left[x - (1+i)\right]\left[x - \left(\boxed{}\right)\right](x-2)(x-3)$$

Multiply the first two factors using FOIL. $= \left[x^2 - (1-i)x - \left(\boxed{}\right)x + (1+i)(1-i)\right](x-2)(x-3)$

Multipy the conjugates. $= \left[x^2 - (1-i)x - (1+i)x + \left(1 - \left(\boxed{}\right)\right)\right](x-2)(x-3)$

Combine like terms. $= \left[x^2 + (-1+i-1-i)x + 2\right](x-2)(x-3)$

Simplify. $= \left(\boxed{}\right)(x-2)(x-3)$

Multipy the binomials. $= (x^2 - 2x + 2)\boxed{}$

Distributive property $= x^2(x^2 - 5x + 6)\boxed{}(x^2 - 5x + 6) + 2(x^2 - 5x + 6)$

Multipy. $= (x^4 - 5x^3 + 6x^2) + (-2x^3 + 10x^2 - 12x) + (2x^2 - 10x + 12)$

Combine like terms. $= \boxed{}$

The polynomial function is $p(x) =$ ______.

Reflect

7. Restate the Irrational Root Theorem in terms of the zeros of polynomial functions.

______

______

______

8. Restate the Complex Conjugates Zero Theorem in terms of the roots of equations.

______

______

Your Turn

Write the polynomial function with the least degree and a leading coefficient of 1 that has the given zeros.

9. $2 + 3i$ and $4 - 7\sqrt{2}$

Explain 3 Solving a Real-World Problem by Graphing Polynomial Functions

You can use graphing to help you locate or approximate any real zeros of a polynomial function. Though a graph will not help you find non-real zeros, it can indicate that the function has non-real zeros. For example, look at the graph of $p(x) = x^4 - 2x^2 - 3$.

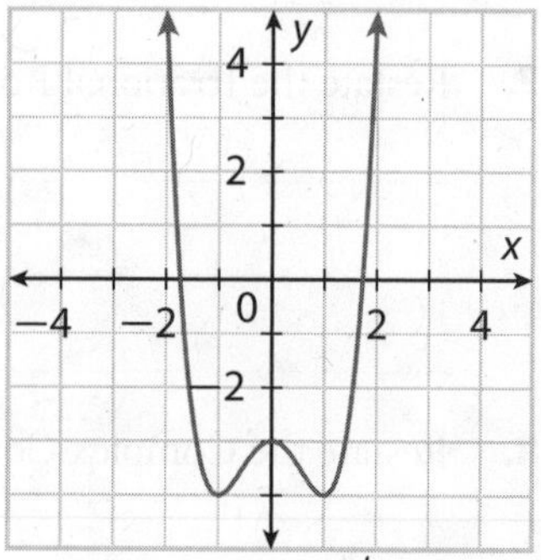

The graph intersects the x-axis twice, which shows that the function has two real zeros. By the corollary to the Fundamental Theorem of Algebra, however, a fourth degree polynomial has four zeros. So, the other two zeros of $p(x)$ must be non-real. The zeros are $-\sqrt{3}$, $\sqrt{3}$, i, and $-i$. (A polynomial whose graph has a turning point on the x-axis has a real zero of even multiplicity at that point. If the graph "bends" at the x-axis, there is a real zero of odd multiplicity greater than 1 at that point.)

Ⓐ The following polynomial models approximate the total oil consumption C (in millions of barrels per day) for North America (NA) and the Asia Pacific region (AP) over the period from 2001 to 2011, where t is in years and $t = 0$ represents 2001.

$$C_{NA}(t) = 0.00494t^4 - 0.0915t^3 + 0.442t^2 - 0.239t + 23.6$$

$$C_{AP}(t) = 0.00877t^3 - 0.139t^2 + 1.23t - 21.1$$

Use a graphing calculator to plot the functions and approximate the x-coordinate of the intersection in the region of interest. What does this represent in the context of this situation? Determine when oil consumption in the Asia Pacific region overtook oil consumption in North America using the requested method.

Graph $Y1 = 0.00494x^4 - 0.0915x^3 + 0.442x^2 - 0.239x + 23.6$ and $Y2 = 0.00877x^3 - 0.139x^2 + 1.23x + 21.1$. Use the "Calc" menu to find the point of intersection. Here are the results for Xmin = 0, Xmax = 10, Ymin = 20, Ymax = 30. (The graph for the Asia Pacific is the one that rises upward on all segments.)

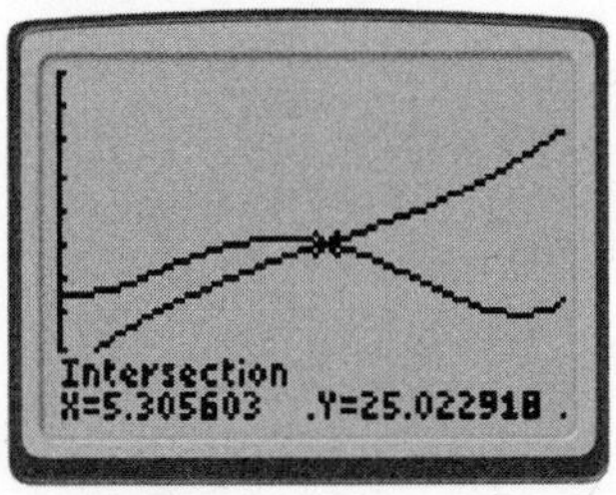

The functions intersect at about $x = 5$, which represents the year 2006. This means that the models show oil consumption in the Asia Pacific equaling and then overtaking oil consumption in North America about 2006.

Ⓑ Find a single polynomial model for the situation in Example 3A whose zero represents the time that oil consumption for the Asia Pacific region overtakes consumption for North America. Plot the function on a graphing calculator and use it to find the x-intercept.

Let the function $C_D(t)$ represent the difference in oil consumption in the Asia Pacific and North America.

A difference of 0 indicates ______________________.

$\boxed{} = \boxed{} - C_{NA}(t)$

$$= -0.00877t^3 - 0.139t^2 + 1.23t + 21.1 - (0.00494t^4 - 0.0915t^3 + 0.442t^2 - 0.239t + 23.6)$$

Remove parentheses and rearrange terms.

$$= -0.00494t^4 + 0.00877t^3 + 0.0915t^3 - 0.139t^2 - 0.442t^2 + 1.23t + 0.239t + 21.1 - 23.6$$

Combine like terms. Round to three significant digits.

$=$

Graph $C_D(t)$ and find the x-intercept. (The graph with Ymin = −4, Ymax = 6 is shown.)

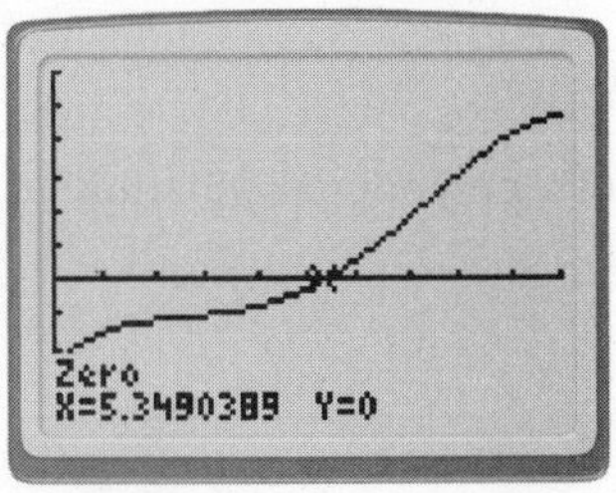

Within the rounding error, the results for the x-coordinate of the intersection of $C_{NA}(t)$ and $C_{AP}(t)$ and the x-intercept of $C_D(t)$ are the same.

Your Turn

10. An engineering class is designing model rockets for a competition. The body of the rocket must be cylindrical with a cone-shaped top. The cylinder part must be 60 cm tall, and the height of the cone must be twice the radius. The volume of the payload region must be 558π cm^3 in order to hold the cargo. Use a graphing calculator to graph the rocket's payload volume as a function of the radius x. On the same screen, graph the constant function for the desired payload. Find the intersection to find x.

Elaborate

11. What does the degree of a polynomial function $p(x)$ tell you about the zeros of the function or the roots of the equation $p(x) = 0$?

12. A polynomial equation of degree 5 has the roots 0.3, 2, 8, and 10.6 (each of multiplicity 1). What can you conclude about the remaining root? Explain your reasoning.

13. Discussion Describe two ways you can use graphing to determine when two polynomial functions that model a real-world situation have the same value.

14. Essential Question Check-In What are possible ways to find all the roots of a polynomial equation?

Evaluate: Homework and Practice

Personal Math Trainer

- Online Homework
- Hints and Help
- Extra Practice

Find all zeros of $p(x)$. Include any multiplicities greater than 1.

1. $p(x) = 3x^3 - 10x^2 + 10x - 4$

2. $p(x) = x^3 - 3x^2 + 4x - 12$

Solve the polynomial equation by finding all roots.

3. $2x^3 - 3x^2 + 8x - 12 = 0$

4. $x^4 - 5x^3 + 3x^2 + x = 0$

Write the polynomial function with least degree and a leading coefficient of 1 that has the given zeros.

5. 0, $\sqrt{5}$, and 2

6. $4i$, 2, and -2

7. 1, -1 (multiplicity 3), and $3i$

8. 3(multiplicity of 2) and $3i$

9. **Forestry** Height and trunk volume measurements from 10 giant sequoias between the heights of 220 and 275 feet in California give the following model, where h is the height in feet and V is the volume in cubic feet.

$$V(h) = 0.131h^3 - 90.9h^2 + 21{,}200h - 1{,}627{,}400$$

The "President" tree in the Giant Forest Grove in Sequoia National Park has a volume of about 45,100 cubic feet. Use a graphing calculator to plot the function $V(h)$ and the constant function representing the volume of the President tree together. (Use a window of 220 to 275 for X and 30,000 to 55,000 for Y.) Find the x-coordinate of the intersection of the graphs. What does this represent in the context of this situation?

10. **Business** Two competing stores, store A and store B, opened the same year in the same neighborhood. The annual revenue R (in millions of dollars) for each store t years after opening can be approximated by the polynomial models shown.

$$R_A(t) = 0.0001(-t^4 + 12t^3 - 77t^2 + 600t + 13{,}650)$$

$$R_B(t) = 0.0001(-t^4 + 36t^3 - 509t^2 + 3684t + 3390)$$

Using a graphing calculator, graph the models from $t = 0$ to $t = 10$, with a range of 0 to 2 for R. Find the x-coordinate of the intersection of the graphs, and interpret the graphs.

11. Personal Finance A retirement account contains cash and stock in a company. The cash amount is added to each week by the same amount until week 32, then that same amount is withdrawn each week. The functions shown model the balance B (in thousands of dollars) over the course of the past year, with the time t in weeks.

$$B_C(t) = -0.12|t - 32| + 13$$

$$B_S(t) = 0.00005t^4 - 0.00485t^3 + 0.1395t^2 - 1.135t + 15.75$$

Use a graphing calculator to graph both models (Use 0 to 50 for the domain and 0 to 20 for the range.). Find the x-coordinate of any points of intersection. Then interpret your results in the context of this situation.

12. Match the roots with their equation.

A. 1 ________ $x^4 + x^3 + 2x^2 + 4x - 8 = 0$

B. -2 ________ $x^4 - 5x^2 + 4 = 0$

C. 2

D. -1

E. $2i$

F. $-2i$

H.O.T. Focus on Higher Order Thinking

13. **Draw Conclusions** Find all of the roots of $x^6 - 5x^4 - 125x^2 + 15{,}625 = 0$. (Hint: Rearrange the terms with a sum of cubes followed by the two other terms.)

14. **Explain the Error** A student is asked to write the polynomial function with least degree and a leading coefficient of 1 that has the zeros $1 + i$, $1 - i$, $\sqrt{2}$, and -3. The student uses these zeros to find the corresponding factors, and multiplies them together to obtain $p(x) = x^4 + (1 - \sqrt{2})x^3 - (4 + \sqrt{2})x^2 + (6 + 4\sqrt{2})x - 6\sqrt{2}$. What error did the student make? What is the correct function?

15. **Critical Thinking** What is the least degree of a polynomial equation that has $3i$ as a root with a multiplicity of 3, and $2 - \sqrt{3}$ as a root with multiplicity 2? Explain.

Lesson Performance Task

In 1984 the MPAA introduced the PG-13 rating to their movie rating system. Recently, scientists measured the incidences of a specific type of violence depicted in movies. The researchers used specially trained coders to identify the specific type of violence in one half of the top grossing movies for each year since 1985. The trend in the average rate per hour of 5-minute segments of this type of violence in movies rated G/PG, PG-13, and R can be modeled as a function of time by the following equations:

$$V_{G/PG}(t) = -0.015t + 1.45$$

$$V_{PG\text{-}13}(t) = 0.000577t^3 - 0.0225t^2 + 0.26t + 0.8$$

$$V_R(t) = 2.15$$

V is the average rate per hour of 5-minute segments containing the specific type of violence in movies, and t is the number of years since 1985.

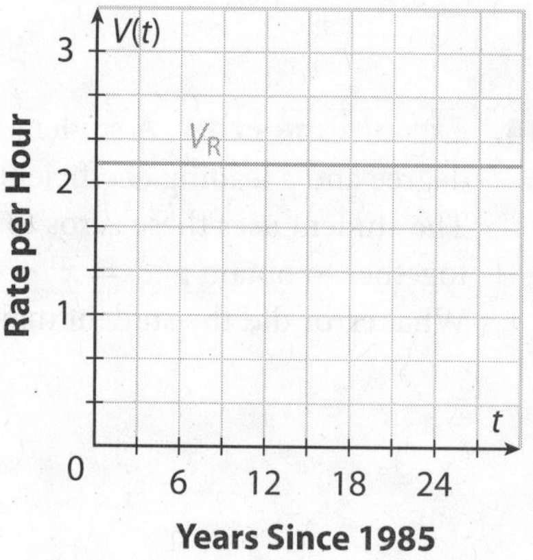

a. Interestingly, in 1985 or $t = 0$, $V_{G/PG}(0) > V_{PG\text{-}13}(0)$. Can you think of any reasons why this would be true?

b. What do the equations indicate about the relationship between $V_{G/PG}(t)$ and $V_{PG\text{-}13}(t)$ as t increases?

c. Graph the models for $V_{G/PG}(t)$ and $V_{PG\text{-}13}(t)$ and find the year in which $V_{PG\text{-}13}(t)$ will be greater than $V_{G/PG}(t)$.

STUDY GUIDE REVIEW

Polynomial Equations

MODULE 7

Essential Question: How can you use polynomial equations to solve real-world problems?

Key Vocabulary

root *(raíz)*

multiplicity *(multiplicidad)*

KEY EXAMPLE (Lesson 7.1)

Find the rational zeros of $f(x) = x^3 + 6x^2 + 11x + 6$; then write the function as a product of factors.

Factors of 6: $\pm1, \pm2, \pm3, \pm6$

Use the Rational Zero Theorem.

$\frac{m}{n}$	1	6	11	6
1	1	7	18	24
2	1	8	27	60
3	1	9	38	120
6	1	12	83	504
−1	1	5	6	0

Test the roots in a synthetic division table.

$(x + 1)(x^2 + 5x + 6)$

Factor the trinomial.

$(x + 1)(x + 2)(x + 3)$

$x = -1, x = -2, x = -3$

KEY EXAMPLE (Lesson 7.2)

Find all the zeros of $m(x) = 2x^4 - 4x^3 + 8x^2 - 16x$.

$2x^4 - 4x^3 - 8x^2 - 16x$

$2x(x^3 - 2x^2 - 4x + 8)$ Factor out the GCF.

$2x((x^3 - 2x^2) - (4x - 8))$ Group the terms.

$2x(x^2(x - 2) - 4(x - 2))$ Factor out common monomials.

$2x(x^2 - 4)(x - 2)$ Factor out the common binomial.

$2x(x + 2)(x - 2)(x - 2)$ Difference of two squares

So, the zeros of $m(x)$ are 0, −2, 2 (mult. 2).

EXERCISES

Rewrite the function as a product of factors, and state all of the zeros.
(Lessons 7.1, 7.2)

1. $r(x) = x^3 + 13x^2 + 48x + 36$

2. $m(x) = 3x^4 - 3x^2$

3. $n(x) = x^3 + 5x^2 - 8x - 12$

4. $p(x) = x^3 - 8$

5. $b(x) = x^4 - 81$

6. $t(x) = 15x^3 + 27x^2 - 6x$

7. Give an example of a fourth-degree polynomial function with all real zeros. Explain how you got your function. *(Lesson 7.1)*

MODULE PERFORMANCE TASK

What Do Polynomials Have to Do With Endangered Species?

A biologist has been studying a particular species of frog in an area for many years and has compiled population data. She used the data to create a model of the population, given here, where x is the years since 2000.

$$P(x) = -x^4 + 27x^3 - 198x^2 + 372x + 1768$$

Describe the trends for the population, and explain what the model predicts for the future population of this species of frog.

Use your own paper to complete the task. Be sure to write down all your data and assumptions. Then use graphs, numbers, words, or algebra to explain how you reached your conclusions.

Ready to Go On?

7.1–7.2 Polynomial Equations

Personal Math Trainer
- Online Homework
- Hints and Help
- Extra Practice

Write the function as a product of factors. *(Lesson 7.1)*

1. $f(x) = 7x^3 - 14x^2 - x + 2$

2. $g(x) = 3x^2 + 2x - 8$

3. $h(x) = 4x^2 - 25$

4. $t(x) = 8x^3 - 512$

List the zeros. *(Lessons 7.1, 7.2)*

5. $m(x) = x^4 + 3x^2 - 18$

6. $r(x) = x^3 + 3x^2 - x - 3$

7. $q(x) = x^3 - 1$

8. $p(x) = 9x^2 - 100$

ESSENTIAL QUESTION

9. Give an example of how factoring polynomials might be used in geometry. *(Lesson 7.1)*

MODULE 7
MIXED REVIEW

Assessment Readiness

1. Look at each equation. Does the polynomial function have all real zeros? Select Yes or No for A–C?

A. $f(x) = x^4 - 2x^2 - 5$ ○ Yes ○ No

B. $g(x) = x^2 - 9$ ○ Yes ○ No

C. $h(x) = x^4 - 256$ ○ Yes ○ No

2. Consider the polynomial function $m(x) = x^4 - 16x^2$. Choose True or False for each statement.

A. There will be both real and imaginary zeros of this function. ○ True ○ False

B. Factoring the polynomial involves the difference of two squares. ○ True ○ False

C. The zeros of the function are 0 (mult. 2), 4, −4. ○ True ○ False

3. Explain why some polynomial functions with real coefficients have non-real zeros.

4. By analyzing a quickly growing oil town, an analyst states that the predicted population P of the town t years from now can be modeled by the function $P(t) = 5t^3 - 2t^2 + 15{,}000$. If we assume the function is true, in approximately how many years will the town have a population of 225,000? How did you get your answer?

Assessment Readiness

Personal Math Trainer
- Online Homework
- Hints and Help
- Extra Practice

1. Identify the transformations of the graph of $f(x) = x^3$ that produce the graph of the function $g(x) = -2(x - 5)^3$. Select True or False for each statement.

A. When compared with f(x), the graph of $g(x)$ is vertically compressed by a factor of $\frac{1}{2}$. ○ True ○ False

B. When compared with f(x), the graph of $g(x)$ is translated 5 units to the right. ○ True ○ False

C. When compared with f(x), the graph of $g(x)$ is reflected across the x-axis. ○ True ○ False

2. Consider the polynomial $3x^3 + 9x^2 - 12x$. Select True or False for each statement.

A. $3x$ can be factored out of every term. ○ True ○ False

B. The polynomial cannot be factored as it is written. ○ True ○ False

C. The completely factored polynomial is $3x(x - 1)(x + 4)$. ○ True ○ False

3. Consider the polynomial operation $3x(x - 2)(5x + 2)$. Is the expression equivalent? Select Yes or No for A–D

A. $(3x^2 - 6x)(5x + 2)$ ○ Yes ○ No

B. $3x(5x^2 - 8x - 4)$ ○ Yes ○ No

C. $15x^3 - 24x^2 - 12x$ ○ Yes ○ No

D. $3x(5x^2 - 5x - 2)$ ○ Yes ○ No

4. Consider the polynomial function $g(x) = 3x^3 + 6x^2 - 9x$. Select True or False for each statement.

A. The polynomial has only real zeros. ○ True ○ False

B. Factoring the polynomial involves a common monomial. ○ True ○ False

C. The zeros of the polynomial are 0, –3, 1, 3. ○ True ○ False

5. Consider the function $m(x) = x^4 - 16$. Are these zeros of the function? Select Yes or No for A–C.

A. $-2i, 2i$ ○ Yes ○ No

B. $2 \pm 2i$ ○ Yes ○ No

C. $-2, 2$ ○ Yes ○ No

6. Use a graphing calculator to graph the function $f(x) = -x(x + 1)(x - 4)^2$, and then use the graph to determine the number of turning points and global maximums and minimums, and local maximums and minimums that are not global.

7. Ms. Flores grows tomatoes on her farm. The price per pound of tomatoes can be modeled by $P(x) = 20x + 4$. If the total income that she wants to earn from tomatoes for one year can be modeled by $I(x) = 60x^3 - 8x^2 + 136x + 28$, write a polynomial that can be used to model the pounds of tomatoes Ms. Flores needs to grow in one year. Explain your answer.

8. During a discussion in class, Hannah stated that she liked the quadratic formula more than completing the square and factoring, because it works on every quadratic equation. The teacher then proposed the equation $-3x(x + 7) = 14$. Explain how Hannah can adjust this equation so she can use the quadratic formula to solve it.

Performance Tasks

★ 9. A bottom for a box can be made by cutting congruent squares from each of the four corners of a piece of cardboard. The volume of a box made from an 8.5-by-11-inch piece of cardboard would be represented by $V(x) = x(11 - 2x)(8.5 - 2x)$, where x is the side length of one square.

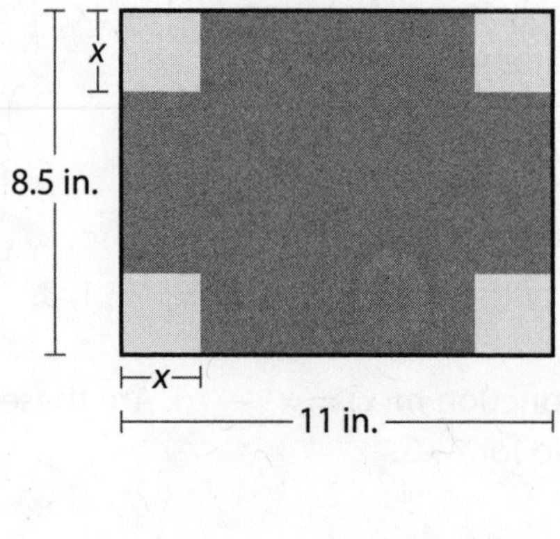

A. Express the volume as a sum of monomials.

B. Find the volume when $x = 1$ inch.

★★10. The volume of several planets in cubic kilometers can be modeled by $v(d) = \frac{1}{6}\pi d^3$, where d is the diameter of the planet in kilometers. The mass of each planet in kilograms in terms of diameter d can be modeled by $M(d) = (3.96 \times 10^{12})d^3 - (6.50 \times 10^{17})d^2 + (2.56 \times 10^{22})d - 5.56 \times 10^{25}$.

A. The density of a planet in kilograms per cubic kilometer can be found by dividing the planet's mass by its volume. Use polynomial division to find a model for the density of a planet in terms of its diameter.

B. Use the model to estimate the density of Jupiter, with diameter $d = 142{,}984$ km.

★★★11. The profit of a small business (in thousands of dollars) since it was founded can be modeled by the polynomial $f(t) = -t^4 + 44t^3 - 612t^2 + 2592t$, where t represents the number of years since 1980.

A. Factor $f(t)$ completely.

B. What was the company's profit in 1985?

C. Find and interpret $f(15)$.

D. What can you say about the company's long-term prospects?

MATH IN CAREERS

Statistician According to data from the U.S. Census Bureau, the total number of people in the United States labor force can be approximated by the function $T(x) = -0.011x^2 + 2x + 107$, where x is the number of years since 1980 and $T(x)$ is the number of workers in millions. The number of women in the United States labor force can be approximated by the function $W(x) = -0.012x^2 + 1.26x + 45.5$.

a. Use the function $T(x)$ to estimate the number of workers in millions in 2010.

b. Write a polynomial function $M(x)$ that models the number of men in the labor force, and explain how you found your function.

c. Use the function found in part *b* to estimate the number of male workers in millions in 2010.

d. Explain how you could have found the answer to part *c* without using the function $M(x)$.

UNIT 4

Rational Functions, Expressions, and Equations

MODULE 8

Rational Functions

MODULE 9

Rational Expressions and Equations

MATH IN CAREERS

Chemist Chemists study the properties and composition of substances. They use the mathematics of ratios and proportions to determine the atomic composition of materials and the quantities of atoms needed to synthesize materials. They use geometry to understand the physical structures of chemical compounds. Chemists also use mathematical models to understand and predict behavior of chemical interactions, including reaction rates and activation energies.

If you are interested in a career as a chemist, you should study these mathematical subjects:

- Geometry
- Algebra
- Calculus
- Differential Equations
- Statistics

Research other careers that require using mathematical models to predict behavior. Check out the career activity at the end of the unit to find out how **Chemists** use math.

Reading Start-Up

Visualize Vocabulary

Use the ✓ words to complete the chart.

	the set of output values of a function or relation
	a linear relationship between two variables, x and y, that can be written in the form $y = kx$, where k is a nonzero constant
	the multiplicative inverse of a number
	the simplest function with the defining characteristics of the function family
	the set of all possible input values of a relation or function
	an algebraic expression whose numerator and denominator are polynomials

Vocabulary

Review Words

✔ direct variation (*variación directa*)
✔ domain (*dominio*)
✔ parent function (*función madre*)
✔ range (*rango*)
✔ rational expression (*expresión racional*)
✔ reciprocal (*recíproco*)

Preview Words

asymptote (*asíntota*)
closure (*cerradura*)
rational function (*función racional*)

Understand Vocabulary

To become familiar with some of the vocabulary terms in the module, consider the following. You may refer to the module, the glossary, or a dictionary.

1. A line that a graph approaches as the value of the variable becomes extremely large or small is a/an ___________.

2. A function whose rule can be written as a rational expression is a/an _________________.

Active Reading

Double-Door Fold Before beginning each lesson, create a double-door fold to compare the characteristics of two expressions, functions, or variations. This can help you identify the similarities and differences between the topics.

Rational Functions

MODULE 8

Essential Question: How can you use rational functions to solve real-world problems?

REAL WORLD VIDEO
As a consumer, you may shop around for the best deal on a new bike helmet. Check out the video to see how sporting goods manufacturers can use rational functions to help set pricing and sales goals.

MODULE PERFORMANCE TASK PREVIEW

What Is the Profit?

Like any business, a manufacturer of bike helmets must pay attention to ways to minimize costs and maximize profit. Businesses use mathematical functions to calculate and predict various quantities, including profits, costs, and revenue. What are some of the ways a business can use a profit function? Let's find out!

Are YOU Ready?

Complete these exercises to review skills you will need for this module.

Personal Math Trainer
- Online Homework
- Hints and Help
- Extra Practice

Graphing Linear Nonproportional Relationships

Example 1

Graph $y = -\frac{1}{2}x - 3$

Plot the y-intercept $(0, -3)$

The slope is $-\frac{1}{2}$, so from $(0, -3)$, plot the next point up 1 and left 2.

Draw a line through the two points.

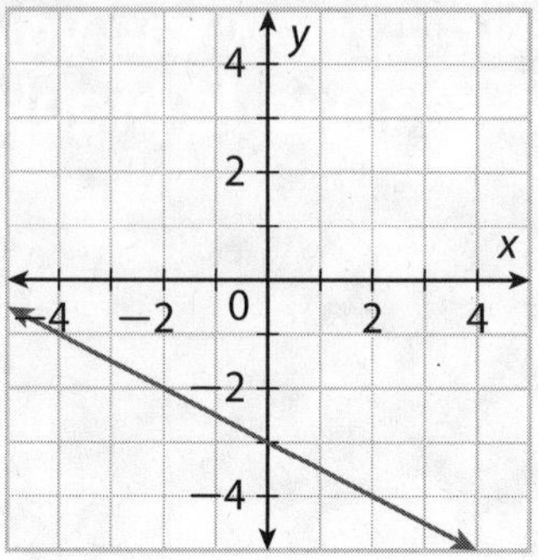

Graph each relationship.

1. $y = 3x - 4$

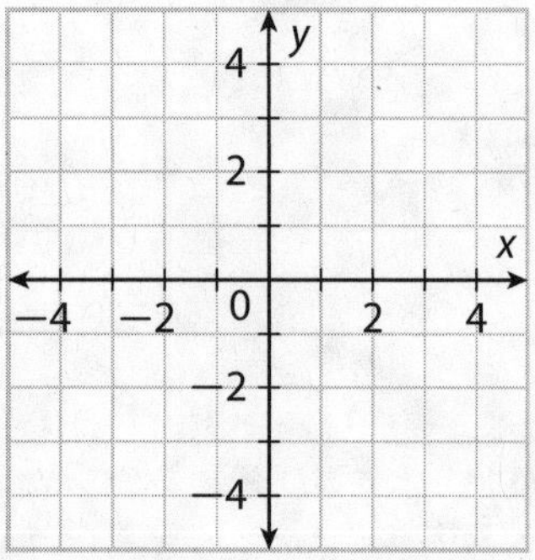

2. $y = -\frac{3}{4}x + 1$

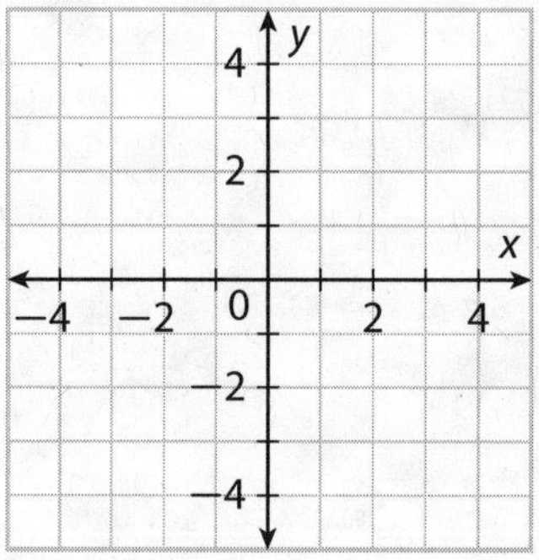

Direct Variation

Example 2

The graph of a direct variation function passes through $(1, 10)$. Write the equation for the function.

$k = \frac{y}{x} = \frac{10}{1} = 10$, so the equation is $y = 10x$.

Write a direct variation equation for the graph that passes through the point.

3. (2, 5) ________ **4.** (3, 6) ________ **5.** (4, 1) ________

6. (8, 1) ________ **7.** (5, 100) ________ **8.** (2, 6) ________

Name ______________________ Class ______________ Date ________

8.1 Graphing Simple Rational Functions

Resource Locker

Essential Question: How are the graphs of $f(x) = a\left(\frac{1}{x-h}\right) + k$ and $f(x) = \frac{1}{\frac{1}{b}(x-h)} + k$ related to the graph of $f(x) = \frac{1}{x}$?

Explore 1 Graphing and Analyzing $f(x) = \frac{1}{x}$

A **rational function** is a function of the form $f(x) = \frac{p(x)}{q(x)}$ where $p(x)$ and $q(x)$ are polynomials. The most basic rational function with a variable expression in the denominator is $f(x) = \frac{1}{x}$.

(A) State the domain of $f(x) = \frac{1}{x}$.

The function accepts all real numbers except ____, because division by ____ is undefined. So, the function's domain is as follows:

- As an inequality: $x <$ ☐ or $x >$ ☐
- In set notation: $\{x \mid x \neq$ ☐ $\}$
- In interval notation (where the symbol ∪ means *union*):

$(-\infty,$ ☐ $) \cup ($ ☐ $, +\infty)$

(B) Determine the end behavior of $f(x) = \frac{1}{x}$.

First, complete the tables.

x Increases without Bound	
x	$f(x) = \frac{1}{x}$
100	
1000	
10,000	

x Decreases without Bound	
x	$f(x) = \frac{1}{x}$
−100	
−1000	
−10,000	

Next, summarize the results.

- As $x \to +\infty$, $f(x) \to$ ☐.
- As $x \to -\infty$, $f(x) \to$ ☐.

(C) Be more precise about the end behavior of $f(x) = \frac{1}{x}$, and determine what this means for the graph of the function.

You can be more precise about the end behavior by using the notation $f(x) \to 0^+$, which means that the value of $f(x)$ approaches 0 from the positive direction (that is, the value of $f(x)$ is positive as it approaches 0), and the notation $f(x) \to 0^-$, which means that the value of $f(x)$ approaches 0 from the negative direction. So, the end behavior of the function is more precisely summarized as follows:

- As $x \to +\infty$, $f(x) \to$ ____.
- As $x \to -\infty$, $f(x) \to$ ____.

The end behavior indicates that the graph of $f(x)$ approaches, but does not cross, the [x-axis/y-axis], so that axis is an asymptote for the graph.

(D) Examine the behavior of $f(x) = \frac{1}{x}$ near $x = 0$, and determine what this means for the graph of the function.

First, complete the tables.

x Approaches 0 from the Positive Direction	
x	$f(x) = \frac{1}{x}$
0.01	
0.001	
0.0001	

x Approaches 0 from the Negative Direction	
x	$f(x) = \frac{1}{x}$
−0.01	
−0.001	
−0.0001	

Next, summarize the results.

- As $x \to 0^+$, $f(x) \to$ ____.
- As $x \to 0^-$, $f(x) \to$ ____.

The behavior of $f(x) = \frac{1}{x}$ near $x = 0$ indicates that the graph of $f(x)$ approaches, but does not cross, the [x-axis/y-axis], so that axis is also an asymptote for the graph.

(E) Graph $f(x) = \frac{1}{x}$.

First, determine the sign of $f(x)$ on the two parts of its domain.

- When x is a negative number, $f(x)$ is a [positive/negative] number.
- When x is a positive number, $f(x)$ is a [positive/negative] number.

Next, complete the tables.

Negative Values of *x*	
x	$f(x) = \frac{1}{x}$
−2	
−1	
−0.5	

Positive Values of *x*	
x	$f(x) = \frac{1}{x}$
0.5	
1	
2	

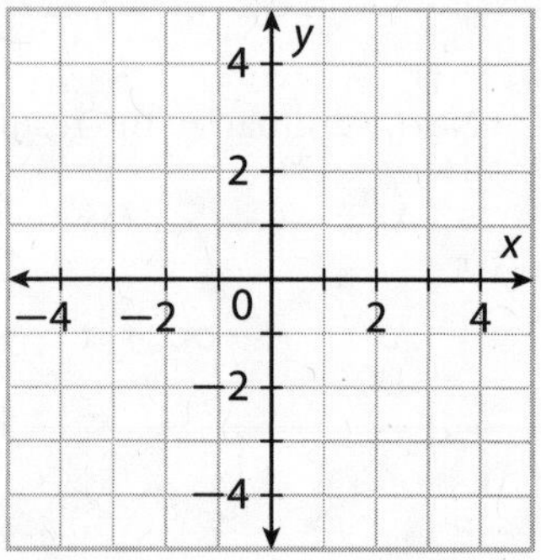

Finally, use the information from this step and all previous steps to draw the graph. Draw asymptotes as dashed lines.

(F) State the range of $f(x) = \frac{1}{x}$.

The function takes on all real numbers except ______, so the function's range is as follows:

- As an inequality: $y <$ ☐ or $y >$ ☐
- In set notation: $\{y \mid y \neq$ ☐ $\}$
- In interval notation (where the symbol ∪ means *union*): $(-\infty,$ ☐ $) \cup ($ ☐ $, +\infty)$

(G) Identify the intervals where the function is increasing and where it is decreasing.

(H) Determine whether $f(x) = \frac{1}{x}$ is an even function, an odd function, or neither.

Reflect

1. How does the graph of $f(x) = \frac{1}{x}$ show that the function has no zeros?

2. **Discussion** A graph is said to be *symmetric about the origin* (and the origin is called the graph's *point of symmetry*) if for every point (x, y) on the graph, the point $(-x, -y)$ is also on the graph. Is the graph of $f(x) = \frac{1}{x}$ symmetric about the origin? Explain.

3. What line is a line of symmetry for the graph of $f(x) = \frac{1}{x}$?

Explain 1 Graphing Simple Rational Functions

When graphing transformations of $f(x) = \frac{1}{x}$, it helps to consider the effect of the transformations on the following features of the graph of $f(x)$: the vertical asymptote, $x = 0$; the horizontal asymptote, $y = 0$; and two reference points, $(-1, -1)$ and $(1, 1)$. The table lists these features of the graph of $f(x)$ and the corresponding features of the graph of $g(x) = a\left(\frac{1}{\frac{1}{b}(x-h)}\right) + k$. Note that the asymptotes are affected only by the parameters h and k, while the reference points are affected by all four parameters.

Feature	$f(x) = \frac{1}{x}$	$g(x) = a\left(\frac{1}{\frac{1}{b}(x-h)}\right) + k$
Vertical asymptote	$x = 0$	$x = h$
Horizontal asymptote	$y = 0$	$y = k$
Reference point	$(-1, -1)$	$(-b + h, -a + k)$
Reference point	$(1, 1)$	$(b + h, a + k)$

Example 1 **Identify the transformations of the graph of $f(x) = \frac{1}{x}$ that produce the graph of the given function $g(x)$. Then graph $g(x)$ on the same coordinate plane as the graph of $f(x)$ by applying the transformations to the asymptotes $x = 0$ and $y = 0$ to the reference points $(-1, -1)$ and $(1, 1)$. Also state the domain and range of $g(x)$ using inequalities, set notation, and interval notation.**

(A) $g(x) = 3\left(\frac{1}{x-1}\right) + 2$

The transformations of the graph of $f(x)$ that produce the graph of $g(x)$ are:

- a vertical stretch by a factor of 3
- a translation of 1 unit to the right and 2 units up

Note that the translation of 1 unit to the right affects only the x-coordinates, while the vertical stretch by a factor of 3 and the translation of 2 units up affect only the y-coordinates.

Feature	$f(x) = \frac{1}{x}$	$g(x) = 3\left(\frac{1}{x-1}\right) + 2$
Vertical asymptote	$x = 0$	$x = 1$
Horizontal asymptote	$y = 0$	$y = 2$
Reference point	$(-1, -1)$	$(-1 + 1, 3(-1) + 2) = (0, -1)$
Reference point	$(1, 1)$	$(1 + 1, 3(1) + 2) = (2, 5)$

Domain of $g(x)$:

Inequality: $x < 1$ or $x > 1$

Set notation: $\{x \mid x \neq 1\}$

Interval notation: $(-\infty, 1) \cup (1, +\infty)$

Range of $g(x)$:

Inequality: $y < 2$ or $y > 2$

Set notation: $\{y \mid y \neq 2\}$

Interval notation: $(-\infty, 2) \cup (2, +\infty)$

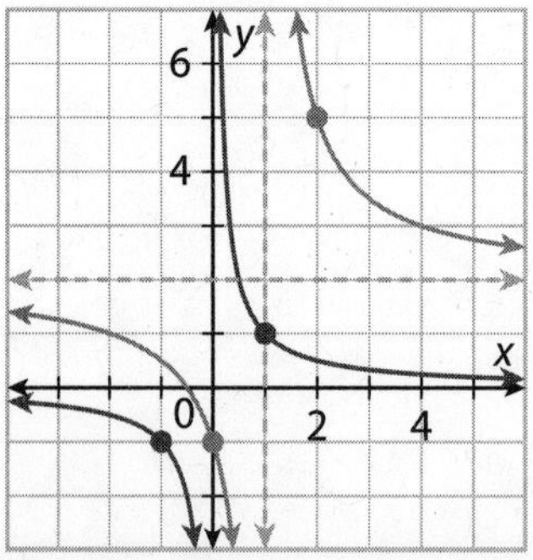

(B) $g(x) = \frac{1}{2(x+3)} - 1$

The transformations of the graph of $f(x)$ that produce the graph of $g(x)$ are:

- a horizontal compression by a factor of $\frac{1}{2}$
- a translation of 3 units to the left and 1 unit down

Note that the horizontal compression by a factor of $\frac{1}{2}$ and the translation of 3 units to the left affect only the x-coordinates of points on the graph of $f(x)$, while the translation of 1 unit down affects only the y-coordinates.

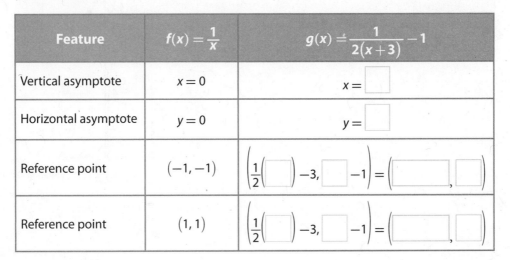

Feature	$f(x) = \frac{1}{x}$	$g(x) = \frac{1}{2(x+3)} - 1$
Vertical asymptote	$x = 0$	$x = \square$
Horizontal asymptote	$y = 0$	$y = \square$
Reference point	$(-1, -1)$	$\left(\frac{1}{2}(\square) - 3, \square - 1\right) = (\square, \square)$
Reference point	$(1, 1)$	$\left(\frac{1}{2}(\square) - 3, \square - 1\right) = (\square, \square)$

Domain of $g(x)$:

Inequality: $x < \square$ or $x > \square$

Set notation: $\{x \mid x \neq \square\}$

Interval notation: $(-\infty, \square) \cup (\square, +\infty)$

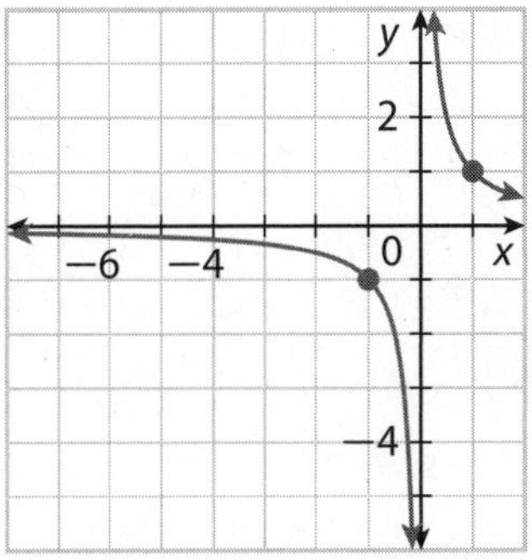

Range of $g(x)$:

Inequality: $y < \square$ or $y > \square$

Set notation: $\{y \mid y \neq \square\}$

Interval notation: $(-\infty, \square) \cup (\square, +\infty)$

Your Turn

Identify the transformations of the graph of $f(x) = \frac{1}{x}$ that produce the graph of the given function $g(x)$. Then graph $g(x)$ on the same coordinate plane as the graph of $f(x)$ by applying the transformations to the asymptotes $x = 0$ and $y = 0$ to the reference points $(-1, -1)$ and $(1, 1)$. Also state the domain and range of $g(x)$ using inequalities, set notation, and interval notation.

4. $g(x) = -0.5\left(\frac{1}{x+1}\right) - 3$

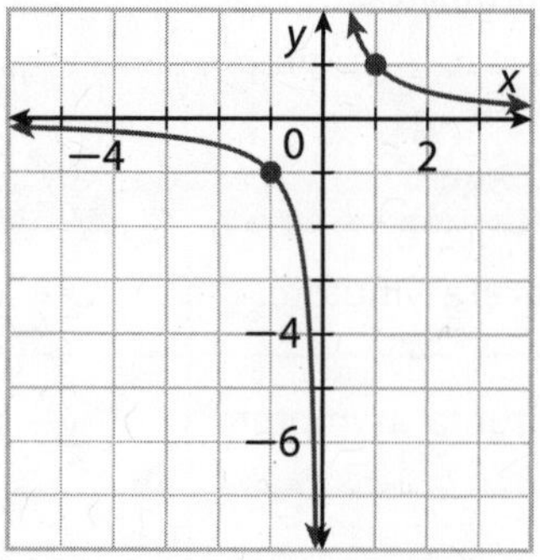

5. $g(x) = \frac{1}{-0.5(x-2)} + 1$

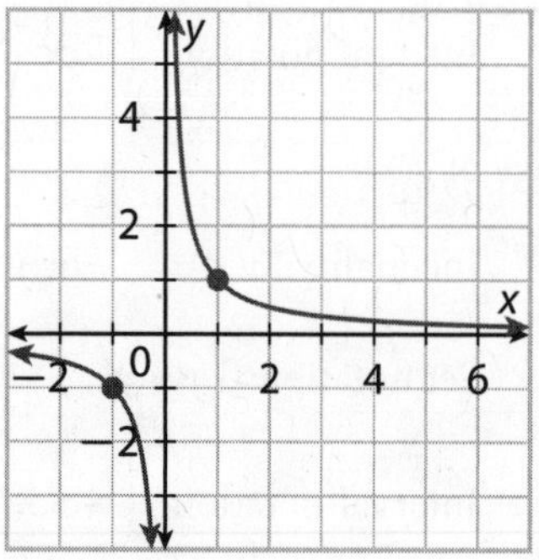

Explain 2 Rewriting Simple Rational Functions in Order to Graph Them

When given a rational function of the form $g(x) = \frac{mx+n}{px+q}$, where $m \neq 0$ and $p \neq 0$, you can carry out the division of the numerator by the denominator to write the function in the form $g(x) = a\left(\frac{1}{x-h}\right) + k$ or $g(x) = \frac{1}{\frac{1}{b}(x-h)} + k$ in order to graph it.

Example 2 **Rewrite the function in the form $g(x) = a\left(\frac{1}{x-h}\right) + k$ or $g(x) = \frac{1}{\frac{1}{b}(x-h)} + k$ and graph it. Also state the domain and range using inequalities, set notation, and interval notation.**

(A) $g(x) = \frac{3x-4}{x-1}$

Use long division.

$$\begin{array}{r} 3 \\ x-1\overline{)\,3x-4} \\ \underline{3x-3} \\ -1 \end{array}$$

So, the quotient is 3, and the remainder is -1. Using the fact that *dividend* = *quotient* + $\frac{\textit{remainder}}{\textit{divisor}}$, you have $g(x) = 3 + \frac{-1}{x-1}$, or $g(x) = -\frac{1}{x-1} + 3$.

The graph of $g(x)$ has vertical asymptote $x = 1$, horizontal asymptote $y = 3$, and reference points $\left(-1+1, -(-1)+3\right) = (0, 4)$ and $(1+1, -(1)+3) = (2, 2)$.

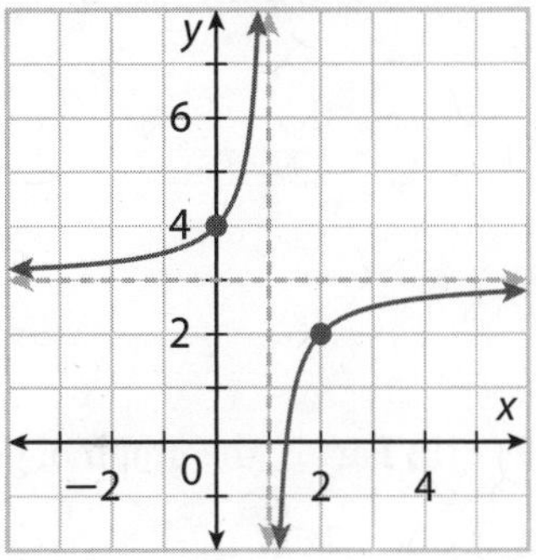

Domain of $g(x)$:

Inequality: $x < 1$ or $x > 1$

Set notation: $\{x \mid x \neq 1\}$

Interval notation: $(-\infty, 1) \cup (1, +\infty)$

Range of $g(x)$:

Inequality: $y < 3$ or $y > 3$

Set notation: $\{y \mid y \neq 3\}$

Interval notation: $(-\infty, 3) \cup (3, +\infty)$

(B) $g(x) = \frac{4x-7}{-2x+4}$

Use long division.

$$\begin{array}{r} -2 \\ -2x+4\overline{)\,4x-7} \\ \underline{4x-8} \\ \square \end{array}$$

So, the quotient is -2, and the remainder is ______. Using the fact that *dividend* = *quotient* + $\frac{\textit{remainder}}{\textit{divisor}}$, you have

$g(x) = -2 + \frac{\square}{-2x+4}$, or $g(x) = \frac{\square}{-2\left(x - \square\right)} - 2$.

The graph of $g(x)$ has vertical asymptote $x = \square$, horizontal asymptote $y = -2$, and reference points

$\left(-\frac{1}{2}(-1) + \square, -1 - 2\right) = \left(\square, -3\right)$ and $\left(-\frac{1}{2}(1) + \square, 1 - 2\right) = \left(\square, -1\right)$.

Domain of $g(x)$:

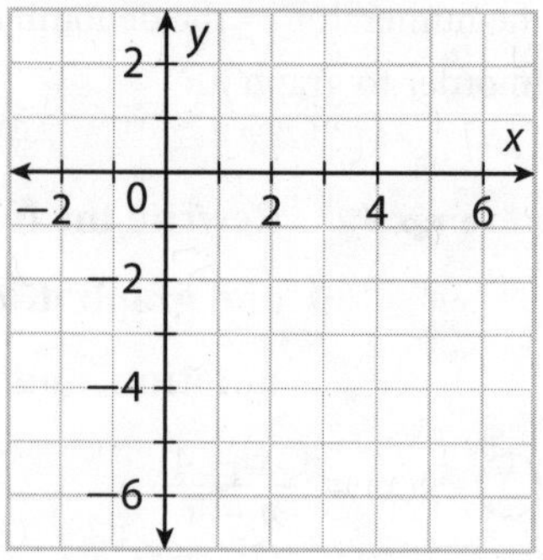

Inequality: $x < \square$ or $x > \square$

Set notation: $\{x \mid x \neq \square\}$

Interval notation: $(-\infty, \square) \cup (\square, +\infty)$

Range of $g(x)$:

Inequality: $y < \square$ or $y > \square$

Set notation: $\{y \mid y \neq \square\}$

Interval notation: $(-\infty, \square) \cup (\square, +\infty)$

6. In Part A, the graph of $g(x)$ is the result of what transformations of the graph of $f(x) = \frac{1}{x}$?

____

____

____

____

7. In Part B, the graph of $g(x)$ is the result of what transformations of the graph of $f(x) = \frac{1}{x}$?

____

____

____

____

Your Turn

Rewrite the function in the form $g(x) = a\left(\frac{1}{x-h}\right) + k$ or $g(x) = \frac{1}{\frac{1}{b}(x-h)} + k$ and graph it. Also state the domain and range using inequalities, set notation, and interval notation.

8. $g(x) = \dfrac{3x + 8}{x + 2}$

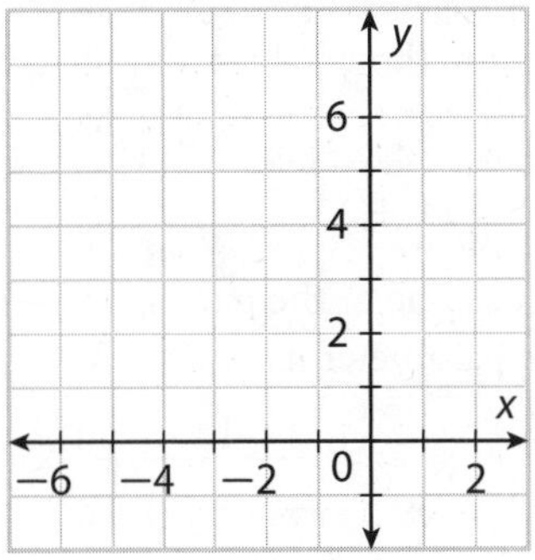

Explain 3 Writing Simple Rational Functions

When given the graph of a simple rational function, you can write its equation using one of the general forms $g(x) = a\left(\frac{1}{x-h}\right) + k$ and $g(x) = \frac{1}{\frac{1}{b}(x-h)} + k$ after identifying the values of the parameters using information obtained from the graph.

Example 3

Ⓐ **Write the function whose graph is shown. Use the form $g(x) = a\left(\frac{1}{x-h}\right) + k$.**

Since the graph's vertical asymptote is $x = 3$, the value of the parameter h is 3. Since the graph's horizontal asymptote is $y = 4$, the value of the parameter k is 4.

Substitute these values into the general form of the function.

$$g(x) = a\left(\frac{1}{x-3}\right) + 4$$

Now use one of the points, such as $(4, 6)$, to find the value of the parameter a.

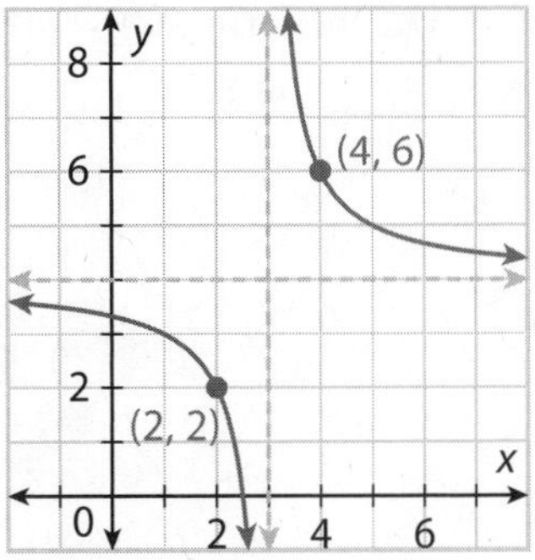

$$g(x) = a\left(\frac{1}{x-3}\right) + 4$$

$$6 = a\left(\frac{1}{4-3}\right) + 4$$

$$6 = a + 4$$

$$2 = a$$

So, $g(x) = 2\left(\frac{1}{x-3}\right) + 4$.

Ⓑ **Write the function whose graph is shown. Use the form $g(x) = \frac{1}{\frac{1}{b}(x-h)} + k$.**

Since the graph's vertical asymptote is $x = -3$, the value of the parameter h is -3. Since the graph's horizontal asymptote is $y = \square$, the value of the parameter k is ____.

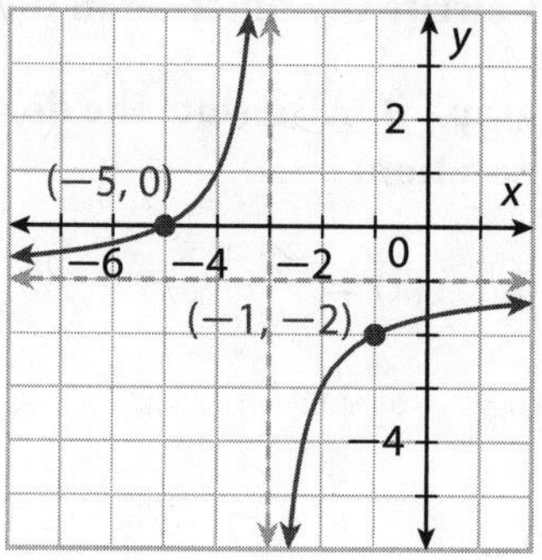

Substitute these values into the general form of the function.

$$g(x) = \frac{1}{\frac{1}{b}(x+3)} + \square$$

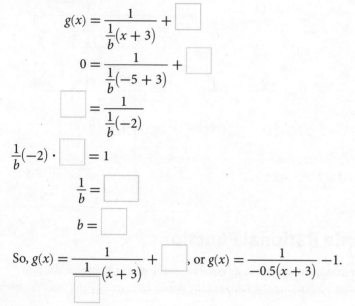

Now use one of the points, such as $(-5, 0)$, to find the value of the parameter a.

$$g(x) = \frac{1}{\frac{1}{b}(x+3)} + \square$$

$$0 = \frac{1}{\frac{1}{b}(-5+3)} + \square$$

$$\square = \frac{1}{\frac{1}{b}(-2)}$$

$$\frac{1}{b}(-2) \cdot \square = 1$$

$$\frac{1}{b} = \square$$

$$b = \square$$

So, $g(x) = \frac{1}{\frac{1}{\square}(x+3)} + \square$, or $g(x) = \frac{1}{-0.5(x+3)} - 1$.

Reflect

9. Discussion In Parts A and B, the coordinates of a second point on the graph of $g(x)$ are given. In what way can those coordinates be useful?

____

____

Your Turn

10. Write the function whose graph is shown. Use the form $g(x) = a\left(\frac{1}{x-h}\right) + k$.

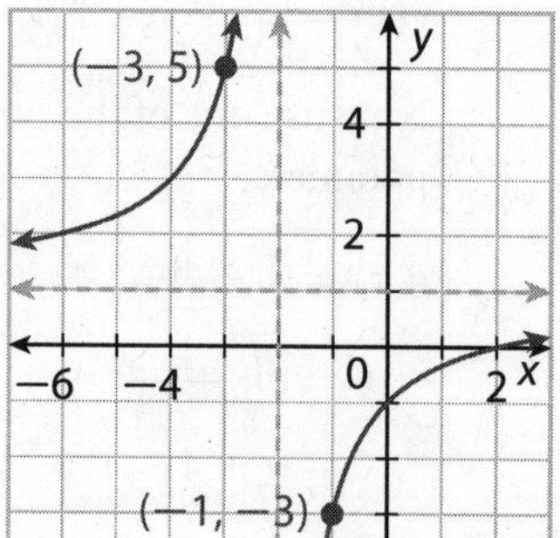

11. Write the function whose graph is shown. Use the form $g(x) = \frac{1}{\frac{1}{b}(x - h)} + k$.

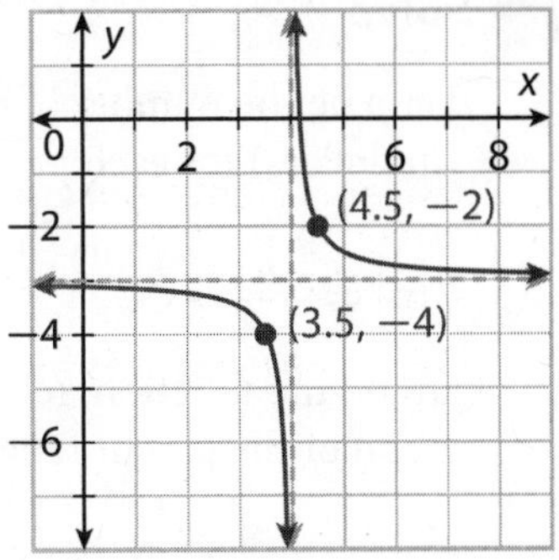

Explain 4 Modeling with Simple Rational Functions

In a real-world situation where there is a shared cost and a per-person or per-item cost, you can model the situation using a rational function that has the general form $f(x) = \frac{a}{x-h} + k$ where $f(x)$ is the total cost for each person or item.

Example 4

(A) **Mary and some of her friends are thinking about renting a car while staying at a beach resort for a vacation. The cost per person for staying at the beach resort is $300, and the cost of the car rental is $220. If the friends agree to share the cost of the car rental, what is the minimum number of people who must go on the trip so that the total cost for each person is no more than $350?**

Analyze Information

Identify the important information.

- The cost per person for the resort is ______.
- The cost of the car rental is ______.
- The most that each person will spend is ______

Formulate a Plan

Create a rational function that gives the total cost for each person. Graph the function, and use the graph to answer the question.

Solve

Let p be the number of people who agree to go on the trip. Let $C(p)$ be the cost (in dollars) for each person.

$$C(p) = \frac{\square}{p} + \square$$

Graph the function, recognizing that the graph involves two transformations of the graph of the parent rational function:

- a vertical stretch by a factor of ______
- a vertical translation of ______ units up

Also draw the line $C(p) = 350$.

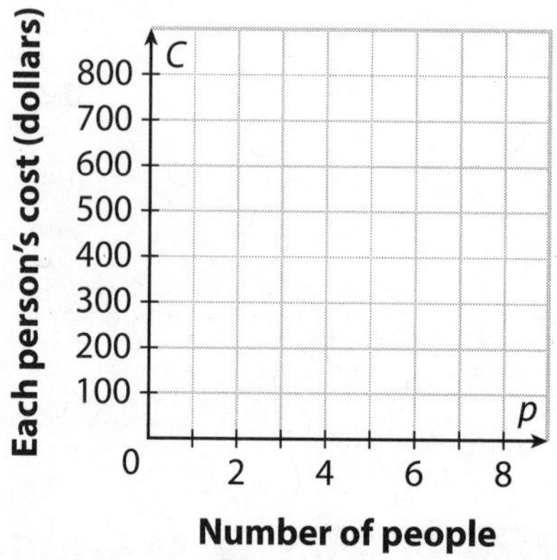

The graphs intersect between $p = \square$ and $p = \square$, so the minimum number of people who must go on the trip in order for the total cost for each person to be no more than $350

is ______.

Justify and Evaluate

Check the solution by evaluating the function $C(p)$. Since $C(4) = \square > 350$ and $C(5) = \square < 350$, the minimum number of people who must go on the trip is ______.

Your Turn

12. Justin has purchased a basic silk screening kit for applying designs to fabric. The kit costs $200. He plans to buy T-shirts for $10 each, apply a design that he creates to them, and then sell them. Model this situation with a rational function that gives the average cost of a silk-screened T-shirt when the cost of the kit is included in the calculation. Use the graph of the function to determine the minimum number of T-shirts that brings the average cost below $17.50.

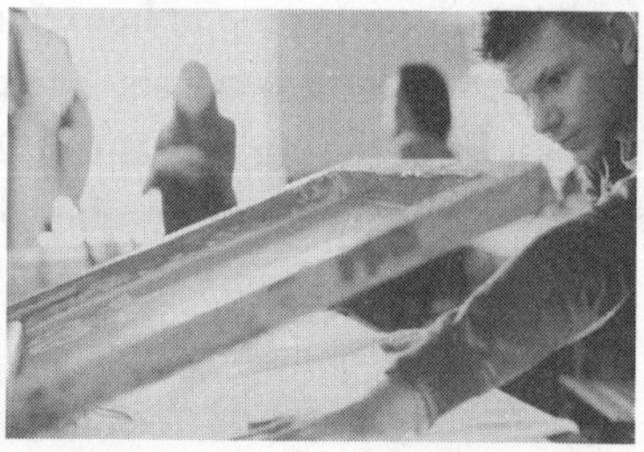

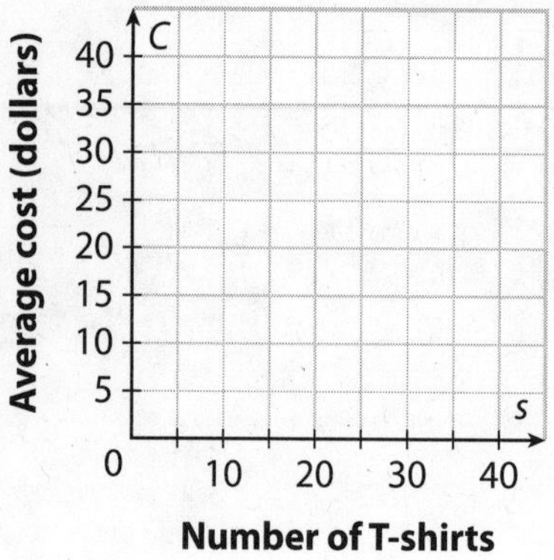

Elaborate

13. Compare and contrast the attributes of $f(x) = \frac{1}{x}$ and the attributes of $g(x) = -\frac{1}{x}$.

14. State the domain and range of $f(x) = a\left(\frac{1}{x-h}\right) + k$ using inequalities, set notation, and interval notation.

15. Given that the model $C(p) = \frac{100}{p} + 50$ represents the total cost C (in dollars) for each person in a group of p people when there is a shared expense and an individual expense, describe what the expressions $\frac{100}{p}$ and 50 represent.

16. Essential Question Check-In Describe the transformations you must perform on the graph of $f(x) = \frac{1}{x}$ to obtain the graph of $f(x) = a\left(\frac{1}{x-h}\right) + k$.

Evaluate: Homework and Practice

Personal Math Trainer

- Online Homework
- Hints and Help
- Extra Practice

Describe how the graph of $g(x)$ is related to the graph of $f(x) = \frac{1}{x}$.

1. $g(x) = \frac{1}{x} + 4$

2. $g(x) = 5\left(\frac{1}{x}\right)$

vertical stretch by 5

3. $g(x) = \frac{1}{x + 3}$

4. $g(x) = \frac{1}{0.1x}$

horizontal stretch by 10

5. $g(x) = \frac{1}{x} - 7$

6. $g(x) = \frac{1}{x - 8}$

horizontal shift to the righ by 8

7. $g(x) = -0.1\left(\frac{1}{x}\right)$

8. $g(x) = \frac{1}{-3x}$

reflection

horizontal stretch by $\frac{1}{3}$

Identify the transformations of the graph of $f(x)$ that produce the graph of the given function $g(x)$. Then graph $g(x)$ on the same coordinate plane as the graph of $f(x)$ by applying the transformations to the asymptotes $x = 0$ and $y = 0$ and to the reference points $(-1, -1)$ and $(1, 1)$. Also state the domain and range of $g(x)$ using inequalities, set notation, and interval notation.

9. $g(x) = 3\left(\frac{1}{x + 1}\right) - 2$

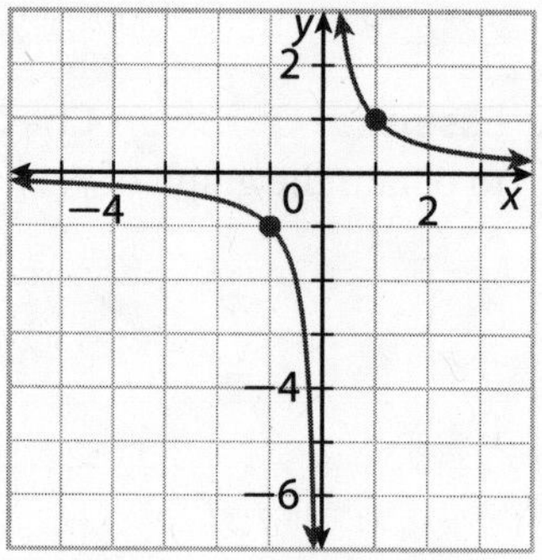

10. $g(x) = \dfrac{1}{-0.5(x-3)} + 1$

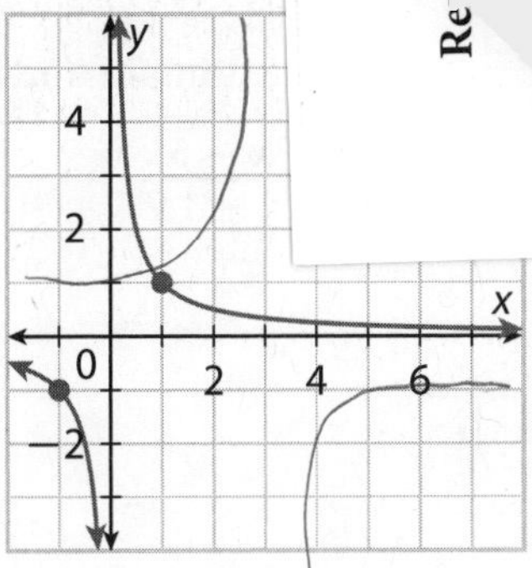

$g(x) = a\left(\frac{1}{x-h}\right) + k$

$g(x) = a\left(\frac{1}{x-3}\right) + 1$

$g(x) = -2\left(\frac{1}{x-3}\right) + 1$

$\frac{1}{\frac{5}{10}}$

$1 \cdot \frac{10}{5}$

3 units right, 1 unit up, reflection, horizontal stretch of 2

D: $(-\infty, 3) \cup (3, \infty)$ R: $(-\infty, 1) \cup (1, \infty)$

11. $g(x) = -0.5\left(\dfrac{1}{x-1}\right) - 2$

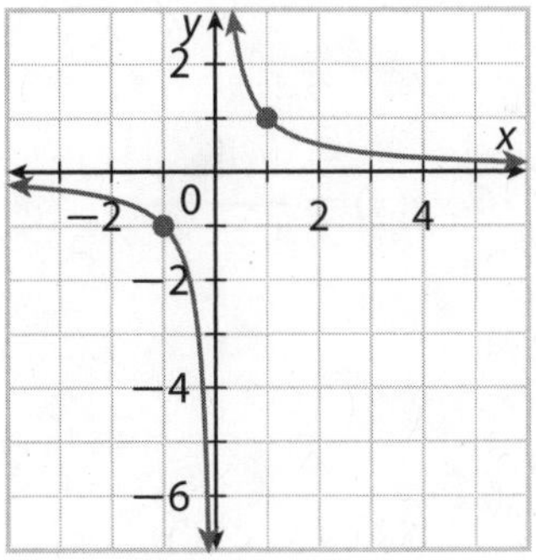

12. $g(x) = \dfrac{1}{2(x+2)} + 3$

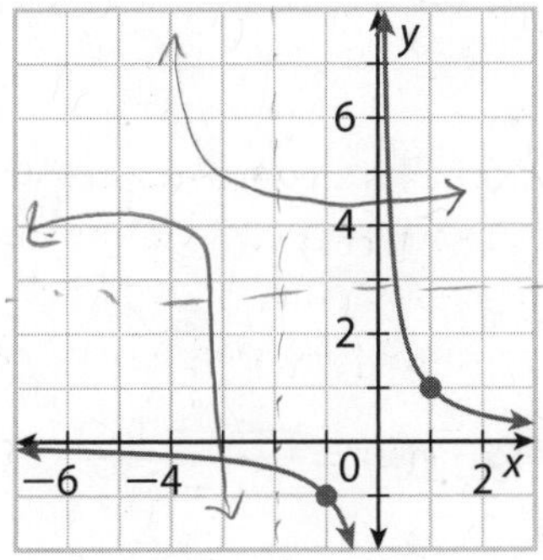

$g(x) = a\left(\frac{1}{x-h}\right) + k$

$g(x) = a\left(\frac{1}{x+2}\right) + 3$

$g(x) = \frac{1}{2}\left(\frac{1}{x+2}\right) + 3$

horizontal stretch by 1/2

vertical shift up 3 units

horizontal shift 2 units right

VA: $x = -2$

HA: $y = 3$

rite the function in the form $g(x) = a\frac{1}{(x-h)} + k$ or $g(x) = \frac{1}{\frac{1}{b}(x-h)} + k$ and graph it. Also state the domain and range using inequalities, set notation, and interval notation.

13. $g(x) = \dfrac{3x-5}{x-1}$

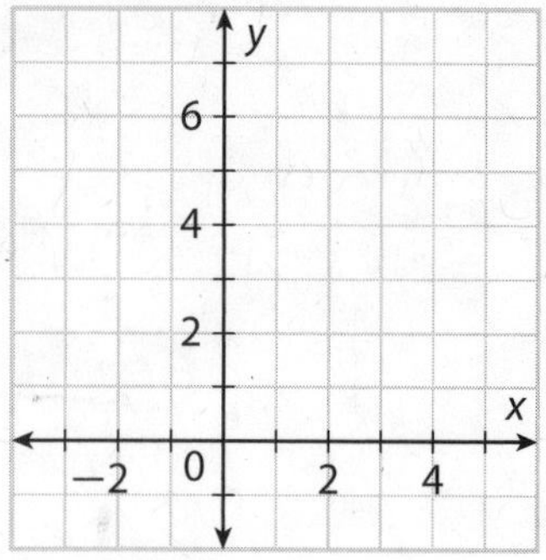

14. $g(x) = \dfrac{x+5}{0.5x+2}$

$g(x) = 2 + \dfrac{1}{0.5x+2}$

$2\left(\dfrac{1}{x+2}\right) + 2$

x	y
−6	1
−5	0
−4	undef
−3	4
−2	3

VA: $0.5x + 2 = 0$

$0.5x = -2$

$x = -4$

HA: 2

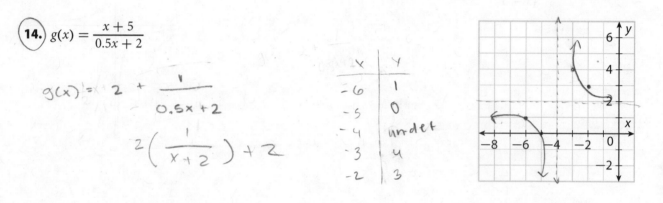

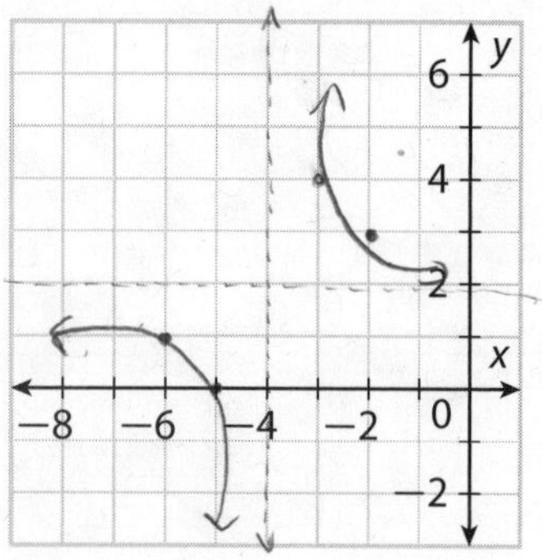

15. $g(x) = \dfrac{-4x+11}{x-2}$

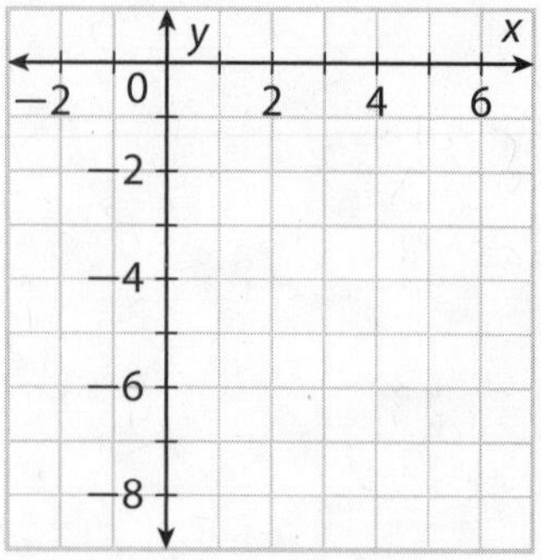

16. $g(x) = \dfrac{4x + 13}{-2x - 6}$

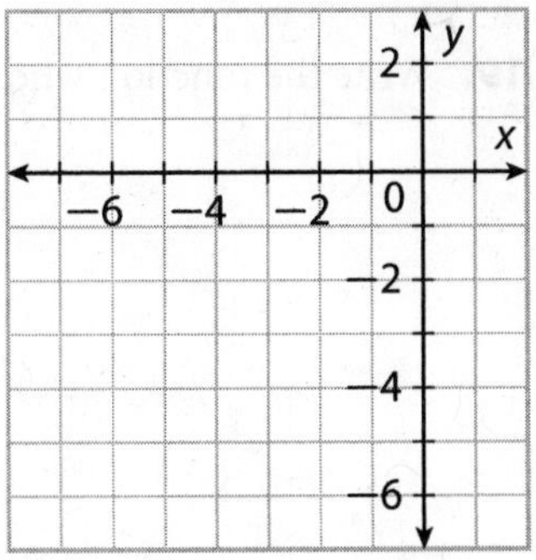

$-2x-6 \overline{)\,4x+13}$ quotient -2; $4x+12$; remainder 1

$g(x) = 2 + \dfrac{1}{-2x-6} + 6$

D: $(-\infty, -6)(-6, \infty)$

R: $(-\infty, 0)(0, -\infty)$

x	g(x)
1	4/4
2	2/10

$-2x + 6 = 0$

$\dfrac{-2x}{2} = \dfrac{6}{2}$

$x = -3, \quad \dfrac{4}{-2} = -2$

17. Write the function whose graph is shown. Use the form $g(x) = a\left(\frac{1}{x - h}\right) + k$.

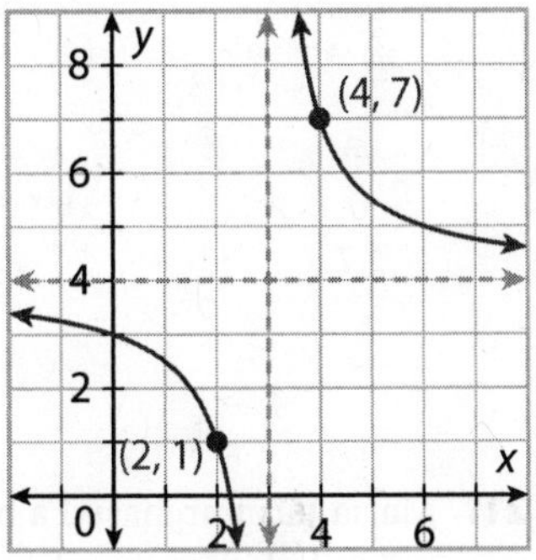

18. Write the function whose graph is shown. Use the form $g(x) = \dfrac{1}{\frac{1}{b}(x - h)} + k$

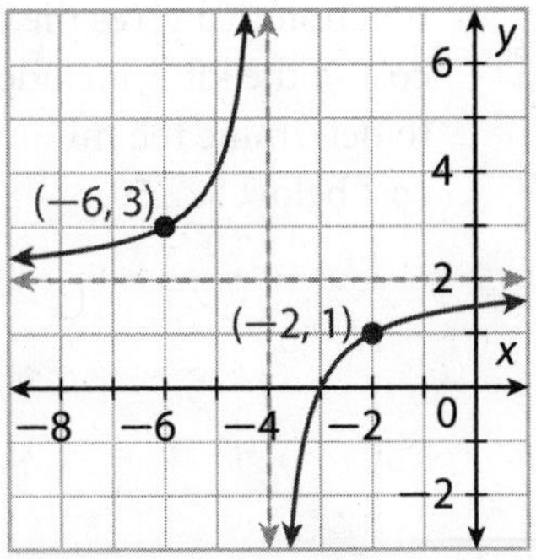

$a\left(\frac{1}{x-h}\right) + k$

$= a\left(\frac{1}{x+4}\right) + 2$

$1 = a\left(\frac{1}{x+4}\right) + 2$

$-1 = \frac{1}{2}$

$a = -2$

$g(x) = -2\left(\frac{1}{x+4}\right) + 2$

19. Write the function whose graph is shown. Use the form $g(x) = \frac{1}{\frac{1}{b}(x-h)} + k$.

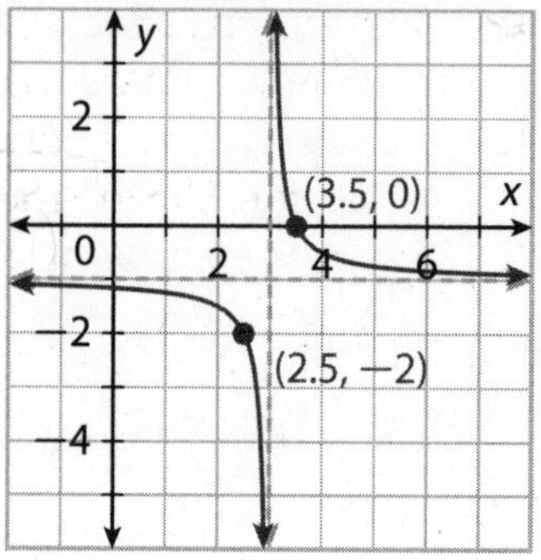

20. Write the function whose graph is shown. Use the form $g(x) = a\left(\frac{1}{x-h}\right) + k$

VA: −2

HA: −4

$g(x) = a\left(\frac{1}{x-h}\right) + k$

$-6 = a\left(\frac{1}{-1+2}\right) - 4$

$a = -2$

$g(x) = -2\left(\frac{1}{x+2}\right) - 4$

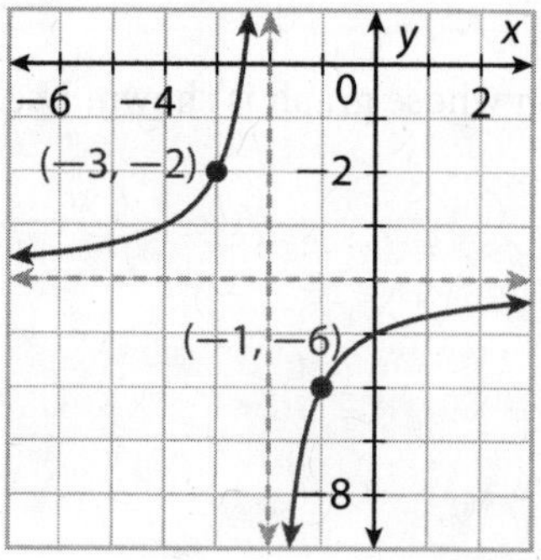

21. Maria has purchased a basic stained glass kit for \$100. She plans to make stained glass suncatchers and sell them. She estimates that the materials for making each suncatcher will cost \$15. Model this situation with a rational function that gives the average cost of a stained glass suncatcher when the cost of the kit is included in the calculation. Use the graph of the function to determine the minimum number of suncatchers that brings the average cost below \$22.50.

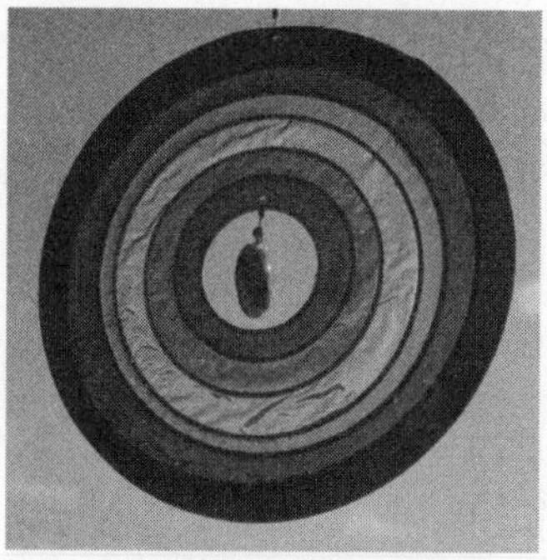

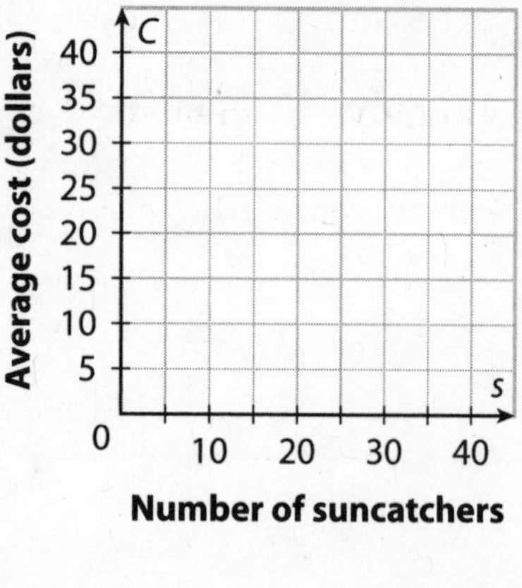

22. Amy has purchased a basic letterpress kit for \$140. She plans to make wedding invitations. She estimates that the cost of the paper and envelope for each invitation is \$2. Model this situation with a rational function that gives the average cost of a wedding invitation when the cost of the kit is included in the calculation. Use the graph of the function to determine the minimum number of invitations that brings the average cost below \$5.

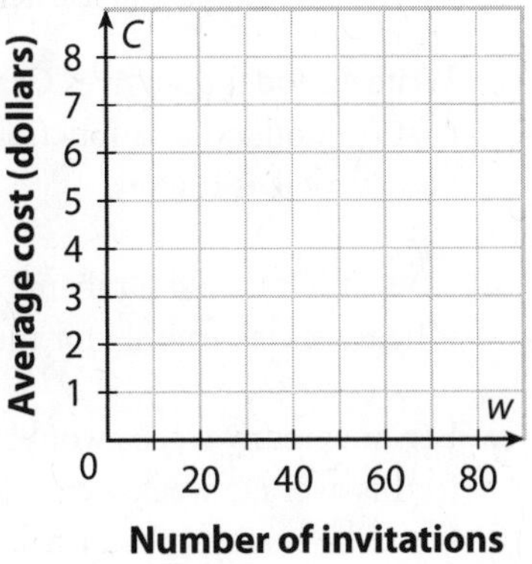

23. **Multiple Response** Select the transformations of the graph of the parent rational function that result in the graph of $g(x) = \frac{1}{2(x-3)} + 1$

A. Horizontal stretch by a factor of 2

B. Horizontal compression by a factor of $\frac{1}{2}$

C. Vertical stretch by a factor of 2

D. Vertical compression by a factor of $\frac{1}{2}$

E. Translation 1 unit up

F. Translation 1 unit down

G. Translation 3 units right

H. Translation 3 units left

H.O.T. Focus on Higher Order Thinking

24. **Justify Reasoning** Explain why, for positive numbers a and b, a vertical stretch or compression of the graph of $f(x) = \frac{1}{x}$ by a factor of a and, separately, a horizontal stretch or compression of the graph of $f(x)$ by a factor of b result in the same graph when a and b are equal.

25. **Communicate Mathematical Ideas** Determine the domain and range of the rational function $g(x) = \frac{mx + n}{px + q}$ where $p \neq 0$. Give your answer in set notation, and explain your reasoning. Assume that there is a remainder when dividing $mx + n$ by $px + q$.

Lesson Performance Task

Graham wants to take snowboarding lessons at a nearby ski resort that charges $40 per week. The resort also charges a one-time equipment-rental fee of $99 for uninterrupted enrollment in classes. The resort requires that learners pay for three weeks of classes at a time.

a. Write a model that gives Graham's average weekly enrollment cost (in dollars) as a function of the time (in weeks) that Graham takes classes.

b. How much would Graham's average weekly enrollment cost be if he took classes only for the minimum of three weeks?

c. For how many weeks would Graham need to take classes for his average weekly enrollment cost to be at most $60? Describe how you can use a graphing calculator to graph the function from part a in order to answer this question, and then state the answer.

Name ______________________ Class ______________ Date ________

8.2 Graphing More Complicated Rational Functions

Essential Question: What features of the graph of a rational function should you identify in order to sketch the graph? How do you identify those features?

Resource Locker

Explore 1 Investigating Domains and Vertical Asympotes of More Complicated Rational Functions

You know that the rational function $f(x) = \frac{1}{x-2} + 3$ has the domain $\{x | x \neq 2\}$ because the function is undefined at $x = 2$. Its graph has the vertical asymptote $x = 2$ because as $x \rightarrow 2^+$ (x approaches 2 from the right), $f(x) \rightarrow +\infty$, and as $x \rightarrow 2^-$ (x approaches 2 from the left), $f(x) \rightarrow -\infty$. In this Explore, you will investigate the domains and vertical asymptotes of other rational functions.

(A) Complete the table by identifying each function's domain based on the x-values for which the function is undefined. Write the domain using an inequality, set notation, and interval notation. Then state the equations of what you think the vertical asymptotes of the function's graph are.

Function	Domain	Possible Vertical Asymptotes
$f(x) = \frac{x+3}{x-1}$		
$f(x) = \frac{(x+5)(x-1)}{x+1}$		
$f(x) = \frac{x-4}{(x+1)(x-1)}$		
$f(x) = \frac{2x^2-3x+9}{x^2-x-6}$		

(B) Using a graphing calculator, graph each of the functions from Step A, and check to see if vertical asymptotes occur where you expect. Are there any unexpected results?

____

____

(C) Examine the behavior of $f(x) = \dfrac{x+3}{x-1}$ near $x = 1$.

First, complete the tables.

x approaches 1 from the right	
x	$f(x) = \dfrac{x+3}{x-1}$
1.1	
1.01	
1.001	

x approaches 1 from the left	
x	$f(x) = \dfrac{x+3}{x-1}$
0.9	
0.99	
0.999	

Next, summarize the results.

- As $x \to 1^+$, $f(x) \to$ ☐.
- As $x \to 1^-$, $f(x) \to$ ☐.

The behaviour of $f(x) = \dfrac{x+3}{x-1}$ near $x = 1$ shows that the graph of $f(x)$ has/does not have a vertical asymptote at $x = 1$.

(D) Examine the behavior of $f(x) = \dfrac{(x+5)(x-1)}{(x+1)}$ near $x = -1$.

First, complete the tables.

x approaches −1 from the right	
x	$f(x) = \dfrac{(x+5)(x-1)}{x+1}$
−0.9	
−0.99	
−0.999	

x approaches −1 from the left	
x	$f(x) = \dfrac{(x+5)(x-1)}{x+1}$
−1.1	
−1.01	
−1.001	

Next, summarize the results.

- As $x \to -1^+$, $f(x) \to$ ☐.
- As $x \to -1^-$, $f(x) \to$ ☐.

The behavior of $f(x) = \dfrac{(x+5)(x-1)}{(x+1)}$ near $x = -1$ shows that the graph of $f(x)$ has/does not have a vertical asymptote at $x = -1$.

(E) Examine the behavior of $f(x) = \dfrac{x-4}{(x+1)(x-1)}$ near $x = -1$ and $x = 1$.

First, complete the tables. Round results to the nearest tenth.

x approaches −1 from the right	
x	$f(x) = \dfrac{x-4}{(x+1)(x-1)}$
−0.9	
−0.99	
−0.999	

x approaches −1 from the left	
x	$f(x) = \dfrac{x-4}{(x+1)(x-1)}$
−1.1	
−1.01	
−1.001	

x approaches 1 from the right	
x	$f(x) = \dfrac{x-4}{(x+1)(x-1)}$
1.1	
1.01	
1.001	

x approaches 1 from the left	
x	$f(x) = \dfrac{x-4}{(x+1)(x-1)}$
0.9	
0.99	
0.999	

Next, summarize the results.

- As $x \to -1^+$, $f(x) \to$ ______.
- As $x \to -1^-$, $f(x) \to$ ______.
- As $x \to 1^+$, $f(x) \to$ ______.
- As $x \to 1^-$, $f(x) \to$ ______.

The behavior of $f(x) = \frac{x-4}{(x+1)(x-1)}$ near $x = -1$ shows that the graph of $f(x)$ has/does not have a vertical asymptote at $x = -1$. The behavior of $f(x) = \frac{x-4}{(x+1)(x-1)}$ near $x = 1$ shows that the graph of $f(x)$ has/does not have a vertical asymptote at $x = 1$.

(F) Examine the behavior of $f(x) = \dfrac{2x^2 - 3x - 9}{x^2 - x - 6}$ near $x = -2$ and $x = 3$.

First, complete the tables. Round results to the nearest ten thousandth if necessary.

x approaches −2 from the right	
x	$f(x) = \dfrac{2x^2 - 3x - 9}{x^2 - x - 6}$
−1.9	
−1.99	
−1.999	

x approaches −2 from the left	
x	$f(x) = \dfrac{2x^2 - 3x - 9}{x^2 - x - 6}$
−2.1	
−2.01	
−2.001	

x approaches 3 from the right	
x	$f(x) = \frac{2x^2 - 3x - 9}{x^2 - x - 6}$
3.1	
3.01	
3.001	

x approaches 3 from the left	
x	$f(x) = \frac{2x^2 - 3x - 9}{x^2 - x - 6}$
2.9	
2.99	
2.999	

Next, summarize the results.

- As $x \to -2^+$, $f(x) \to$ ☐.
- As $x \to -2^-$, $f(x) \to$ ☐.
- As $x \to 3^+$, $f(x) \to$ ☐.
- As $x \to 3^-$, $f(x) \to$ ☐.

The behavior of $f(x) = \frac{2x^2 - 3x - 9}{x^2 - x - 6}$ near $x = -2$ shows that the graph of $f(x)$ has/does not have a vertical asymptote at $x = -2$. The behavior of $f(x) = \frac{2x^2 - 3x - 9}{x^2 - x - 6}$ near $x = 3$ shows that the graph of $f(x)$ has/does not have a vertical asymptote at $x = 3$.

Reflect

1. Rewrite $f(x) = \frac{2x^2 - 3x - 9}{x^2 - x - 6}$ so that its numerator and denominator are factored. How does this form of the function explain the behavior of the function near $x = 3$?

2. **Discussion** When you graph $f(x) = \frac{2x^2 - 3x - 9}{x^2 - x - 6}$ on a graphing calculator, you can't tell that the function is undefined for $x = 3$. How does using the calculator's table feature help? What do you think the graph should look like to make it clear that the function is undefined at $x = 3$?

Explain 1 Sketching the Graphs of More Complicated Rational Functions

As you have seen, there can be breaks in the graph of a rational function. These breaks are called *discontinuities*, and there are two kinds:

1. When a rational function has a factor in the denominator that is not also in the numerator, an *infinite discontinuity* occurs at the value of x for which the factor equals 0. On the graph of the function, an infinite discontinuity appears as a vertical asymptote.

2. When a rational function has a factor in the denominator that is also in the numerator, a *point discontinuity* occurs at the value of x for which the factor equals 0. On the graph of the function, a point discontinuity appears as a "hole."

The graph of a rational function can also have a horizontal asymptote. It is determined by the degrees and leading coefficients of the function's numerator and denominator. If the numerator is a polynomial $p(x)$ in standard form with leading coefficient a and the denominator is a polynomial $q(x)$ in standard form with leading coefficient b, then an examination of the function's end behavior gives the following results.

Relationship between Degree of $p(x)$ and Degree of $q(x)$	Equation of Horizontal Asymptote (if one exists)
Degree of $p(x) <$ degree of $q(x)$	$y = 0$
Degree of $p(x) =$ degree of $q(x)$	$y = \frac{a}{b}$
Degree of $p(x) >$ degree of $q(x)$	There is no horizontal asymptote. The function instead increases or decreases without bound as x increases or decreases without bound. In particular, when the degree of the numerator is 1 more than the degree of the denominator, the function's graph approaches a slanted line, called a *slant asymptote*, as x increases or decreases without bound.

You can sketch the graph of a rational function by identifying where vertical asymptotes, "holes," and horizontal asymptotes occur. Using the factors of the numerator and denominator, you can also establish intervals on the x-axis where either an x-intercept or a discontinuity occurs and then check the signs of the factors on those intervals to determine whether the graph lies above or below the x-axis.

Example 1 **Sketch the graph of the given rational function. (If the degree of the numerator is 1 more than the degree of the denominator, find the graph's slant asymptote by dividing the numerator by the denominator.) Also state the function's domain and range using inequalities, set notation, and interval notation. (If your sketch indicates that the function has maximum or minimum values, use a graphing calculator to find those values to the nearest hundredth when determining the range.)**

Ⓐ $f(x) = \frac{x+1}{x-2}$

Identify vertical asymptotes and "holes."

The function is undefined when $x - 2 = 0$, or $x = 2$. Since $x - 2$ does not appear in the numerator, there is a vertical asymptote rather than a "hole" at $x = 2$.

Identify horizontal asymptotes and slant asymptotes.

The numerator and denominator have the same degree and the leading coefficient of each is 1, so there is a horizontal asymptote at $y = \frac{1}{1} = 1$.

Identify x-intercepts.

An x-intercept occurs when $x + 1 = 0$, or $x = -1$.

Check the sign of the function on the intervals $x < -1$, $-1 < x < 2$, and $x > 2$.

Interval	Sign of $x+1$	Sign of $x-2$	Sign of $f(x) = \frac{x+1}{x-2}$
$x < -1$	−	−	+
$-1 < x < 2$	+	−	−
$x > 2$	+	+	+

Sketch the graph using all this information. Then state the domain and range.

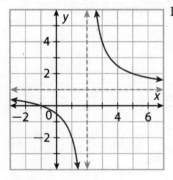

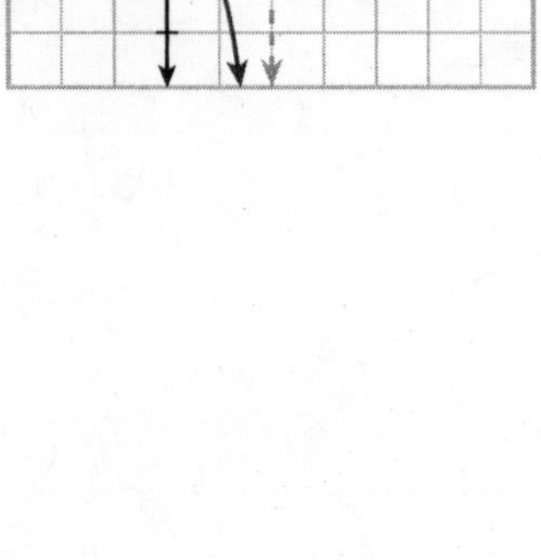

Domain:

Inequality: $x < 2$ or $x > 2$

Set notation: $\{x \mid x \neq 2\}$

Interval notation: $(-\infty, 2) \cup (2, +\infty)$

Range:

Inequality: $y < 1$ or $y > 1$

Set notation: $\{y \mid y \neq 1\}$

Interval notation: $(-\infty, 1) \cup (1, +\infty)$

(B) $f(x) = \dfrac{x^2 + x - 2}{x + 3}$

Factor the function's numerator.

$$f(x) = \frac{x^2 + x - 2}{x + 3} = \frac{(x - 1)(x + 2)}{x + 3}$$

Identify vertical asymptotes and "holes."

The function is undefined when $x + 3 = 0$, or $x = \square$. Since $x + 3$ does not appear in the numerator, there is a vertical asymptote rather than a "hole" at $x = \square$.

Identify horizontal asymptotes and slant asymptotes.

Because the degree of the numerator is 1 more than the degree of the denominator, there is no horizontal asymptote, but there is a slant asymptote. Divide the numerator by the denominator to identify the slant asymptote.

$$\begin{array}{r}
x - \square \\
x + 3\overline{)\,x^2 + x - 2} \\
\underline{x^2 + 3x} \\
-2x - 2 \\
\underline{-2x - 6} \\
4
\end{array}$$

So, the line $y = x - \square$ is the slant asymptote.

Identify x-intercepts.

There are two x-intercepts: when $x - 1 = 0$, or $x = \square$, and when $x + 2 = 0$, or $x = \square$.

Check the sign of the function on the intervals $x < -3$, $-3 < x < -2$, $-2 < x < 1$, and $x > 1$.

Interval	Sign of $x + 3$	Sign of $x + 2$	Sign of $x - 1$	Sign of $f(x) = \dfrac{(x-1)(x+2)}{x+3}$
$x < -3$	$-$	$-$	$-$	$-$
$-3 < x < -2$				
$-2 < x < 1$				
$x > 1$				

Sketch the graph using all this information. Then state the domain and range.

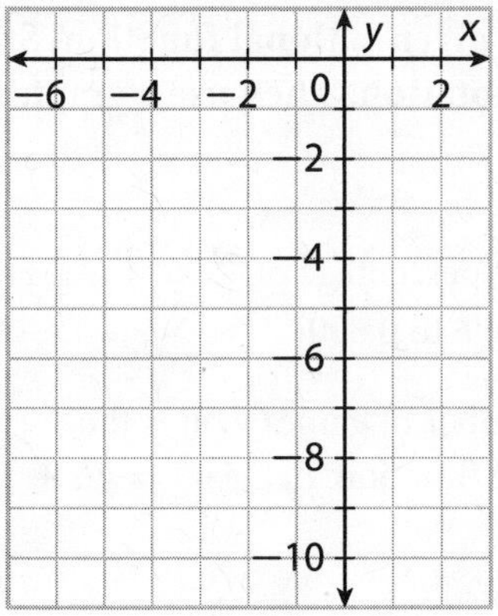

Domain:

Inequality: $x < \square$ or $x > \square$

Set notation: $\{x \mid x \neq \square\}$

Interval notation: $(-\infty, \square) \cup (\square, +\infty)$

The sketch indicates that the function has a maximum value and a minimum value. Using **3:minimum** from the **CALC** menu on a graphing calculator gives -1 as the minimum value. Using **4:maximum** from the **CALC** menu on a graphing calculator gives -5 as the maximum value.

Range: Inequality: $y <$ $\square$ or $y >$ $\square$

Set notation: $\{y \mid y < \square \text{ or } y > \square\}$ Interval notation: $(-\infty, \square) \cup (\square, +\infty)$

Your Turn

Sketch the graph of the given rational function. (If the degree of the numerator is 1 more than the degree of the denominator, find the graph's slant asymptote by dividing the numerator by the denominator.) Also state the function's domain and range using inequalities, set notation, and interval notation. (If your sketch indicates that the function has maximum or minimum values, use a graphing calculator to find those values to the nearest hundredth when determining the range.)

3. $f(x) = \dfrac{x + 1}{x^2 + 3x - 4}$

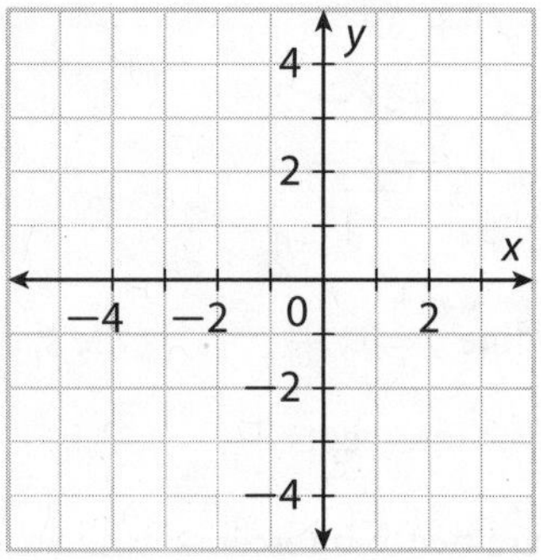

Explain 2 Modeling with More Complicated Rational Functions

When two real-world variable quantities are compared using a ratio or rate, the comparison is a rational function. You can solve problems about the ratio or rate by graphing the rational function.

Example 2 **Write a rational function to model the situation, or use the given rational function. State a reasonable domain and range for the function using set notation. Then use a graphing calculator to graph the function and answer the question.**

(A) A baseball team has won 32 games out of 56 games played, for a winning percentage of $\frac{32}{56} \approx 0.571$. How many consecutive games must the team win to raise its winning percentage to 0.600?

Let w be the number of consecutive games to be won. Then the total number of games won is the function $T_{won}(w) = 32 + w$, and the total number of games played is the function $T_{played}(w) = 56 + w$.

The rational function that gives the team's winning percentage p (as a decimal) is

$p(w) = \frac{T_{\text{won}}(w)}{T_{\text{played}}(w)} = \frac{32 + w}{56 + w}$.

The domain of the rational function is $\{w \mid w \geq 0 \text{ and } w \text{ is a whole number}\}$. Note that you do not need to exclude -56 from the domain, because only nonnegative whole-number values of w make sense in this situation.

Since the function models what happens to the team's winning percentage from consecutive wins (no losses), the values of $p(w)$ start at 0.571 and approach 1 as w increases without bound. So, the range is

$\{p \mid 0.571 \leq p < 1\}$.

Graph $y = \frac{32 + x}{56 + x}$ on a graphing calculator using a viewing window that shows 0 to 10 on the x-axis and 0.5 to 0.7 on the y-axis. Also graph the line $y = 0.6$. To find where the graphs intersect, select **5: intersect** from the **CALC** menu.

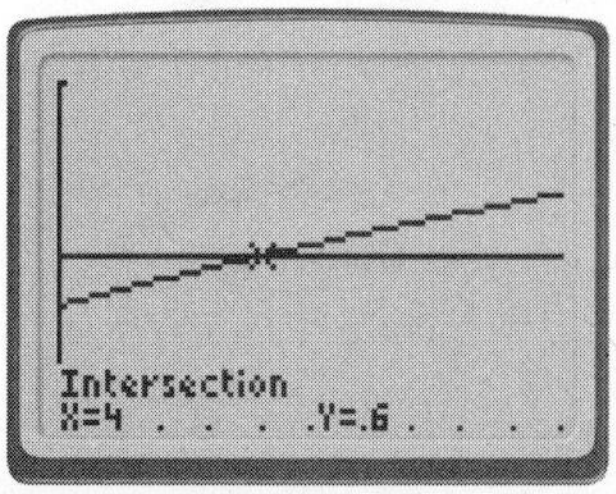

So, the team's winning percentage (as a decimal) will be 0.600 if the team wins 4 consecutive games.

(B) Two friends decide spend an afternoon canoeing on a river. They travel 4 miles upstream and 6 miles downstream. In still water, they know that their average paddling speed is 5 miles per hour. If their canoe trip takes 4 hours, what is the average speed of the river's current? To answer the question, use the rational function $t(c) = \frac{4}{5 - c} + \frac{6}{5 + c} = \frac{50 - 2c}{(5 - c)(5 + c)}$ where c is the average speed of the current (in miles per hour) and t is the time (in hours) spent canoeing 4 miles against the current at a rate of $5 - c$ miles per hour and 6 miles with the current at a rate of $5 + c$ miles per hour.

In order for the friends to travel upstream, the speed of the current must be less than their average paddling speed, so the domain of the function is $\{c \mid 0 \leq c < \square\}$. If the friends canoed in still water ($c = 0$), the trip would take a total of $\frac{4}{5} + \frac{6}{5} = \square$ hours.

As c approaches 5 from the left, the value of $\frac{6}{5 + c}$ approaches $\frac{6}{10} = 0.6$ hour, but the value of $\frac{4}{5 - c}$ ____________________. So, the range of the function is $\{t \mid t \geq \square\}$.

Graph $y = \frac{50 - 2x}{(5 - x)(5 + x)}$ on a graphing calculator using a viewing window that shows 0 to 5 on the x-axis and 2 to 5 on the y-axis. Also graph the line $y = \square$. To find where the graphs intersect, select **5:intersect** from the **CALC** menu. The calculator shows that the average speed of the current is about ______ miles per hour.

Your Turn

Write a rational function to model the situation, or use the given rational function. State a reasonable domain and range for the function using set notation. Then use a graphing calculator to graph the function and answer the question.

4. A saline solution is a mixture of salt and water. A $p\%$ saline solution contains $p\%$ salt and $(100 - p)\%$ water by mass. A chemist has 300 grams of a 4% saline solution that needs to be strengthened to a 6% solution by adding salt. How much salt should the chemist add?

Elaborate

5. How can you show that the vertical line $x = c$, where c is a constant, is an asymptote for the graph of a rational function?

6. How can you determine the end behavior of a rational function?

7. **Essential Question Check-In** How do you identify any vertical asymptotes and "holes" that the graph of a rational function has?

Evaluate: Homework and Practice

- Online Homework
- Hints and Help
- Extra Practice

State the domain using an inequality, set notation, and interval notation. For any x-value excluded from the domain, state whether the graph has a vertical asymptote or a "hole" at that x-value. Use a graphing calculator to check your answer.

1. $f(x) = \dfrac{x+5}{x+1}$

2. $f(x) = \dfrac{x^2+2x-3}{x^2-4x+3}$

Divide the numerator by the denominator to write the function in the form $f(x) = \text{quotient} + \dfrac{\text{remainder}}{\text{divisor}}$ and determine the function's end behavior. Then, using a graphing calculator to examine the function's graph, state the range using an inequality, set notation, and interval notation.

3. $f(x) = \dfrac{3x+1}{x-2}$

4. $f(x) = \dfrac{x}{(x-2)(x+3)}$

VA: x = 2   x = -3   HA: none

D: (-∞, -3) ∪ (-3, 2) ∪ (2, ∞)

R: (-∞, ∞)

x-intercept: (0, 0)

y-intercepr: (0, 0)

5. $f(x) = \dfrac{x^2-5x+6}{x-1}$

6. $f(x) = \dfrac{4x^2-1}{x^2+x-2}$

$x^2+x-2 \overline{)\,4x^2-1}$ quotient 4

$4x^2+4x-8$

$-4x+7$

$f(x) = 4 + \dfrac{-4x+7}{x^2+x-2}$

Sketch the graph of the given rational function. (If the degree of the numerator is 1 more than the degree of the denominator, find the graph's slant asymptote by dividing the numerator by the denominator.) Also state the function's domain and range using inequalities, set notation, and interval notation. (If your sketch indicates that the function has maximum or minimum values, use a graphing calculator to find those values to the nearest hundredth when determining the range.)

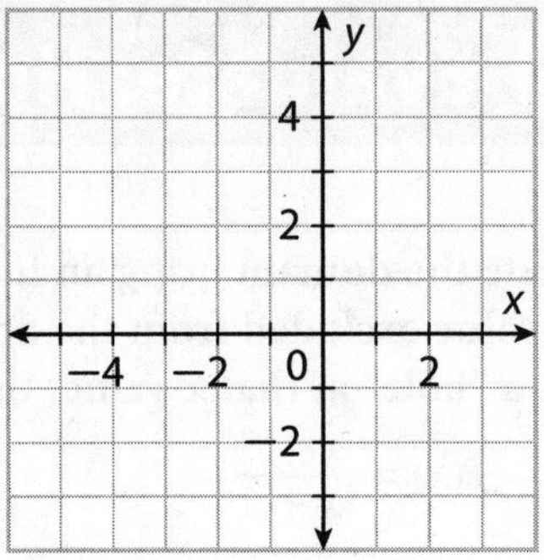

7. $f(x) = \dfrac{x-1}{x+1}$

8. $f(x) = \dfrac{x-1}{(x-2)(x+3)}$

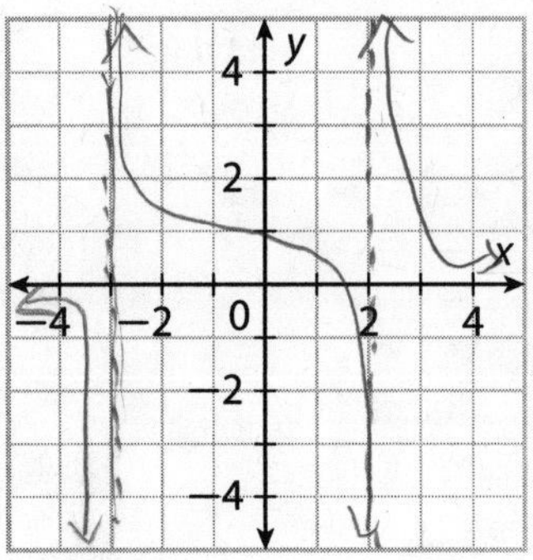

$f(x) = \dfrac{x-1}{(x-2)(x+3)}$

$x - 2 = 0$ $\quad$ $x + 3 = 0$

$x = 2$ $\quad$ $x = -3$

VA: $x = 2, -3$

x	f(x)
-3	undef
-2	3/4
-1	1/3
0	1/6
1	0
2	undef
3	1/3

9. $f(x) = \dfrac{(x+1)(x-1)}{x+2}$

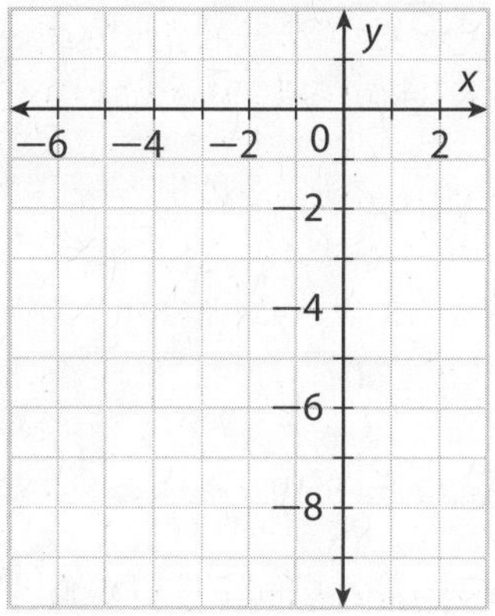

10. $f(x) = \dfrac{-3x(x-2)}{(x-2)(x+2)}$

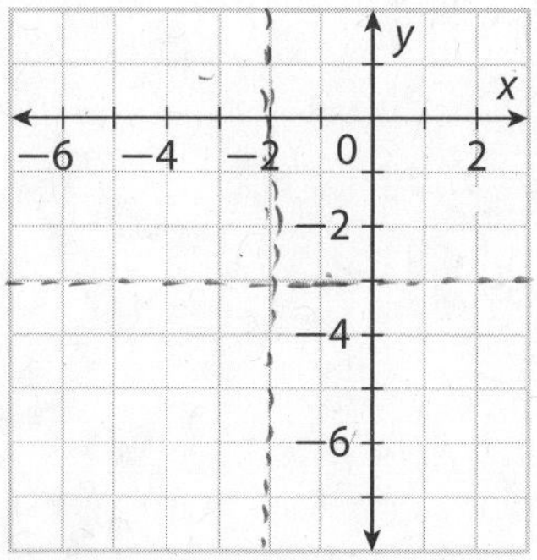

$f(x) = \dfrac{-3x(x-2)}{(x-2)(x+2)}$

$x = 2, -2$

$f(x) = \dfrac{-3x}{x+2}$

$x = -2$

→ Hole at $x = 2$

VA: $x = -2$

HA: $y = -3$

Hole: $x = 2$

X-int: (0, 0)

Y-int: (0, 0)

D:

R:

11. $f(x) = \dfrac{x^2 + 2x - 8}{x - 1}$

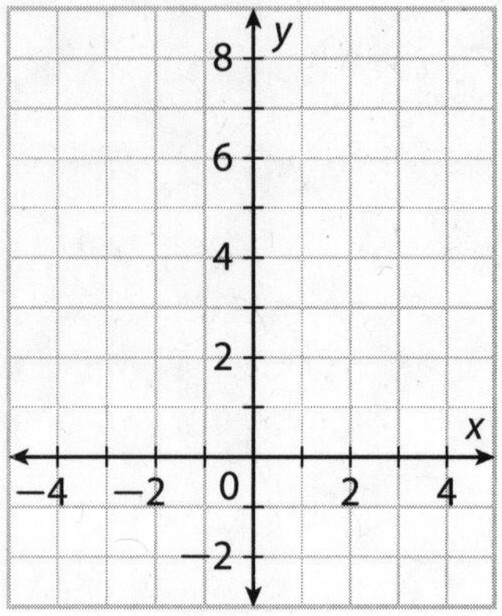

12. $f(x) = \dfrac{2x^2 - 4x}{x^2 + 4x + 4}$

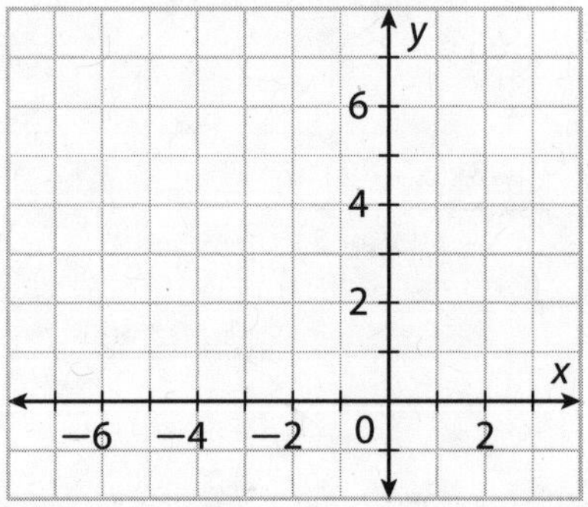

Write a rational function to model the situation, or use the given rational function. State a reasonable domain and range for the function using set notation. Then use a graphing calculator to graph the function and answer the question.

13. A basketball team has won 16 games out of 23 games played, for a winning percentage (expressed as a decimal) of $\frac{16}{23} \approx 0.696$. How many consecutive games must the team win to raise its winning percentage to 0.750?

14. So far this season, a baseball player has had 84 hits in 294 times at bat, for a batting average of $\frac{84}{294} \approx 0.286$. How many consecutive hits must the player get to raise his batting average to 0.300?

15. A kayaker traveled 5 miles upstream and then 8 miles downstream on a river. The average speed of the current was 3 miles per hour. If the kayaker was paddling for 5 hours, what was the kayaker's average paddling speed? To answer the question, use the rational function $t(s) = \frac{5}{s-3} + \frac{8}{s+3} = \frac{13s - 9}{(s-3)(s+3)}$ where s is the kayaker's average paddling speed (in miles per hour) and t is the time (in hours) spent kayaking 5 miles against the current at a rate of $s - 3$ miles per hour and 8 miles with the current at a rate of $s + 3$ miles per hour.

16. In aviation, *air speed* refers to a plane's speed in still air. A small plane maintains a certain air speed when flying to and from a city that is 400 miles away. On the trip out, the plane flies against a wind, which has an average speed of 40 miles per hour. On the return trip, the plane flies with the wind. If the total flight time for the round trip is 3.5 hours, what is the plane's average air speed? To answer this question, use the rational function $t(s) = \frac{400}{s-40} + \frac{400}{s+40} = \frac{800s}{(s-40)(s+40)}$, where s is the air speed (in miles per hour) and t is the total flight time (in hours) for the round trip.

17. Multiple Response Select the statements that apply to the rational function $f(x) = \frac{x - 2}{x^2 - x - 6}$.

A. The function's domain is $\left\{x \mid x \neq -2 \text{ and } x \neq 3\right\}$.

B. The function's domain is $\left\{x \mid x \neq -2 \text{ and } x \neq -3\right\}$.

C. The function's range is $\left\{y \mid y \neq 0\right\}$.

D. The function's range is $\left\{y \mid -\infty < y < +\infty\right\}$.

E. The function's graph has vertical asymptotes at $x = -2$ and $x = 3$.

F. The function's graph has a vertical asymptote at $x = -3$ and a "hole" at $x = 2$.

G. The function's graph has a horizontal asymptote at $y = 0$.

H. The function's graph has a horizontal asymptote at $y = 1$.

H.O.T. Focus on Higher Order Thinking

18. Draw Conclusions For what value(s) of a does the graph of $f(x) = \frac{x + a}{x^2 + 4x + 3}$ have a "hole"? Explain. Then, for each value of a, state the domain and the range of $f(x)$ using interval notation.

19. Critique Reasoning A student claims that the functions $f(x) = \frac{4x^2 - 1}{4x + 2}$ and $g(x) = \frac{4x + 2}{4x^2 - 1}$ have different domains but identical ranges. Which part of the student's claim is correct, and which is false? Explain.

Lesson Performance Task

In professional baseball, the smallest allowable volume of a baseball is 92.06% of the largest allowable volume, and the range of allowable radii is 0.04 inch.

a. Let r be the largest allowable radius (in inches) of a baseball. Write expressions, both in terms of r, for the largest allowable volume of the baseball and the smallest allowable volume of the baseball. (Use the formula for the volume of a sphere, $V = \frac{4}{3}\pi r^3$.)

b. Write and simplify a function that gives the ratio R of the smallest allowable volume of a baseball to the largest allowable volume.

c. Use a graphing calculator to graph the function from part b, and use the graph to find the smallest allowable radius and the largest allowable radius of a baseball. Round your answers to the nearest hundredth.

STUDY GUIDE REVIEW

Rational Functions

MODULE 8

Essential Question: How can you use rational functions to solve real-world problems?

Key Vocabulary

asymptote *(asíntota)*
constant of variation *(constante de variación)*
parent function *(función madre)*
rational function *(función racional)*

KEY EXAMPLE (Lesson 8.1)

Graph $y = -\frac{1}{x-2}$. State the domain, range, y-intercept, and identify any asymptotes.

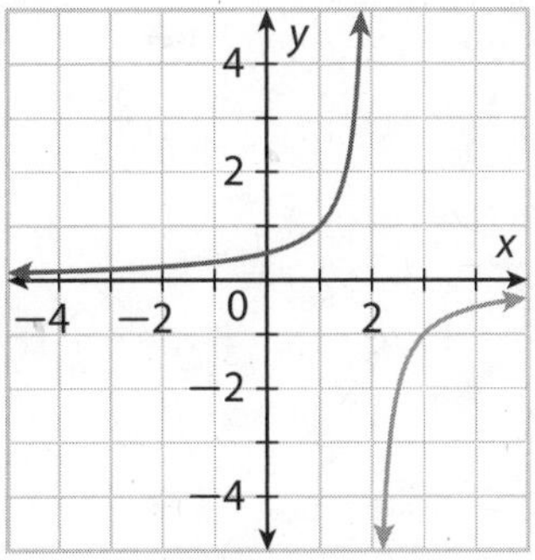

Domain: $x < 2$ or $x > 2$

Range: $y < 0$ or $y > 0$

y-intercept: $\left(0, \frac{1}{2}\right)$

The graph has a vertical asymptote at $x = 2$ and a horizontal asymptote at $y = 0$.

KEY EXAMPLE (Lesson 8.2)

Graph $y = \frac{2x^2}{x+2}$. State the domain, range, x-intercept, and identify any asymptotes.

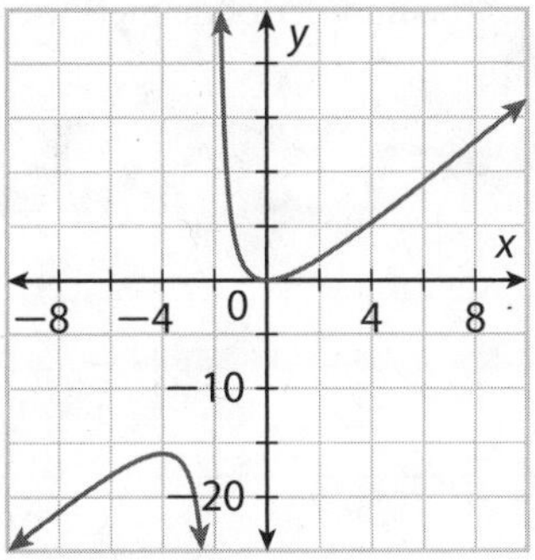

Domain: $x < -2$ or $x > -2$

Range: $y \leq -16$ or $y \geq 0$

The numerator has 0 as its only zero, so the x-intercept is $(0, 0)$.

The denominator has -2 as its only zero, so the graph has a vertical asymptote at $x = -2$.

EXERCISES

Describe how the graph of $g(x)$ is related to the graph of $f(x) = \frac{1}{x}$. (Lesson 8.1)

1. $g(x) = \dfrac{1}{x + 4}$

2. $g(x) = \dfrac{1}{x - 2} + 3$

3. $g(x) = \dfrac{-1}{x + 3}$

Graph the function using a graphing calculator. State the domain, x-intercept(s), and identify asymptotes. (Lesson 8.2)

4. $f(x) = \dfrac{x^2 - 3x}{x + 4}$

5. $f(x) = \dfrac{x - 3}{x^2 + 6x + 5}$

6. $f(x) = -\dfrac{(x^2 - 4)}{(x + 1)}$

MODULE PERFORMANCE TASK

What Is the Profit?

A sporting goods store sells two styles of bike helmets: Style A for \$30 each and Style B for \$40 each. The store is trying to calculate its average profit on each style of helmet, using the rational function $A(x) = \frac{P(x)}{x}$, where $P(x)$ is the profit on the sale of x helmets. The helmet supplier offers a volume discount for orders up to 500 helmets, using the cost formulas shown in the table. For each style, how does per-helmet profit change as the number of helmets increases? What is the maximum per-helmet profit?

Number of Helmets (x)	100	200	300	400	500
Style A					
Revenue					
Cost: $100 + (20 - 0.01x)x$					
Profit					
Style B					
Revenue					
Cost: $250 + (30 - 0.03x)x$					
Profit					

Start by organizing your data in the table. Then use your own paper to complete the task. Use graphs, numbers, words, or algebra to explain how you reached your conclusion.

Ready to Go On?

8.1–8.2 Rational Functions

Personal Math Trainer
- Online Homework
- Hints and Help
- Extra Practice

Describe how the graph of $g(x)$ is related to the graph of $f(x) = \frac{1}{x}$. (Lesson 8.1)

1. $g(x) = \frac{5}{x} - 3$

2. $g(x) = \frac{1}{-0.5(x - 2)} + 4$

3. $g(x) = \frac{-1}{x} + 5$

Graph the function using a graphing calculator. State the domain, x-intercept(s), and identify asymptotes. (Lesson 8.2)

4. $f(x) = \frac{2x - 4}{x + 3}$

5. $f(x) = \frac{x^2 - 9}{x - 2}$

6. $f(x) = -\frac{(x + 2)}{(x^2 + 3x)}$

ESSENTIAL QUESTION

7. How do you identify any linear asymptotes of a rational function?

MODULE 8
MIXED REVIEW

Assessment Readiness

1. Consider the inequality $x^2 - 64 < 0$. Tell whether each of the following is a solution set of the inequality.
Select Yes or No for A–C.

A. $x < -8$ or $x > -8$ ○ Yes ○ No
B. $-8 < x < -8$ ○ Yes ○ No
C. $-64 < x < -64$ ○ Yes ○ No

2. Consider the equation $y = \frac{2x + 5}{x - 1}$. Select True or False for each statement.

A. The line $x = 1$ is an asymptote. ○ True ○ False
B. The point $(0, -5)$ lies on the graph. ○ True ○ False
C. The function is undefined for $x = -1$. ○ True ○ False

3. Consider the function $y = \frac{x^2 + 5x + 4}{x^2 - 9}$. State the domain, range, and x- and y-intercepts, and identify any asymptotes.

4. You have subscribed to a cable television service. The cable company charges a one-time installation fee of \$30 and a monthly fee of \$50. Write a model that gives the average cost per month as a function of months subscribed to the service. After how many months will the average cost be \$56? Explain your thinking and identify any asymptotes on the graph of the function.

Rational Expressions and Equations

MODULE 9

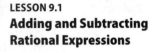

Essential Question: How can you use rational expressions and equations to solve real-world problems?

REAL WORLD VIDEO
Robotic arms and other prosthetic devices are among the wonders of robotics. Check out some of the other cutting-edge applications of modern robotics.

MODULE PERFORMANCE TASK PREVIEW

Robots and Resistors

Robotics engineers design robots and develop applications for them, such as executing high-precision tasks in factories, cleaning toxic waste, and locating and defusing bombs. People who work in robotics are skilled in areas such as electronics and computer programming. How can a rational expression be used to help design the circuitry for a robot? Let's find out!

Are YOU Ready?

Complete these exercises to review skills you will need for this module.

Personal Math Trainer

- Online Homework
- Hints and Help
- Extra Practice

Graphing Linear Proportional Relationships

Example 1

Graph $y = \frac{1}{2}x$.

When $x = 0$, $y = 0$, so plot $(0, 0)$ on the graph.

The slope is $\frac{1}{2}$, so from $(0, 0)$, plot the next point up 1 and over 2.

Draw a line through the two points.

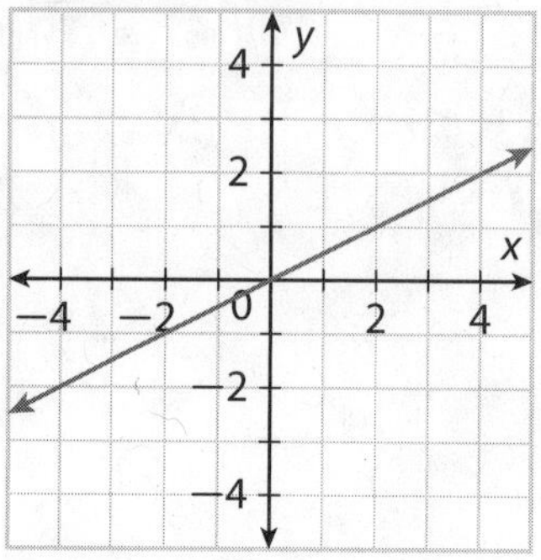

Graph each proportional relationship.

1. $y = 2x$

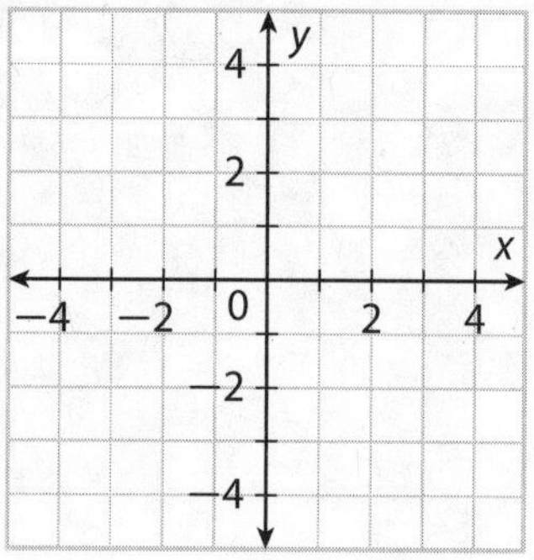

2. $y = \frac{2}{3}x$

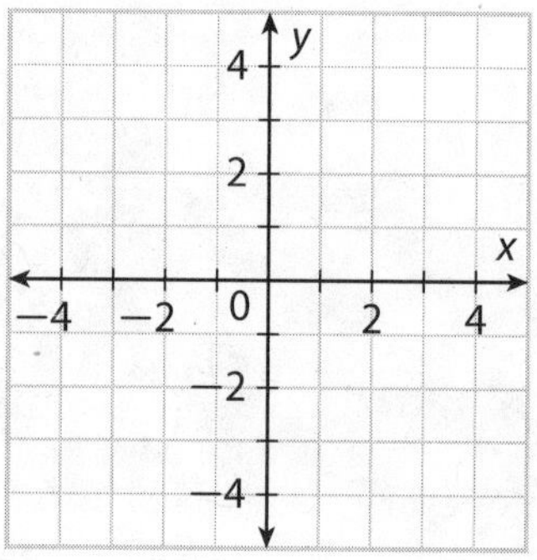

Direct and Inverse Variation

Example 2 In a direct variation the constant is 4 and its graph passes through $(x, 10)$. Find x.

$y = kx \rightarrow 10 = 4x \rightarrow x = 2.5$

Example 3 In an inverse variation the constant is 2.4 and its graph passes through $(6, y)$. Find y.

$k = xy \rightarrow 2.4 = 6y \rightarrow y = 0.4$

Find the missing variable for each direct variation.

3. $k = -1$; $(x, -5)$ ______

4. $k = 3$; $(9, y)$ ______

5. $k = \frac{1}{3}$; $(x, -2)$ ______

Find the missing variable for each inverse variation.

6. $k = 8$; $(x, -10)$ ______

7. $k = -2$; $(5, y)$ ______

8. $k = 6$; $(x, 1.5)$ ______

Name_______________ Class_______________ Date_______________

9.1 Adding and Subtracting Rational Expressions

Essential Question: How can you add and subtract rational expressions?

Resource Locker

Explore Identifying Excluded Values

Given a rational expression, identify the excluded values by finding the zeroes of the denominator. If possible, simplify the expression.

(A) $\frac{(1-x^2)}{x-1}$

The denominator of the expression is ______.

(B) Since division by 0 is not defined, the excluded values for this expression are all the values that would make the denominator equal to 0.

$x - 1 = 0$

$x = \square$

(C) Begin simplifying the expression by factoring the numerator.

$$\frac{(1-x^2)}{x-1} = \frac{(\square)(\square)}{x-1}$$

(D) Divide out terms common to both the numerator and the denominator.

$$\frac{(1-x^2)}{x-1} = \frac{(\square)(\square)}{-(1-x)} = \square = \square$$

(E) The simplified expression is

$$\frac{(1-x^2)}{x-1} = \square, \text{ whenever } x \neq \square$$

(F) What is the domain for this function? What is its range?

____

Reflect

1. What factors can be divided out of the numerator and denominator?

____

Explain 1 Writing Equivalent Rational Expressions

Given a rational expression, there are different ways to write an equivalent rational expression. When common terms are divided out, the result is an equivalent but simplified expression.

Example 1 **Rewrite the expression as indicated.**

(A) Write $\frac{3x}{(x+3)}$ as an equivalent rational expression that has a denominator of $(x+3)(x+5)$.

The expression $\frac{3x}{(x+3)}$ has a denominator of $(x+3)$.

The factor missing from the denominator is $(x+5)$.

Introduce a common factor, $(x+5)$.

$$\frac{3x}{(x+3)} = \frac{3x(x+5)}{(x+3)(x+5)}$$

$\frac{3x}{(x+3)}$ is equivalent to $\frac{3x(x+5)}{(x+3)(x+5)}$.

(B) Simplify the expression $\frac{(x^2+5x+6)}{(x^2+3x+2)(x+3)}$.

Write the expression. $\frac{(x^2+5x+6)}{(x^2+3x+2)(x+3)}$

Factor the numerator and denominator. ____________

Divide out like terms. ______

Your Turn

2. Write $\frac{5}{5x-25}$ as an equivalent expression with a denominator of $(x-5)(x+1)$.

3. Simplify the expression $\frac{(x+x^3)(1-x^2)}{(x^2-x^6)}$.

Explain 2 Identifying the LCD of Two Rational Expressions

Given two or more rational expressions, the least common denominator (LCD) is found by factoring each denominator and finding the least common multiple (LCM) of the factors. This technique is useful for the addition and subtraction of expressions with unlike denominators.

Least Common Denominator (LCD) of Rational Expressions

To find the LCD of rational expressions:

1. Factor each denominator completely. Write any repeated factors as powers.
2. List the different factors. If the denominators have common factors, use the highest power of each common factor.

Example 2 **Find the LCD for each set of rational expressions.**

(A) $\frac{-2}{3x - 15}$ and $\frac{6x}{4x + 28}$

Factor each denominator completely.

$3x - 15 = 3(x - 5)$

$4x + 28 = 4(x + 7)$

List the different factors.

$3, 4, x - 5, x + 7$

The LCD is $3 \cdot 4(x - 5)(x + 7)$,

or $12(x - 5)(x + 7)$.

(B) $\frac{-14}{x^2 - 11x + 24}$ and $\frac{9}{x^2 - 6x + 9}$

Factor each denominator completely.

$x^2 - 11x + 24 =$ ______

$x^2 - 6x + 9 =$ ______

List the different factors.

______ and ______

Taking the highest power of $(x - 3)$,

the LCD is ______.

Reflect

4. **Discussion** When is the LCD of two rational expressions not equal to the product of their denominators?

______

Your Turn

Find the LCD for each set of rational expressions.

5. $\frac{x + 6}{8x - 24}$ and $\frac{14x}{10x - 30}$

6. $\frac{12x}{15x + 60} = \frac{5}{x^2 + 9x + 20}$

Explain 3 Adding and Subtracting Rational Expressions

Adding and subtracting rational expressions is similar to adding and subtracting fractions.

Example 3 **Add or subtract. Identify any excluded values and simplify your answer.**

(A) $\dfrac{x^2 + 4x + 2}{x^2} + \dfrac{x^2}{x^2 + x}$

Factor the denominators. $\dfrac{x^2 + 4x + 2}{x^2} + \dfrac{x^2}{x(x + 1)}$

Identify where the expression is not defined. The first expression is undefined when $x = 0$. The second expression is undefined when $x = 0$ and when $x = -1$.

Find a common denominator. The LCM for x^2 and $x(x + 1)$ is $x^2(x + 1)$.

Write the expressions with a common denominator by multiplying both by the appropriate form of 1. $\dfrac{(x+1)}{(x+1)} \cdot \dfrac{x^2 + 4x + 2}{x^2} + \dfrac{x^2}{x(x + 1)} \cdot \dfrac{x}{x}$

Simplify each numerator. $= \dfrac{x^3 + 5x^2 + 6x + 2}{x^2(x + 1)} + \dfrac{x^3}{x^2(x + 1)}$

Add. $= \dfrac{2x^3 + 5x^2 + 6x + 2}{x^2(x + 1)}$

Since none of the factors of the denominator are factors of the numerator, the expression cannot be further simplified.

(B) $\dfrac{2x^2}{x^2 - 5x} - \dfrac{x^2 + 3x - 4}{x^2}$

Factor the denominators. $\dfrac{2x^2}{\square} - \dfrac{x^2 + 3x - 4}{x^2}$

Identify where the expression is not defined. The first expression is undefined when $x = 0$ and when $x = 5$. The second expression is undefined when $x = 0$.

Find a common denominator. The LCM for $x(x - 5)$ and x^2 is ________.

Write the expressions with a common denominator by multiplying both by the appropriate form of 1. $\square \cdot \dfrac{2x^2}{x(x - 5)} - \dfrac{x^2 + 3x - 4}{x^2} \cdot \dfrac{x - 5}{x - 5}$

Simplify each numerator. $= \dfrac{2x^3}{x^2(x - 5)} - \dfrac{x^3 - 2x^2 - 19x + 20}{x^2(x - 5)}$

Subtract. $= \dfrac{\square + 2x^2 + 19x - 20}{x^2(x - 5)}$

Since none of the factors of the denominator are factors of the numerator, the expression cannot be further simplified.

Your Turn

Add each pair of expressions, simplifying the result and noting the combined excluded values. Then subtract the second expression from the first, again simplifying the result and noting the combined excluded values.

7. $-x^2$ and $\frac{1}{(1 - x^2)}$

8. $\frac{x^2}{(4 - x^2)}$ and $\frac{1}{(2 - x)}$

Explain 4 Adding and Subtracting with Rational Models

Rational expressions can model real-world phenomena, and can be used to calculate measurements of those phenomena.

Example 4 **Find the sum or difference of the models to solve the problem.**

Ⓐ Two groups have agreed that each will contribute \$2000 for an upcoming trip. Group A has 6 more people than group B. Let x represent the number of people in group A. Write and simplify an expression in terms of x that represents the difference between the number of dollars each person in group A must contribute and the number each person in group B must contribute.

$$\frac{2000}{x} - \frac{2000}{x-6} = \frac{2000(x-6)}{x(x-6)} - \frac{2000x}{(x-6)x}$$

$$= \frac{2000x - 12,000 - 2000x}{x(x-6)}$$

$$= -\frac{12,000}{x(x-6)}$$

Ⓑ A freight train averages 30 miles per hour traveling to its destination with full cars and 40 miles per hour on the return trip with empty cars. Find the total time in terms of d. Use the formula $t = \frac{d}{r}$.

Let d represent the one-way distance.

Total time: $\frac{d}{30} + \frac{d}{40} = \frac{d \cdot \square}{30 \cdot \square} + \frac{d \cdot \square}{40 \cdot \square}$

$$= \frac{d \cdot \square + d \cdot \square}{\square}$$

$$= \frac{\square}{\square} d$$

Your Turn

9. A hiker averages 1.4 miles per hour when walking downhill on a mountain trail and 0.8 miles per hour on the return trip when walking uphill. Find the total time in terms of d. Use the formula $t = \frac{d}{r}$.

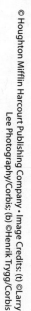

10. Yvette ran at an average speed of 6.20 feet per second during the first two laps of a race and an average speed of 7.75 feet per second during the second two laps of a race. Find her total time in terms of d, the distance around the racecourse.

Elaborate

11. Why do rational expressions have excluded values?

12. How can you tell if your answer is written in simplest form?

13. **Essential Question Check-In** Why must the excluded values of each expression in a sum or difference of rational expressions also be excluded values for the simplified expression?

Evaluate: Homework and Practice

Personal Math Trainer

- Online Homework
- Hints and Help
- Extra Practice

Given a rational expression, identify the excluded values by finding the zeroes of the denominator.

1. $\dfrac{x-1}{x^2+3x-4}$

2. $\dfrac{4}{x(x+17)}$

Write the given expression as an equivalent rational expression that has the given denominator.

3. Expression: $\dfrac{x-7}{x+8}$

Denominator: x^3+8x^2

4. Expression: $\dfrac{3x^3}{3x-6}$

Denominator: $(2-x)(x^2+9)$

Simplify the given expression.

5. $\dfrac{(-4-4x)}{(x^2-x-2)}$

$\dfrac{-4(1+x)}{(x-2)(x+1)}$

$\dfrac{-4}{x+2}$

6. $\dfrac{-x-8}{x^2+9x+8}$

7. $\dfrac{6x^2+5x+1}{3x^2+4x+1}$

$\dfrac{(3x+1)(2x+1)}{(3x+1)(x+1)} \rightarrow \dfrac{2x+1}{x+1}$

8. $\dfrac{x^4-1}{x^2+1}$

Find the LCD for each set of rational expressions.

9. $\dfrac{x}{2x+16}$ and $\dfrac{-4x}{3x-27}$

$(2x+16)(3x-27)$

$= 6x^2-54x+48x+432$

$= 6(x+8)(x-9)$

$x(3x-27)$

10. $\dfrac{x^2-4}{5x-30}$ and $\dfrac{5x+13}{7x-42}$

11. $\dfrac{4x + 12}{x^2 + 5x + 6}$ and $\dfrac{5x + 15}{10x + 20}$

(x+3)(x+2)

10(x+2)

10(x+3)(x+2)

12. $\dfrac{-11}{x^2 - 3x - 28}$ and $\dfrac{2}{x^2 - 2x - 24}$

13. $\dfrac{12}{3x^2 - 21x - 54}$ and $\dfrac{-1}{21x^2 - 84}$

3(x²-7x-18) 21(x⁴-4)

3(x+2)(x-9) 21(x-2)(x+2)

21(x+2)(x-2)(x-9)

14. $\dfrac{3x}{5x^2 - 40x + 60}$ and $\dfrac{17}{-7x^2 + 56x + 84}$

Add or subtract the given expressions, simplifying each result and noting the combined excluded values.

15. $\dfrac{1}{1 + x} + \dfrac{1 - x}{x}$

$\dfrac{x}{x(1+x)} + \dfrac{(1+x)(1-x)}{x(1+x)}$

$\dfrac{x}{x(1+x)} + \dfrac{x - x^2 + 1 - x}{x(1+x)}$

$\dfrac{x}{x(1+x)} - \dfrac{x^2+1}{x(1+x)} - \dfrac{x^2+x+1}{x(1+x)}$

16. $\dfrac{x + 4}{x^2 - 4} + \dfrac{-2x - 2}{x^2 - 4}$

17. $\frac{1}{2+x} - \frac{2-x}{x}$

$\frac{x - (2-x)(2+x)}{x^2 + 2x}$

$\frac{x - (4 - x^2)}{x^2 + 2x}$

$\frac{-x^2 + x + 4}{x^2 + 2x}$

18. $\frac{4x^4 + 4}{x^2 + 1} - \frac{8}{x^2 + 1}$

19. $\frac{x^4 - 2}{x^2 - 2} + \frac{2}{-x^2 + 2}$

$\frac{-x^4 + 2 + 2}{-x^2 + 2} = \frac{-x^4 + 4}{-x^2 + 2}$

20. $\frac{1}{x^2 + 3x - 4} - \frac{1}{x^2 - 3x + 2}$

$(x+5)(x-2)$

$x^2 + 2x + 5x - 10$

$x^2 + 3x - 10$

21. $\frac{3}{x^2 - 4} - \frac{x+5}{x+2}$

$\frac{3 - (x^2 + 3x - 10)}{x^2 - 4}$

$\frac{3 - x^2 - 3x + 10}{x^2 - 4}$

22. $\frac{-3}{9x^2 - 4} + \frac{1}{3x^2 + 2x}$

23. $\frac{x-2}{x+2} + \frac{1}{x^2-4} - \frac{x+2}{2-x}$

LCD: $(x+2)(x-2)$

$\frac{x-2}{x+2} + \frac{1}{x^2-4} - \frac{x+2}{2-x}$

24. $\frac{x-3}{x+3} - \frac{1}{x-3} + \frac{x+2}{3-x}$

25. The owner of store A and store B wants to know the average cost of both stores. Store A has an average cost of $\frac{100+2q}{q}$, and store B has an average cost of $\frac{200+q}{2q}$, where both stores have the same output, q. Find an expression to represent the cost of both stores.

26. An auto race consists of 8 laps. A driver completes the first 3 laps at an average speed of 185 miles per hour and the remaining laps at an average speed of 200 miles per hour. Let d represent the length of one lap. Find the time in terms of d that it takes the driver to complete the race.

27. The junior and senior classes of a high school are cleaning up a beach. Each class has pledged to clean 1600 meters of shoreline. The junior class has 12 more students than the senior class. Let s represent the number of students in the senior class. Write and simplify an expression in terms of s that represents the difference between the number of meters of shoreline each senior must clean and the number of meters each junior must clean.

28. **Architecture** The Renaissance architect Andrea Palladio believed that the height of a room with vaulted ceilings should be the harmonic mean of the length and width. The harmonic mean of two positive numbers a and b is equal to $\frac{2}{\frac{1}{a}+\frac{1}{b}}$. Simplify this expression. What are the excluded values? What do they mean in this problem?

29. Match each expression with the correct excluded value(s).

a. $\frac{3x+5}{x+2}$ ______ no excluded values

b. $\frac{1+x}{x^2-1}$ ______ $x \neq 0, -2$

c. $\frac{3x^4-12}{x^2+4}$ ______ $x \neq 1, -1$

d. $\frac{3x+6}{x^2(x+2)}$ ______ $x \neq -2$

H.O.T. Focus on Higher Order Thinking

30. Explain the Error George was asked to write the expression $2x - 3$ three times, once each with excluded values at $x = 1$, $x = 2$, and $x = -3$. He wrote the following expressions:

a. $\dfrac{2x - 3}{x - 1}$

b. $\dfrac{2x - 3}{x - 2}$

c. $\dfrac{2x - 3}{x + 3}$

What error did George make? Write the correct expressions, then write an expression that has all three excluded values.

31. Communicate Mathematical Ideas Write a rational expression with excluded values at $x = 0$ and $x = 17$.

32. Critical Thinking Sketch the graph of the rational equation $y = \dfrac{x^2 + 3x + 2}{x + 1}$. Think about how to show graphically that a graph exists over a domain except at one point.

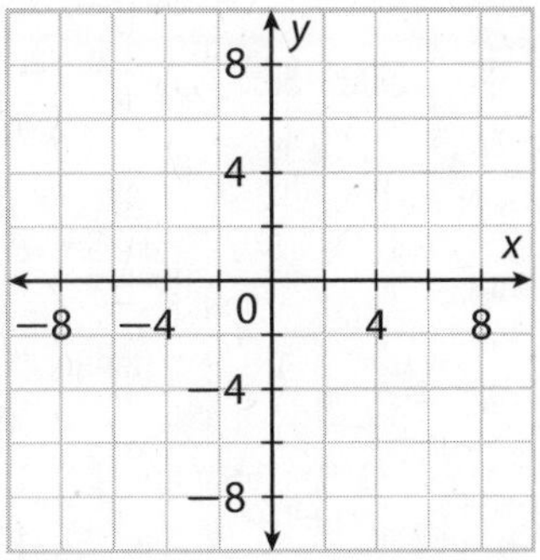

Lesson Performance Task

A kayaker spends an afternoon paddling on a river. She travels 3 miles upstream and 3 miles downstream in a total of 4 hours. In still water, the kayaker can travel at an average speed of 2 miles per hour. Based on this information, can you estimate the average speed of the river's current? Is your answer reasonable?

Next, assume the average speed of the kayaker is an unknown, k, and not necessarily 2 miles per hour. What is the range of possible average kayaker speeds under the rest of the constraints?

Name ____________________ Class __________ Date __________

9.2 Multiplying and Dividing Rational Expressions

Resource Locker

Essential Question: How can you multiply and divide rational expressions?

Explore Relating Multiplication Concepts

Use the facts you know about multiplying rational numbers to determine how to multiply rational expressions.

(A) How do you multiply $\frac{4}{5} \cdot \frac{5}{6}$?

Multiply 4 by ___ to find the __________ of the product, and multiply 5 by ___ to find the __________.

(B) $\frac{4}{5} \cdot \frac{5}{6} = \frac{\square}{\square}$

(C) To simplify, factor the numerator and denominator.

$20 = \square$

$30 = \square$

(D) Cancel common factors in the numerator and denominator to simplify the product.

$\frac{4}{5} \cdot \frac{5}{6} = \frac{20}{30} = \frac{2 \cdot 2 \cdot 5}{2 \cdot 3 \cdot 5} = \frac{\square}{\square}$

(E) Based on the steps used for multiplying rational numbers, how can you multiply the rational expression $\frac{x+1}{x-1} \cdot \frac{3}{2(x+1)}$?

____

____

Reflect

1. **Discussion** Multiplying rational expressions is similar to multiplying rational numbers. Likewise, dividing rational expressions is similar to dividing rational numbers. How could you use the steps for dividing rational numbers to divide rational expressions?

____

____

____

Explain 1 Multiplying Rational Expressions

To multiply rational expressions, multiply the numerators to find the numerator of the product, and multiply the denominators to find the denominator. Then, simplify the product by cancelling common factors.

Note the excluded values of the product, which are any values of the variable for which the expression is undefined.

Example 1 **Find the products and any excluded values.**

(A) $\dfrac{3x^2}{x^2-2x-8} \cdot \dfrac{2x^2-6x-20}{x^2-3x-10}$

$\dfrac{3x^2}{x^2-2x-8} \cdot \dfrac{2x^2-6x-20}{x^2-3x-10} = \dfrac{3x^2}{(x+2)(x-4)} \cdot \dfrac{2(x+2)(x-5)}{(x+2)(x-5)}$ Factor the numerators and denominators.

$= \dfrac{6x^2(x+2)(x-5)}{(x+2)(x-4)(x+2)(x-5)}$ Multiply the numerators and multiply the denominators.

$= \dfrac{6x^2\cancel{(x+2)}\cancel{(x-5)}}{\cancel{(x+2)}(x-4)(x+2)\cancel{(x-5)}}$ Cancel the common factors in the numerator and denominator.

$= \dfrac{6x^2}{(x+2)(x-4)}$

Determine what values of x make each expression undefined.

$\dfrac{3x^2}{x^2-2x-8}$: The denominator is 0 when $x = -2$ and $x = 4$.

$\dfrac{2x^2-6x-20}{x^2-3x-10}$: The denominator is 0 when $x = -2$ and $x = 5$.

Excluded values: $x = -2$, $x = 4$, and $x = 5$

(B) $\dfrac{x^2-8x}{14(x^2+8x+15)} \cdot \dfrac{7x+35}{x+8}$

$\dfrac{x^2-8x}{14(x^2+8x+15)} \cdot \dfrac{7x+35}{x+8} = \dfrac{\square(x-8)}{14(\square)(x+5)} \cdot \dfrac{7(\square)}{x+8}$ Factor the numerators and denominators.

$= \dfrac{7x(x-8)(\square)}{14(\square)(x+5)(x+8)}$ Multiply the numerators and multiply the denominators.

$= \dfrac{\square}{\square}$ Cancel the common factors in the numerator and denominator.

Determine what values of x make each expression undefined.

$\dfrac{x^2-8x}{14(x^2+8x+15)}$: The denominator is 0 when ________.

$\dfrac{7x+35}{x+8}$: The denominator is 0 when ________.

Excluded values: ________

Your Turn

Find the products and any excluded values.

2. $\dfrac{x^2 - 9}{x^2 - 5x - 24} \cdot \dfrac{x - 8}{2x^2 - 18x}$

3. $\dfrac{x}{x - 9} \cdot \dfrac{3x - 27}{x + 1}$

Explain 2 Dividing Rational Expressions

To divide rational expressions, change the division problem to a multiplication problem by multiplying by the reciprocal. Then, follow the steps for multiplying rational expressions.

Example 2 **Find the quotients and any excluded values.**

(A) $\dfrac{(x+7)^2}{x^2} \div \dfrac{x^2 + 9x + 14}{x^2 + x - 2}$

$\dfrac{(x+7)^2}{x^2} \div \dfrac{x^2 + 9x + 14}{x^2 + x - 2} = \dfrac{(x+7)^2}{x^2} \cdot \dfrac{x^2 + x - 2}{x^2 + 9x + 14}$ Multiply by the reciprocal.

$= \dfrac{(x+7)(x+7)}{x^2} \cdot \dfrac{(x+2)(x-1)}{(x+7)(x+2)}$ Factor the numerators and denominators.

$= \dfrac{(x+7)(x+7)(x+2)(x-1)}{x^2(x+7)(x+2)}$ Multiply the numerators and multiply the denominators.

$= \dfrac{\cancel{(x+7)}(x+7)\cancel{(x+2)}(x-1)}{x^2\cancel{(x+7)}\cancel{(x+2)}}$ Cancel the common factors in the numerator and denominator.

$= \dfrac{(x+7)(x-1)}{x^2}$

Determine what values of x make each expression undefined.

$\dfrac{(x+7)^2}{x}$: The denominator is 0 when $x = 0$.

$\dfrac{x^2 + 9x + 14}{x^2 + x - 2}$: The denominator is 0 when $x = -2$ and $x = 1$.

$\dfrac{x^2 + x - 2}{x^2 + 9x + 14}$: The denominator is 0 when $x = -7$ and $x = -2$.

Excluded values: $x = 0$, $x = -7$, $x = 1$, and $x = -2$

(B) $\dfrac{6x}{3x-30} \div \dfrac{9x^2-27x-36}{x^2-10x}$

$\dfrac{6x}{3x-30} \div \dfrac{9x^2-27x-36}{x^2-10x} = \dfrac{6x}{3x-30} \cdot \dfrac{\boxed{}}{\boxed{}}$ Multiply by the reciprocal.

$= \dfrac{6x}{3\left(\boxed{}\right)} \cdot \dfrac{x\left(\boxed{}\right)}{9(x+1)\left(\boxed{}\right)}$ Factor the numerators and denominators.

$= \dfrac{6x^2\left(\boxed{}\right)}{27\left(\boxed{}\right)(x+1)\left(\boxed{}\right)}$ Multiply the numerators and multiply the denominators.

$= \dfrac{\boxed{}}{\boxed{}}$ Cancel the common factors in the numerator and denominator.

Determine what values of x make each expression undefined.

$\dfrac{6x}{3x-30}$: The denominator is 0 when $\boxed{}$.

$\dfrac{9x^2-27x-36}{x^2-10x}$: The denominator is 0 when $\boxed{}$.

$\dfrac{x^2-10x}{9x^2-27x-36}$: The denominator is 0 when $\boxed{}$.

Excluded values: $\boxed{}$

Your Turn

Find the quotients and any excluded values.

4. $\dfrac{x+11}{4x} \div \dfrac{2x+6}{x^2+2x-3}$

5. $\dfrac{20}{x^2-7x} \div \dfrac{5x^2-40x}{x^2-15x+56}$

Explain 3 Activity: Investigating Closure

A set of numbers is said to be closed, or to have **closure**, under a given operation if the result of the operation on any two numbers in the set is also in the set.

(A) Recall whether the set of whole numbers, the set of integers, and the set of rational numbers are closed under each of the four basic operations.

	Addition	Subtraction	Multiplication	Division
Whole Numbers				
Integers				
Rational Numbers				

(B) Look at the set of rational expressions. Use the rational expressions $\frac{p(x)}{q(x)}$ and $\frac{r(x)}{s(x)}$ where $p(x)$, $q(x)$, $r(x)$ and $s(x)$ are nonzero. Add the rational expressions.

$$\frac{p(x)}{q(x)} + \frac{r(x)}{s(x)} = \square$$

(C) Is the set of rational expressions closed under addition? Explain.

(D) Subtract the rational expressions.

$$\frac{p(x)}{q(x)} - \frac{r(x)}{s(x)} = \square$$

(E) Is the set of rational expressions closed under subtraction? Explain.

(F) Multiply the rational expressions.

$$\frac{p(x)}{q(x)} \cdot \frac{r(x)}{s(x)} = \square$$

(G) Is the set of rational expressions closed under multiplication? Explain.

(H) Divide the rational expressions.

$$\frac{p(x)}{q(x)} \div \frac{r(x)}{s(x)} = \square$$

(I) Is the set of rational expressions closed under division? Explain.

Reflect

6. Are rational expressions most like whole numbers, integers, or rational numbers? Explain.

Explain 4 Multiplying and Dividing with Rational Models

Models involving rational expressions can be solved using the same steps to multiply or divide rational expressions.

Example 4 **Solve the problems using rational expressions.**

(A) Leonard drives 40 miles to work every day. One-fifth of his drive is on city roads, where he averages 30 miles per hour. The other part of his drive is on a highway, where he averages 55 miles per hour. The expression $\frac{d_c r_h + d_h r_c}{r_c r_h}$ represents the total time spent driving, in hours. In the expression, d_c represents the distance traveled on city roads, d_h represents the distance traveled on the highway, r_c is the average speed on city roads, and r_h is the average speed on the highway. Use the expression to find the average speed of Leonard's drive.

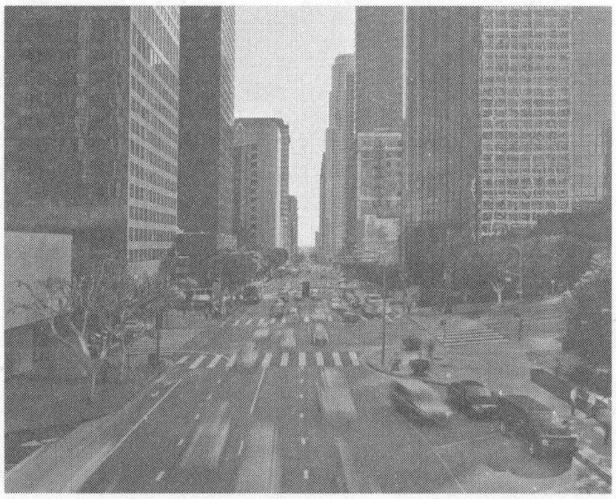

The total distance traveled is 40 miles. Find an expression for the average speed, r, of Leonard's drive.

$$r = \text{Total distance traveled} \div \text{Total time}$$

$$= 40 \div \frac{d_c r_h + d_h r_c}{r_c r_h}$$

$$= 40 \cdot \frac{r_c r_h}{d_c r_h + d_h r_c}$$

$$= \frac{40 r_c r_h}{d_c r_h + d_h r_c}$$

Find the values of d_c and d_h.

$$d_c = \frac{1}{5}(40) = 8 \text{ miles}$$

$$d_h = 40 - 8 = 32 \text{ miles}$$

Solve for r by substituting in the given values from the problem.

$$r = \frac{d r_c r_h}{d_c r_h + d_h r_c}$$

$$= \frac{40 \cdot 55 \cdot 30}{8 \cdot 55 + 32 \cdot 30}$$

$$\approx 47 \text{ miles per hour}$$

The average speed of Leonard's drive is about 47 miles per hour.

(B) The fuel efficiency of Tanika's car at highway speeds is 35 miles per gallon. The expression $\frac{48E - 216}{E(E - 6)}$ represents the total gas consumed, in gallons, when Tanika drives 36 miles on a highway and 12 miles in a town to get to her relative's house. In the expression, E represents the fuel efficiency, in miles per gallon, of Tanika's car at highway speeds. Use the expression to find the average rate of gas consumed on her trip.

The total distance traveled is ☐ miles. Find an expression for the average rate of gas consumed, g, on Tanika's trip.

$g =$ Total gas consumed $\div$ Total distance traveled

$= \frac{48E - 216}{E(E-6)} \div \square$

$= \frac{48E - 216}{\square \, E(E-6)}$

The value of E is ☐.

Solve for g by substituting in the value of E.

$$g = \frac{48(\square) - 216}{48(\square)(\square - 6)}$$

$$= \frac{\square}{\square}$$

$$\approx \square$$

The average rate of gas consumed on Tanika's trip is about ☐ gallon per mile.

Your Turn

7. The distance traveled by a car undergoing constant acceleration, a, for a time, t, is given by $d = v_0t + \frac{1}{2}at^2$, where v_0 is the initial velocity of the car. Two cars are side by side with the same initial velocity. One car accelerates and the other car does not. Write an expression for the ratio of the distance traveled by the accelerating car to the distance traveled by the nonaccelerating car as a function of time.

Elaborate

8. Explain how finding excluded values when dividing one rational expression by another is different from multiplying two rational expressions.

9. **Essential Question Check-In** How is dividing rational expressions related to multiplying rational expressions?

Evaluate: Homework and Practice

Personal Math Trainer

- Online Homework
- Hints and Help
- Extra Practice

1. Explain how to multiply the rational expressions.

$$\frac{x-3}{2} \cdot \frac{x^2-3x+4}{x^2-2x}$$

Find the products and any excluded values.

2. $\frac{x}{3x-6} \cdot \frac{x-2}{x+9}$

3. $\frac{5x^2+25x}{2} \cdot \frac{4x}{x+5}$

$$\frac{5x(x+5)(4x)}{2(x+5)}$$

$$\frac{20x^2}{2} = 10x^2$$

$$x \neq -5$$

4. $\frac{x^2-2x-15}{10x+30} \cdot \frac{3}{x^2-3x-10}$

5. $\frac{x^2-1}{x^2+5x+4} \cdot \frac{x^2}{x^2-x}$

$$\frac{(x-1)(x+1)}{x^2+5x+4} \cdot \frac{x^2}{x(x-1)}$$

$$\frac{x+1}{x^2+5x+4} \cdot \frac{x}{1}$$

$$\frac{x^2+x}{x^2+5x+4}$$

6. $\dfrac{x^2+14x+33}{4x} \cdot \dfrac{x^2-3x}{x+3} \cdot \dfrac{8x-56}{x^2+4x-77}$

7. $\dfrac{9x^2}{x-6} \cdot \dfrac{x^2-36}{3x-6} \cdot \dfrac{3}{4x^2+24x}$

$= \dfrac{9x^2}{x-6} \cdot \dfrac{(x+6)(x-6)}{3(x-2)} \cdot \dfrac{3}{4x(x+6)}$

$= \dfrac{9x^2 \cdot 3}{4x(3x-6)} = \dfrac{27x^2}{12x^2-24x}$

$= \dfrac{9x^2}{4x^2+24x}$

Find the quotients and any excluded values.

8. $\dfrac{5x^2+10x}{x^2+2x+1} \div \dfrac{20x+40}{x^2-1}$

9. $\dfrac{x^2-9x+18}{x^2+9x+18} \div \dfrac{x^2-36}{x^2-9}$

$= \dfrac{(x-3)(x-6)}{(x+3)(x+6)} - \dfrac{(x+6)(x-6)}{(x+3)(x-3)}$

$= \dfrac{(x-3)^2}{(x+6)^2}$ $x \neq -3, -6$

10. $\dfrac{-x^2+x+20}{5x^2-25x} \div \dfrac{x+4}{2x-14}$

11. $\dfrac{x+3}{x^2+8x+15} \div \dfrac{x^2-25}{x-5}$

$= \dfrac{x-3}{x^2+8x+5} \cdot \dfrac{x-5}{x^2-25}$

$= \dfrac{(x-3)}{(x-3)(x+5)} \cdot \dfrac{x-5}{(x+5)(x-5)}$

$= \dfrac{(x+3)(x+5)}{(x+5)(x-3)(x+5)(x-5)}$

$= \dfrac{1}{(x+5)^2}$ where $x \neq -3, 5, 5$

12. $\dfrac{x^2 - 10x + 9}{3x} \div \dfrac{x^2 - 7x - 18}{x^2 + 2x}$

13. $\dfrac{8x + 32}{x^2 + 8x + 16} \div \dfrac{x^2 - 6x}{x^2 - 2x - 24}$

Let $p(x) = \frac{1}{x+1}$ and $q(x) = \frac{1}{x-1}$. Find the result and determine whether the result of performing each operation is another rational expression.

14. $p(x) + q(x)$

15. $p(x) - q(x)$

16. $p(x) \cdot q(x)$

17. $p(x) \div q(x)$

18. The distance a race car travels is given by the equation $d = v_0t + \frac{1}{2}at^2$, where v_0 is the initial speed of the race car, a is the acceleration, and t is the time travelled. Near the beginning of a race, the driver accelerates for 9 seconds at a rate of 4 m/s². The driver's initial speed was 75 m/s. Find the driver's average speed during the acceleration.

19. Julianna is designing a circular track that will consist of three concentric rings. The radius of the middle ring is 6 meters greater than that of the inner ring and 6 meters less than that of the outer ring. Find an expression for the ratio of the length of the outer ring to the length of the middle ring and another for the ratio of the length of the outer ring to length of the inner ring. If the radius of the inner ring is set at 90 meters, how many times longer is the outer ring than the middle ring and the inner ring?

20. Geometry Find a rational expression for the ratio of the surface area of a cylinder to the volume of a cylinder. Then find the ratio when the radius is 3 inches and the height is 10 inches.

H.O.T. Focus on Higher Order Thinking

21. Explain the Error Maria finds an expression equivalent to $\frac{x^2 - 4x - 45}{3x - 15} \div \frac{6x^2 - 150}{x^2 - 5x}$. Her work is shown. Find and correct Maria's mistake.

$$\frac{x^2 - 4x - 45}{3x - 15} \div \frac{6x^2 - 150}{x^2 - 5x} = \frac{(x-9)(x+5)}{3(x-5)} \div \frac{6(x+5)(x-5)}{x(x-5)}$$

$$= \frac{6(x-9)(x+5)(x+5)(x-5)}{3x(x-5)(x-5)}$$

$$= \frac{2(x-9)(x+5)^2}{x(x-5)}$$

22. Critical Thinking Multiply the rational expressions. What do you notice about the expression?

$$\left(\frac{3}{x-4} + \frac{x^3 - 4x}{8x^2 - 32}\right)\left(\frac{3x + 18}{x^2 + 2x - 24} - \frac{x}{8}\right)$$

23. Multi-Step Jordan is making a garden with an area of $x^2 + 13x + 30$ square feet and a length of $x + 3$ feet.

a. Find an expression for the width of Jordan's garden.

b. If Karl makes a garden with an area of $3x^2 + 48x + 180$ square feet and a length of $x + 6$, how many times larger is the width of Jon's garden than Jordan's?

c. If x is equal to 4, what are the dimensions of both Jordan's and Karl's gardens?

Lesson Performance Task

Who has the advantage, taller or shorter runners? Almost all of the energy generated by a long-distance runner is released in the form of heat. For a runner with height H and speed V, the rate h_g of heat generated and the rate h_r of heat released can be modeled by $h_g = k_1H^3V^2$ and $h_r = k_2H^2$, k_1 and k_2 being constants. So, how does a runner's height affect the amount of heat she releases as she increases her speed?

Name________________________ Class______________ Date__________

9.3 Solving Rational Equations

Essential Question: What methods are there for solving rational equations?

Resource Locker

Explore Solving Rational Equations Graphically

A rational equation is an equation that contains one or more rational expressions. The time t in hours it takes to travel d miles can be determined by using the equation $t = \frac{d}{r}$, where r is the average rate of speed. This equation is an example of a rational equation. One method to solving rational equations is by graphing.

Solve the rational equation $\frac{x}{x-3} = 2$ by graphing.

(A) First, identify any excluded values. A number is an excluded value of a rational expression if substituting the number into the expression results in a division by 0, which is undefined. Solve $x - 3 = 0$ for x.

$x - 3 = 0$

$x = $ ☐

(B) So, 3 is an excluded value of the rational equation. Rewrite the equation with 0 on one side.

$\frac{x}{x-3} = 2$

☐ $= 0$

(C) Graph the left side of the equation as a function. Substitute y for 0 and complete the table below.

x	y	(x, y)
0		
1		
2		
4		
5		
9		

(D) Use the table to graph the function.

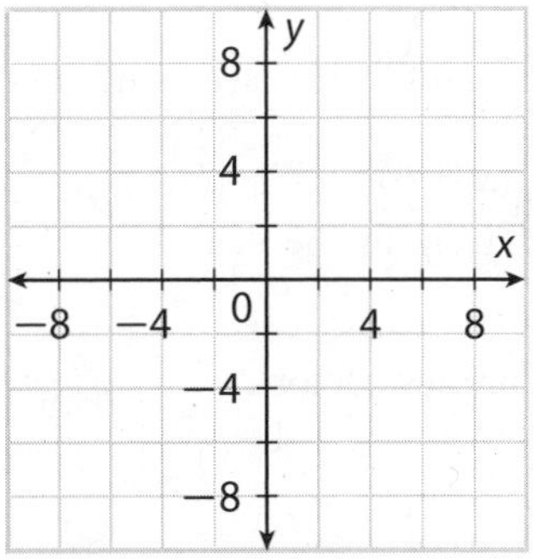

(E) Identify any x-intercepts of the graph.

There is an x-intercept at ☐.

(F) Is the value of x an excluded value? What is the solution of $\frac{x}{x-3} = 2$?

____

____

Reflect

1. **Discussion** Why does rewriting a rational equation with 0 on one side help with solving the equation?

Explain 1 Solving Rational Equations Algebraically

Rational equations can be solved algebraically by multiplying through by the LCD and solving the resulting polynomial equation. However, this eliminates the information about the excluded values of the original equation. Sometimes an excluded value of the original equation is a solution of the polynomial equation, and in this case the excluded value will be an **extraneous solution** of the polynomial equation. Extraneous solutions are not solutions of an equation.

Example 1 **Solve each rational equation algebraically.**

(A) $\frac{3x+7}{x-5} = \frac{5x+17}{2x-10}$

Identify any excluded values.

$x - 5 = 0 \qquad 2x - 10 = 0$

$x = 5 \qquad x = 5$

The excluded value is 5.

Identify the LCD by finding all factors of the denominators.

$2x - 10 = 2(x - 5)$

The different factors are 2 and $x - 5$.

The LCD is $2(x - 5)$.

Multiply each term by the LCD. $\frac{3x+7}{x-5} \cdot 2(x-5) = \frac{5x+17}{2(x-5)} \cdot 2(x-5)$

Divide out common factors. $\frac{3x+7}{\cancel{x-5}} \cdot 2\cancel{(x-5)} = \frac{5x+17}{\cancel{2}\cancel{(x-5)}} \cdot \cancel{2}\cancel{(x-5)}$

Simplify. $(3x + 7)2 = 5x + 17$

Use the Distributive Property. $6x + 14 = 5x + 17$

Solve for x. $x + 14 = 17$

$x = 3$

The solution $x = 3$ is not an excluded value. So, $x = 3$ is the solution of the equation.

(B) $\frac{2x-9}{x-7} + \frac{x}{2} = \frac{5}{x-7}$

Identify any excluded values.

$x - 7 = 0$

$x = \square$

The excluded value is ______.

Identify the LCD.

The different factors are ______.

The LCD is ______.

Multiply each term by the LCD. $\frac{2x-9}{x-7} \cdot \square + \frac{x}{2} \cdot \square = \frac{5}{x-7} \cdot \square$

Divide out common factors. $\frac{2x-9}{\cancel{x-7}} \cdot \square + \frac{x}{\cancel{2}} \cdot \square = \frac{5}{\cancel{x-7}} \cdot \square$

Simplify. $\square(2x-9) + x(\square) = 5(\square)$

Use the Distributive Property. $\square + x^2 - 7x = \square$

Write in standard form. $\square = 0$

Factor. $(\square)(\square) = 0$

Use the Zero Product Property. $x - 7 = 0$ or $\square = 0$

Solve for x. $x = 7$ or $x = \square$

The solution $x = \square$ is extraneous because it is an excluded value. The only solution is $x = \square$.

Your Turn

Solve each rational equation algebraically.

2. $\frac{8}{x+3} = \frac{x+1}{x+6}$

Explain 2 Solving a Real-world Problem with a Rational Equation

Rational equations are used to model real-world situations. These equations can be solved algebraically.

Example 2 **Use a rational equation to solve the problem.**

(A) Kelsey is kayaking on a river. She travels 5 miles upstream and 5 miles downstream in a total of 6 hours. In still water, Kelsey can travel at an average speed of 3 miles per hour. What is the average speed of the river's current?

Analyze Information

Identify the important information:

- The answer will be the average speed of ________________.
- Kelsey spends ________________ kayaking.
- She travels ________________ upstream and ________________ downstream.
- Her average speed in still water is ________________.

Formulate a Plan

Let c represent the speed of the current in miles per hour. When Kelsey is going upstream, her speed is equal to her speed in still water ________ c. When Kelsey is going downstream, her speed is equal to her speed in still water ________ c.

The variable c is restricted to ________________.

Complete the table.

	Distance (mi)	Average speed (mi/h)	Time (h)
Upstream	5		
Downstream	5		

Use the results from the table to write an equation.
total time = time upstream + time downstream

$6 = \square + \square$

Solve

$3 - c = 0 \qquad 3 + c = 0$

$\square = c \qquad c = \square$

Excluded values: ______

LCD: ______

Multiply by the LCD. $6 \cdot \square = \frac{5}{3-c} \cdot \square + \frac{5}{3+c} \cdot \square$

Divide out common factors. $6 \cdot \square = \frac{5}{\cancel{3-c}} \cdot \square + \frac{5}{\cancel{3+c}} \cdot \square$

Simplify. $6 \cdot \square = 5 \cdot \square + 5 \cdot \square$

Use the Distributive Property. $\square = 15 + 5c + \square$

Write in standard form. $0 = \square$

Factor. $0 = 6(c + 2)(\square)$

Use the Zero Product Property. $c + 2 = 0$ or $\square = 0$

Solve for c. $c = \square$ or $c = \square$

There ______ extraneous solutions. The solutions are ______.

Justify and Evaluate

The solution $c = \square$ is unreasonable because the speed of the current cannot be ______ but the solution $c = \square$ is reasonable because the speed of the current can be ______. If the speed of the current is ______, it would take Kelsey ______ hour(s) to go upstream and ______ hour(s) to go downstream, which is a total of ______ hours.

Reflect

3. Why does the domain of the variable have to be restricted in real-world problems that can be modeled with a rational equation?

______

______

Your Turn

4. Kevin can clean a large aquarium tank in about 7 hours. When Kevin and Lara work together, they can clean the tank in 4 hours. Write and solve a rational equation to determine how long, to the nearest tenth of an hour, it would take Lara to clean the tank if she works by herself. Explain whether the answer is reasonable.

Elaborate

5. Why is it important to check solutions to rational equations?

6. Why can extraneous solutions to rational equations exist?

7. **Essential Question Check In** How can you solve a rational equation without graphing?

Evaluate: Homework and Practice

- Online Homework
- Hints and Help
- Extra Practice

Solve each rational equation by graphing using a table of values.

1. $\frac{x}{x+4} = -3$

x	y	(x, y)
−8		
−6		
−5		
−3.5		
−2		
0		

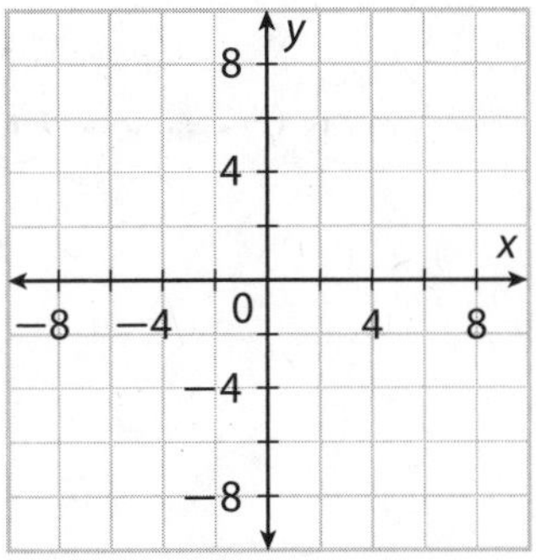

2. $\frac{x}{2x-10} = 3$

x	y	(x, y)
0		
3		
4		
5.5		
7		
10		

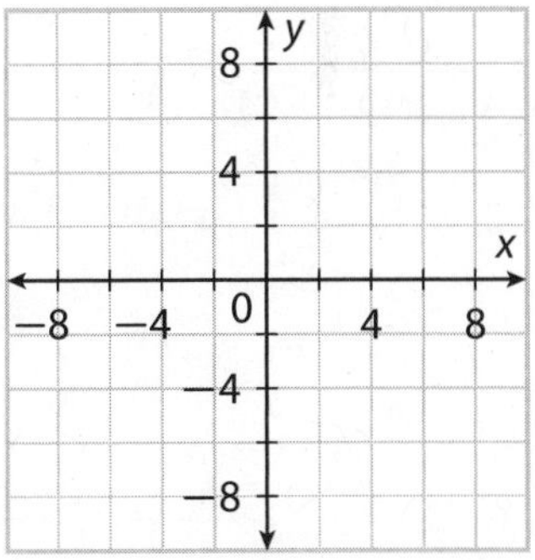

Solve each rational equation algebraically.

3. $\frac{9}{4x} - \frac{5}{6} = -\frac{13}{12x}$

$\frac{9}{4x} - \frac{5}{6} + \frac{13}{12x}$

$\frac{27}{12x} - \frac{10}{12x} + \frac{13}{12x}$

$\frac{40-10x}{12x}$

$\frac{5(4-x)}{6x} = 0 \quad x = 4$

$x \neq 0$

4. $\frac{3}{x+1} + \frac{2}{7} = 2$

$\frac{3}{x+1} + \frac{2}{7} - \frac{2}{1}$

$21 + 2x + 2 - 14x - 14$

$\frac{9-12x}{7(x+1)} = 0$

$12x = 9$

$x = \frac{9}{12}$

$x = \frac{3}{4}$

5. $\frac{56}{x^2 - 2x - 15} - \frac{6}{x + 3} = \frac{7}{x - 5}$

$\frac{56}{(x-5)(x+3)} - \frac{6}{x+3} - \frac{7}{x-5} = 0$

$\frac{56 - 6x + 30 - 7x - 21}{(x-5)(x+3)}$

$= \frac{-13x + 65}{(x-5)(x+3)}$ $x \neq 5, 3$

6. $\frac{x^2 - 29}{x^2 - 10x + 21} = \frac{6}{x - 7} + \frac{5}{x - 3}$

$\frac{x-29}{(x-7)(x-3)} - \frac{6}{(x-7)} - \frac{5}{(x-3)} = 0$

$\frac{x^2 - 29 - 6(x-3) - 5(x-7)}{(x-7)(x-3)}$

$x^2 - 29 - 6x + 18 - 5x + 35$

$\rightarrow \frac{x^2 - 11x + 24}{(x-7)(x-3)} = \frac{(x-8)(x-3)}{(x-7)(x-3)}$

$= \frac{(x-8)}{(x-7)}$

7. $\frac{5}{2x + 6} - \frac{1}{6} = \frac{2}{x + 4}$

$\frac{30}{12x+36} - \frac{2x+6}{12x+36} = \frac{2}{x+4}$

$\frac{-2x+24}{12x+36} = \frac{2}{x+4}$

$(-2x+24)(x+4) = (12x+36)(2)$

$-2x^2 - 8x + 24x + 96 = 24x + 72$

$-2x^2 - 8x = -24$

$x^2 + 4x - 12 = 0$

$(x+6)(x-2) = 0$

$x = -6, 2$

8. $\frac{5}{x^2 - 3x + 2} - \frac{1}{x - 2} = \frac{x + 6}{3x - 3}$

For 9 and 10, write a rational equation for each real-world application. Do not solve.

9. A save percentage in lacrosse is found by dividing the number of saves by the number of shots faced. A lacrosse goalie saved 9 of 12 shots. How many additional consecutive saves s must the goalie make to raise his save percentage to 0.850?

10. Jake can mulch a garden in 30 minutes. Together, Jake and Ross can mulch the same garden in 16 minutes. How much time t, in minutes, will it take Ross to mulch the garden when working alone?

11. **Geometry** A new ice skating rink will be approximately rectangular in shape and will have an area of 18,000 square feet. Using an equation for the perimeter P, of the skating rink in terms of its width W, what are the dimensions of the skating rink if the perimeter is 580 feet?

12. Water flowing through both a small pipe and a large pipe can fill a water tank in 9 hours. Water flowing through the large pipe alone can fill the tank in 17 hours. Write an equation that can be used to find the amount of time t, in hours, it would take to fill the tank using only the small pipe.

13. A riverboat travels at an average of 14 km per hour in still water. The riverboat travels 110 km east up the Ohio River and 110 km west down the same river in a total of 17.5 hours. To the nearest tenth of a kilometer per hour, what was the speed of the current of the river?

14. A baseball player's batting average is equal to the number of hits divided by the number of at bats. A professional player had 139 hits in 515 at bats in 2012 and 167 hits in 584 at bats in 2013. Write and solve an equation to find how many additional consecutive hits h the batter would have needed to raise his batting average in 2012 to be at least equal to his average in 2013.

15. The time required to deliver and install a computer network at a customer's location is $t = 5 + \frac{2d}{r}$, where t is time in hours, d is the distance (in miles) from the warehouse to the customer's location, and r is the average speed of the delivery truck. If it takes 8.2 hours for an employee to deliver and install a network for a customer located 80 miles from the warehouse, what is the average speed of the delivery truck?

16. **Art** A glassblower can produce several sets of simple glasses in about 3 hours. When the glassblower works with an apprentice, the job takes about 2 hours. How long would it take the apprentice to make the same number of sets of glasses when working alone?

17. Which of the following equations have at least two excluded values? Select all that apply.

A. $\frac{3}{x} + \frac{1}{5x} = 1$

B. $\frac{x-4}{x-2} + \frac{3}{x} = \frac{5}{6}$

C. $\frac{x}{x-6} + 1 = \frac{5}{2x-12}$

D. $\frac{2x-3}{x^2-10x+25} + \frac{3}{7} = \frac{1}{x-5}$

E. $\frac{7}{x+2} + \frac{3x-4}{x^2+5x+6} = 9$

H.O.T. Focus on Higher Order Thinking

18. Critical Thinking An equation has the form $\frac{a}{x} + \frac{x}{b} = c$, where a, b, and c are constants and $b \neq 0$. How many solutions could this equation have? Explain.

19. Multiple Representations Write an equation whose graph is a straight line, but with an open circle at $x = 4$.

20. Justify Reasoning Explain why the excluded values do not change when multiplying by the LCD to add or subtract rational expressions.

21. Critical Thinking Describe how you would find the inverse of the rational function $f(x) = \frac{x-1}{x-2}$, $x \neq 2$. Then find the inverse.

Lesson Performance Task

Kasey creates comedy sketch videos and posts them on a popular video website and is selling an exclusive series of sketches on DVD. The total cost to make the series of sketches is $989. The materials cost $1.40 per DVD and the shipping costs $2.00 per DVD. Kasey plans to sell the DVDs for $12 each.

a. Let d be the number of DVDs Kasey sells. Create a profit-per-item model from the given information by writing a rule for $C(d)$, the total costs in dollars, $S(d)$, the total sales income in dollars, $P(d)$, the profit in dollars, and $P_{PI}(d)$, the profit per item sold in dollars.

b. What is the profit per DVD if Kasey sells 80 DVDs? Does this value make sense in the context of the problem?

c. Then use the function $P_{PI}(d)$ from part a to find how many DVDs Kasey would have to sell to break even. Identify all excluded values.

STUDY GUIDE REVIEW

Rational Expressions and Equations

MODULE 9

Essential Question: How can you use rational expressions and equations to solve real-world problems?

Key Vocabulary

closure *(cerradura)*
extraneous solution *(solución extraña)*
rational expression *(expresión racional)*
reciprocal *(recíproco)*

KEY EXAMPLE *(Lesson 9.1)*

Add $\frac{1}{3+x}$ and $\frac{3-x}{x}$, simplify the result, and note the excluded values.

$$\frac{1}{3+x}+\frac{3-x}{x}=\frac{1x}{(3+x)x}+\frac{(3-x)(3+x)}{x(3+x)}$$ Write with like denominators.

$$=\frac{x+(9-x^2)}{x(x+3)}$$ Add.

$$=\frac{-x^2+x+9}{x(x+3)},\ x\neq -3, 0$$ Simplify.

KEY EXAMPLE *(Lesson 9.2)*

Find the quotient $\frac{x+3}{x+2}\div\frac{x^2-9}{2x-4}$ and note any excluded values.

$$\frac{x+3}{x+2}\div\frac{x^2-9}{2x-4}=\frac{x+3}{x+2}\cdot\frac{2x-4}{x^2-9}$$ Multiply by the reciprocal.

$$=\frac{x+3}{x+2}\cdot\frac{2(x-2)}{(x+3)(x-3)}$$ Factor the numerators and denominators.

$$=\frac{2\cancel{(x+3)}(x-2)}{(x+2)\cancel{(x+3)}(x-3)}$$ Multiply and cancel the common factors.

$$=\frac{2(x-2)}{(x+2)(x-3)};\ x\neq \pm 2, \pm 3$$ Simplify.

KEY EXAMPLE *(Lesson 9.3)*

Solve the rational equation algebraically.

$$\frac{x}{x-3}+\frac{x}{2}=\frac{6x}{2x-6}$$

$$2\cancel{(x-3)}\frac{x}{\cancel{x-3}}+\cancel{2}(x-3)\frac{x}{\cancel{2}}=\cancel{2}\cancel{(x-3)}\frac{6x}{\cancel{2x-6}}$$ Multiply each term by the LCD and divide out common factors.

$$2x+x(x-3)=6x$$ Simplify.

$$x^2-7x=0$$ Write in standard form.

$$x(x-7)=0$$ Factor.

$$x=0 \text{ or } x=7$$ Solve for *x*.

EXERCISES

Add or subtract the given expressions, simplify the result, and note the excluded values. *(Lesson 9.1)*

1. $\frac{6x + 6}{x^2 - 9} + \frac{-3x + 3}{x^2 - 9}$

2. $\frac{4}{x^2 - 1} - \frac{x + 2}{x - 1}$

Multiply or divide the given expressions, simplify the result, and note the excluded values. *(Lesson 9.2)*

3. $\frac{x^2 - 4x - 5}{3x - 15} \cdot \frac{4}{x^2 - 2x - 3}$

4. $\frac{x + 2}{x - 4} \div \frac{x}{3x - 12}$

Solve each rational equation algebraically. *(Lesson 9.3)*

5. $x - \frac{10}{x} = 3$

6. $\frac{5}{x + 1} = \frac{2}{x + 4}$

MODULE PERFORMANCE TASK

Robots and Resistors

An engineer is designing part of a circuit that will control a robot. The circuit must have a certain total resistance to function properly. The engineer plans to use several resistors in *parallel,* which means each resistor is on its own branch of the circuit. The resistors available for this project are 20, 50, 80, and 200-ohm.

How can the engineer design a parallel circuit with a total resistance of 10 ohms using a maximum of 5 resistors, at least two of which must be different values? Find at least two possible circuit configurations that meet these criteria.

For another part of the circuit, the engineer wants to use resistors in parallel to create a total resistance of 6 ohms. Can she do it using the available resistor values? If so, how? If not, explain why not.

Begin by listing in the space below all of the information you will need to solve the problem. Then use your own paper to complete the task. Be sure to write down all your data and assumptions. Then use graphs, numbers, words, or algebra to explain how you reached your conclusion.

★★ **9.** The average speed for the winner of the 2002 Indy 500 was 25 mi/h greater than the average speed for the 2001 winner. In addition, the 2002 winner completed the 500 mi race 32 min faster than the 2001 winner.

A. Let s represent the average speed of the 2001 winner in miles per hour. Write expressions in terms of s for the time in hours that it took the 2001 and 2002 winners to complete the race.

B. Write a rational equation that can be used to determine s. Solve your equation to find the average speed of the 2001 winner to the nearest mile per hour.

★★★**10.** The Renaissance architect Andrea Palladio preferred that the length and width of rectangular rooms be limited to certain ratios. These ratios are listed in the table. Palladio also believed that the height of a room with vaulted ceilings should be the harmonic mean of the length and width.

Rooms with a Width of 30 ft		
Length-to-Width Ratio	**Length (ft)**	**Height (ft)**
2:1		
3:2		
4:3		
5:3		
$\sqrt{2}$:1		

A. The harmonic mean of two positive numbers a and b is equal to $\dfrac{2}{\frac{1}{a}+\frac{1}{b}}$. Simplify this expression.

B. Complete the table for a rectangular room with a width of 30 feet that meets Palladio's requirements for its length and height. If necessary, round to the nearest tenth.

C. A Palladian room has a length-to-width ratio of 4:3. If the length of this room is doubled, what effect should this change have on the room's width and height, according to Palladio's principles?

MATH IN CAREERS

Chemist A chemist mixes 5 mL of an acid with 15 mL of water. The concentration of acid in the acid-and-water mix is $\frac{5}{5+15} = \frac{5}{20} = 25\%$. If the chemist adds more acid to the mix, then the concentration C becomes a function of the additional amount a of acid added to the mix.

a. Write a rule for the function $C(a)$.

b. What is a reasonable domain for this function? Explain.

c. What concentration of acid does pure water have? What concentration of acid does pure acid have? So, what are the possible values of $C(a)$?

d. Graph the function. Be sure to label the axes with the quantities they represent and indicate the axis scales by showing numbers for some grid lines.

e. Analyze the function's rule to determine the vertical asymptote of the function's graph. Why is the asymptote irrelevant in this situation?

f. Analyze the function's rule to determine the horizontal asymptote of the function's graph. What is the relevance of the asymptote in this situation?

UNIT 5

Radical Functions, Expressions, and Equations

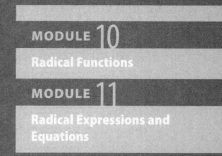

MODULE 10

Radical Functions

MODULE 11

Radical Expressions and Equations

MATH IN CAREERS

Nutritionist Nutritionists provide services to individuals and institutions, such as schools and hospitals. Nutritionists must be able to calculate the amounts of different substances in a person's diet, including calories, fat, vitamins, and minerals. They must also calculate measures of fitness, such as body mass index. Nutritionists must use statistics when reviewing nutritional studies in scientific journals.

If you are interested in a career as a nutritionist, you should study these mathematical subjects:

- Algebra
- Statistics
- Business Math

Research other careers that require proficiency in understanding statistics in scientific articles. Check out the career activity at the end of the unit to find out how **Nutritionists** use math.

Reading Start-Up

Vocabulary

Review Words

✔ composition of functions *(composición de funciones)*
extraneous solution *(solución extraña)*
✔ inverse function *(función inversa)*
✔ many-to-one function *(función muchos a uno)*
✔ one-to-one function *(función uno a uno)*
radical expression *(expresión radical)*

Preview Words

cube root function *(función de raíz cúbica)*
index *(índice)*
square root function *(función de raíz cuadrada)*

Visualize Vocabulary

Use the ✓ words to complete the graphic. Put just one word in each section of the square.

Function Types

The function that results from exchanging the input and output values of a function.	A function where each element of the range may correspond to more than one element of the domain.
A function where each element of the range corresponds to only one element of the domain.	A situation with two functions in which the output of one function is used as the input for the other.

Understand Vocabulary

To become familiar with some of the vocabulary terms in the module, consider the following. You may refer to the module, the glossary, or a dictionary.

1. A function whose rule contains a variable under a square-root sign is a ____________________.

2. A function whose rule contains a variable under a cube-root sign is a ____________________.

3. In the radical expression $\sqrt[n]{x}$, n is the __________.

Active Reading

Pyramid Fold Before beginning a module, create a pyramid fold to help you take notes from each lesson in the module. The three sides of the pyramid can summarize information about function families, their graphs, and their characteristics.

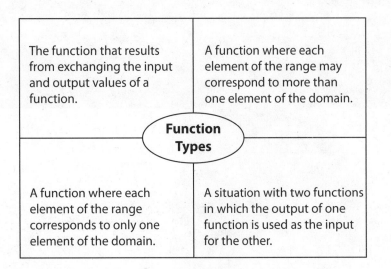

MODULE 10

Radical Functions

Essential Question: How can you use radical functions to solve real-world problems?

REAL WORLD VIDEO
A rocket must generate enough thrust to achieve escape velocity from Earth's gravitational field. Check out some of the calculations and preparations that go into a successful launch.

MODULE PERFORMANCE TASK PREVIEW

We Have Liftoff!

If you throw a ball straight up, it will eventually come back down. But if you could throw it with enough initial velocity, it would escape Earth's surface and go into orbit. If you could throw it even faster, it might even escape the solar system. What is the escape velocity for Earth, the minimum velocity for an object to leave Earth's surface and not return? What about the velocity necessary to escape other planets? Let's take off and find out!

Are YOU Ready?

Complete these exercises to review skills you will need for this module.

Personal Math Trainer

- Online Homework
- Hints and Help
- Extra Practice

Exponents

Example 1 Simplify .

$$x^2 \cdot x^3 - 2x^4 \cdot x = x^{2+3} - 2x^{4+1}$$
$$= x^5 - 2x^5$$
$$= -x^5$$

Simplify each expression.

1. $5x^3 \cdot 2x$

2. $-x^4 \cdot x^3$

3. $4x^2\left(2xy - x^2\right)$

Inverse Linear Functions

Example 2 Write the inverse function of $y = x + 9$.

$y - 9 = x + 9 - 9$ Subtract.

$y - 9 = x$ Simplify.

$x - 9 = y$ Switch *x* and *y*.

The inverse function of $y = x + 9$ is $y = x - 9$.

Example 3 Write the inverse function of $y = \frac{x}{-22}$.

$(-22)y = -\frac{x}{22}(-22)$ Multiply.

$-22y = x$ Simplify.

$-22x = y$ Switch *x* and *y*.

The inverse function of $y = \frac{x}{-22}$ is $y = -22x$.

Write the inverse of each function.

4. $y = x - 6$

5. $y = 7x$

6. $y = \frac{1}{2}x$

7. $y = x + 11$

8. $y = -18x$

9. $y = 21 + x$

Name________________________ Class________________________ Date________________

10.1 Inverses of Simple Quadratic and Cubic Functions

Resource Locker

Essential Question: What functions are the inverses of quadratic functions and cubic functions, and how can you find them?

Explore Finding the Inverse of a Many-to-One Function

The function $f(x)$ is defined by the following ordered pairs: $(-2, 4)$, $(-1, 2)$, $(0, 0)$, $(1, 2)$, and $(2, 4)$.

(A) Find the inverse function of $f(x)$, $f^{-1}(x)$, by reversing the coordinates in the ordered pairs.

____

(B) Is the inverse also a function? Explain.

____

(C) If necessary, restrict the domain of $f(x)$ such that the inverse, $f^{-1}(x)$, is a function.

The domain of $f(x)$ should be restricted to $\{x | x \geq \square\}$

(D) With the restricted domain of $f(x)$, what ordered pairs define the inverse function $f^{-1}(x)$?

____

Reflect

1. **Discussion** Look again at the ordered pairs that define $f(x)$. Without switching the order of the coordinates, how could you have known that the inverse of $f(x)$ would not be a function?

____

2. How will restricting the domain of $f(x)$ affect the range of its inverse?

____

Explain 1 Finding and Graphing the Inverse of a Simple Quadratic Function

The function $f(x) = x^2$ is a many-to-one function, so its domain must be restricted in order to find its inverse function. If the domain is restricted to $x \geq 0$, then the inverse function is $f^{-1}(x) = \sqrt{x}$; if the domain is restricted to $x \leq 0$, then the inverse function is $f^{-1}(x) = -\sqrt{x}$.

The inverse of a quadratic function is a **square root function**, which is a function whose rule involves $\sqrt{x}$. **The parent square root function** is $g(x) = \sqrt{x}$. A square root function is defined only for values of x that make the expression under the radical sign nonnegative.

Example 1 **Restrict the domain of each quadratic function and find its inverse. Confirm the inverse relationship using composition. Graph the function and its inverse.**

Ⓐ $f(x) = 0.5x^2$

Restrict the domain. $\left\{x \mid x \geq 0\right\}$

Find the inverse.

Replace $f(x)$ with y. $\qquad y = 0.5x^2$

Multiply both sides by 2. $\qquad 2y = x^2$

Use the definition of positive square root. $\qquad \sqrt{2y} = x$

Switch x and y to write the inverse. $\qquad \sqrt{2x} = y$

Replace y with $f^{-1}(x)$. $\qquad f^{-1}(x) = \sqrt{2x}$

Confirm the inverse relationship using composition.

$$f^{-1}(f(x)) = f^{-1}(0.5x^2) \qquad f(f^{-1}(x)) = 0.5\left(\sqrt{2x}\right)^2$$

$$= \sqrt{2(0.5x^2)} \qquad = 0.5(2x)$$

$$= \sqrt{x^2} \qquad = x \text{ for } x \geq 0$$

$$= x \text{ for } x \geq 0$$

Since $f^{-1}(f(x)) = x$ for $x \geq 0$ and $f(f^{-1}(x)) = x$ for $x \geq 0$, it has been confirmed that $f^{-1}(x) = \sqrt{2x}$ for $x \geq 0$ is the inverse function of $f(x) = 0.5x^2$ for $x \geq 0$.

Graph $f^{-1}(x)$ by graphing $f(x)$ and reflecting $f(x)$ over the line $y = x$.

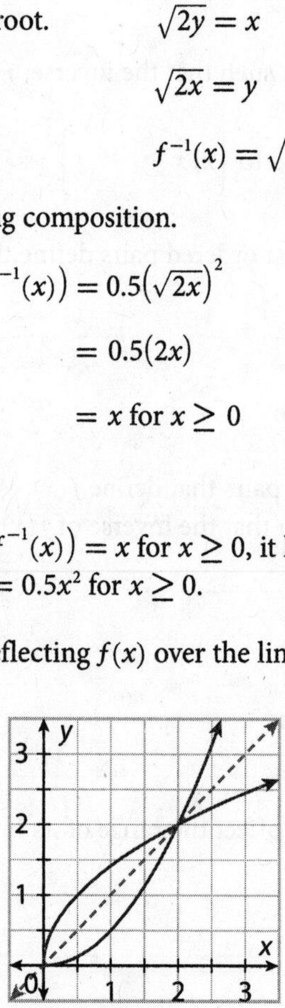

© Houghton Mifflin Harcourt Publishing Company

(B) $f(x) = x^2 - 7$

Find the inverse.

Restract the domain. ________

Replace $f(x)$ with y. $\square = x^2 - 7$

Add 7 to both sides. $\square = x^2$

Use the definition of positive square root. $\square = x$

Switch x and y to write the inverse. ________

Replace y with $f^{-1}(x)$. ________

Confirm the inverse relationship using composition.

$f^{-1}(f(x)) = f^{-1}(\square)$

$= \square$

$= \square$

$= \square$

$f(f^{-1}(x)) = f(\square)$

$= (\square)^2 - 7$

$= \square - 7$

$= \square$

Since $f^{-1}(f(x)) = \square$ for ________ and $f(f^{-1}(x)) = \square$ it has been confirmed that $f^{-1}(x) = \square$ for $\square$ is the inverse function of $f(x) = x^2 - 7$ for ________.

Graph $f^{-1}(x)$ by graphing $f(x)$ and reflecting $f(x)$ over the line $y = x$.

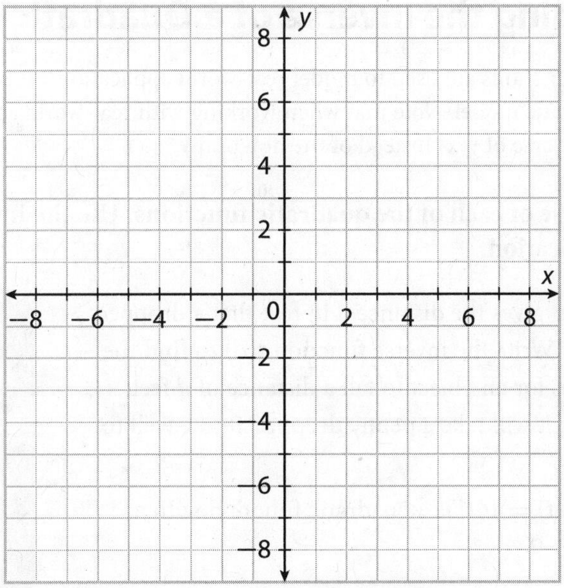

Your Turn

Restrict the domain of each quadratic function and find its inverse. Confirm the inverse relationship using composition. Graph the function and its inverse.

3. $f(x) = 3x^2$

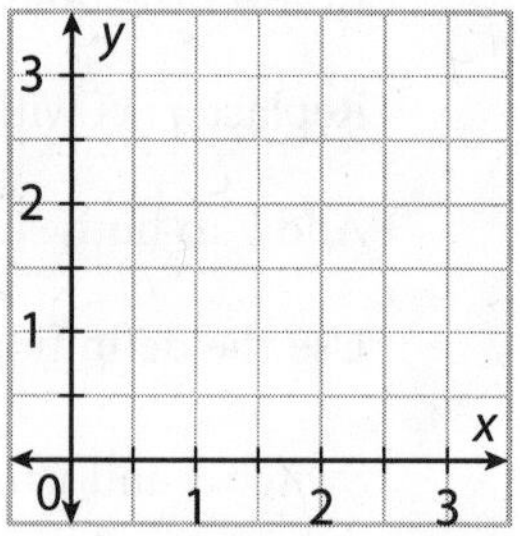

Explain 2 Finding the Inverse of a Quadratic Model

In many instances, quadratic functions are used to model real-world applications. It is often useful to find and interpret the inverse of a quadratic model. Note that when working with real-world applications, it is more useful to use the notation $x(y)$ for the inverse of $y(x)$ instead of the notation $y^{-1}(x)$.

Example 2 **Find the inverse of each of the quadratic functions. Use the inverse to solve the application.**

Ⓐ The function $d(t) = 16t^2$ gives the distance d in feet that a dropped object falls in t seconds. Write the inverse function $t(d)$ to find the time t in seconds it takes for an object to fall a distance of d feet. Then estimate how long it will take a penny dropped into a well to fall 48 feet.

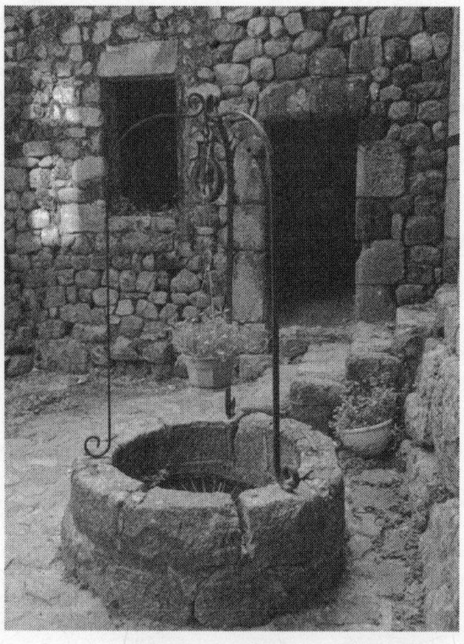

The original function $d(t) = 16t^2$ is a quadratic function with a domain restricted to $t \geq 0$.

Find the inverse function.

Write $d(t)$ as d. $\quad d = 16t^2$

Divide both sides by 16. $\quad \frac{d}{16} = t^2$

Use the definition of positive square root. $\quad \sqrt{\frac{d}{16}} = t$

Write t as $t(d)$. $\sqrt{\frac{d}{16}} = t(d)$

The inverse function is $t(d) = \sqrt{\frac{d}{16}}$ for $d \geq 0$.

Use the inverse function to estimate how long it will take a penny dropped into a well to fall 48 feet. Substitute $d = 48$ into the inverse function.

Write the function. $t(d) = \sqrt{\frac{d}{16}}$

Substitute 48 for d. $t(48) = \sqrt{\frac{48}{16}}$

Simplify. $t(48) = \sqrt{3}$

Use a calculator to estimate. $t(48) \approx 1.7$

So, it will take about 1.7 seconds for a penny to fall 48 feet into the well.

(B) The function $E(v) = 4v^2$ gives the kinetic energy E in Joules of an 8-kg object that is traveling at a velocity of v meters per second. Write and graph the inverse function $v(E)$ to find the velocity v in meters per second required for an 8-kg object to have a kinetic energy of E Joules. Then estimate the velocity required for an 8-kg object to have a kinetic energy of 60 Joules.

The original function $E(v) = 4v^2$ is a ______________ function with a domain restricted to v ______________.

Find the inverse function.

Write $E(v)$ as E. $\square = 4v^2$

Divide both sides by 4. $\square = v^2$

Use the definition of positive square root. $\square = v$

Write v as $v(E)$. ______________

The inverse function is $v(E) =$ ______________ for E ______________.

Use the inverse function to estimate the velocity required for an 8-kg object to have a kinetic energy of 60 Joules.

Substitute $E = 60$ into the inverse function.

Write the function. $v(E) = \square$

Substitute 60 for E. $v(\square) = \square$

Simplify. ______________

Use a calculator to estimate. ______________

So, an 8-kg object with kinetic energy of 60 Joules is traveling at a velocity of ______________ meters per second.

Your Turn

Find the inverse of the quadratic function. Use the inverse to solve the application.

4. The function $A(r) = \pi r^2$ gives the area of a circular object with respect to its radius r. Write the inverse function $r(A)$ to find the radius r required for area of A. Then estimate the radius of a circular object that has an area of 40 cm^2.

Explain 3 Finding and Graphing the Inverse of a Simple Cubic Function

Note that the function $f(x) = x^3$ is a one-to-one function, so its domain does not need to be restricted in order to find its inverse function. The inverse of $f(x) = x^3$ is $f^{-1}(x) = \sqrt[3]{x}$.

The inverse of a cubic function is a **cube root function**, which is a function whose rule involves $\sqrt[3]{x}$. The **parent cube root function** is $g(x) = \sqrt[3]{x}$.

Example 3 **Find the inverse of each cubic function. Confirm the inverse relationship using composition. Graph the function and its inverse.**

(A) $f(x) = 0.5x^3$

Find each inverse. Graph the function and its inverse.

Replace $f(x)$ with y. $y = 0.5x^3$

Multiply both sides by 2. $2y = x^3$

Use the definition of cube root. $\sqrt[3]{2y} = x$

Switch x and y to write the inverse. $\sqrt[3]{2x} = y$

Replace y with $f^{-1}(x)$. $\sqrt[3]{2x} = f^{-1}(x)$

Confirm the inverse relationship using composition.

$$\begin{aligned} f^{-1}(f(x)) &= f^{-1}(0.5x^3) \\ &= \sqrt[3]{2(0.5x^3)} \\ &= \sqrt[3]{x^3} \\ &= x \end{aligned} \qquad \begin{aligned} f(f^{-1}(x)) &= f(\sqrt[3]{2x}) \\ &= 0.5\left(\sqrt[3]{2x}\right)^3 \\ &= 0.5(2x) \\ &= x \end{aligned}$$

Since $f^{-1}(f(x)) = x$ and $f(f^{-1}(x)) = x$, it has been confirmed that $f^{-1}(x) = \sqrt[3]{2x}$ is the inverse function of $f(x) = 0.5x^3$.

Graph $f^{-1}(x)$ by graphing $f(x)$ and reflecting $f(x)$ over the line $y = x$.

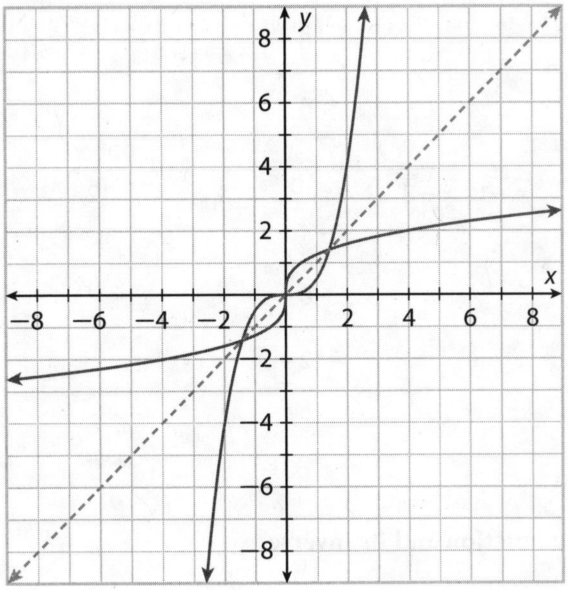

(B) $f(x) = x^3 - 9$

Find the inverse.

Replace $f(x)$ with y. $\boxed{} = x^3 - 9$

Add 9 to both sides. $\boxed{} = x^3$

Use the definition of cube root. $\boxed{} = x$

Switch x and y to write the inverse. ______________

Replace y with $f^{-1}(x)$. ______________

Confirm the inverse relationship using composition.

$f^{-1}(f(x)) = f^{-1}\left(\boxed{}\right)$

$= \boxed{}$

$= \boxed{}$

$= \boxed{}$

$f(f^{-1}(x)) = f\left(\boxed{}\right)$

$= \boxed{}$

$= \boxed{}$

$= \boxed{}$

Since $f^{-1}(f(x)) = \boxed{}$ and $f(f^{-1}(x)) = \boxed{}$, it has been confirmed that $f^{-1}(x) = \boxed{}$ is the inverse function of $f(x) = x^3 - 9$.

Graph $f^{-1}(x)$ by graphing $f(x)$ and reflecting $f(x)$ over the line $y = x$.

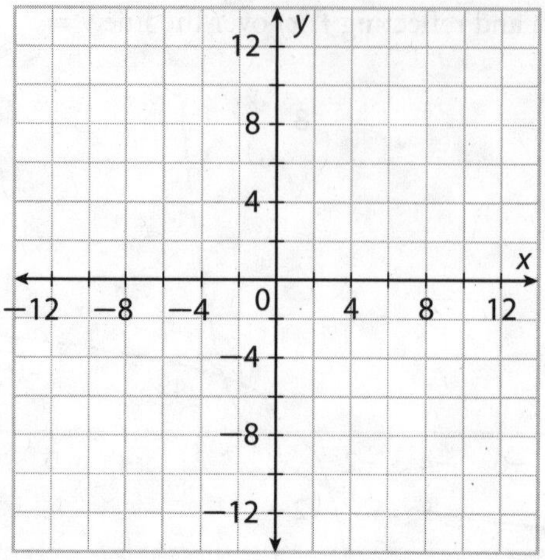

Your Turn

Find each inverse. Graph the function and its inverse.

5. $f(x) = 2x^3$

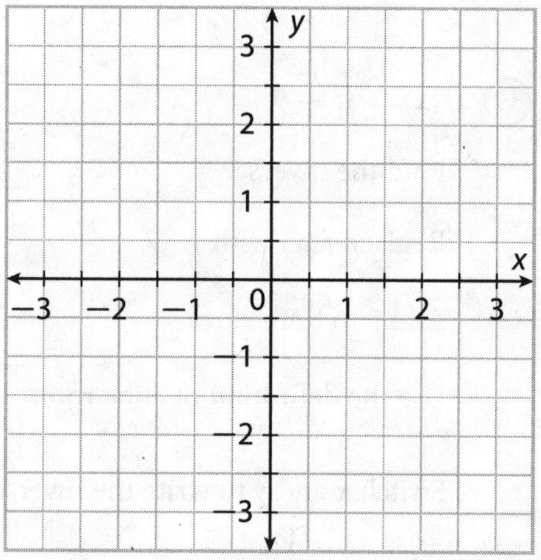

Explain 4 Finding the Inverse of a Cubic Model

In many instances, cubic functions are used to model real-world applications. It is often useful to find and interpret the inverse of cubic models. As with quadratic real-world applications, it is more useful to use the notation $x(y)$ for the inverse of $y(x)$ instead of the notation $y^{-1}(x)$.

Example 4 Find the inverse of each of the following cubic functions.

(A) The function $m(L) = 0.00001L^3$ gives the mass m in kilograms of a red snapper of length L centimeters. Find the inverse function $L(m)$ to find the length L in centimeters of a red snapper that has a mass of m kilograms.

The original function $m(L) = 0.00001L^3$ is a cubic function.

Find the inverse function.

Write $m(L)$ as m. $\qquad m = 0.00001L^3$

Multiply both sides by 100,000. $\qquad 100{,}000m = L^3$

Use the definition of cube root. $\qquad \sqrt[3]{100{,}000m} = L$

Write L as $L(m)$. $\qquad \sqrt[3]{100{,}000m} = L(m)$

The inverse function is $L(m) = \sqrt[3]{100{,}000m}$.

(B) The function $V(r) = \frac{4}{3}\pi r^3$ gives the volume V of a sphere with radius r. Find the inverse function $r(V)$ to find the radius r of a sphere with volume V.

The original function $V(r) = \frac{4}{3}\pi r^3$ is a ________ function.

Find the inverse function.

Write $V(r)$ as V. $\qquad \square = \frac{4}{3}\pi r^3$

Divide both sides by $\frac{4}{3}\pi$. $\qquad \square = r^3$

Use the definition of cube root. $\qquad \square = r$

Write r as $r(V)$. $\qquad$ ________

The inverse function is $r(V) =$ ________.

Your Turn

6. The function $m(r) = \frac{44}{3}\pi r^3$ gives the mass in grams of a spherical lead ball with a radius of r centimeters. Find the inverse function $r(m)$ to find the radius r of a lead sphere with mass m.

Elaborate

7. What is the general form of the inverse function for the function $f(x) = ax^2$? State any restrictions on the domains.

8. What is the general form of the inverse function for the function $f(x) = ax^3$? State any restrictions on the domains.

9. **Essential Question Check-In** Why must the domain be restricted when finding the inverse of a quadratic function, but not when finding the inverse of a cubic function?

Evaluate: Homework and Practice

Personal Math Trainer

- Online Homework
- Hints and Help
- Extra Practice

Restrict the domain of the quadratic function and find its inverse. Confirm the inverse relationship using composition. Graph the function and its inverse.

1. $f(x) = 0.2x^2$

$y = 0.2x^2$

$x = 0.2y^2$

$\sqrt{x} = 0.2y$

$y = \pm\frac{\sqrt{x}}{0.2}$

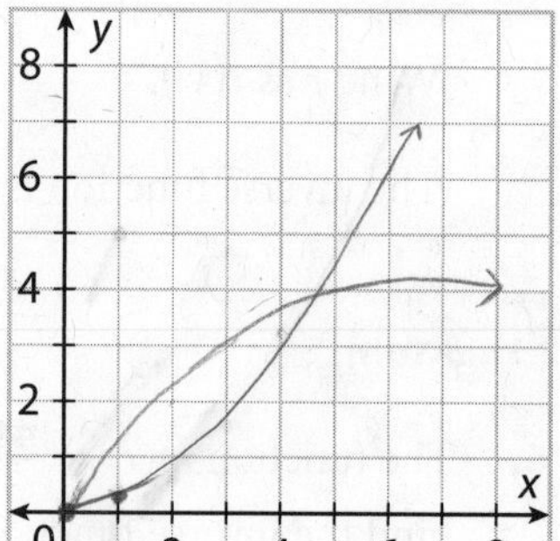

(2.) $f(x) = 8x^2$

$y = 8x^2$

$x = 8y^2$

$\sqrt{x} = 8y$

$y = \pm\frac{\sqrt{x}}{8}$

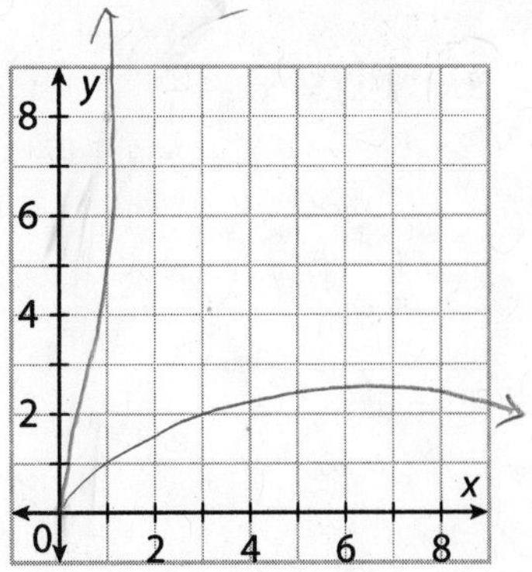

(3.) $f(x) = x^2 + 10$

restrict domain: $[0, \infty)$

inverse: $y = x^2 + 10$

$x = y^2 + 10$

$x - 10 = y^2$

$y = \sqrt{x - 10}$

$f^{-1}(x) = \sqrt{x - 10}$

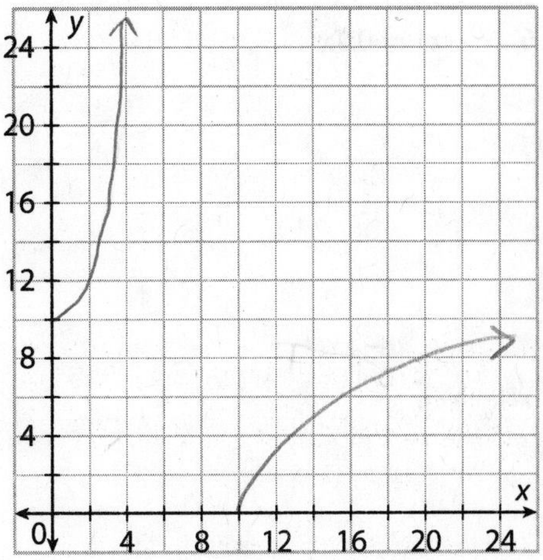

Restrict the domain of the quadratic function and find its inverse. Confirm the inverse relationship using composition.

(4.) $f(x) = 15x^2$

$y = 15x^2$

$x = 15x^2$

$\sqrt{x} = 15y$

$y = \pm\frac{\sqrt{x}}{15}$

Domain: $[0, \infty)$

5. $f(x) = x^2 - \frac{3}{4}$

$x = y^2 - \frac{3}{4}$

$x + \frac{3}{4} = y^2$

$f^{-1}(x) = \sqrt{x + \frac{3}{4}}$

$x + \frac{3}{4} = 0$

Domain: $[-\frac{3}{4}, \infty)$

6. $f(x) = 0.7x^2$

$x = 0.7y^2$

$\sqrt{x} = 7y$

$y = \pm\frac{\sqrt{x}}{7}$

Domain: $[0, \infty)$

7. The function $d(s) = \frac{1}{14.9}s^2$ models the average depth d in feet of the water over which a tsunami travels, where s is the speed in miles per hour. Write the inverse function $s(d)$ to find the speed required for a depth of d feet. Then estimate the speed of a tsunami over water with an average depth of 1500 feet.

8. The function $x(T) = 9.8\left(\frac{T}{2\pi}\right)^2$ gives the length x in meters for a pendulum to swing for a period of T seconds. Write the inverse function to find the period of a pendulum in seconds. The period of a pendulum is the time it takes the pendulum to complete one back-and-forth swing. Find the period of a pendulum with length of 5 meters.

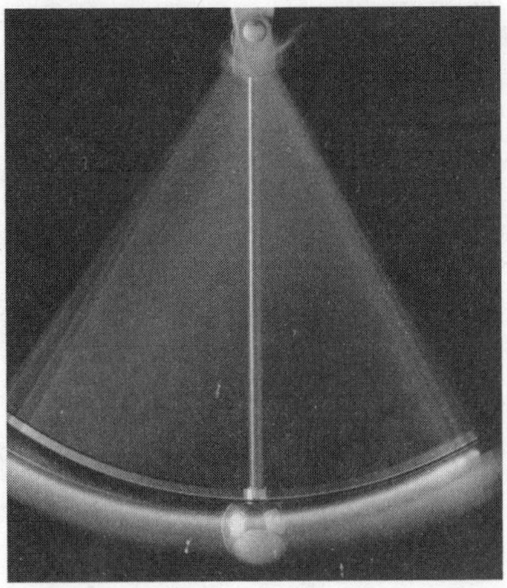

Find the inverse of each cubic function. Confirm the inverse relationship using composition. Graph the function and its inverse.

9. $f(x) = 0.25x^3$

$x = 0.25y^3$

$y^3 = \frac{x}{0.25}$

$y = \sqrt[3]{\frac{x}{0.25}}$

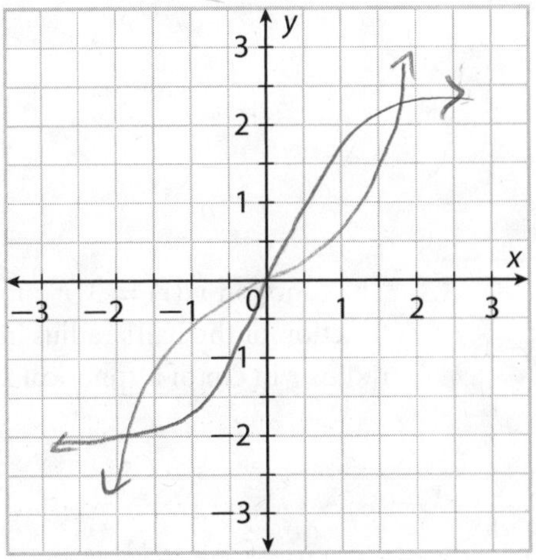

10. $f(x) = -12x^3$

$x = -12y^3$

$y^3 = \frac{x}{-12}$

$y = \sqrt[3]{\frac{x}{-12}}$

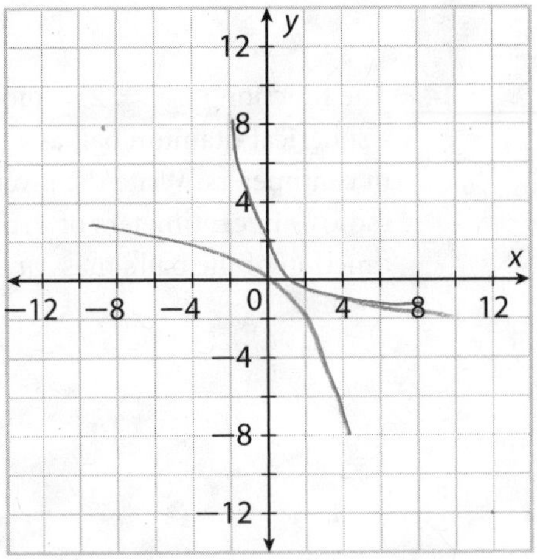

Find the inverse of the cubic function. Confirm the inverse relationship using composition.

11. $f(x) = x^3 - \frac{5}{6}$

$y = x^3 - \frac{5}{6}$

$x = y^3 - \frac{5}{6}$

$y = \sqrt[3]{x + \frac{5}{6}}$

12. $f(x) = x^3 + 9$

$y = x^3 + 9$

$x = y^3 + 9$

$y = \sqrt[3]{x - 9}$

13. The function $m(r) = 31r^3$ models the mass in grams of a spherical zinc ball as a function of the ball's radius in centimeters. Write the inverse model to represent the radius r in cm of a spherical zinc ball as a function of the ball's mass m in g.

14. The function $m(r) = 21r^3$ models the mass in grams of a spherical titanium ball as a function of the ball's radius in centimeters. Write the inverse model to represent the radius r in centimeters of a spherical titanium ball as a function of the ball's mass m in grams.

15. After an initial deposit of \$2000, a bank account pays interest at an annual rate $r\%$ compounded annually. The value V of the account after 3 years can be represented by the model $V(r) = 2000(1 + r)^3$. Write the inverse function $r(V)$ to find the interest rate needed for the account to have value V after the 3 years.

H.O.T. Focus on Higher Order Thinking

16. Explain the Error A student was asked to find the inverse of the function $f(x) = \left(\frac{x}{2}\right)^3 + 9$. What did the student do wrong? Find the correct inverse.

$$f(x) = \left(\frac{x}{2}\right)^3 + 9$$

$$y = \left(\frac{x}{2}\right)^3 + 9$$

$$y - 9 = \left(\frac{x}{2}\right)^3$$

$$2y - 18 = x^3$$

$$\sqrt[3]{2y - 18} = x$$

$$y = \sqrt[3]{2x - 18}$$

$$f^{-1}(x) = \sqrt[3]{2x - 18}$$

17. Multi-Step A framing store uses the function $\left(\frac{c - 0.2}{0.5}\right)^2 = a$ to determine the total area of a piece of glass with respect to the cost before installation of the glass. Write the inverse function for the cost c in dollars of glass for a picture with an area of a in square centimeters. Then write a new function to represent the total cost C the store charges if it costs \$6.00 for installation. Use the total cost function to estimate the cost if the area of the glass is 192 cm^2.

18. Make a Conjecture The function $f(x) = x^2$ must have its domain restricted to have its inverse be a function. The function $f(x) = x^3$ does not need to have its domain restricted to have its inverse be a function. Make a conjecture about which power functions need to have their domains restricted to have their inverses be functions and which do not.

Lesson Performance Task

One method used to irrigate crops is the center-pivot irrigation system. In this method, sprinklers rotate in a circle to water crops. The challenge for the farmer is to determine where to place the pivot in order to water the desired number of acres. The farmer knows the area but needs to find the radius of the circle necessary to define that area. How can the farmer determine this from the formula for the area of a circle $A = \pi r^2$? Find the formula the farmer could use to determine the radius necessary to irrigate a given number of acres, A. (Hint: One acre is 43,560 square feet.) What would be the radius necessary for the sprinklers to irrigate an area of 133 acres?

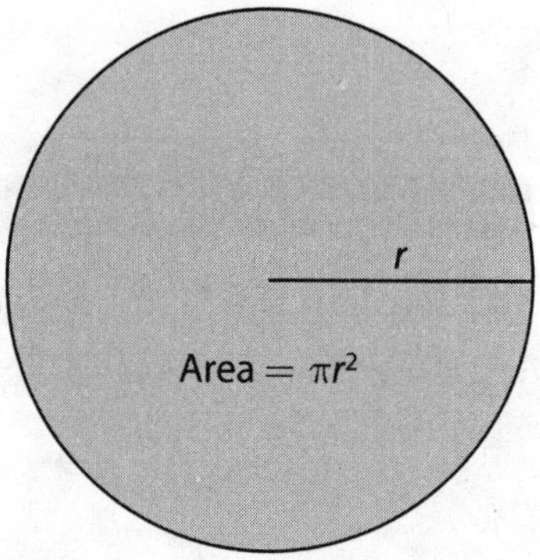

Name______________ Class__________ Date________

10.2 Graphing Square Root Functions

Essential Question: How can you use transformations of a parent square root function to graph functions of the form $g(x) = a\sqrt{(x-h)} + k$ or $g(x) = \sqrt{\frac{1}{b}(x-h)} + k$?

Resource Locker

Explore 1 Graphing and Analyzing the Parent Square Root Function

Although you have seen how to use imaginary numbers to evaluate square roots of negative numbers, graphing complex numbers and complex valued functions is beyond the scope of this course. For purposes of graphing functions based on the square roots (and in most cases where a square root function is used in a real-world example), the domain and range should both be limited to real numbers.

The square root function is the inverse of a quadratic function with a domain limited to positive real numbers. The quadratic function must be a one-to-one function in order to have an inverse, so the domain is limited to one side of the vertex. The square root function is also a one-to-one function as all inverse functions are.

(A) The domain of the square root function (limited to real numbers) is given by $\{x \mid x \geq \square\}$

(B) Fill in the table.

x	$f(x) = \sqrt{x}$
0	
1	
4	
9	

(C) Plot the points on the graph, and connect them with a smooth curve.

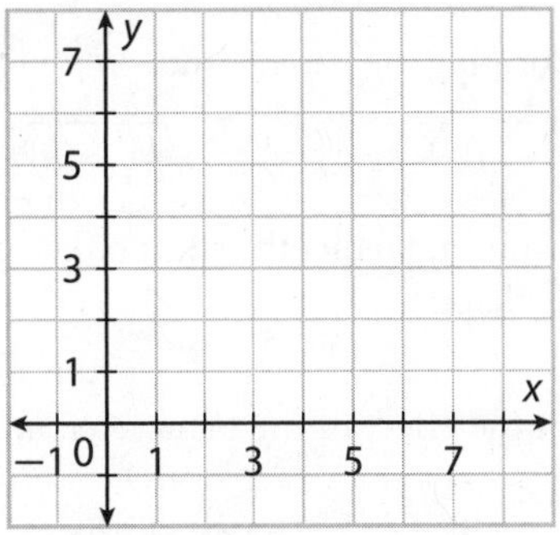

(D) Recall that this function is the inverse of the parent quadratic $(f(x) = x^2)$ with a domain limited to the nonnegative real numbers. Write the range of this square root function:

$\{y \mid y \geq \square\}$.

(E) The graph appears to be getting flatter as x increases, indicating that the rate of change ________ as x increases.

(F) Describe the end behavior of the square root function, $f(x) = \sqrt{x}$. $f(x) \to \square$ as $x \to \square$

Reflect

1. **Discussion** Why does the end behavior of the square root function only need to be described at one end?

2. The solution to the equation $x^2 = 4$ is sometimes written as $x = \pm 2$. Explain why the inverse of $f(x) = x^2$ cannot similarly be written as $g(x) = \pm\sqrt{x}$ in order to use all reals as the domain of $f(x)$.

Explore 2 Predicting the Effects of Parameters on the Graphs of Square Root Functions

You have learned how to transform the graph of a function using reflections across the x- and y-axes, vertical and horizontal stretches and compressions, and translations. Here, you will apply those transformations to the graph of the square root function $f(x) = \sqrt{x}$.

When transforming the parent function $f(x) = \sqrt{x}$, you can get functions of the form

$g(x) = a\sqrt{(x - h)} + k$ or $g(x) = \sqrt{\frac{1}{b}(x - h)} + k$.

For each parameter, predict the effect on the graph of the parent function, and then confirm your prediction with a graphing calculator.

(A) Predict the effect of the parameter, h, on the graph of $g(x) = \sqrt{x - h}$ for each function.

a. $g(x) = \sqrt{x - 2}$: The graph is a ______________ of the graph of $f(x)$ [right/left/up/down] 2 units.

b. $g(x) = \sqrt{x + 2}$: The graph is a ______________ of the graph of $f(x)$ [right/left/up/down] 2 units.

Check your answers using a graphing calculator.

(B) Predict the effect of the parameter k on the graph of $g(x) = \sqrt{x} + k$ for each function.

a. $g(x) = \sqrt{x} - 2$: The graph is a ______________ of the graph of $f(x)$ [right/up/left/down] 2 units.

b. $g(x) = \sqrt{x} - 2$: The graph is a ______________ of the graph of $f(x)$ [right/up/left/down] 2 units.

Check your answers using a graphing calculator.

(C) Predict the effect of the parameter a on the graph of $g(x) = a\sqrt{x}$ for each function.

a. $g(x) = 2\sqrt{x}$: The graph is a ______________ stretch of the graph of $f(x)$ by a factor of ____.

b. $g(x) = \frac{1}{2}\sqrt{x}$: The graph is a ______________ compression of the graph of $f(x)$ by a factor of ____.

c. $g(x) = -\frac{1}{2}\sqrt{x}$: The graph is a ______________ compression of the graph of $f(x)$ by a factor of ____ as well as a ______________ across the ______________.

d. $g(x) = -2\sqrt{x}$: The graph is a ______________ stretch of the graph of $f(x)$ by a factor of ____ as well as a ______________ across the ______________.

Check your answers using a graphing calculator.

(D) Predict the effect of the parameter, b, on the graph of $g(x) = \sqrt{\frac{1}{b}x}$ for each function.

a. $g(x) = \sqrt{\frac{1}{2}x}$: The graph is a ______________ stretch of the graph of $f(x)$ by a factor of ____.

b. $g(x) = \sqrt{2x}$: The graph is a ______________ compression of the graph of $f(x)$ by a factor of ____.

c. $g(x) = \sqrt{-\frac{1}{2}x}$: The graph is a ______________ stretch of the graph of $f(x)$ by a factor of ____ as well as a ______________ across the ______________.

d. $g(x) = \sqrt{-2x}$: The graph is a ______________ compression of the graph of $f(x)$ by a factor of ____ as well as a ______________ across the ______________.

Check your answers using a graphing calculator.

Reflect

3. Discussion Describe what the effect of each of the transformation parameters is on the domain and range of the transformed function.

____

____

____

____

____

Explain 1 Graphing Square Root Functions

When graphing transformations of the square root function, it is useful to consider the effect of the transformation on two reference points, $(0, 0)$ and $(1, 1)$, that lie on the parent function, and where they map to on the transformed function, $g(x)$.

$f(x) = \sqrt{x}$		$g(x) = a\sqrt{x-h}+k$		$g(x) = \sqrt{\frac{1}{b}(x-h)}+k$	
x	y	x	y	x	y
0	0	h	k	h	k
1	1	$h+1$	$k+a$	$h+b$	$k+1$

The reference points can be found by recognizing that the initial point of the graph is translated from $(0, 0)$ to (h, k). From the initial point, find the next reference point by going up or down by $|a|$ or left or right by $|b|$, depending on the parameter used and its sign.

Transformations of the square root function also affect the domain and range. In order to work with real valued inputs and outputs, the domain of the square root function cannot include values of x that result in a negative-valued expression. Negative values of x can be in the domain, as long as they result in nonnegative values of the expression that is inside the square root. Similarly, the value of the square root function is positive by definition, but multiplying the square root function by a negative number, or adding a constant to it changes the range and can result in negative values of the transformed function.

Example 1 **For each of the transformed square root functions, find the transformed reference points and use them to plot the transformed function on the same graph with the parent function. Describe the domain and range using set notation.**

(A) $g(x) = 2\sqrt{x-3} - 2$

To find the domain:

Square root input must be nonnegative. $x - 3 \geq 0$

Solve the inequality for x. $x \geq 3$

The domain is $\{x \mid x \geq 3\}$.

To find the range:

The square root function is nonnegative. $\sqrt{x-3} \geq 0$

Multiply by 2 $2\sqrt{x-3} \geq 0$

Subtract 2. $2\sqrt{x-3} - 2 \geq -2$

The expression on the left is $g(x)$. $g(x) \geq -2$

Since $g(x)$ is greater than or equal to -2 for all x in the domain, the range is $\{y \mid y \geq -2\}$.

$(0, 0) \rightarrow (3, -2)$

$(1, 1) \rightarrow (4, 0)$

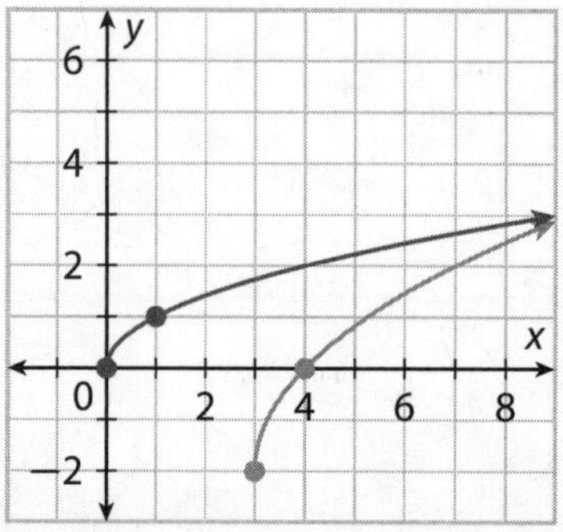

(B) $g(x) = \sqrt{-\frac{1}{2}(x-2)} + 1$

To find the domain:

Square root input must be nonnegative. $-\frac{1}{2}(x-2) \geq$ ☐

Multiply both sides by -2. $x - 2$ ☐ 0

Add 2 to both sides. ☐ ≤ 2

Expressed in set notation, the domain is $\{x \mid$ ☐ $\}$.

To find the range:

The square root function is nonnegative. $\sqrt{-\frac{1}{2}(x-2)}$ ☐ 0

Add 1 both sides $\sqrt{-\frac{1}{2}(x-2)} + 1 \geq$ ☐

Substitute in ☐. $g(x) \geq 1$

Since $g(x)$ is greater than 1 for all x in the domain,

the range (in set notation) is $\{y \mid$ ☐ $\}$.

$(0, 0) \rightarrow$ ☐

$(1, 1) \rightarrow$ ☐

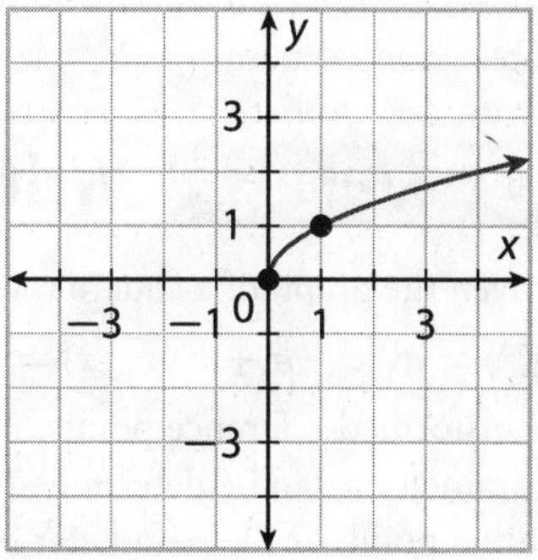

Your Turn

For each of the transformed square root functions, find the transformed reference points and use them to plot the transformed function on the same graph with the parent function. Describe the domain and range using set notation.

4. $g(x) = -3\sqrt{x-2} + 3$

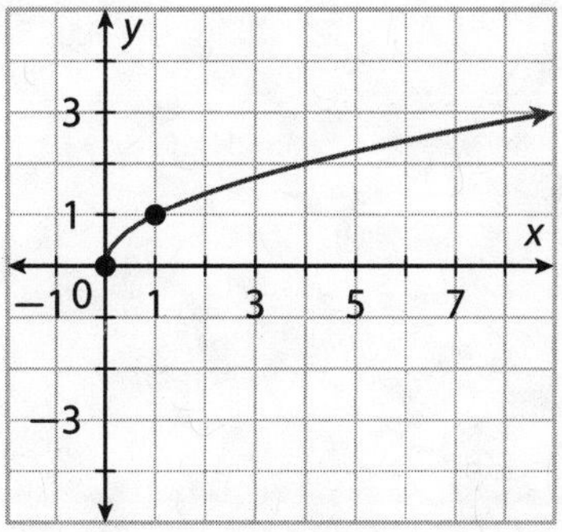

5. $g(x) = \sqrt{\frac{1}{3}(x + 2)} + 1$

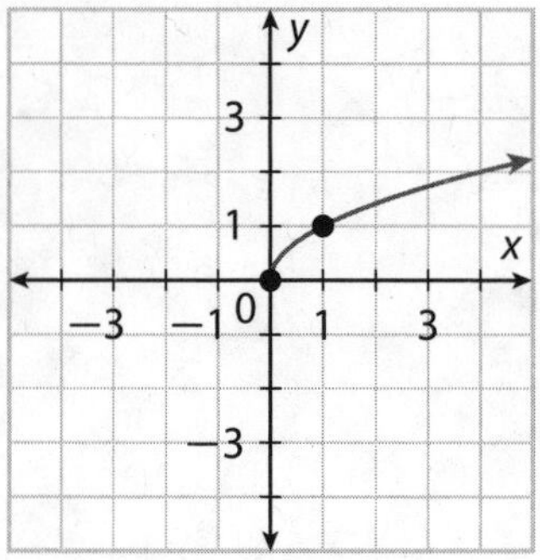

Explain 2 Writing Square Root Functions

Given the graph of a square root function and the form of the transformed function, either $g(x) = a\sqrt{x - h} + k$ or $g(x) = \sqrt{\frac{1}{b}(x - h)} = k$, the transformation parameters can be determined from the transformed reference points. In either case, the initial point will be at (h, k) and readily apparent. The parameter a can be determined by how far up or down the second point (found at $x = h + 1$) is from the initial point, or the parameter b can be determined by how far to the left or right the second point (found at $y = k + 1$) is from the initial point.

Example 2 **Write the function that matches the graph using the indicated transformation format.**

(A) $g(x) = \sqrt{\frac{1}{b}(x - h)} + k$

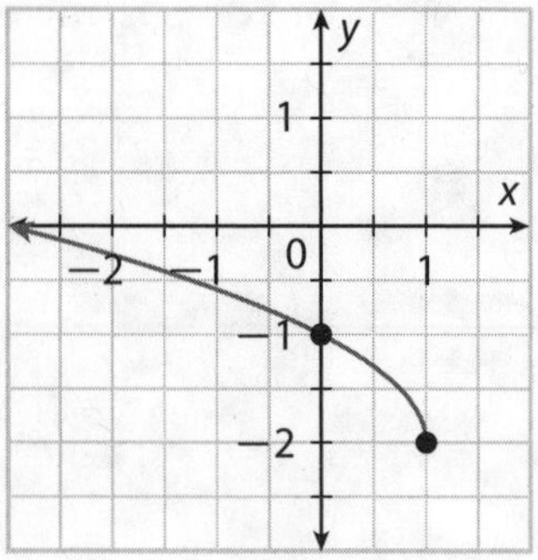

Initial point: $(h, k) = (1, -2)$

Second point:

$$(h + b, k + 1) = (0, -1)$$

$$1 + b = 0$$

$$b = -1$$

The function is $g(x) = \sqrt{-1(x - 1)} - 2$.

(B) $g(x) = a\sqrt{x - h} + k$

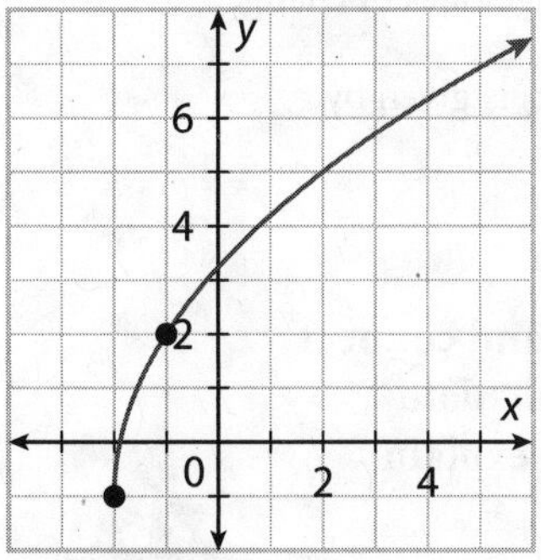

Initial point: $(h, k) = (\square, \square)$

Second point:

$(h + 1, k + \square) = (-1, \square)$

$\square + a = 2$

$a = \square$

The function is $g(x) = \square\sqrt{x \square} 2 - \square$.

Your Turn

Write the function that matches the graph using the indicated transformation format.

6. $g(x) = \sqrt{\frac{1}{b}(x - h)} + k$

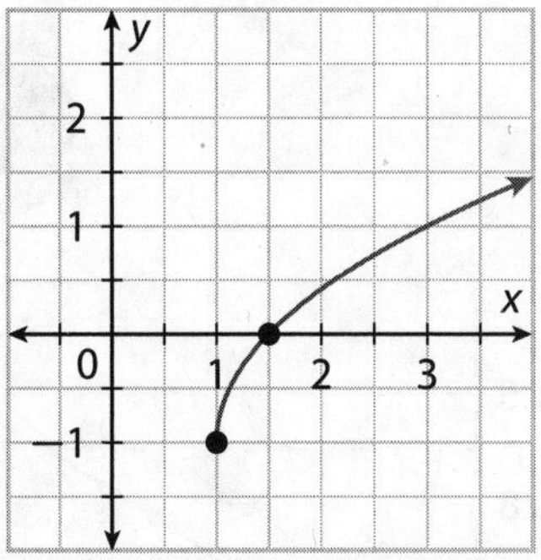

7. $g(x) = a\sqrt{(x - h)} + k$

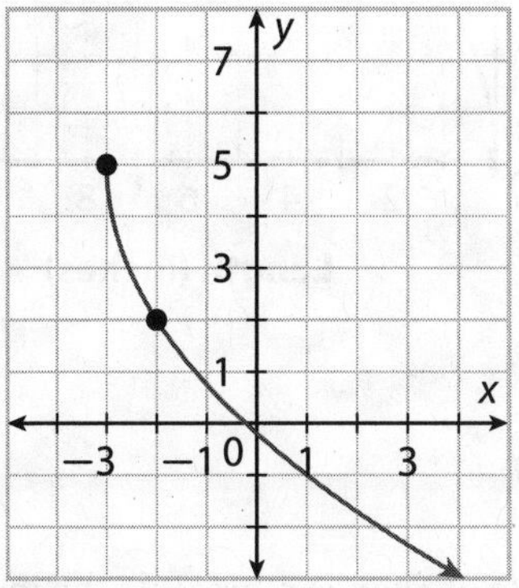

Explain 3 Modeling with Square Root Functions

Square root functions that model real-world situations can be used to investigate average rates of change.

Recall that the average rate of change of the function $f(x)$ over an interval from x_1 to x_2 is given by

$$\frac{f(x_2) - f(x_1)}{x_2 - x_1}.$$

Example 3 **Use a calculator to evaluate the model at the indicated points, and connect the points with a curve to complete the graph of the model. Calculate the average rates of change over the first and last intervals and explain what the rate of change represents.**

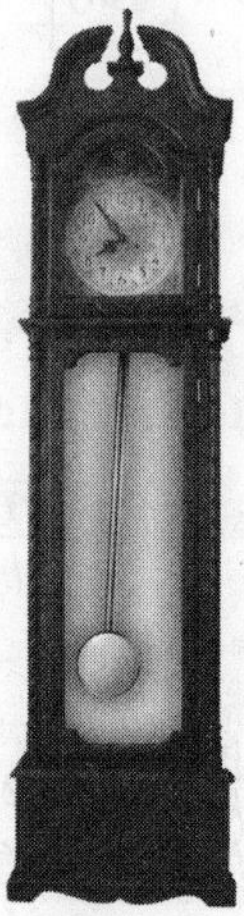

(A) The approximate period T of a pendulum (the time it takes a pendulum to complete one swing) is given in seconds by the formula $T = 0.32\sqrt{\ell}$, where ℓ is the length of the pendulum in inches. Use lengths of 2, 4, 6, 8, and 10 inches.

First find the points for the given x-values.

Length (inches)	Period (seconds)
2	0.45
4	0.64
6	0.78
8	0.91
10	1.01

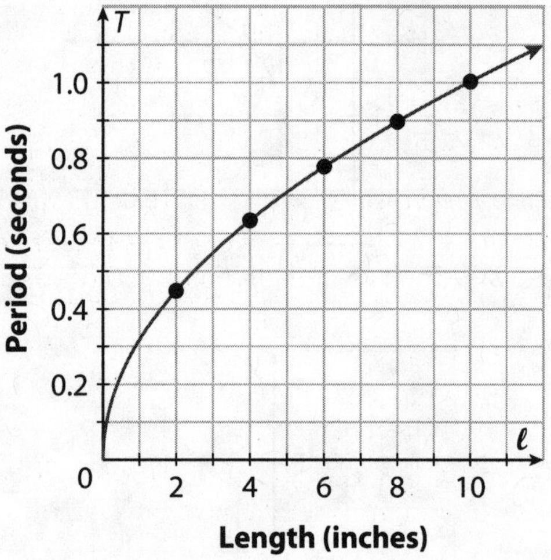

Plot the points and draw a smooth curve through them.

Find the average increase in period per inch increase in the pendulum length for the first interval and the last interval.

First interval:

$$\text{rate of change} = \frac{0.64 - 0.45}{4 - 2}$$
$$= 0.095$$

Last Interval:

$$\text{rate of change} = \frac{1.01 - 0.91}{10 - 8}$$
$$= 0.05$$

The average rate of change is less for the last interval. The average rate of change represents the increase in pendulum period with each additional inch of length. As the length of the pendulum increases, the increase in period time per inch of length becomes less.

(B) A car with good tires is on a dry road. The speed, in miles per hour, from which the car can stop in a given distance d, in feet, is given by $s(d) = \sqrt{96d}$. Use distances of 20, 40, 60, 80, and 100 feet.

First, find the points for the given x-values.

Distance	20	40	60	80	100
Speed					

Plot the points and draw a smooth curve through them.

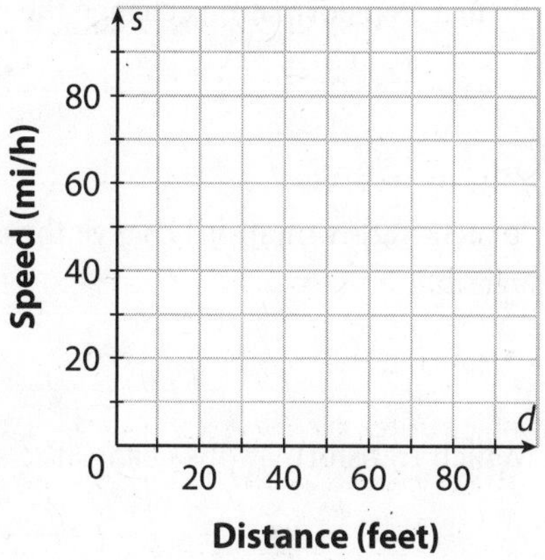

First interval:

$$\text{rate of change} = \frac{\square - \square}{40 - 20} = \square$$

Last Interval:

$$\text{rate of change} = \frac{\square - \square}{100 - 80} = \square$$

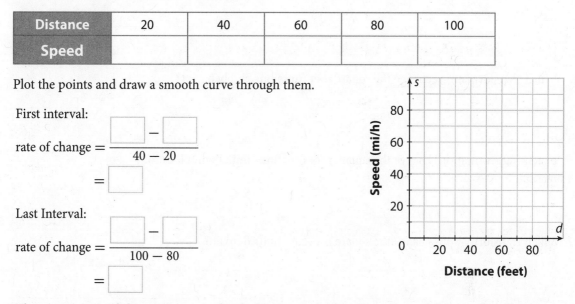

The average rate of change is ______ for the last interval. The average rate of change represents the increase in ______ with each additional ______. As the available stopping distance increases, the additional increase in speed per foot of stopping distance ______.

Your Turn

Use a calculator to evaluate the model at the indicated points, and connect the points with a curve to complete the graph of the model. Calculate the average rates of change over the first and last intervals and explain what the rate of change represents.

8. The speed in miles per hour of a tsunami can be modeled by the function $s(d) = 3.86\sqrt{d}$, where d is the average depth in feet of the water over which the tsunami travels. Graph this function from depths of 1000 feet to 5000 feet and compare the change in speed with depth from the shallowest interval to the deepest. Use depths of 1000, 2000, 3000, 4000, and 5000 feet for the x-values.

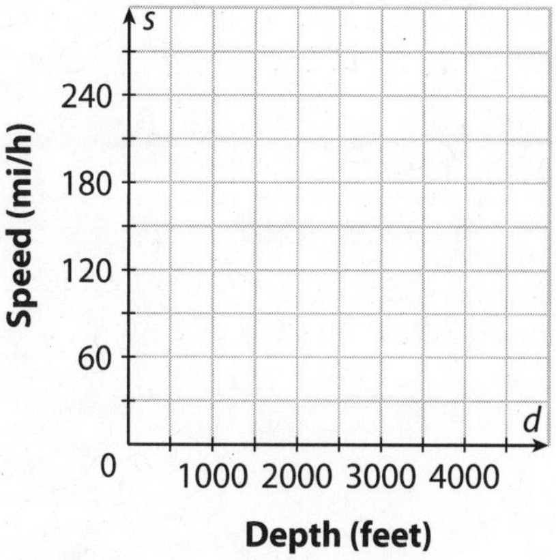

Elaborate

9. What is the difference between the parameters inside the radical (b and h) and the parameters outside the radical (a and k)?

10. Which transformations change the square root function's end behavior?

11. Which transformations change the square root function's initial point location?

12. Which transformations change the square root function's domain?

13. Which transformations change the square root function's range?

14. **Essential Question Check-In** Describe in your own words the steps you would take to graph a function of the form $g(x) = a\sqrt{x - h} + k$ or $g(x) = \sqrt{\frac{1}{b}(x - h)} + k$ if you were given the values of h and k and using either a or b.

Evaluate: Homework and Practice

Personal Math Trainer

- Online Homework
- Hints and Help
- Extra Practice

1. Graph the functions $f(x) = \sqrt{x}$ and $g(x) = -\sqrt{x}$ on the same grid. Describe the domain, range and end behavior of each function. How are the functions related?

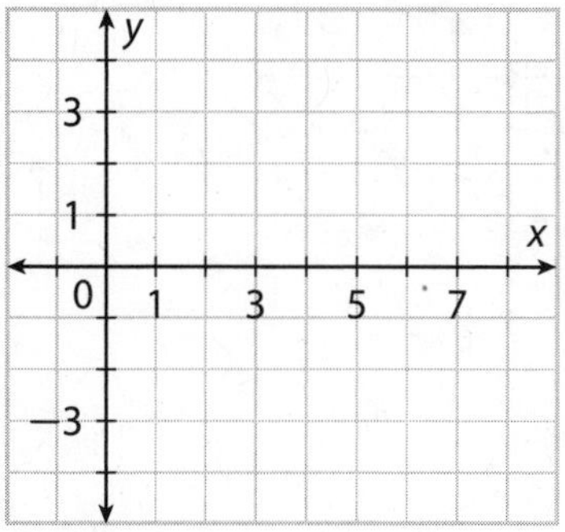

Describe the transformations of $g(x)$ from the parent function $f(x) = \sqrt{x}$.

2. $g(x) = \sqrt{\frac{1}{2}x + 1}$

vertical shrink
by 1/2

3. $g(x) = -5\sqrt{x + 1} - 3$

4. $g(x) = \frac{1}{4}\sqrt{x - 5} - 2$

vertical shrink
by 1/4

5. $g(x) = \sqrt{-7(x - 7)}$

Describe the domain and range of each function using set notation.

6. $g(x) = \sqrt{\frac{1}{3}(x - 1)}$

D: $x - 1 \geq 0$
$x \geq 1$
$[1, \infty)$

R:

7. $g(x) = 3\sqrt{x + 4} + 3$

8. $g(x) = \sqrt{-5(x + 1)} + 2$

D: $x + 1 \geq 0$
$x \geq -1$
$(-\infty, -1]$

9. $g(x) = -7\sqrt{x - 3} - 5$

Plot the transformed function $g(x)$ on the grid with the parent function, $f(x) = \sqrt{x}$. Describe the domain and range of each function using set notation.

10. $g(x) = -\sqrt{x} + 3$

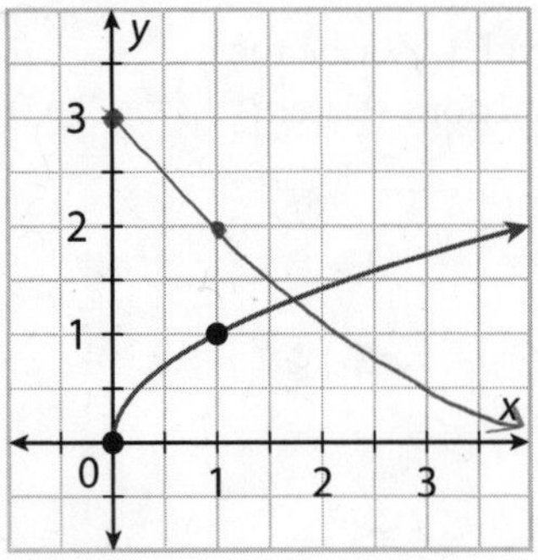

D: [0, ∞)

R: [3, ∞)

11. $g(x) = \sqrt{\frac{1}{3}(x + 4)} - 1$

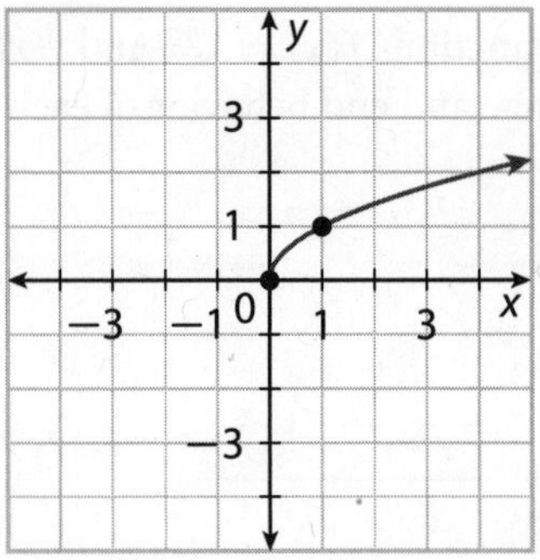

12. $g(x) = \sqrt{-\frac{2}{3}\left(x - \frac{1}{2}\right)} - 2$

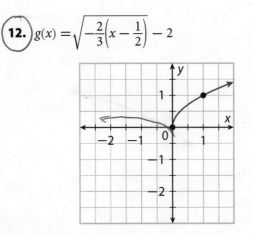

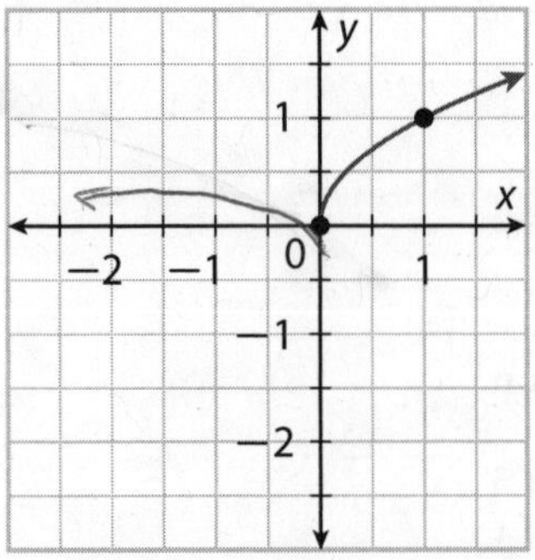

Doman: x ≤ ½

Range: [-½, ∞)

13. $g(x) = 4\sqrt{x + 3} - 4$

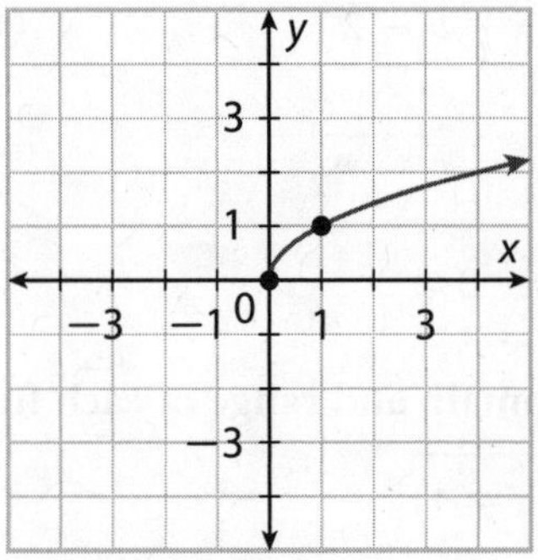

Write the function that matches the graph using the indicated transformation format.

14. $g(x) = \sqrt{\frac{1}{b}(x - h)} + k$

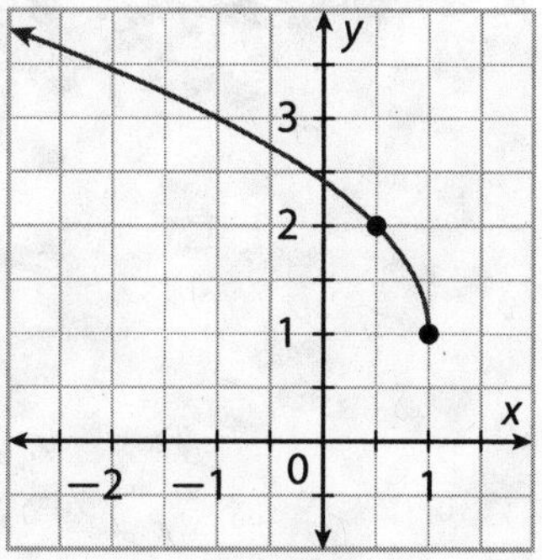

$g(x) = \sqrt{\frac{1}{b}(x-1)} + 1$

$g(x) = \sqrt{\frac{1}{2}(x-1)} + 1$

15. $g(x) = \sqrt{\frac{1}{b}(x - h)} + k$

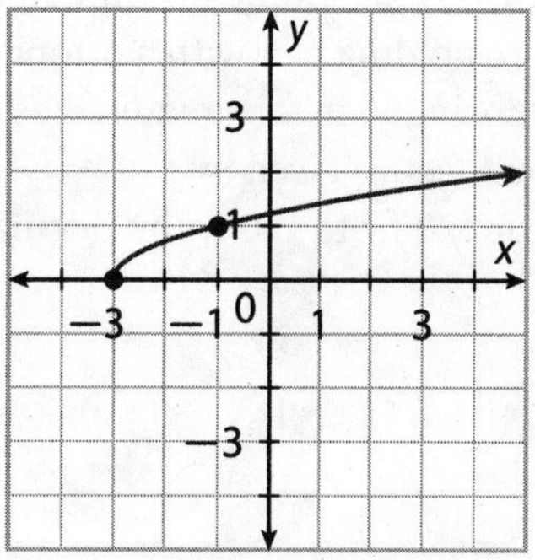

16. $g(x) = a\sqrt{x - h} + k$

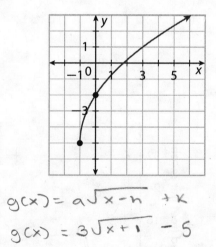

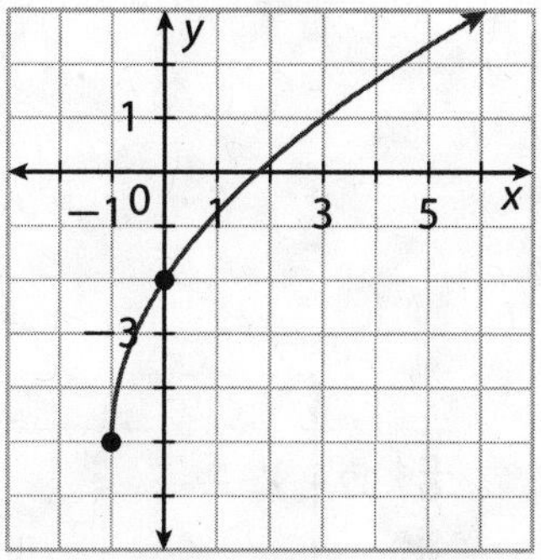

$g(x) = a\sqrt{x-h} + k$

$g(x) = 3\sqrt{x+1} - 5$

17. $g(x) = a\sqrt{x - h} + k$

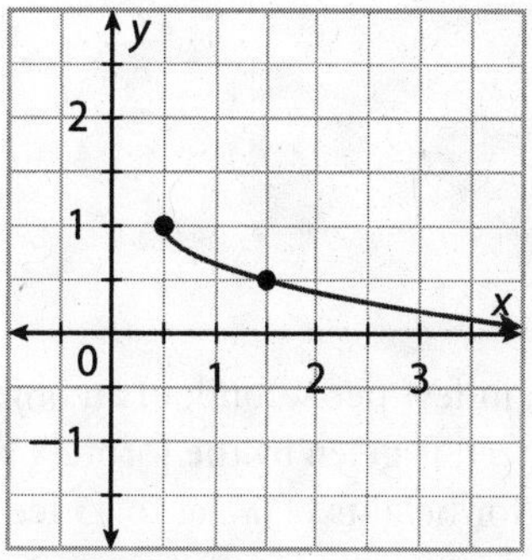

Use a calculator to evaluate the model at the indicated points, and connect the points with a curve to complete the graph of the model. Calculate the average rates of change over the first and last intervals and explain what the rate of change represents.

18. A farmer is trying to determine how much fencing to buy to make a square holding pen with a 6-foot gap for a gate. The length of fencing, f, in feet, required as a function of area, A, in square feet, is given by $f(A) = 4\sqrt{A} - 6$. Evaluate the function from 20 ft^2 to 100 ft^2 by calculating points every 20 ft^2.

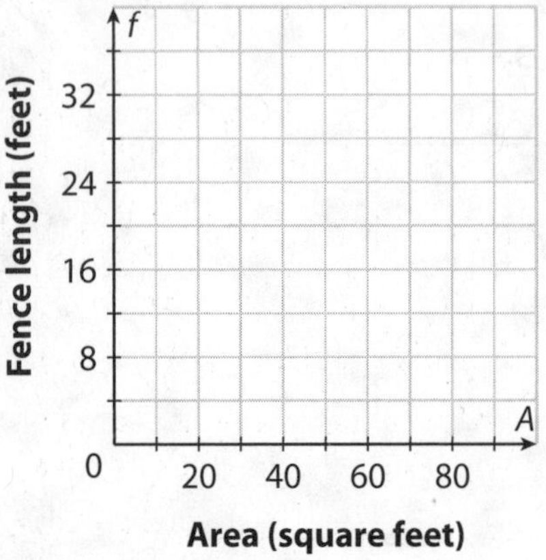

19. The speed, s, in feet per second, of an object dropped from a height, h, in feet, is given by the formula $s(h) = \sqrt{64h}$. Evaluate the function for heights of 0 feet to 25 feet by calculating points every 5 feet.

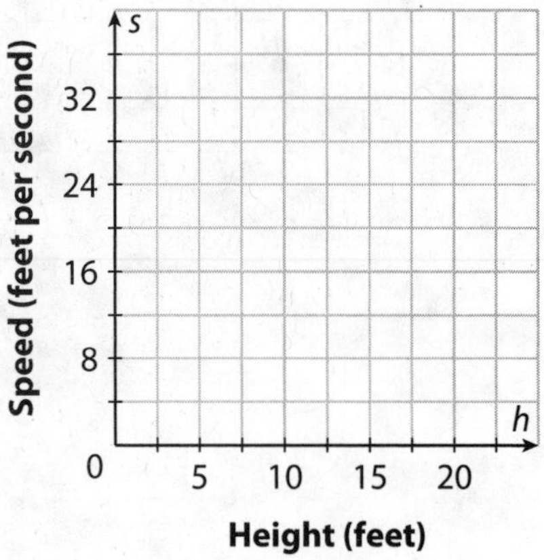

20. Water is draining from a tank at an average speed, s, in feet per second, characterized by the function $s(d) = 8\sqrt{d-2}$, where d is the depth of the water in the tank in feet. Evaluate the function for depths of 2, 3, 4, and 5 feet.

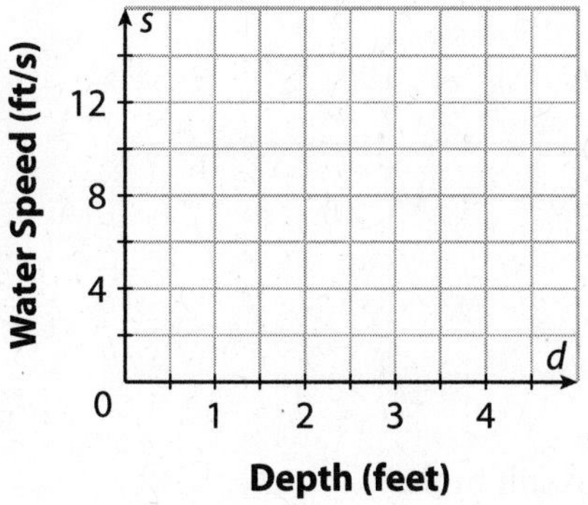

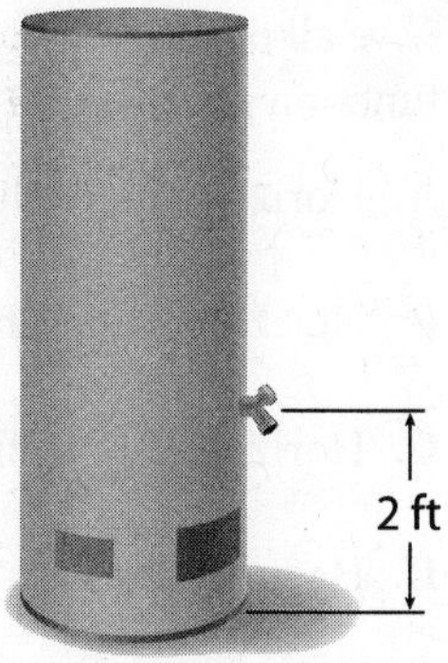

21. A research team studies the effects from an oil spill to develop new methods in oil clean-up. In the spill they are studying, the damaged oil tanker spilled oil into the ocean, forming a roughly circular spill pattern. The spill expanded out from the tanker, increasing the area at a rate of 100 square meters per hour. The radius of the circle is given by the function $r = \sqrt{\frac{100}{\pi}t}$, where t is the time (in hours) after the spill begins. Evaluate the function at hours 0, 1, 2, 3, and 4.

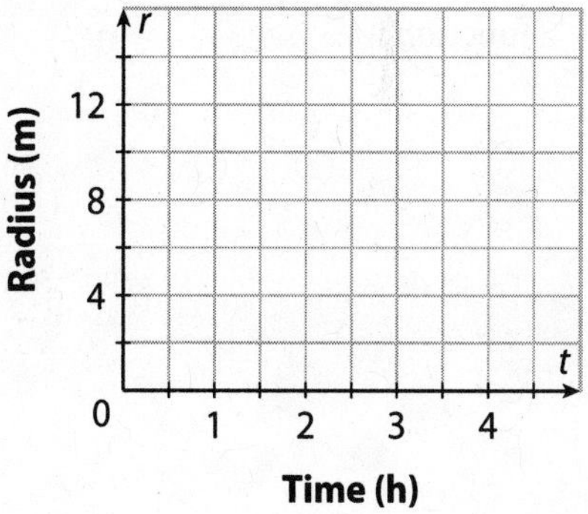

22. Give all of the transformations of the parent function $f(x) = \sqrt{x}$ that result in the function $g(x) = \sqrt{-2(x-3)} + 2$.

A. Horizontal stretch

B. Horizontal compression

C. Horizontal reflection

D. Horizontal translation

E. Vertical stretch

F. Vertical compression

G. Vertical reflection

H. Vertical translation

H.O.T. Focus on Higher Order Thinking

23. Draw Conclusions Describe the transformations to $f(x) = \sqrt{x}$ that result in the function $g(x) = \sqrt{-8x + 16} + 3$.

24. Analyze Relationships Show how a horizontally stretched square root function can sometimes be replaced by a vertical compression by equating the two forms of the transformed square root function.

$$g(x) = a\sqrt{x} = \sqrt{\frac{1}{b}x}$$

What must you assume about a and b for this replacement to result in the same function?

25. Multi-Step On a clear day, the view across the ocean is limited by the curvature of Earth. Objects appear to disappear below the horizon as they get farther from an observer. For an observer at height h above the water looking at an object with a height of H (both in feet), the approximate distance (d) in miles at which the object drops below the horizon is given by $d(h) = 1.21\sqrt{h + H}$.

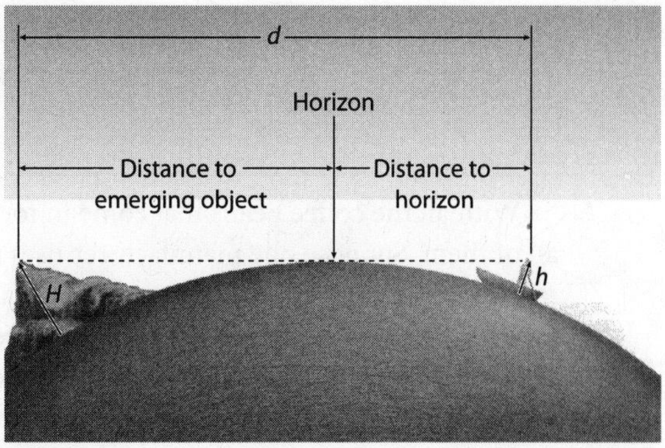

a. What is the effect of the object height, H, on the graph of $d(h)$?

b. What is the domain of the function $d(h)$? Explain your answer.

c. Plot two functions of distance required to see an object over the horizon versus observer height: one for seeing a 2-foot-tall buoy and one for seeing a 20-foot-tall sailboat. Calculate points every 10 feet from 0 to 40 feet.

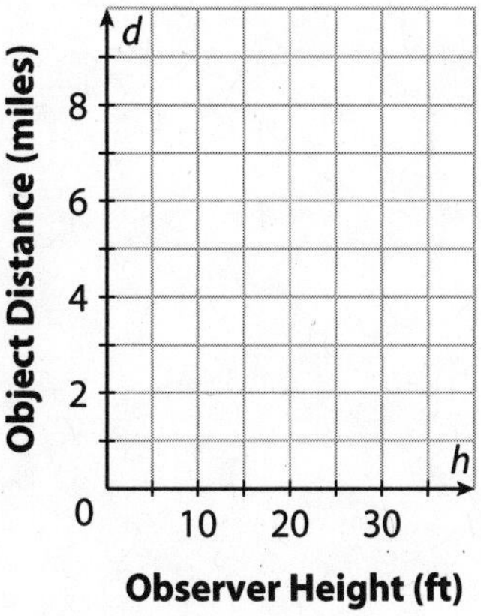

d. Where is the greatest increase in viewing distance with observer height?

Lesson Performance Task

With all the coffee beans that come in for processing, a coffee manufacturer cannot sample all of them. Suppose one manufacturer uses the function $s(x) = \sqrt{x} + 1$ to determine how many samples that it must take from x containers in order to obtain a good representative sampling of beans. How does this function relate to the function $f(x) = \sqrt{x}$? Graph both functions. How many samples should be taken from a shipment of 45 containers of beans? Explain why this can only be a whole number answer.

Name ______________________ Class ______________ Date ________

10.3 Graphing Cube Root Functions

Essential Question: How can you use transformations of the parent cube root function to graph functions of the form $f(x) = a\sqrt[3]{(x - h)} + k$ or $g(x) = \sqrt[3]{\frac{1}{b}(x - h)} + k$?

Resource Locker

Explore Graphing and Analying the Parent Cube Root Function

The cube root parent function is $f(x) = \sqrt[3]{x}$. To graph $f(x)$, choose values of x and find corresponding values of y. Choose both negative and positive values of x.

Graph the function $f(x) = \sqrt[3]{x}$. Identify the domain and range of the function.

(A) Make the table of values.

x	y	x, y
−8		
−1		
0		
1		
8		

(B) Use the table to graph the function.

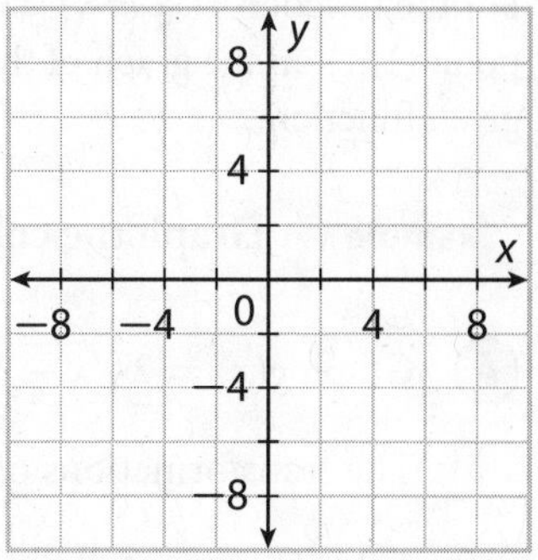

(C) Identify the domain and range of the function.

The domain is the ______________________.

The range is ______________________.

(D) Does the graph of $f(x) = \sqrt[3]{x}$ have any symmetry?

The graph has ______________.

Reflect

1. Can the radicand in a cube root function be negative?

____

Explain 1 Graphing Cube Root Functions

Transformations of the Cube Root Parent Function $f(x) = \sqrt[3]{x}$		
Transformation	**$f(x)$ Notation**	**Examples**
Vertical translation	$f(x) + k$	$y = \sqrt[3]{x} + 3$ 3 units up $y = \sqrt[3]{x} - 4$ 4 units down
Horizontal translation	$f(x - h)$	$y = \sqrt[3]{x - 2}$ 2 units right $y = \sqrt[3]{x + 1}$ 1 units left
Vertical stretch/compression	$af(x)$	$y = 6\sqrt[3]{x}$ vertical stretch by 6 $y = \frac{1}{2}\sqrt[3]{x}$ vertical compression by $\frac{1}{2}$
Horizontal stretch/ compression	$f\left(\frac{1}{b}x\right)$	$y = \sqrt[3]{\frac{1}{5}x}$ horizontal stretch by 5 $y = \sqrt[3]{3x}$ horizontal compression by $\frac{1}{3}$
Reflection	$-f(x)$ $f(-x)$	$y = -\sqrt[3]{x}$ across x-axis $y = \sqrt[3]{-x}$ across y-axis

For the function $f(x) = a\sqrt[3]{x - h} + k$, (h, k) is the graph's point of symmetry. Use the values of a, h, and k to draw each graph. For example, the point $(1, 1)$ on the graph of the parent function becomes the point $(1 + h, a + k)$ on the graph of the given function.

For the function $f(x) = \sqrt[3]{\frac{1}{b}(x - h)} + k$, (h, k) remains the graph's point of symmetry. Note that the point $(1, 1)$ on the graph of the parent function becomes the point $(b + h, 1 + k)$ on the graph of the given function.

Example 1 **Graph the cube root functions.**

(A) Graph $g(x) = 2\sqrt[3]{x - 3} + 5$.

The transformations of the graph of $f(x) = \sqrt[3]{x}$ that produce the graph of $g(x)$ are:

- a vertical stretch by a factor of 2
- a translation of 3 units to the right and 5 units up

Choose points on $f(x) = \sqrt[3]{x}$ and find the transformed corresponding points on $g(x) = 2\sqrt[3]{x - 3} + 5$.

Graph $g(x) = 2\sqrt[3]{x - 3} + 5$ using the transformed points.

(See the table and graph on the next page.)

$f(x) = \sqrt[3]{x}$	$g(x) = 2\sqrt[3]{x-3}+5$
$(-8, -2)$	$(-5, 1)$
$(-1, -1)$	$(2, 3)$
$(0, 0)$	$(3, 5)$
$(1, 1)$	$(4, 7)$
$(8, 2)$	$(11, 9)$

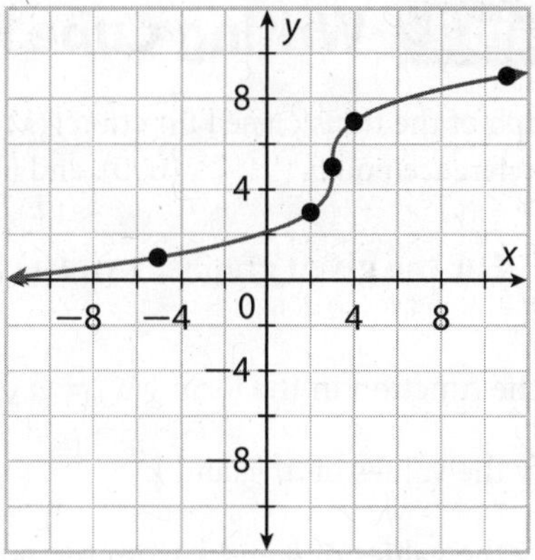

(B) Graph $g(x) = \sqrt[3]{\frac{1}{2}(x-10)} + 4$.

The transformations of the graph of $f(x) = \sqrt[3]{x}$ that produce the graph of $g(x)$ are:

- a horizontal stretch by a factor of 2
- a translation of 10 units to the right and 4 units up

Choose points on $f(x) = \sqrt[3]{x}$ and find the transformed corresponding points on $g(x) = \sqrt[3]{\frac{1}{2}(x-10)} + 4$.

Graph $g(x) = \sqrt[3]{\frac{1}{2}(x-10)} + 4$ using the transformed points.

$f(x) = \sqrt[3]{x}$	$g(x) = \sqrt[3]{\frac{1}{2}(x-10)} + 4$
$(-8, -2)$	
$(-1, -1)$	
$(0, 0)$	
$(1, 1)$	
$(8, 2)$	

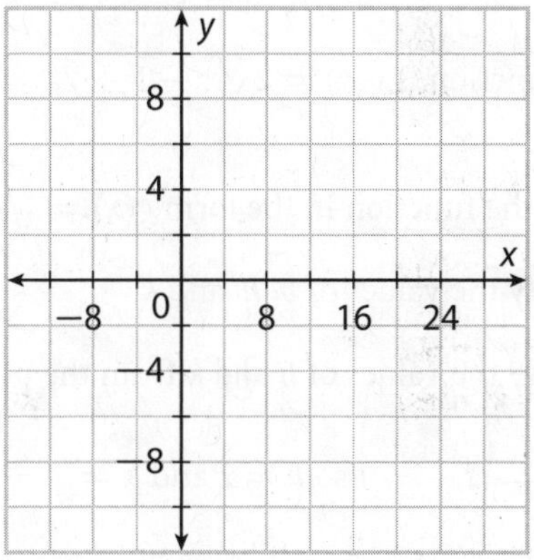

Your Turn

Graph the cube root function.

2. Graph $g(x) = \sqrt[3]{x-3} + 6$.

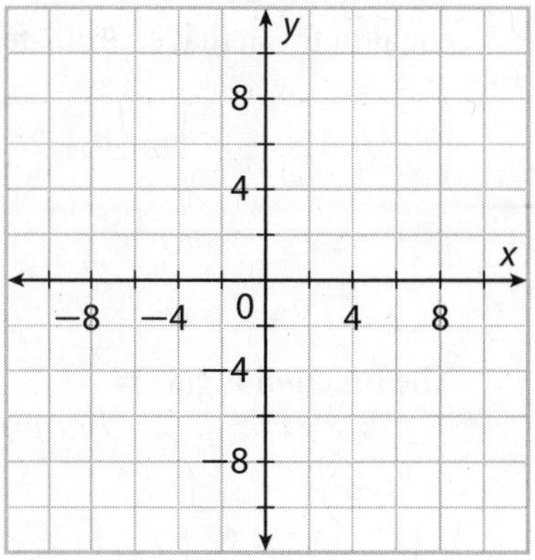

$f(x) = \sqrt[3]{x}$	$g(x) = \sqrt[3]{x-3}+6$
$(-8, -2)$	
$(-1, -1)$	
$(0, 0)$	
$(1, 1)$	
$(8, 2)$	

Explain 2 Writing Cube Root Functions

Given the graph of the transformed function $g(x) = a\sqrt[3]{\frac{1}{b}(x-h)} + k$, you can determine the values of the parameters by using the reference points $(-1, 1)$, $(0, 0)$, and $(1, 1)$ that you used to graph $g(x)$ in the previous example.

Example 2 **For the given graphs, write a cube root function.**

(A) Write the function in the form $g(x) = a\sqrt[3]{x-h} + k$.

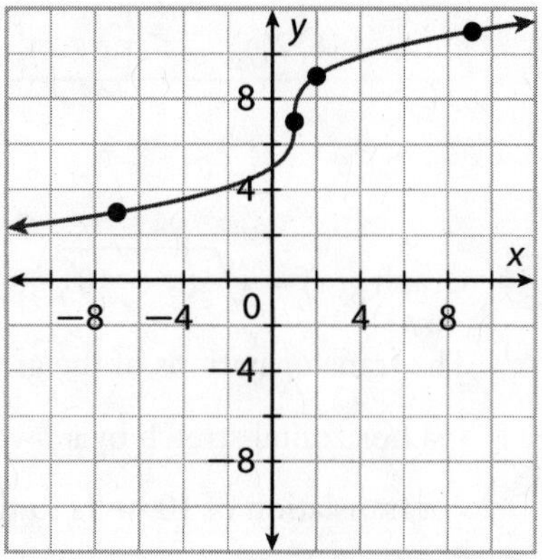

Identify the values of a, h, and k.

Identify the values of h and k from the point of symmetry.

$(h, k) = (1, 7)$, so $h = 1$ and $k = 7$.

Identify the value of a from either of the other two reference points $(-1, 1)$ or $(1, 1)$.

The reference point $(1, 1)$ has general coordinates $(h + 1, a + k)$. Substituting 1 for h and 7 for k and setting the general coordinates equal to the actual coordinates gives this result:

$(h + 1, a + k) = (2, a + 7) = (2, 9)$, so $a = 2$.

$a = 2$ $\quad\quad h = 1$ $\quad\quad k = 7$

The function is $g(x) = 2\sqrt[3]{x-1} + 7$.

(B) Write the function in the form $g(x) = \sqrt[3]{\frac{1}{b}(x-h)} + k$.

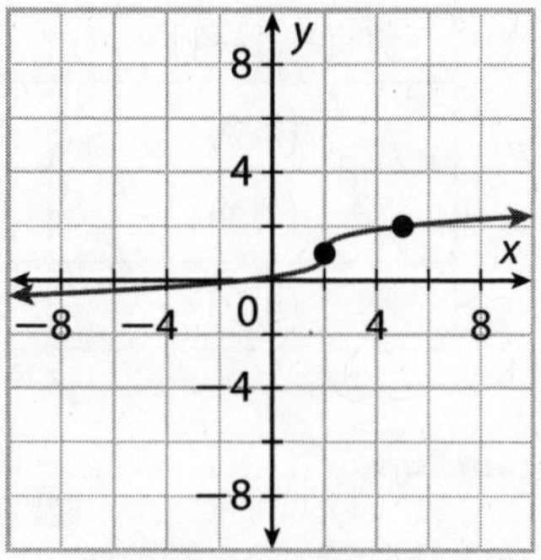

Identify the values of b, h, and k.

Identify the values of h and k from the point of symmetry.

$(h, k) = (2, \square)$ so $h = 2$ and $k = \square$.

Identify the value of b from either of the other two reference points.

The rightmost reference point has general coordinates $(b + h, 1 + k)$. Substituting 2 for h and ____ for k and setting the general coordinates equal to the actual coordinates gives this result:

$(b + h, 1 + \square) = (b + 2, \square) = (5, 2)$, so $b = \square$.

$b = \square$ $\quad\quad h = \square$ $\quad\quad k = \square$

The function is $g(x) =$ ____________.

Your Turn

For the given graphs, write a cube root function.

3. Write the function in the form $g(x) = a\sqrt[3]{x - h} + k$.

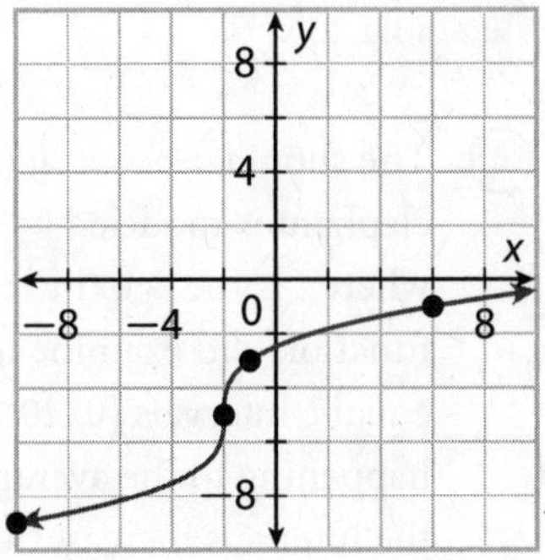

4. Write the function in the form $g(x) = \sqrt[3]{\frac{1}{b}(x - h)} + k$.

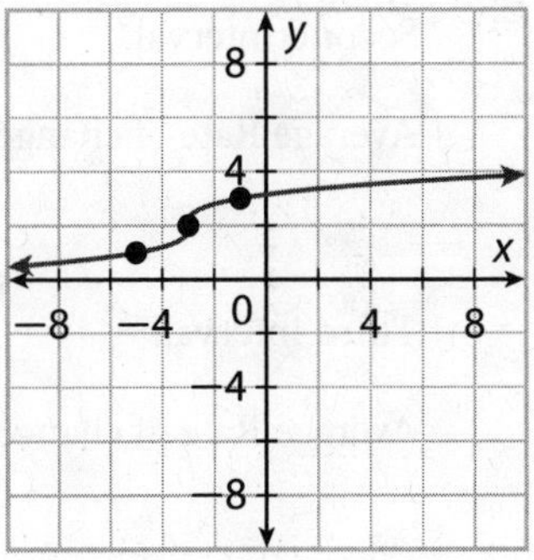

Explain 3 Modeling with Cube Root Functions

You can use cube root functions to model real-world situations.

Example 3

(A) The shoulder height h (in centimeters) of a particular elephant is modeled by the function $h(t) = 62.1\sqrt[3]{t} + 76$, where t is the age (in years) of the elephant. Graph the function and examine its average rate of change over the equal t-intervals $(0, 20)$, $(20, 40)$, and $(40, 60)$. What is happening to the average rate of change as the t-values of the intervals increase? Use the graph to find the height when $t = 35$.

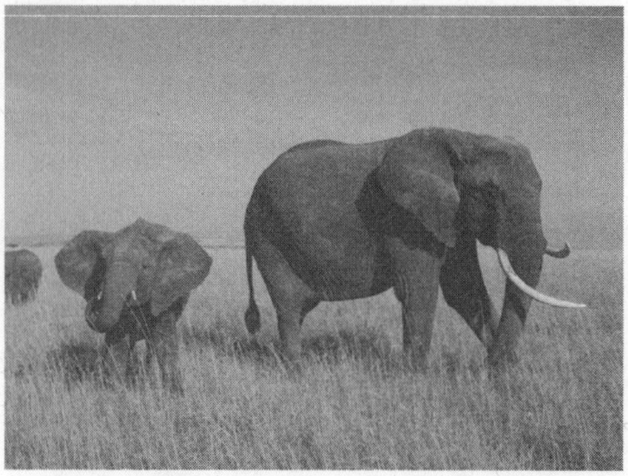

Graph $h(t) = 62.1\sqrt[3]{t} + 76$.

The graph is the graph of $f(x) = \sqrt[3]{x}$ translated up 76 and stretched vertically by a factor of 62.1. Graph the transformed points $(0, 76)$, $(8, 200.2)$, $(27, 262.3)$, and $(64, 324.4)$. Connect the points with a smooth curve.

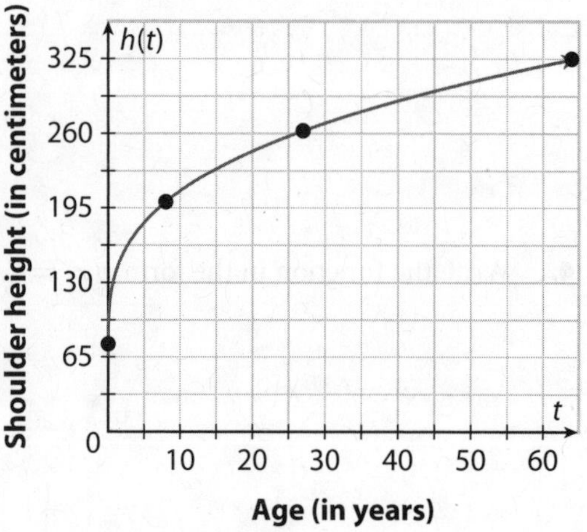

First interval:

$$\text{Average Rate of change} \approx \frac{244.6 - 76}{20 - 0}$$
$$= 8.43$$

Second interval:

$$\text{Average Rate of change} \approx \frac{288.4 - 244.6}{40 - 20}$$
$$= 2.19$$

Third interval:

$$\text{Average Rate of change} \approx \frac{319.1 - 288.4}{60 - 40}$$
$$= 1.54$$

The average rate of change is becoming less.

Drawing a vertical line up from 35 gives a value of about 280 cm.

(B) The velocity of a 1400-kilogram car at the end of a 400-meter run is modeled by the function $v = 15.2\sqrt[3]{p}$, where v is the velocity in kilometers per hour and p is the power of its engine in horsepower. Graph the function and examine its average rate of change over the equal p-intervals $(0, 60)$, $(60, 120)$, and $(120, 180)$. What is happening to the average rate of change as the p-values of the intervals increase? Use the function to find the velocity when p is 100 horsepower.

Graph $V = 15.2\sqrt[3]{p}$.

The graph is the graph of $f(x) = \sqrt[3]{x}$ stretched ________ by a factor of 15.2. Graph the transformed points $(0, 0)$, $(8, \_\_\_\_)$, $(27, \_\_\_\_)$, $(64, \_\_\_\_)$, $(125, \_\_\_\_)$, and $(216, \_\_\_\_)$.

Connect the points with a smooth curve.

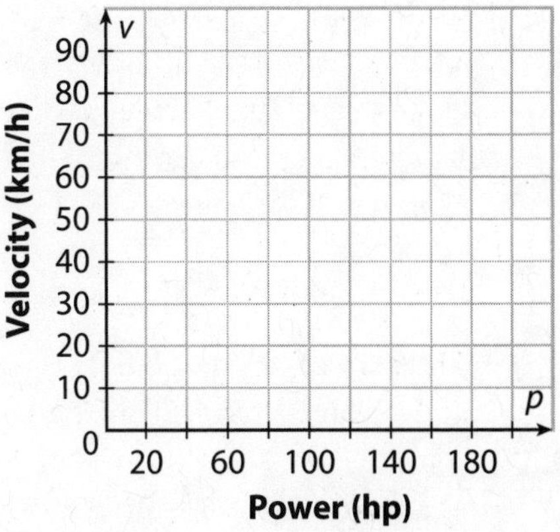

The rate of change over the interval $(0, 60)$ is

$\frac{\square - \square}{60 - 0}$ which is about ________.

The rate of change over the interval $(60, 120)$ is $\frac{\square - \square}{120 - 60}$ whichis about ________.

The rate of change over the interval $(120, 180)$ is $\frac{\square - \square}{180 - 120}$ which is about ________.

The average rate of change is becoming ________.

Substitute $p = 100$ in the function.

$v = 15.2\sqrt[3]{p}$

$v = 15.2\sqrt[3]{\square}$

$v \approx 15.2(\square)$

$v \approx \square$

The velocity is about ________ km/h.

Your Turn

5. The fetch is the length of water over which the wind is blowing in a certain direction. The function $s(f) = 7.1\sqrt[3]{f}$, relates the speed of the wind s in kilometers per hour to the fetch f in kilometers. Graph the function and examine its average rate of change over the intervals $(20, 80)$, $(80, 140)$, and $(140, 200)$. What is happening to the average rate of change as the f-values of the intervals increase? Use the function to find the speed of the wind when $f = 64$.

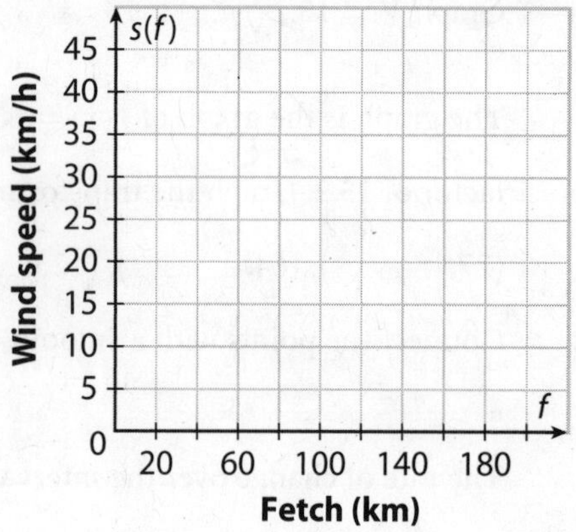

Elaborate

6. Discussion Why is the domain of $f(x) = \sqrt[3]{x}$ all real numbers?

7. Identify which transformations (stretches or compressions, reflections, and translations) of $f(x) = \sqrt[3]{x}$ change the following attributes of the function.

a. Location of the point of symmetry

b. Symmetry about a point

8. Essential Question Check-In How do parameters a, b, h, and k effect the graphs of $f(x) = a\sqrt[3]{(x - h)} + k$ and $g(x) = \sqrt[3]{\frac{1}{b}(x - h)} + k$?

Evaluate: Homework and Practice

Personal Math Trainer

- Online Homework
- Hints and Help
- Extra Practice

1. Graph the function $g(x) = \sqrt[3]{x} + 3$. Identify the domain and range of the function.

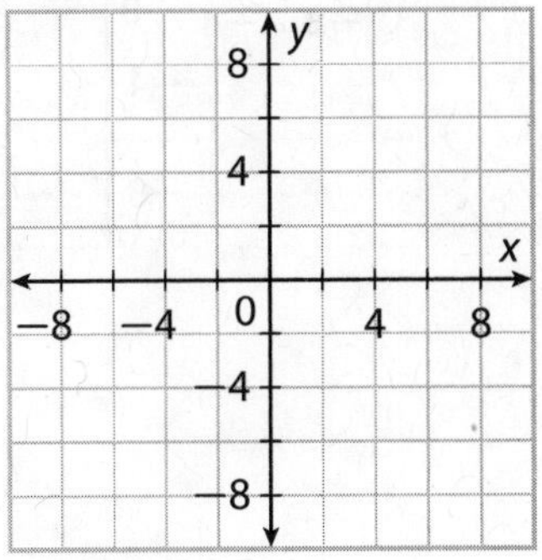

2. Graph the function $g(x) = \sqrt[3]{x} - 5$. Identify the domain and range of the function.

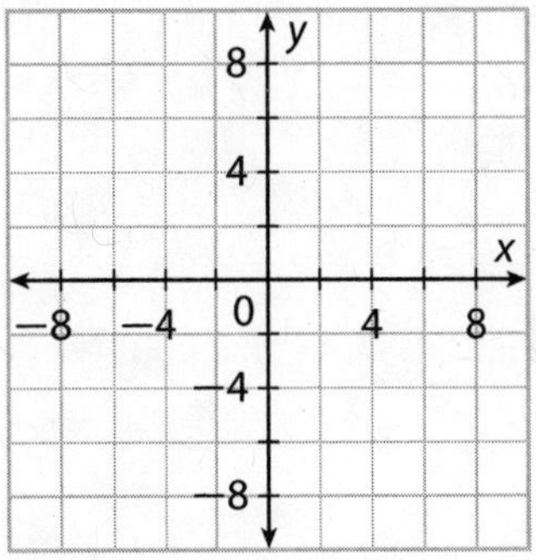

Describe how the graph of the function compares to the graph of $f(x) = \sqrt[3]{x}$.

3. $g(x) = \sqrt[3]{x} + 6$

4. $g(x) = \sqrt[3]{x - 5}$

horizontal shift 5 units to the right.

5. $g(x) = \frac{1}{3}\sqrt[3]{-x}$

6. $g(x) = \sqrt[3]{5x}$

vertical stretch by 5

7. $g(x) = -2\sqrt[3]{x} + 3$

8. $g(x) = \sqrt[3]{x + 4} - 3$

horizontal shift to the right 4
vertical shift up 3

Graph the cube root functions.

9. $g(x) = 3\sqrt[3]{x+4}$

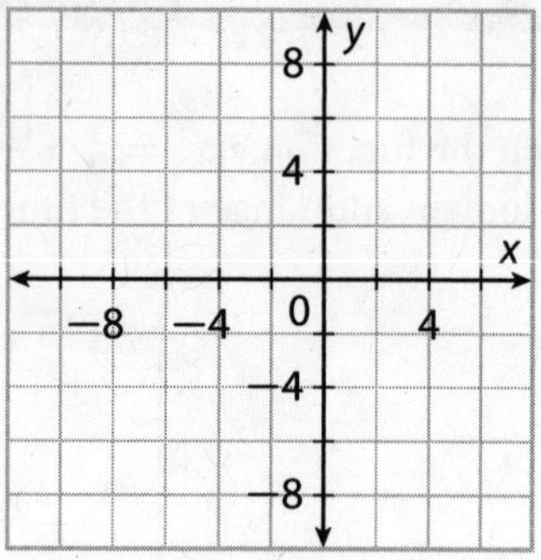

10. $g(x) = 2\sqrt[3]{x} + 3$

(0, 3)

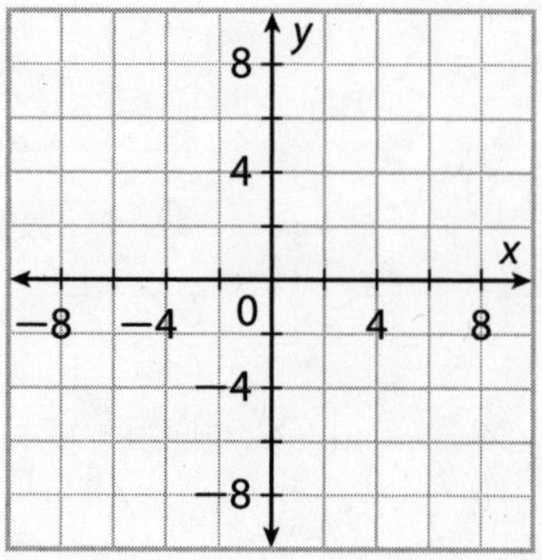

11. $g(x) = \sqrt[3]{x-3} + 2$

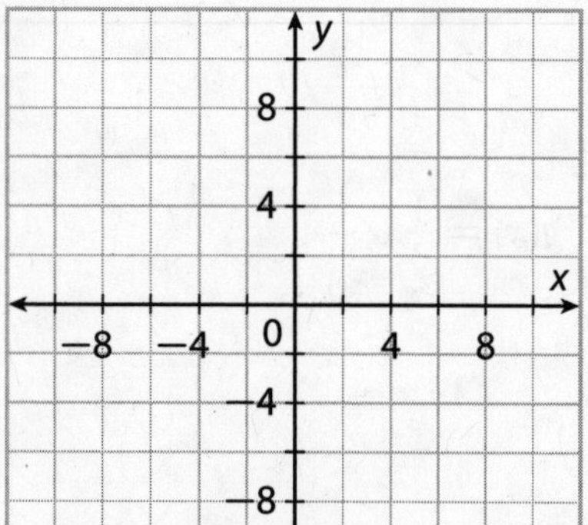

For the given graphs, write a cube root function.

12. Write the function in the form $g(x) = a\sqrt[3]{x - h} + k$.

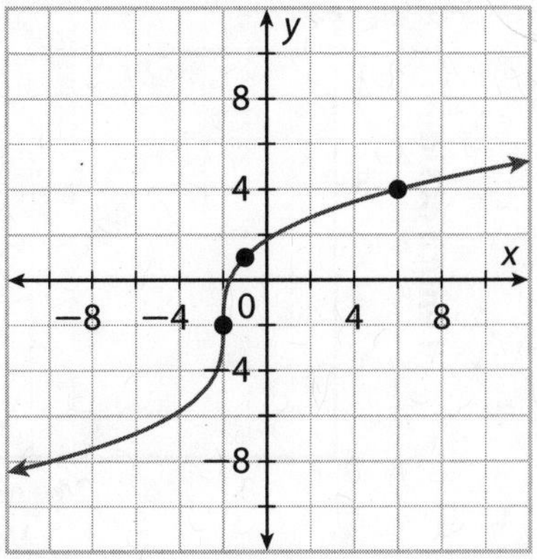

13. Write the function in the form $g(x) = a\sqrt[3]{x - h} + k$.

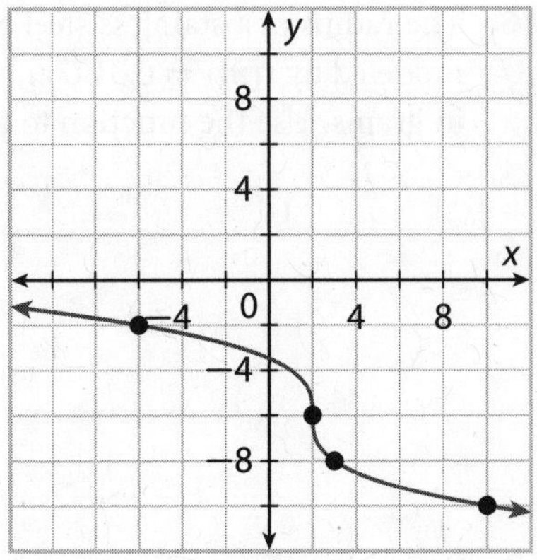

14. Write the function in the form $g(x) = \sqrt[3]{\frac{1}{b}(x - h)} + k$.

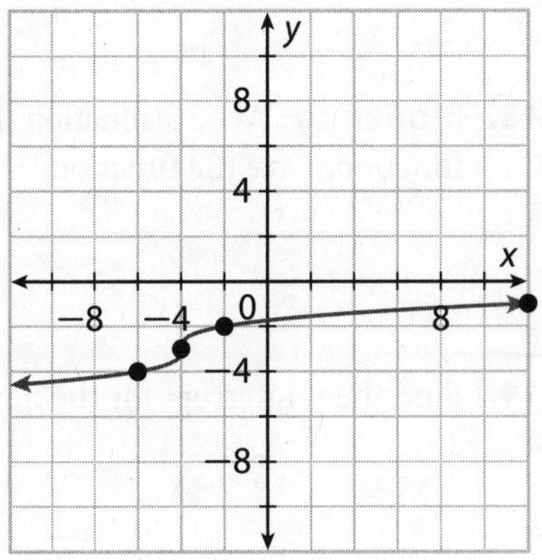

15. The length of the side of a cube is modeled by $s = \sqrt[3]{V}$. Graph the function. Use the graph to find s when $V = 48$.

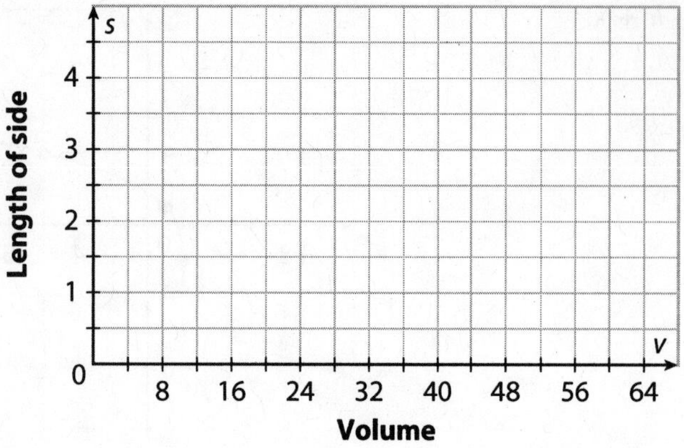

16. The radius of a stainless steel ball, in centimeters, can be modeled by $r(m) = 0.31\sqrt[3]{m}$, where m is the mass of the ball in grams. Use the function to find r when $m = 125$.

17. Describe the steps for graphing $g(x) = \sqrt[3]{x + 8} - 11$.

18. Modeling Write a situation that can be modeled by a cube root function. Give the function.

19. Find the y-intercept for the function $y = a\sqrt[3]{x - h} + k$.

20. Find the x-intercept for the function $y = a\sqrt[3]{x - h} + k$.

21. Describe the translation(s) used to get $g(x) = \sqrt[3]{x - 9} + 12$ from $f(x) = \sqrt[3]{x}$. Select all that apply.

A. translated 9 units right

B. translated 9 units left

C. translated 9 units up

D. translated 9 units down

E. translated 12 units right

F. translated 12 units left

G. translated 12 units up

H. translated 12 units down

H.O.T. Focus on Higher Order Thinking

22. Explain the Error Tim says that to graph $g(x) = \sqrt[3]{x - 6} + 3$, you need to translate the graph of $f(x) = \sqrt[3]{x}$ 6 units to the left and then 3 units up. What mistake did he make?

23. Communicate Mathematical Ideas Why does the square root function have a restricted domain but the cube root function does not?

24. Justify Reasoning Does a horizontal translation and a vertical translation of the function $f(x) = \sqrt[3]{x}$ affect the function's domain or range? Explain.

Lesson Performance Task

The side length of a 243-gram copper cube is 3 centimeters. Use this information to write a model for the radius of a copper sphere as a function of its mass. Then, find the radius of a copper sphere with a mass of 50 grams. How would changing the material affect the function?

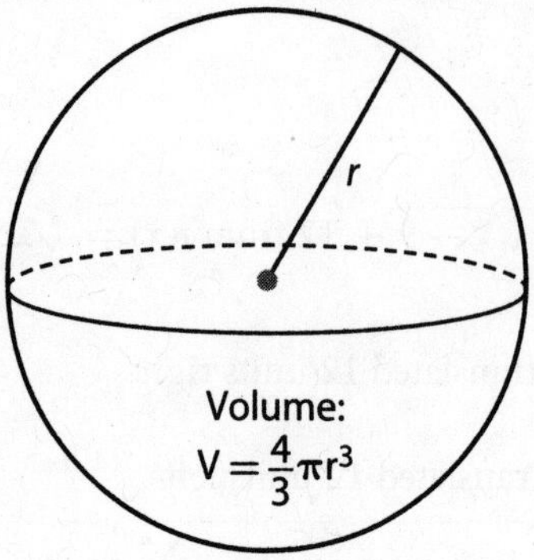

STUDY GUIDE REVIEW

Radical Functions

MODULE 10

Essential Question: How can you use radical functions to solve real-world problems?

Key Vocabulary
cube root function *(función de raíz cúbica)*
index *(índice)*
inverse function *(función inversa)*
square root function *(función de raíz cuadrada)*

KEY EXAMPLE (Lesson 10.1)

Find the inverse function $f^{-1}(x)$ for $f(x) = 2x^3 + 10$.

Replace $f(x)$ with y. $\quad y = 2x^3 + 10$

Solve for x^3. $\quad \frac{y-10}{2} = x^3$

Take the cube root. $\quad \sqrt[3]{\frac{y-10}{2}} = x$

Switch x and y. $\quad y = \sqrt[3]{\frac{x-10}{2}}$

Replace y with $f^{-1}(x)$. $\quad f^{-1}(x) = \sqrt[3]{\frac{x-10}{2}}$

KEY EXAMPLE (Lesson 10.2)

Graph $y = -\sqrt{x-3} + 2$. Describe the domain and range.

Sketch the graph of $y = -\sqrt{x}$.

It begins at the origin and passes through $(1, -1)$.

For $y = -\sqrt{x-3} + 2$, $h = 3$ and $k = 2$.
Shift the graph of $y = -\sqrt{x}$ right 3 units and up 2 units. The graph begins at $(3, 2)$ and passes through $(4, 1)$.

Domain: $\{x \mid x \geq 3\}$ Range: $\{y \mid y \leq 2\}$

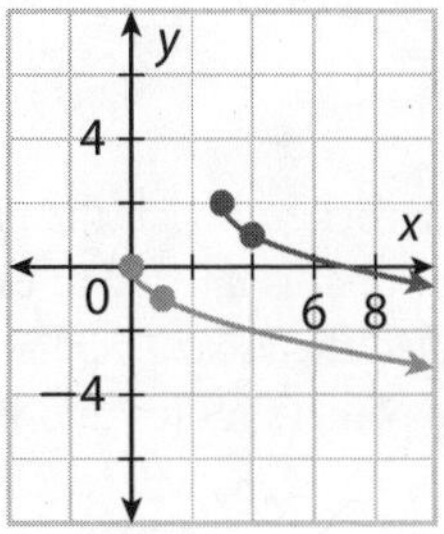

KEY EXAMPLE (Lesson 10.3)

Graph $y = \sqrt[3]{x+2} - 4$.

Sketch the graph of $y = \sqrt[3]{x}$.

It passes through $(-1, -1)$, $(0, 0)$, and $(1, 1)$.

For $y = \sqrt[3]{x+2} - 4$, $h = -2$ and $k = -4$.
Shift the graph of $y = \sqrt[3]{x}$ left 2 units and down 4 units. The graph passes through $(-3, -5)$, $(-2, -4)$, and $(-1, -3)$.

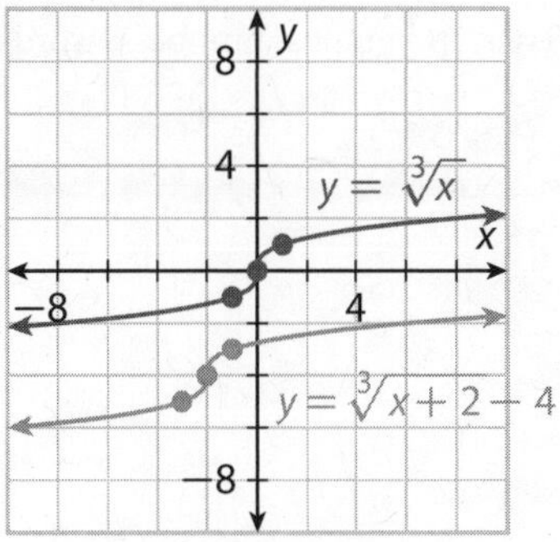

EXERCISES

Find the inverse of each function. Restrict the domain where necessary. (Lesson 10.1)

1. $f(x) = 16x^2$

2. $f(x) = x^3 - 20$

Identify the transformations of the graph $f(x) = \sqrt{x}$ that produce the graph of the function. (Lesson 10.2)

3. $g(x) = -\sqrt{4x}$

4. $h(x) = \frac{1}{2}\sqrt{x} + 1$

Identify the transformations of the graph $f(x) = \sqrt[3]{x}$ that produce the graph of the function. (Lesson 10.3)

5. $g(x) = 4\sqrt[3]{x}$

6. $h(x) = \sqrt[3]{x - 5} + 3$

MODULE PERFORMANCE TASK

We Have Liftoff!

A rocket scientist is designing a rocket to visit the planets in the solar system. The velocity that is needed to escape a planet's gravitational pull is called the escape velocity. The escape velocity depends on the planet's radius and its mass, according to the equation $V_{\text{escape}} = \sqrt{2gR}$, where R is the radius and g is the gravitational constant for the particular planet. The rocket's maximum velocity is exactly double Earth's escape velocity. For which planets will the rocket have enough velocity to escape the planet's gravity?

Planet	Radius (m)	Mass (kg)	g (m/s^2)
Mercury	2.43×10^6	3.20×10^{23}	3.61
Venus	6.07×10^6	4.88×10^{24}	8.83
Mars	3.38×10^6	6.42×10^{23}	3.75
Jupiter	6.98×10^7	1.90×10^{27}	26.0
Saturn	5.82×10^7	5.68×10^{26}	11.2
Uranus	2.35×10^7	8.68×10^{25}	10.5
Neptune	2.27×10^7	1.03×10^{26}	13.3

Begin by listing in the space below any additional information you will need to solve the problem. Then use your own paper to complete the task. Be sure to write down all your data and assumptions. Then use graphs, numbers, words, or algebra to explain how you reached your conclusions.

Ready to Go On?

10.1–10.3 Radical Functions

Personal Math Trainer

- Online Homework
- Hints and Help
- Extra Practice

Find the inverse of each function. State any restrictions on the domain. *(Lesson 10.1)*

1. $f(x) = x^2 + 9$

2. $f(x) = -7x^3$

3. $f(x) = -2x^3 + 1$

4. $f(x) = 5x^2 + 3$

Identify the transformations of the graph $f(x) = \sqrt{x}$ or $h(x) = \sqrt[3]{x}$ that produce the graph of the function. *(Lessons 10.2, 10.3)*

5. $g(x) = \frac{1}{3}\sqrt{x - 5} - 4$

6. $g(x) = \sqrt[3]{4x} + 3$

7. $g(x) = \sqrt{x - 4} - 1$

8. $g(x) = \sqrt[3]{7x + 10}$

ESSENTIAL QUESTION

9. How do you use a parent square root or cube root function to graph a transformation of the function? *(Lessons 10.2, 10.3)*

MODULE 10
MIXED REVIEW

Assessment Readiness

1. Look at each equation. Is it the inverse of $f(x) = x^3 - 16$? Select Yes or No for A–C.

A. $f^{-1}(x) = \sqrt[3]{x - 16}$ ◯ Yes ◯ No

B. $f^{-1}(x) = \sqrt[3]{x + 16}$ ◯ Yes ◯ No

C. $f^{-1}(x) = \sqrt[3]{x} + 16$ ◯ Yes ◯ No

2. Consider the graphed function. Choose True or False for each statement.

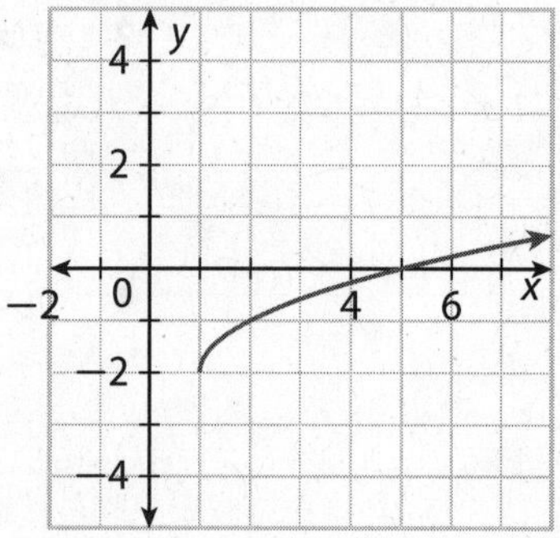

A. The equation for the function is $y = \sqrt{x - 1} - 2$. ◯ Yes ◯ No

B. The function has exactly one *y*-intercept. ◯ Yes ◯ No

C. The range of the function is $y \leq -2$. ◯ Yes ◯ No

3. A plane's average speed when flying from one city to another is 550 mi/h and is 430 mi/h on the return flight. To the nearest mile per hour, what is the plane's average speed for the entire trip? Explain your answer.

4. The kinetic energy *E* (in joules) of a 1250-kilogram compact car is given by the equation $E = 625s^2$, where *s* is the speed of the car (in meters per second). Write an inverse model that gives the speed of the car as a function of its kinetic energy. If the kinetic energy doubles, will the speed double? Explain why or why not.

Radical Expressions and Equations

MODULE 11

Essential Question: How can you use radical expressions and equations to solve real-world problems?

REAL WORLD VIDEO
A field biologist studying howler monkeys can use radical functions to calculate sound intensity, which decreases faster than linearly with distance.

MODULE PERFORMANCE TASK PREVIEW

Don't Disturb the Neighbors!

The loudness of a sound is subjective and depends on the listener's sensitivity to the frequencies of the sound waves. An objective measure, sound intensity, can be used to measure sounds. Sound intensity decreases the farther you get from the source of a sound. How far away do your neighbors have to be so that a loud band does not bother them? Let's find out!

Are YOU Ready?

Complete these exercises to review skills you will need for this module.

Personal Math Trainer

- Online Homework
- Hints and Help
- Extra Practice

Exponents

Example 1 Simplify $(x^3)^2 + x \cdot x^3 + 3x^4$.

$(x^3)^2 + x \cdot x^3 + 3x^4 = (x^3)(x^3) + x \cdot x^3 + 3x^4$ Start with the raised power.

$= x^{3+3} + x^{1+3} + 3x^4$ Add exponents.

$= x^6 + x^4 + 3x^4$ Simplify.

$= x^6 + 4x^4$ Add like terms.

Simplify each expression.

1. $(-x^5)^2$

2. $(3x^2)^3 - x^4 \cdot x^2$

3. $3x(2x)^2$

Inverse Linear Functions

Example 2 Write the inverse function of $y = 10x - 4$.

$y + 4 = 10x$ Isolate the *x*-term.

$\frac{y+4}{10} = \frac{10x}{10}$ Divide.

The inverse function of $y = 10x - 4$ is $y = \frac{x+4}{10}$.

Write the inverse function.

4. $y = 3x + 1$

5. $y = 2(x - 9)$

6. $y = \frac{1}{4}(3x + 4)$

Rational and Radical Exponents

Example 3 Write $\sqrt[9]{a^3}$ using a rational exponent.

$\sqrt[9]{a^3} = a^{\frac{3}{9}} = a^{\frac{1}{3}}$

Write each radical expression using a rational exponent.

7. $\sqrt[2]{x^5}$

8. $\sqrt[4]{a^2b}$

9. $\sqrt[4]{p^8q^2}$

Name ______________________ Class ______________ Date ________

11.1 Radical Expressions and Rational Exponents

Resource Locker

Essential Question: How are rational exponents related to radicals and roots?

Explore Defining Rational Exponents in Terms of Roots

Remember that a number a is an nth root of a number b if $a^n = b$. As you know, a square root is indicated by $\sqrt{\ }$ and a cube root by $\sqrt[3]{\ }$. In general, the nth root of a real number a is indicated by $\sqrt[n]{a}$, where n is the **index** of the radical and a is the radicand. (Note that when a number has more than one real root, the radical sign indicates only the principal, or positive, root.)

A *rational exponent* is an exponent that can be expressed as $\frac{m}{n}$, where m is an integer and n is a natural number. You can use the definition of a root and properties of equality and exponents to explore how to express roots using rational exponents.

(A) How can you express a square root using an exponent? That is, if $\sqrt{a} = a^m$, what is m?

Given	$\sqrt{a} = a^m$
Square both sides.	$(\sqrt{a})^2 = (a^m)^2$
Definition of square root	$\square = (a^m)^2$
Power of a power property	$a = a^{\square}$
Definition of first power	$a^{\square} = a^{2m}$
The bases are the same, so equate exponents.	$\square = \square$
Solve.	$m = \square$
So,	$\sqrt{a} = a^{\square}$.

(B) How can you express a cube root using an exponent? That is, if $\sqrt[3]{a} = a^m$, what is m?

Given	$\sqrt[3]{a} = a^m$
Cube both sides.	$(\sqrt[3]{a})^3 = (a^m)^3$
Definition of cube root	$\square = \square$
Power of a power property	$\square = \square$

Definition of first power $\square = \square$

The bases are the same, so equate exponents. $\square = \square$

Solve. $m = \square$

So, $\sqrt[3]{a} = a^{\square}$.

Reflect

1. **Discussion** Examine the reasoning in Steps A and B. Can you apply the same reasoning for any nth root, $\sqrt[n]{a}$, where n is a natural number? Explain. What can you conclude?

2. For a positive number a, under what condition on n will there be only one real nth root? two real nth roots? Explain.

3. For a negative number a, under what condition on n will there be no real nth roots? one real nth root? Explain.

Explain 1 Translating Between Radical Expressions and Rational Exponents

In the Explore, you found that a rational exponent $\frac{m}{n}$ with $m = 1$ represents an nth root, or that $a^{\frac{1}{n}} = \sqrt[n]{a}$ for positive values of a. This is also true for negative values of a when the index is odd. When $m \neq 1$, you can think of the numerator m as the power and the denominator n as the root. The following ways of expressing the exponent $\frac{m}{n}$ are equivalent.

Rational Exponents

For any natural number n, integer m, and real number a when the nth root of a is real:

Words	Numbers	Algebra
The exponent $\frac{m}{n}$ indicates the mth power of the nth root of a quantity.	$27^{\frac{2}{3}} = (\sqrt[3]{27})^2 = 3^2 = 9$	$a^{\frac{m}{n}} = (\sqrt[n]{a})^m$
The exponent $\frac{m}{n}$ indicates the nth root of the mth power of a quantity.	$4^{\frac{3}{2}} = \sqrt{4^3} = \sqrt{64} = 8$	$a^{\frac{m}{n}} = \sqrt[n]{a^m}$

Notice that you can evaluate each example in the "Numbers" column using the equivalent definition.

$$27^{\frac{2}{3}} = \sqrt[3]{27^2} = \sqrt[3]{729} = 9 \qquad 4^{\frac{3}{2}} = \left(\sqrt{4}\right)^3 = 2^3 = 8$$

Example 1 **Translate radical expressions into expressions with rational exponents, and vice versa. Simplify numerical expressions when possible. Assume all variables are positive.**

(A) a. $(-125)^{\frac{4}{3}}$ b. $x^{\frac{11}{8}}$ c. $\sqrt[5]{6^4}$ d. $\sqrt[4]{x^3}$

a. $(-125)^{\frac{4}{3}} = \left(\sqrt[3]{-125}\right)^4 = (-5)^4 = 625$

b. $x^{11/8} = \sqrt[8]{x^{11}}$ or $\left(\sqrt[8]{x}\right)^{11}$

c. $\sqrt[5]{6^4} = 6^{\frac{4}{5}}$

d. $\sqrt[4]{x^3} = x^{\frac{3}{4}}$

(B) a. $\left(\frac{81}{16}\right)^{\frac{3}{4}}$ b. $(xy)^{\frac{5}{3}}$ c. $\sqrt[3]{11^6}$ d. $\sqrt[3]{\left(\frac{2x}{y}\right)^5}$

a. $\left(\frac{81}{16}\right)^{\frac{3}{4}} = \left(\sqrt[\square]{\frac{81}{16}}\right)^{\square} = \left(\square\right)^3 = \square$

b. $(xy)^{\frac{5}{3}} = \sqrt[\square]{(xy)^{\square}}$ or $\left(\sqrt[\square]{xy}\right)^{\square}$

c. $\sqrt[3]{11^6} = 11^{\square} = 11^{\square} = \square$

d. $\sqrt[3]{\left(\frac{2x}{y}\right)^5} = \left(\frac{2x}{y}\right)^{\square}$

Reflect

4. How can you use a calculator to show that evaluating $0.001728^{\frac{4}{3}}$ as a power of a root and as a root of a power are equivalent methods?

Your Turn

5. Translate radical expressions into expressions with rational exponents, and vice versa. Simplify numerical expressions when possible. Assume all variables are positive.

a. $\left(-\frac{32}{243}\right)^{\frac{2}{5}}$

b. $(3y)^{\frac{b}{c}}$

c. $\sqrt[3]{0.5^9}$

d. $\left(\sqrt[u]{st}\right)^v$

Explain 2 Modeling with Power Functions

The following functions all involve a given power of a variable.

$A = \pi r^2$ (area of a circle)

$V = \frac{4}{3}\pi r^3$ (volume of a sphere)

$T = 1.11 \cdot L^{\frac{1}{2}}$ (the time T in seconds for a pendulum of length L feet to complete one back-and-forth swing)

These are all examples of *power functions*. A power function has the form $y = ax^b$ where a is a real number and b is a rational number.

Example 2 **Solve each problem by modeling with power functions.**

Ⓐ **Biology** The function $R = 73.3\sqrt[4]{M^3}$, known as Kleiber's law, relates the basal metabolic rate R in Calories per day burned and the body mass M of a mammal in kilograms. The table shows typical body masses for some members of the cat family.

Typical Body Mass	
Animal	**Mass (kg)**
House cat	4.5
Cheetah	55
Lion	170

a. Rewrite the formula with a rational exponent.

b. What is the value of R for a cheetah to the nearest 50 Calories?

c. From the table, the mass of the lion is about 38 times that of the house cat. Is the lion's metabolic rate more or less than 38 times the cat's rate? Explain.

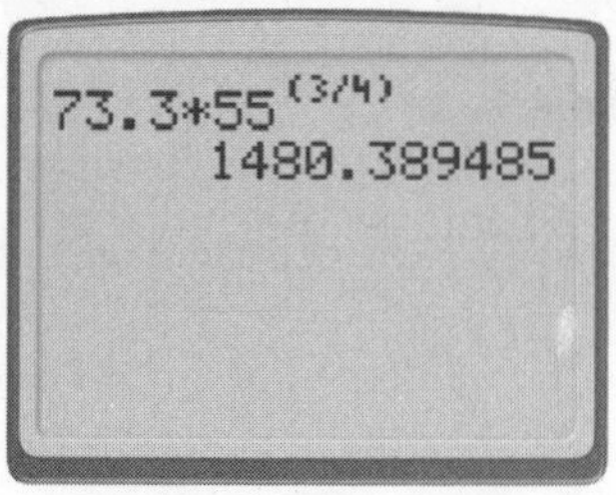

a. Because $\sqrt[n]{a^m} = a^{\frac{m}{n}}$, $\sqrt[4]{M^3} = M^{\frac{3}{4}}$, so the formula is $R = 73.3M^{\frac{3}{4}}$.

b. Substitute 55 for M in the formula and use a calculator.

The cheetah's metabolic rate is about 1500 Calories.

c. Less; find the ratio of R for the lion to R for the house cat.

$$\frac{73.3(170)^{\frac{3}{4}}}{73.3(4.5)^{\frac{3}{4}}} = \frac{170^{\frac{3}{4}}}{4.5^{\frac{3}{4}}} \approx \frac{47.1}{3.1} \approx 15$$

The metabolic rate for the lion is only about 15 times that of the house cat.

(B) The function $h(m) = 241m^{-\frac{1}{4}}$ models an animal's approximate resting heart rate h in beats per minute given its mass m in kilograms.

a. A common shrew has a mass of only about 0.01 kg. To the nearest 10, what is the model's estimate for this shrew's resting heart rate?

b. What is the model's estimate for the resting heart rate of an American elk with a mass of 300 kg?

c. Two animal species differ in mass by a multiple of 10. According to the model, about what percent of the smaller animal's resting heart rate would you expect the larger animal's resting heart rate to be?

a. Substitute ________ for m in the formula and use a calculator.

$$h(m) = 241\left(\square\right)^{-\frac{1}{4}} \approx \square$$

The model estimates the shrew's resting heart rate to be about ________ beats per minute.

b. Substitute ________ for m in the formula and use a calculator.

$$h(m) = 241\left(\square\right)^{-\frac{1}{4}} \approx \square$$

The model estimates the elk's resting heart rate to be about ________ beats per minute.

c. Find the ratio of $h(m)$ for the ________ animal to the ________ animal. Let 1 represent the mass of the smaller animal.

$$\frac{241 \cdot \square^{-\frac{1}{4}}}{241 \cdot 1^{-\frac{1}{4}}} = \square^{-\frac{1}{4}} = \frac{1}{10^{\square}} \approx \square$$

You would expect the larger animal's resting heart rate to be about ________ of the smaller animal's resting heart rate.

Reflect

6. What is the difference between a power function and an exponential function?

7. In Part B, the exponent is negative. Are the results consistent with the meaning of a negative exponent that you learned for integers? Explain.

Your Turn

8. Use Kleiber's law from Part A.

a. Find the basal metabolic rate for a 170 kilogram lion to the nearest 50 Calories. Then find the formula's prediction for a 70 kilogram human.

b. Use your metabolic rate result for the lion to find what the basal metabolic rate for a 70 kilogram human *would* be *if* metabolic rate and mass were directly proportional. Compare the result to the result from Part a.

Elaborate

9. Explain how can you use a radical to write and evaluate the power $4^{2.5}$.

10. When $y = kx$ for some constant k, y varies directly as x. When $y = kx^2$, y varies directly as the square of x; and when $y = k\sqrt{x}$, y varies directly as the square root of x. How could you express the relationship $y = kx^{\frac{3}{5}}$ for a constant k?

11. Essential Question Check-In Which of the following are true? Explain.

- To evaluate an expression of the form $a^{\frac{m}{n}}$, first find the nth root of a. Then raise the result to the mth power.
- To evaluate an expression of the form $a^{\frac{m}{n}}$, first find the mth power of a. Then find the nth root of the result.

☆ Evaluate: Homework and Practice

Personal Math Trainer

- Online Homework
- Hints and Help
- Extra Practice

Translate expressions with rational exponents into radical expressions. Simplify numerical expressions when possible. Assume all variables are positive.

1. $64^{\frac{5}{3}}$

$(\sqrt[3]{64})^5$

$4^5 = 1024$

2. $x^{\frac{p}{q}}$

$\sqrt[q]{x}^{\,p}$

3. $(-512)^{\frac{2}{3}}$

$(\sqrt[3]{-512})^2 = -8^2 = 64$

4. $3^{\frac{2}{7}}$

$\sqrt[7]{3}^{\,2}$

5. $-\left(\frac{729}{64}\right)^{\frac{5}{6}}$

$-\left(\sqrt[6]{\frac{729}{64}}\right)^5 = -\left(\frac{3}{2}\right)^5 = -\frac{243}{32}$

6. $0.125^{\frac{4}{3}}$

$\left(\sqrt[3]{0.125}\right)^4 = 0.5^4 = 0.0625$

7. $vw^{\frac{2}{3}}$

$\sqrt[3]{vw}^{\,2}$

8. $(-32)^{0.6}$

$(-32)^{3/5} \to (\sqrt[5]{-32})^3 \to -2^3 \to -8$

Translate radical expressions into expressions with rational exponents. Simplify numerical expressions when possible. Assume all variables are positive.

9. $\sqrt[7]{y^5}$

$= y^{\frac{5}{7}}$

10. $\sqrt[7]{(-6)^6}$

$= -6^{\frac{6}{7}}$

11. $\sqrt[3]{3^{15}}$

$3^{\frac{15}{3}} = 3^5 = 243$

12. $\sqrt[4]{(\pi z)^3}$

$\pi z^{\frac{3}{4}}$

13. $\sqrt[6]{(bcd)^4}$

$bcd^{\frac{4}{6}}$

14. $\sqrt{6^6}$

$6^{\frac{6}{2}}$

15. $\sqrt[5]{32^2}$

$32^{\frac{2}{5}}$

16. $\sqrt[3]{\left(\frac{4}{x}\right)^9}$

$\frac{4}{x}^{\frac{9}{3}}$

17. Music Frets are small metal bars positioned across the neck of a guitar so that the guitar can produce the notes of a specific scale. To find the distance a fret should be placed from the bridge, multiply the length of the string by $2^{-\frac{n}{12}}$, where n is the number of notes higher than the string's root note. Where should a fret be placed to produce a F note on a B string (6 notes higher) given that the length of the string is 64 cm?

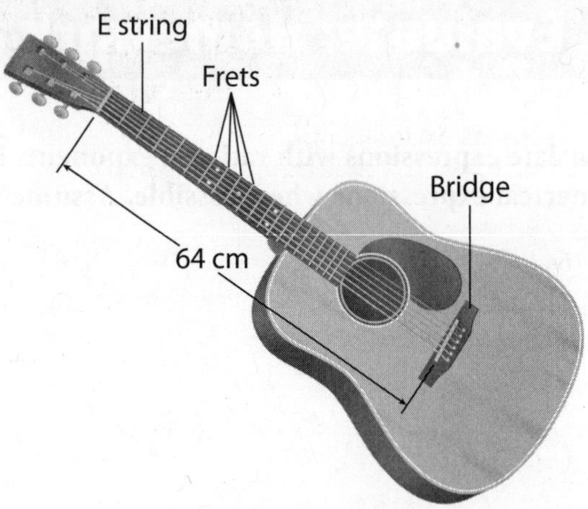

18. Meteorology The function $W = 35.74 + 0.6215T - 35.75V^{\frac{4}{25}} + 0.4275TV^{\frac{4}{25}}$ relates the windchill temperature W to the air temperature T in degrees Fahrenheit and the wind speed V in miles per hour. Use a calculator to find the wind chill temperature to the nearest degree when the air temperature is 28 °F and the wind speed is 35 miles per hour.

19. Astronomy New stars can form inside a cloud of interstellar gas when a cloud fragment, or *clump*, has a mass M greater than the *Jean's mass* M_J. The Jean's mass is $M_J = 100n^{-\frac{1}{2}}(T + 273)^{\frac{3}{2}}$ where n is the number of gas molecules per cubic centimeter and T is the gas temperature in degrees Celsius. A gas clump has $M = 137$, $n = 1000$, and $T = -263$. Will the clump form a star? Justify your answer.

20. Urban geography The total wages W in a metropolitan area compared to its total population p can be approximated by a power function of the form $W = a \cdot p^{\frac{9}{8}}$ where a is a constant. About how many times as great does the model predict the total earnings for a metropolitan area with 3,000,000 people will be as compared to a metropolitan area with a population of 750,000?

21. Which statement is true?

A. In the expression $8x^{\frac{3}{4}}$, $8x$ is the radicand.

B. In the expression $(-16)x^{\frac{4}{5}}$, 4 is the index.

C. The expression $1024^{\frac{n}{m}}$ represents the mth root of the nth power of 1024.

D. $50^{-\frac{2}{5}} = -50^{\frac{2}{5}}$

E. $\sqrt{(xy)^3} = xy^{\frac{3}{2}}$

H.O.T. Focus on Higher Order Thinking

22. Explain the Error A teacher asked students to evaluate $10^{-\frac{3}{5}}$ using their graphing calculators. The calculator entries of several students are shown below. Which entry will give the incorrect result? Explain.

$10^{(-3/5)}$ $\quad \sqrt[5]{10^{-3}}$ $\quad 10^{-.6}$ $\quad 1/10^{5/3}$ $\quad (1/10^{1/5})^3$

23. Critical Thinking The graphs of three functions of the form $y = ax^{\frac{m}{n}}$ are shown for a specific value of a, where m and n are natural numbers. What can you conclude about the relationship of m and n for each graph? Explain.

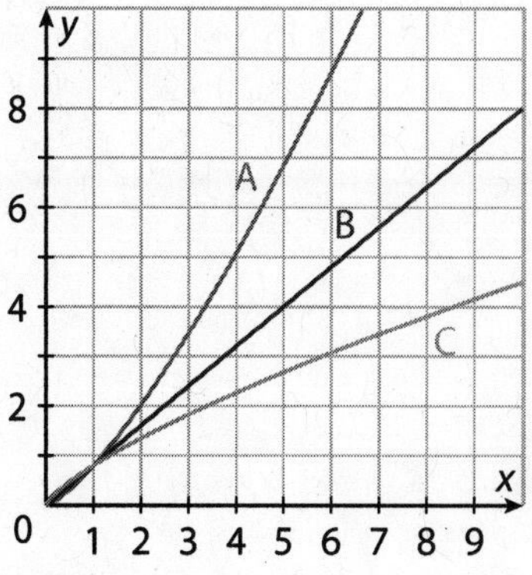

24. Critical Thinking For a negative real number a, under what condition(s) on m and n $(n \neq 0)$ is $a^{\frac{m}{n}}$ a real number? Explain. (Assume $\frac{m}{n}$ is written in simplest form.)

Lesson Performance Task

The formula $W = 35.74 + 0.6215T - 35.75V^{\frac{4}{25}} + 0.4275TV^{\frac{4}{25}}$ relates the wind chill temperature W to the air temperature T in degrees Fahrenheit and the wind speed V in miles per hour. Find the wind chill to the nearest degree when the air temperature is 40 °F and the wind speed is 35 miles per hour. If the wind chill is about 23 °F to the nearest degree when the air temperature is 40 °F, what is the wind speed to the nearest mile per hour?

Name ______________________ Class ____________ Date ________

11.2 Simplifying Radical Expressions

Essential Question: How can you simplify expressions containing rational exponents or radicals involving *n*th roots?

Resource Locker

Explore Establishing the Properties of Rational Exponents

In previous courses, you have used properties of integer exponents to simplify and evaluate expressions, as shown here for a few simple examples:

$$4^2 \cdot 4^3 = 4^{2+3} = 4^5 = 1024$$

$$(4 \cdot x)^2 = 4^2 \cdot x^2 = 16x^2$$

$$(4^2)^3 = 4^{2 \cdot 3} = 4^6 = 4096$$

$$\frac{4^2}{4^3} = 4^{2-3} = 4^{-1} = \frac{1}{4}$$

$$\left(\frac{4}{x}\right)^3 = \frac{4^3}{x^3} = \frac{64}{x^3}$$

Now that you have been introduced to expressions involving rational exponents, you can explore the properties that apply to simplifying them.

(A) Let $a = 64$, $b = 4$, $m = \frac{1}{3}$, and $n = \frac{3}{2}$. Evaluate each expression by substituting and applying exponents individually, as shown.

$64^{\frac{9}{6} - \frac{2}{6}}$

Expression	Substitute	Simplify	Result
$a^m \cdot a^n$	$64^{\frac{1}{3}} \cdot 64^{\frac{3}{2}}$	$4 \cdot 512$	2048
$(a \cdot b)^n$	$(64 \cdot 4)^{\frac{3}{2}}$	$256^{\frac{3}{2}}$	216
$(a^m)^n$	$(64^{\frac{1}{3}})^{\frac{3}{2}}$	$64^{\frac{1}{3} \cdot \frac{3}{2}}$	8
$\frac{a^n}{a^m}$	$\frac{64^{\frac{3}{2}}}{64^{\frac{1}{3}}}$	$64^{\frac{3}{2} - \frac{1}{3}}$	128
$\left(\frac{a}{b}\right)^n$	$\left(\frac{64}{4}\right)^{\frac{3}{2}}$	$(16)^{\frac{3}{2}}$	64

(B) Complete the table again. This time, however, apply the rule of exponents that you would use for integer exponents.

Expression	Apply Rule and Substitute	Simplify	Result
$a^m \cdot a^n$	$64^{\frac{1}{3}+\frac{3}{2}}$	$64^{\frac{11}{6}}$	
$(a \cdot b)^n$			
$(a^m)^n$			
$\frac{a^n}{a^m}$			
$\left(\frac{a}{b}\right)^n$			

Reflect

1. Compare your results in Steps A and B. What can you conclude?

2. In Steps A and B, you evaluated $\frac{a^n}{a^m}$ two ways. Now evaluate $\frac{a^m}{a^n}$ two ways, using the definition of negative exponents. Are your results consistent with your previous conclusions about integer and rational exponents?

Explain 1 Simplifying Rational-Exponent Expressions

Rational exponents have the same properties as integer exponents.

Properties of Rational Exponents

For all nonzero real numbers a and b and rational numbers m and n

Words	Numbers	Algebra
Product of Powers Property To multiply powers with the same base, add the exponents.	$12^{\frac{1}{2}} \cdot 12^{\frac{3}{2}} = 12^{\frac{1}{2}+\frac{3}{2}} = 12^2 = 144$	$a^m \cdot a^n = a^{m+n}$
Quotient of Powers Property To divide powers with the same base, subtract the exponents.	$\frac{125^{\frac{2}{3}}}{125^{\frac{1}{3}}} = 125^{\frac{2}{3}-\frac{1}{3}} = 125^{\frac{1}{3}} = 5$	$\frac{a^m}{a^n} = a^{m-n}$
Power of a Power Property To raise one power to another, multiply the exponents.	$\left(8^{\frac{2}{3}}\right)^3 = 8^{\frac{2}{3}\cdot 3} = 8^2 = 64$	$(a^m)^n = a^{m \cdot n}$
Power of a Product Property To find a power of a product, distribute the exponent.	$(16 \cdot 25)^{\frac{1}{2}} = 16^{\frac{1}{2}} \cdot 25^{\frac{1}{2}} = 4 \cdot 5 = 20$	$(ab)^m = a^m b^m$
Power of a Quotient Property To find the power of a qoutient, distribute the exponent.	$\left(\frac{16}{81}\right)^{\frac{1}{4}} = \frac{16^{\frac{1}{4}}}{81^{\frac{1}{4}}} = \frac{2}{3}$	$\left(\frac{a}{b}\right)^m = \frac{a^m}{b^m}$

Example 1 **Simplify the expression. Assume that all variables are positive. Exponents in simplified form should all be positive.**

(A) **a.** $25^{\frac{3}{5}} \cdot 25^{\frac{7}{5}}$

$= 25^{\frac{3}{5}+\frac{7}{5}}$ Product of Powers Prop.

$= 25^2$ Simplify.

$= 625$

b. $\frac{8^{\frac{1}{3}}}{8^{\frac{2}{3}}}$

$= 8^{\frac{1}{3}-\frac{2}{3}}$ Quotient of Powes Prop.

$= 8^{-\frac{1}{3}}$ Simplify.

$= \frac{1}{8^{\frac{1}{3}}}$ Definition of neg. power

$= \frac{1}{2}$ Simplify.

(B) a. $\left(\dfrac{y^{\frac{4}{3}}}{16y^{\frac{2}{3}}}\right)^{\frac{3}{2}}$ b. $\left(27x^{\frac{3}{4}}\right)^{\frac{2}{3}}$

$= \left(\dfrac{y^{\frac{4}{3}-\frac{2}{3}}}{16}\right)^{\frac{3}{2}}$ ______ Prop. $= \square^{\frac{2}{3}}\left(\square\right)^{\frac{2}{3}}$ Power of a Product Prop.

$= \left(\dfrac{\square}{16}\right)^{\frac{3}{2}}$ Simplify. $= 27^{\frac{2}{3}}\left(x^{\square}\right)$ Power of a Power Prop.

$= \dfrac{\left(y^{\frac{2}{3}}\right)^{\frac{3}{2}}}{16^{\frac{3}{2}}}$ ______ Prop. $= \square$ Simplify.

$= \dfrac{y^{\frac{2}{3}\cdot\frac{3}{2}}}{16^{\frac{3}{2}}}$ ______ Prop.

$= \square$ Simplify.

Your Turn

Simplify the expression. Assume that all variables are positive. Exponents in simplified form should all be positive.

3. $\left(12^{\frac{2}{3}} \cdot 12^{\frac{4}{3}}\right)^{\frac{3}{2}}$

4. $\dfrac{\left(6x^{\frac{1}{3}}\right)^2}{x^{\frac{5}{3}}y}$

Explain 2 Simplifying Radical Expressions Using the Properties of Exponents

When you are working with radical expressions involving *n*th roots, you can rewrite the expressions using rational exponents and then simplify them using the properties of exponents.

Example 2 **Simplify the expression by writing it using rational exponents and then using the properties of rational exponents. Assume that all variables are positive. Exponents in simplified form should all be positive.**

(A) $x\left(\sqrt[3]{2y}\right)\left(\sqrt[3]{4x^2y^2}\right)$

$= x(2y)^{\frac{1}{3}}\left(4x^2y^2\right)^{\frac{1}{3}}$ Write using rational exponents.

$= x\left(2y \cdot 4x^2y^2\right)^{\frac{1}{3}}$ Power of a Product Property

$= x\left(8x^2y^3\right)^{\frac{1}{3}}$ Product of Powers Property

$= x\left(2x^{\frac{2}{3}}y\right)$ Power of a Product Property

$= 2x^{\frac{5}{3}}y$ Product of Powers Property

(B) $\dfrac{\sqrt{64y}}{\sqrt[3]{64y}}$

$= \dfrac{(64y)^{\frac{1}{2}}}{(64y)^{\frac{1}{3}}}$ Write using rational exponents.

$= (64y)^{\square}$ Quotient of Powers Property

$= (64y)^{\square}$ Simplify.

$= \square$ Power of a Product Property

$= \square$ Simplify.

Your Turn

Simplify the expression by writing it using rational exponents and then using the properties of rational exponents.

5. $\dfrac{\sqrt{x^3}}{\sqrt[3]{x^2}}$

6. $\sqrt[6]{16^3} \cdot \sqrt[4]{4^6} \cdot \sqrt[3]{8^2}$

Explain 3 Simplifying Radical Expressions Using the Properties of *nth* Roots

From working with square roots, you know, for example, that $\sqrt{8} \cdot \sqrt{2} = \sqrt{8 \cdot 2} = \sqrt{16} = 4$ and $\dfrac{\sqrt{8}}{\sqrt{2}} \cdot = \sqrt{\dfrac{8}{2}} = \sqrt{4} = 2$. The corresponding properties also apply to *n*th roots.

Properties of *n*th Roots

For a > 0 and b > 0

Words	Numbers	Algebra
Product Property of Roots The *n*th root of a product is equal to the product of the *n*th roots.	$\sqrt[3]{16} = \sqrt[3]{8} \cdot \sqrt[3]{2} = 2\sqrt[3]{2}$	$\sqrt[n]{ab} = \sqrt[n]{a} \cdot \sqrt[n]{b}$
Quotient Property of Roots The *n*th root of a Quotient is equal to the Quotient of the *n*th roots.	$\sqrt{\dfrac{25}{16}} = \dfrac{\sqrt{25}}{\sqrt{16}} = \dfrac{5}{4}$	$\sqrt[n]{\dfrac{a}{b}} = \dfrac{\sqrt[n]{a}}{\sqrt[n]{b}}$

Example 3 **Simplify the expression using the properties of nth roots. Assume that all variables are positive. Rationalize any irrational denominators.**

Ⓐ $\sqrt[3]{256x^3y^7}$

$\sqrt[3]{256x^3y^7}$

$= \sqrt[3]{2^8 \cdot x^3y^7}$ Write 256 as a power.

$= \sqrt[3]{2^6 \cdot x^3y^6} \cdot \sqrt[3]{2^2 \cdot y}$ Product Property of Roots

$= \sqrt[3]{2^6} \cdot \sqrt[3]{x^3} \cdot \sqrt[3]{y^6} \cdot \sqrt[3]{4y}$ Factor out perfect cubes.

$= 4xy^2\sqrt[3]{4y}$ Simplify.

Ⓑ $\sqrt[4]{\frac{81}{x}}$

$\sqrt[4]{\frac{81}{x}}$

$= \frac{\sqrt[4]{81}}{\sqrt[4]{x}}$ [ ]

$= \frac{[\ ]}{\sqrt[4]{x}}$ Simplify.

$= \frac{3}{\sqrt[4]{x}} \cdot \frac{[\ ]}{\sqrt[4]{x^3}}$ Rationalize the denominator.

$= \frac{3\sqrt[4]{x^3}}{\sqrt[4]{x^4}}$ [ ]

$=$ [ ] Simplify.

Reflect

7. In Part B, why was $\sqrt[4]{x^3}$ used when rationalizing the denominator? What factor would you use to rationalize a denominator of $\sqrt[5]{4y^3}$?

Your Turn

Simplify the expression using the properties of *n*th roots. Assume that all variables are positive.

8. $\sqrt[3]{216x^{12}y^{15}}$

9. $\sqrt[4]{\dfrac{16}{x^{14}}}$

Explain 4 Rewriting a Radical-Function Model

When you find or apply a function model involving rational powers or radicals, you can use the properties in this lesson to help you find a simpler expression for the model.

Example 4

(A) **Manufacturing** A can that is twice as tall as its radius has the minimum surface area for the volume it contains. The formula $S = 6\pi\left(\frac{V}{2\pi}\right)^{\frac{2}{3}}$ expresses the surface area of a can with this shape in terms of its volume.

a. Use the properties of rational exponents to simplify the expression for the surface area. Then write the approximate model with the coefficient rounded to the nearest hundredth.

b. Graph the model using a graphing calculator. What is the surface area in square centimeters for a can with a volume of 440 cm³?

a. $S = 6\pi\left(\frac{V}{2\pi}\right)^{\frac{2}{3}}$

Power of a Quotient Property $= 6\pi \cdot \dfrac{V^{\frac{2}{3}}}{(2\pi)^{\frac{2}{3}}}$

Group Powers of 2π. $= \dfrac{3(2\pi)}{(2\pi)^{\frac{2}{3}}} \cdot V^{\frac{2}{3}}$

Quotient of Powers Property $= 3(2\pi)^{1-\frac{2}{3}} \cdot V^{\frac{2}{3}}$

Simplify. $= 3(2\pi)^{\frac{1}{3}} \cdot V^{\frac{2}{3}}$

Use a calculator. $\approx 5.54V^{\frac{2}{3}}$

A simplified model is $S = 3(2\pi)^{\frac{1}{3}} \cdot V^{\frac{2}{3}}$, which gives $S \approx 5.54V^{\frac{2}{3}}$.

b.

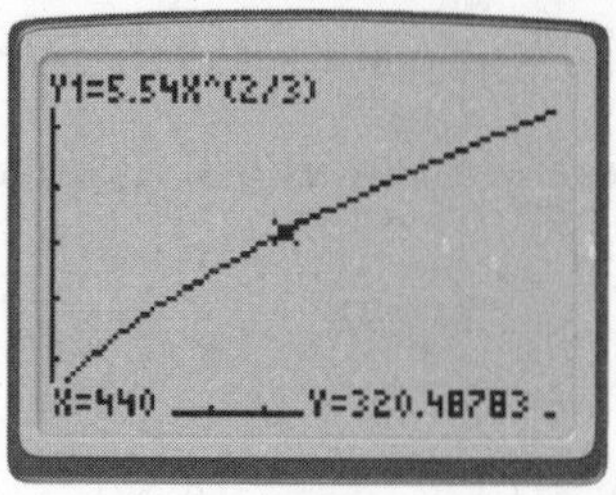

The surface area is about 320 cm^2.

Ⓑ **Commercial fishing** The buoyancy of a fishing float in water depends on the volume of air it contains. The radius of a spherical float as a function of its volume is given by $r = \sqrt[3]{\frac{3V}{4\pi}}$.

a. Use the properties of roots to rewrite the expression for the radius as the product of a coefficient term and a variable term. Then write the approximate formula with the coefficient rounded to the nearest hundredth.

b. What should the radius be for a float that needs to contain 4.4 ft^3 of air to have the proper buoyancy?

a. $r = \sqrt[3]{\frac{3V}{4\pi}}$

Rewrite radicand. $= \sqrt[3]{\frac{3}{4\pi} \cdot \square}$

Product Property of Roots $= \sqrt[3]{\frac{3}{4\pi}} \cdot \square$

Use a calculator $\approx \square$

The rewritten formula is $r = \square$, which gives $r \approx \square$.

b. Substitute 4.4 for V.

$r = 0.62\sqrt[3]{4.4} \approx \square$

The radius is about ____ feet.

Reflect

10. Discussion What are some reasons you might want to rewrite an expression involving radicals into an expression involving rational exponents?

Your Turn

11. The surface area as a function of volume for a box with a square base and a height that is twice the side length of the base is $S = 10\left(\frac{V}{2}\right)^{\frac{2}{3}}$. Use the properties of rational exponents to simplify the expression for the surface area so that no fractions are involved. Then write the approximate model with the coefficient rounded to the nearest hundredth.

Elaborate

12. In problems with a radical in the denominator, you rationalized the denominator to remove the radical. What can you do to remove a rational exponent from the denominator? Explain by giving an example.

13. Show why $\sqrt[n]{a^n}$ is equal to a for all natural numbers a and n using the definition of nth roots and using rational exponents.

14. Show that the Product Property of Roots is true using rational exponents.

15. **Essential Question Check-In** Describe the difference between applying the Power of a Power Property and applying the Power of a Product Property for rational exponents using an example that involves both properties.

Evaluate: Homework and Practice

Personal Math Trainer
- Online Homework
- Hints and Help
- Extra Practice

Simplify the expression. Assume that all variables are positive. Exponents in simplified form should all be positive.

1. $\left(\left(\frac{1}{16}\right)^{-\frac{2}{3}}\right)^{\frac{3}{4}}$

$\frac{1}{16}^{-\frac{2}{3}\cdot\frac{3}{4}} = \frac{1}{16}^{-\frac{6}{12}}$

$= \frac{1}{16}^{-\frac{1}{2}} = 16^{\frac{1}{2}} \to \sqrt{16} = \boxed{4}$

2. $\dfrac{x^{\frac{1}{3}} \cdot x^{\frac{5}{6}}}{x^{\frac{1}{6}}}$

$= \dfrac{x^{\frac{1}{3}+\frac{5}{6}}}{x^{\frac{1}{6}}} = \dfrac{x^{\frac{7}{6}}}{x^{\frac{1}{6}}}$

$= \boxed{x}$

3. $\dfrac{9^{\frac{3}{2}} \cdot 9^{\frac{1}{2}}}{9^{-2}}$

$= \dfrac{(3^2)^{\frac{3}{2}} \cdot (3^2)^{\frac{1}{2}}}{3^{-4}} = \dfrac{3^3 \cdot 3}{3^{-4}}$

$\dfrac{3^4}{3^{-4}} = \boxed{3^8}$

4. $\left(\dfrac{16^{\frac{5}{3}}}{16^{\frac{5}{6}}}\right)^{\frac{9}{5}}$

$16^{\frac{5}{3}-\frac{5}{6}} = \left(16^{\frac{5}{6}}\right)^{\frac{9}{5}}$

$16^{\frac{5}{6}\cdot\frac{9}{5}} = 16^{\frac{3}{2}}$

$(\sqrt{16})^3 = 4^3 = \boxed{64}$

5. $\dfrac{2xy}{\left(x^{\frac{1}{3}}y^{\frac{2}{3}}\right)^{\frac{3}{2}}}$

$= \dfrac{2xy}{x^{\frac{1}{3}\cdot\frac{3}{2}}\,y^{\frac{2}{3}\cdot\frac{3}{2}}} = \dfrac{2xy}{x^{\frac{1}{2}}y} = 2x^{\frac{1}{2}}$

$= 2\sqrt{x}$

6. $\dfrac{3y^{\frac{3}{4}}}{2xy^{\frac{3}{2}}}$

$= \dfrac{3}{2xy^{\frac{3}{2}-\frac{3}{4}}} = \dfrac{3}{2xy^{\frac{3}{4}}} = \dfrac{3}{2x\sqrt[4]{y^3}} \cdot \dfrac{\sqrt[4]{y}}{\sqrt[4]{y}}$

$= \dfrac{3\sqrt[4]{y}}{2x\sqrt[4]{y^3}\sqrt[4]{y}} = \dfrac{3\sqrt[4]{y}}{2xy}$

Simplify the expression by writing it using rational exponents and then using the properties of rational exponents. Assume that all variables are positive. Exponents in simplified form should all be positive.

7. $\sqrt[4]{25} \cdot \sqrt[3]{5}$

$\sqrt[4]{(5)^2}$

$= \sqrt[4]{5^2}$

$= 5^{\frac{2}{4}} = 5^{\frac{1}{2}} \cdot 5^{\frac{1}{3}}$

8. $\dfrac{\sqrt[4]{2^{-2}}}{\sqrt[6]{2^{-9}}}$

9. $\dfrac{\sqrt[4]{3^3} \cdot \sqrt[3]{x^2}}{\sqrt{3x}}$

10. $\dfrac{\sqrt[4]{x^4y^6} \cdot \sqrt{x^6}}{y}$

$\dfrac{xy\sqrt[4]{y^2} \cdot x^3}{y}$ $\qquad y^{\frac{2}{4}} = y^{\frac{1}{2}}$

$x\sqrt[4]{y^2}\,x^3$

$x\sqrt{y}\,x^3$

$x^4\sqrt{y}$

11. $\dfrac{\sqrt[6]{s^4t^9}}{\sqrt[3]{st}}$

$\dfrac{s^{\frac{4}{6}} + \frac{9}{6}}{s^{\frac{1}{3}} + \frac{1}{3}}$

$\dfrac{s^{\frac{4}{6}} + \frac{9}{6}}{s^{\frac{2}{6}} + \frac{2}{6}}$

$s^{\frac{2}{6}} + \frac{7}{6}$

$6\sqrt{s^2+7}$

12. $\sqrt[4]{27} \cdot \sqrt{3} \cdot \sqrt[6]{81^3}$

$3^{\frac{3}{4}}$ $3^{\frac{1}{2}}$, 3^{7}

5^{-5} , $3^{\frac{2}{4}}$, $\frac{8}{4}$

$3^{\frac{15}{4}} = 4\sqrt{3^{15}}$

Simplify the expression using the properties of *n*th roots. Assume that all variables are positive. Rationalize any irrational denominators.

13. $\dfrac{\sqrt[4]{36} \cdot \sqrt[4]{216}}{\sqrt[4]{6}}$

$\dfrac{4\sqrt{7776}}{4\sqrt{6}}$

$4\sqrt{1296}$

6

14. $\sqrt[4]{4096x^6y^8}$

$8xy^2\ 4\sqrt{x^2}$

$8xy^2\sqrt{x}$

15. $\dfrac{\sqrt[3]{x^8y^4}}{\sqrt[3]{x^2y}}$

$3\sqrt{x^6y^3}$

x^2y

16. $\sqrt[5]{\dfrac{125}{w^6}} \cdot \sqrt[5]{25v}$

17. **Weather** The volume of a sphere as a function of its surface area is given by $V = \dfrac{4\pi}{3}\left(\dfrac{S}{4\pi}\right)^{\frac{3}{2}}$.

a. Use the properties of roots to rewrite the expression for the volume as the product of a simplified coefficient term (with positive exponents) and a variable term. Then write the approximate formula with the coefficient rounded to the nearest thousandth.

b. A spherical weather balloon has a surface area of 500 ft². What is the approximate volume of the balloon?

18. Amusement parks An amusement park has a ride with a free fall of 128 feet. The formula $t = \sqrt{\frac{2d}{g}}$ gives the time t in seconds it takes the ride to fall a distance of d feet. The formula $v = \sqrt{2gd}$ gives the velocity v in feet per second after the ride has fallen d feet. The letter g represents the gravitational constant.

a. Rewrite each formula so that the variable d is isolated. Then simplify each formula using the fact that $g \approx 32$ ft/s^2.

b. Find the time it takes the ride to fall halfway and its velocity at that time. Then find the time and velocity for the full drop.

c. What is the ratio of the time it takes for the whole drop to the time it takes for the first half? What is the ratio of the velocity after the second half of the drop to the velocity after the first half? What do you notice?

19. Which choice(s) is/are equivalent to $\sqrt{2}$?

A. $\left(\sqrt[8]{2}\right)^4$

B. $\dfrac{2^3}{2^{-\frac{5}{2}}}$

C. $\left(4^{\frac{2}{3}} \cdot 2^{\frac{2}{3}}\right)^{\frac{1}{4}}$

D. $\dfrac{\sqrt[3]{2^2}}{\sqrt[6]{2}}$

E. $\dfrac{\sqrt{2^{-\frac{3}{4}}}}{\sqrt{2^{-\frac{7}{4}}}}$

20. Home Heating A propane storage tank for a home is shaped like a cylinder with hemispherical ends, and a cylindrical portion length that is 4 times the radius. The formula $S = 12\pi\left(\frac{3V}{16\pi}\right)^{\frac{2}{3}}$ expresses the surface area of a tank with this shape in terms of its volume.

a. Use the properties of rational exponents to rewrite the expression for the surface area so that the variable V is isolated. Then write the approximate model with the coefficient rounded to the nearest hundredth.

b. Graph the model using a graphing calculator. What is the surface area in square feet for a tank with a volume of 150 ft^3 ?

H.O.T. Focus on Higher Order Thinking

21. Critique Reasoning Aaron's work in simplifying an expression is shown. What mistake(s) did Aaron make? Show the correct simplification.

$$625^{-\frac{1}{3}} \div 625^{-\frac{4}{3}}$$
$$= 625^{-\frac{1}{3}-\left(-\frac{4}{3}\right)}$$
$$= 625^{-\frac{1}{3}\left(-\frac{3}{4}\right)}$$
$$= 625^{\frac{1}{4}}$$
$$= 5$$

22. Critical Thinking Use the definition of nth root to show that the Product Property of Roots is true, that is, that $\sqrt[n]{ab} = \sqrt[n]{a} \cdot \sqrt[n]{b}$. (Hint: Begin by letting x be the nth root of a and letting y be the nth root of b.)

23. Critical Thinking For what real values of a is $\sqrt[4]{a}$ greater than a? For what real values of a is $\sqrt[5]{a}$ greater than a?

Lesson Performance Task

You've been asked to help decorate for a school dance, and the theme chosen is "The Solar System." The plan is to have a bunch of papier-mâché spheres serve as models of the planets, and your job is to paint them. All you're told are the volumes of the individual spheres, but you need to know their surface areas so you can get be sure to get enough paint. How can you write a simplified equation using rational exponents for the surface area of a sphere in terms of its volume?

(The formula for the volume of a sphere is $V = \frac{4}{3}\pi r^3$ and the formula for the surface area of a sphere is $A = 4\pi r^2$.)

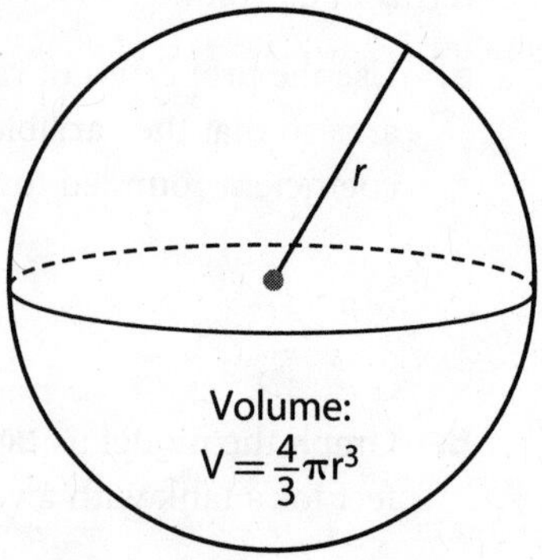

$\sqrt{3b} = 3$

$(x+30)^{1/2} = x$

$\sqrt[3]{4c} = 18$

$\sqrt[4]{27} \cdot \sqrt[4]{3}$

$\frac{\sqrt{x}}{\sqrt{13}} = 5$

$(3^{-2/3} \cdot 3^{1/3})^{-1}$

$\sqrt{4k+6} - \sqrt{6k-14} = 0$

$\frac{\sqrt[3]{3} \cdot \sqrt[3]{18}}{\sqrt[6]{2} \cdot \sqrt[6]{2}}$

p. 204 of robot book

Name ______________________ Class ____________ Date ________

11.3 Solving Radical Equations

Essential Question: How can you solve equations involving square roots and cube roots?

Resource Locker

Explore — Investigating Solutions of Square Root Equations

When solving quadratic equations, you have learned that the number of real solutions depends upon the values in the equation, with different equations having 0, 1, or 2 real solutions. How many real solutions does a square root equation have? In the Explore, you will investigate graphically the numbers of real solutions for different square root equations.

(A) Remember that you can graph the two sides of an equation as separate functions to find solutions of the equation: a solution is any x-value where the two graphs intersect.

The graph of $y = \sqrt{x-3}$ is shown on a calculator window of $-4 \le x \le 16$ and $-2 \le y \le 8$. Reproduce the graph on your calculator. Then add the graph of $y = 2$.

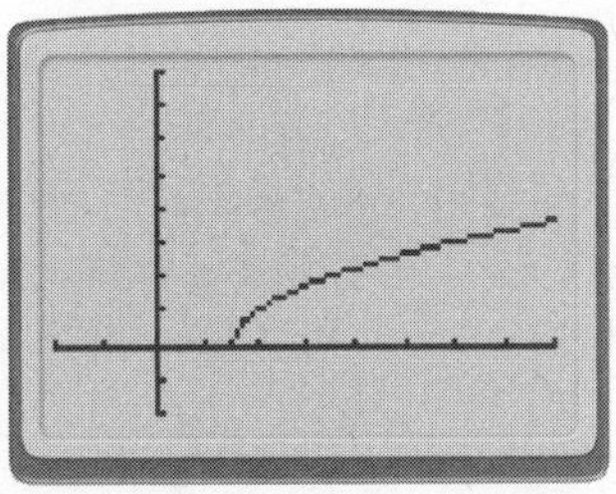

How many solutions does the equation $\sqrt{x-3} = 2$ have? ______ How do you know?

____

On your calculator, replace the graph of $y = 2$ with the graph of $y = -1$.

How many solutions does the equation $\sqrt{x-3} = -1$ have? ______ How do you know?

____

(B) Graph $y = \sqrt{x-3} + 2$ on your calculator (you can use the same viewing window as in Step A).

Add the graph of $y = 3$ to the graph of $y = \sqrt{x-3} + 2$.

How many solutions does $\sqrt{x-3} + 2 = 3$ have? ______

Replace the graph of $y = 3$ with the graph of $y = 1$.

How many solutions does $\sqrt{x-3} + 2 = 1$ have? ______

(C) Graph both sides of $\sqrt{4x - 4} = x + 1$ as separate functions on your calculator.

How many solutions does $\sqrt{4x - 4} = x + 1$ have? ______

Replace the graph of $y = x + 1$ with the graph of $y = \frac{1}{2}x$.

How many solutions does $\sqrt{4x - 4} = \frac{1}{2}x$ have? ______

Replace the graph of $y = \frac{1}{2}x$ with the graph of $y = 2x - 5$.

How many solutions does $\sqrt{4x - 4} = 2x - 5$ have? ______

(D) Graph both sides of $\sqrt{2x - 3} = \sqrt{x}$ as separate functions on your calculator.

How many solutions does $\sqrt{2x - 3} = \sqrt{x}$ have? ______

Replace the graph of $y = \sqrt{x}$ with the graph of $y = \sqrt{2x + 3}$.

How many solutions does $\sqrt{2x - 3} = \sqrt{2x + 3}$ have? ______

Reflect

1. For a square root equation of the form $\sqrt{bx - h} = c$, what can you conclude about the number of solutions based on the sign of c?

2. For a square root equation of the form $\sqrt{bx - h} + k = c$, what can you conclude about the number of solutions based on the values of k and c?

3. For a cube root equation of the form $\sqrt[3]{bx - h} = c$, will the number of solutions depend on the sign of c? Explain.

4. The graphs in the second part of Step D appear to be get closer and closer as x increases. How can you be sure that they never meet, that is, that $\sqrt{2x - 3} = \sqrt{2x + 3}$ really has no solutions?

Explain 1 Solving Square Root and $\frac{1}{2}$-Power Equations

A *radical equation* contains a variable within a radical or a variable raised to a (non-integer) rational power. To solve a square root equation, or, equivalently, an equation involving the power $\frac{1}{2}$, you can square both sides of the equation and solve the resulting equation.

Because opposite numbers have the same square, squaring both sides of an equation may introduce an apparent solution that is not an actual solution (an extraneous solution). For example, while the only solution of $x = 2$ is 2, the equation that is the square of each side, $x^2 = 4$, has two solutions, -2 and 2. But -2 is not a solution of the original equation.

Example 1 **Solve the equation. Check for extraneous solutions.**

(A) $2 + \sqrt{x + 10} = x$

$$2 + \sqrt{x + 10} = x$$

Isolate the radical. $\sqrt{x + 10} = x - 2$

Square both sides. $\left(\sqrt{x + 10}\right)^2 = (x - 2)^2$

Simplify. $x + 10 = x^2 - 4x + 4$

Simplify. $0 = x^2 - 5x - 6$

Factor. $0 = (x - 6)(x + 1)$

Zero Product Property $x = 6$ or $x = -1$

Check:

$2 + \sqrt{x + 10} = x$	$2 + \sqrt{x + 10} = x$
$2 + \sqrt{6 + 10} \stackrel{?}{=} 6$	$2 + \sqrt{-1 + 10} \stackrel{?}{=} -1$
$2 + \sqrt{16} \stackrel{?}{=} 6$	$2 + \sqrt{9} \stackrel{?}{=} -1$
$6 = 6$ ✓	$5 \neq -1$
$x = 6$ is a solution.	$x = -1$ is not a solution.

The solution is $x = 6$.

(B) $(x + 6)^{\frac{1}{2}} - (2x - 4)^{\frac{1}{2}} = 0$

Rewrite with radicals. $\sqrt{x + 6} - \sqrt{2x - 4} = 0$

Isolate radicals on each side. $\sqrt{x + 6} = \square$

Square both sides. $\left(\sqrt{x + 6}\right)^2 = \left(\square\right)^2$

Simplify. $\square = \square$

Solve. $\square = x$

Check:

$$\sqrt{x + 6} - \sqrt{2x - 4} = 0$$

$$\sqrt{10 + 6} - \sqrt{2\left(\square\right) - 4} \stackrel{?}{=} 0$$

$$\square - \square \stackrel{?}{=} 0$$

$$\square = 0$$

The solution is ________.

Reflect

5. The graphs of each side of the equation from Part A are shown on the graphing calculator screen below. How can you tell from the graph that one of the two solutions you found algebraically is extraneous?

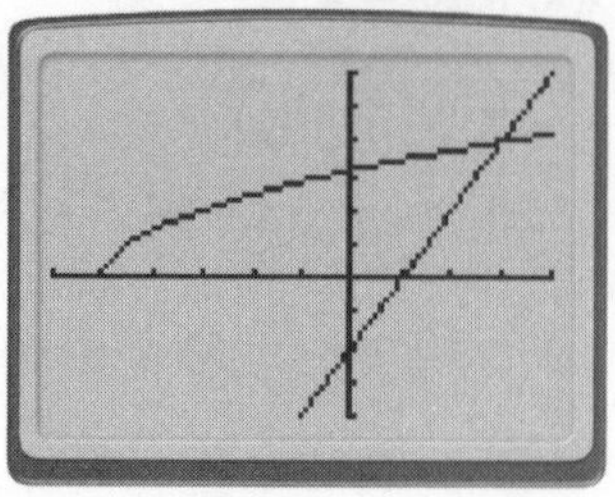

Your Turn

6. Solve $(x+5)^{\frac{1}{2}} - 2 = 1$.

Explain 2 Solving Cube Root and $\frac{1}{3}$-Power Equations

You can solve radical equations that involve roots other than square roots by raising both sides to the index of the radical. So, to solve a cube root equation, or, equivalently, an equation involving the power $\frac{1}{3}$, you can cube both sides of the equation and solve the resulting equation.

Example 2 **Solve the equation.**

Ⓐ $\sqrt[3]{x+2} + 7 = 5$

	$\sqrt[3]{x+2} + 7 = 5$
Isolate the radical.	$\sqrt[3]{x+2} = -2$
Cube both sides.	$\left(\sqrt[3]{x+2}\right)^3 = (-2)^3$
Simplify.	$x + 2 = -8$
Solve for x	$x = -10$

The solution is $x = -10$.

(B) $\sqrt[3]{x-5} = x + 1$

$$\sqrt[3]{x-5} = x + 1$$

Cube both sides. $\left(\sqrt[3]{x-5}\right)^3 = (x+1)^3$

Simplify $\square = \square$

Simplify. $0 = \square$

Begin to factor by grouping. $0 = x^2\left(\square\right) + 2\left(\square\right)$

Complete factoring $0 = \left(x^2 + 2\right)\left(\square\right)$

By the Zero Product Property, $\square = 0$ or $\square = 0$.

Because there are no real values of x for which $x^2 = \square$, the only solution is $\square$.

Reflect

7. Discussion Example 1 shows checking for extraneous solutions, while Example 2 does not. While it is always wise to check your answers, can a cubic equation have an extraneous solution? Explain your answer.

____

____

____

____

Your Turn

8. Solve $2(x - 50)^{\frac{1}{3}} = -10$.

Explain 3 Solving a Real-World Problem

Example 3

(A) **Driving** The speed s in miles per hour that a car is traveling when it goes into a skid can be estimated by using the formula $s = \sqrt{30fd}$, where f is the coefficient of friction and d is the length of the skid marks in feet.

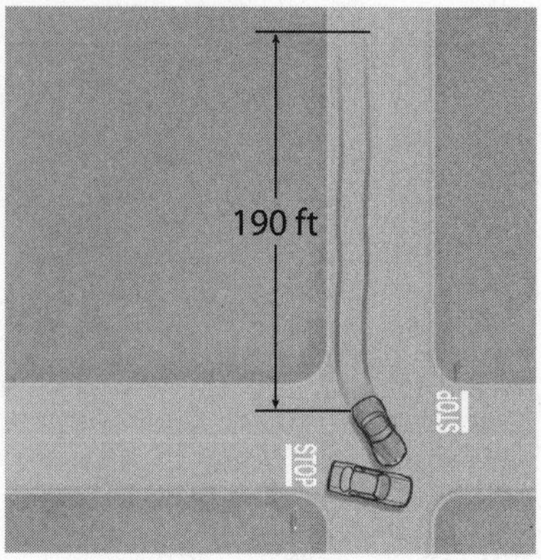

After an accident, a driver claims to have been traveling the speed limit of 55 mi/h. The coefficient of friction under the conditions at the time of the accident was 0.6, and the length of the skid marks is 190 feet. Is the driver telling the truth about the car's speed? Explain.

Use the formula to find the length of a skid at a speed of 55 mi/h. Compare this distance to the actual skid length of 190 feet.

$$s = \sqrt{30fd}$$

Substitute 55 for s and 0.6 for f $\quad 55 = \sqrt{30(0.6)d}$

Simplify. $\quad 55 = \sqrt{18d}$

Square both sides. $\quad 55^2 = \left(\sqrt{18d}\right)^2$

Simplify. $\quad 3025 = 18d$

Solve for d. $\quad 168 \approx d$

If the driver had been traveling at 55 mi/h, the skid marks would measure about 168 feet. Because the skid marks actually measure 190 feet, the driver must have been driving faster than 55 mi/h.

(B) **Construction** The diameter d in inches of a rope needed to lift a weight of w tons is given by the formula $d = \frac{\sqrt{15w}}{\pi}$. How much weight can be lifted with a rope with a diameter of 1.0 inch?

Use the formula for the diameter as a function of weight, and solve for the weight given the diameter.

$$d = \frac{\sqrt{15w}}{\pi}$$

Substitute. $\quad \square = \frac{\sqrt{15w}}{\pi}$

Square both sides. $\quad \square = \square$

Isolate the radical. $\quad \left(\square\right)^2 = \left(\sqrt{15w}\right)^2$

Simplify. $\quad \square = 15w$

Solve for w. $\quad \square \approx w$

A rope with a diameter of 1.0 can hold about ______ ton, or about ______ pounds.

Your Turn

9. **Biology** The trunk length (in inches) of a male elephant can be modeled by $l = 23\sqrt[3]{t} + 17$, where t is the age of the elephant in years. If a male elephant has a trunk length of 100 inches, about what is his age?

Elaborate

10. A student asked to solve the equation $\sqrt{4x + 8} + 9 = 1$ isolated the radical, squared both sides, and solved for x to obtain $x = 14$, only to find out that the apparent solution was extraneous. Why could the student have stopped trying to solve the equation after isolating the radical?

11. When you see a cube root equation with the radical expression isolated on one side and a constant on the other, what should you expect for the number of solutions? Explain. What are some reasons you should check your answer anyway?

12. **Essential Question Check-In** Solving a quadratic equation of the form $x^2 = a$ involves taking the square root of both sides. Solving a square root equation of the form $\sqrt{x} = b$ involves squaring both sides of the equation. Which of these operations can create an equation that is not equivalent to the original equation? Explain how this affects the solution process.

Evaluate: Homework and Practice

Personal Math Trainer

- Online Homework
- Hints and Help
- Extra Practice

Solve the equation.

1. $\sqrt{x-9} = 5$

$x - 9 = 5^2$

$x - 9 = 25$

$x = 34$

2. $\sqrt{3x} = 6$

$3x = 6^2$

$3x = 36$

$x = 12$

3. $\sqrt{x+3} = x + 1$

$x + 3 = (x+1)^2$

$x + 3 = x^2 + 2x + 1$

$0 = x^2 + x - 2$

$x = 1$

4. $\sqrt{(15x + 10)} = 2x + 3$

$15x + 10 = (2x+3)^2$

$15x + 10 = 2x^2 +$

5. $(x+4)^{\frac{1}{2}} = 6$

x + 4 = 36

x = 32

6. $(45-9x)^{\frac{1}{2}} = x - 5$

45 − 9x = x² − 10x + 25

x² − x − 20

(x − 5)(x + 4) = 0

x = 5, −4

7. $(x-6)^{\frac{1}{2}} = x - 2$

x − 6 = x² − 4x + 4

x² − 5x + 10 = 0

8. $4(x-2)^{\frac{1}{2}} = (x+13)^{\frac{1}{2}}$

(4x − 8)½ = (x + 13)½

4√x−2

16x − 32 = x + 13

15x = 45

x = 3

9. $5 - \sqrt[3]{x-4} = 2$

10. $2\sqrt[3]{3x+2} = \sqrt[3]{4x-9}$

11. $\sqrt[3]{69x + 35} = x + 5$

$69x + 35 = (x+5)^3$

$69x + 35 = x^3 + 15x^2 + 75x + 125$

$0 = x^2 + 15x^2 + 6x + 90 = x^2(x+15) + 6(x+15)$

$0 = (x^2+6)(x+15)$

$x = -15, \sqrt{-6}$

12. $\sqrt[3]{x + 5} = x - 1$

13. $(x + 7)^{\frac{1}{3}} = (4x)^{\frac{1}{3}}$

$x + 7 = 4x$

$-x \quad -x$

$\frac{7 = 3x}{3}$

$\left(\frac{7}{3} + 7\right) = 4\left(\frac{7}{3}\right)$

$= \frac{28}{3} = \frac{28}{3}$

14. $(5x + 1)^{\frac{1}{4}} = 4$

$\sqrt[4]{5x+1} = 4$

$5x + 1 = 4^4$

$5x + 256$

$5x = -256$

$x = 51$

15. $(-9x - 54)^{\frac{1}{3}} = -2x + 3$

$-9x - 54 = -2x + 3$

$7x = -57$

$x = \frac{-57}{7}$

16. $2(x - 1)^{\frac{1}{5}} = (2x - 17)^{\frac{1}{5}}$

$2\sqrt[3]{x-1} = \sqrt[6]{2x-17}$

$32(x-1) = 2x - 17$

$32x - 32 = 2x - 17$

$36x = 15$

$x = -\frac{1}{12}$

17. Driving The formula for the speed versus skid length in Example 3A assumes that all 4 wheel brakes are working at top efficiency. If this is not true, another parameter is included in the equation so that the equation becomes $s = \sqrt{30fdn}$ where n is the percent braking efficiency as a decimal. Accident investigators know that the rear brakes failed on a car, reducing its braking efficiency to 60%. On a dry road with a coefficient of friction of 0.7, the car skidded 250 feet. Was the car going above the speed limit of 60 mi/h when the skid began?

18. Anatomy The surface area S of a human body in square meters can be approximated by $S = \sqrt{\frac{hm}{36}}$ where h is height in meters and m is mass in kilograms. A basketball player with a height of 2.1 meters has a surface area of about 2.7 m^2. What is the player's mass?

19. Biology The approximate antler length L (in inches) of a deer buck can be modeled by $L = 9\sqrt[3]{t} + 15$ where t is the age in years of the buck. If a buck has an antler length of 36 inches, what is its age?

20. Amusement Parks For a spinning amusement park ride, the velocity v in meters per second of a car moving around a curve with radius r meters is given by $v = \sqrt{ar}$ where a is the car's acceleration in m/s^2. If the ride has a maximum acceleration of 30 m/s^2 and the cars on the ride have a maximum velocity of 12 m/s, what is the smallest radius that any curve on the ride may have?

21. For each radical equation, state the number of solutions that exist.

A. $\sqrt{x - 4} = -5$

B. $\sqrt{x - 4} + 6 = 11$

C. $4 = -2\sqrt[3]{x + 2}$

D. $\sqrt{x + 40} = 0$

E. $\sqrt[3]{2x + 5} = -18$

H.O.T. Focus on Higher Order Thinking

22. Critical Thinking For an equation of the form $\sqrt{x + a} = b$ where b is a constant, does the sign of a affect whether or not there is a solution for a given value of b? If so, how? If not, why not?

23. Explain the Error Below is a student's work in solving the equation $2\sqrt{3x + 3} = 12$. What mistake did the student make? What is the correct solution?

$$2\sqrt{3x + 3} = 12$$

$$2\left(\sqrt{3x + 3}\right)^2 = 12^2$$

$$2(3x + 3) = 144$$

$$6x + 6 = 144$$

$$x = 23$$

24. Communicate Mathematical Ideas Describe the key difference between solving radical equations for which you solve by raising both sides to an even power and those you solve by raising both sides to an odd power.

25. Critical Thinking How could you solve an equation for which one side is a rational power expression and the other side is a constant? Give an example. Under what condition would you have to be especially careful to check your solutions?

Lesson Performance Task

For many years scientists have used a scale known as the Fujita Scale to categorize different types of tornados in relation to the velocity of the winds produced. The formula used to generate the scale is given by $V = k(F + 2)^{\frac{3}{2}}$. The scale employs a constant, k, and the tornado's category number to determine wind speed. If you wanted to determine the different category numbers, how could you solve the radical equation for the variable F? (The value for k is about 14.1.) Solve the equation for F then verify the different categories using the minimum wind velocity. Do the values seem reasonable given the value for k?

Fujita Tornado Scale			
Damage Level	**Category**	**Minimum Wind Velocity (mi/h)**	**Calculations**
Moderate	F1	73	
Significant	F2	113	
Severe	F3	158	
Devastating	F4	207	
Incredible	F5	261	

Radical Expressions and Equations

Essential Question: How can you use radical expressions and equations to solve real-world problems?

Key Vocabulary
extraneous solution *(solución extraña)*
radical expression *(expresión radical)*
rational exponent *(exponente racional)*

KEY EXAMPLE (Lesson 11.1)

Evaluate the expression.

$$\left(\sqrt[4]{16}\right)^5 = 2^5 = 32$$

$$27^{\frac{4}{3}} = \left(\sqrt[3]{27}\right)^4 = 3^4 = 81$$

KEY EXAMPLE (Lesson 11.2)

Write the expression in simplest form. Assume all variables are positive.

$\sqrt[3]{48} = \sqrt[3]{8 \cdot 6}$ — Factor out a perfect cube.

$= \sqrt[3]{8} \cdot \sqrt[3]{6}$ — Apply the Product Property of Radicals.

$= 2\sqrt[3]{6}$ — Evaluate.

$\left(\frac{x^4}{y^8}\right)^{\frac{1}{2}} = \frac{\left(x^4\right)^{\frac{1}{2}}}{\left(y^8\right)^{\frac{1}{2}}}$ — Apply the Power of a Quotient Property.

$= \frac{x^{4 \cdot \frac{1}{2}}}{y^{8 \cdot \frac{1}{2}}}$ — Apply the Power of a Power Property.

$= \frac{x^2}{y^4}$ — Simplify.

KEY EXAMPLE (Lesson 11.3)

Solve the equation. $\sqrt{x + 15} = x - 5$

$\left(\sqrt{x + 15}\right)^2 = (x - 5)^2$ — Square both sides.

$x + 15 = x^2 - 10x + 25$

$x^2 - 11x + 10 = 0$ — Write in standard form.

$(x - 10)(x - 1) = 0$ — Factor.

$x = 10$ or $x = 1$ — Solve for x.

$\sqrt{10 + 15} \stackrel{?}{=} 10 - 5$ $\quad$ $\sqrt{1 + 15} \stackrel{?}{=} 1 - 5$ — Check.

$5 = 5$ $\quad$ $4 \neq -4$

The solution $x = 1$ is extraneous. The only solution is $x = 10$.

EXERCISES

Evaluate the expression. *(Lesson 11.1)*

1. $\sqrt[3]{-64}$

2. $81^{\frac{1}{4}}$

3. $256^{\frac{3}{4}}$

Write the expression in simplest form. Assume that all variables are positive. *(Lesson 11.2)*

4. $\sqrt[3]{80}$

5. $\left(3^4 \cdot 5^4\right)^{-\frac{1}{4}}$

6. $\left(25a^{10}b^{16}\right)^{\frac{1}{2}}$

7. $\sqrt[5]{\frac{c}{d^8}}$

Solve each equation. *(Lesson 11.3)*

8. $\sqrt[3]{5x - 4} = 2$

9. $\sqrt{x + 6} - 7 = -2$

MODULE PERFORMANCE TASK

Don't Disturb the Neighbors!

The faintest sound an average person can detect has an intensity of 1×10^{-12} watts per square meter, where watts are a unit of power. The intensity of a sound is given by $I = \frac{P}{4\pi d^2}$, where P is the power of the sound and d is the distance from the source. Yolanda wants to throw a party at her house and plans to invite a band to perform. The power of the sound from the band's speakers is typically 3.0 watts. Yolanda's neighborhood has a rule that between 7 p.m. and 11 p.m., a sound intensity up to $I = 5.0 \times 10^{-5}$ W/m^2 is acceptable; after 11 p.m., the acceptable intensity is $I = 5.0 \times 10^{-7}$ W/m^2. How far away would Yolanda's closest neighbors need to be for the band to play till 11 p.m.? How far would they need to be for the band to play all night?

Start by listing in the space below the information you will need to solve the problem. Then use your own paper to complete the task. Be sure to write down all your data and assumptions. Then use graphs, numbers, words, or algebra to explain how you reached your conclusion.

Ready to Go On?

11.1–11.3 Radical Expressions and Equations

Personal Math Trainer

- Online Homework
- Hints and Help
- Extra Practice

Simplify each expression. Assume that all variables are positive. *(Lessons 11.1, 11.2)*

1. $32^{\frac{1}{5}}$

2. $\left(\sqrt[3]{64}\right)^4$

3. $\sqrt[3]{27x^6}$

4. $\sqrt[4]{2x^6y^8}$

Solve each equation. *(Lesson 11.3)*

5. $\sqrt{10x} = 3\sqrt{x+1}$

6. $\sqrt[3]{2x-2} = 6$

7. $(4x+7)^{\frac{1}{2}} = 3$

8. $(x+3)^{\frac{1}{3}} = -6$

ESSENTIAL QUESTION

9. How do you solve a radical equation and identify any extraneous roots?

MODULE 11
MIXED REVIEW

Assessment Readiness

1. Look at each expression. Can the expression be simplified to a rational number? Select Yes or No for A–C.

A. $\sqrt{2} + \sqrt{2}$ ○ Yes ○ No

B. $\sqrt{4} \cdot \sqrt{20}$ ○ Yes ○ No

C. $(\sqrt{12})^2$ ○ Yes ○ No

2. Consider the function $f(x) = \frac{2x^2 - 5x - 3}{x - 3}$. Choose True or False for each statement.

A. This function looks like a straight line when graphed. ○ True ○ False

B. There is a hole in this function at $(3, 7)$. ○ True ○ False

C. There is a hole in this function at $(-0.5, 0)$. ○ True ○ False

3. Explain how to find the product of $(4 - 3i)(2 - i)$, then state the product.

4. The formula $s = \sqrt{\frac{A}{4.828}}$ can be used to approximate the side length s of a regular octagon with area A. A stop sign is shaped like a regular octagon with a side length of 12.4 in. To the nearest square inch, what is the area of the stop sign? Explain how you got your answer.

Assessment Readiness

Personal Math Trainer
• Online Homework
• Hints and Help
• Extra Practice

1. Consider the graph of $g(x) = \frac{1}{3}\sqrt{x - 1}$ as related to the graph of $f(x) = \sqrt{x}$. Select True or False for each statement.

   A. $g(x)$ is a vertical stretching by a factor of $\frac{1}{3}$ and a translation of 1 unit up from $f(x)$. ○ True ○ False

   B. $g(x)$ is a vertical compression by a factor of $\frac{1}{3}$ and a translation 1 unit right from $f(x)$. ○ True ○ False

   C. $g(x)$ is a vertical compression by a factor of $\frac{1}{3}$ and a translation 1 unit left from $f(x)$. ○ True ○ False

2. Consider each transformation in relation to $f(x) = \sqrt[3]{x}$.
   Select True or False for each statement.

   A. $g(x) = 5\sqrt[3]{x + 1} - 2$ is a transformation of $f(x)$ by a vertical stretch by a factor of 5 and a translation 1 unit left and 2 units down. ○ True ○ False

   B. $g(x) = 5\sqrt[3]{x - 1} + 2$ is a transformation of $f(x)$ by a horizontal stretch by a factor of 5 and a translation of 1 unit left and 2 units down. ○ True ○ False

   C. $g(x) = \frac{1}{5}\sqrt[3]{x + 1} - 2$ is a transformation of $f(x)$ by a horizontal stretch by a factor of $\frac{1}{5}$ and a translation of 1 unit left and 2 units down. ○ True ○ False

3. Consider each equation. Is the equation the inverse of $f(x) = \frac{1}{2}x^3 + 5$?
   Choose Yes or No for A–C.

   A. $f^{-1}(x) = \sqrt[3]{2(x - 5)}$ ○ Yes ○ No

   B. $f^{-1}(x) = \sqrt[3]{2(x + 5)}$ ○ Yes ○ No

   C. $f^{-1}(x) = \sqrt[3]{\frac{1}{2}(x - 5)}$ ○ Yes ○ No

4. Consider each expression. Can the expression be simplified to 25?
   Choose Yes or No for A–C.

   A. $\left(\sqrt[2]{125}\right)^3$ ○ Yes ○ No

   B. $\left(\sqrt[3]{125}\right)^2$ ○ Yes ○ No

   C. $\left(\sqrt{125}\right)^{\frac{1}{3}}$ ○ Yes ○ No

5. A company produces canned tomatoes. They want the height h of each can to be twice the diameter d. Write an equation for the surface area A of the can in terms of the radius r. If the company wants to use no more than 90 square inches of metal for each can, what is the maximum radius of the can they will produce?

6. The period T of a pendulum in seconds is given by $T = 2\pi\sqrt{\frac{L}{9.81}}$, where L is the length of the pendulum in meters. If you want to use a pendulum as a clock, with a period of 2 seconds, how long should the pendulum be?

7. Tandra says that $\sqrt[3]{\frac{8x^6}{y}}$ can be simplified to $\frac{2x^2}{\sqrt[3]{y}}$. Elizabeth says that $\sqrt[3]{\frac{6x^6}{y}}$ can be simplified to $\frac{2x^2}{\sqrt[3]{y}}$. Who is correct, or are they both correct? Explain.

Performance Tasks

★ 8. The formula $P = 73.3\sqrt[4]{m^3}$, known as Kleiber's law, relates the metabolism rate P of an organism in Calories per day and the body mass m of the organism in kilograms. The table shows the typical body mass of several members of the cat family.

Typical Body Mass	
Animal	**Mass(kg)**
House cat	4.5
Cheetah	55.0
Lion	170.0

A. What is the metabolism rate of a cheetah to the nearest Calorie per day?

B. Approximately how many more Calories of food does a lion need to consume each day than a house cat does?

★★ 9. On a clear day, the approximate distance d in miles that a person can see is given by $d = 1.2116\sqrt{h}$, where h is the person's height in feet above the ocean.

A. To the nearest tenth of a mile, how far can the captain on a clipper ship 15 feet above the ocean see?

B. How much farther, to the nearest tenth of a mile, will a sailor at the top of a mast 120 feet above the ocean be able to see than will the captain?

C. A pirate ship is approaching the clipper ship at a relative speed of 10 miles per hour. Approximately how many minutes sooner will the sailor be able to see the pirate ship than will the captain?

★★★10. The time it takes a pendulum to make one complete swing back and forth depends on its string length, as shown in the table.

String Length (m)	2	4	6	8	10
Time (s)	2.8	4.0	4.9	5.7	6.3

A. Graph the relationship between string length and time, and identify the parent function which best describes the data.

B. The function $T(x) = 2\pi\sqrt{\frac{x}{9.8}}$ gives the period in seconds of a pendulum of length x. The period of a pendulum is the time it takes the pendulum to complete one back-and-forth swing. Describe the graph of T as a transformation of $f(x) = \sqrt{x}$.

C. By what factor must the length of a pendulum be increased to double its period?

Nutritionist Body mass index (BMI) is a measure used to determine healthy body mass based on a person's height. BMI is calculated by dividing a person's mass in kilograms by the square of his or her height in meters. The median BMI measures for a group of boys, ages 2 to 10 years are given in the chart below.

Age of Boys	2	3	4	5	6	7	8	9	10
Median BMI	16.6	16.0	15.6	15.4	15.4	15.5	15.8	16.2	16.6

a. Create a scatter plot for the data in the table, treating age as the independent variable x and median BMI as the dependent variable y.

b. Use a calculator to find a quadratic regression model for the data. What is your model?

c. Give the domain of $f(x)$ based on the data set. Because $f(x)$ is quadratic, it is not one-to-one and its inverse is not a function. Restrict the domain of $f(x)$ to values of x for which $f(x)$ is increasing so that its inverse will be a function. What is the restricted domain of $f(x)$?

d. Find and graph the inverse of $f(x)$. What does $f^{-1}(x)$ model?

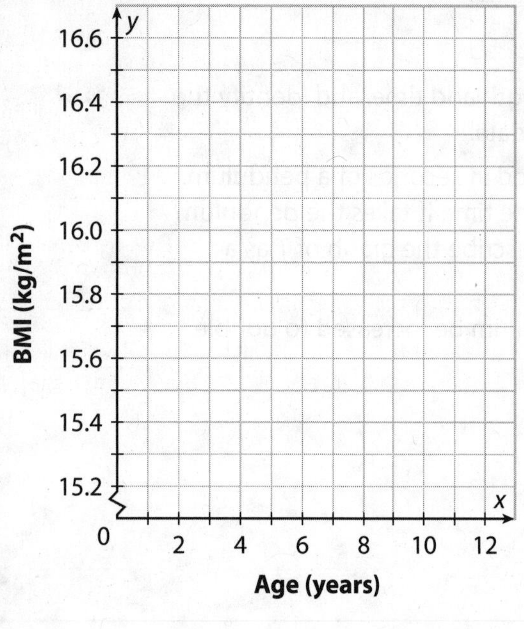

Glossary/Glosario

A

ENGLISH	SPANISH	EXAMPLES
absolute value of a complex number The absolute value of $a + bi$ is the distance from the origin to the point (a, b) in the complex plane and is denoted $\lvert a + bi \rvert = \sqrt{a^2 + b^2}$.	**valor absoluto de un número complejo** El valor absoluto de $a + bi$ es la distancia desde el origen hasta el punto (a, b) en el plano complejo y se expresa $\lvert a + bi \rvert = \sqrt{a^2 + b^2}$.	$\lvert 2 + 3i \rvert = \sqrt{2^2 + 3^2} = \sqrt{13}$
absolute value of a real number The absolute value of x is the distance from zero to x on a number line, denoted $\lvert x \rvert$. $\lvert x \rvert = \begin{cases} x & \text{if } x \geq 0 \\ -x & \text{if } x < 0 \end{cases}$	**valor absoluto de un número real** El valor absoluto de x es la distancia desde cero hasta x en una recta numérica y se expresa $\lvert x \rvert$. $\lvert x \rvert = \begin{cases} x & \text{si } x \geq 0 \\ -x & \text{si } x < 0 \end{cases}$	$\lvert 3 \rvert = 3$ $\lvert -3 \rvert = 3$
absolute-value function A function whose rule contains absolute-value expressions.	**función de valor absoluto** Función cuya regla contiene expresiones de valor absoluto.	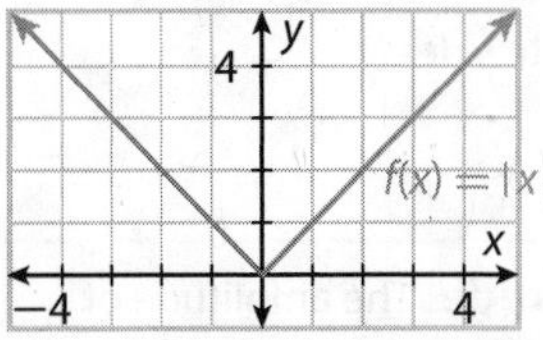
adjacent arcs Two arcs of the same circle that intersect at exactly one point.	**arcos adyacentes** Dos arcos del mismo círculo que se cruzan en un punto exacto.	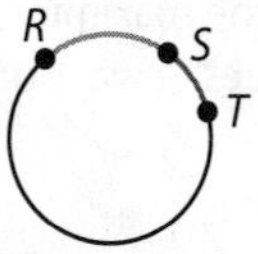 $\overset{\frown}{RS}$ and $\overset{\frown}{ST}$ are adjacent arcs.
alternate exterior angles For two lines intersected by a transversal, a pair of angles that lie on opposite sides of the transversal and outside the other two lines.	**ángulos alternos externos** Dadas dos líneas cortadas por una transversal, par de ángulos no adyacentes ubicados en los lados opuestos de la transversal y fuera de las otras dos líneas.	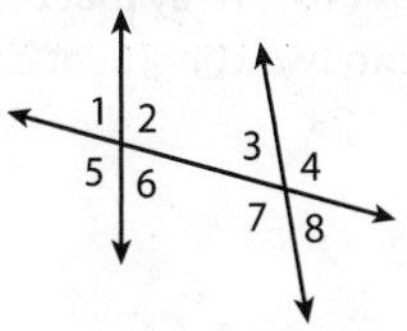 $\angle 4$ and $\angle 5$ are alternate exterior angles.
alternate interior angles For two lines intersected by a transversal, a pair of nonadjacent angles that lie on opposite sides of the transversal and between the other two lines.	**ángulos alternos internos** Dadas dos líneas cortadas por una transversal, par de ángulos no adyacentes ubicados en los lados opuestos de la transversal y entre las otras dos líneas.	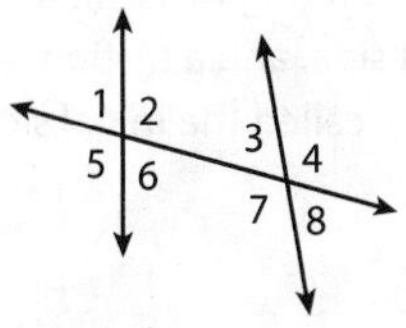 $\angle 3$ and $\angle 6$ are alternate interior angles.

Glossary/Glosario

ENGLISH	SPANISH	EXAMPLES
altitude of a cylinder A segment with its endpoints on the planes of the bases that is perpendicular to the planes of the bases.	**altura de un cilindro** Segmento con sus extremos en los planos de las bases que es perpendicular a los planos de las bases.	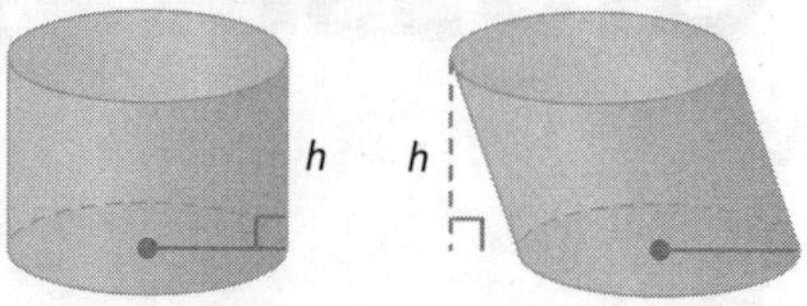
altitude of a prism A segment with its endpoints on the planes of the bases that is perpendicular to the planes of the bases.	**altura de un prisma** Segmento con sus extremos en los planos de las bases que es perpendicular a los planos de las bases.	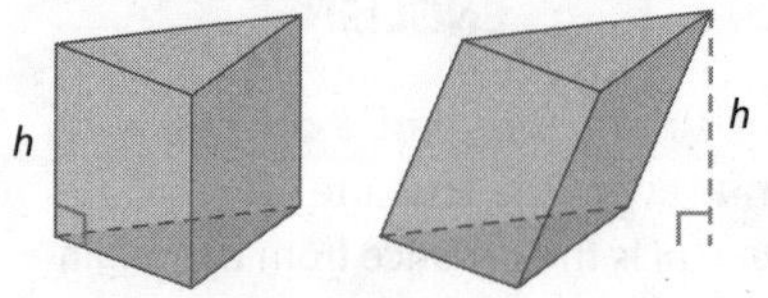
altitude of a pyramid A segment from the vertex to the plane of the base that is perpendicular to the plane of the base.	**altura de una pirámide** Segmento que se extiende desde el vértice hasta el plano de la base y es perpendicular al plano de la base.	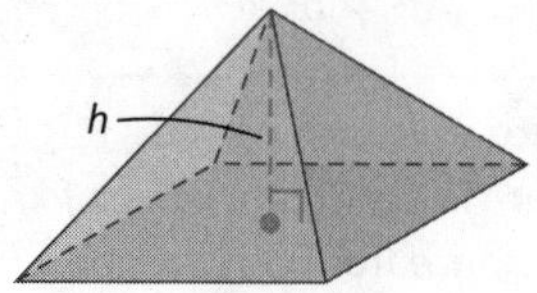
altitude of a triangle A perpendicular segment from a vertex to the line containing the opposite side.	**altura de un triángulo** Segmento perpendicular que se extiende desde un vértice hasta la línea que forma el lado opuesto.	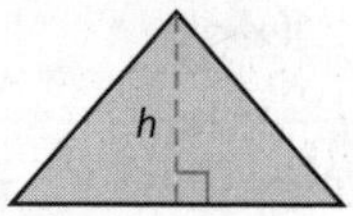
amplitude The amplitude of a periodic function is half the difference of the maximum and minimum values (always positive).	**amplitud** La amplitud de una función periódica es la mitad de la diferencia entre los valores máximo y mínimo (siempre positivos).	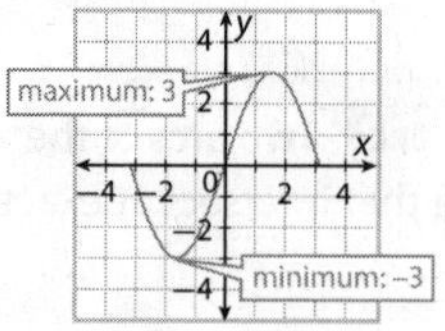 amplitude $= \frac{1}{2}\left[3 - (-3)\right] = 3$
angle bisector A ray that divides an angle into two congruent angles.	**bisectriz de un ángulo** Rayo que divide un ángulo en dos ángulos congruentes.	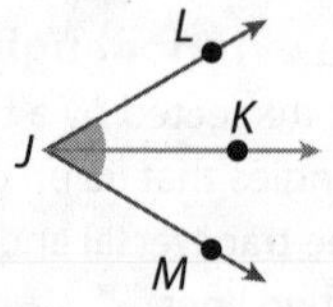 $\overrightarrow{JK}$ is an angle bisector of $\angle LJM$.
angle of rotation An angle formed by a rotating ray, called the terminal side, and a stationary reference ray, called the initial side.	**ángulo de rotación** Ángulo formado por un rayo en rotación, denominado lado terminal, y un rayo de referencia estático, denominado lado inicial.	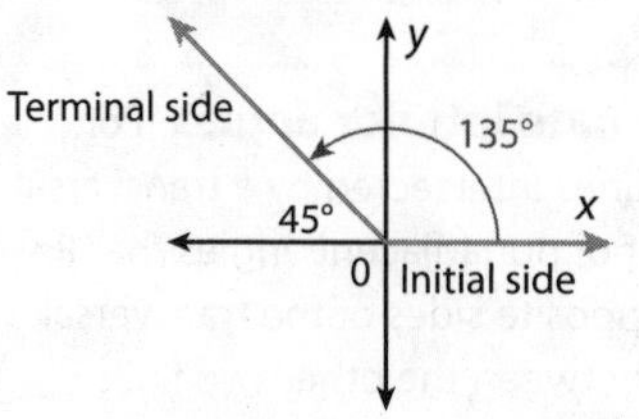
arc length The distance along an arc measured in linear units.	**longitud de arco** Distancia a lo largo de un arco medida en unidades lineales.	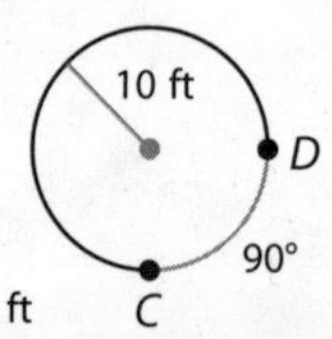 $m\widehat{CD} = 5\pi$ ft

ENGLISH	SPANISH	EXAMPLES
arithmetic sequence A sequence whose successive terms differ by the same nonzero number d, called the *common difference.*	**sucesión aritmética** Sucesión cuyos términos sucesivos difieren en el mismo número distinto de cero d, denominado *diferencia común.*	4, 7, 10, 13, 16, ... + 3 + 3 + 3 + 3 $d = 3$
arithmetic series The indicated sum of the terms of an arithmetic sequence.	**serie aritmética** Suma indicada de los términos de una sucesión aritmética.	$4 + 7 + 10 + 13 + 16 + ...$
asymptote A line that a graph approaches as the value of a variable becomes extremely large or small.	**asíntota** Línea recta a la cual se aproxima una gráfica a medida que el valor de una variable se hace sumamente grande o pequeño.	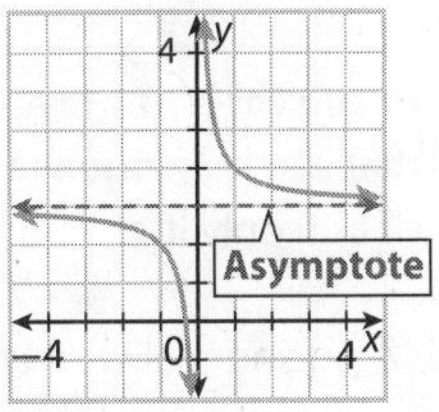
augmented matrix A matrix that consists of the coefficients and the constant terms in a system of linear equations.	**matriz aumentada** Matriz formada por los coeficientes y los términos constantes de un sistema de ecuaciones lineales.	System of equations: $3x + 2y = 5$, $2x - 3y = 1$ Augmented matrix: $\left[\begin{array}{cc\|c} 3 & 2 & 5 \\ 2 & -3 & 1 \end{array}\right]$
average rate of change The ratio of the change in the function values, $f(x_2) - f(x_1)$ to the change in the x-values, $x_2 - x_1$.	**tasa de cambio promedio** Razón entre el cambio en los valores de la función, $f(x_2) - f(x_1)$ y el cambio en los valores de x, $x_2 - x_1$.	
axis of a cone The segment with endpoints at the vertex and the center of the base.	**eje de un cono** Segmento cuyos extremos se encuentran en el vértice y en el centro de la base.	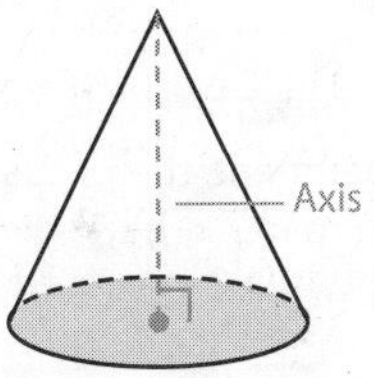
axis of a cylinder The segment with endpoints at the centers of the two bases.	**eje de un cilindro** Segmentos cuyos extremos se encuentran en los centros de las dos bases.	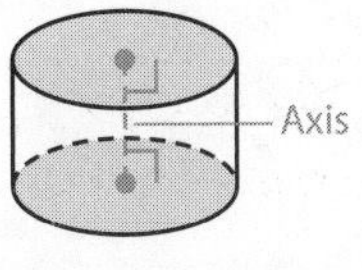
axis of symmetry A line that divides a plane figure or a graph into two congruent reflected halves.	**eje de simetría** Línea que divide una figura plana o una gráfica en dos mitades reflejadas congruentes.	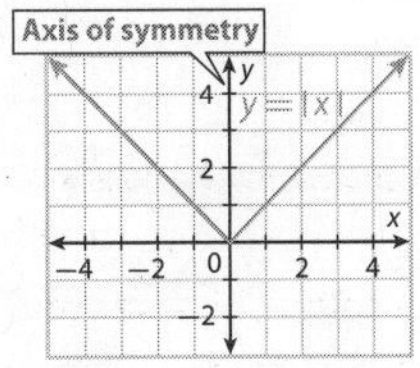

B

base of a geometric figure A side of a polygon; a face of a three-dimensional figure by which the figure is measured or classified.	**base de una figura geométrica** Lado de un polígono; cara de una figura tridimensional por la cual se mide o clasifica la figura.	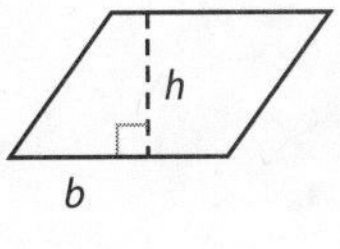 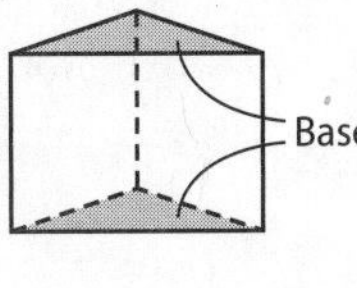

Glossary/Glosario

ENGLISH	SPANISH	EXAMPLES
base of an exponential function The value of b in a function of the form $f(x) = ab^x$, where a and b are real numbers with $a \neq 0$, $b > 0$, and $b \neq 1$.	**base de una función exponencial** Valor de b en una función del tipo $f(x) = ab^x$, donde a y b son números reales con $a \neq 0$, $b > 0$, y $b \neq 1$.	$f(x) = 5(2)^x$ (2 ← base)
biased sample A sample that does not fairly represent the population.	**muestra no representativa** Muestra que no representa adecuadamente una población.	
biconditional statement A statement that can be written in the form "*p* if and only if *q*."	**enunciado bicondicional** Enunciado que puede expresarse en la forma "*p* si y sólo si *q*".	A figure is a triangle if and only if it is a three-sided polygon.
binomial A polynomial with two terms.	**binomio** Polinomio con dos términos.	$x + y$ $2a^2 + 3$ $4m^3n^2 + 6mn^4$
binomial experiment A probability experiment consists of n identical and independent trials whose outcomes are either successes or failures, with a constant probability of success p and a constant probability of failure q, where $q = 1 - p$ or $p + q = 1$.	**experimento binomial** Experimento de probabilidades que comprende n pruebas idénticas e independientes cuyos resultados son éxitos o fracasos, con una probabilidad constante de éxito p y una probabilidad constante de fracaso q, donde $q = 1 - p$ o $p + q = 1$.	A multiple-choice quiz has 10 questions with 4 answer choices. The number of trials is 10. If each question is answered randomly, the probability of success for each trial is $\frac{1}{4} = 0.25$ and the probability of failure is $\frac{3}{4} = 0.75$.
binomial probability In a binomial experiment, the probability of r successes $(0 \leq r \leq n)$ is $P(r) = {}_nC_r \cdot p^r q^{n-r}$.	**probabilidad binomial** En un experimento binomial, la probabilidad de r éxitos $(0 \leq r \leq n)$ es $P(r) = {}_nC_r \cdot p^r q^{n-r}$.	In the binomial experiment above, the probability of randomly guessing 6 problems correctly is $P = {}_{10}C_6\,(0.25)^6\,(0.75)^4 \approx 0.016$.
Binomial Theorem For any positive integer n, $(x+y)^n = {}_nC_0\,x^n y^0 + {}_nC_1\,x^{n-1} y^1 + {}_nC_2\,x^{n-2} y^2 + \ldots + {}_nC_{n-1}\,x^1 y^{n-1} + {}_nC_n\,x^0 y^n$.	**Teorema de los binomios** Dado un entero positivo n, $(x+y)^n = {}_nC_0\,x^n y^0 + {}_nC_1\,x^{n-1} y^1 + {}_nC_2\,x^{n-2} y^2 + \ldots + {}_nC_{n-1}\,x^1 y^{n-1} + {}_nC_n\,x^0 y^n$.	$(x+2)^4 = {}_4C_0\,x^4 2^0 + {}_4C_1\,x^3 2^1 + {}_4C_2\,x^2 2^2 + {}_4C_3\,x^1 2^3 + {}_4C_4 x^0 2^4 = x^4 + 8x^3 + 24x^2 + 32x + 16$
bisect To divide into two congruent parts.	**trazar una bisectriz** Dividir en dos partes congruentes.	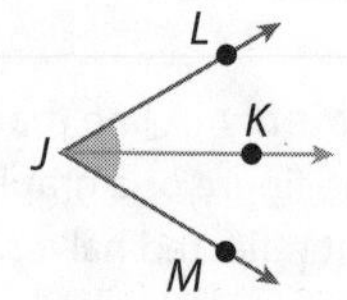 $\overrightarrow{JK}$ bisects $\angle LJM$.
branch of a hyperbola One of the two symmetrical parts of the hyperbola.	**rama de una hipérbola** Una de las dos partes simétricas de la hipérbola.	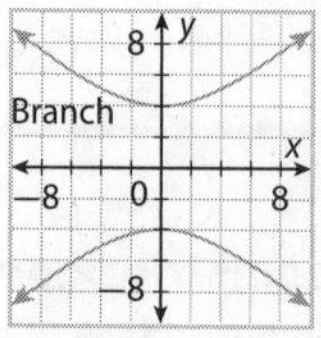

ENGLISH | SPANISH | EXAMPLES

C

census A survey of an entire population.

censo Estudio de una población entera.

---

center of a circle The point inside a circle that is the same distance from every point on the circle.

centro de un círculo Punto dentro de un círculo que se encuentra a la misma distancia de todos los puntos del círculo.

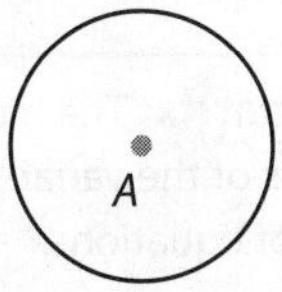

---

center of a sphere The point inside a sphere that is the same distance from every point on the sphere.

centro de una esfera Punto dentro de una esfera que está a la misma distancia de cualquier punto de la esfera.

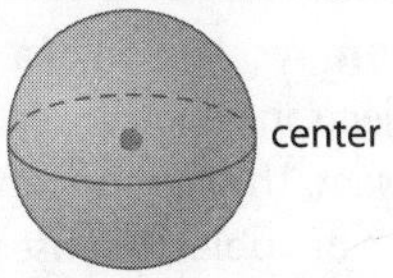

---

center of rotation The point around which a figure is rotated.

centro de rotación Punto alrededor del cual rota una figura.

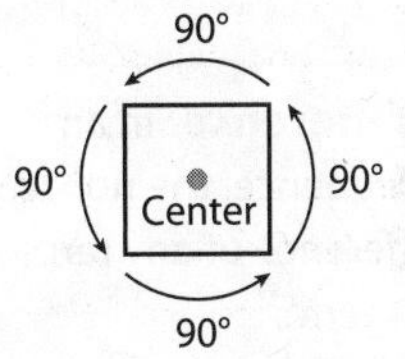

---

central angle of a circle An angle with measure less than or equal to 180° whose vertex is the center of a circle.

ángulo central de un círculo Ángulo con medida inferior o igual a 180° cuyo vértice es el centro de un círculo.

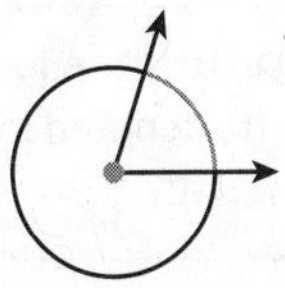

---

chord A segment whose endpoints lie on a circle.

cuerda Segmento cuyos extremos se encuentran en un círculo.

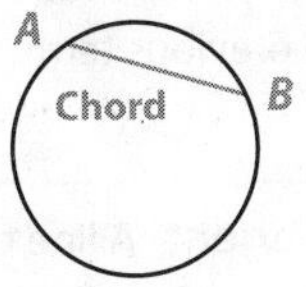

---

circumscribed angle An angle formed by two rays from a common endpoint that are tangent to a circle

ángulo circunscrito Ángulo formado por dos semirrectas tangentes a un círculo que parten desde un extremo común.

---

circumscribed circle Every vertex of the polygon lies on the circle.

círculo circunscrito Todos los vértices del polígono se encuentran sobre el círculo.

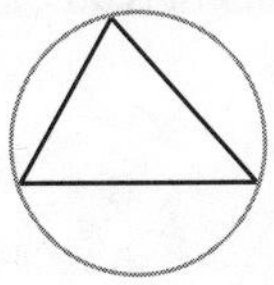

---

circumscribed polygon Each side of the polygon is tangent to the circle.

polígono circunscrito Todos los lados del polígono son tangentes al círculo.

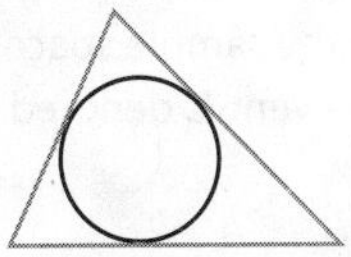

ENGLISH	SPANISH	EXAMPLES

closure A set of numbers is said to be closed, or to have closure, under a given operation if the result of the operation on any two numbers in the set is also in the set.

cerradura Se dice que un conjunto de números es cerrado, o tiene cerradura, respecto de una operación determinada, si el resultado de la operación entre dos numerous cualesquiera del conjunto también está en el conjunto.

The natural numbers are closed under addition because the sum of two natural numbers is always a natural number.

---

coefficient matrix The matrix of the coefficients of the variables in a linear system of equations.

matriz de coeficientes Matriz de los coeficientes de las variables en un sistema lineal de ecuaciones.

System of equations	Coefficient matrix
$2x + 3y = 11$ $5x - 4y = 16$	$\begin{bmatrix} 2 & 3 \\ 5 & -4 \end{bmatrix}$

---

combination A selection of a group of objects in which order is *not* important. The number of combinations of *r* objects chosen from a group of *n* objects is denoted ${}_nC_r$.

combinación Selección de un grupo de objetos en la cual el orden *no* es importante. El número de combinaciones de *r* objetos elegidos de un grupo de *n* objetos se expresa así: ${}_nC_r$.

For 4 objects *A*, *B*, *C*, and *D*, there are ${}_4C_2 = 6$ different combinations of 2 objects: *AB*, *AC*, *AD*, *BC*, *BD*, *CD*.

---

common difference In an arithmetic sequence, the nonzero constant difference of any term and the previous term.

diferencia común En una sucesión aritmética, diferencia constante distinta de cero entre cualquier término y el término anterior.

In the arithmetic sequence 3, 5, 7, 9, 11, ..., the common difference is 2.

---

common logarithm A logarithm whose base is 10, denoted $\log_{10}$ or just log.

logaritmo común Logaritmo de base 10, que se expresa $\log_{10}$ o simplemente log.

$\log 100 = \log_{10} 100 = 2$, since $10^2 = 100$.

---

common ratio In a geometric sequence, the constant ratio of any term and the previous term.

razón común En una sucesión geométrica, la razón constante *r* entre cualquier término y el término anterior.

In the geometric sequence 32, 16,18, 4, 2 ..., the common ratio is $\frac{1}{2}$.

---

common tangent A line that is tangent to two circles.

tangente común Línea que es tangente a dos círculos.

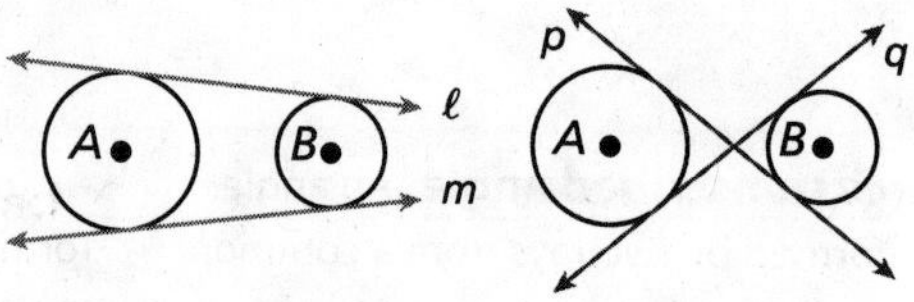

---

complement of an angle The sum of the measures of an angle and its complement is 90°.

complemento de un ángulo La suma de las medidas de un ángulo y su complemento es 90°.

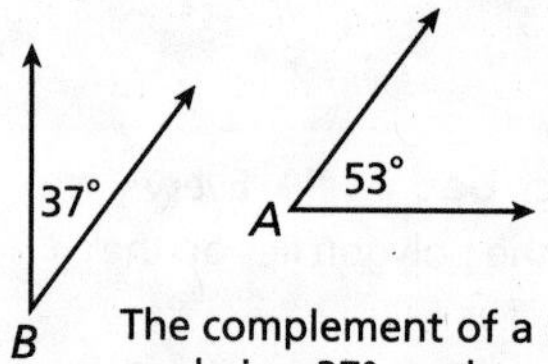

The complement of a 53° angle is a 37° angle.

---

complement of an event All outcomes in the sample space that are not in an event *E*, denoted $\overline{E}$.

complemento de un suceso Todos los resultados en el espacio muestral que no están en el suceso *E* y se expresan $\overline{E}$.

In the experiment of rolling a number cube, the complement of rolling a 3 is rolling a 1, 2, 4, 5, or 6.

ENGLISH	SPANISH	EXAMPLES
complementary angles Two angles whose measures have a sum of 90°.	**ángulos complementarios** Dos ángulos cuyas medidas suman 90°.	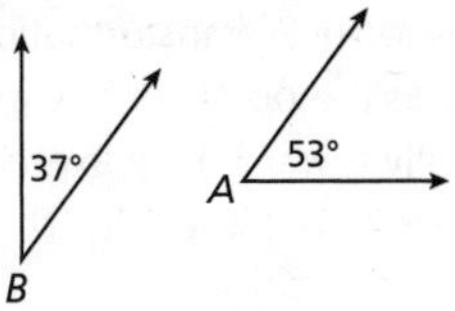
completing the square A process used to form a perfect-square trinomial. To complete the square of $x^2 + bx$, add $\left(\frac{b}{2}\right)^2$.	**completar el cuadrado** Proceso utilizado para formar un trinomio cuadrado perfecto. Para completar el cuadrado de $x^2 + bx$, hay que sumar $\left(\frac{b}{2}\right)^2$.	$x^2 + 6x + \blacksquare$ Add $\left(\frac{6}{2}\right)^2 = 9$. $x^2 + 6x + 9$ $(x + 3)^2$ *is a perfect square.*
complex conjugate The complex conjugate of any complex number $a + bi$, denoted $\overline{a + bi}$, is $a - bi$.	**conjugado complejo** El conjugado complejo de cualquier número complejo $a + bi$, expresado como $\overline{a + bi}$, es $a - bi$.	$\overline{4 + 3i} = 4 - 3i$ $\overline{4 - 3i} = 4 + 3i$
complex fraction A fraction that contains one or more fractions in the numerator, the denominator, or both.	**fracción compleja** Fracción que contiene una o más fracciones en el numerador, en el denominador, o en ambos.	$\dfrac{\frac{1}{2}}{1 + \frac{2}{3}}$
complex number Any number that can be written as $a + bi$, where a and b are real numbers and $i = \sqrt{-1}$.	**número complejo** Todo número que se puede expresar como $a + bi$, donde a y b son números reales e $i = \sqrt{-1}$.	$4 + 2i$ $5 + 0i = 5$ $0 - 7i = -7i$
complex plane A set of coordinate axes in which the horizontal axis is the real axis and the vertical axis is the imaginary axis; used to graph complex numbers.	**plano complejo** Conjunto de ejes cartesianos en el cual el eje horizontal es el eje real y el eje vertical es el eje imaginario; se utiliza para representar gráficamente números complejos.	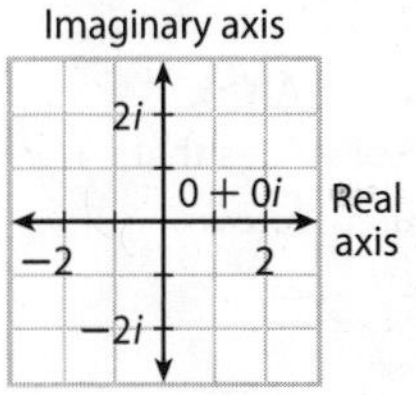
composition of functions The composition of functions f and g, written as $(f \circ g)(x)$ and defined as $f(g(x))$ uses the output of $g(x)$ as the input for $f(x)$.	**composición de funciones** La composición de las funciones f y g, expresada como $(f \circ g)(x)$ y definida como $f(g(x))$ utiliza la salida de $g(x)$ como la entrada para $f(x)$.	If $f(x) = x^2$ and $g(x) = x + 1$, the composite function $(f \circ g)(x) = (x + 1)^2$.
compound event An event made up of two or more simple events.	**suceso compuesto** Suceso formado por dos o más sucesos simples.	In the experiment of tossing a coin and rolling a number cube, the event of the coin landing heads and the number cube landing on 3.
compound interest Interest earned or paid on both the principal and previously earned interest. The formula for compound interest is $A = P\left(1 + \frac{r}{n}\right)^{nt}$, where A is the final amount, P is the principal, r is the interest rate expressed as a decimal, n is the number of times interest is compounded, and t is the time.	**interés compuesto** Interés ganado o pagado tanto sobre el capital inicial como sobre el interés previamente ganado. Se halla usando la fórmula $A = P\left(1 + \frac{r}{n}\right)^{nt}$, donde A es la cantidad final, P es el capital inicial, r es la tasa de interés indicada en forma de número decimal, n es el número de veces que se reinvierte el interés y t es el tiempo.	If \$100 is put into an account with an interest rate of 5% compounded monthly, then after 2 years, the account will have $100\left(1 + \frac{0.05}{12}\right)^{12 \cdot 2} = \$110.49$.

Glossary/Glosario

ENGLISH	SPANISH	EXAMPLES
compression A transformation that pushes the points of a graph horizontally toward the *y*-axis or vertically toward the *x*-axis.	**compresión** Transformación que desplaza los puntos de una gráfica horizontalmente hacia el eje *y* o verticalmente hacia el eje *x*.	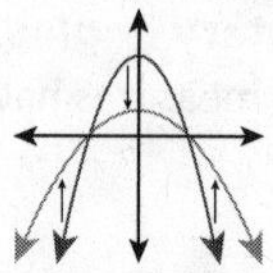
concurrent Three or more lines that intersect at one point.	**concurrente** Tres o más líneas que se cortan en un punto.	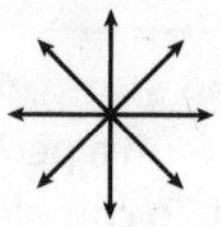
conditional probability The probability of event *B*, given that event *A* has already occurred or is certain to occur, denoted $P(B \mid A)$; used to find probability of dependent events.	**probabilidad condicional** Probabilidad del suceso *B*, dado que el suceso *A* ya ha ocurrido o es seguro que ocurrirá, expresada como $P(B \mid A)$; se utiliza para calcular la probabilidad de sucesos dependientes.	
conditional statement A statement that can be written in the form "if *p*, then *q*," where *p* is the hypothesis and *q* is the conclusion.	**enunciado condicional** Enunciado que se puede expresar como "si *p*, entonces *q*", donde *p* es la hipótesis y *q* es la conclusión.	If $\underbrace{x + 1 = 5}_{\text{Hypothesis}}$, then $\underbrace{x = 4}_{\text{Conclusion}}$.
cone A three-dimensional figure with a circular base and a curved lateral surface that connects the base to a point called the vertex.	**cono** Figura tridimensional con una base circular y una superficie lateral curva que conecta la base con un punto denominado vértice.	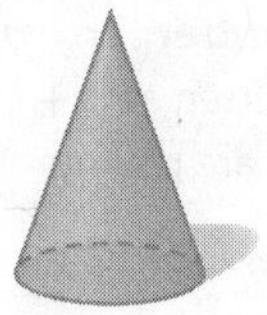
confidence interval An approximate range of values that is likely to include an unknown population parameter.	**intervalo de confianza** Un rango aproximado de valores que probablemente incluirá un parámetro de población desconocido.	
conic section A plane figure formed by the intersection of a double right cone and a plane. Examples include circles, ellipses, hyperbolas, and parabolas.	**sección cónica** Figura plana formada por la intersección de un cono regular doble y un plano. Algunos ejemplos son círculos, elipses, hipérbolas y parábolas.	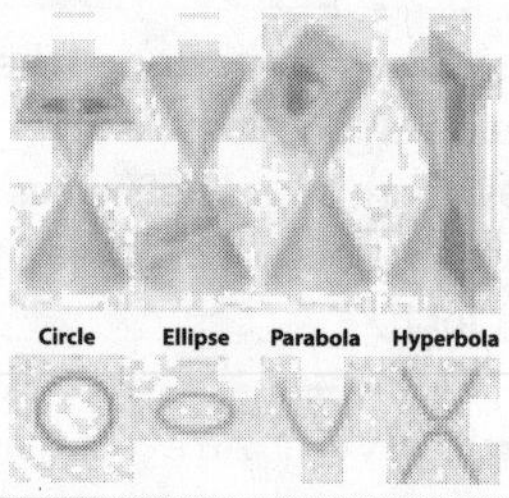
conjecture A statement that is believed to be true.	**conjetura** Enunciado que se supone verdadero.	A sequence begins with the terms 2, 4, 6, 8, 10. A reasonable conjecture is that the next term in the sequence is 12.
conjugate axis The axis of symmetry of a hyperbola that separates the two branches of the hyperbola.	**eje conjugado** Eje de simetría de una hipérbola que separa las dos ramas de la hipérbola.	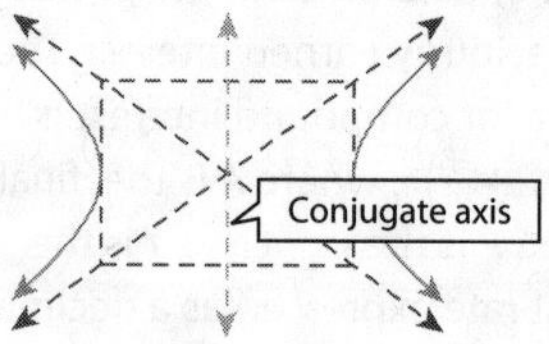

ENGLISH	SPANISH	EXAMPLES
constraint One of the inequalities that define the feasible region in a linear-programming problem.	**restricción** Una de las desigualdades que definen la región factible en un problema de programación lineal.	Constraints: $x > 0$ $y > 0$ $x + y \leq 8$ $3x + 5y \leq 30$ Feasible region 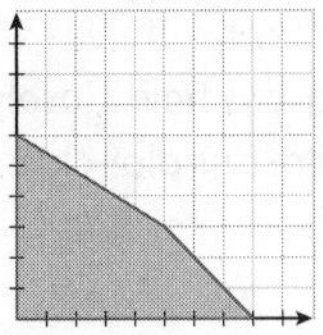
continuous function A function whose graph is an unbroken line or curve with no gaps or breaks.	**función continua** Función cuya gráfica es una línea recta o curva continua, sin espacios ni interrupciones.	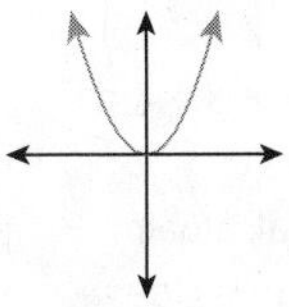
contradiction An equation that has no solutions.	**contradicción** Ecuación que no tiene soluciones.	$x + 1 = x$ $1 = 0x$
contrapositive The statement formed by both exchanging and negating the hypothesis and conclusion of a conditional statement.	**contrarrecíproco** Enunciado que se forma al intercambiar y negar la hipótesis y la conclusión de un enunciado condicional.	Statement: If $n + 1 = 3$, then $n = 2$. Contrapositive: If $n \neq 2$, then $n + 1 \neq 3$.
converse The statement formed by exchanging the hypothesis and conclusion of a conditional statement.	**recíproco** Enunciado que se forma intercambiando la hipótesis y la conclusión de un enunciado condicional.	Statement: If $n + 1 = 3$, then $n = 2$. Converse: If $n = 2$, then $n + 1 = 3$.
coordinate proof A style of proof that uses coordinate geometry and algebra.	**prueba de coordenadas** Tipo de demostración que utiliza geometría de coordenadas y álgebra.	
coplanar Points that lie in the same plane.	**coplanar** Puntos que se encuentran en el mismo plano.	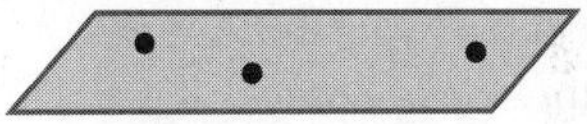
corollary A theorem whose proof follows directly from another theorem.	**corolario** Teorema cuya demostración proviene directamente de otro teorema.	
correlation A measure of the strength and direction of the relationship between two variables or data sets.	**correlación** Medida de la fuerza y dirección de la relación entre dos variables o conjuntos de datos.	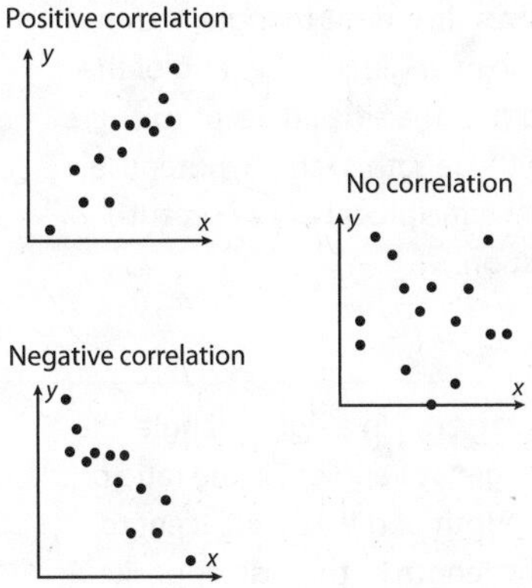

ENGLISH	SPANISH	EXAMPLES

correlation coefficient A number r, where $-1 \leq r \leq 1$, that describes how closely the points in a scatter plot cluster around the least–squares line.

coeficiente de correlación Número r, donde $-1 \leq r \leq 1$, que describe a qué distancia de la recta de mínimos cuadrados se agrupan los puntos de un diagrama de dispersión.

An r–value close to 1 describes a strong positive correlation.
An r–value close to 0 describes a weak correlation or no correlation.
An r–value close to -1 describes a strong negative correlation.

---

corresponding angles of lines intersected by a transversal For two lines intersected by a transversal, a pair of angles that lie on the same side of the transversal and on the same sides of the other two lines.

ángulos correspondientes de líneas cortadas por una transversal Dadas dos líneas cortadas por una transversal, el par de ángulos ubicados en el mismo lado de la transversal y en los mismos lados de las otras dos líneas.

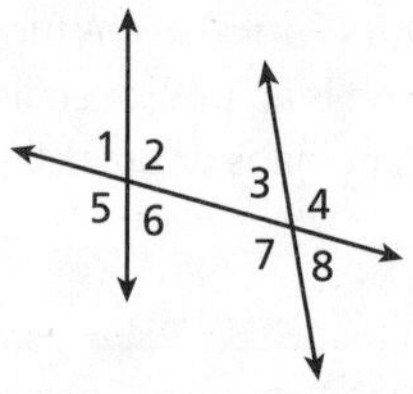

$\angle 1$ and $\angle 3$ are corresponding.

---

corresponding angles of polygons Angles in the same position in two different polygons that have the same number of angles.

ángulos correspondientes de los polígonos Ángulos que tienen la misma posición en dos polígonos diferentes que tienen el mismo número de ángulos.

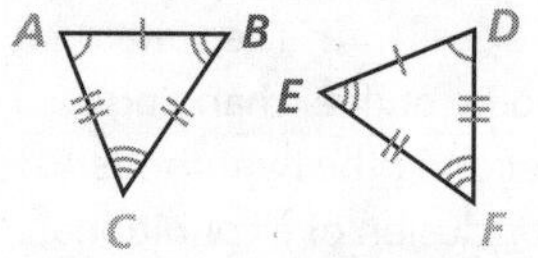

$\angle A$ and $\angle D$ are corresponding angles.

---

corresponding sides of polygons Sides in the same position in two different polygons that have the same number of sides.

lados correspondientes de los polígonos Lados que tienen la misma posición en dos polígonos diferentes que tienen el mismo número de lados.

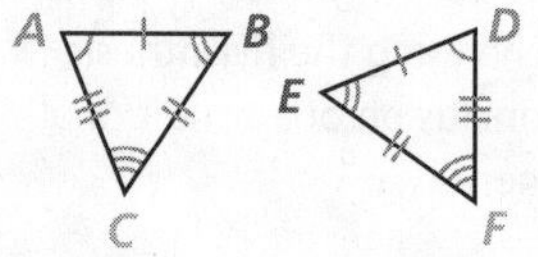

$\overline{AB}$ and $\overline{DE}$ are corresponding sides.

---

cosecant In a right triangle, the cosecant of angle A is the ratio of the length of the hypotenuse to the length of the side opposite A. It is the reciprocal of the sine function.

cosecante En un triángulo rectángulo, la cosecante del ángulo A es la razón entre la longitud de la hipotenusa y la longitud del cateto opuesto a A. Es la inversa de la función seno.

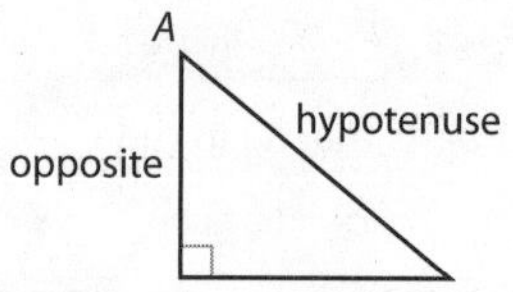

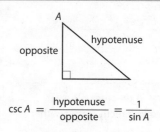

$$\csc A = \frac{\text{hypotenuse}}{\text{opposite}} = \frac{1}{\sin A}$$

---

cosine In a right triangle, the cosine of angle A is the ratio of the length of the side adjacent to angle A to the length of the hypotenuse. It is the reciprocal of the secant function.

coseno En un triángulo rectángulo, el coseno del ángulo A es la razón entre la longitud del cateto adyacente al ángulo A y la longitud de la hipotenusa. Es la inversa de la función secante.

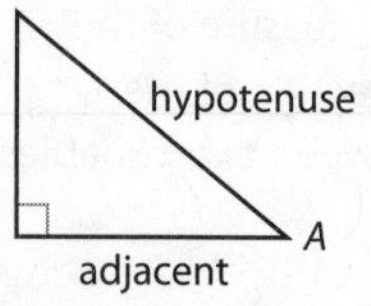

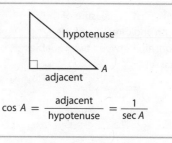

$$\cos A = \frac{\text{adjacent}}{\text{hypotenuse}} = \frac{1}{\sec A}$$

---

cotangent In a right triangle, the cotangent of angle A is the ratio of the length of the side adjacent to A to the length of the side opposite A. It is the reciprocal of the tangent function.

cotangente En un triángulo rectángulo, la cotangente del ángulo A es la razón entre la longitud del cateto adyacente a A y la longitud del cateto opuesto a A. Es la inversa de la función tangente.

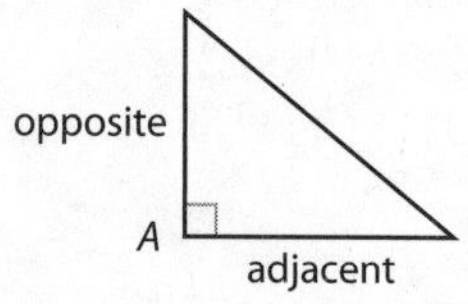

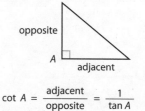

$$\cot A = \frac{\text{adjacent}}{\text{opposite}} = \frac{1}{\tan A}$$

ENGLISH	SPANISH	EXAMPLES

coterminal angles Two angles in standard position with the same terminal side.

ángulos coterminales Dos ángulos en posición estándar con el mismo lado terminal.

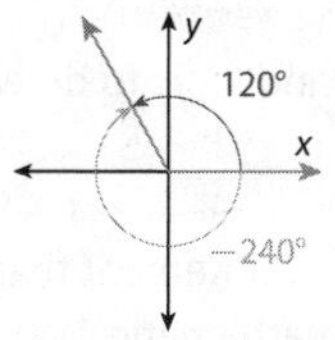

critical values Values that separate the number line into intervals that either contain solutions or do not contain solutions.

valores críticos Valores que separan la recta numérica en intervalos que contienen o no contienen soluciones.

cross section The intersection of a three-dimensional figure and a plane.

sección transversal Intersección de una figura tridimensional y un plano.

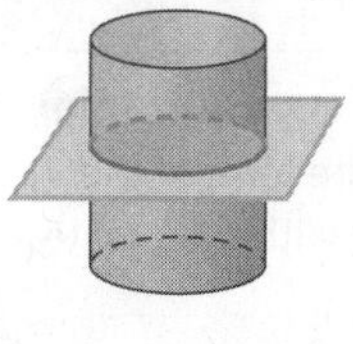

cube-root function The function $f(x) = \sqrt[3]{x}$.

función de raíz cúbica La función $f(x) = \sqrt[3]{x}$.

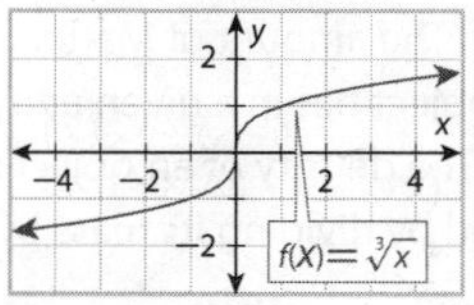

cubic function A polynomial function of degree 3.

función cúbica Función polinomial de grado 3.

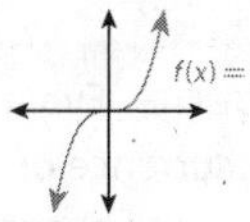

cumulative probability The probability that a random variable is less than or equal to a given value.

probabilidad acumulada La probabilidad de que una variable aleatoria sea menor o igual que un valor determinado.

cycle of a periodic function The shortest repeating part of a periodic graph or function.

ciclo de una función periódica La parte repetida más corta de una gráfica o función periódica.

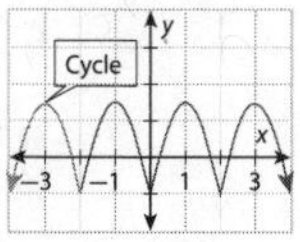

D

decay factor The base $1 - r$ in an exponential expression.

factor decremental Base $1 - r$ en una expresión exponencial.

$2(0.93)^t$

decay factor (representing $1 - 0.07$)

decay rate The constant percent decrease, in decimal form, in an exponential decay function.

tasa de disminución Disminución porcentual constante, en forma decimal, en una función de disminución exponencial.

In the function $f(t) = a(1 - 0.2)^t$, 0.2 is the decay rate.

decreasing A function is decreasing on an interval if $f(x_1) > f(x_2)$ when $x_1 > x_2$ for any x-values x_1 and x_2 from the interval.

decreciente Una función es decreciente en un intervalo si $f(x_1) > f(x_2)$ cuando $x_1 > x_2$ dados los valores de x, x_1 y x_2, pertenecientes al intervalo.

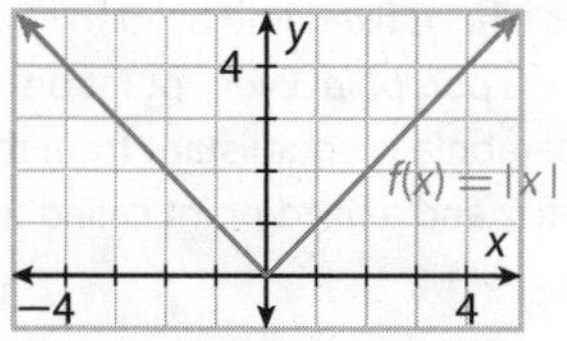

$f(x)$ is decreasing on the interval $x < 0$.

Glossary/Glosario

ENGLISH	SPANISH	EXAMPLES
deductive reasoning The process of using logic to draw conclusions.	**razonamiento deductivo** Proceso en el que se utiliza la lógica para sacar conclusiones.	
definition A statement that describes a mathematical object and can be written as a true biconditional statement.	**definición** Enunciado que describe un objeto matemático y se puede expresar como un enunciado bicondicional verdadero.	
degree of a monomial The sum of the exponents of the variables in the monomial.	**grado de un monomio** Suma de los exponentes de las variables del monomio.	$4x^2y^5z^3$ Degree: $2 + 5 + 3 = 10$ 5 Degree: 0 $(5 = 5x^0)$
degree of a polynomial The degree of the term of the polynomial with the greatest degree.	**grado de un polinomio** Grado del término del polinomio con el grado máximo.	$3x^2y^2 + 4xy^5 - 12x^3y^2$ Degree 6 Degree 4, Degree 6, Degree 5
density The amount of Matter that an object has in a given unit of volume. The density of an object is calculated by dividing its mass by its volume.	**densidad** La cantidad de materia que tiene un objeto en una unidad de volumen determinada. La densidad de un objeto se calcula dividiendo su masa entre su volumen.	$\text{density} = \frac{\text{mass}}{\text{volume}}$
dependent events Events for which the occurrence or nonoccurrence of one event affects the probability of the other event.	**sucesos dependientes** Dos sucesos son dependientes si el hecho de que uno de ellos se cumpla o no afecta la probabilidad del otro.	From a bag containing 3 red marbles and 2 blue marbles, drawing a red marble, and then drawing a blue marble without replacing the first marble.
dependent system A system of equations that has infinitely many solutions.	**sistema dependiente** Sistema de ecuaciones que tiene infinitamente muchas soluciones.	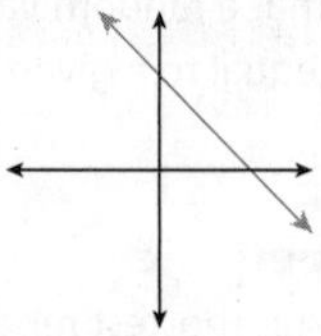 $\begin{cases} x + y = 3 \\ 2x + 2y = 6 \end{cases}$
difference of two squares A polynomial of the form $a^2 - b^2$, which may be written as the product $(a + b)(a - b)$.	**diferencia de dos cuadrados** Polinomio del tipo $a^2 - b^2$, que se puede expresar como el producto $(a + b)(a - b)$.	$x^2 - 4 = (x + 2)(x - 2)$
directed line segment A segment between two points *A* and *B* with a specified direction, from *A* to *B* or from *B* to *A*.	**segmento de una línea con dirección** Un segmento entro dos puntos con una dirección especificada.	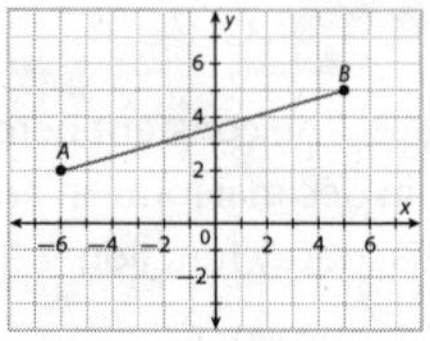
directrix A fixed line used to define a *parabola*. Every point on the parabola is equidistant from the directrix and a fixed point called the *focus*.	**directriz** Línea fija utilizada para definir una *parábola*. Cada punto de la parábola es equidistante de la directriz y de un punto fijo denominado *foco*.	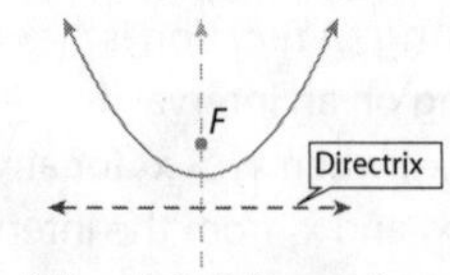 $P_1D_1 = P_1F$ $P_2D_2 = P_2F$

ENGLISH	SPANISH	EXAMPLES
discontinuous function A function whose graph has one or more jumps, breaks, or holes.	**función discontinua** Función cuya gráfica tiene uno o más saltos, interrupciones u hoyos.	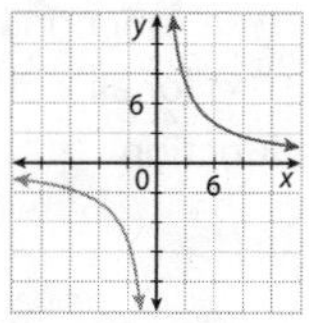
discrete data Data that cannot take on any real-value measurement within an interval.	**datos discretos** Datos que no admiten cualquier medida de valores reales dentro de un intervalo.	the number of pennies in a jar over time
discriminant The discriminant of the quadratic equation $ax^2 + bx + c = 0$ is $b^2 - 4ac$.	**discriminante** El discriminante de la ecuación cuadrática $ax^2 + bx + c = 0$ es $b^2 - 4ac$.	The discriminant of $2x^2 - 5x - 3 = 0$ is $(-5)^2 - 4(2)(-3) = 25 + 24 = 49$.
distribution A set of numerical data that you can graph using a data display that involves a number line, such as a line plot, histogram, or box plot.	**distribución** Un conjunto de datos numéricos que se pueden representar gráficamente mediante una representación de datos que incluye una recta numérica, como un diagrama de puntos, un histograma o un diagrama de cajas.	

E

ENGLISH	SPANISH	EXAMPLES
elementary row operations *See* row operations.	**operaciones elementales de fila** *Véase* operaciones de fila.	
elimination A method used to solve systems of equations in which one variable is eliminated by adding or subtracting two equations of the system.	**eliminación** Método utilizado para resolver sistemas de ecuaciones por el cual se elimina una variable sumando o restando dos ecuaciones del sistema.	
end behavior The trends in the *y*-values of a function as the *x*-values approach positive and negative infinity.	**comportamiento extremo** Tendencia de los valores de y de una función a medida que los valores de *x* se aproximan al infinito positivo y negativo.	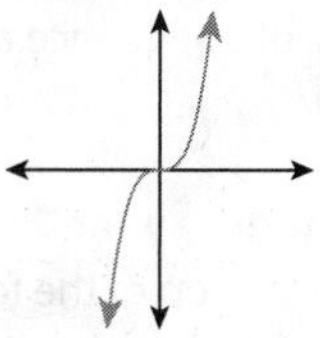 End behavior: $f(x) \to \infty$ as $x \to \infty$; $f(x) \to -\infty$ as $x \to -\infty$
Euclidean geometry The system of geometry described by Euclid. In particular, the system of Euclidean geometry satisfies the Parallel Postulate, which states that there is exactly one line through a given point parallel to a given line.	**geometría euclidiana** Sistema geométrico desarrollado por Euclides. Específicamente, el sistema de la geometría euclidiana cumple con el postulado de las paralelas, que establece que por un punto dado se puede trazar una única línea paralela a una línea dada.	

Glossary/Glosario

ENGLISH	SPANISH	EXAMPLES

even function A function in which $f(-x) = f(x)$ for all x in the domain of the function.

función par Función en la que para todos los valores de x dentro del dominio de la función.

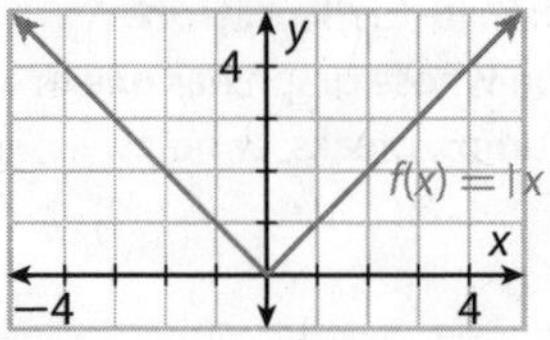

$f(x) = |x|$ is an even function.

---

event An outcome or set of outcomes in a probability experiment.

suceso Resultado o conjunto de resultados en un experimento de probabilidad.

In the experiment of rolling a number cube, the event "an odd number" consists of the outcomes 1, 3, and 5.

---

expected value The weighted average of the numerical outcomes of a probability experiment.

valor esperado Promedio ponderado de los resultados numéricos de un experimento de probabilidad.

The table shows the probability of getting a given score by guessing on a three-question quiz.

Score	0	1	2	3
Probability	0.42	0.42	0.14	0.02

The expected value is a score of $0\,(0.42) + 1\,(0.42) + 2\,(0.14) + 3\,(0.02) = 0.76$.

---

experiment An operation, process, or activity in which outcomes can be used to estimate probability.

experimento Una operación, proceso o actividad cuyo resultado se puede usar para estimar la probabilidad.

Tossing a coin 10 times and noting the number of heads.

---

experimental probability The ratio of the number of times an event occurs to the number of trials, or times, that an activity is performed.

probabilidad experimental Razón entre la cantidad de veces que ocurre un suceso y la cantidad de pruebas, o veces, que se realiza una actividad.

Kendra made 6 of 10 free throws. The experimental probability that she will make her next free throw is

$P(\text{free throw}) = \frac{\text{number made}}{\text{number attempted}} = \frac{6}{10}$.

---

explicit formula A formula that defines the nth term a_n, or general term, of a sequence as a function of n.

fórmula explícita Fórmula que define el enésimo término a_n, o término general, de una sucesión como una función de n.

Sequence: 4, 7, 10, 13, 16, 19, …
Explicit formula: $a_n = 1 + 3n$

---

exponential decay An exponential function of the form $f(x) = ab^x$ in which $0 < b < 1$. If r is the rate of decay, then the function can be written $y = a\,(1 - r)^t$, where a is the initial amount and t is the time.

decremento exponencial Función exponencial del tipo $f(x) = ab^x$ en la cual $0 < b < 1$. Si r es la tasa decremental, entonces la función se puede expresar como $y = a\,(1 - r)^t$, donde a es la cantidad inicial y t es el tiempo.

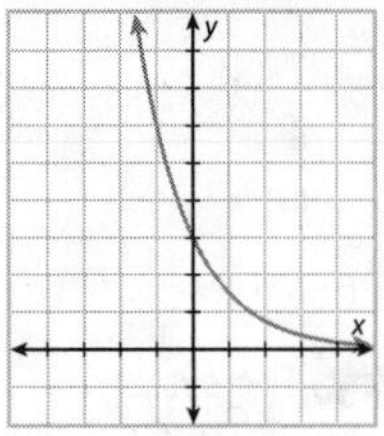

$y = 3\left(\frac{1}{2}\right)^x$

---

exponential equation An equation that contains one or more exponential expressions.

ecuación exponencial Ecuación que contiene una o más expresiones exponenciales.

$2^{x+1} = 8$

---

exponential function A function of the form $f(x) = ab^x$, where a and b are real numbers with $a \neq 0$, $b > 0$, and $b \neq 1$.

función exponencial Función del tipo $f(x) = ab^x$, donde a y b son números reales con $a \neq 0$, $b > 0$ y $b \neq 1$.

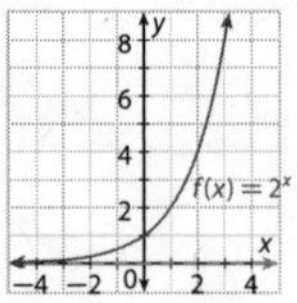

ENGLISH	SPANISH	EXAMPLES
exponential growth An exponential function of the form $f(x) = ab^x$ in which $b > 1$. If r is the rate of growth, then the function can be written $y = a(1 + r)^t$, where a is the initial amount and t is the time.	**crecimiento exponencial** Función exponencial del tipo $f(x) = ab^x$ en la que $b > 1$. Si r es la tasa de crecimiento, entonces la función se puede expresar como $y = a(1 + r)^t$, donde a es la cantidad inicial y t es el tiempo.	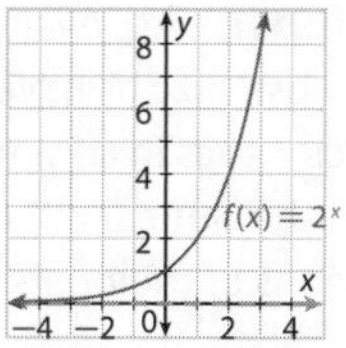
exponential regression A statistical method used to fit an exponential model to a given data set.	**regresión exponencial** Método estadístico utilizado para ajustar un modelo exponencial a un conjunto de datos determinado.	
exterior angle of a polygon An angle formed by one side of a polygon and the extension of an adjacent side.	**ángulo externo de un polígono** Ángulo formado por un lado de un polígono y la prolongación del lado adyacente.	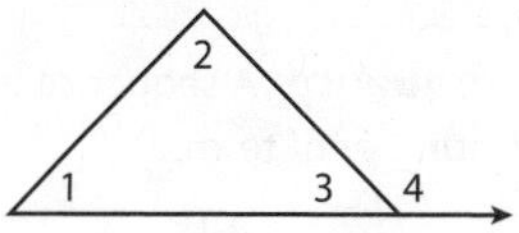 ∠4 is an exterior angle.
external secant segment A segment of a secant that lies in the exterior of the circle with one endpoint on the circle.	**segmento secante externo** Segmento de una secante que se encuentra en el exterior del círculo y tiene un extremo sobre el círculo.	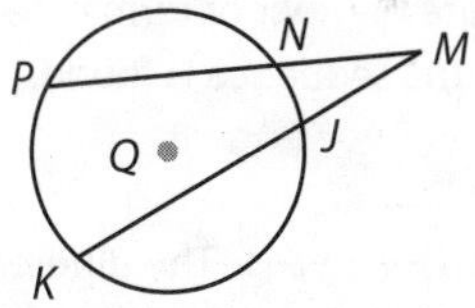 $\overline{NM}$ is an external secant segment.
extraneous solution A solution of a derived equation that is not a solution of the original equation.	**solución extraña** Solución de una ecuación derivada que no es una solución de la ecuación original.	To solve $\sqrt{x} = -2$, square both sides; $x = 4$. ***Check*** $\sqrt{4} = -2$ is false; so 4 is an extraneous solution.

F

Factor Theorem For any polynomial $P(x)$, $(x - a)$ is a factor of $P(x)$ if and only if $P(a) = 0$.	**Teorema del factor** Dado el polinomio $P(x)$, $(x - a)$ es un factor de $P(x)$ si y sólo si $P(a) = 0$.	$(x - 1)$ is a factor of $P(x) = x^2 - 1$ because $P(1) = 1^2 - 1 = 0$.
factorial If n is a positive integer, then n factorial, written $n!$, is $n \cdot (n - 1) \cdot (n - 2) \cdot \ldots \cdot 2 \cdot 1$. The factorial of 0 is defined to be 1.	**factorial** Si n es un entero positivo, entonces el factorial de n, expresado como n!, es $n \cdot (n - 1) \cdot (n - 2) \cdot \ldots \cdot 2 \cdot 1$ Por definición, el factorial de 0 será 1.	$7! = 7 \cdot 6 \cdot 5 \cdot 4 \cdot 3 \cdot 2 \cdot 1 = 5040$ $0! = 1$

ENGLISH	SPANISH	EXAMPLES

family of functions A set of functions whose graphs have basic characteristics in common. Functions in the same family are transformations of their parent function.

familia de funciones Conjunto de funciones cuyas gráficas tienen características básicas en común. Las funciones de la misma familia son transformaciones de su función madre.

Some members of the family of quadratic functions with the parent function $f(x) = x^2$ are:
$f(x) = 3x^2$ $f(x) = x^2 + 1$ $f(x) = (x - 2)^2$

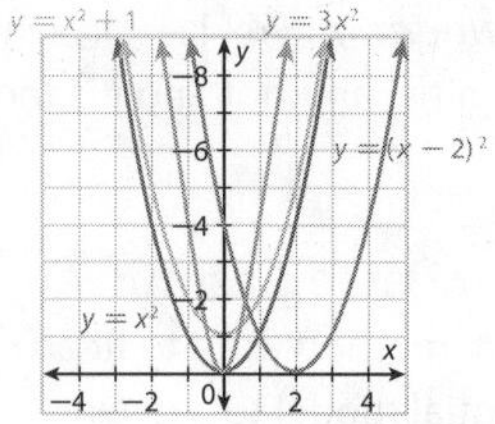

Fibonacci sequence The infinite sequence of numbers beginning with 1, 1 such that each term is the sum of the two previous terms.

sucesión de Fibonacci Sucesión infinita de números que comienza con 1, 1 de forma tal que cada término es la suma de los dos términos anteriores.

1, 1, 2, 3, 5, 8, 13, 21, …

finite sequence A sequence with a finite number of terms.

sucesión finita Sucesión con un número finito de términos.

1, 2, 3, 4, 5

finite geometric series A geometric series in which the sum of a finite number of terms of a geometric sequence is found.

serie geométrica finita Una serie geométrica en la que se halla la suma de un número finito de términos de una secuencia geométrica.

first differences The differences between y-values of a function for evenly spaced x-values.

primeras diferencias Diferencias entre los valores de y de una función para valores de x espaciados uniformemente.

x	0	1	2	3
y	3	7	11	15

first differences +4 +4 +4

first quartile The median of the lower half of a data set, denoted Q_1. Also called *lower quartile.*

primer cuartil Mediana de la mitad inferior de un conjunto de datos, expresada como Q_1. También se llama *cuartil inferior.*

Lower half			Upper half		
18,	(23,)	28,	36,	42,	49,

First quartile

focus (pl. foci) of a parabola A fixed point F used with a *directrix* to define a *parabola.*

foco de una parábola Punto fijo F utilizado con una *directriz* para definir una *parábola.*

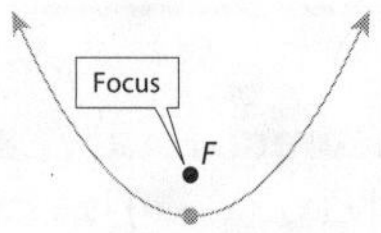

frequency of a data value The number of times the value appears in the data set.

frecuencia de un valor de datos Cantidad de veces que aparece el valor en un conjunto de datos.

In the data set 5, 6, 6, 6, 8, 9, the data value 6 has a frequency of 3.

frequency of a periodic function The number of cycles per unit of time. Also the reciprocal of the period.

frecuencia de una función periódica Cantidad de ciclos por unidad de tiempo. También es la inversa del periodo.

The function $y = \sin(2x)$ has a period of π and a frequency of $\frac{1}{\pi}$.

function rule An algebraic expression that defines a function.

regla de función Expresión algebraica que define una función.

$f(x) = 2x^2 + 3x - 7$
↑
function rule

ENGLISH	SPANISH	EXAMPLES

G

ENGLISH	SPANISH	EXAMPLES
Gaussian Elimination An algorithm for solving systems of equations using matrices and row operations to eliminate variables in each equation in the system.	**Eliminación Gaussiana** Algoritmo para resolver sistemas de ecuaciones mediante matrices y operaciones de fila con el fin de eliminar variables en cada ecuación del sistema.	
general form of a conic section $Ax^2 + Bxy + Cy^2 + Dx + Ey + F = 0$, where A and B are not both 0.	**forma general de una sección cónica** $Ax^2 + Bxy + Cy^2 + Dx + Ey + F = 0$, donde A y B no son los dos 0.	A circle with a vertex at $(1, 2)$ and radius 3 has the general form $x^2 + y^2 - 2x - 4y - 4 = 0$.
geometric mean In a geometric sequence, a term that comes between two given nonconsecutive terms of the sequence. For positive numbers a and b, the geometric mean is $\sqrt{ab}$.	**media geométrica** En una sucesión geométrica, un término que se encuentra entre dos términos no consecutivos dados de la sucesión. Dados los números positivos a y b, la media geométrica es $\sqrt{ab}$.	The geometric mean of 4 and 9 is $\sqrt{4(9)} = \sqrt{36} = 6$.
geometric probability A form of theoretical probability determined by a ratio of geometric measures such as lengths, areas, or volumes.	**probabilidad geométrica** Una forma de la probabilidad teórica determinada por una razón de medidas geométricas, como longitud, área o volumen.	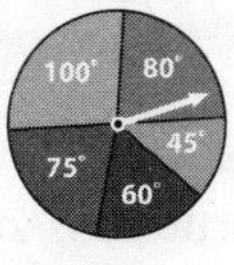 The probability of the pointer landing on 80° is $\frac{2}{9}$.
geometric sequence A sequence in which the ratio of successive terms is a constant r, called the common ratio, where $r \neq 0$ and $r \neq 1$.	**sucesión geométrica** Sucesión en la que la razón de los términos sucesivos es una constante r, denominada razón común, donde $r \neq 0$ y $r \neq 1$.	1, 2, 4, 8, 16, ... $\cdot 2$ $\cdot 2$ $\cdot 2$ $\cdot 2$ $r = 2$
geometric series The indicated sum of the terms of a geometric sequence.	**serie geométrica** Suma indicada de los términos de una sucesión geométrica.	$1 + 2 + 4 + 8 + 16 + \ldots$
great circle A circle on a sphere that divides the sphere into two hemispheres.	**círculo máximo** En una esfera, círculo que divide la esfera en dos hemisferios.	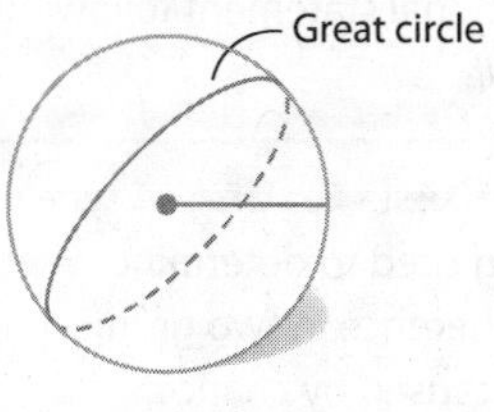
greatest-integer function A function denoted by $f(x) = [x]$ or $f(x) = \lfloor x \rfloor$ in which the number x is rounded down to the greatest integer that is less than or equal to x.	**función de entero mayor** Función expresada como $f(x) = [x]$ o $f(x) = [x]$ en la cual el número x se redondea hacia abajo hasta el entero mayor que sea menor que o igual a x.	$[4.98] = 4$ $[-2.1] = -3$

Glossary/Glosario

ENGLISH	SPANISH	EXAMPLES
growth factor The base $1 + r$ in an exponential expression.	**factor de crecimiento** La base $1 + r$ en una expresión exponencial.	$12{,}000\,(1 + 0.14)^t$ ↑ growth factor
growth rate The constant percent increase, in decimal form, in an exponential growth function.	**tasa de crecimiento** Aumento porcentual constante, en forma decimal, en una función de crecimiento exponencial.	In the function $f(t) = a(1 + 0.3)^t$, 0.3 is the growth rate.

H

ENGLISH	SPANISH	EXAMPLES
hemisphere Half of a sphere.	**hemisferio** Mitad de una esfera.	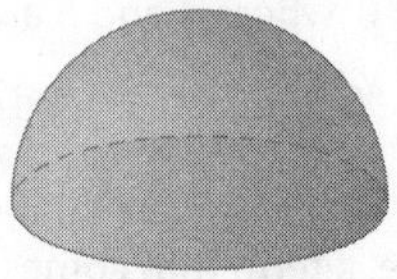
Heron's Formula A triangle with side lengths *a*, *b*, and *c* has area $A = \sqrt{s(s-a)(s-b)(s-c)}$, where *s* is one-half the perimeter, or $s = \frac{1}{2}(a + b + c)$.	**fórmula de Herón** Un triángulo con longitudes de lado *a*, *b* y *c* tiene un área $A = \sqrt{s(s-a)(s-b)(s-c)}$, donde *s* es la mitad del perímetro ó $s = \frac{1}{2}(a + b + c)$.	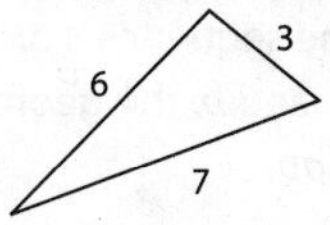 $s = \frac{1}{2}(3 + 6 + 7) = 8$ $A = \sqrt{8(8-3)(8-6)(8-7)}$ $= \sqrt{80} = 4\sqrt{5}$ square units
hole (in a graph) An omitted point on a graph. If a rational function has the same factor $x - b$ in both the numerator and the denominator, and the line $x = b$ is not a vertical asymptote, then there is a hole in the graph at the point where $x = b$.	**hoyo (en una gráfica)** Punto omitido en una gráfica. Si una función racional tiene el mismo factor $x - b$ tanto en el numerador como en el denominador, y la línea $x = b$ no es una asíntota vertical, entonces hay un hoyo en la gráfica en el punto donde $x = b$.	$f(x) = \frac{(x-2)(x+2)}{(x+2)}$ has a hole at $x = -2$. 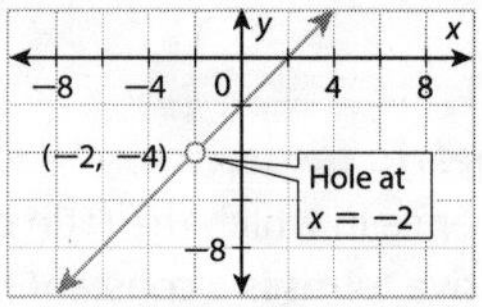
hypotenuse The side opposite the right angle in a right triangle.	**hipotenusa** Lado opuesto al ángulo recto de un triángulo rectángulo.	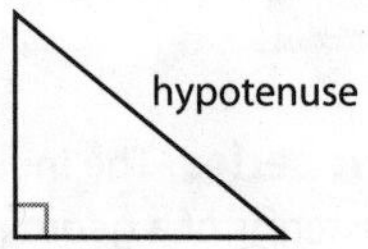
hypothesis The part of a conditional statement following the word *if*.	**hipótesis** La parte de un enunciado condicional que sigue a la palabra *si*.	If $x + 1 = 5$, then $x = 4$. Hypothesis
hypothesis testing A type of testing used to determine whether the difference in two groups is likely to be caused by chance.	**comprobación de hipótesis** Tipo de comprobación que sirve para determinar si el azar es la causa probable de la diferencia entre dos grupos.	

Glossary/Glosario

I

imaginary axis The vertical axis in the complex plane, it graphically represents the purely imaginary part of complex numbers.

eje imaginario Eje vertical de un plano complejo. Representa gráficamente la parte puramente imaginaria de los números complejos.

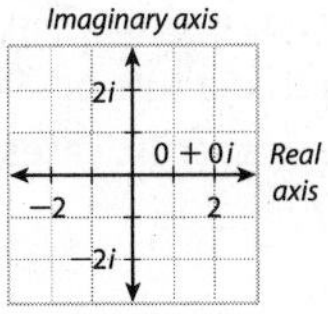

imaginary number The square root of a negative number, written in the form bi, where b is a real number and i is the imaginary unit, $\sqrt{-1}$. Also called a *pure imaginary number*.

número imaginario Raíz cuadrada de un número negativo, expresado como bi, donde b es un número real e i es la unidad imaginaria, $\sqrt{-1}$. También se denomina *número imaginario puro*.

$\sqrt{-16} = \sqrt{16} \cdot \sqrt{-1} = 4i$

imaginary unit The unit in the imaginary number system, $\sqrt{-1}$.

unidad imaginaria Unidad del sistema de números imaginarios, $\sqrt{-1}$.

$\sqrt{-1} = i$

incircle *See* inscribed circle.

incírculo *Véase* círculo inscrito.

inconsistent system A system of equations or inequalities that has no solution.

sistema inconsistente Sistema de ecuaciones o desigualdades que no tiene solución.

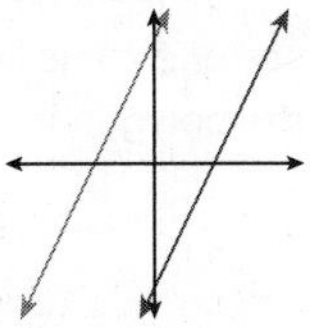

$\begin{cases} y = 2.5x + 5 \\ y = 2.5x - 5 \end{cases}$ is inconsistent.

Increasing A function is increasing on an interval if $f(x_1) < f(x_2)$ when $x_1 < x_2$ for any x-values x_1 and x_2 from the interval.

creciente Una función es creciente en un intervalo si $f(x_1) < f(x_2)$ cuando $x_1 < x_2$ dados los valores de x, x_1 y x_2, pertenecienlos al intervalo.

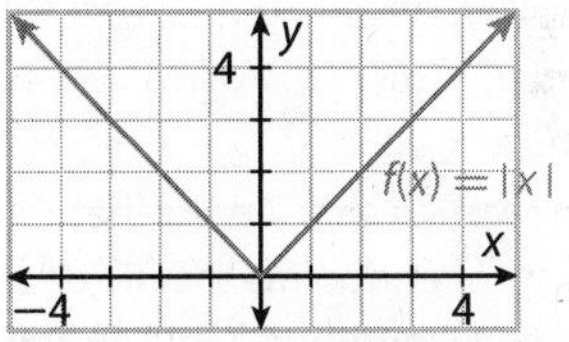

$f(x)$ is increasing on the interval $x > 0$.

independent system A system of equations that has exactly one solution.

sistema independiente Sistema de ecuaciones que tiene exactamente una solución.

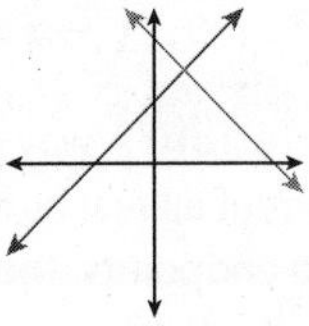

$\begin{cases} y = -x + 4 \\ y = x + 2 \end{cases}$ Solution: $(1, 3)$

independent variable The input of a function; a variable whose value determines the value of the output, or dependent variable.

variable independiente Entrada de una función; variable cuyo valor determina el valor de la salida, o variable dependiente.

$y = 2x + 1$
↑
independent variable

indirect proof A proof in which the statement to be proved is assumed to be false and a contradiction is shown.

demostración indirecta Prueba en la que se supone que el enunciado a demostrar es falso y se muestra una contradicción.

ENGLISH	SPANISH	EXAMPLES
indirect reasoning *See* indirect proof.	**razonamiento indirecto** *Ver* demostración indirecta.	
inductive reasoning The process of reasoning that a rule or statement is true because specific cases are true.	**razonamiento inductivo** Proceso de razonamiento por el que se determina que una regla o enunciado son verdaderos porque ciertos casos específicos son verdaderos.	
initial side The ray that lies on the positive x-axis when an angle is drawn in standard position.	**lado inicial** El rayo que se encuentra en el eje positivo x cuando se traza un ángulo en la posición estándar.	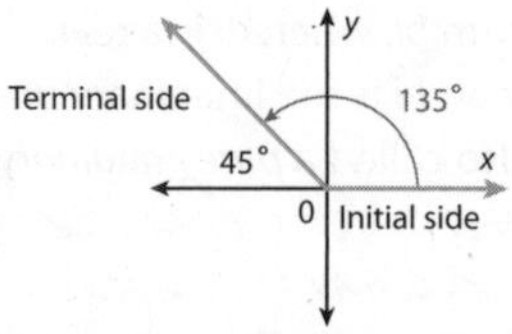
inscribed angle An angle whose vertex is on a circle and whose sides contain chords of the circle.	**ángulo inscrito** Ángulo cuyo vértice se encuentra sobre un círculo y cuyos lados contienen cuerdas del círculo.	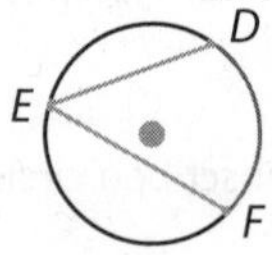
inscribed circle A circle in which each side of the polygon is tangent to the circle.	**círculo inscrito** Círculo en el que cada lado del polígono es tangente al círculo.	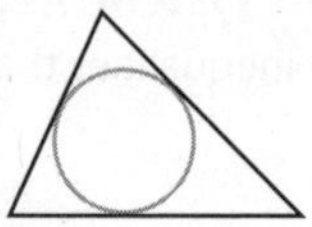
inscribed polygon A polygon in which every vertex of the polygon lies on the circle.	**polígono inscrito** Polígono cuyos vértices se encuentran sobre el círculo.	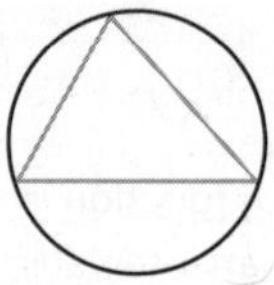
intercepted arc An arc that consists of endpoints that lie on the sides of an inscribed angle and all the points of the circle between the endpoints.	**arco abarcado** Arco cuyos extremos se encuentran en los lados de un ángulo inscrito y consta de todos los puntos del círculo ubicados entre dichos extremos.	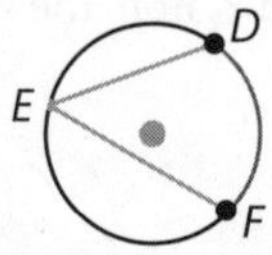 $\widehat{DF}$ is the intercepted arc.
interval notation A way of writing the set of all real numbers between two endpoints. The symbols [and] are used to include an endpoint in an interval, and the symbols (and) are used to exclude an endpoint from an interval.	**notación de intervalo** Forma de expresar el conjunto de todos los números reales entre dos extremos. Los símbolos [y] se utilizan para incluir un extremo en un intervalo y los símbolos (y) se utilizan para excluir un extremo de un intervalo.	Interval notation / Set-builder notation: (a, b) — $\{x \mid a < x < b\}$; $(a, b]$ — $\{x \mid a < x \leq b\}$; $[a, b)$ — $\{x \mid a \leq x < b\}$; $[a, b]$ — $\{x \mid a \leq x \leq b\}$
inverse cosine function If the domain of the cosine function is restricted to $[0, \pi]$, then the function $\text{Cos}\,\theta = a$ has an inverse function $\text{Cos}^{-1}\,a = \theta$, also called *arccosine.*	**función coseno inverso** Si el dominio de la función coseno se restringe a $[0, \pi]$, entonces la función $\text{Cos}\,\theta = a$ tiene una función inversa $\text{Cos}^{-1}\,a = \theta$, también llamada *arco coseno.*	$\text{Cos}^{-1}\frac{1}{2} = \frac{\pi}{3}$

ENGLISH	SPANISH	EXAMPLES

inverse function The function that results from exchanging the input and output values of a one-to-one function. The inverse of $f(x)$ is denoted $f^{-1}(x)$.

función inversa Función que resulta de intercambiar los valores de entrada y salida de una función uno a uno. La función inversa de $f(x)$ se expresa $f^{-1}(x)$

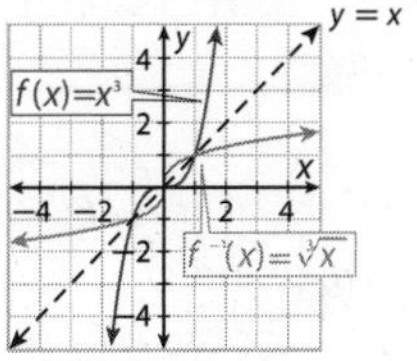

inverse relation The inverse of the relation consisting of all ordered pairs (x, y) is the set of all ordered pairs (y, x). The graph of an inverse relation is the reflection of the graph of the relation across the line $y = x$.

relación inversa La inversa de la relación que consta de todos los pares ordenados (x, y) es el conjunto de todos los pares ordenados (y, x). La gráfica de una relación inversa es el reflejo de la gráfica de la relación sobre la línea $y = x$.

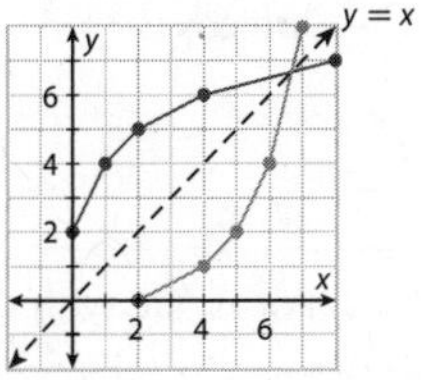

inverse sine function If the domain of the sine function is restricted to $\left[-\frac{\pi}{2}, \frac{\pi}{2}\right]$ then the function Sin $\theta = a$ has an inverse function, $\text{Sin}^{-1}\, a = \theta$, also called *arcsine.*

función seno inverso Si el dominio de la función seno se restringe a $\left[-\frac{\pi}{2}, \frac{\pi}{2}\right]$, entonces la función Sen $\theta = a$ tiene una función inversa, $\text{Sen}^{-1}\, a = \theta\theta$, también llamada *arco seno.*

$\text{Sin}^{-1}\frac{\sqrt{3}}{2} = \frac{\pi}{3}$

inverse tangent function If the domain of the tangent function is restricted to $\left(-\frac{\pi}{2}, \frac{\pi}{2}\right)$, then the function Tan $\theta = a$ has an inverse function, $\text{Tan}^{-1}\, a = \theta$, also called *arctangent.*

función tangente inversa Si el dominio de la función tangente se restringe a $\left(-\frac{\pi}{2}, \frac{\pi}{2}\right)$ entonces la función Tan$\theta = $ a tiene una función inversa, $\text{Tan}^{-1}\, a = \theta$, también llamada *arco tangente.*

$\text{Tan}^{-1}\sqrt{3} = \frac{\pi}{3}$

inverse variation A relationship between two variables, x and y, that can be written in the form $y = \frac{k}{x}$, where k is a nonzero constant and $x \neq 0$.

variación inversa Relación entre dos x e y, que puede expresarse en la forma $y = \frac{k}{x}$ donde k es una constante distinta de cero $y\ x \neq 0$.

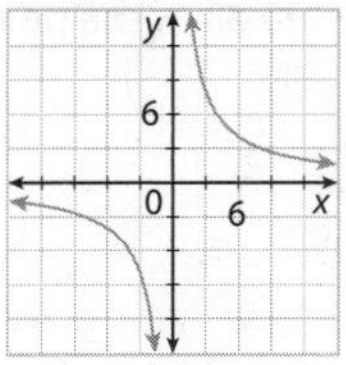

$y = \frac{24}{x}$

irreducible factor A factor of degree 2 or greater that cannot be factored further.

factor irreductible Factor de grado 2 o mayor que no se puede seguir factorizando.

$x^2 + 7x + 1$

J

joint relative frequency The ratio of the frequency in a particular category divided by the total number of data values.

frecuencia relativa conjunta La razón de la frecuencia en una determinada categoría dividida entre el número total de valores.

Glossary/Glosario

ENGLISH	SPANISH	EXAMPLES

L

Law of Cosines For $\triangle ABC$ with side lengths a, b, and c,
$a^2 = b^2 + c^2 - 2bc \cos A$
$b^2 = a^2 + c^2 - 2ac \cos B$
$c^2 = a^2 + b^2 - 2ab \cos C$.

Ley de cosenos Dado $\triangle ABC$ con longitudes de lado a, b y c,
$a^2 = b^2 + c^2 - 2bc \cos A$
$b^2 = a^2 + c^2 - 2ac \cos B$
$c^2 = a^2 + b^2 - 2ab \cos C$

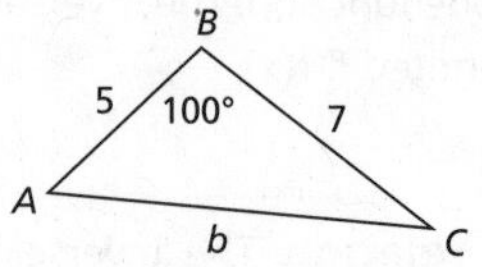

$b^2 = 7^2 + 5^2 - 2(7)(5)\cos 100°$
$b^2 \approx 86.2$
$b \approx 9.3$

Law of Sines For $\triangle ABC$ with side lengths a, b, and c,
$\frac{\sin A}{a} = \frac{\sin B}{b} = \frac{\sin C}{c}$.

Ley de senos Dado $\triangle ABC$ con longitudes de lado a, b y c,
$\frac{\text{sen}A}{a} = \frac{\text{sen}B}{b} = \frac{\text{sen}C}{c}$.

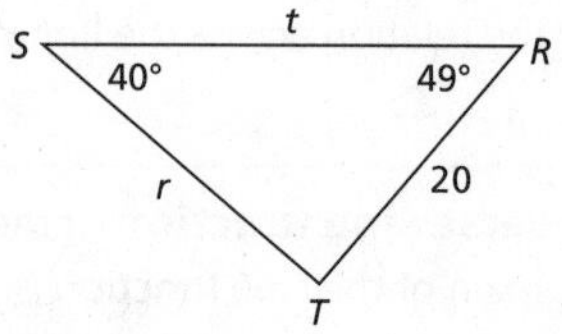

$\frac{\sin 49°}{r} = \frac{\sin 40°}{20}$
$r = \frac{20 \sin 49°}{\sin 40°} \approx 23.5$

leading coefficient The coefficient of the first term of a polynomial in standard form.

coeficiente principal Coeficiente del primer termino de un polinomio en forma estandar

$3x^2 + 7x - 2$
↑
Leading coefficient

limit For an infinite arithmetic series that converges, the number that the partial sums approach.

límite Para un serie que coverge, el número que se aproximan las sumas.

The series $\frac{1}{2} + \frac{1}{4} + \frac{1}{8} + \frac{1}{16} + \ldots$ has a limit of 1.

line of best fit The line that comes closest to all of the points in a data set.

línea de mejor ajuste Línea que más se acerca a todos los puntos de un conjunto de datos.

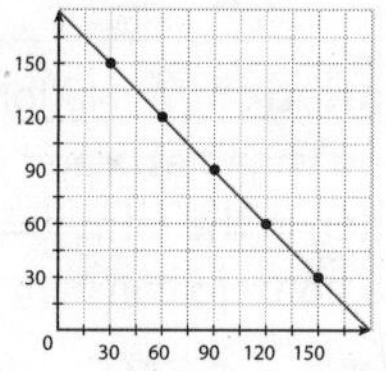

linear equation in three variables An equation with three distinct variables, each of which is either first degree or has a coefficient of zero.

ecuación lineal en tres variables Ecuación con tres variables diferentes, sean de primer grado o tengan un coeficiente de cero.

$5 = 3x + 2y + 6z$

linear regression A statistical method used to fit a linear model to a given data set.

regresión lineal Método estadístico utilizado para ajustar un modelo lineal a un conjunto de datos determinado.

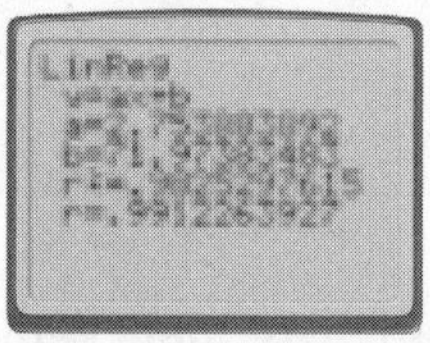

linear system A system of equations containing only linear equations.

sistema lineal Sistema de ecuaciones que contiene sólo ecuaciones lineales.

$\begin{cases} y = 2x + 1 \\ x + y = 8 \end{cases}$

local maximum For a function f, $f(a)$ is a local maximum if there is an interval around a such that $f(x) < f(a)$ for every x-value in the interval except a.

máximo local Dada una función f, $f(a)$ es el máximo local si hay un intervalo en a tal que $f(x) < f(a)$ para cada valor de x en el intervalo excepto a.

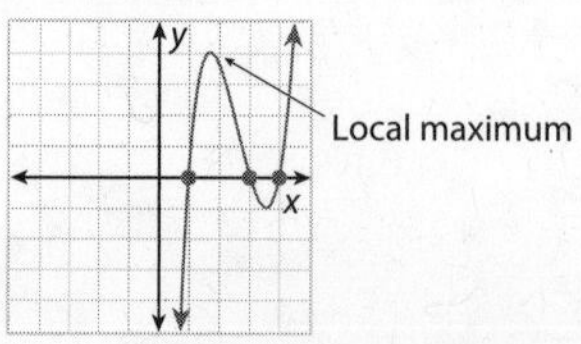

ENGLISH	SPANISH	EXAMPLES

local minimum For a function f, $f(a)$ is a local minimum if there is an interval around a such that $f(x) > f(a)$ for every x-value in the interval except a.

mínimo local Dada una función f, $f(a)$ es el mínimo local si hay un intervalo en a tal que $f(x) > f(a)$ para cada valor de x en el intervalo excepto a.

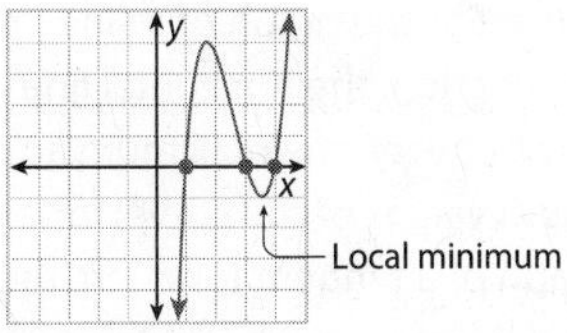

---

logarithm The exponent that a specified base must be raised to in order to get a certain value.

logaritmo Exponente al cual debe elevarse una base determinada a fin de obtener cierto valor.

$\log_2 8 = 3$, because 3 is the power that 2 is raised to in order to get 8; or $2^3 = 8$.

---

logarithmic equation An equation that contains a logarithm of a variable.

ecuación logarítmica Ecuación que contiene un logaritmo de una variable.

$\log x + 3 = 7$

---

logarithmic function A function of the form $f(x) = \log_b x$, where $b \neq 1$ and $b > 0$, which is the inverse of the exponential function $f(x) = b^x$.

función logarítmica Función del tipo $f(x) = \log_b x$, donde $b \neq 1$ y $b > 0$, que es la inversa de la función exponencial $f(x) = b^x$.

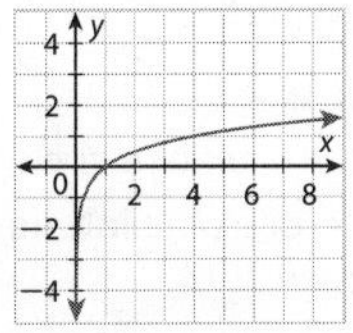

$f(x) = \log_4 x$

---

logarithmic regression A statistical method used to fit a logarithmic model to a given data set.

regresión logarítmica Método estadístico utilizado para ajustar un modelo logarítmico a un conjunto de datos determinado.

M

major arc An arc of a circle whose points are on or in the exterior of a central angle.

arco mayor Arco de un círculo cuyos puntos están sobre un ángulo central o en su exterior.

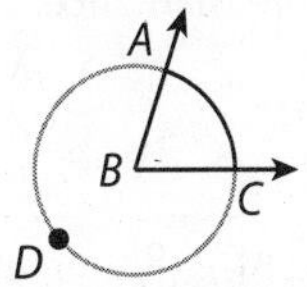

$\overparen{ADC}$ is a major arc of the circle.

---

margin of error In a random sample, it defines an interval, centered on the sample percent, in which the population percent is most likely to lie.

margen de error En una muestra aleatoria, define un intervalo, centrado en el porcentaje de muestra, en el que es más probable que se encuentre el porcentaje de población.

---

matrix A rectangular array of numbers.

matriz Arreglo rectangular de números.

$$\begin{bmatrix} 1 & 0 & 3 \\ -2 & 2 & -5 \\ 7 & -6 & 3 \end{bmatrix}$$

---

maximum value of a function The y-value of the highest point on the graph of the function.

máximo de una función Valor de y del punto más alto en la gráfica de la función.

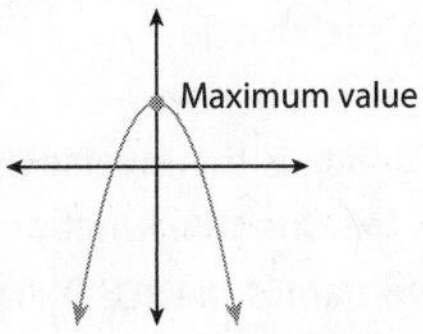

ENGLISH	SPANISH	EXAMPLES

midline For the graph of a sine or cosine function, the horizontal line halfway between the maximum and minimum values of the curve; for the graph of a tangent function, the horizontal line through the point of each cycle that is midway between the asymptotes.

línea media En la gráfica de una función seno o coseno, la línea horizontal a medio camino entre los valores máximo y mínimo de la curva; en la gráfica de una función tangente, la línea horizontal que atraviesa el punto de cada ciclo que está a medio camino entre las asíntotas.

---

minimum value of a function The y-value of the lowest point on the graph of the function.

mínimo de una función Valor de y del punto más bajo en la gráfica de la función.

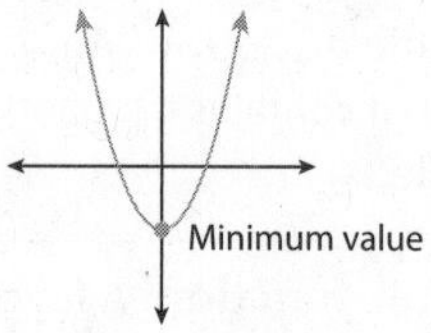

---

minor arc An arc of a circle whose points are on or in the interior of a central angle.

arco menor Arco de un círculo cuyos puntos están sobre un ángulo central o en su interior.

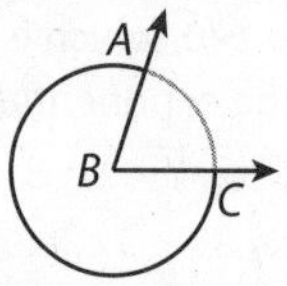

$\overset{\frown}{AC}$ is a minor arc of the circle.

---

monomial A number or a product of numbers and variables with whole-number exponents, or a polynomial with one term.

monomio Número o producto de números y variables con exponentes de números cabales, o polinomio con un término.

$8x, 9, 3x^2y^4$

---

multiple root A root r is a multiple root when the factor $(x - r)$ appears in the equation more than once.

raíz múltiple Una raíz r es una raíz múltiple cuando el factor $(x - r)$ aparece en la ecuación más de una vez.

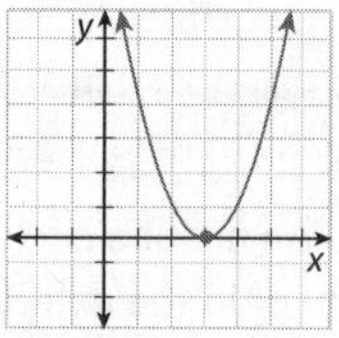

3 is a multiple root of $P(x) = (x - 3)^2$.

---

multiplicity If a polynomial $P(x)$ has a multiple root at r, the multiplicity of r is the number of times $(x - r)$ appears as a factor in $P(x)$.

multiplicidad Si un polinomio $P(x)$ tiene una raíz múltiple en r, la multiplicidad de r es la cantidad de veces que $(x - r)$ aparece como factor en $P(x)$.

For $P(x) = (x - 3)^2$, the root 3 has a multiplicity of 2.

N

natural logarithm A logarithm with base e, written as ln.

logaritmo natural Logaritmo con base e, que se escribe ln.

$\ln 5 = \log_e 5 \approx 1.6$

---

natural logarithmic function The function $f(x) = \ln x$, which is the inverse of the natural exponential function $f(x) = e^x$. Domain is $\{x \mid x > 0\}$; range is all real numbers

función logarítmica natural Función $f(x) = \ln x$, que es la inversa de la función exponencial natural $f(x) = e^x$. El dominio es $\{x \mid x > 0\}$; el rango es todos los números reales.

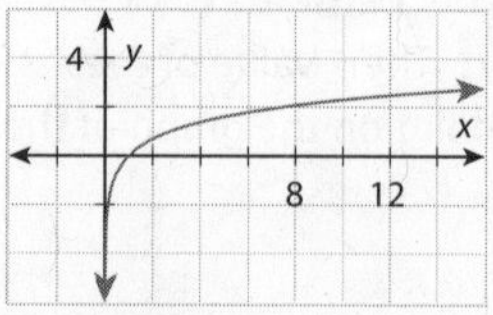

ENGLISH	SPANISH	EXAMPLES
net A diagram of the faces of a three-dimensional figure arranged in such a way that the diagram can be folded to form the three-dimensional figure.	**plantilla** Diagrama de las caras de una figura tridimensional que se puede plegar para formar la figura tridimensional.	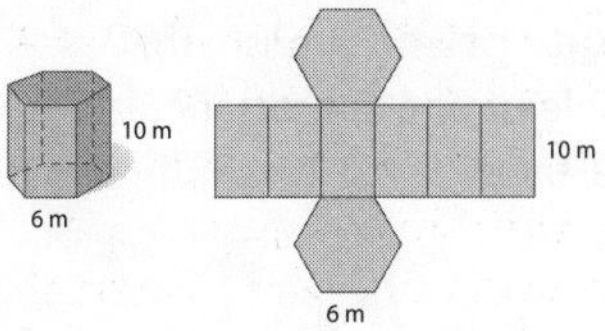
non-Euclidean geometry A system of geometry in which the Parallel Postulate, which states that there is exactly one line through a given point parallel to a given line, does not hold.	**geometría no euclidiana** Sistema de geometría en el cual no se cumple el postulado de las paralelas, que establece que por un punto dado se puede trazar una única línea paralela a una línea dada.	In spherical geometry, there are no parallel lines. The sum of the angles in a triangle is always greater than 180°.
nonlinear system of equations A system in which at least one of the equations is not linear.	**sistema no lineal de ecuaciones** Sistema en el cual por lo menos una de las ecuaciones no es lineal.	$\begin{cases} y = 2x^2 \\ y = -3^2 + 5 \end{cases}$
normal distribution A distribution that is mounded in the middle with symmetric "tails" at each end, forming a bell shape.	**distribución normal** Una distribución que está elevada en el centro con "colas" simétricas en los extremos, lo que forma la figura de una campana.	
***n*th root** The *n*th root of a number a, written as $\sqrt[n]{a}$ or $a^{\frac{1}{n}}$, is a number that is equal to a when it is raised to the *n*th power.	**enésima raíz** La enésima raíz de un número a, que se escribe como $\sqrt[n]{a}$ or $a^{\frac{1}{n}}$, es un número igual a a cuando se eleva a la enésima potencia.	$\sqrt[5]{32} = 2$, because $2^5 = 32$.
null hypothesis The assumption made that any difference between the control group and the treatment group in an experiment is due to chance, and not to the treatment.	**hipótesis nula** La suposición de que cualquier diferencia entre el grupo de control y el grupo de tratamiento en un experimento se debe al azar, no al tratamiento.	
numerical data Data that represent quantities or observations that can be measured.	**datos numéricos** Datos que representan cantidades u observaciones que pueden medirse.	

O

ENGLISH	SPANISH	EXAMPLES
oblique cone A cone whose axis is not perpendicular to the base.	**cono oblicuo** Cono cuyo eje no es perpendicular a la base.	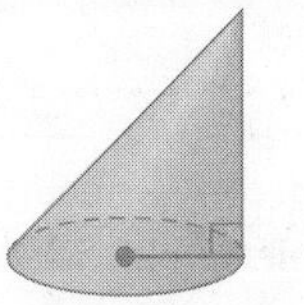
oblique cylinder A cylinder whose axis is not perpendicular to the bases.	**cilindro oblicuo** Cilindro cuyo eje no es perpendicular a las bases.	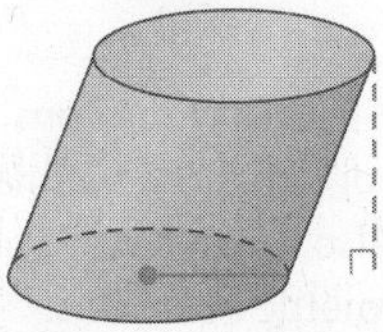

ENGLISH	SPANISH	EXAMPLES
oblique prism A prism that has at least one nonrectangular lateral face.	**prisma oblicuo** Prisma que tiene por lo menos una cara lateral no rectangular.	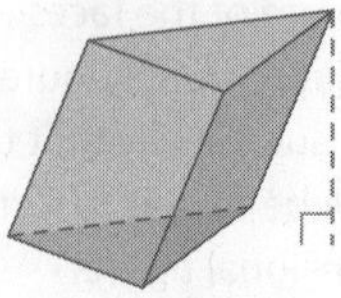
observational study A study that observes individuals and measures variables without controlling the individuals or their environment in any way.	**estudio de observación** Estudio que permite observar a individuos y medir variables sin controlar a los individuos ni su ambiente.	
odd function A function in which $f(-x) = -f(x)$ for all x in the domain of the function.	**función impar** Función en la que $f(-x) = -f(x)$ para todos los valores de x dentro del dominio de la función	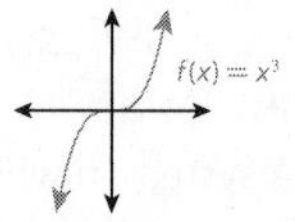 $f(x) = x^3$ is an odd function.
one-to-one function A function in which each y-value corresponds to only one x-value. The inverse of a one-to-one function is also a function.	**función uno a uno** Función en la que cada valor de y corresponde a sólo un valor de x. La inversa de una función uno a uno es también una función.	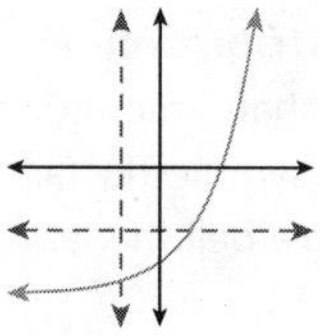
ordered triple A set of three numbers that can be used to locate a point (x, y, z) in a three-dimensional coordinate system.	**tripleta ordenada** Conjunto de tres números que se pueden utilizar para ubicar un punto (x, y, z) en un sistema de coordenadas tridimensional.	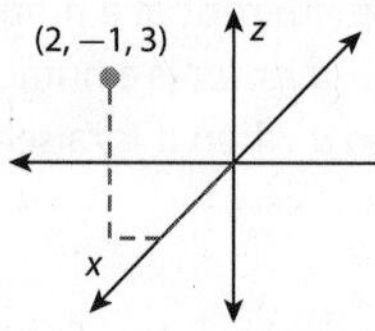

P

ENGLISH	SPANISH	EXAMPLES
parabola The shape of the graph of a quadratic function. Also, the set of points equidistant from a point F, called the focus, and a line d, called the *directrix*.	**parábola** Forma de la gráfica de una función cuadrática. También, conjunto de puntos equidistantes de un punto F, denominado *foco*, y una línea d, denominada *directriz*.	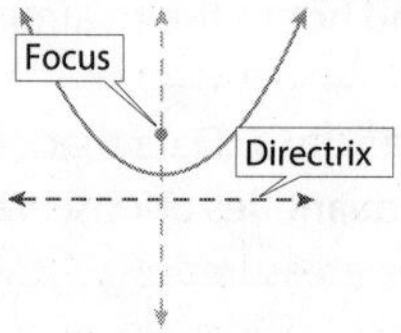
parallel lines Lines in the same plane that do not intersect.	**líneas paralelas** Líneas rectas en el mismo plano que no se cruzan.	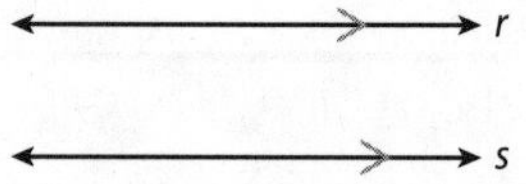 $r \parallel s$
parallelogram A quadrilateral with two pairs of parallel sides.	**paralelogramo** Cuadrilátero con dos pares de lados paralelos.	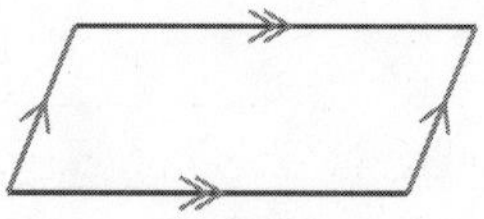
parameter One of the constants in a function or equation that may be changed. Also the third variable in a set of parametric equations.	**parámetro** Una de las constantes en una función o ecuación que se puede cambiar. También es la tercera variable en un conjunto de ecuaciones paramétricas.	$y = (x - h)^2 + k$ parameters

ENGLISH	SPANISH	EXAMPLES
parent cube root function The function $f(x) = \sqrt[3]{x}$.	**función madre de la raíz cúbica** Función del tipo $f(x) = \sqrt[3]{x}$.	$f(x) = \sqrt[3]{x}$
parent function The simplest function with the defining characteristics of the family. Functions in the same family are transformations of their parent function.	**función madre** La función más básica con las características de la familia. Las funciones de la misma familia son transformaciones de su función madre.	$f(x) = x^2$ is the parent function for $g(x) = x^2 + 4$ and $h(x) = 5(x+2)^2 - 3$.
parent square root function The function $f(x) = \sqrt{x}$, where $x \geq 0$.	**función madre de la raíz cuadrada** Función del tipo $f(x) = \sqrt{x}$, donde $x \geq 0$.	$f(x) = \sqrt{x}$
partial sum Indicated by $S_n = \sum_{i=1}^{n} a_i$, the sum of a specified number of terms n of a sequence whose total number of terms is greater than n.	**suma parcial** Expresada por $S_n = \sum_{i=1}^{n} a_i$, la suma de un número específico n de términos de una sucesión cuyo número total de términos es mayor que n.	For the sequence $a_n = n^2$, the fourth partial sum of the infinite series $\sum_{k=1}^{\infty} k^2$ is $\sum_{k=1}^{4} k^2 = 1^2 + 2^2 + 3^2 + 4^2 = 30$.
Pascal's triangle A triangular arrangement of numbers in which every row starts and ends with 1 and each other number is the sum of the two numbers above it.	**triángulo de Pascal** Arreglo triangular de números en el cual cada fila comienza y termina con 1 y cada uno de los demás números es la suma de los dos números que están encima de él.	1 1 1 1 2 1 1 3 3 1 1 4 6 4 1
perfect-square trinomial A trinomial whose factored form is the square of a binomial. A perfect-square trinomial has the form $a^2 - 2ab + b^2 = (a-b)^2$ or $a^2 + 2ab + b^2 = (a+b)^2$.	**trinomio cuadrado perfecto** Trinomio cuya forma factorizada es el cuadrado de un binomio. Un trinomio cuadrado perfecto tiene la forma $a^2 - 2ab + b^2 = (a-b)^2$ o $a^2 + 2ab + b^2 = (a+b)^2$.	$x^2 + 6x + 9$ is a perfectsquare trinomial, because $x^2 + 6x + 9 = (x+3)^2$.
period of a periodic function The length of a cycle measured in units of the independent variable (usually time in seconds). Also the reciprocal of the frequency.	**periodo de una función periódica** Longitud de un ciclo medido en unidades de la variable independiente (generalmente el tiempo en segundos). También es la inversa de la frecuencia.	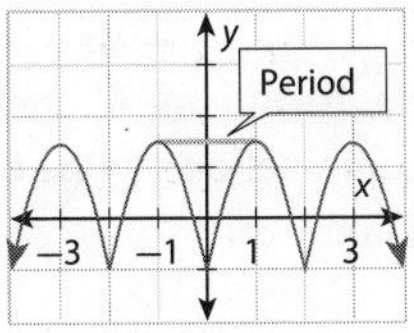
periodic function A function that repeats exactly in regular intervals, called *periods*.	**función periódica** Función que se repite exactamente a intervalos regulares denominados *periodos*.	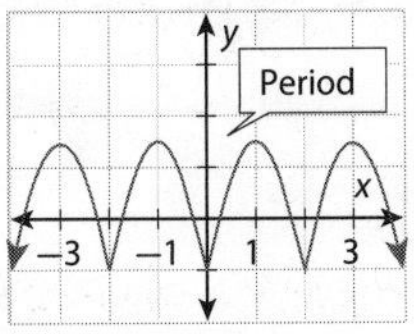
permutation An arrangement of a group of objects in which order is important. The number of permutations of r objects from a group of n objects is denoted ${}_nP_r$.	**permutación** Arreglo de un grupo de objetos en el cual el orden es importante. El número de permutaciones de r objetos de un grupo de n objetos se expresa ${}_nP_r$.	For 4 objects *A*, *B*, *C*, and *D*, there are ${}_4P_2 = 12$ different permutations of 2 objects: *AB*, *AC*, *AD*, *BC*, *BD*, *CD*, *BA*, *CA*, *DA*, *CB*, *DB*, and *DC*.

Glossary/Glosario

ENGLISH	SPANISH	EXAMPLES
permutation test A significance test performed on the results of an experiment by forming every possible regrouping of all the data values taken from the control and treatment groups into two new groups, finding the distribution of the differences of the means for all of the new group pairings, and then finding the likelihood, given that the null hypothesis is true, of getting a difference of means at least as great as the original experimental difference.	**prueba de permutación** Una prueba de significancia realizada sobre los resultados de un experimento al formar todos los reagrupamientos posibles de todos los valores de datos tomados de los grupos de control y de tratamiento en dos nuevos grupos, hallar la distribución de las diferencias de las medias para todos los emparejamientos nuevos, y luego hallar la probabilidad, suponiendo que la hipótesis nula es verdadera, de obtener una diferencia de medias al menos tan grande como la diferencia experimental original.	
perpendicular bisector of a segment A line perpendicular to a segment at the segment's midpoint.	**mediatriz de un segmento** Línea perpendicular a un segmento en el punto medio del segmento.	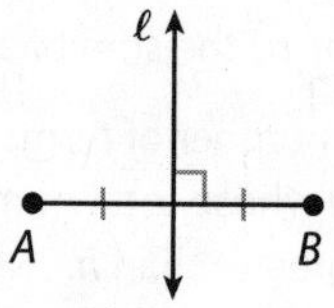 ℓ is the perpendicular bisector of $\overline{AB}$.
perpendicular lines Lines that intersect at 90° angles.	**líneas perpendiculares** Líneas que se cruzan en ángulos de 90°.	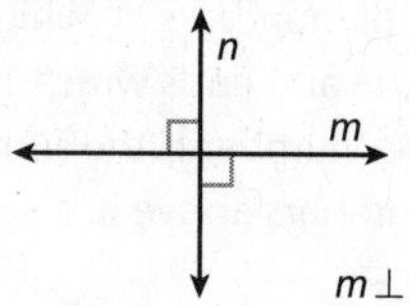 $m \perp n$
phase shift A horizontal translation of a periodic function.	**cambio de fase** Traslación horizontal de una función periódica.	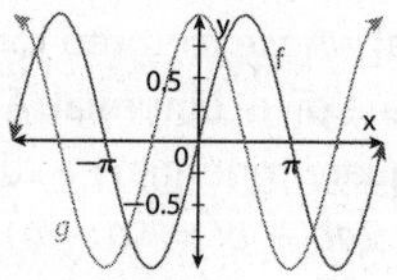 g is a phase shift of f $\frac{\pi}{2}$ units left.
piecewise function A function that is a combination of one or more functions.	**función a trozos** Función que es una combinación de una o más funciones.	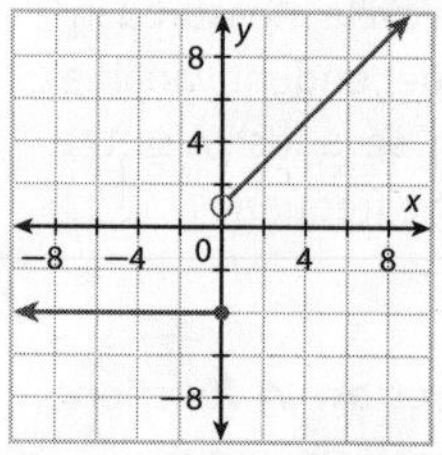 $f(x) = \begin{cases} -4 & \text{if } x \leq 0 \\ x+1 & \text{if } x > 0 \end{cases}$
point of tangency The point of intersection of a circle or sphere with a tangent line or plane.	**punto de tangencia** Punto de intersección de un círculo o esfera con una línea o plano tangente.	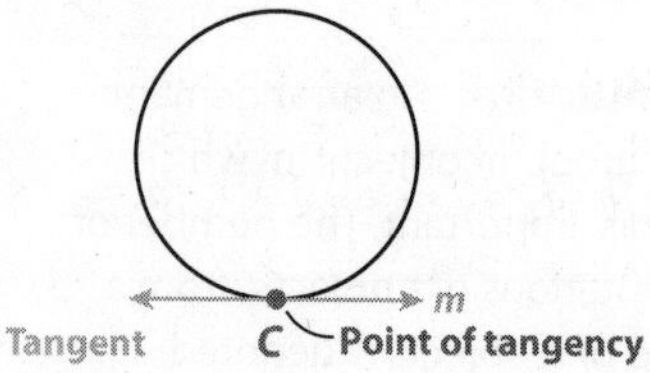
polynomial A monomial or a sum or difference of monomials.	**polinomio** Monomio o suma o diferencia de monomios.	$2x^2 + 3x - 7$

ENGLISH	SPANISH	EXAMPLES
polynomial function A function whose rule is a polynomial.	**función polinomial** Función cuya regla es un polinomio.	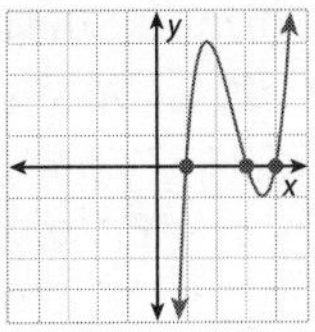 $f(x) = x^3 - 8x^2 + 19x - 12$
polynomial identity A mathematical relationship equating one polynomial quantity to another.	**identidad de polinomios** Relación matemática que iguala una cantidad polinomial con otra.	$(x^4 - y^4) = (x^2 + y^2)(x^2 - y^2)$
population The entire group of objects or individuals considered for a survey.	**población** Grupo completo de objetos o individuos que se desea estudiar.	In a survey about the study habits of high school students, the population is all high school students.
probability A number from 0 to 1 (or 0% to 100%) that is the measure of how likely an event is to occur.	**probabilidad** Número entre 0 y 1 (o entre 0% y 100%) que describe cuán probable es que ocurra un suceso.	A bag contains 3 red marbles and 4 blue marbles. The probability of choosing a red marble is $\frac{3}{7}$.
probability distribution for an experiment The function that pairs each outcome with its probability.	**distribución de probabilidad para un experimento** Función que asigna a cada resultado su probabilidad.	A number cube is rolled 10 times. The results are shown in the table.
probability sample A sample in which every member of the population being sampled has a nonzero probability of being selected.	**muestra de probabilidad** Muestra en la que cada miembro de la población que se estudia tiene una probabilidad distinta de cero de ser elegido.	
pure imaginary number *See* imaginary number.	**número imaginario puro** Ver número imaginario.	$3i$
Pythagorean Theorem If a right triangle has legs of lengths a and b and a hypotenuse of length c, then $a^2 + b^2 = c^2$.	**Teorema de Pitágoras** Dado un triángulo rectángulo con catetos de longitudes a y b y una hipotenusa de longitud c, entonces $a^2 + b^2 = c^2$.	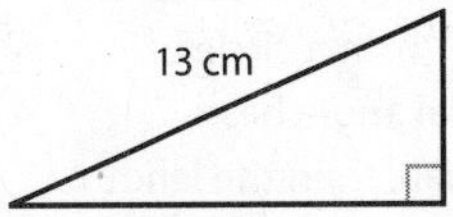 $5^2 + 12^2 = 13^2$ $25 + 144 = 169$

Table for probability distribution example:

Outcome	1	2	3	4	5	6
Probability	$\frac{1}{10}$	$\frac{1}{5}$	$\frac{1}{5}$	0	$\frac{3}{10}$	$\frac{1}{5}$

Q

quadratic equation An equation that can be written in the form $ax^2 + bx + c = 0$, where a, b, and c are real numbers and $a \neq 0$.	**ecuación cuadrática** Ecuación que se puede expresar como $ax^2 + bx + c = 0$, donde a, b y c son números reales y $a \neq 0$.	$x^2 + 3x - 4 = 0$ $x^2 - 9 = 0$

Glossary/Glosario

ENGLISH	SPANISH	EXAMPLES

Quadratic Formula The formula $x = \frac{-b \pm \sqrt{b^2 - 4ac}}{2a}$, which gives solutions, or roots, of equations in the form $ax^2 + bx + c = 0$, where $a \neq 0$.

fórmula cuadrática La fórmula $x = \frac{-b \pm \sqrt{b^2 - 4ac}}{2a}$, que da soluciones, o raíces, para las ecuaciones del tipo $ax^2 + bx + c = 0$, donde $a \neq 0$.

The solutions of $2x^2 - 5x - 3 = 0$ are given by

$$x = \frac{-(-5) \pm \sqrt{(-5)^2 - 4(2)(-3)}}{2(2)}$$

$$= \frac{5 \pm \sqrt{25 + 24}}{4} = \frac{5 \pm 7}{4};$$

$x = 3$ or $x = -\frac{1}{2}$.

---

quadratic function A function that can be written in the form $f(x) = ax^2 + bx + c$, where a, b, and c are real numbers and $a \neq 0$, or in the form $f(x) = a(x - h)^2 + k$, where a, h, and k are real numbers and $a \neq 0$.

función cuadrática Función que se puede expresar como $f(x) = ax^2 + bx + c$, donde a, b y c son números reales y $a \neq 0$, o como $f(x) = a(x - h)^2 + k$, donde a, h y k son números reales y $a \neq 0$.

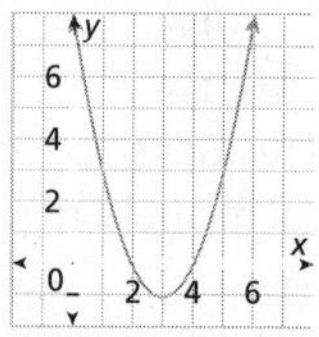

$f(x) = x^2 - 6x + 8$

---

quadratic model A quadratic function used to represent a set of data.

modelo cuadrático Función cuadrática que se utiliza para representar un conjunto de datos.

x	4	6	8	10
$f(x)$	27	52	89	130

A quadratic model for the data is $f(x) = x^2 + 3.3x - 2.6$.

---

quadratic regression A statistical method used to fit a quadratic model to a given data set.

regresión cuadrática Método estadístico utilizado para ajustar un modelo cuadrático a un conjunto de datos determinado.

---

quadrilateral A four-sided polygon.

cuadrilátero Polígono de cuatro lados.

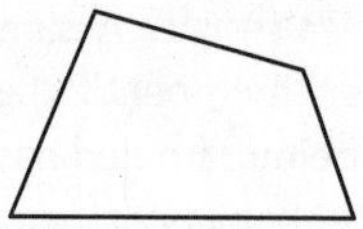

R

radian A unit of angle measure based on arc length. In a circle of radius r, if a central angle has a measure of 1 radian, then the length of the intercepted arc is r units.

2π radians $= 360°$
1 radian $\approx 57°$

radián Unidad de medida de un ángulo basada en la longitud del arco. En un círculo de radio r, si un ángulo central mide 1 radián, entonces la longitud del arco abarcado es r unidades.

2π radianes $= 360°$
1 radián $\approx 57°$

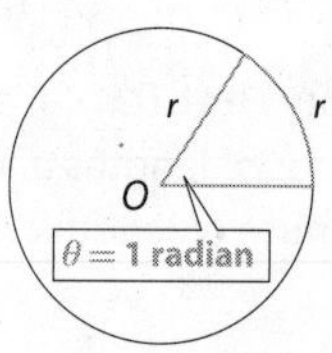

---

radical An indicated root of a quantity.

radical Raíz indicada de una cantidad.

$\sqrt{36} = 6$, $\sqrt[3]{27} = 3$

---

radical equation An equation that contains a variable within a radical.

ecuación radical Ecuación que contiene una variable dentro de un radical.

$\sqrt{x + 3} + 4 = 7$

ENGLISH	SPANISH	EXAMPLES
radical function A function whose rule contains a variable within a radical.	**función radical** Función cuya regla contiene una variable dentro de un radical.	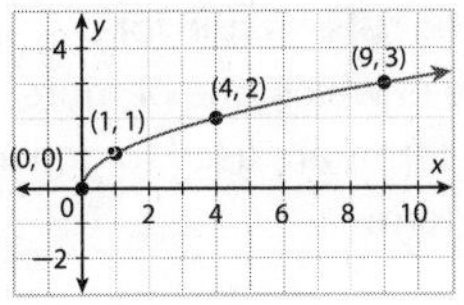 $f(x) = \sqrt{x}$
radicand The expression under a radical sign.	**radicando** Número o expresión debajo del signo de radical.	$\sqrt{x+3} - 2$ ↑ Radicand
random variable A variable whose value is determined by the outcome of a probability experiment.	**variable aleatoria** Una variable cuyo valor viene determinado por el resultado de un experimento de probabilidad	
randomized comparative experiment An experiment in which the individuals are assigned to the control group or the treatment group at random, in order to minimize bias.	**experimento comparativo aleatorizado** Experimento en el que se elige al azar a los individuos para el grupo de control o para el grupo experimental, a fin de minimizar el sesgo.	
range of a data set The difference of the greatest and least values in the data set.	**rango de un conjunto de datos** La diferencia del mayor y menor valor en un conjunto de datos.	The data set $\{3, 3, 5, 7, 8, 10, 11, 11, 12\}$ has a range of $12 - 3 = 9$.
range of a function or relation The set of output values of a function or relation.	**rango de una función o relación** Conjunto de los valores desalida de una función o relación.	The range of $y = x^2$ is $\{y \mid y \geq 0\}$.
rational equation An equation that contains one or more rational expressions.	**ecuación racional** Ecuación que contiene una o más expresiones racionales.	$\frac{x+2}{x^2+3x-1} = 6$
rational exponent An exponent that can be expressed as $\frac{m}{n}$ such that if m and n are integers, then $b^{m/n} = \sqrt[n]{b^m} = \left(\sqrt[n]{b}\right)^m$.	**exponente racional** Exponente quese puede expresar como $\frac{m}{n}$ tal que, si m y n son números enteros, entonces $b^{m/n} = \sqrt[n]{b^m} = \left(\sqrt[n]{b}\right)^m$	$4^{\frac{2}{2}} = \sqrt{4^3} = \sqrt{64} = 8$ $4^{\frac{2}{2}} = \left(\sqrt{4}\right)^3 = 2^3 = 8$
rational expression An algebraic expression whose numerator and denominator are polynomials and whose denominator has a degree ≥ 1.	**expresión racional** Expresión algebraica cuyo numerador y denominador son polinomios y cuyo denominador tiene un grado ≥ 1.	$\frac{x+2}{x^2+3x-1}$
rational function A function whose rule can be written as a rational expression.	**función racional** Función cuya regla se puede expresar como una expresión racional.	$f(x) = \frac{x+2}{x^2+3x-1}$
real axis The horizontal axis in the complex plane; it graphically represents the real part of complex numbers.	**eje real** Eje horizontal de un plano complejo. Representa gráficamente la parte real de los números complejos.	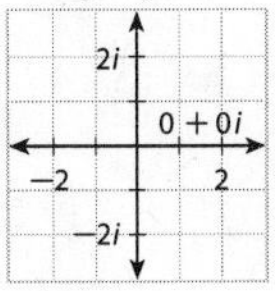

Glossary/Glosario

ENGLISH	SPANISH	EXAMPLES
recursive rule A rule for a sequence in which one or more previous terms are used to generate the next term.	**Regla recurrente** Regla para una sucesión en la cual uno o más términos anteriores se utilizan para generar el término siguiente.	For the sequence 5, 7, 9, 11, ..., a recursive rule is $a_1 = 5$ and $a_n = a_{n-1} + 2$.
reduced row-echelon form A form of an augmented matrix in which the coefficient columns form an identity matrix.	**forma escalonada reducida por filas** Forma de matriz aumentada en la que las columnas de coeficientes forman una matriz de identidad.	$\left[\begin{array}{cc\|c} 1 & 0 & -1 \\ 0 & 1 & 3 \end{array}\right]$
reference angle For an angle in standard position, the reference angle is the positive acute angle formed by the terminal side of the angle and the *x*-axis.	**ángulo de referencia** Dado un ángulo en posición estándar, el ángulo de referencia es el ángulo agudo positivo formado por el lado terminal del ángulo y el eje *x*.	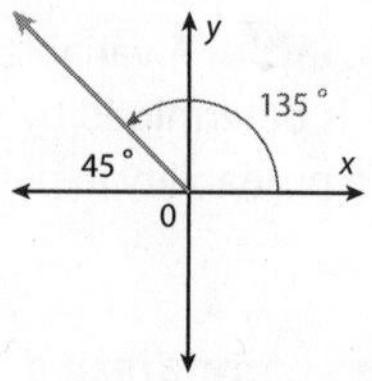
reflection A transformation that reflects, or "flips," a graph or figure across a line, called the line of reflection, such that each reflected point is the same distance from the line of reflection but is on the opposite side of the line.	**reflexión** Transformación que refleja, o invierte, una gráfica o figura sobre una línea, llamada la línea de reflexión, de manera tal que cada punto reflejado esté a la misma distancia de la línea de reflexión pero que se encuentre en el lado opuesto de la línea.	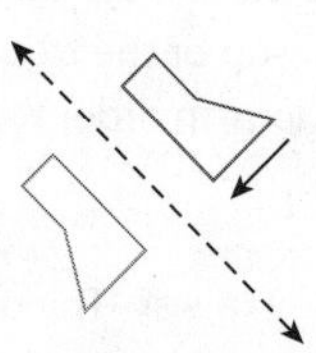
regression The statistical study of the relationship between variables.	**regresión** Estudio estadístico de la relación entre variables.	
regular pyramid A pyramid whose base is a regular polygon and whose lateral faces are congruent isosceles triangles.	**pirámide regular** Pirámide cuya base es un polígono regular y cuyas caras laterales son triángulos isósceles congruentes.	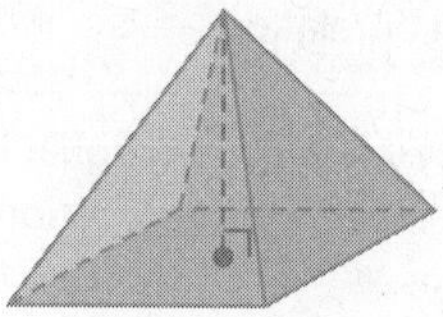
Remainder Theorem If the polynomial function $P(x)$ is divided by $x - a$, then the remainder r is $P(a)$.	**Teorema del resto** Si la función polinomial $P(x)$ se divide entre $x - a$, entonces, el residuo r será $P(a)$.	
representative sample A sample that is a good estimator for its corresponding population parameter.	**muestra representativa** Una muestra que es un buen estimador para su parámetro de población correspondiente.	
right cone A cone whose axis is perpendicular to its base.	**cono recto** Cono cuyo eje es perpendicular a su base.	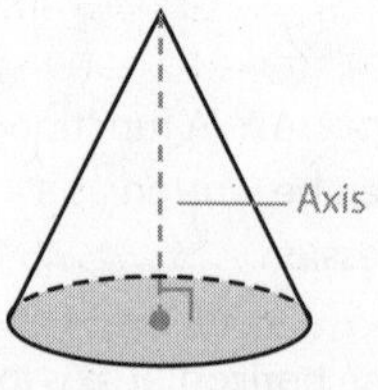

ENGLISH	SPANISH	EXAMPLES
right cylinder A cylinder whose axis is perpendicular to its bases.	**cilindro recto** Cilindro cuyo eje es perpendicular a sus bases.	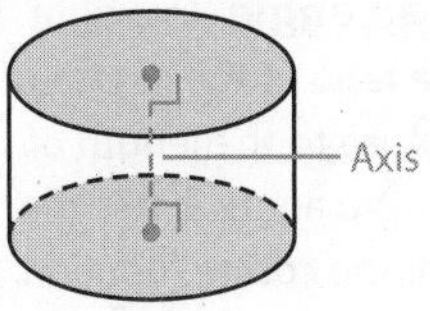
right prism A prism whose lateral faces are all rectangles.	**prisma recto** Prisma cuyas caras laterales son todas rectángulos.	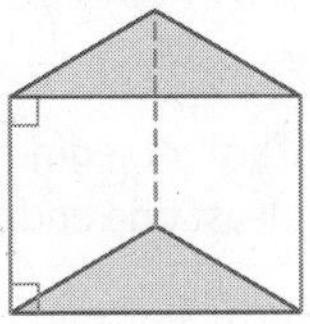
rotation A transformation that rotates or turns a figure about a point called the center of rotation.	**rotación** Transformación que hace rotar o girar una figura sobre un punto llamado centro de rotación.	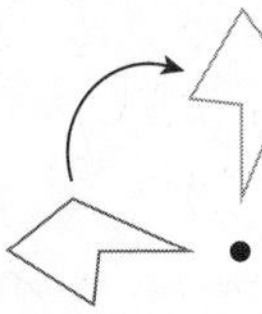
row operation An operation performed on a row of an augmented matrix that creates an equivalent matrix.	**operación por filas** Operación realizada en una fila de una matriz aumentada que crea una matriz equivalente.	$\left[\begin{array}{cc:c}2&0&-2\\0&1&3\end{array}\right] = \left[\begin{array}{cc:c}\frac{1}{2}(2)&\frac{1}{2}(0)&\frac{1}{2}(-2)\\0&1&3\end{array}\right] = \left[\begin{array}{cc:c}1&0&-1\\0&1&3\end{array}\right]$
row-reduction method The process of performing elementary row operations on an augmented matrix to transform the matrix to reduced row echelon form.	**método de reducción por filas** Proceso por el cual se realizan operaciones elementales de filas en una matriz aumentada para transformar la matriz en una forma reducida de filas escalonadas.	$\left[\begin{array}{cc:c}2&0&-2\\0&1&3\end{array}\right] = \left[\begin{array}{cc:c}\frac{1}{2}(2)&\frac{1}{2}(0)&\frac{1}{2}(-2)\\0&1&3\end{array}\right] = \left[\begin{array}{cc:c}1&0&-1\\0&1&3\end{array}\right]$

S

sample A part of the population.	**muestra** Una parte de la población.	In a survey about the study habits of high school students, a sample is a survey of 100 students.
sample space The set of all possible outcomes of a probability experiment.	**espacio muestral** Conjunto de todos los resultados posibles en un experimento de probabilidades.	In the experiment of rolling a number cube, the sample space is 1, 2. 3, 4, 5, 6.
sampling distribution A distribution that shows how a particular statistic varies across all samples of *n* individuals from the same population.	**distribución de muestreo** Una distribución que muestra de qué manera una determinada estadística varía a lo largo de todas las muestras de n individuos de la misma población.	
secant of a circle A line that intersects a circle at two points.	**secante de un círculo** Línea que corta un círculo en dos puntos.	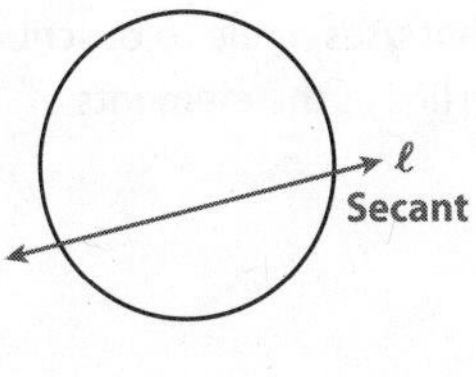

Glossary/Glosario

Glossary/Glosario

ENGLISH	SPANISH	EXAMPLES

secant of an angle In a right triangle, the ratio of the length of the hypotenuse to the length of the side adjacent to angle *A*. It is the reciprocal of the cosine function.

secante de un ángulo En un triángulo rectángulo, la razón entre la longitud de la hipotenusa y la longitud del cateto adyacente al ángulo *A*. Es la inversa de la función coseno.

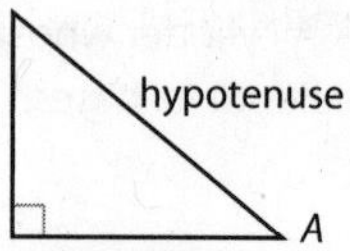

$$\sec A = \frac{\text{hypotenuse}}{\text{adjacent}} = \frac{1}{\cos A}$$

---

secant segment A segment of a secant with at least one endpoint on the circle.

segmento secante Segmento de una secante que tiene al menos un extremo sobre el círculo.

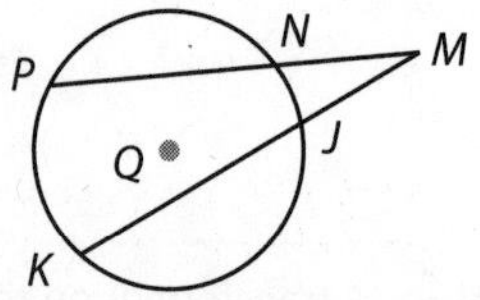

$\overline{NM}$ is an external secant segment.
$\overline{JK}$ is an internal secant segment.

---

second-degree equation in two variables An equation constructed by adding terms in two variables with powers no higher than 2.

ecuación de segundo grado en dos variables Ecuación compuesta por la suma de términos en dos variables con potencias no mayores a 2.

$$ax^2 + by^2 + cx + dy + e = 0$$

---

second differences Differences between first differences of a function.

segundas diferencias Diferencias entre las primerasdiferencias de una función.

x	0	1	2	3
y	1	4	9	16

first differences +3 +5 +7
second differences +2 +2

---

self-selected sample A sample in which members volunteer to participate.

muestra de voluntarios Muestra en la que los miembros se ofrecen voluntariamente para participar.

---

semicircle An arc of a circle whose endpoints lie on a diameter.

semicírculo Arco de un círculo cuyos extremos se encuentran sobre un diámetro.

---

sequence A list of numbers that often form a pattern.

sucesión Lista de números que generalmente forman un patrón.

1, 2, 4, 8, 16, ...

---

series The indicated sum of the terms of a sequence.

serie Suma indicada de los términos de una sucesión.

1 + 2 + 4 + 8 + 16 + ...

---

set A collection of items called elements.

conjunto Grupo de componentes denominados elementos.

$\{1, 2, 3\}$

---

set-builder notation A notation for a set that uses a rule to describe the properties of the elements of the set.

notación de conjuntos Notación para un conjunto que se vale de una regla para describir las propiedades de los elementos del conjunto.

$\{x \mid x > 3\}$ read, "The set of all *x* such that *x* is greater than 3."

ENGLISH	SPANISH	EXAMPLES
simple event An event consisting of only one outcome.	**suceso simple** Suceso que contiene sólo un resultado.	In the experiment of rolling a number cube, the event consisting of the outcome 3 is a simple event.
simulation A model of an experiment, often one that would be too difficult or time-consuming to actually perform.	**simulación** Modelo de un experimento; generalmente se recurre a la simulación cuando realizar dicho experimento sería demasiado difícil o llevaría mucho tiempo.	A random number generator is used to simulate the roll of a number cube.
sine In a right triangle, the ratio of the length of the side opposite $\angle A$ to the length of the hypotenuse.	**seno** En un triángulo rectángulo, razón entre la longitud del cateto opuesto a $\angle A$ y la longitud de la hipotenusa.	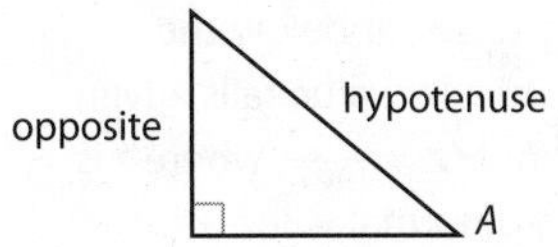 $\sin A = \frac{\text{opposite}}{\text{hypotenuse}}$.
skewed distribution A distribution that is mounded but not symmetric because one "tail" is much longer than the other.	**distribución sesgada** Una distribución que está elevada pero no es simétrica porque una de las "colas" es mucho más larga que la otra.	
square-root function A function whose rule contains a variable under a square-root sign.	**función de raíz cuadrada** Función cuya regla contiene una variable bajo un signo de raíz cuadrada.	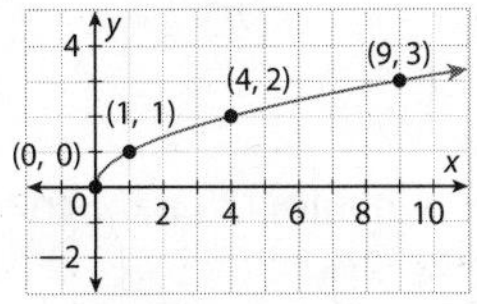 $f(x) = \sqrt{x}$
standard deviation A measure of dispersion of a data set. The standard deviation σ is the square root of the variance.	**desviación estándar** Medida de dispersión de un conjunto de datos. La desviación estándar σ es la raíz cuadrada de la varianza.	Data set: $\{6, 7, 7, 9, 11\}$ Mean: $\frac{6+7+7+9+11}{5} = 8$ Variance: $\frac{1}{5}(4+1+1+1+9) = 3.2$ Standard deviation: $\sigma = \sqrt{3.2} \approx 1.8$
standard error of the mean The standard deviation of the sampling distribution of the sample mean, denoted $\sigma_{\bar{x}}$.	**error estándar de la media** La desviación estándar de la distribución de muestreo de la media de la muestra, que se indica así: $\sigma_{\bar{x}}$.	
standard error of the proportion The standard deviation of the sampling distribution of the sample proportion, denoted $\sigma_{\hat{p}}$.	**error estándar de la proporción** La desviación estándar de la distribución de muestreo de la proporción de la muestra, que se indica así: $\sigma_{\hat{p}}$.	
standard form of a polynomial A polynomial in one variable is written in standard form when the terms are in order from greatest degree to least degree.	**forma estándar de un polinomio** Un polinomio de una variable se expresa en forma estándar cuando los términos se ordenan de mayor a menor grado.	$3x^3 - 5x^2 + 6x - 7$

ENGLISH	SPANISH	EXAMPLES
standard form of a quadratic equation $ax^2 + bx + c = 0$, where a, b, and c are real numbers and $a \neq 0$.	**forma estándar de una ecuación** cuadrática $ax^2 + bx + c = 0$, donde a, b y c son números reales y $a \neq 0$.	$2x^2 + 3x - 1 = 0$
standard normal distribution A normal distribution that has a mean of 0 and a standard deviation of 1.	**distribución normal estándar** Una distribución normal que tiene una media de 0 y una desviación estándar de 1.	
standard normal value A value that indicates how many standard deviations above or below the mean a particular value falls, given by the formula $z = \frac{x - \mu}{\sigma}$, where z is the standard normal value, x is the given value, μ is the mean, and σ is the standard deviation of a standard normal distribution.	**valor normal estándar** Valor que indica a cuántas desviaciones estándar por encima o por debajo de la media se encuentra un determinado valor, dado por la fórmula $z = \frac{x - \mu}{\sigma}$, donde z es el valor normal estándar, x es el valor dado, μ es la media y σ es la desviación estándar de una distribución normal estándar.	
standard position An angle in standard position has its vertex at the origin and its initial side on the positive x-axis.	**osición estándar** Ángulo cuyo vértice se encuentra en el origen y cuyo lado inicial se encuentra sobre el eje x.	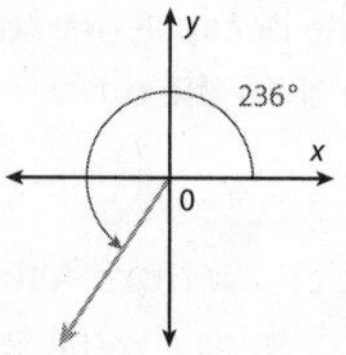
statistic A number that describes a sample.	**estadística** Número que describe una muestra.	
statistical significance A determination that the likelihood that an experimental result occurred by chance is so low that a conclusion in favor of rejecting the null hypothesis is justified.	**significación estadística** Una determinación de que la probabilidad de que un resultado experimental ocurriera por azar es tan reducida que está justificada una conclusión a favor de rechazar la hipótesis nula.	
step function A piecewise function that is constant over each interval in its domain.	**función escalón** Función a trozos que es constante en cada intervalo en su dominio.	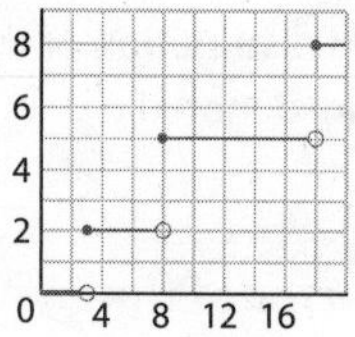
stretch A transformation that pulls the points of a graph horizontally away from the y-axis or vertically away from the x-axis.	**estiramiento** Transformación que desplaza los puntos de una gráfica en forma horizontal alejándolos del eje y o en forma vertical alejándolos del eje x.	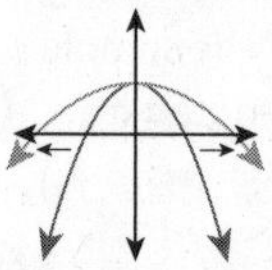
summation notation A method of notating the sum of a series using the Greek letter $\sum$ (capital *sigma*).	**notación de sumatoria** Método de notación de la suma de una serie que utiliza la letra griega $\sum$ (SIGMA mayúscula).	$\sum_{n=1}^{5} 3k = 3 + 6 + 9 + 12 + 15 = 45$

ENGLISH	SPANISH	EXAMPLES
supplementary angles Two angles whose measures have a sum of 180°.	**ángulos suplementarios** Dos ángulos cuyas medidas suman 180°.	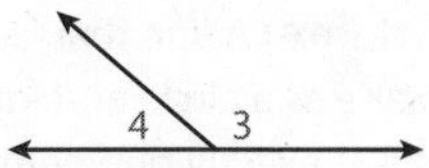 $\angle 3$ and $\angle 4$ are supplementary angles.
surface area The total area of all faces and curved surfaces of a three-dimensional figure.	**área total** Área total de todas las caras y superficies curvas de una figura tridimensional.	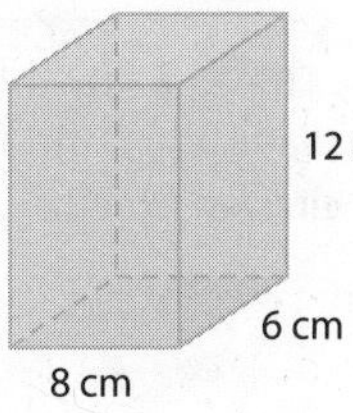 Surface area $= 2(8)(12) + 2(8)(6) + 2(12)(6) = 432\text{ cm}^2$
survey A data collection tool that uses questions to measure characteristics of interest about a population using a sample selected from the population.	**encuesta** Una herramienta para recopilar datos que usa preguntas para medir las características de interés sobre una población mediante una muestra seleccionada de entre la población.	
synthetic division A shorthand method of dividing by a linear binomial of the form $(x - a)$ by writing only the coefficients of the polynomials.	**división sintética** Método abreviado de división que consiste en dividir por un binomio lineal del tipo $(x - a)$ escribiendo sólo los coeficientes de los polinomios.	$(x^3 - 7x + 6) \div (x - 2)$ $\begin{array}{r\|rrrr} 2 & 1 & 0 & -7 & 6 \\ & & 2 & 4 & 6 \\ \hline & 1 & 2 & -3 & \boxed{0} \end{array}$ $(x^3 - 7x + 6) \div (x - 2) = x^2 + 2x - 3$
synthetic substitution The process of using synthetic division to evaluate a polynomial $p(x)$ when $x = c$.	**sustitución sintética** Proceso que consiste en usar la división sintética para evaluar un polinomio $p(x)$ cuando $x = c$.	
system of equations A set of two or more equations that have two or more variables.	**sistema de ecuaciones** Conjunto de dos o más ecuaciones que contienen dos o más variables.	$\begin{cases} 2x + 3y = -1 \\ x^2 = 4 \end{cases}$
system of linear inequalities A system of inequalities in two or more variables in which all of the inequalities are linear.	**sistema de desigualdades lineales** Sistema de desigualdades en dos o más variables en el que todas las desigualdades son lineales.	$\begin{cases} 2x + 3y \geq -1 \\ x - 3y < 4 \end{cases}$

T

ENGLISH	SPANISH	EXAMPLES
tangent circles Two coplanar circles that intersect at exactly one point. If one circle is contained inside the other, they are *internally tangent*. If not, they are *externally tangent*.	**círculos tangentes** Dos círculos coplanares que se cruzan únicamente en un punto. Si un círculo contiene a otro, son *tangentes internamente*. De lo contrario, son *tangentes externamente*.	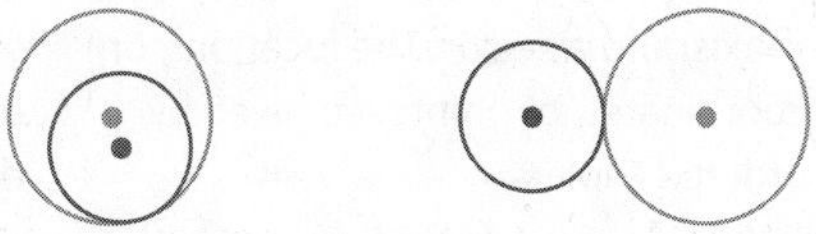

ENGLISH | **SPANISH** | **EXAMPLES**

tangent line A line that is in the same plane as a circle and intersects the circle at exactly one point.

línea tangente Línea que está en el mismo plano que un círculo y corta al círculo en exactamente un punto.

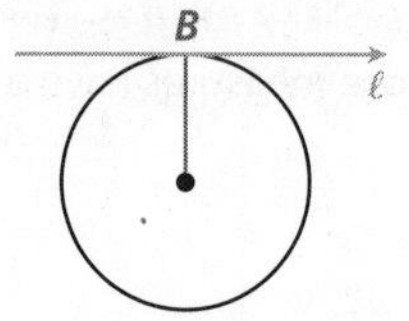

---

tangent of a circle A line that is in the same plane as a circle and intersects the circle at exactly one point.

tangente de un círculo Línea que se encuentra en el mismo plano que un círculo y lo cruza únicamente en un punto.

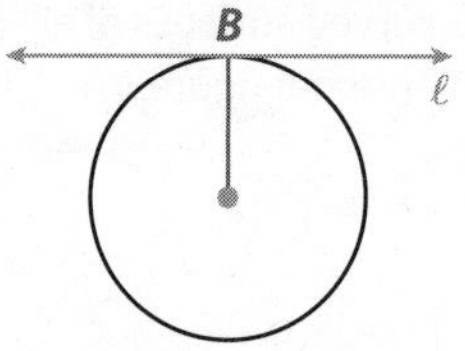

---

tangent of a sphere A line that intersects the sphere at exactly one point.

tangente de una esfera Línea que toca la esfera únicamente en un punto.

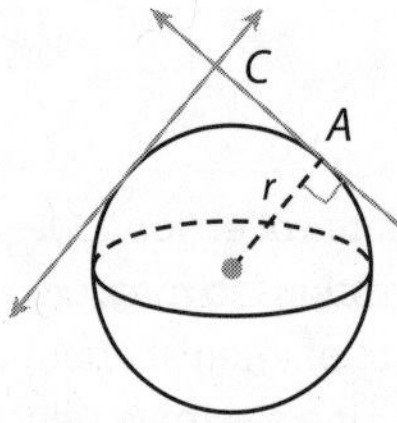

---

tangent of an angle In a right triangle, the ratio of the length of the leg opposite $\angle A$ to the length of the leg adjacent to $\angle A$.

tangente de un ángulo En un triángulo rectángulo, razón entre la longitud del cateto opuesto a $\angle A$ y la longitud del cateto adyacente a $\angle A$.

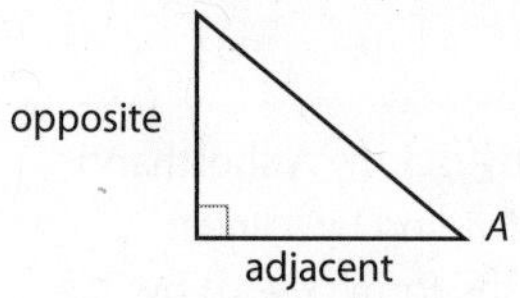

$$\tan A = \frac{\text{opposite}}{\text{adjacent}}$$

---

term of a sequence An element or number in the sequence.

término de una sucesión Elemento o número de una sucesión.

5 is the third term in the sequence 1, 3, 5, 7, . . .

---

terminal side For an angle in standard position, the ray that is rotated relative to the positive *x*–axis.

lado terminal Dado un ángulo en una posición estándar, el rayo que rota en relación con el eje positivo *x*.

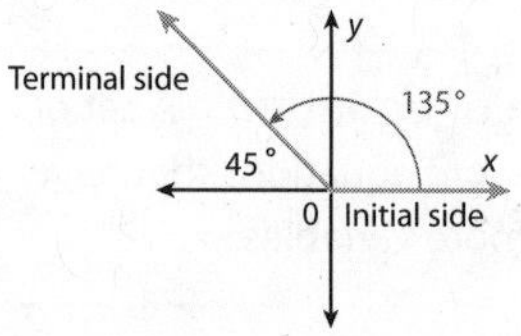

---

theoretical probability The ratio of the number of equally likely outcomes in an event to the total number of possible outcomes.

probabilidad teórica Razón entre el número de resultados igualmente probables de un suceso y el número total de resultados posibles.

The theoretical probability of rolling an odd number on a number cube is $\frac{3}{6} = \frac{1}{2}$.

---

three-dimensional coordinate system A space that is divided into eight regions by an *x*–axis, a *y*–axis, and a *z*–axis. The locations, or coordinates, of points are given by ordered triples.

sistema de coordenadas tridimensional Espacio dividido en ocho regiones por un eje *x*, un eje *y* y un eje *z*. Las ubicaciones, o coordenadas, de los puntos son dadas por tripletas ordenadas.

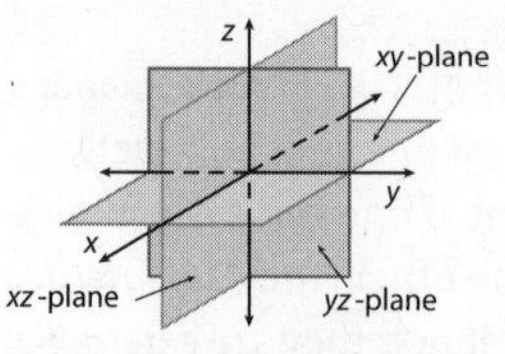

ENGLISH	SPANISH	EXAMPLES
transformation A change in the position, size, or shape of a figure or graph.	**transformación** Cambio en la posición, tamaño o forma de una figura o gráfica.	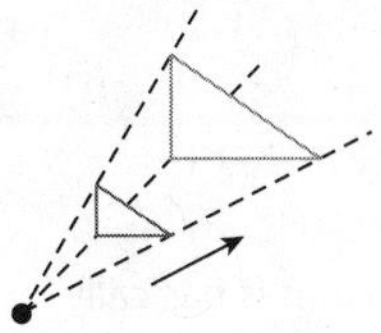
translation A transformation that shifts or slides every point of a figure or graph the same distance in the same direction.	**traslación** Transformación en la que todos los puntos de una figura se mueven la misma distancia en la misma dirección.	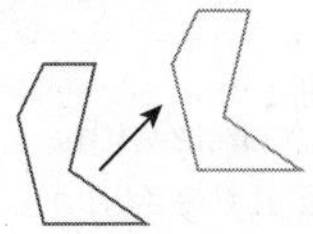
transversal A line that intersects two coplanar lines at two different points.	**transversal** Línea que corta dos líneas coplanares en dos puntos diferentes.	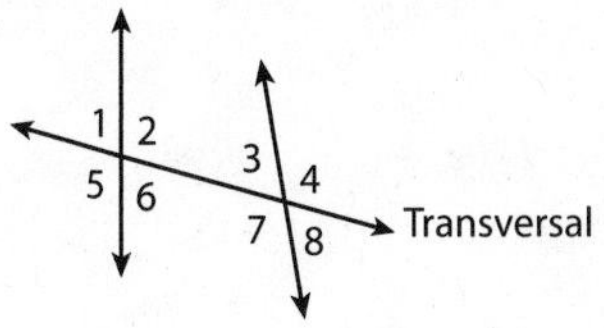
trapezoid A quadrilateral with at least one pair of parallel sides.	**trapecio** Cuadrilátero con al menos un par de lados paralelos.	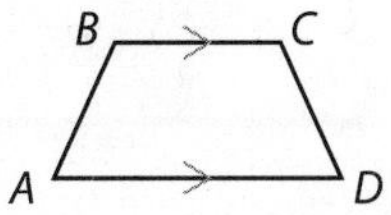
trial In probability, a single repetition or observation of an experiment.	**prueba** En probabilidad, una sola repetición u observación de un experimento.	In the experiment of rolling a number cube, each roll is one trial.
trigonometric function A function whose rule is given by a trigonometric ratio.	**función trigonométrica** Función cuya regla es dada por una razón trigonométrica.	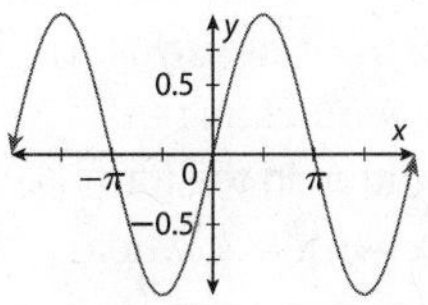 $f(x) = \sin x$
trigonometric ratio Ratio of the lengths of two sides of a right triangle.	**razón trigonométrica** Razón entre dos lados de un triángulo rectángulo.	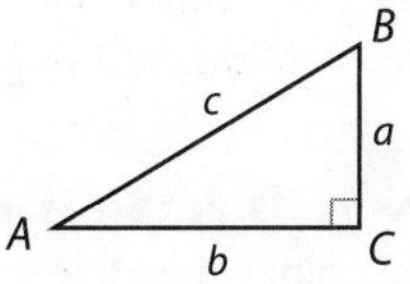 $\sin A = \frac{a}{c}$, $\cos A = \frac{b}{c}$, $\tan A = \frac{a}{b}$
trigonometry The study of the measurement of triangles and of trigonometric functions and their applications.	**trigonometría** Estudio de la medición de los triángulos y de las funciones trigonométricas y sus aplicaciones.	
trinomial A polynomial with three terms.	**trinomio** Polinomio con tres términos.	$4x^2 + 3xy - 5y^2$
turning point A point on the graph of a function that corresponds to a local maximum (or minimum) where the graph changes from increasing to decreasing (or vice versa).	**punto de inflexión** Punto de la gráfica de una función que corresponde a un máximo (o mínimo) local donde la gráfica pasa de ser creciente a decreciente (o viceversa).	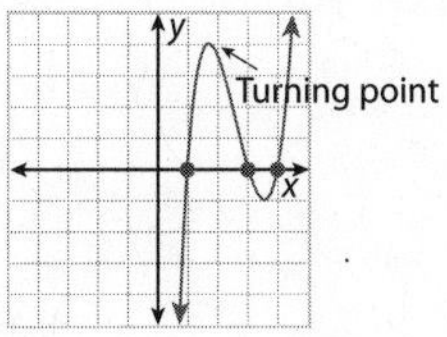

Glossary/Glosario

ENGLISH | **SPANISH** | **EXAMPLES**

U

uniform distribution A distribution that is basically level, forming a shape that looks like a rectangle.

distribución uniforme Una distribución que es básicamente llana, formando una figura similar a un rectángulo.

unit circle A circle with a radius of 1, centered at the origin.

círculo unitario Círculo con un radio de 1, centrado en el origen.

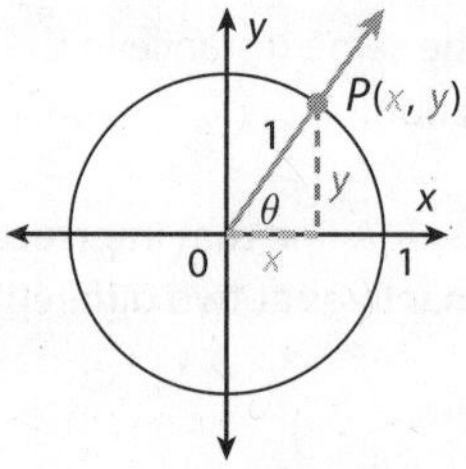

Unit circle

V

variance The average of squared differences from the mean. The square root of the variance is called the *standard deviation*.

varianza Promedio de las diferencias cuadráticas en relación con la media. La raíz cuadrada de la varianza se denomina *desviación estándar*.

Data set: is $\{6, 7, 7, 9, 11\}$

Mean: $\frac{6 + 7 + 7 + 9 + 11}{5} = 8$

Variance: $\frac{1}{5}(4 + 1 + 1 + 1 + 9) = 3.2$

vertex form of a quadratic function A quadratic function written in the form $f(x) = a(x - h)^2 + k$, where a, h, and k are constants and (h, k) is the vertex.

forma en vértice de una función cuadrática Una función cuadrática expresada en la forma $f(x) = a(x - h)^2 + k$, donde a, h y k son constantes y (h, k) es el vértice.

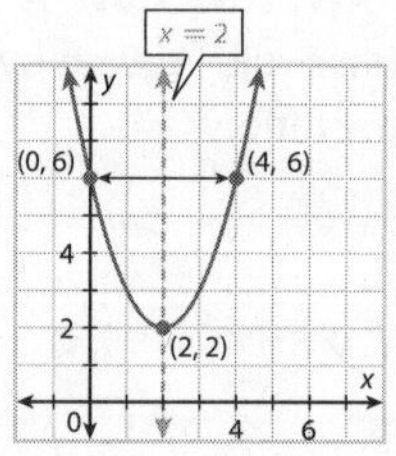

$f(x) = (x - 2)^2 + 2$

vertex of an absolute-value graph The point where the axis of symmetry intersects the graph.

vértice de una gráfica de valor absoluto Punto donde en el eje de simetría interseca la gráfica.

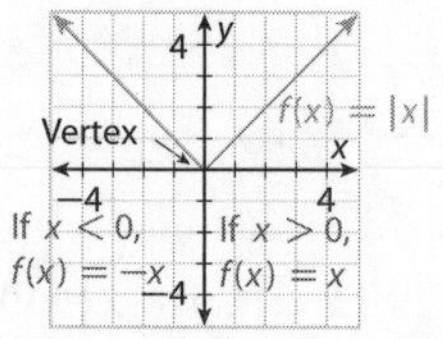

vertex of a parabola The highest or lowest point on the parabola.

vértice de una parábola Punto más alto o más bajo de una parábola.

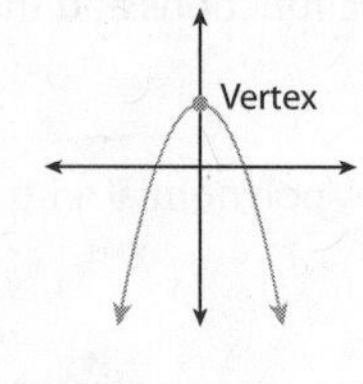

ENGLISH | SPANISH | EXAMPLES

Z

z-axis The third axis in a three-dimensional coordinate system.

eje z Tercer eje en un sistema de coordenadas tridimensional.

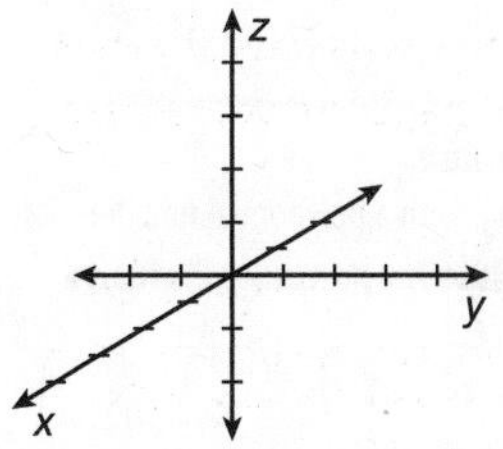

z-score A standardized data value from a normal distribution with mean μ and standard deviation σ found by using the formula $z = \frac{x-\mu}{\sigma}$ where x is the original data value.

puntaje z Un valor de datos estandarizado de una distribución normal con una media μ y una desviación estándar σ que se halla usando la fórmula $z = \frac{x-\mu}{\sigma}$, donde x es el valor de datos original.

zero of a function For the function f, any number x such that $f(x) = 0$.

cero de una función Dada la función f, todo número x tal que $f(x) = 0$.

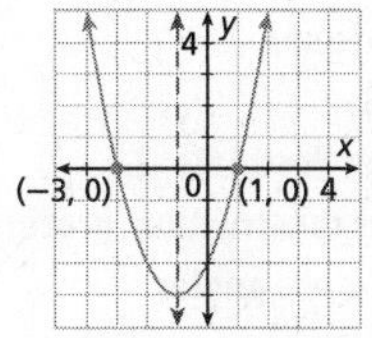

The zeros of $f(x) = x^2 + 2x - 3$ are −3 and 1.

Index

Index locator numbers are in Module. Lesson form. For example, 2.1 indicates Module 2, Lesson 1 as listed in the Table of Contents.

Index

D

E

F

G

H

I

L

M

N

O

P

Index

Q

R

S

T

Index

Table of Measures

LENGTH

1 inch = 2.54 centimeters

1 meter = 39.37 inches

1 mile = 5,280 feet

1 mile = 1760 yards

1 mile = 1.609 kilometers

1 kilometer = 0.62 mile

MASS/WEIGHT

1 pound = 16 ounces

1 pound = 0.454 kilograms

1 kilogram = 2.2 pounds

1 ton = 2000 pounds

CAPACITY

1 cup = 8 fluid ounces

1 pint = 2 cups

1 quart = 2 pints

1 gallon = 4 quarts

1 gallon = 3.785 liters

1 liter = 0.264 gallons

1 liter = 1000 cubic centimeters

Symbols

$\neq$	is not equal to
$\approx$	is approximately equal to
10^2	ten squared; ten to the second power
$2.\overline{6}$	repeating decimal 2.66666...
$\lvert -4 \rvert$	the absolute value of negative 4
$\sqrt{}$	square root
π	pi: (about 3.14)
$\perp$	is perpendicular to
$\parallel$	is parallel to
$\overleftrightarrow{AB}$	line *AB*
$\overrightarrow{AB}$	ray *AB*
$\overline{AB}$	line segment *AB*
$m\angle A$	measure of $\angle A$

Formulas

FACTORING	
Perfect square trinomials	$a^2 + 2ab + b^2 = (a + b)^2$
	$a^2 - 2ab + b^2 = (a - b)^2$
Difference of squares	$a^2 - b^2 = (a - b)(a + b)$
Sum of cubes	$a^3 + b^3 = (a + b)(a^2 - ab + b^2)$
Difference of cubes	$a^3 - b^3 = (a - b)(a^2 + ab + b^2)$

PROPERTIES OF EXPONENTS	
Product of powers	$a^m a^n = a^{(m+n)}$
Quotient of powers	$\frac{a^m}{a^n} = a^{(m-n)}$
Power of a power	$(a^m)^n = a^{mn}$
Rational exponent	$a^{\frac{m}{n}} = \sqrt[n]{a^m}$
Negative exponent	$a^{-n} = \frac{1}{a^n}$

QUADRATIC EQUATIONS	
Standard form	$f(x) = ax^2 + bx + c$
Vertex form	$f(x) = a(x - h)^2 + k$
Parabola	$(x - h)^2 = 4p(y - k)$ $(y - k)^2 = 4p(x - h)$
Quadratic formula	$x = \frac{-b \pm \sqrt{b^2 - 4ac}}{2a}$
Axis of symmetry	$x = \frac{-b}{2a}$